# FROM THIRD
# WORLD
# TO FIRST

# FROM THIRD WORLD TO FIRST

## THE SINGAPORE STORY:
## 1965–2000

Lee Kuan Yew

SINGAPORE AND THE
ASIAN ECONOMIC BOOM

HarperCollins*Publishers*

HarperCollins books may be purchased for educational, business, or sales
promotional use. For information please write: Special Markets Department,
HarperCollins Publishers Inc., 10 East 53rd Street, New York, NY 10022.


Designed by North Market Street Graphics

Library of Congress Cataloging-in-Publication Data is available.

ISBN 0-06-019776-5

06 07 08 09  RRD  20 19 18 17 16 15 14 13 12 11

*To Goh Keng Swee, S. Rajaratnam, Hon Sui Sen,*
*Lim Kim San, Eddie Barker, Toh Chin Chye,*
*Ong Pang Boon, and Othman Wok,*
*my old-guard colleagues who together made possible*
*The Singapore Story.*

# Contents

# Foreword

*Dr. Henry A. Kissinger*

In the second half of the twentieth century, the emergence of scores of new states has made international politics and economics truly global for the first time in history. At the same time, technology has made it possible for nearly every country to participate in events in every part of the world as they occur.

Unfortunately, the explosion in information has not been accompanied by a similar increase in knowledge. The continents interact, but they do not necessarily understand each other. The uniformity of technology is accompanied by an implicit assumption that politics, and even cultures, will become homogenized. Especially, the long-established nations of the West have fallen prey to the temptation of ignoring history and judging every new state by the criteria of their own civilizations. It is often overlooked that the institutions of the West did not spring full-blown from the brow of contemporaries but evolved over centuries which shaped frontiers and defined legitimacy, constitutional provisions, and basic values.

But history does matter. The institutions of the West developed gradually while those of most new states were put into place in elaborated form immediately. In the West, a civil society evolved side-by-side with the maturation of the modern state. This made possible the growth of representative institutions which confined the state's power to those matters which society could not deal with by its own arrangements. Political conflicts were moderated by overriding purposes.

Many postcolonial states have no comparable history. Tasks, which, in the West, were accomplished over centuries, must be completed in a decade or two and under much more complex circumstances. Where the common national experience is colonial rule, especially when the state comprises diverse ethnic groups, political opposition is often considered an assault on the political validity of the state rather than of a particular government.

Singapore is a case in point. As the main British naval base in the Far East, it had neither prospect nor aspiration for nationhood until the collapse of European power in the aftermath of the Second World War redrew the political map of Southeast Asia. In the first wave of decolonization, Singapore was made part of Malaya until its largely Chinese population proved too daunting for a state attempting to define its national identity by a Malay majority. Malaya extruded Singapore because it was not yet ready to cope with so large a Chinese population or, less charitably, to teach Singapore the habits of dependence if it was forced back into what later became the Malaysian Federation.

But history shows that normally prudent, ordinary calculations can be overturned by extraordinary personalities. In the case of Lee Kuan Yew, the father of Singapore's emergence as a national state, the ancient argument whether circumstance or personality shapes events is settled in favor of the latter. Circumstances could not have been less favorable. Located on a sandbar with nary a natural resource, Singapore had in the 1950s a polyglot population of slightly over a million (today over 3 million), of which 75.4 percent was Chinese, 13.6 percent Malay, and 8.6 percent Indian. It adjoined in the south with Indonesia, with a population of over 100 million (now nearly double that), and in the north with Malaya (later Malaysia), with a then-population of 6.28 million. By far the smallest country in Southeast Asia, Singapore seemed destined to become a client state of more powerful neighbors, if indeed it could preserve its independence at all.

Lee Kuan Yew thought otherwise. Every great achievement is a dream before it becomes reality, and his vision was of a state that would not simply survive but prevail by excelling. Superior intelligence, discipline, and ingenuity would substitute for resources. Lee Kuan Yew summoned his compatriots to a duty they had never previously perceived: first to clean up their city, then to dedicate it to overcome the initial hostility of their neighbors and their own ethnic divisions by superior performance. The Singapore of today is his testament. Annual per capita income has grown from less than $1,000 at the time of independence to nearly $30,000 today. It is the high-tech leader of Southeast Asia, the commercial entrepôt, the scientific center. Singapore plays a major role in the politics and economics of Southeast Asia and beyond.

This volume is Lee Kuan Yew's account of his extraordinary achievement. He navigated this passage by understanding not only the requirements of his own society but the needs and motives of his neighbors. A thoughtful discussion of Indonesia and the fall of its President Suharto is matched by Lee Kuan Yew's account of his encounters with China and its leaders. His narrative of Singapore's abortive venture into creating a satellite city in Suzhou is particularly instructive on the challenge of melding the market economics of even so friendly an interlocutor as Singapore with the political and social realities of a China midway between Mao and reform.

Lee Kuan Yew would not be true to himself were he less than frank about his analysis of the difference between the individualism of the West and the priority for social cohesion in countries such as his and in much of the rest of Asia. He does not ask us to change our patterns, only to refrain from imposing them on societies with different histories and necessities.

These views have subjected Lee Kuan Yew to considerable criticism in the West. Those of us who prize our values while understanding the complexities of a new country in a different culture are prepared to leave it to history to pass judgment as to whether there were other options available to him. But, for a generation, every American leader who has dealt with Lee Kuan Yew has benefited from the fact that, on international issues, he has identified the future of his country with the fate of the democracies. And he has done so not passively but by making a seminal political contribution to the struggles of our time.

# Preface

I wrote this book for a younger generation of Singaporeans who took stability, growth, and prosperity for granted. I wanted them to know how difficult it was for a small country of 640 sq. km with no natural resources to survive in the midst of larger, newly independent nations all pursuing nationalistic policies.

Those who have been through the trauma of war in 1942 and the Japanese occupation, and have taken part in building a new economy for Singapore, are not so sanguine. We cannot afford to forget that public order, personal security, economic and social progress, and prosperity are not the natural order of things, that they depend on ceaseless effort and attention from an honest and effective government that the people must elect.

In my earlier book, I described my formative years in prewar Singapore, the Japanese occupation, and the communist upheavals followed by racial problems during our two years in Malaysia.

The Japanese occupation (1942–1945) filled me with hatred for the cruelties they inflicted on their fellow Asians, aroused my nationalism and self-respect, and my resentment at being lorded over. My four years as a student in Britain after the war strengthened my determination to get rid of British colonial rule.

I returned to Singapore in 1950, confident of my cause, but ignorant of the pitfalls and dangers that lay ahead. An anticolonial wave swept me and many others of my generation. I involved myself with trade unions and politics, formed a political party, and at the age of 35 assumed office in 1959 as the first prime minister of an elected government of self-governing Singapore. My friends and I formed a united front with the communists. From the start we knew that there would have to be a parting of the ways and a time for reckoning. When it came, the fight was bitter, and we were fortunate not to have been defeated.

We believed the long-term future for Singapore was to rejoin Malaya, so we merged with it to form Malaysia in September 1963. Within a year, in July 1964, we suffered Malay-Chinese race riots in Singapore. We were trapped in an intractable struggle with Malay extremists of the ruling party, United Malay National Organisation (UMNO), who were intent on a Malay-dominated Malaysia. To counter their use of communal riots to cow us, we rallied the non-Malays and Malays throughout Malaysia in the Malaysian Solidarity Convention to fight for a Malaysian Malaysia. By August 1965 we were given no choice but to leave.

The communal bullying and intimidation made our people willing to endure the hardships of going it alone. That traumatic experience of race riots also made my colleagues and me even more determined to build a multiracial society that would give equality to all citizens, regardless of race, language, or religion. It was an article of faith which guided our policies.

This book covers the long, hard slog to find ways of staying independent and making a living without Malaysia as our hinterland. We had to work against seemingly insuperable odds to make it from poverty to prosperity in three decades.

The years after 1965 were hectic and filled with anxiety, as we struggled to find our feet. We were relieved when we found in 1971 that we had created enough jobs to avoid heavy unemployment even though the British withdrew their forces from Singapore. But only after we weathered the international oil crisis in 1973, with the quadrupling of oil prices, were we confident that we could make it on our own. Thereafter, it was hard work, planning, and improvising to establish ourselves as a viable nation linked by trade and investments to the major industrial countries, and as a successful hub for the dissemination of goods, services, and information in our region.

Our climb from a per capita GDP of US$400 in 1959 (when I took office as prime minister) to more than US$12,200 in 1990 (when I stepped down) and US$22,000 in 1999 took place at a time of immense political and economic changes in the world.

In material terms, we have left behind our Third World problems of poverty. However, it will take another generation before our arts, culture, and social standards can match the First World infrastructure we have installed. During the Cold War in the 1960s and 1970s, when it was far from clear which side would win, we aligned ourselves with the West. The Cold War divide made for a simpler international environment. Because our immediate neighbors were against the communists, we enjoyed both regional solidarity and international support from America, Western Europe, and Japan. By the late 1980s it was clear we were on the side of the victors.

This is not a how-to book, whether to build an economy, an army, or a nation. It is an account of the problems my colleagues and I faced, and how we set about solving them. I wrote my earlier book as a chronological narrative. To do so for this volume would have made the book too long. I have written by themes, to compress 30 years into 700 pages.

# Acknowledgments

Andrew Tan Kok Kiong started research for these memoirs in 1995. He was an officer in the Singapore administrative service, seconded to Singapore Press Holdings (SPH) to help me. The prime minister, Goh Chok Tong, allowed me access to all records and documents in the government ministries and in the archives. The registry officer in the prime minister's office, Florence Ler Chay Keng, and her assistants, Wendy Teo Kwee Geok and Vaijayanthimala, were tireless and thorough in tracing files and documents. With the help of Pang Gek Choo, who worked for the *Straits Times*, and Alan Chong, a young political science graduate, Andrew searched through government records, minutes of important meetings, correspondence, and other relevant documents. Most useful were the notes I dictated immediately after meetings and conversations.

Andrew Tan was able and resourceful. He coordinated the work of the researchers, organized the material, and made my task easier. Pang Gek Choo was quick and efficient in tracing reports of events and speeches in the *Straits Times'* library and archives. In 1997, when the work expanded, Walter Fernandez and Yvonne Lim from SPH and Dr. Goh Ai Ting from the National University of Singapore (NUS) joined my researchers.

Panneer Selvan from the ministry of foreign affairs helped retrieve records of my dealings with foreign leaders. Lily Tan, director of the National Archives, produced many useful documents and oral history transcripts of those who had allowed me to read them. The staffs at the

NUS library, the National Library, and the *Straits Times* editorial library were always helpful.

John Dickie, former diplomatic correspondent of the *Daily Mail,* gave much valuable advice, especially on what would interest a British reader. My good friend Gerald Hensley, New Zealand's former high commissioner in Singapore and later secretary for defence, gave good suggestions.

*Straits Times* writers, Cheong Yip Seng (editor in chief), Han Fook Kwang, Warren Fernandez, Zuraidah Ibrahim, Irene Ng, and Chua Mui Hoong proposed many changes, making the book easier to read, especially for those without background knowledge of the events I described.

Lim Jin Koon, editor of *Zaobao,* read through the whole draft before its translation into Chinese. Seng Han Thong, formerly of *Zaobao,* now in the National Trades Union Congress (NTUC), went through many versions of the drafts before finally settling the Chinese translation.

Guntor Sadali, editor of *Berita Harian,* minister for community development, Abdullah Tarmugi, senior parliamentary secretary Zainul Abidin Rasheed, and parliamentary secretaries Mohamad Maidin and Yaacob Ibrahim gave their views on all the chapters relating to Malays. I wanted to avoid unintentionally hurting Malay sensitivities and have tried hard not to do so.

Old friends and colleagues, Goh Keng Swee, Lim Kim San, Ong Pang Boon, Othman Wok, Lee Khoon Choy, Rahim Ishak, Maurice Baker, Sim Kee Boon, S. R. Nathan (now our president), and Ngiam Tong Dow, read various parts of my drafts and corrected or confirmed my recollection of events.

My drafts were also read by Kishore Mahbubani (permanent representative to the United Nations), Chan Heng Chee (ambassador to Washington), Bilahari Kausikan (deputy secretary, ministry of foreign affairs), Tommy Koh (ambassador at large), and Lee Tsao Yuan (director of the Institute of Policy Studies). Their valuable advice as diplomats, writers, and academics helped me give the book a better focus.

Shova Loh, line editor in Times Editions, meticulously cleaned up the final draft.

My three personal assistants, Wong Lin Hoe, Loh Hock Teck, and Koh Kiang Chay, worked tirelessly, often late into the evenings, to take in every amendment and check for accuracy. They went well beyond the call of duty. To all of them and others too numerous to name, I express my grateful thanks. The errors and shortcomings that remain are mine.

As with the first volume, my wife, Choo, went through every page many times until she was satisfied that what I had written was clear and easy to read.

The line editor at HarperCollins, New York, has meticulously Americanized my English. She has also made me politically gender correct. Wherever I wrote "man," he has become "person" or "people." I thank her for making me appear less of a male chauvinist to Americans.

# PART I

# Getting the Basics Right

# 1. Going It Alone

There are books to teach you how to build a house, how to repair engines, how to write a book. But I have not seen a book on how to build a nation out of a disparate collection of immigrants from China, British India, and the Dutch East Indies, or how to make a living for its people when its former economic role as the entrepôt of the region is becoming defunct.

I never had expected that in 1965, at 42, I would be in charge of an independent Singapore, responsible for the lives of its 2 million people. From 1959, when I was 35, I was prime minister of a self-governing state of Singapore. We joined the Federation of Malaysia in September 1963. There were fundamental disagreements over policies between Singapore and the federal government. All of a sudden, on 9 August 1965, we were out on our own as an independent nation. We had been asked to leave Malaysia and go our own way with no signposts to our next destination.

We faced tremendous odds with an improbable chance of survival. Singapore was not a natural country but man-made, a trading post the British had developed into a nodal point in their worldwide maritime empire. We inherited the island without its hinterland, a heart without a body.

Foreign press comments immediately after independence, all predicting doom, added to my gloom. One writer compared Britain's withdrawal from its colonies to the decline of the Roman Empire when law and order collapsed as the Roman legions withdrew and barbarian hordes took over. Denis Warner wrote in the *Sydney Morning Herald* (10 August 1965), "An independent Singapore was not regarded as viable three years ago. Nothing in the current situation suggests that it is more viable today." In the London *Sunday Times* (22 August 1965), Richard Hughes wrote, "Singapore's economy would collapse if the British bases—costing more than 100 million pounds sterling—were closed." I shared these fears but did not express them: My duty was to give the people hope, not demoralize them.

Indeed one question uppermost in my mind was how long the British would or could keep their bases in Singapore. Would their stay be shortened because of the way separation had taken place? Harold Wilson was already facing opposition from his backbenchers. The "east of Suez" policy was costly and did not help the Labour government win votes. They needed the money for welfare and other vote-winning programs. The only guarantor of security and stability in East Asia, the United States, was deeply mired in a guerrilla war in Vietnam which was extremely unpopular with their European allies and with African and Asian governments. Anti-American propaganda by the Soviets and the People's Republic of China was most effective in the Third World. I felt it would be politically costly, if not impossible, for Singapore to have the Americans take over the role of the British. Australia and New Zealand on their own would not be credible guarantors.

I feared that slowly but inexorably British influence would decline, and American influence expand. For my generation born and bred in empire, it was not an easy change. I had to come to terms with American power without a British buffer. The British had enforced their will with a certain civility. The Americans were different, as I could see from the way they dealt with South Vietnamese leaders, and even with Thai and Filipino leaders who were not in as parlous a position as those in Saigon. America was a power on the ascendant, with bulging muscles and a habit of flexing them.

There was the personal burden of tighter security. It was irksome. Immediately after separation, the police officer in charge of my security had warned me that I had become the number one hate object in the Malaysian Malay-language newspapers and radio and television broadcasts then circulating and receivable in Singapore. He advised me to move from my home on Oxley Road until they had made certain alterations to the house. I had a thick layer of security men instead of just one officer. He also extended discreet security cover for my wife Choo and the children. The threat from racial fanatics was unpredictable, unlike that from the communists who were rational and calculating and would see no benefit in going for Choo or our children. For three to four months, Choo and I stayed at Changi Cottage, a government chalet by the sea, near the RAF Changi airfield and inside a "protected" area. During that time, I held cabinet meetings irregularly, for the drive to my office at City Hall caused traffic disruption with the unaccustomed motorcycle outriders and a security car. I took urgent decisions by telephone conference with the relevant ministers which gave me relief from interminable office meetings. My personal assistants and Wong Chooi Sen, my trusted cabinet secretary, came every day to the cottage from where I worked. Within walking distance was a nine-hole RAF golf course that provided a welcome break from the daily grind of papers and minutes. I would play nine holes, sometimes with a friend, at other times on my own, with Choo walking to keep me company.

Our three children had to attend school, so they stayed at home and put up with the inconvenience of workers erecting a wall of bricks set in honeycomb pattern to screen off our front porch from the road. As a temporary measure, until bullet-proof glass could be obtained, they also blocked our windows with steel plates. This made the rooms feel like prisons, and the whole family felt a tremendous sense of relief when the glass windows were finally installed months later. When I returned to Oxley Road, Gurkha policemen (recruited by the British from Nepal) were posted as sentries. To have either Chinese policemen shooting Malays or Malay policemen shooting Chinese would have caused widespread repercussions. The Gurkhas, on the other hand, were neutral, besides having a reputation for total discipline and loyalty. All this heightened my sense of insecurity and underlined the urgency of building an army to protect our fragile independence.

I had many pressing concerns: first, to get international recognition for Singapore's independence, including our membership in the United Nations (UN). I chose Sinnathamby Rajaratnam (affectionately called Raja by all of us) as foreign minister. He was eminently suitable, with anticolonial nationalist credentials from his student days in London before and during the war, but no rabid radical. Friendly, urbane, sincere, he had the right balance between standing up for principles and the need for diplomatic compromise. He was to be much liked and respected by all those he worked with at home and abroad. As messages of recognition flowed in, Toh Chin Chye, the deputy prime minister, and Raja as foreign minister set off to New York to take our seat at the UN that September of 1965.

My next concern was to defend this piece of real estate. We had no army. Our two battalions were under the command of a Malaysian brigadier. How were we to build up some defense forces quickly, however rudimentary? We had to deter and, if need be, prevent any wild move by the Malay Ultras (extremists) in Kuala Lumpur (KL) to instigate a coup by the Malaysian forces in Singapore and reverse the independence we had acquired. Many Malay leaders in KL believed that Singapore should never have been allowed to leave Malaysia, but should have been clobbered into submission. If anything were to happen to Tunku Abdul Rahman, the prime minister of Malaysia, Tun Abdul Razak would become the prime minister and he could be made to reverse the Tunku's decision by strong-minded Ultra leaders. It was a time of great uncertainty.

While wrestling with these major concerns, I had to attend to another pressing need—keeping law and order. We feared that pro-UMNO Malays would run amok when they realized they had been abandoned by the Malaysian government and were once again a minority. Our policemen were mostly Malays from the kampongs of Malaya and their loyalty would be strained if they had to take action against Malay rioters who wanted to rejoin Malaysia. Our troops, two battalions, were also mostly Malays from Malaya.

To my relief, Goh Keng Swee was willing and eager to take on the task of building up the forces. I decided to have him take charge of home affairs and defense, put together into one ministry called MID (ministry of interior and defense). This would allow him to use the police force to help in the basic training of army recruits. (To this day, license plates of Singapore Armed Forces vehicles carry the letters MID.) Keng Swee's transfer left a void in the finance ministry. I discussed this with him and decided on Lim Kim San as finance minister. Kim San had a practical approach to problems. Moreover, he could work closely with Keng Swee without friction, thus allowing Keng Swee to contribute informally to policies on finance.

My third and biggest headache was the economy—how to make a living for our people? Indonesia was "confronting" us and trade was at a standstill. The Malaysians wanted to bypass Singapore and deal direct with all their trading partners, importers, and exporters, and only through their own ports. How was an independent Singapore to survive when it was no longer the center of the wider area that the British once governed as one unit? We needed to find some answers and soon, for unemployment was alarming at 14 percent and rising. Furthermore, we had to make a living different from that under British rule. I used to see our godowns [warehouses] filled with rubber sheets, pepper, copra, and rattan and workers laboriously cleaning and grading them for export. There would be no more imports of such raw materials from Malaysia and Indonesia for processing and grading. We had to create a new kind of economy, try new methods and schemes never tried before anywhere else in the world, because there was no other country like Singapore. Hong Kong was the one island most like us, but it was still governed by the British and it had China as its hinterland. Economically, it was very much a part of China, acting as China's contact with the capitalist world for trade with noncommunist countries.

After pondering these problems and the limited options available, I concluded an island city-state in Southeast Asia could not be ordinary if it was to survive. We had to make extraordinary efforts to become a tightly knit, rugged, and adaptable people who could do things better and cheaper than our neighbors, because they wanted to bypass us and render obsolete our role as the entrepôt and middleman for the trade of the region. We had to be different.

Our greatest asset was the trust and confidence of the people. These we had earned by the fight we had put up on their behalf against the communists and the Malay Ultras, our refusal to be browbeaten and cowed at a time when the police and the army were both in the hands of the central government. The communists had jeered at my colleagues and me as running dogs of the colonialist imperialists, and cursed us as lackeys and henchmen of the Malay feudalists. But when things got bad, even the skeptical Chinese-speaking left-leaning types saw us, a group of bourgeois English-educated leaders, stand up for them and defend their interests. We were careful not to squander this newly gained trust by misgovernment and corruption. I needed this political strength to maximize what use we could make of our few assets, a natural world-class harbor sited in a strategic location astride one of the busiest sea-lanes of the world.

The other valuable asset we had was our people—hardworking, thrifty, eager to learn. Although divided into several races, I believed a fair and even-handed policy would get them to live peacefully together, especially if such hardships as unemployment were shared equally and not carried mainly by the minority groups. It was crucial to keep united Singapore's multilingual, multicultural, multireligious society, and make it rugged and dynamic enough to compete in world markets. But how to get into this market? I did not know the answer. Nobody had asked us to push the British out. Driven by our visceral urges, we had done so. Now it was our responsibility to provide for the security and livelihood of the 2 million people under our care. We had to succeed, for if we failed, our only survival option would be a remerger, but on Malaysian terms, as a state like Malacca or Penang.

I did not sleep well. Choo got my doctors to prescribe tranquilizers, but I found beer or wine with dinner better than the pills. I was then in my early forties, young and vigorous; however hard and hectic the day had been, I would take two hours off in the late afternoon to go on the practice tee to hit 50 to 100 balls and play nine holes with one or two friends. Still, I was short of sleep. Late one morning, when the newly arrived British high commissioner, John Robb, had an urgent message for me from his government, I received him at home lying in bed, physically exhausted. Harold Wilson, the British prime minister, must have been told of this for he expressed his concern. On 23 August 1965, I replied, "Do not worry about Singapore. My colleagues and I are sane, rational people even in our moments of anguish. We weigh all possible consequences before we make any move on the political chessboard. . . . Our people have the will to fight and the stuff that makes for survival."

While brooding over these daunting problems, on the night of 30 September 1965, alarm bells rang with the news of a coup in Indonesia. Pro-

communist officers had killed six Indonesian generals. A bloodbath followed as General Suharto moved to put down the coup. These further
uncertainties deepened my concerns.


On that 9th day of August 1965, I had started out with great trepidation
on a journey along an unmarked road to an unknown destination.

# 2. Building an Army from Scratch

When Parliament was due to open in December 1965, four months after our separation from Malaysia, Brigadier Syed Mohamed bin Syed Ahmad Alsagoff, who was in charge of a Malaysian brigade stationed in Singapore, called on me and insisted that his motorcycle outriders escort me to Parliament. Alsagoff was a stout, heavy-built Arab Muslim with a moustache, a Singaporean by birth who had joined the Malayan Armed Forces. To my amazement, he acted as if he was the commander in chief of the army in Singapore, ready at any time to take over control of the island. At that time the First and Second Singapore Infantry Regiments (1 and 2 SIR) of about 1,000 men each were under Malaysian command. The Malaysian government had placed 700 Malaysians in 1 and 2 SIR, and posted out 300 Singaporean soldiers to various Malaysian units.

I weighed the situation and concluded that the Tunku wanted to remind us and the foreign diplomats who would be present that Malaysia was still in charge in Singapore. If I told him off for his presumptuousness, Alsagoff would report this back to his superiors in Kuala Lumpur and they would take other steps to show me who wielded real power in Singapore. I decided it was best to acquiesce. So, for the ceremonial opening of the first Parliament of the Republic of Singapore, Malaysian army outriders "escorted" me from my office in City Hall to Parliament House.

Not long after this problem, at 4:00 P.M. on Tuesday, 1 February 1966, Keng Swee suddenly came to my office at City Hall with the troubling news that rioting had broken out at an army training depot at Shenton

Way, next to the Singapore Polytechnic. When he learned to his astonishment that 80 percent of recent recruits to all units were Malays, Keng Swee had given instructions that all recruitment and training should cease and the position be frozen. The army commander misinterpreted this and, on his own initiative, had instructed the Chinese major to discharge all Malay recruits. The major assembled everyone in the parade square, asked the non-Malays to fall out, and told the Malays that they were dismissed. For a few minutes, the Malays were dumbfounded at this discrimination. When they recovered from the shock, bedlam broke out as they attacked the non-Malays with poles, sticks, and aerated water bottles; burnt two motorcycles; damaged a scooter; and overturned a van. A police patrol car responding to an emergency call drove into a barrage of bottles and could not get past the overturned van. A fire engine that arrived later was similarly attacked.

A huge crowd gathered along Shenton Way to watch. Polytechnic students left their classes for a bird's-eye view of the mêlée from the balconies and rooftop. At about 2:45 P.M., the riot squad arrived in their vans and lobbed tear-gas canisters into the crowd. Then specially trained riot police moved in, captured the rioters, bundled them into police vans, and took them across the road to the CID (Criminal Investigation Department) building. They were held at the CID quadrangle pending instructions on whether to charge them and refuse bail, or to let them off on bail.

Keng Swee feared that if they were allowed to go, they would start a riot between Malays and Chinese when they got home to Geylang Serai and other Malay areas and spread the story of how they had been dismissed. I immediately called the British high commissioner, John Robb, to my office. I asked him to alert the British military commander in case intercommunal riots got out of hand as the Singapore police and army were still nearly all Malays who would sympathize with the rioters. I told him that I intended to go to the CID building to sort the problem out myself. If it was possible to defuse it, I would let them go home; otherwise, they might have to be charged and held on remand. In that case, some 365 families would miss their sons that night and rumors would spread throughout Singapore of the Malays being oppressed.

John Robb said he would report the matter but was careful to point out that British forces could not interfere in an internal security problem.

I said the commander in chief or the officer in charge of the British garrison should ensure that British troops were ready to prevent rioters from becoming uncontrollable and turning against the white families as they did in the religious riot involving a Dutch girl in 1950.

I tested out my approach on Othman Wok, the minister for social affairs, and had him accompany Keng Swee and me to meet the men at the CID. At the quadrangle, speaking to them in Malay through a hand-held battery-powered loudspeaker, I said that the major had misunderstood his orders, which were to take on only Singapore citizens. He mistakenly thought this meant no Malays were to be recruited whereas Malays who were Singapore citizens were eligible. Ten of them identified as ringleaders of the riots would be detained and charged by the police, but the rest could go home. They were not to spread rumors when they got home. If any one of those allowed to go home was subsequently identified as a rioter, he would also be charged. I added that all those who were Singapore citizens had to report back to camp the following day for normal training. Only citizens were eligible and those who were not had to seek employment in Malaysia. The prospect of jobs brought applause and cheers. I had to make a decision on the spot; the least risky option was to hold and punish a few ringleaders but allow the majority to go home. I hoped they would behave themselves because of the prospect of jobs.

At a press briefing, I asked the reporters to report the matter tactfully, especially in the Malay paper. When I read the newspapers the next morning, I heaved a sigh of relief. Fourteen men were charged with rioting but the attorney general later decided that it was best to withdraw the charges. This was a sharp reminder to the government that we had to deal with matters of race with the utmost sensitivity.

We had another anxious time in November 1967 when Chinese-Malay clashes broke out in Penang and Butterworth, a town on the peninsula opposite Penang island. The racial situation had deteriorated rapidly in Malaysia after Singapore's separation. Chinese anger and resentment were mounting against their government's Malay-language policy. It was sufficiently alarming for us to form a ministerial committee, with Goh Keng Swee as chairman and top officials from the police and the army as members, to prepare contingency plans in case racial riots broke out in peninsular Malaysia and spilled over to Singapore.

Tan Siew Sin, the Malaysian finance minister, had unwisely decided after the British pound was devalued that even for small change there would have to be an adjustment between the old coins issued by the British colonial government, which had been devalued by about 14 percent, and the new Malaysian coins. This led to sporadic hartals (stoppage of work in protest), which in turn led to racial clashes. Chinese from rural areas were moving into the towns and we feared that if widespread racial conflicts broke out, the Malaysian armed forces would have difficulty dealing with trouble in many towns.

Concern that these riots could involve Singapore forced us to build up our armor quickly. In January 1968, we decided to buy French-made AMX-13 light tanks that the Israelis were selling at discounted prices because they were upgrading their armor. Thirty refurbished tanks arrived by June 1969 and another 42 in September 1969. We also bought 170 four-wheeled V200 armored vehicles.

The British had made no offer to help us build an army as they had done with the Malayans in the 1950s. They had worked behind the scenes to get a fair deal for Singapore in Malaysia and incurred the displeasure of the Malaysians. Now they had to deal with a Malaysia more than a little unhappy with them. And because the Malaysians had sponsored us for membership both to the Commonwealth and the United Nations, the British must have guessed that the Malaysians would also want to be our military instructors, if for no other reason than to make sure we were not taught more than they knew about defense.

We had to get back our two regiments and restore their Singapore identity to ensure their loyalty. Goh Keng Swee, then finance minister, had offered to be defense minister immediately at independence. He was willing to build an army from scratch, although all he knew of military matters was learned as a corporal in the British-led Singapore Volunteer Corps until it surrendered in February 1942. I told him to get going. Keng Swee contacted Mordecai Kidron, the Israeli ambassador in Bangkok, for help. A few days after separation on 9 August, Kidron flew in from Bangkok to offer assistance in military training, and Keng Swee brought him to see me. Kidron had approached me several times in 1962–1963 to ask for an Israeli consulate in Singapore. He had assured me the Tunku had agreed and that we need not wait until Malaysia was established. I replied that if the Tunku had agreed, there should be no trouble in setting it up after Malaysia was formed, but if I did so before that, I would create an issue that would excite the Malay Muslim grassroots and upset my plans for merger. He was disappointed. As I had expected, when Malaysia came about, the Tunku could not and did not allow an Israeli consulate.

I listened to Kidron's proposal on military training but told Keng Swee to put it on hold until Lal Bahadur Shastri, the prime minister of India, and President Nasser of Egypt replied to my letters seeking their urgent help to build up our armed forces.

I had written to Shastri for a military adviser to help us build up five battalions. Two days later, Shastri replied sending "sincere good wishes for the happiness and prosperity of the people of Singapore" but did not mention my request. Nasser, in his reply, extended recognition to Singapore as an independent and sovereign state, but he too did not refer to my request for a naval adviser to build up our coastal defense. I had half expected the Indian government might not want to take sides against Malaysia. India was after all a relatively close neighbor in Asia. But I was disappointed when Nasser, a good friend, opted out. Perhaps it was a case of Muslim solidarity with Malaysia's Muslim leaders.

I told Keng Swee to proceed with the Israelis, but to keep it from becoming public knowledge for as long as possible so as not to provoke grassroots antipathy from Malay Muslims in Malaysia and Singapore. A small group of Israelis led by Colonel Jak Ellazari arrived in November 1965, followed by a team of six in December. To disguise their presence, we called them "Mexicans." They looked swarthy enough.

We had to have a credible force to protect ourselves. I had no fear of the Tunku changing his mind but other powerful Malay leaders, like Syed Ja'afar Albar who so strongly opposed separation that he had resigned as secretary-general of UMNO, might persuade Brigadier Alsagoff it was his patriotic duty to reverse separation. The brigadier with his brigade based in Singapore could have captured me and all my ministers without difficulty. So we maintained a quiet, nonchallenging posture, while Keng Swee as defense minister worked feverishly to build up some defense capability.

We faced another security risk from the racial composition of our army and police. Independent Singapore could not continue the old British practice of having a city three-quarters Chinese policed and guarded by Malay police and soldiers. The British had recruited mostly Malays born in Malaya, who traditionally had come to Singapore to enlist. Malays liked soldiering whereas the Chinese shunned it, a historical legacy of the predatory habits of soldiers during the years of rebellions and warlords in China. The question was whether the army and police would be as loyal to a government no longer British or Malay, but one the Malays perceived as Chinese. We had to find some way to induct more Chinese and Indians into the police and armed forces to reflect the population mix.

Shortly after separation, at the request of the Malaysian government, we had sent the 2nd battalion SIR to Sabah for Confrontation duties. We wanted to demonstrate our good faith and solidarity with Malaysia even though a formal defense treaty had not been concluded. This left their barracks, Camp Temasek, vacant. We then agreed to a Malaysian proposal that one Malaysian regiment be sent down to Camp Temasek. The 2nd battalion SIR was due to return from its duties in Borneo in February 1966, and arrangements were made at staff level for the Malaysian regiment to withdraw. The Malaysian defense minister requested that instead of reoccupying Camp Temasek, one Singapore battalion should be sent to the Malayan mainland to enable the Malaysian regiment to remain where it was. Keng Swee did not agree. We wanted both our own battalions in Singapore. We believed the Malaysians had changed their minds because they wanted to keep one battalion of Malaysian forces in Singapore to control us.

The Malaysians refused to move out, so the SIR advance party had to live under canvas at Farrer Park. Keng Swee saw me to urgently warn that if our troops were under canvas for too long, with poor facilities for their mess and toilets, there was the risk of a riot or a mutiny. He compared himself to a British general in charge of troops the majority of whom were Italians. The Malaysians could take advantage of this and, through Brigadier Alsagoff, mount a coup. He advised me to move from my home on Oxley Road into the Istana Villa in the Istana domain and to post Gurkha police guards around just in case. For the next few weeks, my family and I stayed there with a company of Gurkhas on standby.

Shortly afterward, the British vacated a camp called Khatib in the north of Singapore, near Sembawang. We offered it to the Malaysians and they agreed in mid-March 1966 to move out of our camp to Khatib, where they remained for 18 months before withdrawing of their own accord in November 1967.

Their unreasonableness only made us more determined to build up the Singapore Armed Forces (SAF) so that they could not intimidate us in this way. It stiffened our resolve and made us dig our heels in.

Keng Swee, ever the intrepid fighter, had written in his paper to Defco (Defence Council):

> It is foolish to allow ourselves to be hypnotised by the disparity in the population ratios between Singapore and her neighbours. What counts is the fighting strength of the armed forces, not the size of populations. . . . After five years of conscription we can field an army of 150,000 by mobilising those on the reserve service. By using older persons and women for non-combatant duties we should eventually be able to field an army with a combat strength of 250,000 consisting of men between the ages of 18 and 35. The war-making potential of a small, vigorous, well-educated and highly motivated population should never be underestimated.

This was an ambitious plan based on the Israeli practice of mobilizing the maximum number possible in the shortest time possible. We thought it important for people in and outside Singapore to know that despite our small population, we could mobilize a large fighting force at short notice.

Ours was no easy task. We had to reorientate people's minds to accept the need for a people's army and overcome their traditional dislike for soldiering. Every Chinese parent knew the saying *hao han bu dang bing, hao tie bu da ding* (a good lad does not become a soldier, good steel does not become nails). We set up national cadet corps and national police cadet corps in all secondary schools so that parents would identify the army and police with their sons and daughters. We wanted the people to regard our soldiers as their protectors—a reversal from the days when army and police uniforms aroused fear and resentment as symbols of colonial coercion.

People must admire military valor. As Keng Swee said in sorrow, "The Spartan approach to life does not come about naturally in a community that lives by buying and selling." I had to get people to change their attitudes. We also had to improve the physical condition of our young by getting them to participate in sports and physical activity of all kinds, and to develop a taste for adventure and strenuous, thrilling activities that were not without danger to themselves. Persuasion alone was not enough. We needed institutions, well organized, well staffed, and well directed to follow up the exhortations and stirring speeches. The prime responsibility was that of the ministry of education. Only if we changed people's thinking and attitudes could we raise a large citizen army like Switzerland's or Israel's. We gave ourselves a decade to accomplish this.

On the first anniversary of independence we mustered what little we had to boost our people's morale. We had organized the People's Defence Force (PDF) under the leadership of a motley collection of civil servants, members of parliament (MPs), and ministers who had been put through a crash officer-training course. The soldiers were civilians, mostly Chinese-educated, recruited through the community centers. Several PDF platoons marched on our first National Day celebrations, 9 August 1966. They put up a brave show and were cheered enthusiastically by those behind the saluting dais and by the crowds lining the streets as they recognized their suntanned ministers and MPs in uniform, eager in their stride if lacking in martial bearing.

Our community leaders representing all races took part in the parade bearing banners or slogans. Chinese, Indian, Malay, and British business leaders joined in the contingent that marched past the president in front of City Hall. They were lustily cheered. There were units from the trade unions, the PAP, and the statutory boards. The police and fire brigade were brought in to add to the uniforms on display. The Malaysians might not have been in awe of our military capability, but they could not but be impressed by the determination and the spirit with which we were building up our defense forces to protect our fledgling state.

Keng Swee's original plan was to build up a regular army of 12 battalions between 1966 and 1969. Disagreeing with this plan, I proposed a small standing army plus the capacity to mobilize the whole civilian population who should be trained and put into reserves. Keng Swee argued that we had first to train a good number of regular officers and noncommissioned officers in his 12 battalions before we could train civilians on such a large scale.

I did not want money spent on the recurrent costs of a large army: It was better spent on the infrastructure we needed to raise and train national service battalions. National service would bring political and social benefits. Keng Swee took the professional military view that an immediate threat from Malaysia had to be countered by a solid regular fighting force raised in the next three years. I said the Malaysians were unlikely to attack us while British and Commonwealth forces were in Singapore. Their presence would be a deterrent even without a defense treaty. I wanted the defense plan to aim at mobilizing as large a part of the population as possible, in order to galvanize the people in their own defense while they had this strong feeling of patriotism as a result of their recent experiences.

A revised plan Keng Swee put up in November 1966 would mobilize a large section of the population and keep the regular component of the armed forces at 12 battalions. I was keen to have our women do national service as Israeli women did, because that would reinforce the people's will to defend themselves. But Keng Swee did not want his new ministry to carry this extra burden. As the other ministers in Defco were also not anxious to draft our women, I did not press my point.

The best deterrent to any Malaysian plan to regain control over Singapore was their knowledge that even if they could subdue our armed forces, they would have to keep down a whole people well trained in the use of arms and explosives. Besides integrating the people into a more united community through equal treatment of recruits regardless of their social background or race, we needed to attract and retain some of the best talents in the highest echelons of the SAF. Most important of all, we had to ensure that the SAF remained subordinate to the political leadership by keeping important functions such as manpower and finance under civilian officers in the defense ministry. Defco endorsed all these objectives.

In February 1967, I tabled legislation to amend the National Service Ordinance which had been passed by the British in 1952. Those who enlisted in the SAF as a full-time career would be guaranteed jobs in the government, statutory boards, or the private sector when they left full-time service to go into the reserves. There was full public support when the bill was passed a month later. I recalled the first call-up in 1954 under this same ordinance and the riots by Chinese middle-school students. This time we had no problems getting 9,000 young men registered in the first batch. I was right about the changed public attitude.

Meanwhile, Keng Swee assembled a team and, with Israeli help, started the buildup. He made use of police personnel, communications equipment, and other assets to kick-start the process. The assistant commissioner for police, Tan Teck Khim, became director general staff.

We began training a select group in August 1967, the top 10 percent of the batch registered. To counter the traditional prejudice against soldiery, we held send-off ceremonies for the recruits from community centers in every constituency. MPs, ministers, and community leaders would attend and make short speeches before the recruits mounted the military trucks that took them to basic training camps. Over the years, we gradually broke down the resistance to soldiering.

It was a crash program with everybody on crash courses. There was much confusion. Arrangements were never 100 percent prepared and crisis management was the order of the day, but it was an urgent and crucial task that had to be accomplished in the shortest possible time. We had to achieve it with men of little experience and unexceptional ability. But the esprit de corps was excellent and they made progress.


While we made haste in the buildup, we had another uneasy period in October 1968, after two Indonesian commandos were hanged for killing three Singapore citizens when they exploded a bomb at the Hongkong & Shanghai Bank in Orchard Road in 1964. When their appeals were dismissed by the Privy Council in London, Indonesian President Suharto sent his close aide, a brigadier general, to petition our president for clemency and to commute the death sentence to imprisonment.

The cabinet had met earlier to decide what advice to give the president. We had already released 43 Indonesians detained for offenses committed during Confrontation. In response to Indonesian pleas we had also released two Indonesians convicted and sentenced to death for carrying a time bomb in Singapore. But these persons had been arrested before they could do harm, unlike the other case, where three civilians had been killed. We were small and weak. If we yielded, then the rule of law not only within Singapore but between our neighbors and Singapore would become meaningless as we would always be open to pressure. If we were afraid to enforce the law while British forces were still in Singapore, even though they had announced that they would be withdrawing by 1971, then our neighbors, whether Indonesia or Malaysia, could walk over us with impunity after 1971. So we decided not to abort the due process of law by acceding to the petition. The two men were hanged on 17 October. I was in Tokyo then on an official visit. Some 20 to 30 Indonesians gathered near the Geihinkan (the Japanese government guesthouse) carrying placards and banners in protest when I drove by.

In Jakarta, an Indonesian crowd rampaged through the Singapore embassy, shattering pictures of the president of Singapore and generally wreaking havoc, but did not burn the embassy as they had done to the British. Our ambassador, P. S. Raman, formerly the director of Radio & Television Singapore, was a stout-hearted Tamil Brahmin and a Christian convert. He and his staff held themselves up with the same aplomb and defiance as Andrew Gilchrist, the British ambassador, had done when Indonesians rampaged through the British embassy in 1963. But unlike Gilchrist, the Singapore embassy staff did not have a bagpiper to add panache to a display of sangfroid.

The next day, ABRI, the Indonesian armed forces, announced that they would hold maneuvers in their territorial waters off the Riau islands close to Singapore. The Indonesian marine commander said that he would personally lead a task force to invade Singapore. A thousand student demonstrators called on the commander of the Indonesian East Java forces to take revenge against Singapore. The press reported that the Indonesian army believed communist China had pressured Singapore to hang the two men. A week later, the Indonesian government announced a curtailment of trade with Singapore, imposing restrictions on exports. Our intelligence assessed that while there would be no open aggression, sabotage was probable. In any event, none took place.

It was a more serious crisis when a tense racial situation enveloped Singapore following bloody race riots in Kuala Lumpur on 13 May 1969, a few days after their general election. It spread alarm among both Chinese and Malays in Singapore; everyone feared that the racial clashes would spill into Singapore, and they did. Malaysian Chinese who had fled to Singapore recounted stories of brutalities inflicted on their relatives there. As news spread of Malay atrocities and the bias of the Malaysian armed forces in dealing with the situation, anger and alarm rose in Singapore.

Taking advantage of their greater numbers in Singapore, the Chinese took revenge for what had happened in Kuala Lumpur. On 19 May, 20 to 30 Chinese youths assaulted several Malays in a Malay area near Sultan Mosque at Sultan Gate. When I returned to Singapore from America on 20 May, I was told that a Malay had been shot and killed by a group of thugs not very far from Raffles Institution. The clashes went on intermittently for several weeks.

On 1 June, I visited the Malay settlement at Geylang Serai, the site of serious race clashes. Lim Kim San as minister of defense accompanied me in a Land Rover driven by a Malay policeman, with the police superintendent for the area sitting beside the driver. Both Kim San and I immediately noticed the sullen, unfriendly looks of our SIR Malay soldiers deployed on the ground. Even the police superintendent, a Malay officer I had known personally for several years, looked sour. I felt strongly that something was amiss. I sensed that the Malays were terrified. The situation was different from the 1964 race riots when the police and army, largely Malays, were controlled by Malay leaders in Kuala Lumpur and had been especially protective of the Malays and punitive toward the Chinese. This time the Malays in Singapore were fearful. Although the police were still largely Malay, Singapore's Chinese leaders who were now in charge of the government might be against them and direct the police and army accordingly. I was determined to make it clear to all, in particular the Chinese, now the majority, that the government would enforce the law impartially regardless of race or religion.

Because of strong police action, 684 Chinese and 349 Malays were arrested but there was not enough evidence to proceed against all. Only 36 persons were charged in court, 18 Chinese and 18 Malays. The most serious charge was against a Chinese for attempted murder. He was found guilty and sentenced to 10 years' imprisonment. One Chinese and 3 Malays had been killed, 11 Chinese and 49 Malays injured.

We were shocked to find how race relations in Singapore had become so polarized. Even Malays who had served in our police and armed forces for many years had become very race conscious, easily swayed by racial pulls during the race riots in Malaysia.

I wanted to be sure that the police and army were not weakened by communal pulls. I also wanted an explanation why so many Malay soldiers were deployed in Geylang Serai where a Chinese minority would have been more reassured by a mixed-race force. I decided we had to review the racial mix of new recruits in the SAF.

Kim San looked into this and found that in spite of the 1966 incident at the Shenton Way army training depot, we had overrecruited Malays into the SAF. George Bogaars, then permanent secretary of the defense ministry and one of our most trusted officers, had been director of Special Branch where he learned to distrust the Chinese-educated because nearly all communists were Chinese-educated. He preferred Malays when recruiting noncommissioned officers and warrant officers for the SAF to train our national servicemen, believing the Chinese-educated were prone to Chinese chauvinism and communism. This bias had to be redressed, a sensitive task that we entrusted to a team headed by Bogaars. A young lieutenant colonel, Edward Yong, implemented a plan that over several years reduced the proportion of Malays, mainly by recruiting more non-Malays.


I had invited the five-power Commonwealth defense ministers (Malaysia, Britain, Australia, New Zealand) to attend our celebrations for the 150th anniversary of the founding of Singapore. Razak, representing Malaysia, attended our National Day parade on 9 August 1969. Kim San arranged for a squadron of AMX-13 tanks and V200 armored vehicles to roll past in the parade. It had a dramatic effect on the people in Johor when they saw it on television that night, and elsewhere in Malaysia the following day in their newspapers which carried photos of the tanks. The Malaysians had no tanks then. At my dinner that night, Razak told Keng Swee that many people in Malaysia were concerned over our armor, but he himself was not. He said there was anxiety in Johor whether Singapore intended to invade the state and suggested that Kim San as defense minister should go to Kuala Lumpur to convince people that Singapore's intentions toward Malaysia were not hostile. Keng Swee's note to Defco concluded, "One bright spot in this whole melancholy episode [the race riots in Kuala Lumpur] is the salutary effect our armour has had on the Malay political base."

It was as well that we had decided to buy tanks and armored vehicles. The 13 May 1969 race riots in Kuala Lumpur polarized race relations in Malaysia, resurrecting my fear that with Tun Abdul Razak now in charge and the Malay Ultras on the ascendant, the Tunku could be shunted aside, and the Ultra leaders could decide to send the army marching down to take Singapore back into the Federation forcibly. I asked Yong Pung How (my friend from Cambridge days then living in Kuala Lumpur, later chief justice of Singapore) when he visited Singapore what the Malaysian public's perception of the SAF was. He said that in 1966, people thought it was all a joke. But this was no longer the case. Word had passed round the cocktail circuit in Kuala Lumpur that the Singapore Armed Forces Training Institute (SAFTI) trained good soldiers and British high commission officials had confirmed this.

By 1971, we had 17 national service battalions (16,000 men), with 14 battalions (11,000 men) in the reserves. We had infantry and commando units; artillery units with mortars; a battalion each of tanks, armored personnel carriers, field engineers, signals, field maintenance, field hospital, and field supply; and a heavy transport company. We had established schools for basic military training and officer cadets, the artillery, engineers, bomb disposal units, and naval training. Our air force had a squadron each of Hunters, Strikemaster trainer aircraft, Alouette helicopters, and transport aircraft.

Until we could achieve a credible defense capability in the 1970s, we had to rely on the British military presence. We had hoped they would stay on for 5 to 10 years, to provide a shield behind which we could build up our own forces. But the British announced their withdrawal in January 1968. This forced us to try to build up one fighter squadron and a small navy capable of coastal defense against infiltrators before they left in 1971. These modest objectives drew down considerable resources from our strapped economy with limited trained manpower. We sent our first batch of six trainee pilots to Britain for training in August 1968, seven months after the withdrawal announcement. By September 1970, we had one squadron of 16 fighter planes (Hawker Hunters) operational in Singapore.

The Israelis helped us plan our naval buildup and the New Zealanders trained our sailors for our fast patrol boats. Two squadrons of three boats each were operational in less than two years. Then we progressed to missile gunboats.

While the Israelis were competent, not only in transmitting military skills but also in imparting the doctrines upon which they based their training, their methods were the exact opposite of the British who had built 1 and 2 SIR in a gradual step-by-step approach, training the officer corps from platoon commanders to company commanders and finally, after 15 or 20 years, to battalion commanders and lieutenant colonels. The Israelis insisted from the very start that our officers learn from them and take over as instructors as soon as possible. Unlike the Americans who, under President Kennedy, sent about 3,000 to 6,000 men in the first batch of "advisers" to help Vietnamese President Ngo Dinh Diem build up the South Vietnamese army, the Israelis sent us only 18 officers. Every job they did was understudied by a Singaporean counterpart, from platoon commanders to company commander, up to director general staff. We co-opted police officers and former Singapore Volunteer Corps officers from British days, those with some military or paramilitary experience. Some were government servants, others were from the private sector. We offered them full-time appointments. The British army placed great store on spit and polish and square bashing to inculcate discipline and obedience to orders from superiors. The Israelis emphasized military skills and high motivation. Smartness on parade and military tattoo, the SAF never learned from the "Mexicans." Whatever smartness the SAF had came from British officers in charge of 1 and 2 SIR in their early years.

Once the Israeli officers led by Ellazari had started work and he had us hooked, Kidron demanded a quid pro quo, that Singapore recognize Israel officially and exchange ambassadors. He was persistent in pressing for this. I told Keng Swee that this was a nonstarter. We would anger the Malay Muslims in Singapore and Malaysia whose sympathies were with their Muslim brothers, the Palestinians and the Arabs. We could not agree to do this even if the Israelis decided to withdraw. When they knew that it was a nonstarter, Tel Aviv sent a message that they understood our position and they would be helpful, but that they hoped we would eventually allow them an embassy in Singapore.

When the Arab-Israeli Six-Day War broke out in June 1967, we were relieved the Israelis were not defeated or our SAF would have lost confidence in their Israeli instructors. When the UN General Assembly was debating the resolution to condemn Israel, Rajaratnam, our foreign minister and an Afro-Asian champion, was all for it. Keng Swee saw me to press Raja to direct our UN delegate not to vote in favor of the resolution or the Israelis would leave.

As I could not attend the cabinet meeting, I stated my position in a note. We had to stand up for the right of small nations to exist. Freedom of navigation of all international highways, such as the Straits of Tiran and the Straits of Malacca, were vital and the UN should play a role in preserving peace or resolving the problem after hostilities. I added that I did not believe the Israeli advisers would leave even if we were to vote for the Afro-Asian resolution. I was in favor of abstaining in the vote. The cabinet agreed with my view. We abstained and the Israelis did not leave. However, now that the Israeli presence in Singapore was well known, we allowed them a diplomatic mission. They wanted an embassy. We decided to allow them a trade representative office first, in October 1968. The following May, after Malay Muslims in Singapore and the region had become accustomed to an Israeli presence, we allowed them to upgrade it to an embassy.

Our reservists had to be ever ready for combat. We changed their title in 1994 from "reservists" to "operationally ready NS men" to emphasize their combat readiness. For a few weeks each year, they do in-camp training in their same units to build up camaraderie. Once every few years, they are sent to Taiwan, Thailand, Brunei, or Australia for brigade-level field exercises or battalion-level live firing exercises. Annual in-camp training is taken seriously by everyone, including employers who have to lose the services of their executives and men for a few weeks each year.

To be effective, the SAF has to mobilize and involve the whole society in defense activities. So, school principals, teachers, parents, employers, and community leaders are brought into a supporting network under a concept called "Total Defense." This keeps morale high.

National service has had a profound impact on Singapore society over the last 30 years. It has become a rite of passage for our young men and a part of our way of life that has helped to unify our people. They learn to live and work closely with each other, regardless of race, language, or religion. Food taboos of Muslims and Hindus are respected, as are all religious rites, from Buddhist, Hindu, Muslim, Sikh to Christian and Zoroastrian. Whether your father is a minister, banker, professional, laborer, taxi driver, or hawker, your military standing depends on your performance.

To have both brains and brawn, Keng Swee and I started to induct some of our ablest students into the SAF in 1971. We selected some of the best officer cadets each year for SAF overseas scholarships to study at Oxbridge and other universities in Britain where they did a full academic course in the humanities, sciences, engineering, or the professions. During their student years they received full pay as lieutenants, besides a scholarship that paid for all fees, board and lodging, and other needs abroad. They had to sign a bond to serve for eight years after graduation. But within that period, they would be sent to America or Britain on two, often three courses: first, specialist training whether in artillery, armor, or signals; in midcareer, staff and command in America or Britain; and finally a course in public or business administration at a top American university such as Harvard or Stanford.

At the end of eight years, they could opt to stay in the SAF, transfer to the public service as administrative officers, the top grade of civil servants, join a statutory board, or leave for the private sector. They would do their annual national service training of two to three weeks. Through this scheme, which I proposed and Keng Swee refined, we recruited some of our best students into the SAF. Without a yearly intake of about 10 of our best students, the SAF would have the military hardware but without the brainpower to use them to best advantage.

The quality of the early batches was reassuring. By 1995, four former SAF scholars, having risen to senior positions, entered politics and later became cabinet ministers: my son, Brigadier General Lee Hsien Loong, Brigadier General George Yeo, Lieutenant Colonel Lim Hng Kiang, and Rear Admiral Teo Chee Hean.

Singapore's limited size was a severe constraint. As our buildup expanded, we needed training areas overseas to deploy a brigade, and later a division. I made a breakthrough in 1975 when President Chiang Ching-kuo allowed our infantry, armor, and artillery to train in Taiwan. We also held combined arms exercises in Taiwan with Siegfried Schulz, a retired general of the Federal Republic of Germany, who accompanied our senior officers on "staff rides" to teach them the finer points of field maneuvers.

President Marcos and the U.S. Defense Department allowed the Republic of Singapore Air Force to use U.S. training facilities at Clark Air Base in the late 1970s. When the Americans left Clark in the 1990s, we moved our training to Australia and America. We had to find unconventional solutions to our problems.

A country's defense capability has to be continually upgraded as new technology, especially information technology, is incorporated into weapons systems. This requires a sound economy that can afford to pay for new weaponry and a highly educated and trained people who can integrate the various arms into one system and operate them efficiently and effectively.

A credible defense capability helps to lower the risk of rash political acts. Whenever they were displeased with us, Malaysian leaders regularly uttered threats in the press to cut off our water supply.

In 1990, when I stepped down as prime minister, *Military Technology,* an international defense journal, wrote, "In 1965, when Singapore became an independent nation, it had virtually nothing in the way of armed forces to defend itself. By 1990, the Singapore Armed Forces (SAF) had grown into a respected and professional force operating modern defence systems that was capable of defending the territorial integrity and independence of the state." Since then, the SAF's capability and readiness have continued to be rated highly by defense journals including *Jane's* and *Asia Pacific Defence Reporter.*

Such an outcome was far from my thoughts in April 1966 when I flew to London hoping for assurance from Prime Minister Harold Wilson that British forces would remain in Singapore for some years.

# 3. Britain Pulls Out

Denis Healey laughed when Keng Swee and I asked him in October 1966 to sell us a squadron of Hawker Hunter fighter aircraft. He wagged his finger at us and asked what we were up to; British forces would look after us. We left London reassured that the Royal Air Force (RAF) would stay in Singapore.

We badly needed the confidence British forces generated. If they were to leave suddenly before we had any capacity to defend ourselves, I did not think we could survive. Their presence gave people a sense of security, without which we would not get investments and be able to export our goods and services. That was the only way we could create enough jobs to absorb our school leavers and prevent massive unemployment. In January that year I had met Harold Wilson, the British prime minister, at an emergency Commonwealth prime ministers' conference in Lagos on Rhodesia's unilateral declaration of independence. In between meetings, we discussed the future of British forces in Singapore. He told me that he might have to take away 25,000 of the 50,000 troops guarding Malaysia. Although he said no decision had yet been made, my impression was that he was moving toward troop reduction.

To get a better understanding of British intentions, I visited London in April 1966 to discuss their defense planning. It was disturbing to discover a growing lobby for withdrawal from east of Suez, both in the Labour and Conservative parties and among their top leader writers and commentators. Healey (corroborated by the British press) said that there were strong advocates in the cabinet for a quick phased withdrawal, with George Brown, no. 2 to Wilson, leading the group. Paul Johnson, the *New Statesman* editor, went so far as to name the year, 1968. This point of view would easily win support from the Labour Party and Labour MPs. Iain MacLeod, a former Conservative minister and now the shadow minister for finance and economic affairs, told me that there were many "Europeans" (those favoring integration with Europe) in his party who were keen on withdrawal.

Wilson, I felt, was committed, at least over this term of office, to carry on with Singapore and Malaysia, and there must have been a quid pro quo from the Americans for Britain to stay. Friendly ambassadors told me that the Americans were helping the British to support the value of the pound sterling, on condition that the British continued to maintain their presence east of Suez. The Americans had good reasons to want the British to stay. By January 1966, their forces in South Vietnam had reached 150,000, and the U.S. Air Force was bombing selected targets in North Vietnam. Later George Brown confirmed to me that the "quid" was U.S. support for the British pound sterling, then overvalued and under pressure.

Denis Healey, the defense secretary, was the most important leader I had to meet after Wilson. I liked him personally. He had a powerful intellect, like a computer which kept on putting out new solutions as more data was fed in, ready to abandon fundamental positions taken earlier. His supple mind and facility with words made him a congenial dinner companion, full of interesting and useful gossip about people I wanted to know more about. But he could be biting in his assessments. He once said of a Commonwealth prime minister, pointing to both sides of his forehead, "He is wood from here to here."

From him I had a good rundown of the position of the Labour ministers. He believed it was possible but difficult for the British government to maintain its military presence in the Far East into the 1970s. In the cabinet, most ministers favored a phased withdrawal within the next five years; only Harold Wilson, Michael Stewart, and Healey himself—"a formidable combination"—were keen on keeping British forces east of Suez in the next decade. I was reassured, for I had met Michael Stewart, the foreign secretary, and found him a steady, dependable man.

Healey said there was a strong body of opinion in the Labour Party that wanted complete withdrawal of British forces from their overseas commitments, believing these forces in the Far East to be less an instrument for the maintenance of peace and security, and more a cat's-paw in the squabbles of regional governments. He warned that Britain's military policy on the Far East might well change in the life of the present government. This uncertainty over the duration of their military presence was a constant worry. Keng Swee and I agreed that whatever the British finally decided, we had to build up a visible defense capability as soon as possible, to make it apparent to our people and our neighbors that we were not defenseless.

The day before my departure, on Monday, 25 April, I had a final meeting with Harold Wilson. He asked about the contribution of British bases to the economy of Singapore. I assessed it at about 20 percent of the gross domestic product (GDP). A rundown of the bases would result in the repatriation of appreciable numbers of Malaysians and Indians. This would be a dislocation of the economy, but I feared most the effect on the morale of our people. It had taken immense effort to get them "off the fence" and to convince them that communism was not the inexorable wave of the future. The withdrawal of British troops and the closure of the bases would lead to a serious erosion of morale. People could be resigned to the inevitability of China's might.

I concluded that Wilson and his government could not do much to help Singapore settle its defense and economic treaty with Malaysia. Their influence had declined, especially with the easing of Confrontation by Indonesia. The visit was as satisfactory as I could have hoped. All the British leaders, particularly Wilson and Healey, stressed that they were badly shaken by the separation, that we should not have taken so drastic a step without consulting them, and at a time when they were defending us against Indonesia's Confrontation. There was a great deal of heart searching then as to whether they should stay on in Southeast Asia. They underlined it to emphasize the gravity of the situation. For the immediate future, I was reassured that Singapore had friends in the Labour government and in the opposition Conservative Party leadership. It would give us a few years—time, I hoped, to get some defense forces built up, revive our economy, resume trade with Indonesia, and, most important of all, get investments in industry.

Wilson showed friendliness in every way during the week I spent in London that April. He had given me lunch at 10 Downing Street with key cabinet ministers and Opposition House of Lords leader, Peter Carrington, and their wives present. In an impromptu speech, he spoke in the warmest terms. In reply I thanked him for his friendship and support.

Soon after I left London, Wilson came under pressure from his Labour Party to cut back on overseas defense commitments. At a Parliamentary Labour Party meeting in June 1966, he had to appeal to their socialist sentiments:

Frankly if we had only ourselves to think of, we would be glad to leave Singapore as quickly as possible. We cannot, however, say, as we do in Aden, that we are not wanted by the local government and local population. Lee Kuan Yew, as good a left-wing and democratic socialist as any in this room, certainly wants us to stay there. Let us remember in the political battles of Southeast Asia and in his own electoral struggles he has shown tremendous courage in fighting communism in an area the communists would dearly like to control.

The government of Singapore as we understand it, is the only democratic socialist government, as we understand the phrase, in Southeast Asia.

His social record, in his housing programme for example, defies challenge in anything that has been done in the most advanced social democratic communities.

After London, I attended a Socialist International conference in Stockholm to keep in touch with British and European socialist party leaders. There I met George Brown over lunch. He spoke in frank and blunt terms; he wanted to pull out from Southeast Asia, the sooner the better. He admitted that he was in a minority, but he intended to persist. Brown said Wilson and Healey had a warm regard for me and the Singapore government, but he was fed up that this was made an excuse for British policy east of Suez. He had wanted to include a firm declaration to pull out in a defense review published in October 1965, but had been outvoted. I argued that if Britain had pulled out, the Americans would not have backed sterling. Then the pound would have been devalued and Labour would have lost the second election. He muttered resentfully that the Lyndon Johnson–Harold Wilson agreement would do Britain no good in the long run.

In July 1966, Healey visited Singapore and told me that troop levels in Singapore and Malaysia would be cut to the position they would have been if there were no Confrontation. He had been to Kuala Lumpur. With a straight face, he said he had told the press that there was no anti-British feeling there and no reason other than Britain's economic difficulties had prevented aid to Malaysia. He winked and said the Malaysians had learned that what he called their "Hate Britain Month" had caused a bad impression and was counterproductive. The Malaysian leaders had reacted angrily to criticism in the British media of their race and language policies and they had gone sour over the British. By the time he arrived, it was "Love Britain Month."

He was jovial, full of bonhomie, and reassuring. There were times when I felt that the British would be able to stay for a decade, into the 1970s. At other moments, I feared that time was fast running out on Wilson and Healey. The mood among British Labour MPs was strongly in favor of cutting defense spending overseas to concentrate resources on Britain itself.

Healey made a second visit to Singapore on 22 April 1967. He made clear that Britain would be out of mainland Asia by the late 1970s. I urged that confidence in the general security of the area be maintained and that there should be no sudden changes.

Healey explained that the decision to pull out had been made for economic, not military, reasons and was therefore unlikely to be changed. There was no other way of resolving Britain's financial problem. There was also fear of Britain becoming involved in a "Vietnam" war. The British were aghast at the bloodletting in Vietnam.

At another meeting, two days later, he tried to soften the blow by talking of significant aid to Singapore; after all, he was talking about cuts, not total withdrawal. He realized the significance of the confidence factor and would try to persuade his colleagues on this. But he had to make long-term plans for British defense and it was not possible to do that bit by bit. He asked about our plans for the naval dockyard. I told him of our intention to have Swan & Hunter (a British firm of shipbuilders) take over and "civilianize" it and that I had already persuaded them to take over our civilian Keppel dockyard, to familiarize themselves with our conditions.

Both Harold Holt, the prime minister of Australia, and Keith Holyoake, the prime minister of New Zealand, had cabled to warn me that heavy reductions in British forces were under consideration and that this would lead to disengagement and dismantlement of the existing framework of Commonwealth defense arrangements.

Among the British military commanders in Singapore there was no expectation of a precipitate withdrawal. In May, a month after Healey's visit, Keng Swee and I had a working dinner with Sir Michael Carver, British commander in chief Far East. Carver was most reassuring. He said the principal role of Singapore's defense forces should be the prevention of a coup from within or from the outside. In the event of sustained hostilities, we would have to depend on allies. His attitude assured me that he expected British forces to stay in Singapore for some time.

In case Carver's political masters were thinking otherwise or were under pressure to do the unthinkable, I wrote to Harold Wilson on 26 May that any talk about "significant aid" had ominous implications. The danger of economic dislocation was secondary compared to the grave danger of damaged confidence when it became known that the British had decided to move out by the mid-1970s. Wilson sent a comforting reply and then invited me to London for preliminary talks.

When Keng Swee and I met Healey in June 1967, he gave a detailed list of the force reductions up to 31 March 1968 and the rundown from 1968 to 1971. After 1971, Britain would have an amphibious force in Southeast Asia, a sort of "policeman on the beat."

Discussions on the economic implications were handled by Keng Swee. Like me, he was more worried over the security than the economic implications of a rundown of British forces. We both felt that we could somehow manage the economic rundown if we had security and confidence was not shaken. I asked an official from the ministry of overseas development who had dealt with problems related to the rundown of British forces in Malta whether abandoned airfields could be put to civilian use. In British experience, he said, abandoned airfields were either reverted to agriculture or in a few instances made available for light industry. I did not think agriculture or light industry at all promising for Singapore and asked that our Economic Development Board be given early access to the three British airfields, Tengah, Seletar, and Changi, to decide how we could use them later.

British military regulations required them to destroy surplus military equipment, but Healey agreed to revise the regulations so that such equipment could be handed over to Singapore for training and other uses. He and his team bent over backward to help. These two meetings were a great relief. We felt confident we could sort out our problems by the mid-1970s. I could not have asked for more. Swan & Hunter had confirmed that the prospects for the naval dockyard at Sembawang were very good, and a committee comprising the Navy Department, Swan & Hunter, and the Singapore government could plan its conversion to commercial use.

In a private discussion on 26 June 1967, Wilson promised that this would be the last defense review for the present Parliament. Healey separately also promised that there would be no further defense reviews. My impression was that Wilson, even more than Healey, wanted to keep open Britain's options east of Suez. What he wanted of me in London was not so much to argue the merits of staying east of Suez but to work on Labour backbenchers and those cabinet ministers who were against staying.

I spoke to Labour backbenchers at the House of Commons later that afternoon. The Afro-Asian scene had changed rapidly, I said. Nehru was dead, Sukarno was discredited, and Mao was involved in the madness of the cultural revolution. Half a million American troops were in South Vietnam. The days of the white man's control of Asia had passed. Instead, some Asians insisted upon Asian solutions to Asian problems so that the big Asian countries could settle their problems with the smaller ones. The smaller ones had the right to ask their friends from the West to help redress the balance.

I spent hours talking to Wilson's ministers. A scheduled half-hour meeting with Jim Callaghan, then chancellor of the exchequer (whom I had met several times over the previous 15 years), went on to one and a half hours. From time to time, whenever the division bells rang, he went out to the lobby to vote but asked me to stay. At the end, he said, "I was for naming a date by which Britain should be off but I will think over what you have told me. At the moment I have an open mind." He asked me to see Roy Jenkins, then home secretary. Roy Jenkins listened to me quietly and said that he would support naming no dates, but that Britain must be off the mainland by 1975.

The minister most opposed to our position was Dick Crossman, then Leader of the House. For one hour, he hectored and berated me for misleading and beguiling his colleagues into staying east of Suez. He set out to shock me by being deliberately rude. He wanted Britain to get out quickly, by 1970. He and his group of MPs wanted savings for more old-age pensions, cheaper interest for home loans, and more votes. In his frustration, he said, "You don't have to worry about me for I am a minority voice in the cabinet for the time being but I am winning, and more and more the Party is coming around to my point of view." Our high commissioner, A. P. Rajah, who was present, thought Crossman was letting off steam because my arguments had strengthened the hand of those who wanted to stay.

I believed we were all right this time, but there was no guarantee there would be no further knocks on the pound, which would lead to another fit of depression in the British cabinet, another defense review, and further watering down of their forces. This danger was one beyond the control even of the British government. The sad fact was the malaise of the British people, and the leadership was not inspiring their people. Both Labour ministers and backbenchers were despondent that they had had to do all the things they had said they did not want to do, including the stop-go economic policy for which they had criticized the Conservative government.

President Lyndon Johnson's papers showed that he had urged Wilson in Washington in June 1967 "not to take any steps which would be contrary to British or American interest and to the interest of the free nations of Asia." But Johnson did not push as hard as his aides had urged in their submissions to him before the meeting. Robert McNamara, Johnson's defense secretary, had written to Johnson as early as December 1965 that America placed a higher value on British presence and commitment in the Far East than in Europe.

The British Defense White Paper published in July 1967 announced their intention to reduce forces in Southeast Asia by 50 percent by

1970–1971 and to withdraw completely by the mid-1970s. A dismayed Harold Holt wrote to Wilson and made his views known to me: "We see the U.K. government as having taken historic decisions to reduce its world role and contract, to a significant degree, from any kind of international responsibility that Britain has carried for many, many years" and that the Australians must now "rethink our whole situation."

Soon afterward, Wilson invited me to speak at his Labour Party annual conference in October 1967. I agreed, knowing he wanted me to talk his party into not opposing his staying on in Singapore. I was their main guest speaker, a fraternal delegate at their eve-of-conference rally on Sunday, 1 October, at Scarborough. I expressed the hope that Singapore's long association with the British over a period of 150 years could allow them to make the disengagement in a way "to give us the best chance of continuing security and stability," and that given a little time and no little effort, we would live as well in the mid-1970s without British base expenditure as we were doing then. I knew the delegates would be preoccupied with Vietnam. Since I could not ignore the subject, I said, "I do not want to sound like a hawk or a dove. If I have to choose a metaphor from the aviary, I would like to think of the owl. Anyone looking at what is happening in Vietnam must have baleful eyes. It need never have been thus. And perhaps it was not the wisest place, nor the safest ground in Asia to have made a stand. But enormous sacrifices have already been expended and in blood, both Vietnamese and American." For that anti-Vietnam audience this was the furthest I could go to hint that if the Americans pulled out, there would be severe repercussions for the rest of Southeast Asia.

Barely six weeks later, without any warning, on Sunday, 18 November 1967, Keng Swee received a message from Callaghan, as chancellor of the exchequer, similar to one he must have sent to all Commonwealth finance ministers, that the British were devaluing the pound sterling from US$2.80 to US$2.40. That meant we had lost 14.3 percent of the reserves we kept in London in sterling. Britain's currency came under selling pressure soon after the Labour government took office in 1964 but we had not moved out our reserves. Their forces were defending us against Indonesian

Confrontation, and we did not want to be blamed for precipitating a deval-uation. Wilson, in a television broadcast that same Sunday evening, said, "We are now on our own; it means Britain first." This was ominous. But Healey was reassuring when he said in the House of Commons on 27 No-vember, "I believe that the whole government share my view, that we must, above all, keep faith with our forces and with our allies in making these cuts. We can have no reversal of the July decisions. . . . That is why my Rt Hon Friend the chancellor [Callaghan] said last Monday that the reductions must be made within the framework of the defence policies announced last summer. Let me tell the Rt Hon Gentleman that these cuts mean no acceleration in the run-down or the redeployment of our forces."

I wrote to thank Healey for his assurance. I was wrong: Healey could not speak for the government. Wilson, the prime minister, was out to save his government. He meant it when he said it was "Britain first." Wilson also said "no area of expenditure can be regarded as sacrosanct." I wrote to Wilson on 18 December to recount how the Singapore government had faithfully supported sterling and lost S$157 million as a result of this devaluation (the Currency Board S$69 million, the Singapore government S$65 million, statutory boards S$23 million). My letter ended: "I would be loath to believe that temporary difficulties could disrupt the trust and confidence we have in each other's good intentions, goodwill and good faith. I shall stand by my statement at Scarborough and on our part we shall see that the last of the British forces will be given a ceremonial send-off when they leave their bases in the mid-70s."

This was a forlorn hope. In the first major crisis of his government, Wilson had no time to save friends and allies, however faithful. Instead of replying, he sent George Thomson, the Commonwealth relations secretary, to see me on 9 January 1968. Thomson was apologetic and defensive. Devaluation, he said, had given the British government a chance once and for all to put the economy right. The defense cuts would mean a fundamen-tal change in the historic role of Britain and its long-term defense structure. The British would remain in Europe, though their capability could be used to help allies outside Europe. I asked about Healey's statement about an amphibious capability in Singapore. That was to be scrapped. No naval forces would be stationed in Southeast Asia after 1971. Asked how firm the decision to pull out by 1971 was, Thomson said it was very firm but they would take into account the views of their Commonwealth partners. Thomson was gentle and friendly in his demeanor. His sympathies were with us. It was an unpleasant task Wilson had given him. To soften the blow, Wilson invited me for discussions at Chequers, the official country home of the prime minister.

In my frustration and anger at this total disregard for undertakings given solemnly, I said that we too could put Singapore's interests first and foremost and protect our sterling balances by moving them out of London. Nevertheless, I decided to go to London and see Wilson at Chequers.

Wilson changed the venue from Chequers to 10 Downing Street on a Sunday. When I arrived at 5:30 P.M., his three senior ministers were present: Denis Healey (defense), George Brown (foreign affairs), and George Thomson (Commonwealth relations). Wilson held out some hope by saying that the cabinet had agreed not to make a final decision until I had met him.

I said any precipitate announcement that all British troops would be off the mainland of Asia by 1971 would shake the confidence of investors, especially those from Hong Kong, and make them go further afield. To restore confidence, Singapore would have to go for massive arms expenditure to make its defense credible. I argued that the British armed services owned valuable real estate in Singapore, homes and barracks worth over £55 million. If the rundown took place over three years, they would not fetch half this price on the open market.

Wilson reiterated what Healey had told me a year earlier in Singapore, that the decision to withdraw was made on economic grounds and could not be altered. The decision on timing, March 1971, was fairly unanimous and his ministers present represented the cabinet view. He was anxious to discuss aid to give real economic relief to Singapore. I replied that security was my main concern, for without it there would be no investments, which we needed much more than aid.

Wilson left the arguments for early withdrawal to Healey while he sat back, sucked at his pipe and looked on sympathetically. From Wilson's body language, I knew it would be impossible to keep him to his original undertaking to stay till the mid-1970s.

The British ministers sympathized with my plight. The most supportive was George Brown. Remembering his strong views when we met in Stockholm in 1966, that British forces should be out of Singapore, I was surprised when he asked how much time I needed. I named 31 March 1973. Years later he told me that U.S. President Johnson had persuaded him that while the Vietnam War continued, America could not replace British forces in the Arabian Gulf and Singapore, and that the British contribution was politically invaluable.

At about 7:00 P.M., Roy Jenkins, who had replaced Callaghan as chancellor of the exchequer, joined us. He pitched in on a related subject, that Singapore's economic position stood out from those of other countries in the region. We were doing well. The position in Britain was quite serious. He compared British and Singapore reserves to show that, per capita, the figure for Britain was smaller than Singapore's. He criticized the Singapore government for investing its budgetary surplus elsewhere without informing the British government. He was on the offensive. We had never taken any of our reserves out of sterling. But we had not given any undertaking to put our budgetary surpluses into sterling. He had scored a point, that we were not as helpful as we could have been and could not expect special consideration now.

We talked through dinner, repeating arguments again and again as we drank liberal glasses of claret—Jenkins's favorite wine. We finished at 10:50 P.M. after five and a half hours. Wilson, summing up, said the British government accepted the need to help maintain confidence in Singapore. But he emphasized that there could be no permanent security for Singapore except in the framework of a wider regional defense agreement with other Commonwealth countries concerned. It was inadvisable for Singapore to make hasty decisions on the purchase of military equipment before the possibility of such an arrangement had been explored in greater detail. His government would do all they reasonably could, consistent with their overriding aim (total withdrawal by 1971), to help Singapore maintain security and hoped that the Singapore government would take full account of British advice.

The next day, Monday, 15 January 1968, in the House of Commons, Healey announced that British forces east of Suez would withdraw in 1971, but he shifted the actual date for final withdrawal from March to December 1971. This difference of nine months was significant because a general election would have to be held before December 1971. In other words, the decision on the final date of withdrawal could either be confirmed by a new Labour government or postponed by a Conservative government. I had to be satisfied with this concession. Defense correspondents reporting Healey's speech noted that he had left this opening. My trip to London had not been altogether in vain.

But Wilson knew this was the end of an era. In the debate he quoted from Kipling's "Recessional":

> *Far-called our navies melt away*
> *On dune and headland sinks the fire*
> *Lo, all our pomp of yesterday*
> *Is one with Nineveh and Tyre.*

During those five days in London in January 1968 I worked hard to prolong the British presence. Besides discussions with Wilson, I took my case to Conservative Party leaders, primarily Ted Heath, Reginald Maudling, and Iain MacLeod. They were most sympathetic and supportive; if they were the government, they would have wished to stay longer without naming a withdrawal date. That made a difference to the actual final outcome. British television and press gave me extensive coverage. I was able to put across a reasoned, not an angry, case. I tugged at the heartstrings of the British people, that our long and fruitful association should not end in an unseemly way which would damage Singapore's future. I had put on the best face possible. But Keng Swee, who flew back to Singapore ahead of me, voiced his frustrations to the press at Singapore airport: "The Labour Party has gone back on its word—a disgraceful breach of an undertaking given to us."

I saw no point in venting my spleen. My other colleagues, including Raja, Chin Chye, and Sui Sen, were deeply disappointed and apprehensive of the implications for our security and economy. But they did not berate the British. Angry words would only annoy British ministers and ruffle British service commanders in Singapore who, after all, were loyal Britishers. I needed goodwill and cooperation from the British to execute the withdrawal with the minimum of friction and the maximum of goodwill, and not have military workshops stripped bare as had happened in Guinea (West Africa) when the French left in the 1960s.

This sudden turn of events added to the pressure on us. Our economic problems would mount, as would unemployment. Our defense problems had widened with the need for an air force. How were we to build up an air force from scratch and have a squadron of fighter aircraft operational by the end of 1971? When we saw Healey a second time about buying a squadron of Hawker Hunters, he readily agreed. He would also help build up our capability to operate them, a total change from his attitude in October 1966, less than two years earlier, when he had wagged his finger at us for harboring "mischievous" thoughts.

The British media were sympathetic but on the whole pessimistic about Singapore's future. Singapore would lose about 20 percent of its GDP with the end of British military spending, and without British military protection, they saw the future as precarious. The chairman of the Daily Mirror Group, Cecil King, was at my press conference on my return to Singapore from London in January. He told my press secretary, Alex Josey, that his heart went out to me but the situation was hopeless. With high unemployment and no security after the withdrawal of the British, the economy must decline. King was not alone in holding such a pessimistic view of Singapore's prospects.

To fill the vacuum that followed the ending of the Anglo-Malayan Defense Agreement (AMDA), the British had proposed a Five-Power Defense Arrangement (FPDA) that would be consultative, not a binding defense obligation. I knew the Australians were fearful that the Indonesians would have the wrong impression, that the five powers—the United Kingdom, Australia, New Zealand, Malaysia, and Singapore—were ganging up against Indonesia. In February 1968, Paul Hasluck, Australia's external affairs minister, when in Singapore, had told me that Australia would maintain its force levels till the end of 1971, after which his government was uncertain. In other words, the Australian forces could leave together with the British. I stressed to him that it was necessary to make clear to everyone that it was not the intention of the Western allies to leave a vacuum in the area after 1971, which could be filled by either Russia or China or anybody else. He stressed that Malaysia-Singapore cooperation was fundamental to Australian defense planning. I assured him that we regarded any attack on Malaysia as a threat to Singapore, but I encouraged him to make it clear to the Malaysians that any bilateral agreement with Australia that excluded Singapore was simply not on. I described how on my trip to Melbourne for Prime Minister Harold Holt's memorial service in December 1967, Razak was on the same aircraft but virtually ignored me. But after McEwen, the Australian deputy prime minister who was acting as prime minister before John Gorton took over, had rebuffed him in blunt terms when he tried for a bilateral agreement between Australia and Malaysia, Razak was all reasonableness and accommodation as he spent three hours in the aircraft with me discussing Malaysia's defense and security. Singapore-Malaysia bilateral relations on defense improved considerably after this.

Indeed, Razak told Kim San and Keng Swee in March 1968 that the security of both countries was inseparable, that Malaysia could not afford heavy military expenditure and Singapore, being a small island and very vulnerable to sneak attacks, should concentrate on its air defense capability while Malaysia with its long coastline would concentrate on its navy. This way we would complement each other. "As two separate territories, we talk to one another as equals. Wherever we can agree, we work together. If we cannot agree, well, we wait a while."

Shortly after the race riots in Kuala Lumpur in May 1969, followed by the suspension of the Malaysian Parliament, Razak had to represent Malaysia in Canberra at a meeting of prime ministers of the five powers, to discuss defense arrangements after the British pullout in 1971. Before the conference started, the Australian permanent secretary of defense told us that his prime minister, John Gorton, would not be attending the conference. In a private discussion, the permanent secretary in their external affairs department said Gorton doubted the Malaysian government's ability to contain the situation and believed further racial trouble would break out and Singapore would be "sucked into" the conflict. Gorton had totally lost confidence in Malaysia. He did not want to commit Australia to any defense arrangement with Malaysia. The Australians were already most unhappy that the British were leaving the region and they did not want to be saddled with responsibility for the defense of Malaysia and

Singapore. Gorton foresaw disaster and was fearful of the electorate's reaction to any new commitments Australia might make for the defense of Malaysia and Singapore.

At the last moment, however, he came to open the conference but left immediately after his speech. He stressed the need for racial harmony in the area and for a categorical assurance from Malaysia and Singapore that their defense was "indivisible." Razak and his Malaysian officials looked extremely depressed.

That night I talked to Razak in his hotel room. I decided to set aside my reservations and support his bid that, after 1971, the commander for the Five-Power Defense Arrangement should be responsible to representatives of the five powers and not just to Singapore and Malaysia as Australia proposed. This cheered Razak. Toward the end of the conference Gordon Freeth, the Australian external affairs minister, clarified that if Malaysia were attacked, Australian troops could be deployed in either East or West Malaysia.

The Conservatives in Britain had been aghast at withdrawing their forces east of Suez. In January 1970, Edward Heath, as Leader of the Opposition, visited Singapore. I arranged for him to have discussions with all key ministers to get a comprehensive view of our economic development, the progress in our defense buildup and an overview of the political and social situation. I arranged for the RAF to give him a bird's-eye view of the island from a helicopter. He was impressed and told the press he would "halt" Labour's policy of withdrawal from east of Suez. He said, "There won't be any question of British forces having been withdrawn and British forces coming back. It will be a question that British forces are still here and we as a Conservative government will halt the withdrawal." He added he was "immensely impressed with the really remarkable achievements which had been brought to the island. . . . The basis for all of this is confidence in the future and peace and stability in the whole area." I hoped the British service commanders would take note and not be too hurried in their withdrawal.

Five months later, in June 1970, the Conservative Party won the general election and Edward Heath became prime minister. His defense minister, Peter Carrington, visited Singapore that same month to announce that withdrawal would proceed as planned, but that Britain would retain some of its forces in Singapore on an equal basis with the Australians and New Zealanders. Privately, Carrington told me that Britain would not leave behind any fighter or transport squadrons. There would be only four Nimrod surveillance aircraft, a flight of Whirlwind helicopters, and a battalion would be stationed at Nee Soon, one of their camps. There would be five frigates/destroyers stationed throughout east of Suez and the Anglo-Malayan Defense Agreement would be replaced by a "political commitment of a consultative nature." The British made it clear they wanted to participate, not as the leader, but as a partner "on an equal basis" in the Five-Power Defense Arrangement being planned.

In mid-April 1971, the five prime ministers met in London to finalize the political arrangements to replace AMDA. The operative words read, "In the event of any form of armed attack externally organised or supported, or the threat of such attack against Malaysia or Singapore, the governments would immediately consult together for the purpose of deciding what measure should be taken jointly or separately in relation to such attack or threat." To "immediately consult" was better than not consulting.

On 1 September 1971, the integrated air defense system was established. On 31 October 1971, the AMDA was replaced by the FPDA. The old era of underwritten security had ended. From now on we had to be responsible for our own security.

But security was not our only concern. We had to make a living, to persuade investors to put their money into manufacturing plants and other businesses in Singapore. We had to learn to survive, without the British military umbrella and without a hinterland.

# 4. Surviving Without a Hinterland

In 1965, a few months after independence, an economic planner whom the Indian government had seconded to us presented me with a thick volume of his report. I scanned the summary to confirm that his plans were based on a common market with Malaysia. I thanked him, and never read it again. He did not understand that if Malaysia was not willing to have a common market while Singapore was a part of it, it was hardly likely to agree now we were independent. We were stripped of our role as the administrative, commercial, and military hub of the British Empire in Southeast Asia. Unless we could find and attach ourselves to a new hinterland, the future was bleak.

A few weeks earlier, I had met Dr. Albert Winsemius, our Dutch economic adviser. He painted a grim but not hopeless picture. Because of Confrontation by Indonesia, unemployment had risen. If we continued with no common market with Malaysia and no trade with Indonesia, by the end of 1966 unemployment would exceed 14 percent. This would mean social unrest. "Singapore is walking on a razor's edge," he said. He recommended a common market agreement with Malaysia (which was a nonstarter) and a resumption of barter trade with Indonesia. He also advised that we seek more favorable entry for Singapore-manufactured goods into the United States, the United Kingdom, Australia, and New Zealand.

Winsemius first came to Singapore in 1960 when he led a United Nations Development Program (UNDP) mission to advise us on industri-

alization. I remember his first report to me in 1961 when he laid two preconditions for Singapore's success: first, to eliminate the communists who
made any economic progress impossible; second, not to remove the statue
of Stamford Raffles. To tell me in 1961, when the communist united
front was at the height of its power and pulverizing the PAP government
day after day, that I should eliminate the communists left me speechless
as I laughed at the absurdity of his simple solution. To keep Raffles'
statue was easy. My colleagues and I had no desire to rewrite the past and
perpetuate ourselves by renaming streets or buildings or putting our faces
on postage stamps or currency notes. Winsemius said we would need
large-scale technical, managerial, entrepreneurial, and marketing know-
how from America and Europe. Investors wanted to see what a new socialist government in Singapore was going to do to the statue of Raffles.
Letting it remain would be a symbol of public acceptance of the British
heritage and could have a positive effect. I had not looked at it that way,
but was quite happy to leave this monument because he was the founder
of modern Singapore. If Raffles had not come here in 1819 to establish a
trading post, my great grandfather would not have migrated to Singapore
from Dapu county in Guangdong province, southeast China. The British
created an emporium that offered him, and many thousands like him, the
opportunity to make a better living than in their homeland which was
going through turmoil and chaos as the Qing dynasty declined and disintegrated.

Now, in 1965, we too faced a future so bleak that I asked Kim San,
then minister of finance, to send a trade delegation from our four chambers of commerce and the manufacturers' association to Africa on "the off-
chance of picking up some business." The delegation went to East and
West African countries, but little trade followed.

After grappling with the problem of unemployment for years since we
first took office in 1959, all of us in the cabinet knew that the only way to
survive was to industrialize. We had reached the limits of our entrepôt
trade. The outlook was a further decline. Confrontation from Indonesia
was still on and the Malaysians were determined to bypass Singapore. We
cast around for solutions and were willing to try any practical idea that
could create jobs and enable us to pay our way. One of our soft drink manufacturers suggested to me that we promote tourism; it was labor-

intensive, needing cooks, maids, waiters, laundrymen, drycleaners, tour guides, drivers, and makers of souvenir handicraft. Best of all, it required little capital. We formed the Singapore Tourist Promotion Board and appointed our film magnate, Runme Shaw of Shaw Brothers, as chairman. He was the right man for the job. He was in the film and entertainment industry and knew all about the packaging and selling of sights and sounds, and how to keep visitors amused while in a strange country. He had a logo designed, the "merlion," a lion with a mermaid's tail. I launched the logo erected in concrete at the mouth of the Singapore River. I did little else for the tourist industry except to speak at the occasional convention of visiting professionals or businesspeople. To my relief it did create many jobs and put coins into many empty pockets. It reduced but did not solve the unemployment problem.

For that, we concentrated on getting factories started. Despite our small domestic market of 2 million, we protected locally assembled cars, refrigerators, air conditioners, radios, television sets, and tape-recorders, in the hope that they would later be partly manufactured locally. We encouraged our own businesspeople who set up small factories to manufacture vegetable oils, cosmetics, mosquito coils, hair cream, joss paper, and even mothballs! And we were able to attract Hong Kong and Taiwanese investors to build factories for toys, textiles, and garments.

It was an unpromising start. The Jurong industrial estate in the west of Singapore was empty in spite of the vast sums we had spent on infrastructure. We had more than our share of failures. Short of water and too small to tolerate heavy pollution of coastal waters, the Economic Development Board (EDB) nevertheless went into a joint venture to recycle paper products, with a businessman who had no manufacturing experience. It also invested in ceramics when we did not have the technical know-how. Both ventures failed. We had a joint venture with IHI (Ishikawajima-Harima Heavy Industries) in Jurong Shipyard for shipbuilding and ship repairing and started to build 14,000-dwt (dead-weight tons) Freedom-type vessels and later 90,000-dwt tankers. But Singapore produced neither steel plates nor engines and had to import them from Japan. After 16 Freedom-type vessels and three tankers, we stopped building ships, except for small vessels of 10,000 dwt. It was not profitable, unlike ship repairing for which the labor content was high.

In the early years any factory was welcome. For example, when I was in London in January 1968 to discuss the British withdrawal, Marcus Sieff, the chairman of Marks & Spencer's, saw me at my London hotel. He had seen me on BBC television. He suggested that as Chinese had nimble fingers, Singapore could go into making fishhooks and lures for trout fishing. This was high-value work because the feathers had to be skillfully attached to the hooks. There were other such products that did not require much capital equipment but created many jobs. His retail network could help market the goods. I must have looked forlorn on television for him to have taken the time to see me. I thanked him but nothing came of it. Not long after, a Norwegian manufacturer of fishhooks, Mustad, set up a factory in Singapore, employing several hundred workers to make millions of fishhooks of all shapes and sizes, though not with feathers for trout fishing.

The loss of British military expenditure between 1968 and 1971 was a blow to our economy. It was some 20 percent of our GDP, providing over 30,000 jobs in direct employment and another 40,000 in support services. I was determined that our attitude to British aid, indeed any aid, should be the opposite of Malta's. When I visited Malta in 1967 to see how it had sorted out its problems after the rundown of the British forces, I was astounded. The Suez Canal had been closed as a result of the Arab-Israeli Six-Day War three months earlier, in June. Ships were no longer going through the Canal, hence the dockyard in Malta was closed, but dockworkers on full pay were playing water polo in the dry dock which they had filled with water! I was shaken by their aid dependency, banking on continuing charity from the British. The British had given fairly generous redundancy payments, including five weeks' salary for each year of service, and had also covered the cost of three months' retraining in Maltese government institutions. This nurtured a sense of dependency, not a spirit of self-reliance.

Healey in 1967 had promised "significant aid" to offset the loss from the rundown of British forces. I was convinced our people must never have an aid-dependent mentality. If we were to succeed we had to depend on ourselves. Even before talks on British aid commenced, I had said in

Parliament on 9 September 1967, "There was a thriving Singapore before the bases were built and manned. If we set about it intelligently and in good heart, there will be a bigger and economically more self-reliant Singapore after the bases have been run down." My attitude was that we wanted the British to give us the earliest notice of those facilities, like the naval dockyard, they would find redundant and hand them over to civilian management while still in military use. Next, assistance should provide Singapore with jobs through industries and not make us dependent on perpetual injections of aid. I warned our workers, "The world does not owe us a living. We cannot live by the begging bowl."

Hon Sui Sen, our most capable permanent secretary, drew up a list of British assets that could be converted to civilian use. The British outlined their approach to the 15,000 acres of real estate they occupied, 11 percent of Singapore's total area. Land to be used for economic or defense purposes would be made available without charge. The Singapore government was to help sell the remaining land on the open market. But in January 1968, before the negotiations were concluded, the British announced their total withdrawal by 1971.

On my return to Singapore that January, I said in a broadcast, "If we were a soft society then we would already have perished. A soft people will vote for those who promised a soft way out, when in truth there is none. There is nothing Singapore gets for free, even our water we pay for. . . . There will be a throbbing and humming industrial, commercial and communication centre long after the British have gone." I felt strongly that the people's morale and confidence would be decisive in the coming battle for Singapore's survival.

That February, we formed the Bases Economic Conversion Department with Sui Sen in charge. I placed it under my portfolio in the Prime Minister's Office to give Sui Sen more clout when dealing with other ministries. His job was to retrain and redeploy redundant workers, take possession of land and other assets the British were vacating, put them to the best use, and negotiate mitigatory aid.

It was important we did not generate rancor and friction over the handover of properties or the provision of aid. To do so would undermine confidence, and whatever aid we might get could never make up for the loss of confidence if relations with the British soured. Moreover, I still hoped for some residual presence of British, Australian, and New Zealand forces after 1971. I told the newly arrived British high commissioner, Sir Arthur de la Mare, in February 1968 that Singapore would accept whatever his government gave, but would not press them. I asked that his government leave whatever it had no further use for instead of destroying it as was the practice. This would create goodwill and sustain pro-British sentiments in Singapore.

By March 1968 the discussions concluded with a £50 million aid package to be spent on British goods and services. Of this, 25 percent were grants, 75 percent loans. We spent half on development projects and half on British defense equipment. The British agreed to hand over the naval dockyard at Sembawang including two valuable floating docks the Royal Navy could easily have towed away, provided the Singapore government appointed Swan & Hunter as managing agents under a five-year contract. I had met Sir John Hunter when I was in London in June 1967, and again in October when I visited his dockyards on Tyneside after the Labour Party conference in Scarborough. The Americans, who were anxious to keep the naval dockyard viable, sent army and navy teams in January and February to inspect the facilities. In April 1968 Sui Sen told me the United States would test-use Sembawang's ship-repair facilities from April to June 1968 and provide S$4 to 5 million of business. That was most encouraging.

This conversion of the naval dockyard to civilian use was successful. Swan & Hunter prospered both at Keppel, our civilian dockyard, and at Sembawang. When two 5-year contracts ended in 1978, one of their top managers, Neville Watson, stayed on with Sembawang Shipyard Limited, the company we had formed to run the dockyard. Eventually he became its chief executive. The company prospered and grew to become SembCorp Industries, a conglomerate listed on the Stock Exchange of Singapore.

Blakang Mati (behind death), an island off Singapore's harbor housing a British Gurkha battalion, became "Sentosa" (tranquillity), a tourist resort. Dr. Winsemius got me to stop it from becoming a military training area, a casino, or an oil refinery, proposals put up by various ministries to the Bases Economic Conversion unit under Sui Sen. I did not need persuading to veto these proposals. Fort Canning, with all its tunnels and bunkers, the British Army headquarters before the Japanese capture of Singapore, has also been preserved, the buildings turned into a clubhouse for leisure and recreation. Seletar military airfield was converted to civilian use for small cargo planes and small commercial aircraft. The RAF Changi air base has been expanded by land reclamation and developed into Changi International Airport with two runways. The Pasir Panjang military complex is now the National University of Singapore campus at Kent Ridge with 26,000 students.

In his quiet, methodical way Sui Sen converted the real estate to economic use, and his EDB staff attracted investors from around the world to set up industries on former British army land. It was our good fortune that the real estate handover started in 1968 and was completed by 1971, before the oil crisis in 1973. A buoyant world economy, with world trade expanding at about 8 to 10 percent per annum, made it easier to convert them to civilian use.

The withdrawal was carried out with goodwill on both sides. The 30,000 retrenched workers were absorbed by industries we attracted from abroad. When the withdrawal was completed in 1971, our people were quietly confident. There was no unemployment, and no land or building was left idle or derelict. The single British battalion with a squadron of helicopters, together with the Australian and New Zealand battalions that formed the FPDA, contributed to stability and security.

After I had settled policies to counter the loss of British military spending, in the autumn of 1968, I took a short sabbatical at Harvard. I had been in office for nine years and needed to recharge my batteries, get some fresh ideas and reflect on the future. The Kennedy School of Government made me an honorary fellow and arranged breakfasts, lunches, dinners, and seminars for me to meet a host of distinguished scholars. During the exchanges, they sparked off many useful and interesting ideas. I learned much about American society and economy by reading and talking to Harvard Business School professors such as Professor Ray Vernon. Vernon gave me a valuable lesson on the ever-changing nature of technology, industry, and markets, and how costs, especially wages in labor-intensive industries, determined profits. That was how Hong Kong entrepreneurs were able to build up such a successful textile and garments industry. They had been nimble, changing their product lines, patterns, and designs with changing fashions. It was a never-ending competition against other equally agile and lower-cost producers in Taiwan and South Korea. And their sales promoters were frequently flying to consult their buyers in New York and other big cities. He dispelled my previous belief that industries changed gradually and seldom moved from an advanced country to a less-developed one. Reliable and cheap air and sea transport made it possible to move industries into new countries, provided their people were disciplined and trained to work the machines, and there was a stable and efficient government to facilitate the process for foreign entrepreneurs.

On my first official visit to America in October 1967, I recounted to 50 businesspeople at a luncheon in Chicago how Singapore had grown from a village of 120 fishermen in 1819 to become a metropolis of 2 million. This was because its philosophy was to provide goods and services "cheaper and better than anyone else, or perish." They responded well because I was not putting my hand out for aid, which they had come to expect of leaders from newly independent countries. I noted their favorable reaction to my "no begging bowl" approach.

In November 1968, I went to New York to address some 800 top decisionmakers at the Economic Club of New York. My hard-headed and realistic analysis of Singapore's problems and the dangers in the region, especially the war in Vietnam, was well received. I took pains to end on a sober but upbeat note, painting a silver lining on somber clouds. I answered their difficult questions frankly and directly. Several of the executives wrote to congratulate me, and after that night Chan Chin Bock, our EDB chief in New York, found it much easier to get access to top American executives. Thereafter, every time I visited America, he would arrange for me to meet 20 to 50 executives. The usual format was drinks before lunch or dinner, conversation at the main table with the important CEOs, then a 20-minute speech followed by questions and answers. Chin Bock explained that most American CEOs had no time to visit Singapore, but they wanted to see and assess the man in charge before they set up a factory there. My meetings were productive because Winsemius had told me how their minds worked; his son was working for a large American business consultancy firm and knew exactly how Americans weighed business risks. They looked for political, economic, and financial stability and sound labor relations to make sure that there would be no disruption in production that supplied their customers and subsidiaries around the world.

That December, I met another group of American executives in the Far East American Council. Originally only 100 were to attend. After that Economic Club dinner, word got around that I was worth listening to, and the numbers swelled to 200. In a note to the cabinet I grumbled, "Eating and talking through the meal while conserving energy and not letting myself go and drink in case I lose my sharp cutting edge is quite a strain. It is part of the price to promote American investments."

After several years of disheartening trial and error, we concluded that Singapore's best hope lay with the American multinational corporations (MNCs). When the Taiwanese and Hong Kong entrepreneurs came in the 1960s, they brought low technology such as textile and toy manufacturing, labor-intensive but not large-scale. American MNCs brought higher technology in large-scale operations, creating many jobs. They had weight and confidence. They believed that their government was going to stay in Southeast Asia and their businesses were safe from confiscation or war loss.

I gradually crystallized my thoughts and settled on a two-pronged strategy to overcome our disadvantages. The first was to leapfrog the region, as the Israelis had done. This idea sprang from a discussion I had with a UNDP expert who visited Singapore in 1962. In 1964, while on a tour of Africa, I met him again in Malawi. He described to me how the Israelis, faced with a more hostile environment than ours, had found a way around their difficulties by leaping over their Arab neighbors who boycotted them, to trade with Europe and America. Since our neighbors were out to reduce their ties with us, we had to link up with the developed world—America, Europe, and Japan—and attract their manufacturers to produce in Singapore and export their products to the developed countries.

The accepted wisdom of development economists at the time was that MNCs were exploiters of cheap land, labor, and raw materials. This "dependency school" of economists argued that MNCs continued the colonial pattern of exploitation that left the developing countries selling raw materials to and buying consumer goods from the advanced countries. MNCs controlled technology and consumer preferences and formed alliances with their host governments to exploit the people and keep them down. Third World leaders believed this theory of neocolonialist exploitation, but Keng Swee and I were not impressed. We had a real-life problem to solve and could not afford to be conscribed by any theory or dogma. Anyway, Singapore had no natural resources for MNCs to exploit. All it had were hard-working people, good basic infrastructure, and a government that was determined to be honest and competent. Our duty was to create a livelihood for 2 million Singaporeans. If MNCs could give our workers employment and teach them technical and engineering skills and management know-how, we should bring in the MNCs.

The second part of my strategy was to create a First World oasis in a Third World region. This was something Israel could not do because it was at war with its neighbors. If Singapore could establish First World standards in public and personal security, health, education, telecommunications, transportation, and services, it would become a base camp for entrepreneurs, engineers, managers, and other professionals who had business to do in the region. This meant we had to train our people and equip them to provide First World standards of service. I believed this was possible, that we could reeducate and reorientate our people with the help of schools, trade unions, community centers, and social organizations. If the communists in China could eradicate all flies and sparrows, surely we could get our people to change their Third World habits.

We had one simple guiding principle for survival, that Singapore had to be more rugged, better organized, and more efficient than others in the region. If we were only as good as our neighbors, there was no reason for businesses to be based here. We had to make it possible for investors to operate successfully and profitably in Singapore despite our lack of a domestic market and natural resources.

We had established the Economic Development Board by statute in August 1961. Winsemius had recommended a one-stop agency so that an investor need not deal with a large number of departments and ministries. This agency would sort out all an investor's requirements whether relating to land, power, water, or environmental and work safety. For the first few months, the EDB had experts from the UNDP and the International Labour Office to help it. The EDB's main efforts were in investment promotion, concentrating on the four industries Winsemius had named in his report—ship breaking and repair, metal engineering, chemicals, and electrical equipment and appliances.

Hon Sui Sen was picked by Keng Swee as the first chairman of the EDB and given the choice of the brightest and best of our scholars who had returned from universities in Britain, Canada, Australia, and New Zealand. These young men were inspired by Sui Sen, a quiet, outstanding administrator with an amazing ability to get the best out of those who worked for him. He shaped the culture of the EDB—the enthusiasm, the unflagging spirit, the ingenious ways they got around obstacles—to promote investments and create jobs. He made the EDB so successful and large that he had to break off different components of the organization, turning the industrial estates section into the Jurong Town Corporation and the development finance section into the Development Bank of Singapore (DBS). Both became leaders in their own fields. DBS helped finance our entrepreneurs who needed venture capital because our established banks had no experience outside trade financing and were too conservative and reluctant to lend to would-be manufacturers.

It was hard legwork for our young EDB officers to interest foreign investors in the opportunities in Singapore, to persuade them to send missions here to see for themselves. When Chin Bock first began visiting corporate offices, the CEOs did not even know where Singapore was. He had to point it out on their globes, a little dot at the tip of the Malay peninsula in Southeast Asia. EDB officers would sometimes call on 40 to 50 companies before getting one to visit Singapore. They worked with inexhaustible energy because they felt the survival of Singapore depended upon them. Ngiam Tong Dow, a young EDB director, later permanent secretary of the ministry of trade and industry, remembered what Keng Swee told him, that every time he drove by a school and saw hundreds of children streaming out, he felt downhearted, wondering how to find jobs for them when they left school.

The EDB officers had imbibed the values and attitudes of the ministers, a willingness to learn from others and a readiness to accept assistance from any quarter. They were helped by their English-language education. We had inherited the English language from the British and had adopted it as our common working language. From the able team in the EDB, I later found three cabinet ministers, S. Dhanabalan, Lee Yock Suan, and Yeo Cheow Tong. Several EDB officers, including Joe Pillay and Ngiam Tong Dow, became outstanding permanent secretaries. In addition Pillay was chairman of Singapore Airlines where his financial and business skills made it the most profitable airline in Asia, while Ngiam became chairman of the Development Bank of Singapore.

Winsemius played a crucial role as economic adviser, serving for 23 years until 1984. He visited Singapore twice a year, each time for about three weeks. We paid for his air tickets and hotel bills in Singapore but for nothing else. To keep him up to date, Ngiam, his EDB liaison officer, sent him regular reports and daily copies of the *Straits Times.* His practice was to spend his first week in Singapore in discussions with our officials, the next with executives of MNCs and some Singapore companies, and also with NTUC (National Trades Union Congress) leaders. He would submit his report and recommendations to the minister of finance and to me. Then I would have a working lunch with him alone.

The top executives of the MNCs soon appreciated the value of his role and spoke freely to him of their problems: overregulation by the government, the rising value of the Singapore dollar, too much job-hopping, too restrictive a policy on employing foreign workers, and so on. Winsemius had a pragmatic, hands-on approach, a good head for figures, and a knack for getting to grips with the basic issues, ignoring the mass of details. Most of all he was wise and canny. I learned much from him especially about how European and American CEOs think and operate.

In between his visits to Singapore, he would meet me whenever my work took me to London, Paris, Brussels, or Amsterdam. He had to endure one hardship: He was a chain-smoker and I was allergic to smoke, so for him our working meals were a real deprivation. Whenever possible, the lunch or dinner would be alfresco, to let him smoke. He spoke English fluently if ungrammatically and with a heavy Dutch accent. He had a deep, guttural voice, a leathery face with deeply lined forehead and cheeks, horn-rimmed glasses, and hair combed straight back. He once told me he could not explain why he felt a great affinity with Sui Sen and me and could only conclude that there was a "congruence of the Calvinistic and Confucian philosophy of life." Whatever the reason, it was Singapore's good fortune that he enjoyed working with us.

The government played a key role in attracting foreign investments; we built the infrastructure and provided well-planned industrial estates, equity participation in industries, fiscal incentives, and export promotion. Most important, we established good labor relations and sound macroeconomic policies, the fundamentals that enable private enterprise to operate successfully. Our largest infrastructure development was the Jurong industrial estate, which eventually covered 9,000 acres, with roads, sewers, drainage, power, gas, and water all laid out. It had a slow start. By 1961, we had issued only 12 pioneer certificates. (During 1963–1965, our years in Malaysia, none were issued by the central government in Kuala Lumpur.) As finance minister, Keng Swee used to attend the foundation-laying ceremony and later the official opening of the factory, to create two occasions for publicity over one factory. He did this even for the smallest factory employing a mere handful of workers, like the one making mothballs. When Jurong lay largely empty, people called it "Goh's Folly," as Keng Swee himself recalled after investments had flowed in. He was not that self-deprecatory when Jurong was barren.

By the end of 1970, however, we had issued 390 pioneer certificates giving investors tax-free status for up to five years, extended to 10 years for those issued after 1975. Jurong was humming with activity. Our break came with a visit by Texas Instruments in October 1968. It wanted to set up a plant to assemble semiconductors, at that time a high-technology product, and was able to start production within 50 days of its decision. Close on its heels came National Semiconductor.

Soon after, its competitor, Hewlett-Packard (HP), sent out a scout. Our EDB officer had worked on him, getting him any information he needed immediately, and would not give up until he agreed to visit Singapore to see for himself. He was as impressed as Texas Instruments. An EDB project officer was assigned to look after his delegation and everything was made convenient and swift. While HP negotiated to acquire a site for its own factory, it decided to lease the top two floors of a six-story building. The elevator to lift the heavy machinery needed a big transformer for electricity, but there was none in place in time for the visit of Mr. Hewlett himself. Rather than have him walk up six flights of stairs, the EDB got a gigantic cable extended from a neighboring building, and on the day of the visit the elevator worked. Hewlett-Packard invested. These stories went through the boardrooms of the American electronics industry, and other American electronics companies soon followed. During this period, China was in the mad throes of Mao's Cultural Revolution. Most investors thought Taiwan and Hong Kong too close to China and headed for Singapore. We welcomed everyone, but when we found a big investor with potential for growth, we went out of our way to help it get started.

By the 1970s, glowing reports on Singapore had appeared in American magazines, including *US News & World Report, Harper's,* and *Time.* In 1970, General Electric (GE) set up six different facilities for electrical and electronic products, circuit breakers, and electric motors. By the late 1970s, GE was to become the largest single employer of labor in Singapore. American MNCs laid the foundations for Singapore's large high-tech electronics industry. Although we did not know it then, the electronics industry was to mop up our unemployment and turn Singapore into a major electronics exporter in the 1980s. From Singapore they were later to expand into Malaysia and Thailand.

Visiting CEOs used to call on me before they made their investment decisions. I thought the best way to convince them was to ensure that the roads from the airport to their hotel and to my office were neat and spruce, lined with shrubs and trees. When they drove into the Istana domain, they would see right in the heart of the city a green oasis, 90 acres of immaculate rolling lawns and woodland, and nestling between them a nine-hole golf course. Without a word being said, they would know that Singaporeans were competent, disciplined, and reliable, a people who would learn the skills they required soon enough. American manufacturing investments soon overtook those of the British, Dutch, and Japanese.

We had carried the burden of unemployment from the time we first took office in 1959—so many young people seeking jobs that were not there. But by 1971, when the British forces left, I felt we had turned a corner. The number of unemployed did not rise although the British had discharged their 30,000 workers and left another 40,000 without jobs, people who had served them. The American electronics companies had generated so many jobs that unemployment was no longer an issue. Then suddenly the Arab oil embargo struck, following the Arab-Israeli war of October 1973. The quadrupling of the price of oil set back the world economy. We urged our people to conserve energy and reduce consumption of fuel and electricity. There was belt-tightening but no hardship. Economic growth slowed down significantly from 13 percent (1972) to 4 percent (1975) while inflation rose from 2.1 percent (1972) to 22 percent (1974). To my relief, we did not suffer a big loss of jobs; our unemployment rate remained around 4.5 percent.

After recovery in 1975, we could afford to be more selective. When our EDB officer asked how much longer we had to maintain protective tariffs for the car assembly plant owned by a local company, the finance director of Mercedes-Benz said brusquely, "Forever," because our workers were not as efficient as Germans. We did not hesitate to remove the tariffs and allow the plant to close down. Soon afterward we also phased out protection for the assembly of refrigerators, air conditioners, television sets, radios, and other consumer electrical and electronic products.

By the late 1970s, we had left our old problems of unemployment and lack of investments behind us. The new problem was how to improve the quality of the new investments and with it the education and skill levels of our workers. We had found our new hinterland in America, Europe, and Japan. Modern communications and transportation made it possible for us to link up with these once faraway countries.

In 1997, we had nearly 200 American manufacturing companies with over S$19 billion worth of investments at book value. Not only were they the largest of our foreign investors, they constantly upgraded their technology and products. This reduced their unit labor costs, enabling them to pay higher wages without losing competitiveness.

Japanese investments were modest in the 1960s and 1970s, well behind those of the British and the Dutch. I tried hard to get the Japanese interested, but they were not moving in strength into Southeast Asia to manufacture for export. In the 1960s and 1970s, the Japanese invested overseas merely to sell in domestic markets and did not invest much in Singapore because of our small market. But the success of the American MNCs later encouraged the Japanese to manufacture in Singapore for export to the United States, then Europe, and only much later to Japan. China opened up in the 1980s and Japanese investments started to trickle in. When the Japanese yen appreciated against all other major currencies as a result of the Plaza Accord in 1985, Japanese manufacturers relocated their middle-technology factories to Taiwan, Korea, Hong Kong, and Singapore and their lower-technology ones to Indonesia, Thailand, and Malaysia. When they discovered that their investments in Asia yielded much higher returns than those in America and Europe, East Asia became their major destination. By the mid-1990s, they had become the largest investors in manufacturing in East Asia.

Our earliest investors had been the British. After the British forces withdrew from Singapore, many of their companies also left, following their flag. I had tried hard to get them to invest but they were suffering from a withdrawal syndrome, retreating from empire back to the security of their home base, which for them was then not productive because of trade union problems. Only after Singapore showed it could make the grade did the British come back in earnest in the late 1970s, this time not to process or trade in raw materials, but to manufacture high-value-added products such as pharmaceuticals. Beecham Pharmaceuticals set up a technologically advanced operation to manufacture semisynthetic penicillin for the Asian market, especially Japan.

It was the British, Dutch, and French who first came and incorporated these countries into the world economies through their empires. These former imperial powers, however, were slow to adjust to the new trade and investment patterns of the postcolonial era, and left the fields they had ploughed to be sown by the Americans and the Japanese.


Several well-established MNCs in Singapore were victims of worldwide restructuring, technological discoveries, or market shifts. One example stands out in my memory. After several years the EDB finally convinced Rollei, the German camera manufacturer, to relocate in Singapore. High

German wages had made them uncompetitive. I visited Rollei-Werke in Brunswick in 1970 just before Rollei started to transfer its entire production to Singapore to manufacture cameras, flash guns, projectors, lenses, and shutters, and to produce cameras for other famous German camera brands. Together with the EDB, Rollei set up a center to train workers in precision mechanics, precision optics, toolmaking, and electromechanics. Rollei (Singapore) made excellent cameras but changes in the market and in technology caused poor sales. Its R&D was in Germany, its production base in Singapore. This led to poor planning and coordination. It concentrated its R&D on the slower-moving, professional photographic equipment area, whereas the Japanese moved into ever simpler cameras with viewfinders and other gadgets like auto focus and talking range finders, all made possible by the computer chip the Germans were slow to develop. After 11 years, Rollei, both in Germany and Singapore, went into receivership.

Rollei's failure was a great blow for Singapore because European investors interpreted it as a failure in the transfer of technology from Europeans to Singaporeans. The EDB had a difficult time explaining that Rollei's failure was because of changes in technology and markets. One consolation was that the 4,000 workers trained in precision engineering became a valuable base for the disk drive industry that arrived in Singapore in the 1980s.

The EDB has been our primary agency to attract a steady flow of ever higher value-added investments. This has enabled Singapore to remain competitive in spite of rising wages and other costs. The officers are still some of the brightest of our graduates, mostly from universities in America, Britain, and Europe. The EDB's present chairman, Philip Yeo, is well known to CEOs of MNCs as energetic and dependable, able to deliver whatever the EDB has promised.

Looking back, I cannot claim that our economic development and industrialization worked as we had planned. The early plans before separation were made on the assumption of a common market with Malaysia. Guinness had already paid a deposit for a site in Jurong for a brewery when Tan Siew Sin, the Malaysian finance minister, told Alan Lennox-Boyd, the Guinness chairman, that he would not allow even one bottle of stout to be imported. So Lennox-Boyd set up his brewery in Kuala Lumpur and offered to allow us to forfeit his deposit. We returned it. Years later we repaid Tan Siew Sin's compliment when we refused to reduce the import duty on stout from Malaysia. Guinness settled on a Singapore brewery to produce it for them under license.

We left most of the picking of winners to the MNCs that brought them to Singapore. A few, such as ship-repairing, oil-refining and petrochemicals, and banking and finance, were picked by the EDB or Sui Sen, our minister of finance, or myself personally. Our ministry of trade and industry believed there could be breakthroughs in biotechnology, computer products, specialty chemicals, and telecommunication equipment and services. When we were unsure how new research and development would turn out, we spread our bets.

Our job was to plan the broad economic objectives and the target periods within which to achieve them. We reviewed these plans regularly and adjusted them as new realities changed the outlook. Infrastructure and the training and education of workers to meet the needs of employers had to be planned years in advance. We did not have a group of ready-made entrepreneurs such as Hong Kong gained in the Chinese industrialists and bankers who came fleeing from Shanghai, Canton, and other cities when the communists took over. Had we waited for our traders to learn to be industrialists we would have starved. It is absurd for critics to suggest in the 1990s that had we grown our own entrepreneurs, we would have been less at the mercy of the rootless MNCs. Even with the experienced talent Hong Kong received in Chinese refugees, its manufacturing technology level is not in the same class as that of the MNCs in Singapore.

The government took the lead by starting new industries such as steel mills (National Iron and Steel Mills) and service industries such as a shipping line, Neptune Orient Lines (NOL), and an airline, Singapore Airlines (SIA). Two ministers were outstanding in their versatility. Hon Sui Sen seeded the Development Bank of Singapore, the Insurance Corporation of Singapore, and the Singapore Petroleum Company. Goh

Keng Swee conceived of our shipping line, NOL, and through the Pakistani government, recruited Captain M. J. Sayeed to start it up. With the help of Sir Lawrence Hartnett, an Australian expert in ordnance production, Keng Swee set up Chartered Industries of Singapore (CIS), a mint, and a factory for small ammunition, placed together because both required tight security and good production tooling. With a practical and resourceful executive director, Ong Kah Kok, CIS succeeded. Philip Yeo, a young permanent secretary, and later chairman of the EDB, took over CIS from Ong Kah Kok and added new activities that later spun off into Singapore Technologies, a high-tech company that, among other things, set up wafer fabrication plants in joint venture with top MNCs.

We had to put our faith in our young officers who had integrity, intellect, energy, drive, and application but no record of business acumen. Our top scholars had been chosen from the best of each year's crop of students and sent to the top universities in Britain, Canada, Australia, New Zealand, Germany, France, Italy, and Japan, and later, when we could afford it, America. We made them our entrepreneurs to start up successful companies like NOL and SIA. I was fearful that these enterprises would result in subsidized and loss-making nationalized corporations as had happened in many new countries. Sui Sen, who knew his young officers, assured me that it was possible to succeed, that they could match our competitors in these businesses. And he had given clear instructions that the enterprises had to be profitable or be shut down. Both Keng Swee and Kim San, with whom I discussed these bold plans, thought it worth the risk, given the dearth of entrepreneurs. I relied on the judgment of Sui Sen who had picked the officers for the jobs. The projects succeeded. As a result, many new companies sprang up under the auspices of other ministers and their ministries. When these also were successful, we turned state monopolies such as the PUB (Public Utilities Board), the PSA (Port of Singapore Authority), and Singapore Telecom into separate entities, free from ministerial control, to be run as companies, efficient, profitable, and competitive.

The key to success was the quality of the people in charge. Not all our top administrators possess business acumen, an intangible gift. Several did. National Iron and Steel Mills with Howe Yoon Chong as chairman,

Keppel Corporation with Sim Kee Boon, and Singapore Airlines with Joe Pillay became household names, leading stocks on the main board of the Stock Exchange of Singapore. When SIA was privatized, we had difficulty finding top-quality executives to replace Joe Pillay, such was the scarcity of entrepreneurial talent.

If I have to choose one word to explain why Singapore succeeded, it is *confidence.* This was what made foreign investors site their factories and refineries here. Within days of the oil crisis in October 1973, I decided to give a clear signal to the oil companies that we did not claim any special privilege over the stocks of oil they held in their Singapore refineries. If we blocked export from those stocks, we would have enough oil for our own consumption for two years, but we would have shown ourselves to be completely undependable. I met the CEOs or managing directors of all the oil refineries—Shell, Mobil, Esso, Singapore Petroleum, and British Petroleum on 10 November 1973. I assured them publicly that Singapore would share in any cuts they imposed on the rest of their customers, on the principle of equal misery. Their customers were in countries as far apart as Alaska, Australia, Japan, and New Zealand, besides those in the region.

This decision increased international confidence in the Singapore government, that it knew its long-term interest depended on being a reliable place for oil and other business. As a result, the oil industry confidently expanded into petrochemicals in the late 1970s. By the 1990s, with a total refining capacity of 1.2 million barrels per day, Singapore had become the world's third largest oil-refining center after Houston and Rotterdam, the third largest oil trading center after New York and London, and the largest fuel oil bunker market in volume terms. Singapore is also a major petrochemical producer.

To overcome the natural doubts of investors from advanced countries over the quality of our workers, I had asked the Japanese, Germans, French, and Dutch to set up centers in Singapore with their own instructors to train technicians. Some centers were government-financed, others were jointly formed with such corporations as Philips, Rollei, and Tata.

After 4 to 6 months of training, these workers, who were trained in a factory-like environment, became familiar with the work systems and cultures of the different nations and were desirable employees. These training institutes became useful points of reference for investors from these countries to check how our workers compared with theirs. They validated the standards of Singapore workers.

# 5. Creating a Financial Center

Anyone who predicted in 1965 when we separated from Malaysia that Singapore would become a financial center would have been thought mad. How did it happen, the gleaming modern office blocks in the city center with banks of computers linking Singapore with London, New York, Tokyo, Frankfurt, Hong Kong, and other major financial centers?

It had a most improbable start in 1968. In his oral history, Dr. Winsemius recalls his telephone call to his friend, the vice president of the Bank of America branch in Singapore, who was then in London. "Look here, Mr. Van Oenen, we [Singapore] want, within 10 years, to be the financial center in Southeast Asia." Van Oenen replied, "All right, you come to London. In five years you can develop it." Winsemius immediately went to London where Van Oenen took him to a large globe standing in a board-room, and said, "Look here, the financial world begins in Zurich. Zurich banks open at 9 o'clock in the morning, later Frankfurt, later London. In the afternoon Zurich closes, then Frankfurt and London. In the meantime, New York is open. So London hands over financial money traffic to New York. In the afternoon New York closes; they had already handed over to San Francisco. When San Francisco closes in the afternoon, the world is covered with a veil. Nothing happens until next day, 9:00 A.M. Swiss time, then the Swiss banks open. If we put Singapore in between, before San Francisco closes, Singapore would have taken over. And when Singapore closes, it would have handed over to Zurich. Then, for the first time since creation, we will have a 24-hour round-the-world service in money and banking."

At Winsemius's request, Van Oenen wrote a paper on the subject and sent it to Hon Sui Sen, chairman of the EDB, and Winsemius's special link to me. Sui Sen saw me to propose that we lift foreign exchange control restrictions on all currency transactions between Singapore and territories outside the sterling area. We were still part of the sterling area that required exchange controls on the movement of money. When Sui Sen sounded out a Bank of England official on the possibility of setting up a foreign currency pool like Hong Kong's, which would allow us to have an Asian dollar market, he was told that Hong Kong's arrangement was allowed for historical reasons, and warned that Singapore might have to leave the sterling area. I decided the risk was worth taking and told Sui Sen to go ahead. The Bank of England did not force the issue and Singapore did not have to leave the sterling bloc. In any case, Britain dissolved it four years later.

Unlike Hong Kong, Singapore could neither ride on the reputation of the City of London, an established financial center with its long history of international banking, nor depend on the backing of the Bank of England, a symbol of financial expertise, reliability, and trustworthiness. In 1968, Singapore was a Third World country. Foreign bankers needed to be assured of stable social conditions, a good working and living environment, efficient infrastructure, and a pool of skilled and adaptable professionals. We also had to convince them that our currency board and the Monetary Authority of Singapore (MAS) were capable of supervising the banking industry. Both Keng Swee and I had decided in 1965, soon after independence, that Singapore should not have a central bank that could issue currency and create money. We were determined not to allow our currency to lose its value against the strong currencies of the big nations, especially the United States. So we retained our currency board which issued Singapore dollars only when backed by its equivalent value in foreign exchange. The MAS has all the powers of a central bank except the authority to issue currency notes.

The MAS has been professional in its financial supervision, working according to laws, rules, and regulations that were periodically reviewed and revised to keep pace with developments in financial services. We had to fight every inch of the way to establish confidence in our integrity, competence, and judgment. The history of our financial center is the story of how we built up credibility as a place of integrity, and developed the officers with the knowledge and skills to regulate and supervise the banks, security houses, and other financial institutions so that the risk of systemic failure is minimized.

We made a modest start with an offshore Asian dollar market. It was the counterpart of the Eurodollar market; we called it "the Asian dollar market." Initially, this market was mainly an interbank market in Singapore that obtained foreign currency funds from banks abroad for lending to banks in the region, and vice versa. Later the Asian dollar market traded in foreign exchange and financial derivatives in foreign currency denominated securities, and undertook loan syndication, bond issuance, and fund management. The Asian dollar market in 1997 exceeded US$500 billion, nearly three times the size of our domestic banking market. The growth was stupendous because it fulfilled a market need. International financial transactions increased exponentially as trade and investments spread across the globe to cover East Asia, with Singapore as one of its key nodes.

In the early years from 1968 to 1985, we had the field all to ourselves in the region. We attracted international financial institutions by abolishing withholding tax on interest income earned by nonresident depositors. All Asian dollar deposits were exempted from statutory liquidity and reserve requirements. By the 1990s, Singapore had become one of the larger financial centers of the world, with its foreign exchange market ranking fourth in size after London, New York, and only slightly behind Tokyo. Because of our success after the mid-1980s, other countries in the region vied to develop international financial centers, some offering tax incentives more generous than ours. The foundations for our financial center were the rule of law, an independent judiciary, and a stable, competent, and honest government that pursued sound macroeconomic policies, with budget surpluses almost every year. This led to a strong and stable Singapore dollar, with exchange rates that dampened imported inflation.

In the 1970s, we had a brush against a big name in the city of London. In March 1972, Jim Slater, a highly regarded British investor who specialized in asset stripping, came to see me in Singapore. When Ted Heath became prime minister, the press reported that he had placed his assets and stockholdings with Jim Slater to manage in a blind trust. Therefore, Slater had strong credentials. I had met him a year earlier at a 10

Downing Street dinner hosted by Ted Heath. I welcomed Slater's participation in our stock market.

Later, in 1975, Sui Sen, then our finance minister, told me that Slater Walker Securities had engaged in manipulating the shares of Haw Par Brothers International, a public-listed company in Singapore. They had been siphoning off the assets of Haw Par and its subsidiaries illegally for the benefit of certain directors and themselves, conduct which amounted to criminal breach of trust: They were cheating the shareholders of Haw Par and the other companies. Investigation into a big name in the London Stock Exchange, if not justified, would give us a bad reputation. Should he proceed against Jim Slater? I decided that we had to if we were to maintain our standing as a well-managed stock exchange.

The investigation revealed a conspiracy to systematically strip off the Haw Par assets, and this was only the tip of a much larger and wider swindle. Slater Walker's criminal activities extended from Singapore to Malaysia, Hong Kong, and London, the final repository of the loot. They had used Haw Par subsidiaries in Hong Kong to purchase listed shares in Hong Kong then sold them to Spydar Securities, which was wholly owned by Slater Walker executives who shared these ill-gotten profits. The men responsible were Jim Slater, Richard Tarling, the chairman of Haw Par, and Ogilvy Watson, the managing director. Watson had returned to Britain before fleeing to Belgium with whom we did not have an extradition treaty. Slater and Tarling were resident in London. We sought the extradition of Tarling and Slater, but the British establishment did not extradite Slater. Instead, in 1979, after a three-year struggle through the London courts, the British home secretary ordered Tarling's extradition on only 5 of the 17 charges, the 5 carrying the lowest penalties. Tarling was prosecuted and sent to jail for six months on each of three charges of willful nondisclosure of material facts in Haw Par's 1972 consolidated profit and loss account. Years later, after he had ceased to be governor of the Bank of England, Gordon Richardson mumbled his regrets to me in my office that he could not help Singapore bring Slater to justice.


The MAS's reputation for being thorough and uncompromising in admitting only financial institutions of repute was put to the test in the

1970s and 1980s when it denied a license to the Bank of Credit and Commerce International (BCCI). The BCCI swindle affected nearly all the big financial centers by the time it finally ended. Incorporated in Luxembourg by a Pakistani, the bank's shareholders included members of the royal families of Saudi Arabia, Bahrain, Abu Dhabi, and Dubai. It had about 400 branches or offices in 73 countries in Europe, the Middle East, Africa, and America. It applied for an offshore banking license in Singapore in 1973. We rejected the application because the bank was too new (it started only in 1972) and low in capitalization. It resubmitted its application in 1980. Again the MAS would not approve; its international standing was poor.

The BCCI did not give up. In 1982, Van Oenen, who had helped us establish the Asian dollar market, enquired about its application. Koh Beng Seng, who had taken over as manager of the banking and financial institutions department of the MAS, had been told by several central bankers that they had reservations about the BCCI. So when Van Oenen saw me, I decided it was best to support Koh Beng Seng.

Not deterred, the BCCI tried again, this time through Harold Wilson. There was something strange about his letter. His practice had been to sign off in his own hand, "Yours sincerely Harold." This time the "Yours sincerely" was typewritten and he signed himself "(Harold) Wilson of Rievaulx." I decided he was writing pro forma, to oblige a friend.

Dishonest operations of the BCCI led to enormous losses for other banks. When it was closed down in July 1991, depositors and creditors had claims for US$11 billion. Singapore escaped unscathed because we refused to compromise standards.

The MAS also denied a license to the National Bank of Brunei which was run by a prominent Singapore Chinese businessman, Khoo Teck Puat. Khoo bought the National Bank of Brunei and arranged for the sultan's brother, Prince Mohamed Bolkiah, as the bank's president to write to the MAS in 1975 asking for a branch in Singapore. Another letter a few months later informed us that his brother, Prince Sufri Bolkiah, had been appointed executive deputy president. Because of Khoo's apparent political backing by the Brunei royal family, the matter was referred to me by the MAS. I backed the MAS decision to turn it down in 1975 and again in 1983 when the bank reapplied.

In 1986, the sultan issued an emergency order to close the National Bank of Brunei. There was a run on its deposits and suspicion of irregularities in loans of S$1.3 billion to Khoo's group of companies. He had used the funds of this bank for his own activities, among them an attempt to get a controlling interest in Standard Chartered Bank of London. His eldest son, who was chairman of the bank, was arrested in Brunei. Banks in Singapore, mainly foreign banks, had lent a total of S$419 million to the National Bank of Brunei. Khoo took two years to repay these debts.

Through strict rules and rigorous supervision, the MAS under Koh Beng Seng helped Singapore to develop as a financial center. To meet the competition from international banks, the MAS encouraged the four largest local banks (known as the "Big Four") to acquire and merge with the smaller local banks to become bigger and stronger. The Big Four were ranked by Moody's, the U.S. rating agency, as financially among the strongest and best capitalized in the world.

In 1985, the MAS had to help manage a crisis in the Stock Exchange of Singapore (SES). Malaysian speculators, particularly Tan Koon Swan, had deposited the shares of Pan Electric Industries and several Malaysian companies with our stockbrokers as security for loans at a higher price than their actual market value, with an undertaking to redeem the shares by a certain date at an even higher price. When the stock market went down and they ran out of money, they were unable to redeem their shares at the price agreed. This caused several large firms of stockbrokers, members of the SES, to become insolvent. The SES was closed for three days while MAS officials, led by Koh Beng Seng, worked around the clock with the Big Four banks to arrange an emergency "lifeboat" fund of S$180 million to rescue the stockbrokers. Koh's efforts enabled the SES to avoid systemic market failure and to restore investor confidence. It was a messy business.

To avoid a recurrence of such a crisis, we revised the Securities Industry Act to strengthen prudential requirements of stockbroking companies. This gave their clients better protection from default by SES member firms, which in turn incorporated themselves to increase their capital. We allowed foreign participation in SES member companies, and also wholly foreign-owned companies that brought in essential expertise.

Because of these prudent changes we had made, the SES was able to ride the Black Monday global stock market crash on 19 October 1987, when Hong Kong's stock exchange had to close down for four days.

Another advance for Singapore's financial center was the Singapore International Monetary Exchange (SIMEX). In 1984, the Gold Exchange of Singapore expanded its trade in gold futures to include financial futures and renamed itself SIMEX. To win the confidence of international financial institutions, we modeled SIMEX after the Chicago Mercantile Exchange (CME) with its open outcry trading system. We also convinced the CME to adopt a mutual offset system with SIMEX that enabled round-the-clock trading. This revolutionary concept allowed an investor to establish a position at CME in Chicago and close off at SIMEX in Singapore, and vice versa, without paying additional margins. The U.S. Commodity Futures Trading Commission approved this arrangement. The mutual offset arrangement has functioned without hitches since the inception of SIMEX. In 1995, when a SIMEX trader, Nick Leeson of Barings, a venerable London bank, lost over a billion U.S. dollars speculating on Nikkei Index Futures, he brought disaster upon Barings but did not affect SIMEX or cause losses to other SIMEX members or their customers.

In 1984, SIMEX started trading in Eurodollar interest rate futures contracts and soon afterward, the Euroyen. By 1998, SIMEX had listed a range of regional contracts including stock index futures of Japan, Taiwan, Singapore, Thailand, and Hong Kong. The London-based *International Financing Review* bestowed upon SIMEX the International Exchange of the Year award in 1998, the only Asian exchange ever to win this title, and the fourth time SIMEX had achieved this award.


As our financial reserves grew with increased Central Provident Fund (CPF) savings (Singapore's pension scheme) and yearly public sector surpluses, the MAS was not investing these funds long term for best returns. I asked Keng Swee to review this. He formed the Government of Singapore Investment Corporation (GIC) in May 1981 with me as chairman, himself as deputy chairman, and Sui Sen and several ministers as board members. Through Keng Swee's links with David Rothschild, we appointed N. M.

Rothschild & Sons as consultants. They sent an experienced officer to work with us for several months to set up the GIC organization. We also employed American and British investment managers to help us develop our systems for the different kinds of investments. To lead the management team, we appointed Yong Pung How as the GIC's first managing director. He secured James Wolfensohn, who later became the World Bank president, as adviser on investment strategy. Gradually, they built up a core of Singaporean professionals led by Ng Kok Song and Teh Kok Peng, who came over from the MAS. By the late 1980s, they and their staff had assumed the key management and investment responsibilities.

At first, the GIC managed only the government's financial reserves. By 1987, it was able to manage the reserves of the Board of Commissioners for Currency of Singapore and the long-term assets of the MAS as well. It was managing assets worth more than S$120 billion in 1997. The GIC's most important responsibility was to allocate our investments between equities (stocks and shares), bonds (mainly bonds issued by the governments of developed countries), and cash. There are books to explain the principles upon which the markets work, but they offer no certain guide to predicting future price movements, much less to making assured returns. In the volatile world of 1997–1998, the GIC could make or lose a few billion dollars just by the yen falling or the German mark rising dramatically against the U.S. dollar. Investing is a hazardous business. My cardinal objective was not to maximize returns but to protect the value of our savings and get a fair return on capital. In the 15 years since 1985, the GIC has outperformed relevant global investment benchmarks and more than preserved the value of our assets.


However, Singapore's financial center was considered over-regulated compared to Hong Kong's. Critics wrote, "In Hong Kong, what is not expressly forbidden is permitted; in Singapore, what is not expressly permitted is forbidden." They forgot that Hong Kong enjoyed the backing of the British flag and the Bank of England. Singapore, with no such safety net, could not have recovered from so dramatic a fall as easily. It had first to establish its reputation on its own. Visiting foreign bankers used to tell me that Singapore's financial market would grow faster if we allowed them to introduce new financial products without having to wait until they had been tried and tested elsewhere. I would listen carefully but did not intervene because I believed we needed more time to establish our standing and reputation.

After I stepped down as prime minister in 1990, I had more time to delve into our banking sector and had working lunches with our Singapore bankers. One of them was Lim Ho Kee, a shrewd and successful foreign exchange dealer who was managing a major foreign bank in Singapore. He persuaded me to reexamine our policies which he said were overcautious and prevented our financial center from expanding and catching up with the activities of the more developed centers. I also had several brainstorming sessions in mid-1994 with other top Singaporean managers of foreign financial institutions. They convinced me that we had too much of our national savings locked up in the Central Provident Fund and that our statutory boards and government-linked companies were too conservative, placing their surpluses in bank deposits. They could have higher returns investing through experienced and well-qualified international fund managers in Singapore. This would expand the fund management industry and bring in more fund managers who in turn would attract foreign funds for investment in the region.

My views on our regulatory environment and banking practices began to change after 1992 when former U.S. secretary of state, George Shultz, who was chairman of the international advisory board of J. P. Morgan, a blue-ribbon U.S. bank, had me invited to be a member of this board. Through briefings and interaction with J. P. Morgan bankers in biannual meetings, I gained insights into their workings and saw how they were preparing themselves for globalized banking. I was struck by the quality of the members of this board which included the bank's directors. There were able and successful CEOs as well as former political leaders from every major economic region of the world to give them different inputs. I was useful to them because of my personal knowledge of our region. Other members brought intimate knowledge of their own regions or their specialties. I learned how they viewed Southeast Asia compared to other emerging markets: Latin America, Russia, other members of the Soviet Union, and the other countries of Eastern Europe. I was impressed by the way they welcomed and prepared for innovation and change in banking especially with developments in information technology (IT). I concluded that Singapore was light-years behind them.

As chairman of the GIC, I had discussions on a range of banking issues with CEOs of the big American, European, and Japanese banks, and learned how they saw the future of global banking. By comparison, Singapore banks were inward-looking. Their boards of directors were mainly Singaporeans, as were the principal bank executives. I expressed my concerns to the chairmen of three of our big banks—Oversea-Chinese Banking Corporation, United Overseas Bank, and Overseas Union Bank. From their responses I concluded they were not awake to the dangers of being inbred and of failing to be outward- and forward-looking in an age of rapid globalization. They were doing well, protected from competition. They wanted the government to continue to restrict foreign banks from opening more branches or even ATMs (automatic teller machines). I cautioned them that, sooner or later, because of bilateral agreements with the United States or possibly World Trade Organization (WTO) agreements, Singapore would have to open up its banking industry and remove protection for local banks.

I decided in 1997 to break this old mold. Singapore banks needed an infusion of foreign talent and a different mindset. If these three big banks would not move, then the DBS Bank, in which the government had a stake, should set the pace. After talent scouting in 1998, DBS Bank engaged John Olds, an experienced senior executive who was about to leave J. P. Morgan. He took over as deputy chairman and CEO to make the bank a major Asian player. Soon, Oversea-Chinese Banking Corporation appointed as CEO a Hong Kong banker, Alex Au.

For over three decades, I had supported Koh Beng Seng on restricting the access of foreign banks to the local market. Now I believed the time had come for the tough international players to force our Big Four to upgrade their services or lose market share. There is a real risk that they may not be able to compete, in which case we may end up with no Singapore-owned and managed banks to depend on in a financial crisis.

Gradually I concluded that Koh, deputy managing director of the banking and financial institutions group in the MAS, was not keeping up with the enormous changes sweeping the banking industry worldwide. He was too protective of our investors. I sought advice from Gerald

Corrigan, formerly president of the Federal Reserve Bank of New York, and Brian Quinn, formerly of the Bank of England. They advised me separately that Singapore could change its style and method of supervising the banks without any loss of rigor, and without increasing the risk of systemic failure. Major financial centers such as New York and London concentrated on protecting not the different market players or the individual investors, but the system itself. Corrigan and Quinn convinced us that stronger and better-managed institutions should be given more leeway to assume risk.

As I did not want to revamp the MAS myself, early in 1997, with the prime minister's permission, I involved Loong in the work. He began meeting bankers and fund managers and mastered the workings of our financial sector. On 1 January 1998, when the prime minister appointed him chairman of the MAS, he was ready to move. With the help of a few key officers, he reorganized and refocused the MAS, to implement the new approach to regulating and developing the financial sector.

Loong and his team changed the MAS's approach to financial supervision; they did it with a lighter touch and were more open to industry proposals and views. With advice from management consultants and industry committees, they made policy changes that affected all parts of the financial sector. They took steps to promote the asset management industry and amended the rules on the internationalization of the Singapore dollar, to promote the growth of the capital market. The MAS encouraged the SES (stock exchange) and SIMEX (futures exchange) to merge and free up commission rates and access to the exchanges.

The MAS liberalized access to the domestic banking sector by allowing qualifying foreign full banks to open more branches and ATMs. It lifted limits on foreign ownership of local bank shares while requiring the banks to set up nominating committees in their boards, modeled on similar arrangements in many U.S. banks. These committees vet nominations to the board and key management appointments, to ensure that capable people are appointed who will look after the interests of all shareholders, not just the controlling shareholders.

The banks believed that a lighter touch in MAS supervision would enable them to be more innovative in introducing new financial products. Perhaps we should have made these changes earlier. But only after the

MAS had demonstrated the strength of its system to weather the financial crisis of 1987 and 1997–1998 did I feel confident enough to move closer to a position where what is not expressly forbidden is permitted. Our cautious approach helped us weather the 1997–1998 East Asian financial crisis. Our banks were sound and not overextended. No bubble puffed up our stock market. It has taken us 30 years from the time we first launched the Asian dollar market in 1968 to establish our credentials as a soundly managed international financial center.

From July 1997, when the financial crisis broke out in East Asia with the devaluation of the Thai baht, disasters devastated the currencies, stock markets, and economies of the region. But no bank in Singapore faltered. Investors were rushing to get out of emerging markets, under which Singapore was classified. When fund managers were fearful of hidden traps, withholding information was not an intelligent response. We decided on the maximum disclosure of information. To enable the investor to judge the value of our assets, we persuaded our banks to abandon their practice of maintaining hidden reserves and not disclosing their nonperforming loans. Our banks disclosed their regional loan exposures. They made substantial additional general provisions for their regional loans, dealing with the potential problems upfront instead of waiting for loans to turn bad. Because of the competent steps the MAS had taken to deal with the crisis, Singapore consolidated its position as a financial center.

# 6. Winning Over the Unions

I started my political life fighting for the unions as their legal adviser and negotiator. By the mid-1950s, the communists had gained control of most of them, and both communist and noncommunist unions had turned combative. To attract investments, we had to free unions from communist control and educate union leaders and workers on the need to create new jobs by getting investments. This was easier said than done.

Given the communist hold on our unions, it was inevitable that we suffered endless strikes, slowdowns, and riots from the late 1940s to the 1960s. Between July 1961 and September 1962, we had 153 strikes, a record for Singapore. In 1969, for the first time since before the war, we had no strikes or work stoppages. How did we do this?

Singapore's British-style trade union practices had been the bane of our labor movement. To counter communist influence, the colonial government brought in such advisers as Jack Brazier from the British Trade Union Congress. To draw noncommunist union leaders away from communist influence, these advisers taught them all the bad habits and practices of how to squeeze employers for more pay and benefits regardless of the consequences to the company. At a meeting in July 1966 of the Army Civil Service Union of workers employed by the British forces, I urged them to abandon these British union practices which had ruined Britain's economy. I admitted that I had been responsible for many of them when I was negotiating for the unions. At that time there was too much exploitation of our workers. But the consequences were so bad, adding to our unemployment, that I regretted having done this. For example, triple pay on public holidays had led to cleansing workers deliberately allowing garbage to accumulate before public holidays to ensure that they would have to work on these holidays. The purpose of public holidays was to give the workers leisure, but our workers wanted more pay, not more leisure. So I asked union leaders to update our trade union practices.

To stress how strongly I held these views, I repeated them in the presence of International Labour Organisation officials and union leaders from the rest of Asia at a meeting of its Asian advisory committee in November 1966. I told our union leaders that they must not kill the goose whose golden eggs we needed. Our unions, I said, had been part of a political movement against the British. Political leaders—and I was one of them—had offered workers the carrot of independence, saying, "Come with me to freedom and I will give you what the British employer gives to his British workers." That promise we must now fulfill, but to do so, we had to reestablish "supervision, discipline, and working norms" to get efficiency.

Each year 30,000 school leavers sought work. Our union practices, I explained, were forcing employers to become capital-intensive, investing in expensive machines to get the work done with the minimum of workers, as in Britain. This had created a small group of privileged unionized workers getting high pay and a growing band of underpaid and underemployed workers. If we maintained our cohesiveness and stability, and did not repeat past stupidities that had shaken confidence, we should overcome these problems. We needed new attitudes, the most important of which was that pay must accord with performance, not time spent on the job.

The unions and workers were so shaken by separation and fearful at the prospect of British withdrawal that they accepted my hard-headed approach. They knew we faced an emergency that could threaten our existence as an independent nation.

The National Trades Union Congress (NTUC) secretary-general, Ho See Beng, a PAP MP and an old colleague from my trade union days, protested against my policies, such as the abolition of triple pay for work on public holidays. He and his union colleagues had to respond to ground pressure to keep the rank and file on their side and not be outflanked by the communist union leaders. I had to override his protests but took care to meet the union leaders privately to explain my worries. These off-the-record meetings made them understand why I had to get a new framework in place, one that would make for a trim and lean workforce.

There was one landmark confrontation with an irrational and ignorant trade union leader who did not understand the changed circumstances. K. Suppiah was president of the Public Daily Rated Employees' Unions Federation. In an ultimatum to the government on 18 October 1966, he demanded settlement of all outstanding grievances arising out of an alleged nonimplementation of a collective agreement made in 1961, wanting S$1 per day increase for his 15,000 daily rated workers.

Suppiah and I had worked together for many years from the 1950s in the old City Council days. He was an uneducated man born in India, a rabble-rouser in Tamil (the language of Madras), and a determined and stubborn leader. Negotiating with him was disconcerting because he was squint-eyed and did not seem to be looking at you. He led a union, the majority of whose members were immigrant Indian unskilled laborers brought over from Madras by the British to do cleansing work. He did not understand that we were no longer in the happy, riotous 1950s when union power was waxing; that in newly independent Singapore, on its own and highly vulnerable, the government could not allow any union to jeopardize Singapore's survival. I met him and his union leaders. In a 40-minute exchange, I said I could consider a wage increase for the 1968 budget, but not for 1967. I warned that 7,000 of his members were Indian nationals who now needed work permits to continue working. If they went on strike they could well lose their jobs and would have to return to India. Suppiah was not impressed. Only 2,000 or 3,000, he said, were on work permits and he would go on with the strike. If the union was broken, then let it be broken by Mr. Lee. He accused me of having forgotten that I owed my position as prime minister largely to the trade union movement.

Suppiah called for a strike by the Public Daily Rated Employees' Unions Federation on 29 December, just before the New Year festivities. I asked them to reconsider their decision, and referred the dispute to the Industrial Arbitration Court. This made any strike by the workers unlawful and I issued a statement to draw their attention to this.

The ministry of health implemented their new work system for cleansing workers in January 1967. On 1 February 1967, about 2,400 workers of the Public Daily Rated Cleansing Workers' Union, a member of Suppiah's federation, went on a wildcat strike. A defiant Suppiah warned the government that if the cleansing workers' grievances were not settled within a week, all 14,000 workers in his federation's other daily rated unions would go on sympathy strike.

The police arrested and charged Suppiah and 14 other leaders of the cleansing workers' union with calling an illegal strike. The registrar of trade unions issued notices to the union and the federation to show cause why they should not be deregistered. At the same time, the ministry of health declared that the strikers had sacked themselves; those who wished to be reemployed could apply the next day. This coordinated firmness panicked the strikers. Ninety percent of them applied for reemployment. Two months later, both the Public Daily Rated Cleansing Workers' Union and Suppiah's federation of unions were deregistered.

This strike was a turning point in Singapore's industrial history. The way the government met it head-on won the support of the public. It triggered a change in union culture, from a defiant flouting of the law to reasonable give-and-take. I was able to swing public opinion round further. In a series of speeches to the unions, I prepared the workers for the changes we planned to make to the labor laws. We banned all strikes in certain essential services and made each statutory board have its own union.

At an NTUC Delegates' Conference in early 1968, I convinced them that industrial relations between employers and workers were more important for our survival than wage increases, and that together we had to get the labor movement into better shape by cutting out restrictive practices and the abuse of fringe benefits. I depended on them as leaders to create a new labor movement with a reputation for realistic policies that benefited workers. Recounting Britain's prodigal years of crippling dock strikes which led to the devaluation of the pound sterling in 1967, I warned, "If that happens here at our harbour I will declare this high treason. I will move against the strike leaders. Charges will be brought in court later. I will get the port going straight away. The Singapore dollar will never be devalued and I think the people of Singapore expect this of their government." I spotlighted the "selfishness of established labour." Cargo handled by the Port of Singapore Authority in 1967 increased by over 10 percent, but the number of workers employed did not go up because the extra work was all taken up by overtime. This was immoral at a time of high unemployment. I told the union delegates that we must rid ourselves of pernicious British-style trade union practices.

For balance, I told a meeting of employers that they had to be fair to their workers if they wanted maximum effort from them, that where unions and employers were not in agreement on basic objectives, the result had been ruinous for the economy. I urged our employers to do their part so that our workers would put in their maximum effort to get maximum rewards: direct rewards in their wages and benefits, and indirect returns through government revenue by way of homes, health, education, and social benefits.

Britain's announcement in January 1968 of the withdrawal of its military forces heightened people's anxieties. I seized that moment to make radical reforms to rid us of those union practices that had usurped employers' prerogatives and eroded management's ability to conduct its own business. After we won reelection in April 1968 with an overwhelming mandate, Parliament passed the Employment Act and the Industrial Relations (Amendment) Act that same year. Later, the Trade Unions Act was amended. These laws spelled out minimum employment conditions and placed limits on retrenchment benefits, overtime bonuses, and fringe benefits. They set out uniform provisions for rest days, public holidays, working days, annual leave, maternity leave, and sick leave. They restored to management the right to hire and fire, to promote and transfer, functions the unions had encroached upon during the years of industrial strife. They laid the foundation for industrial peace.

We made it illegal for a trade union to take strike or industrial action without a secret ballot. If it did so, the union and its officers would be liable to prosecution. This stopped the practice of voting by an open show of hands where dissenters were intimidated into acquiescence.

Seah Mui Kok, a union leader and PAP MP, another old friend from my time with the unions, objected to the wide latitude given to employers to hire and fire, but accepted the need for unions to be less confrontational to create a better climate for foreign investments. I included safeguards against misuse of these powers. These changes in employment and industrial relations laws and practices brought tangible benefits. Within a year, in 1969, 52 new factories were built, creating 17,000 new jobs. In 1970, new investments added 20,000 jobs. Incomes increased.

In 1972, we set up the National Wages Council (NWC), with representatives from unions, management, and government. Every year, using facts and figures available to the government, the NWC reached a wide consensus recommendation on wage increases and other terms and conditions of service for the coming year that would be affordable and would promote further economic growth. Its joint recommendations were accepted as general guidelines, with variations for the different sectors, for all union-management negotiations. From its early years, all parties agreed on the principle that wage increases must not exceed productivity increases.

The deep sense of crisis that prevailed made it possible for me to turn around union attitudes in a few years. The danger of an economic collapse because British forces were about to leave altered the mood and attitudes of the people. They realized that unless we made a U-turn from strikes and violence toward stability and economic growth, we would perish.

I got management to undertake their new role of winning worker cooperation, without which productivity could not increase. Strict laws and tough talk alone could not have achieved this. It was our overall policy that convinced our workers and union leaders to support our key objective: to establish international confidence in Singapore and attract investments and create jobs. But ultimately it was the trust and confidence they had in me, gained over long years of association, that helped transform industrial relations from one of militancy and confrontation to cooperation and partnership.

In 1969, Devan Nair returned to Singapore from Kuala Lumpur at my urging, to lead the NTUC again. He had stayed on there after being elected to the Malaysian Parliament in 1964. I needed him in Singapore to play a key role in maintaining industrial peace and persuading our workers to increase productivity and efficiency. It was an enormous advantage for me to have Devan as secretary-general of the NTUC. He coordinated and fine-tuned my policies and inculcated positive work attitudes in the unions. As NTUC leader from 1970 to 1981, when Parliament elected him president of Singapore, he got union leaders to face the challenge of competition in world markets. Each time Winsemius visited Singapore, he with his liaison officer, Ngiam Tong Dow, would brief Devan on the economic and employment situation. Devan taught the union leaders the basic principles of economics and helped make the tripartite NWC a success.

One problem he faced was the decline in union membership because of reduced union militancy. To counter this trend, Devan held a modernization seminar in November 1969 and convinced the union delegates of the need to modernize their functions to meet the changed environment. They set up several union cooperative enterprises. In 1970, the NTUC set up a taxi cooperative called NTUC Comfort which helped to break the pirate (unlicensed) taxi racket rampant in the 1960s. It started with 200 Morris Oxford taxis and 200 British Austin minibuses paid for out of British loans from their aid package. By 1994, with 10,000 taxis and 200 school buses, it was corporatized and listed on the Stock Exchange of Singapore as Comfort Group Limited. To lower the cost of living for its members, the NTUC started a consumer cooperative in 1973 called NTUC Welcome to run shops, stores, and supermarkets. Later, as NTUC Fairprice, it became a successful supermarket chain that kept prices of basic consumer goods near wholesalers' costs. NTUC Income, an insurance cooperative, began in 1970 with life insurance, then went on to motor insurance and other fields. It employed professional actuaries and experienced managers. Union leaders sat on the boards of directors to oversee the professional managers of these enterprises and soon understood that good management was critical for success.


Renewing its leadership has enabled the NTUC to keep itself relevant to a younger generation of workers. When Devan resigned in 1981 to become president, Lim Chee Onn, a 37-year-old political secretary, took over as secretary-general. He had worked under Devan after becoming a member of Parliament in 1977. A first-class graduate in naval architecture from the University of Glasgow, he brought sound management methods to his union work. However, his interpersonal skills were not as good as Devan's, and misunderstanding arose between him and older union leaders who claimed they found him somewhat unapproachable.

This was a problem I faced each time there was a change of generation between leaders. Chee Onn was more than 20 years younger than Devan. The union leaders of Devan's generation were used to Devan and did not take to Chee Onn's different work style. The basic problem was that the old leaders did not welcome a sudden infusion of young blood. At my suggestion, Chee Onn had brought in several young graduates to help him. This added to the discomfort of the older union leaders. I concluded that it would be difficult for him to get on with them. Chee Onn took this as a personal failure and resigned from politics in 1982. He went into the private sector, joining Keppel Corporation, one of our largest government-linked companies. He was a success as a corporate leader, and a tower of strength to Sim Kee Boon, who had retired as head of the civil service to be chairman of the corporation.

Devan and I agreed that Ong Teng Cheong, then minister for communications and concurrently minister for labor, would get on with the older union leaders. He was in his forties, nine years older than Chee Onn, and I believed there would be less of a generational difference. I persuaded Teng Cheong to work with the unions. He agreed and by 1983 was elected NTUC secretary-general. He remained in the cabinet; it worked well since the unions had their interests represented and the government was able to take their views into consideration when discussing policies. Teng Cheong, an architect trained in Adelaide University, has a good command of English. Being Chinese-educated, he is also fluent in Mandarin and Hokkien, his mother tongue. He got on well with both union leaders and the rank-and-file workers. He took the NTUC into new fields, providing members with better leisure and recreational facilities. I had encouraged him in this, but he needed little encouragement. What he required were financial resources and political support, which I gave him.

The NTUC expanded into health services, child care, a broadcasting station, a seaside resort hotel for workers called Pasir Ris Resort, and a country club, the Orchid Country Club with a golf course by Seletar reservoir. It also developed quality condominiums its members could buy. These new cooperative enterprises gave more union leaders hands-on experience in running enterprises. Successive generations of new leaders learned about good management. These clubs, resorts, and other facilities provided workers with lifestyles previously available only to the better-off. I believed these facilities would reduce the feeling that workers belonged to a lower order, excluded from lifestyles which only the successful enjoyed. To make them affordable, the government provided state land at nominal prices.

For many years I had been urging the NTUC to set up a labor college. In 1990, with help from the principal of Ruskin College, Teng Cheong established an Institute of Labour Studies to teach industrial relations and leadership development.

When Teng Cheong was elected president of Singapore in 1993, Lim Boon Heng, 12 years younger, then second minister for trade and industry, took over as secretary-general of the NTUC. He graduated in naval architecture from the University of Newcastle-upon-Tyne and had worked with the unions since 1981, where his good interpersonal skills had been a great asset. He brought in well-educated and talented young men in their twenties and thirties who had done well in universities abroad and had fresh ideas. This input of new blood rejuvenated the thinking and attitudes of union leaders and produced results for the unions. Like Teng Cheong, Boon Heng remained a cabinet minister, formalizing a pattern of cooperation between the unions and the government that has served Singapore well.

I launched a productivity movement in the early 1980s because I was impressed by Japanese practitioners. I encouraged NTUC leaders to work with management to introduce quality control circles (QCCs), groups of workers who together put up suggestions on how to improve work, save time and costs, and achieve zero defects. Progress was slow. Following Japanese company practice, QCCs whose suggestions resulted in savings or improvements had their photos displayed and were awarded small prizes or bonuses. The Japan Productivity Centre helped with experts, training fellowships, training materials, equipment, and software. Every now and again I would speak at award ceremonies and present the annual productivity prizes.

On one occasion, in 1987, after presenting a prize to the managing director of a Japanese company, I asked why his local workers were less productive than his Japanese workers although they used the same machines. His honest reply was that Japanese workers were more skilled, more multiskilled, more flexible, and more adaptable, with less absenteeism and job-hopping. Singapore technicians, group leaders, and supervisors were unwilling to undertake work that would soil their hands. In contrast, their Japanese counterparts considered themselves not as white- or blue-collar workers, but as grey-collar workers; they would readily help operate and maintain machines and so better understood the problems of workers.

Devan had been struck by the achievements of Japanese unions. He got two octopus-like general unions to reorganize themselves into nine industrial unions. In 1982, Chee Onn, who was then NTUC secretary-general, initiated the change from industrial to house unions. It made for better communication between union leaders and workers, and leaders could focus on the specific issues and problems of their own company with management. In 1984, the NTUC, convinced of the benefits, adopted a resolution to support house unions.

In most cases, house unions increased union membership. They encouraged openness and trust, and were good for labor-management relations. However, in the 1990s, Boon Heng found that house unions did not function as well as they did in Japan. Singapore companies are too small, most with less than a thousand workers, compared with tens of thousands in Japanese companies. Furthermore, unlike Singapore, in Japan, executives, university graduates, and other professionals can join unions. Singapore house unions do not have enough well-educated members for leadership positions. They have to depend on the NTUC for help when negotiating with employers. We have to find a solution to this problem without re-creating the disadvantages of omnibus unions.

These changes to unionism in Singapore were achieved with few strikes or industrial disputes. The maturing of the trade union movement and its leaders was helped by several dedicated and able officers I had seconded from the government administrative service to the NTUC Labour Research Unit in 1962, after the communist unions broke away in 1961 from the Singapore Trade Union Congress to form their own union feder-

ation, leaving the noncommunist unions without sufficient skilled negotiators. One of the officers I sent was S. R. Nathan, who had been a social
worker. He had good judgment and worked well with the union leaders.
Nathan later became permanent secretary of the foreign affairs ministry
and our ambassador in Washington. In 1999, he became president of
Singapore. Another was Hsu Tse Kwang, an energetic "doer" who later
became our income tax commissioner. They helped the noncommunist
union leaders in their collective bargaining and in presenting their cases
in the Industrial Arbitration Court. They educated union leaders on the
realities of economic survival for Singapore and in the process forged an
NTUC leadership that was realistic and practical. Later, in the 1990s, I
encouraged promising returned scholars to take up full-time careers in
the NTUC to beef up its research and negotiating capabilities. With universal education and numerous scholarships, by then all the bright children of poor parents had made it to university. Able union leaders who
rose from the ranks became few and far between.

To maintain the symbiotic relationship between the PAP government
and the NTUC, I encouraged the NTUC to get some MPs to work full-
time with the unions, and to appoint others as advisers to various unions.
These MPs raised union issues in Parliament. Such additions to the
unions' manpower capabilities made a qualitative difference. Without
their disciplined intellectual input and their easy access to ministers, the
case for the unions would not be put across in a way that would command
attention and from time to time bring about a revision of policies.

We have put in place a fair framework to govern industrial relations.
Restrictions on unions' excesses are balanced by consultative and arbitration procedures through which the unions can protect the interests of the
workers. The key to peace and harmony in society is a sense of fair play,
that everyone has a share in the fruits of our progress.

The NTUC's positive approach to problems helped reduce unemployment from 14 percent in 1965 to 1.8 percent in 1997. For 25 years, from
1973 to 1997, average real wages increased yearly by just under 5 percent.
We suffered a reverse in the Asian financial crisis of 1997: Unemployment
increased to 3.2 percent in 1998. To regain our competitiveness, the
unions and government agreed and implemented a package of measures
that reduced wages and other costs by 15 percent from 1 January 1999.

# 7. A Fair, Not Welfare, Society

We believed in socialism, in fair shares for all. Later we learned that personal motivation and personal rewards were essential for a productive economy. However, because people are unequal in their abilities, if performance and rewards are determined by the marketplace, there will be a few big winners, many medium winners, and a considerable number of losers. That would make for social tensions because a society's sense of fairness is offended.

A competitive, winner-takes-all society, like colonial Hong Kong in the 1960s, would not be acceptable in Singapore. A colonial government did not have to face elections every five years; the Singapore government did. To even out the extreme results of free-market competition, we had to redistribute the national income through subsidies on things that improved the earning power of citizens, such as education. Housing and public health were also obviously desirable. But finding the correct solutions for personal medical care, pensions, or retirement benefits was not easy. We decided each matter in a pragmatic way, always mindful of possible abuse and waste. If we over-re-distributed by higher taxation, the high performers would cease to strive. Our difficulty was to strike the right balance.

My primary preoccupation was to give every citizen a stake in the country and its future. I wanted a home-owning society. I had seen the contrast between the blocks of low-cost rental apartments, badly misused and poorly maintained, and those of house-proud owners, and was convinced that if every family owned its home, the country would be more stable. After we won the general election in September 1963, while Singapore was in Malaysia, I had the Housing and Development Board (HDB) announce a home ownership scheme. We had set up the HDB in 1960 as a statutory authority to build low-cost housing for workers. The HDB offered buyers housing loans in 1964, at a low interest rate with repayment periods of up to 15 years, but the scheme did not take off. Prospective buyers could not raise the down payment of 20 percent of the selling price.

After independence in 1965, I was troubled by Singapore's completely urban electorate. I had seen how voters in capital cities always tended to vote against the government of the day and was determined that our householders should become home owners, otherwise we would not have political stability. My other important motive was to give all parents whose sons would have to do national service a stake in the Singapore their sons had to defend. If the soldier's family did not own their home, he would soon conclude he would be fighting to protect the properties of the wealthy. I believed this sense of ownership was vital for our new society which had no deep roots in a common historical experience. On this, Keng Swee as defense minister was my strongest supporter. Other ministers thought home ownership desirable but not that vital.

The colonial government had started the Central Provident Fund (CPF) as a simple savings scheme for retirement: 5 percent of wages contributed by the employee with a matching 5 percent by the employer, to be withdrawn at age 55. As a pension scheme it was inadequate. Keng Swee and I decided to expand this compulsory savings scheme into a fund that would enable every worker to own a home. In 1968, after we passed an amendment to the CPF Act to raise the rate of contribution, the HDB launched a revised home ownership scheme. Workers were allowed to use their accumulated CPF savings to pay the 20 percent down payment and service the housing loan for the balance by monthly installments over 20 years.

I had earlier discussed my plan with NTUC leaders. Because they placed their confidence in me, I felt I had to overcome all difficulties to fulfill my promise to the unions that every worker would be given the opportunity to own a home. I therefore gave this scheme my constant attention, making adjustments from time to time as market conditions affected wages, construction costs, and the price of land. Every year, the National Wages Council recommended an increase in wages based on the previous year's economic growth. Once workers got used to a higher take-home pay, I knew they would resist any increase in their CPF contribution that would reduce their spendable money. So, almost yearly I increased the rate of CPF contributions, but such that there was still a net increase in take-home pay. It was painless for the workers and kept inflation down. This was only made possible by high growth year after year. And because the government fulfilled its promise of fair shares for workers through the ownership of their homes, industrial peace prevailed.

From 1955 to 1968, the CPF contribution had remained unchanged. I raised it in stages from 5 percent to a maximum of 25 percent in 1984, making a total savings rate of 50 percent of wages. This was later reduced to 40 percent. The minister for labor was usually most anxious to have the worker's take-home pay increased and would urge me to put less into the CPF. I regularly overruled him. I was determined to avoid placing the burden of the present generation's welfare costs onto the next generation.

In 1961, a big fire completely destroyed a squatter settlement on 47 acres of land at Bukit Ho Swee, making some 16,000 families homeless. I immediately amended the law to allow the government, after a fire, to acquire the fire site at the price without vacant possession, as if the land still had squatters on it. This meant, at that time, about one-third of its market value with vacant possession. In moving the bill, I argued, "It is heinous in the extreme to allow any profit to be made out of this fire. In fact, if any profit is allowed to be made, then it will only be an inducement, a temptation to arson by those who possess land with squatters on it."

Later, I further amended the law to give the government power to acquire land for public purposes at its value on a date then fixed at 30 November 1973. I saw no reason why private landowners should profit from an increase in land value brought about by economic development and the infrastructure paid for with public funds. As we became more prosperous, we moved the base year to January 1986, January 1992, and then to January 1995, closer to market rates.

The number who wanted to buy new HDB apartments rose rapidly from about 3,000 in 1967 to 70,000 in 1996. More than half of these buyers in the 1990s already owned HDB homes, but wanted to upgrade to bigger ones. In 1996, we had $725,000 HDB apartments, out of which only 9 percent were rented out; the rest were owner-occupied, ranging in value from $150,000 for the smallest three-room apartments to $450,000 for executive apartments.

From time to time I intervened directly, as in May 1974 when I asked the chief executive officer to improve the quality and vary the apartment designs and landscaping of new towns so that they would not look so uniform. The architectural variations that followed gave distinctiveness and character to the new towns by exploiting unique site features such as undulating terrain and ponds.

In the first decade from 1965, the new housing estates were sited on the fringes of the central area, in Tiong Bahru, Queenstown, Toa Payoh, and MacPherson. After 1975, they were built further afield, in then rural or farming areas. Following my discussions with EDB officers, I asked the HDB to set aside land in these estates for clean industries which could then tap the large pool of young women and housewives whose children were already schooling. This proved successful when Philips built its first factory in 1971 in Toa Payoh. After this, most new towns had clean air-conditioned factories set up by MNCs producing computer peripherals and electronics—Hewlett-Packard, Compaq, Texas Instruments, Apple Computer, Motorola, Seagate, Hitachi, Mitsubishi, Aiwa, and Siemens. They provided over 150,000 jobs for more women than men, most living nearby; this helped to double or triple family incomes.

Compressing 30 years into a few pages makes it all appear simple and straightforward. There were enormous problems, especially in the early stages when we resettled farmers and others from almost rent-free wooden squatter huts with no water, power, or modern sanitation, and therefore no utility bills, into high-rise dwellings with all these amenities but also a monthly bill to pay. It was a wrenching experience for them in personal, social, and economic terms.

Difficult adjustments were inevitable and there were comic, even absurd, results. Several pig farmers could not bear to part with their pigs and reared them in their high-rise apartments. Some were seen coaxing their pigs up the stairs! One family, a couple with 12 children moving from a hut to a new HDB apartment at Old Airport Road, brought a dozen chickens and ducks to rear in the kitchen. The mother built a wooden gate at the kitchen entrance to stop them from entering the living room. In the evenings, the children would look for earthworms and insects at the grass patches outdoors for feed. They did this for 10 years until they moved into another apartment.

The Malays preferred to be closer to the ground. They planted vegetables around the high-rise as they used to do in their kampongs. For a long while, many Chinese, Malays, and Indians walked up the stairs instead of taking the elevators, not because they wanted the exercise but because they were afraid of elevators. There were people who continued to use kerosene lamps instead of electric bulbs. Others carried on their old business as before, selling cigarettes, sweets, and sundry goods from their front rooms on the ground floor. They all suffered from culture shock.

Success brought new problems. Those waiting for their homes noticed that prices of apartments went up year by year with rising costs of labor and imported materials and appreciating land value. They became impatient and wanted their apartments as soon as possible. There was a limit to what we could do well. We made one of our more grievous mistakes in 1982–1984 by more than doubling the number of apartments we had previously built. I had appointed Teh Cheang Wan minister for national development in 1979. Before that, he had been the CEO of the HDB. He assured me that he could meet the demand for more homes. He did, but the contractors could not cope with the enlarged workload, and poor workmanship caused great unhappiness when defects surfaced a few years later. They had to be put right at considerable cost to the HDB and inconvenience to the owner occupants.

I should have known that it does not pay to yield to popular pressure beyond our capacity to deliver. Yet I was party to a similar mistake in the early 1990s. As property prices rose, everybody wanted to make a profit on the sale of their old home and then upgrade to a new one, the biggest they could afford. Instead of choking off demand by charging a levy to reduce their windfall profits, I agreed that we accommodate the voters by increasing the number of homes built. That aggravated the real estate bubble and made it more painful when the currency crisis struck in 1997. Had we choked off demand earlier, in 1995, we would have been immensely better off.

To prevent older estates from looking like slums, I suggested to the minister for national development in 1989 that it was time to upgrade old housing with public funds to make them approximate the quality of the new. He agreed and sent missions abroad to study how such improvements could be made while the occupants remained in residence. The missions found examples in Germany, France, and Japan. The HDB started with a demonstration phase for older apartments, spending S$58,000 per home to upgrade the estates and build additional space for a utility room, bathroom, or kitchen extension, but charging the owner only S$4,500. The facade and surroundings were refurbished to match the standard of the newer estates and the facilities of private condominiums, with covered linkways, common covered areas for social functions, and landscaping. The value of the upgraded homes rose substantially.

Another intractable problem was health care. I was a student in Britain when the Labour government in 1947 implemented the National Health Service. Their belief that all people were equal and no one should be denied the best of medical services was idealistic but impractical and led to ballooning costs. The British National Health Service was a failure. American-style medical insurance schemes are expensive, with high premiums because of wasteful and extravagant diagnostic tests paid for out of insurance. We had to find our own solution.

The ideal of free medical services collided against the reality of human behavior, certainly in Singapore. My first lesson came from government clinics and hospitals. When doctors prescribed free antibiotics, patients took their tablets or capsules for two days, did not feel better, and threw away the balance. They then consulted private doctors, paid for their antibiotics, completed the course, and recovered. I decided to impose a charge of 50 cents for each attendance at outpatient dispensaries. This fee was gradually increased over the years to keep pace with rising incomes and inflation.

I wrestled with the problem of preventing our health budget from growing out of control. In 1975, I discussed with a few cabinet colleagues my proposal to set aside part of each person's monthly CPF contribution for co-payment of that person's medical bills. Keng Swee, the deputy prime minister, supported a contribution of 2 percent for hospital charges. He agreed it was better than a generalized health insurance system, because expenses would be charged against an individual; this would prevent abuse.

Toh Chin Chye, then the minister for health, wanted the proposal shelved. He had just returned from China, where he had visited some hospitals in Beijing, and was impressed by the excellent medical services which were free, providing the same treatment for all, from the highest to the lowest in the land. I said I did not believe they had such medical standards for everyone in Beijing, let alone for all in China.

I decided not to make an issue of it. Instead, I asked the permanent secretary of the health ministry, Dr. Andrew Chew Guan Khuan, to work out how much of a person's CPF contribution would have to be set aside to enable that person to meet part of his or her health costs. He reported that it would require between 6 and 8 percent of a person's CPF contribution. From 1977, I made all CPF members set aside 1 percent of their monthly income in a special account that could be used to co-pay medical expenses for themselves and their families. It was gradually increased to 6 percent.

After the 1980 election, I put Goh Chok Tong in charge of the health ministry. He had been elected an MP in 1976 and was equal to the job. I explained my thinking on health services and gave him some research reports and other articles on health care costs to read. He understood what I wanted: good health services, with waste and costs kept in check by requiring co-payments from the user. Subsidies for health care were necessary, but could be extremely wasteful and ruinous for the budget.

When Medisave was implemented in 1984, each CPF "special account" had accumulated a tidy sum. We increased the monthly contributions for the Medisave account to 6 percent of wages, with an upper limit of S$15,000 in 1986. The limit was increased at regular intervals. Savings above this limit were transferred to a member's general CPF account which could be used for home mortgage payments or other investments. To reinforce family solidarity and responsibility, Medisave accounts could be used to pay medical costs for a member's immediate family: grandparents, parents, spouse, and children.

Co-payment by patients did prevent waste. A patient in a government hospital pays fees subsidized at rates up to 80 percent, depending on the type of ward he or she chooses. As incomes increased, fewer patients chose the lower-cost wards, which had the highest government subsidies, and opted for wards with more comfort but lower subsidies. We considered but rejected a means test to determine which wards patients were entitled to use; it would have been difficult to implement. Instead we encouraged people to upgrade to the ward they could afford by making clear differences in comfort between different types of wards. It was in effect a self-administered means test. Rising incomes resulting in high Medisave savings made people feel wealthy enough to choose the better-fitted wards.

We allowed the use of Medisave for private hospital fees, subject to price limits for various procedures. This competition put pressure on government hospitals to improve their service quality. But we disallowed the use of Medisave for visits to outpatient clinics or private GPs. We believed more people would see a doctor unnecessarily for minor ailments if they could pay from Medisave than if they had to pay from their monthly budget.

In 1990, we added MediShield, an optional insurance against the cost of catastrophic illnesses. Premiums could be paid out of the Medisave account. In 1993, we set up Medifund with money from government revenue to cover those who had exhausted their Medisave and MediShield and had no immediate family to rely on. They could apply for a total waiver of all fees which would then be paid from Medifund. Thus, while no one is deprived of essential medical care, we do not have a massive drain on resources, nor long queues waiting for operations.

A universal problem we had to resolve was retirement benefits or pensions when a worker became too old to work. In Europe and America, the government provided these pensions, paid for by taxpayers. We decided that all workers should accumulate their own savings in the CPF for old age. In 1978, we allowed the CPF to be used as a personal savings fund for investments. Early that year the government had revamped Singapore's bus services. We then formed the Singapore Bus Services (SBS), listed it on the stock exchange, and allowed members to use up to S$5,000 of their CPF to buy SBS shares on its first listing. I wanted it to have the widest share ownership so that profits would go back to the workers, the regular users of public transport. There would also be less incentive to demand cheaper bus fares and government subsidies for public transport.

After this success, we liberalized the use of the CPF to allow investment in private, commercial, and industrial properties, trustee shares, unit trusts or mutual funds, and gold. If their investments outperformed the CPF interest rate, they could take the surplus out of the CPF. We had safeguards to prevent members from losing all their savings. By 1997, 1.5 million CPF members had invested in stocks and shares, mostly blue chips on the main board of the Stock Exchange of Singapore.

When we floated Singapore Telecom in 1993, we sold a large portion of its shares at half their market value to all adult citizens. We did this to redistribute part of the surpluses the government had accumulated over the years of our steady growth. We wanted our people to hold shares in a major Singapore company and have a tangible stake in the country's success.

To discourage "stagging," the immediate sale for cash gains, which happened when the British privatized British Telecom, we offered shareholders the right to bonus shares after the first, second, fourth, and sixth years, provided they had not sold the original shares. This resulted in 90 percent of the workforce owning Singapore Telecom shares, probably the highest in the world.

After observing how differently people maintained their own apartments as against rented ones, I believed that a deep sense of property was instinctive in a person. During the riots of the 1950s and early 1960s, people would join in the rioting, stone windshields, overturn cars, and burn them. When riots broke out in the mid-1960s, after they owned homes and property, they acted differently. I saw young men carrying their scooters parked on the roads to safety up the stairs of their HDB blocks. I was strengthened in my resolve to give every family solid assets which I was confident they would protect and defend, especially their home. I was not wrong.

We chose to redistribute wealth by asset enhancement, not by subsidies for consumption. Those who are not winners of top prizes in the free market will still get valuable consolation prizes for competing in the marathon of life. Those who want to spend can sell some of their assets. Significantly, few have consumed their assets. Instead they have invested and increased their assets, spending only the derived income. They want to conserve their capital for a rainy day, and later leave it to their children and grandchildren.

The CPF grew from 420,000 members in 1965, to over 2.8 million members worth S$85 billion in 1998, excluding S$80 billion withdrawn to pay for HDB homes, private properties, and investments in shares. Almost every worker carries his or her own pension fund. At his or her death, the balance of a worker's CPF savings will be paid according to the worker's written wishes without the delays and formality of applying to court.

Watching the ever-increasing costs of the welfare state in Britain and Sweden, we decided to avoid this debilitating system. We noted by the 1970s that when governments undertook primary responsibility for the basic duties of the head of a family, the drive in people weakened. Welfare undermined self-reliance. People did not have to work for their families' well-being. The handout became a way of life. The downward spiral was relentless as motivation and productivity went down. People lost the drive to achieve because they paid too much in taxes. They became dependent on the state for their basic needs.

We thought it best to reinforce the Confucian tradition that a man is responsible for his family—his parents, wife, and children. We used to face frequent criticism and attacks from opposition parties and the Western media, through their correspondents in Singapore, for pursuing such hard-hearted policies and refusing subsidies for consumption. It was difficult to counter the seductiveness of welfare promises by the opposition during elections. In the 1960s and 1970s, the failure of the European welfare state was not yet self-evident. It took two generations for the harm to work its way through and be seen in lowered performance of individuals, sluggish growth rates, and growing budget deficits. We needed time to build up substantial CPF savings, and have many own their homes. Only then would people not want their individual savings put into a common pool for everyone to have the same welfare "entitlement," own the same kind of home, or enjoy the same level of comfort in hospitals. I was certain they would prefer to make that additional effort to pay for the extras they sought, either in the size and quality of their homes or in the level of comfort in hospitals. It was fortunate that I was able to withstand these criticisms in successive elections until the 1980s, when the failure of the welfare state was acknowledged by the Western media.

The CPF has made for a different society. People who have substantial savings and assets have a different attitude to life. They are more conscious of their strength and take responsibility for themselves and their families. They are not attracted to the "buffet syndrome" where, after paying a health insurance premium, you consume as much in medical investigations and procedures as you or your doctor can think of.

To ensure a member's savings will be enough for his retirement, neither his CPF balance nor his assets bought with CPF money can be levied upon or attached for any debt or claim. Nor is his HDB apartment bought with CPF money available to his creditors. Only the HDB can execute against an owner for mortgage installments unpaid on the home.

The CPF has provided workers with a comprehensive self-financing social security fund equal to any old-age pension system or entitlement program, without shifting the burden to the next generation of workers. It is fairer and sounder to have each generation pay for itself and each person save for his own pension fund.

The CPF and home ownership have ensured political stability, the foundation upon which Singapore grew and developed without interruption for more than 30 years. Singaporeans are unlike their counterparts in Hong Kong, Taipei, Seoul, or Tokyo, who have high wages but pay vast rents for tiny rooms which they will never own. Such an electorate would not have reelected the PAP with solid majorities in successive elections.

To work a social security system like the CPF, an economy needs to have low inflation and interest rates above inflation rates. People must be confident their savings will not melt away through inflation or devaluation against other currencies. In other words, sound fiscal and budget policies are the preconditions for the success of the CPF.

If we had not redistributed the wealth generated by our people competing in a free-market economy, we would have weakened Singaporeans' sense of solidarity, the feeling that they are one people sharing a common destiny. I can best explain the need for balance between individual competition and group solidarity by using the metaphor of the oriental yin and yang symbol, two fishlike shapes forming a circle. Yin represents the female element; yang, the male. The more yang (male) competitiveness in society, the higher the total performance. If winner takes all, competition will be keen, but group solidarity weak. The more yin (female) solidarity, with rewards evenly redistributed, the greater the group solidarity, but the weaker the total performance because of reduced competition.

In Singapore's Asian society, parents want their children to have a better start in life than they themselves had. Because nearly all Singaporeans are of immigrant stock, their desire for security, especially for their children, is intense. Owning assets, instead of subsisting on welfare, has given people the power and the responsibility to decide what they want to spend their money on.

There will always be the irresponsible or the incapable, some 5 percent of our population. They will run through any asset, whether a house or shares. We try hard to make them as independent as possible and not end up in welfare homes. More important, we try to rescue their children from repeating the feckless ways of their parents. We have arranged help but in such a way that only those who have no other choice will seek it. This is the opposite of attitudes in the West, where liberals actively encourage people to demand their entitlements with no sense of shame, causing an explosion of welfare costs.

Our policies kept people keen to achieve their best. Monetary stability, a balanced budget, and low taxes encouraged ample investments and high productivity. On top of their high CPF compulsory savings of 40 percent of their wages, many have additional voluntary savings in the Post Office Savings Bank, later called POSBank. All these helped the government to pay for infrastructure: roads, bridges, airports, container ports, power stations, reservoirs, and a mass rapid transit system. By avoiding wasteful expenditure, we kept inflation low and did not need to borrow foreign funds. Since the 1960s, we had annual budget surpluses, except for the years 1985 to 1987, when we were in recession. Government expenditure has averaged 20 percent of GDP, compared to an average of 33 percent in the G7 economies. On the other hand, our development expenditure has consistently been much higher than that of the G7 countries.

We aimed in most years to raise sufficient revenue to finance both operating and development expenditure, and also to be internationally competitive in our tax structure. In 1984, direct taxes accounted for two-thirds of our total tax revenue. We progressively reduced income tax, both personal and corporate, until direct taxes in 1996 made up about half of total tax revenue, compared to three-quarters in the G7 economies. We moved from taxing income to taxing consumption. The top marginal income tax rate for individuals was reduced from 55 percent in 1965 to 28 percent in 1996. The corporate tax rate of 40 percent was reduced to 26 percent in the same period. Singapore has no capital gains tax. Our GST (goods and services tax, the equivalent of VAT) is 3 percent. Our import tariff is about 0.4 percent.

Initially we had punishing rates of estate duty, based on the British socialist philosophy of soaking the rich. But good tax lawyers and accountants left little for the tax collector. In 1984, we cut estate duty from a maximum of 60 percent to between 5 percent and 10 percent, depending on the value of the estate. We collected more revenue as the wealthy no longer found it worthwhile to avoid estate duty. We have nontax revenue from a wide range of user charges. Our aim is to have partial or total cost recovery for goods and services provided by the state. This checks over-consumption of subsidized public services and reduces distortions in the allocation of resources.

Sustained growth ensures stability, which encourages investments that create wealth. Because we made the difficult decisions early, we have established a virtuous cycle—low expenditure, high savings; low welfare, high investments. We have accumulated assets during the last 30 years of strong growth with a relatively youthful workforce. In the next 20 years, our economic growth will slow down as our population ages. Private savings rates will decline, and health care costs will rise sharply with more old people, just when taxpayers as a percentage of the population will decrease. We can partly meet this problem by taking steps early to ensure the old will have larger Medisave savings; the better answer is to attract educated and skilled immigrants to enlarge our talent pool and increase both GDP and revenue. The government must give increased financial and administrative support to more community welfare projects, as many as there are social volunteers to drive and supervise them.

All this fine-tuning to rev up the economy would never have been possible had the communists retained their baleful influence. Instead their open-front leaders fumbled and faltered after Singapore became independent in 1965. They removed themselves from the constitutional arena and left the PAP to set the agenda. We seized the opportunity and reshaped the politics of Singapore.

# 8. The Communists Self-Destruct

On the morning of 17 November 1965, the superintendent of Changi Prison noticed that Lim Chin Siong, who normally greeted him, was strangely silent. The leader of the communist united front in the 1950s and 1960s, and once PAP member of the Legislative Assembly, had been detained since a 1963 security operation. Lim was trembling. His clothes were dishevelled, his trousers torn, and he appeared to have been in a fight. He wanted to be transferred to another part of the prison. His fellow detainees asked and were allowed to interview Lim in the superintendent's presence. Looking upset, Lim muttered, "They will beat me up, they will poison . . . I will finish myself or they will. . . . Ideological differences." He again asked to be moved and was transferred to another section of the prison.

He was taken ill the next day and was brought first to the prison hospital, then to the General Hospital. At about 3:00 A.M. a detective saw him near a medical trolley looking for something. Questioned, he replied he was looking for a knife. At 6:15 A.M. Lim got up and went to the toilet. A warder and a detective waited outside. When Lim did not come out after 3 minutes, they knocked on the door. There was no response. The warder looked into the toilet from an adjacent one and saw Lim hanging from a cistern. He kicked the door open, rushed in and lowered him. Lim had used his pyjamas to hang himself. The doctors resuscitated him.

The communists in detention were confused and divided by the reverses they had suffered: first, their setback in September 1962 when they lost the referendum on merger with Malaysia, and second, their defeat in the September 1963 elections. The Barisan Sosialis, their united-front party, won only 13 out of 51 seats and 33 percent of the votes and emerged as the second largest party. When Singapore was separated from Malaysia, Dr. Lee Siew Choh, the Barisan Sosialis chairman, denounced Singapore's independence as "phoney." He had lost his seat in the 1963 election and was not a member of Parliament when it met in December 1965. On behalf of the Barisan MPs, he declared that they would boycott Parliament. A short while later he announced that they would abandon constitutional politics and "take the battle to the streets." He was imitating the madness of the Cultural Revolution in China gleaned from Radio Beijing broadcasts. As Red Guards took to the streets in China, he ordered his Barisan cohorts to mount demonstrations at hawker centers and mobile night bazaars (*pasar malam*), and wherever there were crowds. Like the Red Guards, they too carried banners and placards and clashed with the police. The police broke up their assemblies and charged the demonstrators in court for mischief and rioting.

Instead of winning public support, these tactics further split and destroyed the Barisan. On 1 January 1966, Lim Huan Boon, the Barisan opposition leader in Parliament, announced his resignation as MP. He said that Singapore was independent; the Barisan's policies were irrelevant and in the interests of international communism, not of the people. The following day the party expelled him. He responded that the Barisan had broken faith not only with the democratic system but also with the people who had elected them. A week later two more Barisan MPs resigned, declaring that the party under Lee Siew Choh's leadership was at a dead-end, and it was a fallacy to think that Singapore's independence was "phoney." Two days after that another Barisan MP, S. T. Bani, then in detention, resigned, renounced communism, and quit politics for good. The communist united front was in total disarray.

Lee Siew Choh had not only rendered the communist united front ineffective, he had in effect surrendered the constitutional arena to the PAP. It was a costly mistake, one that gave the PAP unchallenged dominance of Parliament for the next 30 years.

I sensed a fundamental change in the attitudes of the people. They realized Singapore was on its own. The British would soon leave; the

Malaysians had no love for us; the Indonesians wanted to destroy us. Politics was now no longer a game of mass rallies and demonstrations. It had become a matter of life and death. All Chinese know the saying: Big fish eat small fish, small fish eat shrimp. Singapore was a shrimp. People worried over their survival. They knew only the PAP had been tried and tested and had the experience to lead them out of danger.

In the Bukit Merah by-election in January 1966, the PAP won with an overwhelming majority of 7,000 out of 11,000 votes. The Barisan call for blank votes got less than 400. In succession we won six more by-elections, all unopposed, to fill Barisan resignations, and brought in higher-quality, better-qualified MPs, many of them Chinese-educated Nanyang University graduates. They helped to move the Chinese-speaking toward the political center.

In January 1968, soon after the British announced their decision to withdraw their forces, I called for a general election. The Barisan boycotted the election. It was another major mistake, one that was to keep them out of Parliament for good. We were returned unopposed in 51 constituencies and won the remaining seven with over 80 percent of valid votes cast. Singapore's future looked so bleak that the opposition parties abandoned the field to us. After winning all the seats, I set out to widen our support in order to straddle as broad a middle ground as possible. I intended to leave the opposition only the extreme left and right. We had to be careful not to abuse the absolute power we had been given. I was sure that if we remained honest and kept faith with the people, we would be able to carry them with us, however tough and unpalatable our policies.

It is impossible in Singapore's political climate of the 1990s to imagine the psychological grip the communists had on the Chinese-speaking in the Singapore and Malaya of the 1950s and 1960s. The communists made these people believe that what had happened in China would also come to pass in Malaya, that communism was the wave of the future and those who opposed them would be buried by history. They had then a hardcore following of some 20 to 30 percent of the electorate that we could not win over for many years, despite the economic benefits we brought them over the next decade.

We had formed and shaped our political strategies and tactics during our struggles as the opposition party from 1954 to 1959, and in govern-

ment from 1959 to 1965. The skillful and tough methods of the unyielding communists, followed by the equally ruthless communal methods of
the UMNO Ultras, were unforgettable lessons in political infighting.
Street fighting with them was like unarmed combat with no holds barred,
in a contest where winner took all. We learned not to give hostages to our
adversaries or they would have destroyed us. Even after we had reduced
the communist strength in the united-front organization, their lurking
presence in the underground had to be taken into our political calculations. At any time they could resort to violence or choose to rebuild their
open-front organizations, or both. Weekly intelligence reports from the
Internal Security Department made us ever mindful of their presence in
Singapore and their secret network that linked them to armed groups in
peninsular Malaya.

After the Barisan became ineffective, the communists reverted to violence and terror. They reappeared as the Malayan National Liberation
Front (MNLF), an adjunct of the Malayan Communist Party (MCP),
exploding several bombs in Jurong and Changi, two ends of Singapore, in
the 1970s. Among those killed was the six-year-old daughter of a British
serviceman.

By the 1970s, they had been reduced to some 2,000 guerrillas on the
Thai side of the Thai-Malaysian border, a few hundred scattered in the
jungles of peninsular Malaysia, and some terrorist squads in the towns.
Could we have defeated them if we had allowed them habeas corpus and
abjured the powers of detention without trial? I doubt it. Nobody dared
speak out against them, let alone in open court. Thousands were held in
detention camps in Malaya, and hundreds in Singapore. The British had
banished thousands to China in the 1940s and 1950s.

Among those not banished was Lim Chin Siong. The price he paid when
communism failed him was his attempted suicide. This was recounted in
detail by the superintendent of prisons in December 1965 during the trial
of two Barisan Sosialis editors of the party's Chinese-language tabloid.
They were charged with sedition because they wrote that the "PAP
regime" was "plotting to murder comrade Lim Chin Siong." The defense

brought many witnesses to give false evidence to support their absurd allegation that there had been a conspiracy to murder Lim at the General Hospital. The two editors were convicted.

In July 1969, three and a half years after his suicide attempt, Lim asked to see me. I had not met him since he led the Barisan split from the PAP in June 1961. When he came to Sri Temasek, my official residence, on the evening of 23 July, he looked a disillusioned man. He had decided to give up politics for good and wanted to leave for studies in London. He would like his girlfriend and fellow detainee, a former trade union worker of the Singapore Factory and Shop Workers' Union in the 1950s who had been released earlier, to accompany him. I readily agreed and wished him well in his new life in London. He had wasted the best years of his life, ending up disgusted with his former comrades and bitter at their blinkered and unthinking refusal to face reality.

In an open letter to Lee Siew Choh, he wrote, "I have completely lost confidence in the international communist movement," and resigned from all posts in the Barisan. Lee immediately denounced Lim as a "spineless and barefaced renegade traitor" and expelled him from the party. Lim's unhappy break from the party he had founded marked the final disintegration of the Barisan as a political force.

After more than a decade in Britain Lim returned to Singapore in the 1980s. We never met again although we exchanged greetings in New Year cards. When he died in 1996, his former comrades forgave him. Although in 1969 they had denounced him as a "spineless and barefaced renegade traitor," hundreds of former communists and their supporters attended his wake. At the funeral service he was praised as "a hero of the people and nation." Some 500 other sympathizers held another memorial service in Kuala Lumpur, more to show the world that they were still strong and firm in their beliefs than to honor him. Lim had been the wiser to have acknowledged earlier than they did that communism was a lost cause. In an open letter of condolence to his wife, I expressed my respect for his personal honesty and his dedication to his cause.

The communist battle in Singapore and Malaysia was lost years before the collapse of communism in the Soviet Union and well before China abandoned them in the 1980s. However, one communist activist held out after more than 20 years in detention, a believer who refused to give up even after communism collapsed worldwide—Chia Thye Poh. He was a determined man with stubborn if misguided convictions. Although a member of the MCP, he strenuously denied having any links with or sympathy for communism in spite of his membership being confirmed to our Internal Security Department (ISD) by several MCP members, two of whom he directly reported to.

He was released in 1989 to reside on Sentosa, a resort island, where he worked as a part-time translator, and was finally freed from all restrictions in 1998. He was not able to accept that his vision of the future had failed. He continued to deny his communist links, playing on the human rights sentiments of the Western media. His detention, in spite of Western media pressure, served to discourage other communist cadres from reactivating their cause under cover of exercising their democratic rights. They were formidable opponents. We had to be as resolute and unyielding in this contest of wills.

We were reminded from time to time that the communists never give up. The switch to English in our schools had dried up their supply of Chinese-educated recruits so they tried hard to enlist the English-educated. Knowing how skillful, resourceful, and tenacious the communists were in their methods of infiltration and manipulation, we were determined that they should not be given any chance to make a comeback by rebuilding their front organizations, especially in the trade unions. Their ability to penetrate an organization with a cadre of influential activists and take control of it was fearsome.

A small group of English-educated pro-Marxist activists made use of the Workers' Party in 1985, writing articles for the party paper, the *Hammer,* and helping to produce it from behind the scenes. They declined to take charge of the publication openly although requested by the party to do so. This put the ISD on alert. The group included some University of Singapore graduates associated with Tan Wah Piow, a pro-communist student activist who had fled to London in 1976. Others in Tan's group had gone to China to work for the CPM clandestine radio. The ISD considered these pro-Marxist English-educated activists an incipient security problem and in 1987 recommended that they be detained. I accepted the recommendation. I did not want a couple of pro-communist cadres including Tan, on whom we had hard evidence of links with the CPM, to rebuild their influence using innocent but disaffected activists. Their new united front included a Roman Catholic who had given up becoming a priest to dabble in liberation theology.

Because of Singapore's experience of communist infiltration and subversion, the ISD is always alert to any clandestine penetration of open organizations, especially trade unions and old boys' associations. To make it difficult for them to manipulate nonpolitical bodies, we require all who enter the political arena to form their legitimate vehicle, a political party. This forces them out into the open and makes them easy to monitor. In this way we have prevented our trade unions from being infiltrated and kept our social, cultural, and trade organizations free from communist influence. One important reason why we will not allow the remnant communist cadres in Thailand to come back without squaring their accounts with the ISD is so they will not pass their infiltration and subversion skills to a younger generation of activists, now English-educated.

The most prominent and senior communist leader we allowed to return to Singapore from China was Eu Chooi Yip, Keng Swee's old friend and contemporary in Raffles College. Keng Swee had met him on many occasions when he went to China in the late 1980s and was convinced he had given up communism. Keng Swee asked me whether I would allow Chooi Yip to return. I did, and in 1989 he returned to Singapore with his wife and two daughters. Soon after that P. V. Sharma also asked to return from China where he had been living after he was banished. He was a former president of the Singapore Teachers' Union who had been arrested in 1951, at the same time as Devan Nair and Samad Ismail, and banished to India where he was born. From India, Sharma had gone to China. Sharma also returned with his wife and children.

Eu Chooi Yip was the direct superior in the MCP of Fang Chuang Pi, the leader of the communists in Singapore whom I had met in the 1950s and named the Plen, short for "plenipotentiary" of the communists. In mid-1990, Chooi Yip asked through Keng Swee if I would allow the Plen's son to work in Singapore. I agreed after Keng Swee assured me the son was not a security risk. An ISD officer interviewed the young man and confirmed that he was no communist. He was born in late 1965 in the Riau islands where his father was in hiding after leaving Singapore in 1962. At the age of 5, he was sent to China and grew up and attended schools in Changsha, Hunan province, where the MCP radio station, "The Voice of the Malayan Revolution," was sited. He did engineering in Qinghua University, one of the best in China. He and his father must have believed he would have a better future in Singapore than in China. He came to Singapore in November 1990 to take a job that Keng Swee had secured for him as an engineer in a government-linked company.

Shortly after his son arrived in Singapore, the Plen sent me a letter through a Singapore Chinese journalist "to seek reconciliation." He also sent me a video documentary entitled *Glorious Peace Settlement.* It was typical MCP propaganda: Surrender and the laying down of arms were called a "glorious peace settlement." I watched the Plen in uniform with a red star cap talking to his uniformed men about the success of peace talks, then the CPM leader Chin Peng visiting the camp, watching a dreadful concert. After that, the Plen made a speech and interrupted himself to lead the applause. I turned off the video.

The Plen followed up with another letter about his return to Singapore. I replied in March 1992 that I was no longer prime minister but knew the government's policy was not to deal with the CPM as a group. Any member of the CPM who wanted to come back to Singapore must cut his links with the party, make a full disclosure of his past CPM activities, and satisfy the Internal Security Department that he had done so. I added that it was on these terms that the government had allowed Eu Chooi Yip, his superior in the party, to return to Singapore from China. The Plen replied immediately to express his disappointment. He found this unacceptable, and there the matter rested. His end game had come when the CPM formally stopped their armed insurrection by signing an agreement with the Malaysian government's representative in Haadyai in south Thailand, and the Thai government allowed him and his followers to reside in a "peace village" near there.

However, some 15 or 20 of the Plen's followers quietly returned, gave a full account of their past activities to our ISD, and settled down to a new life in a very different Singapore. Like Eu Chooi Yip, Sharma, and the Plen's son, they too felt they would be better off here than in China or Thailand.

When I arrived in Beijing in August 1995, our ambassador handed me a letter from the Plen. He wanted to meet me. Our first meeting had been in 1958 when I was just an assemblyman. Through an emissary, he had asked to see me, so I met him quietly on a road next to the Legislative Assembly and took him into a committee room. He assured me his party supported me and wanted to work together with the PAP. I asked for evidence that he was in charge of the MCP organization in Singapore. He said I had to take his word for it. I suggested he prove his credentials by getting a city councillor of the Workers' Party I believed to be a communist activist to resign. He agreed and asked for time. A few weeks later, the councillor resigned. It was an impressive display of his capacity to control his members even while he was on the run from the police. We met again on three other occasions before I formed the government. Our final meeting was on 11 May 1961, when I was already prime minister. He promised me support and cooperation if I gave the communists more room to organize. I gave him no such undertaking and he ordered his united-front organizations to bring down the PAP government before vanishing.

That final meeting was in an unfurnished apartment in an uncompleted HDB building in Whampoa, lighted only by a candle. This time I received him at Diaoyutai, in the VIP state guesthouse of the People's Republic of China, on 23 August at 9:00 P.M. I wondered whether he saw the irony of the situation, that he was calling on me in Beijing where I was the honored guest of the communist government and party that had been the inspiration for his life's struggle.

It was an older and stouter Plen, no longer the gaunt features, the lean and hungry look of an angry, hunted revolutionary from the underground. At our last meeting, he served me warm beer. On this occasion I offered him a choice of beer, wine, or maotai. He thanked me but said that for health reasons he would drink plain Chinese tea. We spoke in Mandarin. He complimented me on my fluency. I returned the compliment over his command of English. He thanked me for allowing his son into Singapore in 1990 and letting him take a job. Choo and my principal private secretary, Alan Chan, sat in, and the Plen agreed to my tape-recording our conversation.

He spoke as though his position was still that of the 1950s and wanted to discuss the terms on which he and his 30 or so comrades could return to Singapore. First he tried the friendly approach, that I had a duty to resolve the old problems. As the CPM and PAP had been friends, could they not be friends again? I said we could, but as individuals. He said there must be some justice for his people. It was unfair that he could not return to Singapore. I said he could, but he must first close his accounts with the ISD by demonstrating that he had cut off his links with the CPM.

When the soft approach failed, he talked tough, reminding me that he had been responsible for my safety and had done much to protect me. I replied that it was a risk I had to take; his men could have killed me but the price would have been high. Moreover, I had been fair in giving him notice in a public speech to leave before Malaysia Day, September 1963, because after that the Malaysians would be in charge of security.

He said the Malaysian Special Branch had invited him to return; why could I not be as generous as the Malaysian government? I told him the obvious: The CPM could not win over its Malay mass base, unlike Singapore's Chinese base. I suggested he accept the Malaysian government's offer. He was not amused.

When I asked how he knew I was coming, he said it was a coincidence, that he had come to see his uncle and had learned of my visit from television. This was most improbable. A retired official of the Chinese foreign ministry had given his letter to our ambassador. The Plen must have been told by a Chinese comrade of my visit and awaited my arrival. He also denied what Lim Chin Siong had already revealed to the ISD, that after our final meeting in 1961, he had personally met and ordered Lim to break up the PAP and bring down the government.

Before leaving, he produced a camera and asked for pictures to be taken with my wife and me. I was happy to have a memento of the mysterious underground leader who from his hideout in Singapore could direct his subordinates in the open front with such total command. He had once inspired awe and fear in me. Shorn of the mystery and power of the underground, he looked a harmless, elderly man.


Despite ruthless methods where the ends justified the means, the communists failed, but not before destroying many who stood up against them, and others who after joining them decided that their cause was mistaken.

# 9.  Straddling the Middle Ground

The PAP has won 10 successive general elections since 1959, a period of 40 years. It has not gone flabby or effete. How did we do it? Between 1959 and 1965, we had fearful clashes, first with the communists and then the Malay communalists. On independence, we faced dire threats, Indonesia confronting us and Malaysia determined to bypass us. This series of events forged a bond of trust between that generation of voters and the old guard PAP leaders.

Our critics believed we stayed in power because we have been hard on our opponents. This is simplistic. If we had betrayed the people's trust, we would have been rejected. We led them out of the depths of despair in the 1960s into an era of unprecedented growth and development. We took advantage of the expansion in world trade and investments to move from Third World to First World standards in one generation.

We had learned from our toughest adversaries, the communists. Present-day opposition leaders go on walkabouts to decide where they will do well, based on the way people respond to them at hawker centers, coffee shops, food courts, and supermarkets, and whether people accept the pamphlets they hand out. I have never believed this. From many unhappy encounters with my communist opponents, I learned that while overall sentiment and mood do matter, the crucial factors are institutional and organizational networks to muster support. When we went into communist-dominated areas, we found ourselves frozen out. Key players in a constituency, including union leaders and officials of retailers' and hawkers' associations, and clan and alumni organizations, would all have been brought into a network by communist activists and made to feel part of a winning team. We could make little headway against them however hard we tried during elections. The only way we could counter their grip of the ground was to work on that same ground for years between elections.

To compete against the self-improvement night classes at the procommunist unions and associations, we formed the People's Association (PA). We brought into the PA, as corporate members, many clan associations, chambers of commerce, recreational clubs, and arts, leisure, and social activity groups. They provided advice and services in more than a hundred community centers we set up to conduct literacy classes in Chinese and English, and courses in sewing, cooking, and repairing automobiles, electrical instruments, radios, and television sets. By competing against and outdoing the communists, we gradually won back part of the ground they had cultivated.

During my constituency tours in 1962 and 1963, I had assembled activists in smaller towns and villages all over the island. They were the local leaders of various associations and clubs who constituted themselves as welcoming committees for their area to discuss with me and my team of officials road improvements, street lights, standpipes, and drains to alleviate flooding. After my visits, work teams would follow up, providing the funds to execute such projects.

While in Malaysia, after the race riots in 1964, we formed "goodwill committees" to keep communal relations from boiling over. Committee members were drawn from grassroots leaders of the different communities in the area.

I built on these "welcoming" and "goodwill" committees by co-opting their more active and promising members into management committees (MCs) of community centers and into citizens' consultative committees (CCCs). MCs of the community centers organized recreational, educational, and other activities. CCCs, with funds we provided, did local improvement projects, the smaller public works. They also raised their own funds to provide welfare grants and scholarships for the needy.

Community leaders at that time were reluctant, even fearful, to identify themselves openly with a political party. They preferred to be associated with the government. It was a holdover from the colonial period, especially during the years of the Emergency when the communists were active and any identification with political parties competing against the MCP could bring retribution. By creating semi-government institutions such as the MCs and CCCs we mobilized a wide spectrum of elders who were respected in their own communities. They worked with our MPs between elections, and during election time their influence and support flowed through into the voting, even though some of them stayed neutral rather than campaign actively.

Later, as the population moved into HDB high-rise blocks, I formed residents' committees (RCs), each serving a precinct of 6 to 10 blocks. This made for closer interaction between leaders and the residents of these blocks. Hence, in our HDB new towns, there is a network that leads from the RCs to the MCs and CCCs on to the prime minister's office, the nerve center. Opposition leaders on walkabouts go through well-tended PAP ground. Naturally there are floating voters. But there is a hard core of local leaders who know that their PAP MP, backed by the government, will attend to their needs whether during or between elections.

A turning point was the general election in 1968, soon after the British had announced the withdrawal of their forces. We won all seats by an overwhelming majority. By 1972, four years later, the people were relieved and happy that we had accomplished a near miracle. In spite of the withdrawal of British forces, and with it the loss of 20 percent of our GDP and some 50,000 jobs, we had high economic growth and lower unemployment. American multinational companies were creating thousands of jobs in electrical and electronic factories. When I called for elections in September 1972, 57 out of 65 seats were contested. We won them all, scoring 70 percent of the votes.

We were to repeat this total sweep again in 1976, winning 37 seats uncontested and all the 38 contested seats. The standing of the PAP leadership and the progress we had achieved made it difficult for the opposition. People had full confidence in the PAP leadership and were not interested in having an opposition. They wanted to get on with economic growth, leave their squatter huts for new homes they would buy with rising incomes from well-paid jobs, and send their children to the better schools we were building. The tide was rising for all. We had a fourth clean sweep in 1980—37 seats unopposed, and the remaining 38 contested seats with 77.5 percent of votes cast.

The noncommunist opposition politicians who emerged to fill the vacuum left by the communists were mostly opportunist types. During elections, they espoused programs that would appeal to their pro-communist following. But as long as they were not led by English-educated professionals who could lend respectability to a communist front, as David Marshall's old Workers' Party had done, they posed no danger. It was in this context that J. B. Jeyaretnam, a lawyer, appeared in a revived Workers' Party. As its candidate in the 1972 election, he advocated abolishing the Internal Security Act. Earlier, in the late 1960s, he had promised remerger with Malaya. He aspired to be Marshall's successor but was not as sharp or as eloquent.

But Jeyaretnam did break the PAP's spell of unprecedented total support in a by-election in 1981, a year after the general election. Devan Nair had resigned his Anson seat to become the president. I left the arrangements for the campaign to the new assistant secretary-general, Goh Chok Tong. Our candidate, a keen PAP activist, was not a good public speaker. I did not take part in the by-election campaign, leaving it completely to Goh and the younger leaders. They were confident we would win, but when the votes were counted on polling day, we had lost. It was quite a shock. I was disturbed, not by the defeat, but because I had had no signal from Goh that we might lose. I worried about his political sensitivity. James Fu, my press secretary, told me that people on the ground resented the overconfident attitude of the party leaders in the campaign. One reason for the loss was obvious. A large number of Singapore port workers in several blocks of apartments had to be moved to make way for a container-holding area but were not given alternative accommodation. The Port of Singapore Authority and the Housing and Development Board pushed this responsibility to each other.

Jeyaretnam (JBJ) was all sound and fury. He made wild allegations of police high-handedness and repeated every grievance disgruntled people channelled through him without checking the facts. That he had no principled stand suited us, because he was unlikely to become a credible alternative. I decided he was useful as a sparring partner for the new MPs who had not gone through the fight with the communists and the UMNO

Ultras. Besides, he filled up space on the opposition side of the political arena and probably kept better opponents out. His weakness was his sloppiness. He rambled on and on, his speeches apparently unprepared. When challenged on the detailed facts, he crumbled.

People, however, wanted an opposition voice in Parliament. The sense of crisis of the 1960s and 1970s had passed. Singaporeans were now more confident and wanted the PAP to know that they could not be taken for granted. In the 1984 election, we lost two seats, to JBJ in Anson and to Chiam See Tong, another lawyer and the secretary-general of the Singapore Democratic Party (SDP), in Potong Pasir. Chiam took a shrewder line than JBJ, more in tune with the sentiments of the population, that the PAP was doing a fair job, but could do better and should listen more to criticism. He improved his public standing. He and the people who made up the SDP were not the types to be used by the communists for their front activities. We treated him differently, extending him respect and latitude. We hoped that if he expanded, those who opposed us could gravitate toward a nonsubversive opposition.

These opposition figures were unlike the formidable adversaries we had met in Lim Chin Siong and his comrades who were serious men, committed to their cause. Jeyaretnam was a poseur, always seeking publicity, good or bad.


Without much of an opposition in Parliament, I missed a foil to project issues. I made up for it with a major annual speech. On a Sunday evening a week or so after my eve-of-National-Day telecast, I would speak at an indoor National Day rally of about 1,200 community leaders. It was televised live. With only notes, I would speak for one to two hours on the important issues of the day. But I would have read extensively on the subjects days before and mulled over how to simplify my presentation. Television polls showed I had high viewership. I had learned how to hold the audience, both those at the National Theatre and over television, and get them to follow my thought processes. I would speak first in Malay, then Hokkien (later Mandarin), and last in English, my master language. I had better rapport with my audience when I expressed my thoughts as they formed and flowed in my mind, whereas if I had a script, I could not get my message across with the same conviction and passion. This annual speech was an important occasion when I set out to move the people to work together with the government and overcome our problems.

During election time in the 1970s and 1980s, I spoke in the evenings at mass rallies in the constituencies, and at Fullerton Square in the heat of the tropical sun at 1 to 2 P.M., to reach out to office workers. Sometimes there would be a heavy shower and I would be drenched while the crowds sheltered under umbrellas or took cover on the "five-foot-way" (covered walkway) of offices around the square. The people stayed and I carried on. Although wet, I never felt the cold; my adrenaline was pouring out. The spoken word on television made a far greater impact than the written script in newspapers. My dominance of the public platform was my strength throughout my political life.

When dealing with the opposition, I had two preoccupations: Were they being used by the communists? And was this a "black operation," one funded and run by a foreign intelligence agency to cause mischief? It was this latter concern that led to our investigation of Francis Seow, a former solicitor general. The Marxist group described earlier had gained influence in the Law Society. They canvassed for him and got him elected as president. With Seow as president, the Law Society became politicized, criticizing and attacking government legislation not on professional but on political grounds, something it had never done as a professional organization constituted by law to maintain discipline and standards in the legal profession.

Around that time, in 1987, a counsellor in the U.S. embassy (called Hendrickson) met Seow to encourage him to lead an opposition group at the next election. The ISD recommended that we detain and interrogate Seow to get to the bottom of the matter. I agreed. We had to put a stop to this foreign interference in Singapore's domestic politics and show that it was off-limits to all, including the United States. Under interrogation, Seow admitted in a sworn affidavit that he had been asked by Hendrickson to lead a group of lawyers to contest the elections against the PAP. He also admitted that he had been to Washington to meet Hendrickson's superior in the U.S. State Department, who had assured him of refuge in

America were he to run into difficulties with the government. We published his admissions made in the sworn affidavit. Then we released Seow, two months before the general election. He contested but lost. He was on a charge for fraudulent income tax returns at that time but we gave him permission to travel to the United States to consult a cardiologist in New York and to attend a human rights conference. He did not return for his trial; instead his lawyers submitted several medical reports from two doctors: The first, Dr. Jonathan E. Fine, who signed himself as "Executive Director" on letter paper headed "Physicians for Human Rights," stated that it was inadvisible for Seow to travel internationally; the second doctor stated that Seow was unable to undertake any air travel until treated for his heart condition. When the prosecution produced evidence that Seow had made at least seven air trips from December through January, the court directed that Seow submit more detailed medical reports. When Seow failed to provide further medical reports, his lawyers, an English Queens Counsel (QC) and a Singapore advocate, asked the court to discharge them. One doctor later admitted that in fact he had not examined him and that he had not renewed his medical license to practice. Seow had no standing at the Bar, having been disciplined by the Law Society for financial misconduct. What was left of his credibility in Singapore was destroyed. When human rights groups in America puffed him up as a major dissident figure, Singaporeans were not impressed. Several years later we learned that the U.S. government had indeed given Seow political asylum.

We had good reason for wanting to investigate Francis Seow. We knew he owed a Singapore bank some S$350,000. The loan was not repaid for many years. In 1986, as the date for election approached, the bank demanded payment. He was able to pay. Where did the money come from? We had seized his books to check for income tax and it was clear that he did not have the funds to settle this loan. He swore in an affidavit that it was paid by his girlfriend, or his fiancée as he called her, Mei Siah. She told Keng Swee in Bangkok in 1989, after Seow had fled from Singapore, that she was asked to lend Seow the money by a Singapore businessman. A CEO of a major company who kept Mei Siah as his mistress for a number of years told us that she was extremely tight with money and would never have parted with S$350,000 for anyone, and that she still owed him more than that sum. This suggested that the money came from some interested agency.

One imperative is to confront directly those who accuse me of corruption or misusing the power of my office. I have always met head-on all such allegations. At election time in many developing countries, allegations of bribery and corruption are standard fare and are never confronted for fear of greater damage if the minister who sues cannot stand up to cross-examination in court. I proceed only after taking the opinions of counsel both in Singapore and in London because, should my action fail, I have personally to carry the heavy costs: my own lawyers' and those of my opponents. On the other hand, I have never been sued for defamation because I have not made any false defamatory statements. When I said something disparaging about my opponents, I had ample evidence to back my statements and my opponents knew that.

My first libel action to uphold the office of prime minister was in 1965 against Syed Ja'afar Albar, then secretary-general of UMNO. We were then still in Malaysia. He had said in the *Utusan Melayu,* a Malay newspaper owned by UMNO, "The Prime Minister of Singapore, Lee Kuan Yew, is an agent of the communists and the Djakarta regime who have the evil intention to destroy Malaysia. Lee Kuan Yew has the evil intention to destroy Malaysia and to pit the Malays and Chinese in Malaysia against each other." Albar and the *Utusan Melayu* had no defense, apologized in court, and paid my legal costs.

I also brought actions against opposition candidates who accused me of corruption in election speeches. An example was in 1972 when one of them said in Chinese that whenever people wanted to buy or transfer their HDB homes, they went to Lee & Lee, the law firm where my wife was a senior partner. Most of these candidates were men without assets, who did not defend themselves and accepted bankruptcy.

J. B. Jeyaretnam, a lawyer, was an exception. At an election rally in 1976 he alleged that I had procured the grant of favors to Lee & Lee and to my family, that I had been guilty of nepotism and corruption and was unfit to be prime minister. I was awarded damages and costs. Jeyaretnam appealed all the way to the Privy Council in London, and lost.

More than a decade later, in 1988, again at an election rally, Jeyaretnam insinuated that I had advised Teh Cheang Wan (a minister of national development) to commit suicide; that I wanted to avoid a full investigation into allegations of corruption because they would have discredited me. He could have raised Teh's suicide two years earlier but waited until election time. I won damages and costs.

I took action against an American-owned weekly based in Hong Kong, the *Far Eastern Economic Review,* and its editor Derek Davies. He had refused to withdraw and apologize for quoting a renegade priest, Edgar D'Souza, who said that the government had attacked the Catholic Church by detaining 16 Marxist conspirators. I went into the witness box and was aggressively cross-examined by the *Review*'s QC for over two days. When it was the turn of the editor to reply, Derek Davies did not give evidence because he would have been cross-examined. Nor did he call D'Souza to support what he had printed. The judge found against the *Review* and its editor.

Another case was against the *International Herald Tribune* (*IHT*), a newspaper owned by the *New York Times* and the *Washington Post,* for publishing on 2 August 1994 a libelous article by Philip Bowring, a columnist formerly from the *Far Eastern Economic Review.* Bowring wrote, "In the Chinese case, history almost seems to consist of a battle between the corporatist needs of the state and the interests of the families who operate it. Dynastic politics is evident in 'Communist' China already, *as in Singapore* [my italics], despite official commitments to bureaucratic meritocracy." My son Loong had been elected to Parliament in 1984 and it was clear what Bowring meant. The *IHT* admitted in its paper that the words were defamatory, and meant that I was advancing the interests of the Lee family at the expense of the corporatist needs of the state. It apologized and paid damages and costs.

On 2 June 1996, the Chinese-language *Yazhou Zhoukan* (*Asian Weekly*) quoted a lawyer, Tang Liang Hong, alleging corruption in my purchase of two apartments. The weekly immediately admitted liability and paid a large sum in settlement. But Tang refused to apologize and retract his allegation. Six months later, at a rally right at the end of the election campaign, Tang aggravated the libel by saying that once he had entered Parliament, he would raise the same issue and that "this is their death blow." The trial judge noted that the day after the libel was published, Tang transferred a substantial sum of money from his wife's bank account to his bank account in Johor Bahru, which was out of Singapore's jurisdiction, to exhaust her overdraft facility. The judge said, "It was a clear piece of evidence of a devious mind." As Tang had absconded from Singapore and did not appear at the trial, judgment was in my favor. On the appeal, Tang's London QC did not challenge the defamatory meaning of the words. The appeal was dismissed.

My opponents waited for elections to get under way before they uttered their slanders, hoping to inflict maximum damage. Had I not sued, these allegations would have gained credence. Western liberal critics argue that my reputation is so unassailable that nobody will believe the outrageous things that are said about me, so I should ignore them magnanimously instead of suing vindictively. But outrageous statements are disbelieved only because they are vigorously refuted. If I failed to sue, that would be cited as proof that there was something in it.

In Tang's case, my purchase of the two apartments had for a time been a hot political issue. Had I not sued Tang after his statements in *Yazhou Zhoukan,* in the subsequent general election he would have gone to town with more wild claims. By then it would have been too late to rebut him, and even PAP supporters would have wondered whether I had done something wrong. But because Singaporeans knew I would challenge any defamatory untruth, when Tang defamed me, he immediately prepared for its consequences by moving all his funds out of Singapore.

There is another important reason for suing those who have defamed me. Since the 1950s we have established a political climate under which politicians have to defend any allegation of misconduct or wrongdoing.

Opposition MPs also sued when they were defamed. Chiam See Tong won damages against two PAP ministers, Howe Yoon Chong and S. Dhanabalan, who settled the cases out of court. Jeyaretnam sued Goh Chok Tong, then minister for trade and industry, in 1981, but failed. He appealed to the Privy Council but lost. Voters have come to expect any allegation of impropriety or dishonesty to be challenged in the courts. PAP ministers have been able to command the respect of people because they are ready to be scrutinized and cross-examined in court for any alleged wrongdoing. Those who allege that my libel actions were designed to silence the opposition do not understand how readily an allegation of dishonesty or corruption would be believed in a region where corruption, cronyism, and nepotism are still a plague.

Some critics have alleged that our judges were compliant. The judges who heard these cases were senior members of the bench with their standing and reputation to uphold. Their judgments were published in the law reports and cited as precedents that can stand the scrutiny of over 2,000 lawyers at the Bar, and of teachers and students at the National University of Singapore law faculty.

The allegation that we use the judiciary in defamation suits to bankrupt our political opponents came to a head when the *International Herald Tribune* of 7 October 1994 carried an article by Christopher Lingle, an American lecturer at the National University of Singapore, attacking me: "Intolerant regimes in the region reveal considerable ingenuity in their methods of suppressing dissent. . . . Others are more subtle: relying upon a compliant judiciary to bankrupt opposition politicians." I sued the editor, the publisher, and the writer. With the foreign media present in strength to give them wide publicity, both the editor and publisher, through their lawyers, admitted it was untrue and apologized for it. The court awarded damages and costs against the *IHT.* To avoid being cross-examined in court, Lingle fled from Singapore when the writ was issued.

Far from oppressing the opposition or the press that unjustly attacked my reputation, I have put my private and public life under close scrutiny whenever I appeared as a plaintiff in court. Without a clear record, it would have been an unnecessary hazard. Because I did this and also gave the damages awarded to deserving charities, I kept my standing with our people.

To straddle the middle ground and win elections, we have to be in charge of the political agenda. This can only be done by not being beaten in the argument with our critics. They complain that I come down too hard on their arguments. But wrong ideas have to be challenged before they influence public opinion and make for problems. Those who try to be clever at the expense of the government should not complain if my replies are as sharp as their criticisms.

At the same time, the PAP has sought to reach out to those outside the party, to a new generation of Singaporeans who are better-educated and informed, and who want to participate in the national debate. The large PAP majorities in Parliament, and the poor quality of opposition MPs, led the public to feel that alternative views were not being adequately aired in Parliament. We changed the constitution in 1990 to provide for a small number of nonelected MPs, called Nominated MPs (or NMPs), to reflect independent and nonpartisan views. The scheme has turned out well. It has enabled non-PAP people who are of good quality to enter Parliament. The NMPs have played a constructive role airing carefully considered criticisms of government policies, and the government has taken them seriously. One, Walter Woon, moved a private member's bill, which Parliament passed to become the Maintenance of Parents Act.

After the 1984 election, we created a Feedback Unit to give the public a channel to express opinions on policies through forums and feedback sessions. MPs with a sympathetic ear chair these meetings to solicit views, not to persuade people. This encouraged people to speak up. Not all contrary opinions led to reversals of policies, but the feedback helped the government to improve its policies.

After separation from Malaysia in 1965 and as British forces started to withdraw in 1968, elections were referenda on the level of our support, not whether we would win. The percentage of votes for the PAP began to trend downward in the mid-1980s, mainly because the younger voters, whose number was increasing, had not been through the early struggles and were not so committed to the PAP. They wanted an opposition to check the PAP, to pressure the government for more concessions and to soften hard policies. It was bound to lead to less than adequate people getting elected, as indeed happened.

When Prime Minister Goh called general elections in 1991, the opposition changed tactics. Instead of fielding more candidates of poor ability, they allowed the PAP to win a majority of seats uncontested on nomination day. They knew that the people wanted some opposition MPs, but also wanted to be sure they had a PAP government. They called it their by-election strategy. It worked. Low Thia Khiang of the Workers' Party, a Nanyang University graduate and a Teochew, won the mainly Teochew constituency of Hougang. He turned out to be a good grassroots leader. The SDP led by Chiam won three seats, becoming the largest party in the opposition, with Chiam the official leader of the opposition. The new SDP MPs were lackluster and did not measure up. Chiam was constructive and could have built up a sizeable political party had he been a shrewder judge of people. In 1992, he proudly produced a plausible young lecturer as his prize candidate for a by-election. Within two years, his protégé had ousted him as the leader and forced him to form a new party.

In the 1997 election, out of 83 seats, the PAP lost only to Low Thia Khiang and Chiam, who by then represented a new party. The PAP's share of valid votes cast rose by 4 percent to 65 percent, reversing the downward trend. We defeated the two SDP MPs who had won in 1991 but had disappointed their voters. The PAP had countered the opposition's "by-election" strategy with the electoral carrot that priority for upgrading of public housing in a constituency would be in accord with the strength of voter support for the PAP in that constituency. This was criticized by American liberals as unfair, as if pork barrel politics did not exist elsewhere.

The present PAP leaders are in the process of forging their bonds with a younger generation. The regional financial meltdown of 1997–1999 was a test for this generation that has not known hardship. Together, people and leaders overcame the problems and emerged the stronger. This crisis and the periodic difficulties with Malaysia have made Singaporeans acutely aware of the realities of life in Southeast Asia.

Will the political system that my colleagues and I developed work more or less unchanged for another generation? I doubt it. Technology and globalization are changing the way people work and live. Singaporeans will have new work styles and lifestyles. As an international hub of a knowledge-based economy in the information technology age, we will be ever more exposed to external influences.

Will the PAP continue to dominate Singapore's politics? How big a challenge will a democratic opposition pose in the future? This will depend on how PAP leaders respond to changes in the needs and aspirations of a better-educated people, and to their desire for greater participation in decisions that shape their lives. Singapore's options are not that numerous that there will be unbridgeable differences between differing political views in working out solutions to our problems.

# 10. Nurturing and Attracting Talent

On the night of 14 August 1983, I dropped a bombshell in my annual National Day Rally address. Live on both our television channels, with maximum viewership, I said it was stupid for our graduate men to choose less-educated and less-intelligent wives if they wanted their children to do as well as they had done. The press named it the "Great Marriage Debate." As I had expected, the speech stirred a hornet's nest. My wife Choo had warned me there were many more women with only O levels (an equivalent to a high school education) than women with university degrees. It caused a drop of 12 percentage points in votes for the PAP in the election the following year, more than I had anticipated.

It had taken me some time to see the obvious, that talent is a country's most precious asset. For a small resource-poor country like Singapore, with 2 million people at independence in 1965, it is the defining factor. The Chinese here were mostly the descendants of agricultural laborers from the southern provinces of China, many brought in by labor contractors as indentured workers to do heavy manual work such as loading and unloading cargo and pulling rickshaws. Early Indian immigrants also came as indentured laborers to work on rubber estates, build roads, and dig trenches and drains. Most were from the lower castes. There were small groups of Indian merchants and clerks. The ablest were Sindhi merchants and Hindu Brahmins, in particular their priests. Their descendants have high ability. Malays as a rule were better in the arts than the sciences.

It was our good fortune that under the British, Singapore had been the regional center for education, with good schools, training for teachers, King Edward VII Medical College, and Raffles College (teaching arts and science). These two colleges, both of a high standard, were later merged to form the University of Malaya in Singapore. The brightest of the English-educated students in Malaya and the Borneo territories studied at Singapore institutions, staying in boarding schools run by the Christian missions. The best students trained in Singapore as doctors, teachers, and administrators. They were the cream of some 6 million Chinese and Indians from Malaya, the Borneo territories, and even the Dutch East Indies, which later became Indonesia. Singapore also had the best Chinese schools in the region, and successful Chinese parents in the region sent their sons here for schooling and later to Nanyang University, when it was teaching in Chinese. Until the Japanese Occupation and the rise of independent governments after the war, the Chinese moved freely between the countries of *Nanyang* (South Seas or Southeast Asia). Many stayed on for the better jobs. They added an extra layer of talent.

After several years in government I realized that the more talented people I had as ministers, administrators, and professionals, the more effective my policies were, and the better the results. My mind flashed back to Prince Sihanouk. He was talented. When he made his films, he had to be author, scriptwriter, director, actor, and producer. Cambodia did not have enough educated and talented people and the few they had, Pol Pot later killed. That was one reason for the tragedy in Cambodia.

What made me decide to make that Great Marriage Debate speech was a report on my desk analyzing the 1980 census figures. It showed that our brightest women were not marrying and would not be represented in the next generation. The implications were grave. Our best women were not reproducing themselves because men who were their educational equals did not want to marry them. About half of our university graduates were women; nearly two-thirds of them were unmarried. The Asian man, whether Chinese, Indian, or Malay, preferred to have a wife with less education than himself. Only 38 percent of graduate men were married to graduate women in 1983.

This lopsided marriage and procreation pattern could not be allowed to remain unmentioned and unchecked. I decided to shock the young men out of their stupid, old-fashioned, and damaging prejudices. I quoted studies of identical twins done in Minnesota in the 1980s which showed that these twins were similar in so many respects. Although they had been brought up separately and in different countries, about 80 percent of their vocabulary, IQ, habits, likes, and dislikes in food and friends, and other character and personality traits were identical. In other words, nearly 80 percent of a person's makeup is from nature, and about 20 percent the result of nurture.

The capabilities of most children were between those of their two parents, with a few having lower or higher intelligence than either. Therefore, male graduates who married less-educated women were not maximizing the chances of having children who make it to university. I urged them to marry their educational equals, and encouraged educated women to have two or more children.

Graduate women were upset that I had spotlighted their plight. Nongraduate women and their parents were angry with me for dissuading graduate men from marrying them. I was attacked in a flood of comments and letters to the press for being an elitist because I believed intelligence was inherited and not the result of education, food, and training. A professional couple challenged my alleged assumption that low-income families would produce less-brainy children. (I had made no such claim.) "Look at Lee Pan Hon, the violinist. He came out of the slums of Chinatown. If he hadn't been given the opportunity, he would never have developed his creativity." (Lee Pan Hon, a Chinatown kid, was talent-spotted by Yehudi Menuhin for his school in Britain. Later he became a first violinist in the Manchester Orchestra.) "This whole thing smacks of elitism." A woman wrote, "I am an unmarried, successful professional woman aged 40. I have remained single because I prefer it this way. I am deeply insulted by the suggestion that some miserable financial incentives will make me jump into bed with the first attractive man I meet and proceed to produce a highly talented child for the sake of Singapore's future." Even Toh Chin Chye, then a PAP backbencher, derided my views, saying that his mother never went to school, his father was a clerk with only secondary school education, and if he had to depend on his parents' educational background, he would have had no chance.

I supported my views by releasing analyses of statistics for the past few years of the educational background of parents of the top 10 percent of our students in examinations at ages 12, 16, and 18. These figures left little doubt that the decisive factor for high performance was a pair of well-educated parents. I also put out 1960 and 1970 data analyses that showed most of our top students who won scholarships for universities abroad had parents who were not well-educated: storekeepers, hawkers, taxi drivers, and laborers. I compared them to the 1980 and 1990 data that revealed over 50 percent of the best 100 scholarship winners had at least one parent who was a professional or self-employed. The conclusion was obvious, that the parents of these scholarship winners of the 1960s and 1970s would have made it to university had they been born a generation later when education was universal and scholarships, stipends, and study loans were freely available to bright students.

This controversy was widely reported by the Western media. Liberal Western writers and commentators mocked me for my ignorance and prejudice. But one academic spoke up for me—R. H. Herrnstein, professor of psychology at Harvard. In an article, "IQ and Falling Birth Rates," in the *Atlantic Monthly* of May 1989, he wrote, "In our time Prime Minister Lee Kuan Yew of Singapore has said, 'Levels of competence will decline, our economy will falter, our administration will suffer, and society will decline' because so many educated men are failing to find educated women to marry and are instead marrying uneducated women or remaining unmarried. But Lee is an exception, for few modern political leaders dare to talk in public about the qualitative aspect of low fertility." A few years later, Herrnstein coauthored *The Bell Curve,* which set out the data that showed intelligence to be inherited.

To help ease this problem of unmarried graduate women, we set up a Social Development Unit (SDU) to facilitate socializing between men and women graduates. I personally chose Dr. Eileen Aw, a doctor at the National University of Singapore. Then in her late forties, she was married to a doctor and had two children at the university. Soft-spoken and approachable, with a knack for putting young people at ease, she was just the person for the job. The SDU was initially received with disdain by graduates, both men and women. The international press had another field day ridiculing our matchmaking efforts and SDU activities, from symposiums, seminars, and computer classes to cruises and Club Med holidays.

The fact was that parents were alarmed at the swelling numbers of their graduate daughters remaining unmarried and were desperate for help. One night in 1985, after a reception at the Istana, Choo told me that the women of her generation were discussing the plight of their professionally trained daughters and commiserating with each other. They lamented the passing of the age when women had marriages arranged by their parents with the help of professional matchmakers. When most women received little formal education, the bright women and the less bright had equal chances of being "married off" since there were no O levels or university degrees to grade them. This practice of arranged marriages was no longer acceptable to educated women.

It was as much the fault of mothers of graduate sons as of the sons themselves. Nongraduate mothers preferred nongraduate daughters-in-law who would be less intimidating. It was most difficult to erase this cultural prejudice, that a male who was not seen to be the main breadwinner and head of the household was to be pitied and ridiculed. This was so with the Chinese, more so with the Indians, and most of all with the Malays.

The same problem extended through all educational levels. A large number of A level (or SAT-qualified) women could not find college or A level men to marry. So too with O level women. Women want to marry up, men want to marry down. The result was that the least-educated men could find no women to marry, because the women who remained unmarried were all better-educated and would not marry them. To complement the SDU, I asked the executive director of the People's Association to form a Social Development Section (SDS) for those with secondary education. Membership rapidly expanded and by 1995 was 97,000. Thirty-one percent of SDS members who met through its activities got married. Traditional methods of choosing marriage partners had been ruptured by universal education: The government had to provide alternatives to the family matchmakers of old.

The 1980 census figures also revealed that better-educated women had compounded our problem by having much fewer children than the less-educated. The tertiary-educated had 1.6, the secondary-educated, also 1.6, the primary-educated, 2.3, and the unschooled, 4.4. To replace themselves, parents must have 2.1 children. We were more than doubling our less-educated, and not replacing our better-educated.

To reverse this reproductive trend, Keng Swee, then minister for education, and I decided in 1984 to give to graduate mothers who have a third child priority in choosing the best schools for all their three children, a much-prized objective of all parents. It was a sensitive and divisive issue. The egalitarians in cabinet led by Raja were outraged. He disputed that brighter parents had brighter children. Even if it were true, he argued, why should we hurt people's self-esteem? Eddie Barker was unhappy not because he agreed with Raja, but because it was offensive to less-bright parents and their children. The younger ministers were divided between these three views of their older colleagues. Keng Swee, ever the hard-headed realist, agreed with me that we had to jolt male graduates from their outdated cultural prejudices into recognizing the folly of marrying down. We carried a majority in cabinet.

Keng Swee and I had expected nongraduate mothers to be angry because they would be discriminated against. Instead, we were taken aback when graduate mothers protested. They did not want this privilege. However, the message to young men did sink in: More married their equals though the progress was slow. After the elections, I agreed that Tony Tan, who had taken over from Keng Swee as the new minister for education, reverse this decision and cancel the priority for graduate mothers. I had awakened our people, especially tertiary-educated young men and women, to the starkness of our plight. But since women graduates were embarrassed by this privilege, it was best to remove it.

In its place, I gave special income tax concessions to married women—this time to graduate, polytechnic, A level, and O level mothers, enlarging the pool and lessening the sense of elitism. They qualified for substantial income tax rebates on either their or their husband's income for their third and fourth child. These concessions did encourage more third and fourth births.

Many critics blamed the government for thoughtlessly implementing the "Stop-at-Two" policy in the 1960s. Was it wrong? Yes and no. Without that policy, family planning might never have brought population growth down, and we would not have solved our unemployment and schooling problems. But we should have foreseen that the better-educated would have two or fewer children, and the less-educated four or more. Western writers on family planning had not drawn attention to this already familiar though less stark outcome in their own mature countries because it was not politically correct to do so. Had we found out on our own sooner, we would have refined and targeted our campaign differently, encouraging with incentives the better-educated women to have three or more children right from the start of the family planning drive in the 1960s. Unfortunately, we did not know and did not change our policy until 1983 when analysis of the 1980 census revealed the reproductive patterns of the different socioeconomic groups.

Since that speech in 1983, I have regularly released the statistical analysis of the educational backgrounds of parents of the top 10 percent of students in national examinations. Singaporeans now accept that the better-educated and more able the parents, the more likely are the children to achieve similar levels. My speech was intended to shake up our young men and women and their parents, and make them do something to redress the seriousness of the situation. The open discussion it stimulated made some difference. However, Keng Swee, the trained statistician, after studying the figures for a couple of years after my shock tactics, told me dolefully that we would not be able to solve this problem soon enough to save most of our graduate women from their fate. The figures, although improving, revealed it would take many years to reverse the trend. Our bright women would suffer, and so would Singapore. By 1997, 63 percent of graduate men married fellow graduates, as against 38 percent in 1982. Also, more graduate women were marrying nongraduates rather than remaining single. It is difficult to override a deep-rooted cultural bias. Intellectually, I agreed with Keng Swee that overcoming this cultural lag would be a slow adjustment process, but emotionally I could not accept that we could not jolt the men out of their prejudices sooner.

Difficulties over our talent pool were aggravated when the rich Western countries changed their policies on Asian immigration. In the 1960s, when the United States was fighting the war in Vietnam, it did not want to be seen as anti-Asian. It decided to accept Asian immigrants, reversing more than a century of its whites-only policy. Canada, Australia,

and New Zealand, the big countries with small populations, soon followed suit. They had long barred Asian immigration. When they
changed their rules to admit better-qualified Asians, we lost a large part
of the inflow of Chinese and Indians from Malaysia. Many middle-class
professional Chinese and Indian Malaysians migrated permanently to
Australia, New Zealand, and Canada. Fewer foreigners also came to
Singapore for their education. They now had their own universities, and
many could afford to study in Australia, New Zealand, Britain, the
United States, and Canada.

Not all leaders shared my view of the bad effects of this change in policy. When I told Malaysian Prime Minister Tun Razak in the early 1970s
that Malaysia was suffering a brain drain, losing many well-educated
Chinese and Indians to Australia and New Zealand, he replied, "This is
not a 'brains drain.' It is a 'trouble drain'; it drains trouble out of
Malaysia."

Our shortage of talent was aggravated from the late 1970s when some
5 percent of our better-educated began emigrating. Too many of our
bright students became doctors. Many emigrated because they felt they
did not have the success their level of professionalism deserved. Some students who had studied in Australia, New Zealand, and Canada migrated
there because their careers in Singapore were not advancing rapidly
enough. Unlike Japanese or Koreans, Singaporeans were educated in
English and faced negligible language or cultural problems when they
settled overseas.

To get enough talent to fill the jobs our growing economy needed, I
set out to attract and retain talent—entrepreneurs, professionals, artistes,
and highly skilled workers. In 1980, we formed two committees, one to
get them placed into jobs, another to integrate them socially. With the
help of our student counsellors in our missions in Britain, the United
States, Australia, New Zealand, and Canada, a team of officers would
meet promising Asian students at their universities to interest them in
jobs in Singapore. We concentrated on recruiting Asian students because
Singapore offered an Asian society with a higher standard of living and
quality of life than their own countries, and they could assimilate easily
into our society. This systematic search for talent worldwide brought in a
few hundred graduates each year. It made up for the loss each year

through emigration of 5 to 10 percent of our better-educated to the industrialized countries.

For the exceptionally bright, the committee tried to "green harvest," an American corporate practice of offering jobs even before graduation, on the basis of their performance before their final examinations. By the 1990s, this inflow through active recruitment was three times the outflow. We began offering a few hundred scholarships to bright students from China, India, and the region in the hope that some would remain because of the better job opportunities; those who returned to their countries could still be useful for our companies that went abroad.

We also set up two task forces specially to attract talent from India and from the region, but were more successful in attracting Indian than Malay talent. There were too many privileges for bumiputras and pribumis (indigenous Malays and Indonesians) in their home countries for them to consider leaving.

A new phenomenon is the increasing number of Caucasian men marrying our women, especially the tertiary-educated. Singapore graduate men were fearful of marrying them but Caucasian graduates were not. Many of these women were forced to emigrate by our rules that allowed a Singapore male citizen to bring in a foreign bride, but not the other way around. We gave that permission only if the foreign husband had regular employment. We changed this policy in January 1999: This will add to the cosmopolitan character of Singapore. Furthermore, quite a number of our men who were educated abroad have married Caucasian, Japanese, and other Asian girls they met at university. Their children are valuable additions to our talent pool. The old clear-cut barriers to interracial marriage have been breached by the intermingling of people as they travel to and work in countries not their own. We have to change our attitudes and take advantage of what was once considered foreign and not assimilable talent. We cannot allow old prejudices to hamper our development as an international center for trade, industry, and services.

Besides natural conservatism, the other problem is fear of competition for jobs. Both at professional and lower levels there is resistance to the inflow of talent. Singaporeans know that more foreign talent will create more jobs. But they want this to happen in some other sector, not their own.

Without foreign talent, we would not have done as well. In my first cabinet of 10, I was the only one born and educated in Singapore. Keng Swee and Chin Chye were born in Malaya, Raja in Ceylon. Our present chief justice, Yong Pung How, came from Malaysia, as did our attorney general, Chan Sek Keong. So the list could roll on. Thousands of engineers, managers, and other professionals who came from abroad have helped us to grow. They are the extra megabytes in Singapore's computer. If we do not top up with foreign talent, we will not make it into the top league.

# 11. Many Tongues, One Language

Both Choo and I had been educated in English-language schools. When we met students from China while studying in England, we became conscious of how deculturalized we were, almost like the Chinese students from the Caribbean. We felt a sense of loss at having been educated in a stepmother tongue, not completely accepting the values of a culture not our own. I felt separated from the mass of the ordinary Chinese who spoke dialect and Mandarin. My world of textbooks and teachers was totally unrelated to the world I lived in. We were like hundreds of Raffles College graduates, not formally tutored in their own Asian cultures, but not belonging to British culture either, lost between two cultures.

Choo and I decided we should not inflict this cultural handicap on our three children, and sent them to Chinese schools to become a part of this vibrant, vigorous, self-confident community, even if their English suffered. We remedied this by having Choo speak to them in English while I spoke to them in Mandarin, to improve my Mandarin!

It turned out well for all three, educated in Chinese, imbued with the values that made them filial children and good citizens, and equally fluent in English. They did well in school, winning prizes that their schools and the Chinese press publicized to encourage other parents to send their children to Chinese schools. This convinced the Chinese-speaking that I would not exterminate Chinese education in Singapore. Those born and bred in homogeneous societies may not understand why the language medium in which I chose to educate my children had political implications.

Singapore never had one common language. It was a polyglot community under colonial rule. The British left people to decide how to educate their children. The government provided a limited number of English-language schools to train people to be clerks, storekeepers, draftsmen, and such subordinate workers, and Malay-language primary schools for Malays. Indians ran their own Tamil and other Indian-language schools or classes. The Chinese set up schools financed by successful members of their community, to teach in Chinese. Because the different races were taught their own languages, their emotional attachment to their mother tongue was deep. They were like the 5 million people in Quebec tenaciously holding on to French in a continent of 300 million English speakers.

When we formed the government in 1959 we decided on Malay as the national language, to prepare the way for merger with Malaya. We realized English had to be the language of the workplace and the common language. As an international trading community, we would not make a living if we used Malay, Chinese, or Tamil. With English, no race would have an advantage. But it was too sensitive an issue for us to make immediate changes. To announce that all had to learn English when each race was intensely and passionately committed to its own mother tongue would have been disastrous. So we left the position as it was, with four official languages—Malay, Chinese (Mandarin), Tamil, and English.

The necessity for a common language was vividly highlighted in the Singapore Armed Forces. We were saddled with a hideous collection of dialects and languages and faced the prospect of going into battle without understanding each other in any of the four official languages. Many could only speak dialects, requiring special Hokkien-speaking platoons. The Chinese were speaking one of more than seven different Chinese dialects at home but learning Mandarin and English in school, neither of which they used at home.

Not wanting to start a controversy over language, I introduced the teaching of three mother tongues, Mandarin, Malay, and Tamil, into English schools. This was well received by all parents. To balance this, I introduced the teaching of English in Chinese, Malay, and Tamil schools. Malay and Indian parents welcomed this but increasing numbers preferred to send their children to English schools. A hard core of the Chinese-educated did not welcome what they saw as a move to make English the common working language, and they expressed their unhappiness in the Chinese newspapers.

Barely eight weeks after separation, the Chinese Chamber of Commerce publicly asked the government to guarantee the status of the Chinese language as one of the official languages in Singapore. The Chamber's treasurer, Kheng Chin Hock, a Chinese-language champion from pre-Malaysia days, stressed that Chinese was used by more than 80 percent of the population in Singapore. I scotched this move before it could grow into a campaign, for once the Chinese Chamber got going, every Chinese school management committee and the two Chinese teachers' unions would surely work up the ground. On 1 October, I restated that all four major languages in Singapore were official and equal. I reminded activists like Kheng in the Chinese Chamber that they had been conspicuous by their silence on language and other vital issues when Singapore was controlled by the Malaysian police and the Malay Regiment. Five days later, under the full glare of television lights, I met the committees of all four chambers of commerce. I left the Chinese representatives in no doubt that I would not allow anyone to exploit the Chinese language as a political issue. That put an end to their attempts to elevate the status of the Chinese language.

Nevertheless, opposition continued to come from students at the Chinese-language Nanyang University and Ngee Ann College. In October 1966, when I declared open a library built at Nanyang University (shortened in Chinese to "Nantah"), 200 students protested. Several days later, Ngee Ann College students demonstrated outside my office and clashed with the police, after which they staged a sit-in at their college. After I deported the Malaysian leaders of the two demonstrations, student agitation diminished.

We waited patiently as year by year parents in increasing numbers chose to send their children to English schools, in the face of determined opposition from the Chinese teachers' unions, Chinese school management committees, Chinese newspaper owners, editors, and journalists, leaders of clan associations, and the Chinese Chamber of Commerce. Every year, around the time when parents had to register their children, these groups would mount a campaign to get parents to enroll their children in Chinese schools for the sake of their culture and identity. They berated those who chose English schools as money-minded and short-sighted.

Many Chinese-speaking parents were deeply attached to their language and culture. They could not understand why their children were allowed to be educated completely in Chinese under the British, yet under their own elected government had also to learn English. But for better job prospects, many sent their children to English schools. These conflicting pulls provided fertile ground for agitation.

Toward the end of 1970, the major Chinese paper, *Nanyang Siang Pau,* turned rabidly pro-communist and pro-Chinese language and culture. It mounted an attack on the government, accusing it of trying to suppress Chinese language, education, and culture, and portraying me as the oppressor in a government of "pseudo foreigners who forget their ancestors." We had to arrest Lee Mau Seng, the general manager, Shamsuddin Tung Tao Chang, the editor in chief, and Ly Singko, the senior editorial writer, for glamorizing communism and stirring up chauvinistic sentiments over Chinese language and culture. Proof that they were doing so only for Singapore came from the Malaysian editions of the same paper that did not carry this campaign.

Nantah graduates were another source of opposition. In both the 1972 and 1976 general elections they raised the issue of Chinese language and culture. When I tried to get the medium of instruction in Nantah changed from Chinese to English, Ho Juan Thai, the president of their students' union, instigated his fellow students to use Chinese instead of English in their examination papers. The university removed him from his post as union leader. After graduating, he contested the 1976 general election as a Workers' Party candidate, accusing the government of exterminating Chinese education and urging the Chinese-speaking to oppose the government or risk losing their cultural identity. He knew we would not act against him during the campaign. When he lost, getting only 31 percent of the votes, he fled to London.

The opposition to English as the one common language was unremitting. The irony was that I was as keen and anxious as anyone to retain the best features of Chinese education. When I acted as legal adviser for the Chinese middle school student leaders in the 1950s, I was impressed by their vitality, dynamism, discipline, and social and political commitment.

By contrast, I was dismayed at the apathy, self-centeredness, and lack of self-confidence of the English-educated students. The crux of the problem was that in our multiracial and multilingual society, English was the only acceptable neutral language, besides being the language that would make us relevant to the world. But it did seem to deculturalize our students and make them apathetic.

However, my education in the English school system gave me one political advantage—it made me at home in the world of both the English- and the Malay-educated, and I was not confined to the Chinese-speaking. It made it easier for me to be accepted as a leader of more than just the Chinese because I was perceived by the Malays and Indians as a Malayan (later Singaporean) nationalist, not a Chinese chauvinist. And because I learned Chinese later, and they saw my intense efforts to master both Mandarin and the Hokkien dialect, I was able to relate to the Chinese-educated and have them accept me as their leader.

In the 1950s, the Chinese-educated felt a burst of pride at the resurgence of China and the Chinese language. The merchants in the Chinese Chamber of Commerce were prosperous with the rubber boom that resulted from the Korean War. In 1953, the chamber proposed a Chinese-language university in Singapore for Chinese students in Southeast Asia. Since Chinese high school graduates were forbidden from going to communist China for further studies, they believed such an institution in Singapore would attract many students. It drew support from Chinese merchants in Singapore, Malaya, and the Borneo territories. The leading spirit was a wealthy rubber merchant, Tan Lark Sye, who personally donated S$5 million, but the project involved the whole Chinese community and generated so much spontaneous enthusiasm that taxi drivers, hawkers, and trishaw riders all contributed one day's earnings. When Nanyang University was opened by the British governor in March 1956, traffic crawled bumper to bumper all the way from the city to its campus in Jurong, 20 miles to the northwest. It became the symbol of Chinese language, culture, and education—a symbol the communists captured through their influence with sympathizers in the Chinese Chamber of Commerce, the clan associations, and school management committees.

But Nantah faced problems. There were few jobs for its graduates. As students switched to English schools, they increasingly went to the

University of Singapore, which taught in English. Better students from the Chinese schools took the English-language Cambridge school certificate examinations as private candidates, to be eligible for admission to the University of Singapore or some overseas university on a government scholarship. Nantah responded by lowering requirements for both admission and pass standards for graduation, further diminishing its academic reputation and the market value of its graduates. What finally propelled me to action was a report from the People's Association that when applying for jobs, Nantah graduates had produced their school certificates and not their Nantah degrees.

I decided to make English the language of instruction at Nantah. With the unanimous agreement of the Nanyang University Council, in 1975 I sent the minister for education, Dr. Lee Chiaw Meng, to be vice chancellor. He was Chinese-educated, but had a Ph.D. in engineering from London University. His task was to convert Nantah into an English-language university. It proved too difficult; the staff were basically Chinese-educated and could not teach in English. Although they had gotten their Ph.D.s in American universities, they had reverted to using Chinese and lost their English fluency.

The situation was so bad that in 1978 our MPs who were Nantah graduates asked me to intervene before the university disintegrated. The one whose judgment I had learned to depend upon was Ch'ng Jit Koon, a minister of state. He had excellent interpersonal skills and had worked closely with me for many years, including helping to look after my constituency. He convinced me that to allow Nantah to continue as it was would make for a bigger problem. With the careers of so many students blighted, the Chinese-speaking would blame the government for not doing more to save them, and also for allowing Nantah to collapse. Ho Kah Leong, Chin Harn Tong, Lee Yiok Seng, all parliamentary secretaries and Nantah graduates, strongly supported Ch'ng's views.

Most of my cabinet colleagues were against intervention as politically too costly. Chin Chye and Eddie Barker were set against it. Even Keng Swee, usually robust and strong-minded, and Kim San, a pragmatist, were not enthusiastic. They would go along with me if I chose to intervene, but why stir up a hornet's nest? They remembered our troubles with the Chinese schools and Nantah in the sixties. I was taken aback when

Ong Pang Boon, Chinese-educated from Confucian High School, Kuala Lumpur, also expressed doubts. He agreed with our Nantah graduate MPs on the seriousness of the situation but was concerned over the political backlash from Nantah donors and supporters in Singapore and Malaysia. But I could not accept the prospect of several hundred students each year wasting their future. Since Nantah could not convert its teaching from Mandarin into English, I persuaded the Nantah council and senate members to move the whole university—staff and students—into the campus of the University of Singapore. Both teachers and students would be forced to use English, subsumed within the larger numbers of English-speaking staff and students at its Bukit Timah campus.

Whatever their misgivings, Nantah staff and students were immersed in an English-speaking environment from the beginning of the 1978 academic year. The majority of the Chinese-speaking parents and students accepted this change from a Chinese-language to an English-language university as unavoidable. The most emotional opposition came from Nantah alumni. Those in Singapore understood, even if they did not openly support the change. The Malaysian alumni were angry and bitter in their denunciation of what they deemed an act of betrayal. On my part I was sad not to have been able to move earlier, thereby saving several thousand Nantah graduates from their poor economic status, handicapped by their inadequate command of English.

It was a painful adjustment, more for the students than for the staff. University of Singapore staff took over the bulk of the teaching until Nantah staff revived their English fluency. I spoke to the students twice to sympathize with their difficulties and encourage them to persevere. About 70 percent of them eventually passed their final joint campus examinations. I had a survey conducted among the graduates, whether they would prefer to receive a University of Singapore degree, a Nantah degree, or a joint degree. The overwhelming majority wanted a University of Singapore degree. I decided to merge the two universities as the National University of Singapore (NUS) and award them NUS degrees. The Nantah campus became the Nanyang Technological Institute attached to the NUS. In 1991, it became the Nanyang Technological University (NTU). Some Nantah alumni wanted it renamed Nanyang University. This is no longer an issue of great moment. The old name can be restored if that is the wish of the graduates of Nantah and NTU. Employers know that the present NTU graduates are up to standard whatever the name of their institution.

I had the political strength to make those changes in Nantah because, unlike many champions of the Chinese language who sent their children to English schools, my three children were completely educated in Chinese schools. When I addressed students and staff of Nantah on the campus in the late 1960s, I could say that I never sacrificed my children's education for a political purpose. I was convinced that Chinese schools were good for them because they were able to master English at home. However, for their university education, I said I would not send them to a Chinese-language university. Their future depended upon a command of the language of the latest textbooks which would be in English. Every parent, whether Chinese- or English-educated, would come to this same conclusion. Because I said this at Nantah and had it reported in the press, I was able to influence the choice of parents and Chinese school students when they sought university places.

Had my children not done well in Chinese schools, I could not have spoken with that same authority. Years later I asked the three of them whether they regretted having gone to a Chinese, not an English, school. They were unanimous that they were better off for having been in Chinese schools.

Nantah produced a total of 12,000 graduates. Had all of them been educated in English, they would have had more satisfying careers and made bigger contributions to Singapore and Malaysia. The problem was one of face. Such high hopes had been pinned on Nantah at its founding, but the tide of history was against it. No country in Southeast Asia wanted a Chinese-language university. On the contrary, they were phasing out Chinese-language schools. Employment opportunities for Chinese-educated high school and university graduates were rapidly declining. Even Chinese banks were switching to English to remain in business.

After the two universities were merged, I made all Chinese schools switch to English as their main language of instruction, with Chinese as their second language. This caused soul-searching among the Chinese-educated, including PAP MPs. None could accept the need to reduce the teaching hours of Chinese in these schools, yet all agreed that the students had to master English to be able to continue their studies in the polytechnics and university without spending an extra year for remedial English. I sympathized with them in their dilemma, but once they accepted English as our working language, these consequences had to follow.

As these changes were taking place, I feared we were losing something valuable in the Chinese school system. I wanted to preserve what was good in the Chinese schools: the discipline, self-confidence, and moral and social values they instilled in their students, based on Chinese traditions, values, and culture. We had to transmit these same values to students in the new bilingual schools or we would deculturalize them. When we use English as the medium of instruction, Confucian values of the family could not be reinforced in schools because both teachers and students were multiracial and the textbooks were not in Chinese.

In addition, the traditional moral values of our students were being eroded by increasing exposure to the Western media, interaction with foreign tourists in Singapore, and their own overseas travel. The values of America's consumer society were permeating Singapore faster than the rest of the region because of our education in the English language.

The changed values and attitudes of younger teachers compounded this problem. The older generation of teachers had known hardship and had seen how difficult it was to bring stability and harmony to Singapore's multiracial society. As I wrote to Keng Swee when he took over the education ministry in 1979, "They teach a philosophy of life, imbue their students with a sense of determination, duty and responsibility, and their teachers have got greater drive and thrust than the majority of the English-medium teachers." The younger teachers, all educated in English with Chinese as their second language, were no longer as steeped in these traditional values.

We wanted to preserve the distinctive traditional values of our different cultures. The Japanese have been able to absorb American influence and remain basically Japanese. Their young, having grown up in affluence, appear less dedicated to the companies they work for than their parents, but they are essentially Japanese and more hardworking and committed to the greater good of their society than Europeans or Americans. I believed that if the Japanese could do this, so could we.

I decided to preserve the best nine of the Chinese schools under a special assistance plan, or SAP. These SAP schools would admit students in the top 10 percent passing the primary school leaving examination. They would teach Chinese at the first language level but have English as the medium of instruction as in other schools. We provided them with additional teachers to enable the pupils to learn English and Chinese through special immersion programs. The SAP schools succeeded in retaining the formality, discipline, and social courtesies of traditional Chinese schools. The ethos in these schools was, and still is, superior to that of the English-language schools, which tended to be more slack in these matters. Today most SAP schools, including the once communist-controlled Chinese High School, are premier institutions with modern facilities to match their proud history and traditions.

After the Nanyang and Singapore University joint campus solution in 1978, I decided the time was right to encourage our Chinese to use Mandarin instead of dialects. It would make it easier for students to master English and Mandarin in school if they spoke Mandarin at home and were not burdened by dialects. I launched a "speak Mandarin" campaign for a month every year.

To emphasize the importance of Mandarin, I stopped making speeches in Hokkien. We stopped all dialect programs on television and radio, but for the older generation, we still broadcast the news in dialects. Unfortunately, at election time we had to speak in dialects, or opposition candidates would have an advantage. As late as the run-up to the January 1997 general election, some of the most rousing responses were to speeches in Hokkien. Dialects are the real mother tongues for the older generation.

It was difficult to change the language habits of Chinese families that interfered with the learning of Mandarin. Until the 1970s, about 80 percent still spoke dialect at home. Young workers interviewed on television were not fluent in Mandarin because they reverted to dialect at home and in their workplace. I used my standing with the people to persuade them to make the switch. They knew that my three children had mastered Mandarin, English, and Malay and respected my views on how to educate children. During our walks in public parks and gardens, parents would often be talking to their children in dialect until they noticed Choo and me, when they would look embarrassed and switch to Mandarin, abashed for not heeding my advice. The switch was especially difficult for the grandparents, but most managed speaking to their grandchildren in dialect and understanding their replies in Mandarin. Without this active promotion of Mandarin, our bilingual policy would have failed for Chinese students. Mandarin-speaking families increased from 26 percent in 1980 to over 60 percent in 1990, and are still increasing. However, English-speaking homes increased from 20 percent in 1988 to 40 percent in 1998.

The opening of China brought a decisive change in the attitudes of Chinese to learning Mandarin. Professionals and supervisors who knew both English and Mandarin commanded a premium: There were no more grumbles about speaking Mandarin and not dialects. We had made the right decision in 1965 at independence to teach Mandarin as a second language. The seven different major south Chinese dialects spoken in Singapore made it easier to persuade all to convert to Mandarin. Had we been like Hong Kong with 95 percent speaking Cantonese, it would have been difficult if not impossible. For many Chinese Singaporeans, dialect is the real mother tongue and Mandarin a stepmother tongue. However, in another two generations, Mandarin can become their mother tongue.

Bilingualism in English and Malay, Chinese, or Tamil is a heavy load for our children. The three mother tongues are completely unrelated to English. But if we were monolingual in our mother tongues, we would not make a living. Becoming monolingual in English would have been a setback. We would have lost our cultural identity, that quiet confidence about ourselves and our place in the world. In any case, we could not have persuaded our people to give up their mother tongues.

Hence, in spite of the criticism from many quarters that our people have mastered neither language, it is our best way forward. English as our working language has prevented conflicts arising between our different races and given us a competitive advantage because it is the international language of business and diplomacy, of science and technology. Without it, we would not have many of the world's multinationals and over 200 of the world's top banks in Singapore. Nor would our people have taken so readily to computers and the Internet.

# 12. Keeping the Government Clean

When the PAP government took office in 1959, we set out to have a clean administration. We were sickened by the greed, corruption, and decadence of many Asian leaders. Fighters for freedom for their oppressed peoples had become plunderers of their wealth. Their societies slid backward. We were swept up by the wave of revolution in Asia, determined to get rid of colonial rule, but angry at and ashamed of the Asian nationalist leaders whose failure to live up to their ideals had disillusioned us.

In England after the war, I met students from China whose burning ambition was to rid China of the corruption and incompetence of the Nationalist Chinese leaders. Hyperinflation and wholesale looting had led to their ignominious defeat and retreat to Taiwan. It was disgust with the venality, greed, and immorality of those men that made so many Chinese school students in Singapore pro-communists. The students saw the communists as exemplars of dedication, sacrifice, and selflessness, the revolutionary virtues displayed in the spartan lives of the Chinese communist leaders. Those were the prevailing beliefs of the time.

One important decision we made before the May 1959 general election highlighted our position on corruption. Lim Yew Hock's government (1956–1959) had started to go corrupt. His education minister, Chew Swee Kee, had received S$1 million, money from an American source to fight the communists in the coming elections. There was widespread market talk of smaller amounts paid for less ideological reasons. We had grave reservations over fighting the election to win because we felt unprepared and not sufficiently organized to take on the communists whom we expected to turn on us once we were the government. But to allow this group of scoundrels another five-year term would corrupt the public servants who were on the whole still honest, and once this happened we would not be able to work the system. We decided to fight to win.

There were temptations everywhere, not only in Singapore. For example, the first official contacts foreigners have when entering a country are immigration and customs officers. At many airports in Southeast Asia, travellers often find themselves delayed at customs clearance until a suitable inducement (often hard cash) is forthcoming. The same tiresome practice is found among traffic police; when stopped for alleged speeding, drivers have to hand over their driving license together with the ongoing rate in dollars to avoid further action. The superior officers do not set a good example. In many cities in the region, even hospital admission after a traffic accident needs a bribe to get prompt attention. Petty power invested in men who cannot live on their salaries is an invitation to misuse that power.

We had a deep sense of mission to establish a clean and effective government. When we took the oath of office at the ceremony in the city council chamber in June 1959, we all wore white shirts and white slacks to symbolize purity and honesty in our personal behavior and our public life. The people expected this of us, and we were determined to live up to their expectations. The pro-communists paraded their working-class credentials in their dress style (rumpled shirt sleeves and slacks), travel mode (buses and taxis), sleeping quarters (back rooms of unions offices), and Chinese school education. They derided my air-conditioned office and home, my large American Studebaker car, my golf and beer drinking, my bourgeois family background, and my Cambridge education. But they could not accuse my colleagues and me of making money out of the workers and unions we helped.

All my ministers except one were university graduates. Out of office, we were confident of getting by and professionals like myself had every expectation of doing so. There was no need to put by something extra for that eventuality. More important, most of us had working wives who could support the family if we were imprisoned or not around. This shaped the attitudes of my ministers and their wives. When ministers commanded the respect and confidence of the people, public servants were also able to hold their heads high and make decisions with confidence. It made a critical difference in our battle against the communists.

We made sure from the day we took office in June 1959 that every dollar in revenue would be properly accounted for and would reach the beneficiaries at the grass roots as one dollar, without being siphoned off along the way. So, from the very beginning we gave special attention to the areas where discretionary powers had been exploited for personal gain and sharpened the instruments that could prevent, detect, or deter such practices.

The principal agency charged with this task was the Corrupt Practices Investigation Bureau (CPIB) set up by the British in 1952 to deal with increasing corruption, especially at lower and middle levels of the police, hawker inspectors, and land bailiffs who had to take action against the many who broke the law by occupying public roads for illegal hawking, or state land for building their squatter huts. These inspectors could either issue a summons or look the other way for an appropriate bribe.

We decided to concentrate on the big takers in the higher echelons and directed the CPIB on our priorities. For the smaller fish we set out to simplify procedures and remove discretion by having clear published guidelines, even doing away with the need for permits or approvals in less important areas. As we ran into problems in securing convictions in prosecutions, we tightened the law in stages.

In 1960, we changed the outdated 1937 anticorruption law and widened the definition of gratuity to include anything of value. The amendments gave wide powers to investigators, including arrest and search and investigation of bank accounts and bank books of suspected persons and their wives, children, or agents. It became unnecessary to prove that the person who accepted a bribe was in a position to carry out the required favor. The comptroller of income tax was obliged to give information concerning anyone investigated. The existing law that the evidence of an accomplice was unworthy of credit unless corroborated was changed to allow the judge to accept the evidence of an accomplice.

The most effective change we made in 1960 was to allow the courts to treat proof that an accused was living beyond his or her means or had property his or her income could not explain as corroborating evidence that the accused had accepted or obtained a bribe. With a keen nose to the ground and the power to investigate every officer and every minister, the director of the CPIB, working from the Prime Minister's Office, developed a justly formidable reputation for sniffing out those betraying the public trust.

In 1963, we made it compulsory for witnesses summoned by the CPIB to present themselves to give information. In 1989, we increased the maximum fine for corruption from S$10,000 to S$100,000. Giving false or misleading information to the CPIB became an offense subject to imprisonment and a fine of up to S$10,000, and the courts were empowered to confiscate the benefits derived from corruption.

Corruption used to be organized on a large scale in certain areas. In 1971, the CPIB broke up a syndicate of over 250 mobile squad policemen who received payments ranging from S$5 to S$10 per month from truck owners whose vehicles they recognized by the addresses painted on the sides of the trucks. Those owners who refused to pay would be constantly harassed by having summonses issued against them.

Customs officers would receive bribes to speed up the checking of vehicles smuggling in prohibited goods. Personnel in the Central Supplies Office (the government's procurement department) provided information on tender bids for a fee. Officers in the import and export department received bribes to hasten the issue of permits. Contractors bribed clerks of works to allow short-piling. Public health laborers were paid by shopkeepers and residents to do their job of clearing refuse. Principals and teachers in some Chinese schools received commissions from stationery suppliers. Human ingenuity is infinite when translating power and discretion into personal gain.

It was not too difficult to clean up these organized rackets. Isolated opportunistic acts of corruption were more difficult to detect, and when discovered had to be squashed.

High-profile cases made the headlines. Several ministers were guilty of corruption, one in each of the decades from the 1960s to the 1980s. Tan Kia Gan was the minister for national development until he lost the 1963 election. We were close colleagues from the early 1950s when he was the leader of the Malayan Airways engineers' union and I was its legal adviser. We appointed him a director on the board of Malaysian Airways. At a board meeting of the company in August 1966, Tan took strong objection to the purchase of Boeing aircraft. A few days later a Mr. Lim contacted First National City Bank, Boeing's bankers, to offer his services for a consideration. He was Tan Kia Gan's business friend. The bank knew of the government's strict stand against corruption and reported the matter. Lim refused to implicate Tan Kia Gan and Tan could not be prosecuted. But I was convinced Tan was behind it. Unpleasant and painful as the decision was, I issued a statement to say that as the government's representative on the board of Malaysian Airways, he had not discharged his duties beyond reproach. I removed him from the board and from all his other appointments. Kim San told me later that Tan was down at heel, unable to do much because he was ostracized. I was sad but there was no other course I could have taken.

Wee Toon Boon was minister of state in the ministry of the environment in 1975 when he took a free trip to Indonesia for himself and his family members, paid for by a housing developer on whose behalf he made representations to civil servants. He also accepted a bungalow worth S$500,000 from this developer and took two overdrafts totalling S$300,000 in his father's name against the personal guarantee of the developer, to speculate in shares. He was a loyal noncommunist trade union leader from the 1950s. It was painful to confront him and hear his unconvincing protestations of innocence. He was charged, convicted, and sentenced to four years and six months in jail. He appealed. The convictions were upheld but the sentence was reduced by 18 months.

In December 1979, we suddenly faced a serious setback. Phey Yew Kok, then president of the NTUC and a PAP MP, was charged on four counts of criminal breach of trust involving a total sum of S$83,000. He was also charged on two counts under the Trade Unions Act for investing S$18,000 of trade union money in a private supermarket without the approval of the minister. As was normal in such cases, he was released on bail.

Devan Nair, as secretary-general of the NTUC, was close to Phey Yew Kok and believed in his innocence. He wanted the CPIB to review the case, saying that an innocent man was being destroyed on false charges. I did not agree because I had seen the investigation reports and had allowed the CPIB to proceed. He was so convinced of Phey's innocence and concerned at losing a valuable aide in the trade union movement that he spoke vehemently to me over lunch one Saturday. In his presence, I rang up the director of the CPIB and told him to show Devan Nair in strict confidence the evidence he had against Phey Yew Kok immediately after that lunch. After he read the evidence, Devan did not contact me. Phey Yew Kok decided to jump bail, and his two sureties lost their S$50,000 when he never returned. He was last heard of in Thailand, eking out a miserable existence as a fugitive, subject to blackmail by immigration and police authorities.

The most dramatic downfall was that of Teh Cheang Wan, then minister for national development. In November 1986, one of his old associates admitted under questioning by the CPIB that he had given Teh two cash payments of S$400,000 each, in one case to allow a development company to retain part of its land which had been earmarked for compulsory government acquisition, and in the second to assist a developer in the purchase of state land for private development. These bribes had taken place in 1981 and 1982. He denied receiving the money and tried to bargain with the senior assistant director of the CPIB for the case not to be pursued. The cabinet secretary reported this and said Teh had asked to see me. I replied that I could not until the investigations were over. A week later, on the morning of 15 December 1986, my security officer reported that Teh had died and left me a letter:

> Prime Minister
>
> I have been feeling very sad and depressed for the last two weeks. I feel responsible for the occurrence of this unfortunate incident and I feel I should accept full responsibility. As an honourable oriental gentleman I feel it is only right that I should pay the highest penalty for my mistake.
>
> Yours faithfully,
> Teh Cheang Wan

I visited the widow and viewed his body lying in his bed. She said he had served the government all his life and wanted to preserve his honor. She asked if it was possible not to have a coroner's inquiry. That was only possible if she got a death certificate from his doctor that he had died of natural causes. Inevitably there was a coroner's inquiry that found he had taken his life with a massive overdose of sodium amytal. The opposition took it up in Parliament and demanded a commission of inquiry. I immediately agreed. This created more painful publicity for his wife and daughter. Soon afterward they left Singapore and never returned. They had lost too much face.

We had established a climate of opinion that looked upon corruption in public office as a threat to society. Teh preferred to take his life rather than face disgrace and ostracism. I never understood why he took this S$800,000. He was an able and resourceful architect and could have made many millions honestly in private practice.

It is easy to start off with high moral standards, strong convictions, and determination to beat down corruption. But it is difficult to live up to these good intentions unless the leaders are strong and determined enough to deal with all transgressors, and without exceptions. CPIB officers must be supported without fear or favor to enforce the rules.

The Institute of Management Development's World Competitiveness Yearbook 1997 ranked the least corrupt countries in the whole world giving 10 points as the perfect score for the country with no corruption. Singapore was ranked as the least corrupt country in Asia with a score of 9.18, ahead of Hong Kong, Japan, and Taiwan. Transparency International (based in Berlin) placed Singapore in seventh place worldwide in 1998 for absence of corruption.

The percentage, kickback, baksheesh, slush, or whatever the local euphemism is a way of life in Asia: People openly accept it as a part of their culture. Ministers and officials cannot live on their salaries to the standard of their office. The higher they are, the bigger their homes and more numerous their wives, concubines, or mistresses, all bedecked in jewelry appropriate to the power and position of their men. Singaporeans who do business in these countries have to take care not to bring home such practices.

When the Chinese communists came to power they made a great play of their total honesty and dedication. Waiters and chambermaids in the

China of the 1950s and 1960s would return every scrap of property left behind in the hotel, even things the guests had intended to discard. It was an ostentatious display of their total disinterest in material possessions. But during the height of the Cultural Revolution, 1966–1976, the system broke down. Favoritism, nepotism, and covert corruption infected high places. The whole society was degraded as opportunists masqueraded as revolutionaries and achieved "helicopter promotions" by betraying and persecuting their peers or superiors. Corruption became worse when China embarked on its open-door policy in 1978. Many communist activists who felt they had been deceived and had wasted the best years of their lives set out to make up for lost time and enrich themselves in every way they could. The same happened with communists in Vietnam. After they opened up to foreign investments and the free market in the late 1980s, corruption infected the Communist Party. Both regimes, once justly proud of their total selflessness and dedication to the communist cause, are bedeviled by worse corruption than the decadent capitalist Asian countries they used to revile and despise.

A precondition for an honest government is that candidates must not need large sums of money to get elected, or it must trigger off the cycle of corruption. The bane of most countries in Asia has been the high cost of elections. Having spent a lot to get elected, winners must recover their costs and also accumulate funds for the next election. The system is self-perpetuating. To be elected to Taiwan's legislative *yuan* in the 1990s, some KMT candidates spent as much as US$10–20 million. Once elected, they had to recoup and prepare for the next round by using their influence with government ministers and officials to get contracts awarded, or to convert land use from agricultural to industrial or urban development. In Thailand, a former government minister described it as "commercial democracy, the purchased mandate." In 1996, some 2,000 candidates spent about 30 billion bahts (US$1.2 billion). One prime minister was called Mr. ATM (Automatic Teller Machine) because he was renowned for dispensing cash to candidates and voters. He retorted that he was not the only ATM.

In Malaysia, UMNO leaders call it "money politics." In his speech to party delegates in October 1996, Prime Minister Dr. Mahathir Mohamad noted that some candidates vying for higher positions had been "offering bribes and gifts to delegates" in exchange for votes. Dr. Mahathir deplored the practice of money politics and was moved to tears as he urged party delegates "not to let bribery destroy the Malay race, religion and nation." According to Malaysian news reports, Bank Negara ran out of RM1,000 and RM5,000 notes at the height of the campaign leading to the UMNO party delegates' conference in 1993.

Indonesia was a celebrated example of corruption on such a grand scale that Indonesian media coined the acronym "KKN" for *Kolusi* (Collusion), *Korupsi* (Corruption), and *Nepotisme* (Nepotism). President Suharto's children, friends, and cronies set examples that made KKN an irreducible part of Indonesian culture. The American media assessed the Suharto family to be worth US$42 billion before the financial crisis reduced their value. Corruption was worse under President Habibie. Ministers and officials, uncertain of their positions after the election for a new president, made the most of the time left. Habibie's aides accumulated huge funds to buy votes in the MPR (People's Consultative Assembly) to get elected. The going rate reportedly was more than a quarter million U.S. dollars for each vote.

The most expensive of all election systems is Japan's. Japanese ministers and Diet members (MPs) are paid modest salaries and allowances. A Japanese MP requires over US$1 million a year to maintain his support staff both in Tokyo and in his constituency as well as to provide gifts to voters for birthdays, births, marriages, and funerals. In an election year, the candidate needs over US$5 million. He depends on his faction leader for funds. Since a leader's power depends on the number of Diet members who support and depend on him, he has to amass vast sums to finance his followers during and between elections.

Singapore has avoided the use of money to win elections. As leader of the opposition, I had persuaded Chief Minister Lim Yew Hock in 1959 to make voting compulsory and prohibit the practice of using cars to take voters to the polls. After winning power, we cleaned up triad (secret society) influence from politics. Our most formidable opponents, the communists, did not use money to win voters. Our own election expenses were small, well below the amount allowed by law. There was no need for the party to replenish its coffers after elections, and between elections there were no gifts for voters. We got them to vote for us again and again by providing jobs, building schools, hospitals, community centers, and, most important of all, homes which they owned. These are substantial benefits that changed their lives and convinced them that their children's future lay with the PAP. Opposition parties also did not need money. They defeated our candidates because the electorate wanted an opposition MP to pressure the government for more concessions.

Western liberals have argued that a completely unfettered press will expose corruption and make for clean, honest government. Yet uninhibited and freewheeling press and television in India, the Philippines, Thailand, Taiwan, South Korea, and Japan have not stopped the pervasive and deeply embedded corruption in these countries, while the most telling example of a free media being part and parcel of its owner's corruption is former Italian Prime Minister Silvio Berlusconi. He owns a large media network but was himself investigated and charged for corrupt practices committed before he became prime minister.

On the other hand Singapore has shown that a system of clean, no-money elections helps to preserve an honest government. But Singapore will remain clean and honest only if honest and able men are willing to fight elections and assume office. They must be paid a wage commensurate with what men of their ability and integrity are earning for managing a big corporation or a successful legal or other professional practice. They have to manage a Singapore economy that yielded an annual growth rate of 8 to 9 percent in the last two decades, giving its citizens a per capita GDP that the World Bank rated in 1995 as the ninth highest in the world.

With the founder generation of leaders, honesty had become a habit. My colleagues would spurn any attempt to suborn them. They had put their lives in jeopardy to achieve power, not to enrich themselves, but to change society. However, this group could not be replicated because it was not possible to recreate the conditions that made them different. Our successors have become ministers as one of many career options, and not the most attractive one. If we underpay men of quality as ministers, we cannot expect them to stay long in office earning a fraction of what they could outside. With high economic growth and higher earnings in the private sector, ministers' salaries have to match their counterparts' in the private sector. Underpaid ministers and public officials have ruined many governments in Asia. Adequate remuneration is vital for high standards of probity in political leaders and high officials.

In a debate on the budget in March 1985, I took the opposition to task for opposing ministerial pay increases. J. B. Jeyaretnam of the Workers' Party had contrasted my monthly salary of S$29,000 with that of the prime minister of Malaysia who was paid S$10,000, but took only S$9,000. I went further to compare the salaries of Philippines President Marcos at 100,000 pesos yearly, or just over S$1,000 a month, and the president of Indonesia, governing 150 million people at a monthly salary of 1.2 million rupiahs or S$2,500. However, they were all wealthier than I was. An Indonesian leader retained his official residence on retirement. A Malaysian prime minister was given a house or land to build his private residence. My official residence belonged to the government. I had no perks, no cars with chauffeurs thrown in, or ministerial quarters with gardeners, cooks, and other servants in attendance. My practice was to have all benefits expressed in a lump sum and let the prime minister and ministers themselves decide what they wanted to spend it on.

I referred to the wage scales of the People's Republic of China. Their lowest wage was 18 yuan and the highest 560 yuan, a ratio of 1:31. But this did not reflect the difference in the quality of life between the lowest and the highest in the land who lived behind the walls of the Zhongnanhai near the Forbidden City. Nor did it take into account the access to different foods and goods, with cooks, other domestic staff, and medical services that made for a different quality of life.

Ostentatious egalitarianism is good politics. For decades in Mao's China, the people wore the same-style Mao jacket and trousers, ostensibly of the same material with the same ill-fitting cut. In fact there were different grades of Mao jackets. A provincial leader in charge of tourism explained to one of my ministers that while they might look alike, they were of different quality cloth. To emphasize his point, he unbuttoned his jacket to show that it was fur-lined.

The need for popular support makes governments who have to be elected into office, as a rule, underpay ministers in their official salaries. But semihidden perks in housing, an expense account, a car, travel, children's education, and other allowances often make up more than their salaries.

In successive debates in Parliament in the 1980s and 1990s, I pointed out that the remuneration of ministers and political appointees in Britain, the United States, and most countries in the West had not kept pace with their economic growth. They had assumed that people who went into politics were gentlemen with private means. Indeed, in prewar Britain, people without private incomes were seldom found in Parliament. While this is no longer the case in Britain or the United States, most successful people are too busy and doing too well to want to be in government.

In the United States, highly paid persons from the private sector are appointed by the president for brief periods of one or two terms. Then they return to their private sector occupations as lawyers, company chairpersons, or lobbyists with enhanced value because they now enjoy easy access to key people in the administration. I thought this "revolving door" system undesirable.

After independence I had frozen ministerial salaries and kept public service wage increases at a low level to be sure that we would cope with the expected unemployment and slowdown in the economy and to set an example of restraint. When we had no serious unemployment by 1970, and everybody breathed a little easier, I increased ministers' salaries from S$2,500 to S$4,500 per month but kept my own fixed at S$3,500 to remind the public service that some restraint was still necessary. Every few years I had to increase ministerial salaries to narrow the widening gap with private sector rewards.

In 1978, Dr. Tony Tan was general manager of the Oversea-Chinese Banking Corporation, a big local bank, on a salary scale that would have taken him to S$950,000 per year. I had persuaded him to resign to become minister of state, for which he was paid less than a third of his former salary, apart from losing his perks, the most valuable of which was a car with a driver. Ong Teng Cheong, the minister for communications, had also made a sacrifice by giving up a successful practice as an architect during a building boom.

When I was senior minister, I proposed in Parliament in 1994 that the government settle a formula so that revisions to salaries of ministers, judges, and top civil servants were automatic, linked to the income tax returns of the private sector. With the Singapore economy growing at 7 to 10 percent per annum for over two decades, public sector salaries were always lagging two or three years behind the private sector. In 1995, Prime Minister Goh decided on a formula I had proposed that would peg the salaries of ministers and senior public officers to those of their private sector counterparts. This would automatically entitle them to an increase as incomes in the private sector increased. This change to a formula, pegged at two-thirds of the earnings of their private sector equivalents as disclosed in their income tax returns, caused an enormous stir, especially with the professionals who felt that it was completely out of proportion to what ministers were paid in advanced countries. People had for so long been accustomed to having public servants paid modest salaries that the idea that ministers not only exercised power but were also paid in accordance with the importance of the job upset their sense of propriety. I was able to help the prime minister justify this change and rebut the arguments that ministers were more than adequately compensated by the honor of high office and the power they wielded, and that public service should entail sacrifice of income. I believed this high-minded approach was unrealistic and the surest way to make ministers serve only briefly, whereas continuity in office and the experience thus gained have been a great advantage and strength in the Singapore government. Our ministers have provided the experience and judgment the government has shown in its decisions, the result of their ability to think and plan long-term.

In the general election 18 months later, the prime minister carried the electorate although the opposition made ministerial salaries an issue. People want a good, honest, clean government that produced results. That was what the PAP provided. It is now less difficult to recruit talent from the private sector. Before the salary formula was implemented top litigation lawyers were earning S$1 to 2 million a year, while judges were paid less than S$300,000. Without this change, we would never have been able to appoint some of our best practicing lawyers to the judiciary. We also had the salaries of doctors and other professionals in government service linked to the incomes of their counterparts in private practice.

This salary formula does not mean increments every year, because the private sector incomes go up and down. When they went down in 1995, the salaries of all ministers and senior officials were reduced accordingly in 1997.

To guard against a freak election of a less than honorable and honest group into government, I had proposed at a National Day Rally in August 1984 that we have an elected president to safeguard the nation's reserves. He would also have powers to override a prime minister who held up investigations for corruption against himself, his ministers, or senior officials, and to veto unsuitable appointments to high positions like chief justice, chief of defense staff, or commissioner of police. Such a president would need an independent mandate from the electorate. Many believed I was preparing a position for myself after I stepped down as prime minister. In fact, I had no interest in this high office as it would be too passive for my temperament. This proposal and its implications were debated as a white paper in Parliament in 1988. Several years later, in 1992, the constitution was amended by Prime Minister Goh Chok Tong to provide for an elected president. We had to keep the right balance between the president's powers and the legitimate discretionary powers of the prime minister and his cabinet.

When the countries of East Asia from South Korea to Indonesia were devastated by the financial crisis in 1997, corruption and cronyism aggravated their woes. Singapore weathered the crisis better because there was no corruption and cronyism that had cost the other countries many billions in losses.

It was the high standards we maintained that made Prime Minister Goh Chok Tong order an investigation into purchases in 1995 of two properties each made by my wife on my behalf and by my son Lee Hsien Loong, the deputy prime minister. They had both enjoyed discounts for the property purchases. The developer had given the same unsolicited 5 to 7 percent discounts on these purchases as he had given to 5 to 10 percent of his other buyers at a soft launch to test the market. Immediately after their purchase, in the heat of the property boom, the properties escalated in price. Those who had not been given a chance to buy at the soft launch made complaints to the committee of the Stock Exchange of Singapore (SES). (The developer was a public-listed company.) After investigations the SES found that the developer had acted within its rights. Because my brother was a nonexecutive director of the company, a rumor went around that my son and I had gained an unfair advantage when purchasing these properties. The Monetary Authority of Singapore investigated and reported to Prime Minister Goh that there was nothing improper in the discounts given to us.

Choo was indignant at the charge of impropriety. She had been a conveyancing lawyer for 40 years, and knew that giving discounts in sales was a common practice by all developers. I was equally angry and decided to scotch suspicions of improper dealings by going public with our purchases and the unsolicited discounts. We paid over the value of the discounts, which amounted to a total of S$1 million, to the finance minister (i.e., the government). The prime minister ordered this sum to be returned to us because he agreed there had been no impropriety and the government was not entitled to the money. Loong and I did not want to appear to have benefited from my brother being a director of the developer company and decided to give the S$1 million to charity.

I asked the prime minister to take the matter to Parliament for a thorough airing of the issue. In the debate, opposition MPs, including two lawyers, one of them the leader of the opposition, said that in their experience the giving of such discounts was standard marketing practice and there was nothing improper in our purchases. This open and complete disclosure of a perceived unfair advantage made it a nonissue in the general election a year later. As I told the House, the fact that the system I had set in place could investigate and report upon my conduct proved that it was impersonal and effective, and that no one was above the law.

# 13.  Greening Singapore

On my first visit to the Great Hall of the People in Beijing in 1976, there were spittoons in the meeting rooms where they greeted us. Some of the Chinese leaders actually used them. When Deng Xiaoping visited Singapore in 1978, we provided a Ming blue and white spittoon. Although we placed it next to his chair in the conference room, he did not use it. He might have noticed that Chinese Singaporeans did not spit. On my next visit to Beijing in 1980, I saw that spittoons had been removed from the Great Hall. A few years later, when I gave dinner in Singapore to Gu Mu, a state councillor in charge of economics, I mentioned that they had stopped using spittoons in the Great Hall of the People. He chuckled and said they had removed them from the meeting rooms but still used them in their offices—it was too old a habit to eradicate.

I had introduced antispitting campaigns in the 1960s. But even in the 1980s some taxi drivers would spit out of their car windows and some people were still spitting in markets and food centers. We persisted and disseminated the message through schools and the media that spitting spread diseases such as tuberculosis. Now people seldom see spitting in public. We are an immigrant people who have uprooted ourselves from our ancient homelands and are prepared to abandon old habits to make good in a new country. This progress encouraged me to alter other bad habits.

After independence, I searched for some dramatic way to distinguish ourselves from other Third World countries. I settled for a clean and green Singapore. One arm of my strategy was to make Singapore into an oasis in Southeast Asia, for if we had First World standards then business-people and tourists would make us a base for their business and tours of the region. The physical infrastructure was easier to improve than the rough and ready ways of the people. Many of them had moved from shanty huts with a hole in the ground or a bucket in an outhouse to high-rise apartments with modern sanitation, but their behavior remained the same. We had to work hard to be rid of littering, noise nuisance, and rudeness, and get people to be considerate and courteous.

We started from a low base. In the 1960s, long queues would form at our "Meet the People" sessions, clinics where ministers and MPs helped solve the problems of their constituents. The unemployed, many accom-panied by wives and children, would plead for jobs, taxi or hawker licenses, or permission to sell food in school cafeterias. These were the human faces behind the unemployment statistics. Thousands would sell cooked food on the pavements and streets in total disregard of traffic, health, or other considerations. The resulting litter and dirt, the stench of rotting food, and the clutter and obstructions turned many parts of the city into slums.

Many became "pirate taxi" drivers, unlicensed and without insurance cover, exploited by businesspeople who rented them junk private cars. They charged slightly more than the buses and much less than licensed taxis. They stopped without signalling to pick up or drop off passengers at will and were a menace to other road users. Hundreds, eventually thou-sands, of pirate taxis clogged our streets and destroyed bus services.

For years we could not clean up the city by removing these illegal hawkers and pirate taxi drivers. Only after 1971, when we had created many jobs, were we able to enforce the law and reclaim the streets. We licensed the cooked food hawkers and moved them from the roads and pavements to properly constructed nearby hawker centers, with piped water, sewers, and garbage disposal. By the early 1980s we had resettled all hawkers. Some were such excellent cooks that they became great tourist attractions. A few became millionaires who drove to work in their Mercedes-Benz and employed waiters. It was the enterprise, drive, and talent of such people that made Singapore. Pirate taxi drivers were ban-ished from the roads only after we had reorganized bus services and could provide them with alternative employment.

The city became scruffy while we were in Malaysia, after two communal riots in July and September 1964. Morale went down and discipline slackened. Two incidents stirred me to action. One morning in November 1964 I looked across the Padang from my office window at City Hall to see several cows grazing on the Esplanade! A few days later a lawyer driving on a main road just outside the city hit a cow and died. The Indian cowherds were bringing their cows into the city to graze on the roadsides and on the Esplanade itself. I called a meeting of public health officers and spelt out an action plan to solve this problem. We gave owners of cows and goats a grace period until 31 January 1965, after which all such stray animals would be taken to the slaughterhouses and the meat given to welfare homes. By December 1965, we had seized and slaughtered 53 cows. Very quickly, all cattle and goats were back in their sheds.

To achieve First World standards in a Third World region, we set out to transform Singapore into a tropical garden city. I had been planting trees at the opening of community centers, during my visits to various establishments and at traffic roundabouts to commemorate the completion of a road junction. Some thrived, many did not. Revisiting a community center, I would find a new sapling, just transplanted for my visit. I concluded that we needed a department dedicated to the care of trees after they had been planted. I established one in the ministry of national development.

After some progress, I met all senior officers of the government and statutory boards to involve them in the "clean and green" movement. I recounted how I had visited almost 50 countries and stayed in nearly as many official guesthouses. What impressed me was not the size of the buildings but the standard of their maintenance. I knew when a country and its administrators were demoralized from the way the buildings had been neglected—washbasins cracked, taps leaking, water closets not functioning properly, a general dilapidation, and, inevitably, unkempt gardens. VIPs would judge Singapore the same way.

We planted millions of trees, palms, and shrubs. Greening raised the morale of people and gave them pride in their surroundings. We taught them to care for and not vandalize the trees. We did not differentiate between middle-class and working-class areas. The British had superior white enclaves in Tanglin and around Government House that were neater, cleaner, and greener than the "native" areas. That would have been politically disastrous for an elected government. We kept down flies and mosquitoes, and cleaned up smelly drains and canals. Within a year there was a distinct spruceness of public spaces.

Perseverance and stamina were needed to fight old habits: People walked over plants, trampled on grass, despoiled flowerbeds, pilfered saplings, or parked bicycles or motorcycles against the larger ones, knocking them down. And it was not just the poorer people who were the offenders. A doctor was caught removing from a central road divider a newly planted valuable Norfolk Island pine which he fancied for his garden. To overcome the initial indifference of the public, we educated their children in schools by getting them to plant trees, care for them, and grow gardens. They brought the message home to their parents.

Nature did not favor us with luscious green grass as it has New Zealand and Ireland. An Australian plant expert and a New Zealand soil expert came in 1978 at my request to study our soil conditions. Their report caught my interest and I asked to see them. They explained that Singapore was part of the equatorial rainforest belt, with strong sunshine and heavy rainfall throughout the year. When trees were cut down, heavy rainfall would wash off the topsoil and leach the nutrients. To have grass green and lush, we had to apply fertilizers regularly, preferably compost, which would not be so easily washed away, and lime, because our soil was too acidic. The Istana curator tested this on our lawns. Suddenly the grass became greener. We had all school and other sports fields and stadiums similarly treated. The bare patches around the goal posts with sparse, tired-looking yellow grass were soon carpeted green. Gradually, the whole city greened up. A visiting French minister, a guest at our National Day reception in the 1970s, was ecstatic as he congratulated me in French; I did not speak it, but understood the word "verdure." He was captivated by the greenness of the city.

Most countries in Asia then paid little or no attention to greening. That Singapore was different, and had taken tough action against stray cattle, made news in the American *Look* magazine of November 1969. Enthused after a visit, Hong Kong's director of information services announced that he would put up a two-year antilitter campaign based on our experience.

For the Commonwealth prime ministers' conference set for mid-January 1971, I rallied our officials to make that extra effort and give visitors a better impression of Singapore. We briefed the service industry, shopkeepers, taxi drivers, and workers in hotels and restaurants to exert themselves to be courteous and friendly. They responded and the feedback from visiting prime ministers, presidents, and their staff was good. Encouraged by this, the tourist promotion board launched a campaign for courteous and gracious service from salespeople and others in the service trade. I intervened. It was absurd if our service personnel were courteous to tourists but not to Singaporeans. I got the ministry of defense in charge of national servicemen, the ministry of education with half a million students under its care, and the National Trades Union Congress with several hundred thousand workers to spread the message that courtesy must be our way of life, to make Singapore a pleasanter place for ourselves, quite apart from the tourist trade.

Our biggest dividend was when Asean leaders decided to compete in the greening of their cities. Malaysia's Dr. Mahathir, who had stayed at the Istana Villa in the 1970s, asked me how I got the Istana lawns to be so green. When he became prime minister, he greened up Kuala Lumpur. President Suharto pushed greening in Jakarta, as did President Marcos in Manila and Prime Minister Thanin in Bangkok, all in the late 1970s. I encouraged them, reminding them that they had a greater variety of trees and a similar favorable climate.

No other project has brought richer rewards to the region. Our neighbors have tried to out-green and out-bloom each other. Greening was positive competition that benefitted everyone—it was good for morale, for tourism, and for investors. It was immensely better that we competed to be the greenest and cleanest in Asia. I can think of many areas where competition could be harmful, even deadly.

On the first Sunday in November 1971, we launched an annual Tree Planting Day that involved all MPs, community centers, and their leaders. We have not missed a single tree planting day since. Saplings planted in November need minimum watering as the rainy season begins then.

Because our own suitable varieties of trees, shrubs, and creepers were limited, I sent research teams to visit botanical gardens, public parks, and arboreta in the tropical and subtropical zones to select new varieties from countries with a similar climate in Asia, Africa, the Caribbean, and Central America. They brought back many free-flowering plants and trees to test on our soil and climate. Unfortunately, beautiful free-flowering trees from the Caribbean will not flower in Singapore because we do not have their cool winters. Those from India and Myanmar (formerly Burma) seldom flowered in Singapore because they needed the annual long dry season between monsoons of their native habitat. Our botanists brought back 8,000 different varieties and got some 2,000 to grow in Singapore. They propagated the successful sturdy ones and added variety to our greenery.

A key implementer of my green policy was an able officer, Wong Yew Kwan. A Malaysian, he had been trained in silviculture, intending to work for rubber and oil palm plantations in Malaysia. He brought his expertise to bear on the problems of roadside trees, shrubs, and other greenery and created parks and park-connectors in Singapore. I showered him with memos, endless wish lists that he assiduously responded to, successfully implementing many of them. His successor, Chua Sian Eng, was an agriculturist who made himself a tree expert and kept up the good work.

Every time I return to Singapore after a few weeks' absence, and see the trees, palms, green grass, and free-flowering shrubs as I drive along East Coast Parkway from the airport into the city, my spirits rise. Greening is the most cost-effective project I have launched.

One compelling reason to have a clean Singapore is our need to collect as much as possible of our rainfall of 95 inches a year. I put Lee Ek Tieng, a civil engineer, then the head of the Anti-Pollution Unit, in charge of a plan to dam up all our streams and rivers. The plan took about 10 years to implement. He had to ensure that all sewage, sullage, and other soiled water from homes and factories emptied into the sewers. Only clean rainwater runoff from the roofs, gardens, and open spaces was allowed into the open drains that flowed into dammed-up rivers. By 1980, we were able to provide some 63 million gallons of water per day, about half of our daily water consumption then.

My most ambitious plan was to clean up the Singapore River and Kallang Basin and bring fish back to the rivers. When I first proposed it in February 1977, many, especially industrialists, asked, "Why clean up? The Rochore Canal {which flows into Kallang Basin}, and the Singapore River have always been filthy; part of Singapore's heritage!" I would have none of this. They smelled putrid. A blind telephone operator in Choo's law office knew when his bus was approaching Singapore River by its distinctive stench. Trade effluents were responsible for half of our water pollution problem. Every stream, culvert, and rivulet had to be free from pollution. Teh Cheang Wan, then chief executive officer of the HDB, quipped, "It will be a lot cheaper for you to buy fish and put them in the river every week."

Lee Ek Tieng was not deterred. He had worked closely with me and was confident of my support. Cleaning up the Singapore River and Kallang Basin was a massive engineering job. He laid underground sewers for the whole island, which was especially difficult in the heavily built-up city center. We moved people from some 3,000 backyard and cottage industries and resettled them in industrial estates with sullage traps for oil and other wastes. Since the founding of Singapore in 1819, lighters and open barges had plied the river. Their workers lived, cooked, and did their ablutions on these vessels. They had to move to Pasir Panjang on the west coast, while boatyards along the Kallang River were relocated at Tuas and the Jurong River. Five thousand street vendors of cooked food and market produce had to go into properly designed centers. Accustomed to doing business on the road rent-free and easily accessible to customers, they resisted moving to centers where they would have to pay rent and water and electricity charges. We gently but firmly moved them and subsidized their rentals. Even so, some failed.

We phased out the rearing of over 900,000 pigs on 8,000 farms because pig waste polluted our streams. We also shut down many food-fish ponds, leaving only 14 in agrotechnology parks and a few for leisure fishing. Food-fish are now farmed offshore in shallow net-cages in the Straits of Johor as well as in deep-sea net-cages off deeper waters near our southern islands.

We had a resettlement unit to deal with the haggling and bargaining involved in every resettlement, whether of hawkers, farmers, or cottage industrialists. They were never happy to be moved or to change their business. This was a hazardous political task that unless carefully and sympathetically handled would lose us votes in the next election. A committee of officials and MPs whose constituencies were affected helped to limit the political fallout.

Resettling farmers was the toughest. We paid compensation based on size of farm structures, the cemented area of open space within their farm holding, and the number of fruit trees and fishponds. As our economy thrived, we increased the amount, but even the most generous payment was not enough. Older farmers did not know what to do with themselves and their compensation money. Living in apartments, they missed their pigs, ducks, chickens, fruit trees, and vegetable plots which had provided them with free food. Fifteen to 20 years after being resettled in HDB new towns, many still voted against the PAP. They felt the government had destroyed their way of life.

In November 1987, I found great satisfaction in going by launch up a clean Kallang Basin and Singapore River, until then the open sewers of Singapore. At the Clean River ceremony, I presented the men responsible with gold medals to commemorate the achievement. We later built eight new estuarine reservoirs, several of them open for boating and recreational fishing. The yield of potable water rose to 120 million gallons per day. Behind each successful project was a dedicated and able officer, trained in that discipline and applying himself to our unique problems. There would have been no clean and green Singapore without Lee Ek Tieng. I could spell out broad conceptual objectives, but he had to work out the engineering solutions. He later became head of the civil service.

In 1993, Winsemius went fishing on the Singapore River and had the satisfaction of catching a fish. Clean rivers made possible a different quality of life. The value and use of land rose significantly, especially in the city and at sites abutting rivers and canals. We bought sand from Indonesia to lay a beach along the banks of the Kallang Basin where people sunbathe and water ski today. Waterside high-rise condominiums have taken over from unsightly small shipyards. For those who remember the Singapore River when it was a sewer, it is a dream to walk along the banks. Shophouses and warehouses have been restored and turned into cafés, restaurants, shops, and hotels, and people wine and dine al fresco by the river or on traditional Chinese barges parked alongside.

You can tell how polluted a city is by its greenery. Where exhaust fumes from poorly maintained cars, buses, and diesel trucks are excessive, the shrubs, covered in black soot particles, wilt and die. In Boston during the autumn of 1970, I was surprised to see lines of cars heading for gas stations. My driver explained that it was the last day for cars to renew their license for the following year, and they had first to be tested and certified roadworthy by authorized gas stations. I decided to set up an Anti-Pollution Unit as part of my office. We had monitoring instruments placed along busy roads to measure dust particles and smoke density and the concentration of sulphur dioxide emitted by motor vehicles. Other cities had clean and green suburbs that gave their residents respite from city centers. Singapore's size forced us to work, play, and reside in the same small place, and this made it necessary to preserve a clean and gracious environment for rich and poor alike.

In the heart of Jurong Town, surrounded by hundreds of factories, we built a bird park in 1971. Without strict antipollution standards, these birds from the world over could not have thrived as they are doing. We also had greening in Jurong itself. All factories had to landscape their grounds and plant trees before they could commence operations.

Although we have solved our domestic air pollution, the whole of Singapore and the surrounding region was covered in haze from forest fires in Sumatra and Borneo in 1994 and 1997. Plantation companies, after extracting the valuable timber, set fire to the rest of the forest to clear the land for oil palms and other crops. In the dry season, the fires raged for months. In mid-1997, a thick poisonous haze spread over Malaysia, Singapore, Thailand, and the Philippines, causing airports to close and thousands to fall ill.

I also had to deal with noise pollution which the old Singapore suffered from vehicles, pile-driving on construction sites, loudspeakers from open-air entertainment, and television sets and radios. Slowly and methodically, we brought the decibels down by enforcing new rules. Noisiest and most dangerous was the custom of firing crackers during the Chinese New

Year season. Many, especially children, suffered serious burns and injuries. Whole squatter villages of wooden buildings had been burnt down. After a massive fire on the last day of the 1970 Chinese New Year festivities, when five persons were killed and many injured, I stopped this age-old Chinese tradition of firing crackers, making it an offense. Nevertheless, two years later, two unarmed policemen were brutally attacked when they tried to prevent a group from firing crackers. We took it one step further and banned the importation of firecrackers altogether. When we live in high-rises 10 to 20 storys high, incompatible traditional practices had to stop.

In the 1960s, the pace of urban renewal had quickened. We went through a phase when we recklessly demolished the old rundown city center to build anew. By late 1970, we felt disquiet over the speed at which we were erasing our past, so we set up a Preservation of Monuments Board in 1971 to identify and preserve buildings of historic, traditional, archaeological, architectural, or artistic interest, and civic, cultural, and commercial buildings significant in Singapore's history. The buildings designated include old Chinese temples, Indian temples, mosques, Anglican and Catholic churches, Jewish synagogues, nineteenth century traditional Chinese architecture, and former colonial government offices in the old civic center. The pride of the colonial past was Government House, once the seat of British governors, now the Istana where the president and prime minister have their offices.

We tried to retain Singapore's distinctive character and identity to remind us of our past. Fortunately we had not demolished the historic districts of Kampong Glam, the historical seat of Malay royalty, Little India, Chinatown, and the old warehouses along the Singapore River.

From the 1970s, to save the young from a nasty and dangerous addiction, we banned all advertising for cigarettes. Progressively, we banned smoking from all public places—elevators, buses, MRT (Mass Rapid Transit) trains and stations, and, eventually, all air-conditioned offices and restaurants. I followed the Canadians who blazed the trail. The Americans were far behind because their tobacco lobby was too powerful.

We had a "Smoke-Free Week" every year. As part of this campaign, I recounted on television my personal experience, how I used to smoke about 20 cigarettes a day until 1957, when after three weeks of campaigning in the city council election, I lost my voice and could not even thank the voters. Since I could not keep my addiction within limits, I stopped smoking altogether. I suffered for a fortnight. In the 1960s I became allergic to tobacco smoke and disallowed smoking in my air-conditioned office and the cabinet room. Within a few years most ministers had given up smoking except two chainsmokers, Raja and Eddie Barker. They would slip out of cabinet meetings for about 10 minutes to light up and satisfy their craving on the open veranda.

It is a relentless battle that we are still waging. The American tobacco industry's wealth and advertising power make it a formidable enemy. The number of older smokers has decreased but the young, including girls, are still being trapped into addiction. We cannot afford to lose this battle.

A ban on chewing gum brought us much ridicule in America. As early as 1983, the minister for national development had proposed that we ban it because of the problems caused by spent chewing gum inserted into keyholes and mailboxes and on elevator buttons. Spitting of chewing gum on floors and common corridors increased the cost of cleaning and damaged cleaning equipment. At first I thought a ban too drastic. Then vandals stuck chewing gum onto the sensors of the doors of our MRT trains and services were disrupted. I was no longer prime minister but Prime Minister Goh and his other colleagues decided on a ban in January 1992. Several ministers who had studied in American universities recounted how the underside of lecture theater seats were filthy with chewing gum stuck to them like barnacles. The ban greatly reduced the nuisance, and after stocks in the shops had been removed the gum problem at MRT stations and trains was negligible.

Foreign correspondents in Singapore have no big scandals of corruption or grave wrongdoings to report. Instead they reported on the fervor and frequency of these "do good" campaigns, ridiculing Singapore as a "nanny state." They laughed at us. But I was confident we would have the last laugh. We would have been a grosser, ruder, cruder society had we not made these efforts to persuade our people to change their ways. We did not measure up as a cultivated, civilized society and were not ashamed to set about trying to become one in the shortest time possible. First, we educated and exhorted our people. After we had persuaded and won over a majority, we legislated to punish the willful minority. It has made Singapore a more pleasant place to live in. If this is a "nanny state," I am proud to have fostered one.

# 14. Managing the Media

In the 40 years since 1959, the Singapore press has evolved away from the norms set by the colonial government. We brought this about by laying down out-of-bounds markers, mostly for our English-language media. They had been influenced by the British editors and reporters who used to be their superiors in the Straits Times group. It took many years before a younger generation of journalists in the 1980s recognized that the political culture of Singapore was and will stay different from the Western norm. However, our journalists are exposed to and influenced by the reporting styles and political attitudes of the American media, always skeptical and cynical of authority. The Chinese and Malay press do not model themselves on newspapers in the West. Their cultural practice is for constructive support of policies they agree with, and criticism in measured terms when they do not.

By the 1990s, our journalists aged below 40 had all gone through similar Singapore schools. Yet differences between the English, Chinese, and Malay press continue; the cultural gap has not been bridged. These differences are evident in their editorial comments, headlines, selection of news, and choice of readers' letters for publication. Chinese-educated readers do not have the same political and social values as the English-educated. They place greater emphasis on the interests of the group than those of the individual.

The main English newspaper, the *Straits Times,* when owned by the British, openly promoted their interests. It enjoyed the patronage of

British commercial firms which fed it with advertisements and of the colonial government which provided it with news and revenue from publishing official notices. No local English-language newspaper could ever reach even a fraction of its circulation and influence.

The Chinese-language newspapers were left to their own devices. Their owners, wealthy Chinese merchants, used them to advance their interests. To attract readers, they played up news about China, Chinese education and culture, and the war in China. The two main papers, the *Nanyang Siang Pau* and the *Sin Chew Jit Poh,* were owned by two wealthy Chinese families with right-wing but opportunistic editors working through young Chinese journalists of whom most were left-wing and quite a few were Communist Party activists.

The vernacular papers—Chinese, Tamil, and other languages—catered to their readers' communal interests and did not have any Singapore identity. The Malay paper, *Utusan Melayu,* printed in the Arabic script (Jawi), made itself the vehicle of pan-Malay-Indonesian nationalism.

Almost from the start, the *Straits Times* was bitterly hostile to the PAP. It saw the noncommunist leadership as a Trojan horse for the Chinese-speaking communists. The *Nanyang Siang Pau, Sin Chew Jit Poh,* and several smaller Chinese papers strongly supported the PAP because of its left-wing policy and the united front we had with the communists. Many of the Chinese journalists were pro-communist. The *Utusan Melayu* was friendly in spite of our links with Chinese-speaking communists because Yusof Ishak, its owner and managing editor, was my friend and had appointed me the paper's lawyer. He was later to become the first president of Singapore. My early experiences in Singapore and Malaya shaped my views about the claim of the press to be the defender of truth and freedom of speech. The freedom of the press was the freedom of its owners to advance their personal and class interests.

As the first general election for a self-governing Singapore approached in May 1959, the *Straits Times* became vehemently anti-PAP to prevent us from winning and forming the government. We decided to meet it head-on. Raja had worked for the *Straits Times* as a senior writer. He confirmed our view that the paper was run for British interests. It was managed by a big, burly, thuggish-looking but competent English newspaperman called Bill Simmons. Simmons took seriously my open threat to settle scores with the paper if, in spite of its opposition, we won. It was preparing to move its editorial staff to Kuala Lumpur after the election should this happen. I fired my first salvo in mid-April, two weeks before polling day: "It is an open secret that *Straits Times* editorial staff would scoot to Kuala Lumpur." I listed the flagrantly biased reporting by its white expatriate journalists, warning that we would give it to them as hard as they were giving it to us.

Next day, Raja followed up with an attack on the English-language *Singapore Standard,* owned by the two Chinese millionaire Aw brothers of Tiger Balm (an ointment panacea for all aches and pains) fame. The *Standard* had turned against the PAP. Raja, who had been its associate editor for five years, was told either to change policy or quit. He quit.

I said we had to tolerate locally owned newspapers that criticized us; we accepted their bona fides, because they had to stay and suffer the consequences of their policies. Not so "the birds of passage who run the *Straits Times*": They would run to Malaya from where they would proclaim their readiness to die for the freedom of the press in Singapore. They used their most senior local man, Leslie Hoffman, a Eurasian, to rebut me: "I am no bird of passage. I, who am responsible for the policy and editorial content of this newspaper, intend to remain in Singapore, even if Mr. Lee and the People's Action Party came to power, and even if they use the Preservation of Public Security Ordinance against me. . . . My home will be in Singapore."

Brave words indeed. Before polling day, Hoffman had left for Kuala Lumpur. A few days earlier, addressing an IPI (International Press Institute) annual assembly in West Berlin, he said that my threats were "the outpourings of a group of power-mad politicians." He claimed the *Straits Times* was "written, produced and controlled by Malayans who were born there, who had been there all their lives and who are genuine in their nationalism and loyalty to their country." He knew this was totally untrue. He called upon the IPI "to stop once and for all an attempt by a party to get popular support and backing for its declared intention to curtail press freedom." That was exactly what we had the right to do, to seek a mandate to deal firmly with foreign, in this case colonial, interests in the press. It was our declared policy that newspapers should not be owned by foreigners.

We won the election. The *Straits Times,* its owners and senior editors moved to Kuala Lumpur. They proved our point that they were cowardly, out to preserve British interests, not to uphold press freedom or the right to information. After we became independent in 1965, the *Straits Times* moved back to Singapore, did a complete turnaround and supported the PAP. This did not increase my respect for it. When Malaysia's pro-Malay policies forced the Straits Times group to sell its Kuala Lumpur operations to UMNO, the ruling party, it was the PAP government that allowed the British shareholders to continue owning and publishing the newspaper in Singapore. Simmons came to make peace, and the paper became a purely commercial concern, now without a political agenda. Leslie Hoffman did not return to Singapore but settled in Australia.

Because I wanted competition, I encouraged other newspapers to set up. Several did but failed. After more than a hundred years of British rule, the *Straits Times* dominated the market. The *Singapore Standard* had folded in the 1960s. A newspaper called the *Eastern Sun* was launched in 1966 by Aw Kow, the son of one of the Tiger Balm Aw brothers, known more as a playboy than a serious newspaper baron. After secret negotiations with high-ranking officials of an agency of the People's Republic of China based in Hong Kong, they lent him S$3 million. It was repayable over five years, with interest at the ludicrous rate of 0.1 percent per annum. The undeclared condition was that the newspaper would not oppose the People's Republic of China on major issues and would remain neutral on minor ones. The *Eastern Sun* incurred heavy losses because of poor management. In 1968, it received a further subvention of S$600,000. In 1971, we exposed this "black operation" funding by a foreign power. Aw Kow admitted it was true. His outraged and humiliated editorial staff resigned, and the paper closed down.

The *Singapore Herald* was another black operation. This time the money came from a noncommunist source. It started in 1970 as a wholly foreign-owned newspaper employing Singaporean editors and local and foreign journalists. At the start I wondered why two foreigners, nominal owners, wanted to start an English-language newspaper to work up issues against the government through its editorials and its news presentation on matters like national service, press restraint, and freedom of speech. It was losing money. The ISD reported that the largest shareholder was a

Hong Kong firm, Heeda & Company, a registered partnership with two dummy names. The paper soon exhausted its S$2.3 million working capital, and Chase Manhattan Bank in Singapore extended to it unsecured loans of S$1.8 million. Pressed for an explanation, the bank's chairman, David Rockefeller, phoned me from New York to claim that his second vice president and manager of his branch in Singapore was unaware of the bank's standing rule not to lend money to newspapers! I was skeptical.

I queried the paper's newly appointed Singaporean editor who had put up the money in the name of Heeda & Company of Hong Kong. He said he thought I knew it was Donald Stephens, the Malaysian high commissioner to Canberra and former chief minister of the state of Sabah, Malaysia. I asked whether he believed Stephens, who had become Fuad Stephens after his conversion to Islam, would risk losing a million and a half dollars in a newspaper that took on the Singapore government. He agreed this was difficult to believe.

When I disclosed this conversation in a public speech in mid-May 1971, Stephens, whom I knew well from our Malaysia days, wrote to me from Canberra: "I feel I should tell you that my only motive in putting money into the *Herald* is because I have been in the newspaper business before and because I believe Singapore to be a country where my investments would be safe. . . . I am not getting younger and I thought if I were to retire before very long I will be able to get a living out of my investments in the *Herald*." He did not explain why he did not first inform me about his investment and seek my support and blessings. A newspaper influences the politics of a country. When a foreigner, British newspaper baron Roy Thomson, considered starting a newspaper in Singapore in the mid-1960s, he first discussed it with me. I discouraged him because I did not want a foreigner not rooted in Singapore to decide our political agenda.

As the *Herald* was running out of funds, a Hong Kong newspaperwoman, Aw Sian, Aw Kow's sister but unlike him a serious businessperson, mysteriously came to the rescue with S$500,000. She was a hardheaded woman who owned a Hong Kong Chinese newspaper. She produced to me receipts for the money she remitted, but had no share certificates. I asked whether she intended to put more money into the paper. She replied "no," and immediately left for Hong Kong.

The Press Foundation of Asia, an affiliate of the International Press Institute, issued a statement asking us not to cancel the paper's license and invited me to speak at the IPI annual assembly at Helsinki in June 1971. Before leaving for Helsinki, I cancelled the printing license of the *Singapore Herald.*

Had I not attended, the assembly would have passed resolutions condemning Singapore in my absence. I stated my position on the role of the media in a new and young country like Singapore. I needed the media "to reinforce, not to undermine, the cultural values and social attitudes being inculcated in our schools and universities. The mass media can create a mood in which people become keen to acquire the knowledge, skills and disciplines of advanced countries. Without these, we can never hope to raise the standards of living of our people."

I recounted how, with Singapore's different races, languages, cultures, and religions, press reports and photographs had caused riots with loss of lives, and cited two examples. In the "jungle girl" riots in 1950, the *Singapore Standard* had headlined a report of a Dutch girl, converted to Islam by her Malay foster mother, kneeling before an image of the Virgin Mary. The anti-Chinese riots on Prophet Mohammed's birthday in July 1964 resulted from a sustained campaign by a Malay newspaper, falsely alleging day after day that the Malay minority were oppressed by the Chinese majority.

I said I did not accept that newspaper owners had the right to print whatever they liked. Unlike Singapore's ministers, they and their journalists were not elected. My final words to the conference were: "Freedom of the press, freedom of the news media, must be subordinated to the overriding needs of Singapore, and to the primacy of purpose of an elected government." I stayed resolutely polite in response to provocative questions.

A few years later, in 1977, we passed laws to prohibit any person or his or her nominee from holding more than 3 percent of the ordinary shares of a newspaper, and created a special category of shares called management shares. The minister had the authority to decide which shareholders would have management shares. He gave management shares to Singapore's four major local banks. They would remain politically neutral and protect stability and growth because of their business interests. I do not subscribe to the Western practice that allows a wealthy press baron to decide what voters should read day after day.

In the 1980s, Western-owned English-language publications became a significant presence in Singapore. Our English-reading public was expanding with the teaching of English in our schools. We have always banned communist publications; no Western media or media organization has ever protested against this. We have not banned any Western newspaper or journal. Yet they frequently refused us the right of reply when they misreported us. We decided in 1986 to enact a law to restrict the sale or distribution of foreign publications that had engaged in the domestic politics of Singapore. One of our tests for "engaging in the politics of Singapore" was whether, after they had misreported or slanted stories on Singapore, they refused to publish our reply. We did not ban them, only restricted the number of copies they sold. Those who could not buy copies could get them photocopied or faxed. This would reduce their advertising revenue but did not stop their reports from circulating. They could not accuse us of being afraid to have their reports read.

The first publication to breach this law was the American weekly *Time* magazine. In an article in October 1986, it reported that an opposition MP had been found guilty by Singapore courts on charges of disposing of assets to defraud creditors and of giving false evidence. My press secretary sent a letter to correct three errors of fact in the report. *Time* refused to publish it and instead proposed two versions, both of which changed its meaning. My press secretary wanted the letter published unedited. When it refused, we restricted the sale of *Time* magazine from 18,000 to 9,000 and then subsequently to 2,000 copies. After this, *Time* published our reply in full. We lifted the restriction—eight months later.

The *Asian Wall Street Journal* (*AWSJ*) in December 1986 printed an untrue story about our proposed second securities market, SESDAQ (Stock Exchange of Singapore Dealing in Automated Quotation Systems). It alleged that the government was setting it up in order to dispose of dud government-owned companies to its citizens. The Monetary Authority of Singapore (MAS) wrote to rebut these false allegations. The *AWSJ* not only refused to print this letter but claimed its article was fair and accurate, that such a dud company did exist and that our letter had defamed its correspondent. The MAS wrote again to point out further errors in the journal's letter, and asked it to name the dud company and to indicate which specific passages in our letter had defamed its correspondent. We asked that it publish the correspondence so that readers could judge for themselves. It refused to name the dud company or point out the supposedly defamatory passages. In February 1987, the government restricted the *AWSJ*'s circulation from 5,000 to 400 copies and released the letters between the MAS and the *AWSJ*. The Singapore newspapers published them. We invited the journal's correspondent to sue if he had indeed been defamed. He did not.

To our amazement, a U.S. State Department spokesman, as reported in the *AWSJ*, expressed regret at the restrictions on both the *AWSJ* and *Time* magazine. Our ministry of foreign affairs asked the State Department to confirm the reported remarks which, if true, represented "an unprecedented interference in Singapore's internal affairs." Its spokesman did so, but maintained the U.S. government did not take sides in either of these two cases. We asked the State Department whether, on the same grounds of impartiality, it would express regret over the refusal of the *AWSJ* to publish the exchange of letters. The State Department repeated that it did not take sides; it was merely expressing concern because of its "fundamental and long-standing commitment to the principles of a free and unrestricted press"—which meant that "the press is free to publish or not publish what it chooses however irresponsible or biased its actions may seem to be."

Our ministry of foreign affairs pointed out that we were not obliged to follow U.S. laws on the press. Singapore had its own laws and reserved the right to reply to wrong reporting. Foreign publications had no right of sale and circulation in Singapore. We gave them this privilege, but on our terms, one of which was the right of reply. The State Department did not reply.

Two weeks later, the *AWSJ* wrote to our ministry of communications and information offering to distribute its journal free of charge to all paying subscribers who had been deprived by its restriction. It was willing to "forego its sales revenue in the spirit of helping Singapore businessmen who had complained of lack of access to the journal." The ministry agreed, provided it left out the advertisements to prove that the journal's motive was not to increase circulation but to justify its higher advertising charges. It declined the offer, arguing that advertisements were an integral part of a paper, and that there would be additional costs and scheduling problems. We offered to defray one-half of the additional costs of removing the advertisements. The *AWSJ* rejected our offer. We responded, "You are not interested in the business community getting information. You want the freedom to make money selling advertisements." It did not reply.

In September 1987, American-owned *Asiaweek* cocked a snook at us. The press secretary to the minister for home affairs had written to point out errors in an article in its magazine. *Asiaweek* printed parts of this letter as an article ("A Distortion of Facts, You Say?"), attributing it to the press secretary. It not only deleted significant parts but added more than 470 words of its own, lengthening it by more than half, without the press secretary's consent and without disclosing this to its readers. The press secretary wrote to protest against this alteration of his letter and asked that his original and subsequent letters be published unaltered. *Asiaweek* refused. We restricted the magazine's circulation from 11,000 copies to 500. A month later, it published the letters unaltered. We lifted the restriction, after a year.

In December 1987, the American-owned *Far Eastern Economic Review* published an account of a meeting between me and the Catholic archbishop of Singapore regarding the arrest of 22 persons involved in a Marxist conspiracy. The article was based on statements made by a renegade priest who had not been present at the meeting. The *Review* alleged that I had called a press conference without the archbishop's knowledge, tricked him into attending it and prevented a comment by him from being publicized. It said the arrest constituted an attack on the Catholic Church.

My press secretary wrote to ask why it published an article based on statements of a person not present at the meeting without checking the facts with the archbishop or me. The editor, Derek Davies, printed this letter but did not answer the question. We wrote to repeat the question. The editor printed the letter and added at the same time that what the priest had said was true. He claimed that a newspaper could legally print anything it wished, true or false, so long as it was able to quote a source who had actually made the statement. It was under no obligation to check its facts to satisfy itself as to the truthfulness of its source, or to verify the assertions with other witnesses, nor could it be held answerable for any lies and libels thereby published. Davies was brazen and defiant. We restricted the *Review* from 9,000 to 500 copies, and I took out a writ for libel against him and the weekly.

He then published another letter from the renegade priest giving a new account of my meeting with the archbishop. We wrote to ask which of its two versions of the meeting was correct. The weekly printed an edited version of my press secretary's letter, suppressing much of it, claiming the subject matter was sub judice. However, when the Singapore government bought advertisement space in the *Review* for the letter, it was published, the sub judice excuse abandoned.

I won my libel action in 1989 when Davies did not go into the witness box to give evidence and be cross-examined. Davies left the *Review* soon afterward.

Before our issue with the *AWSJ* was settled, I was invited to speak to the American Society of Newspaper Editors at a meeting in Washington, D.C., in April 1988. I accepted. I quoted the U.S. State Department's aide-mémoire, "that where the media are free, the marketplace of ideas sorts the irresponsible from the responsible and rewards the latter," and pointed out that the U.S. model was not universally valid. The Philippine press was based on the U.S. model. It enjoyed all the freedoms but it had failed the Filipino people. "A partisan press helped Filipino politicians to flood the marketplace of ideas with junk, and confused and befuddled the people so that they could not see what their vital interests were in a developing country." I stated my position:

Singapore's domestic debate is a matter for Singaporeans. We allow American journalists in Singapore in order to report Singapore to their fellow countrymen. We allow their papers to sell in Singapore so that we can know what foreigners are reading about us. But we cannot allow them to assume a role in Singapore that the American media play in America, that is, that of invigilator, adversary and inquisitor of the administration. No foreign television station had claimed the right to telecast its programmes in

Singapore. Indeed America's Federal Communications Commission regulations bar foreigners from owning more than 25 percent of a TV or radio station. Only Americans can control a business which influences opinion in America. Thus Rupert Murdoch took up US citizenship before he purchased the independent TV stations of the Metromedia group in 1985.

Through these cases, Singaporeans realized that what the foreign press wanted was to sell their papers to our growing English-reading public. They did this by being tendentious at the expense of the facts. Naturally they did not like their slanted articles straightened out. When they discovered that if they twisted our arm, we could tweak their noses in reply, biased reporting became less frequent.

In July 1993, the *Economist,* an influential British weekly, published an article that criticized us for prosecuting a government officer and the editor and a reporter of a newspaper under the Official Secrets Act. We sent a letter to the editor to correct errors in the article. It published the letter, claiming it had "virtually not been touched, practically in full." But it left out a key sentence: "The government will not acquiesce in breaches of the Official Secrets Act, nor allow anyone to flout, challenge and gradually change the law, as has happened in Britain with Clive Ponting's case and Peter Wright's book, *Spycatcher."*

This was the whole point of the letter; we were not going to allow our press to challenge and gradually alter by precedent the law governing official secrets. The British press had succeeded in doing this when Clive Ponting, a civil servant, released secret information about the sinking during the Falklands war, of the *Belgrano,* an Argentinean warship, and when Wright, an MI6 officer, broke their secrecy rules by publishing his book. We sent a letter asking the editor to remedy the omission. The editor quibbled and refused. We gazetted the publication and capped its circulation at 7,500 copies. We made clear that circulation would be progressively restricted and released the exchange of letters. Then the *Economist* published our letter, including this sentence. After a decent interval, we lifted the restriction.

Apart from replying to attacks in the media itself, I was ready to meet my critics face to face. In 1990, Bernard Levin of the London *Times* wrote a bitter attack on me and criticized the Singapore judiciary. He alleged "misrule" and a "frenzied determination to allow no one in his realm to defy him." To sue Levin in England, where I was not widely known and did not have any voters, would have been pointless. Instead, I wrote to invite him to a live television debate in London on his allegations. Levin's editor replied that no television station would be interested. I had taken the precaution of first writing to the chairman of the BBC, my friend Marmaduke Hussey, who had agreed to provide half an hour and a neutral moderator. When I informed the London *Times* of this offer, the editor on Levin's behalf backed off, arguing that my response should be in the same medium in which Levin had attacked me, namely the *Times.* I wrote to regret Levin's unwillingness to confront me. When the *Times* refused to publish my letter, I bought a half-page advertisement in the British daily, the *Independent.* Interviewed on the BBC World Service, I said, "Where I come from, if an accuser is not prepared to face the person he has attacked, there is nothing more to be said." Levin has not written about Singapore or me since.

In another instance, I readily agreed to a tape-recorded exchange with a vehement critic, William Safire, who, over many years, had repeatedly denounced me as a dictator like Saddam Hussein. In January 1999, when we were both at Davos, he questioned me for an hour. He wrote two articles in the *New York Times* based on the interview and also published the transcripts verbatim on the *Times'* Internet Web site. Singapore newspapers reprinted his articles. From the recorded comments of Americans and others who read the full text on the Internet, I did not lose in the exchange.

If we do not stand up to and answer our critics from the foreign media, Singaporeans, especially journalists and academics, will believe that their leaders are afraid of or unequal to the argument, and will lose respect for us.

Advances in information technology, satellite broadcasting, and the Internet will enable Western media networks to saturate our domestic audience with their reports and views. Countries that try to block the use of IT will lose. We have to learn to manage this relentless flood of information so that the Singapore government's point of view is not smothered by the foreign media. The turmoil in Indonesia and the disorders in

Malaysia in 1998 following the currency crisis are examples of the prominent role played by the foreign media networks, both electronic and print, in their domestic debate. We must work out ways to make sure that in the midst of this cacophony of voices, that of the Singapore government is heard. It is important for Singaporeans to know the official position of their government on major issues.

# 15.  Conductor of an Orchestra

My ministers and I remained friends and political colleagues for three to four decades. Several of us had been together since we met as students in England to discuss the future of Malaya and Singapore, then returned home and worked together to build mass support in the trade unions and in the PAP. Our commitment to a common cause and to each other was deep. We had abiding political convictions, or we would not have undertaken the risk of challenging both the British and the communists at the same time, and later the Malay Ultras. The strongest bonds that bound us were forged during our early struggles when often it looked like we'd be swept away by overwhelming forces. Differences on policy we kept within the cabinet until we had resolved them and reached a consensus. Then we would put forth a clear line which people could understand and accept. Once a decision had been made in the cabinet, we made a point of abiding by it.

We knew each other's strong and weak points, and worked well as a team. When the old guard ministers were in agreement, the rest in the cabinet would usually concur. I had an easy relationship with my colleagues. I was able to put my views on matters within their portfolios without ruffling their feathers. At the end of the day, they knew that I would have to stand before the voters to persuade them to give us a mandate for another term and I needed a convincing case to present.

Running a government is not unlike conducting an orchestra. No prime minister can achieve much without an able team. While he himself need not be a great player, he has to know enough of the principal instruments from the violin to the cello to the French horn and the flute, or he would not know what he can expect from each of them. My style was to appoint the best man I had to be in charge of the most important ministry at that period, usually finance, except at independence when defense became urgent. That man was Goh Keng Swee. The next best would get the next most important portfolio. I would tell the minister what I wanted him to achieve, and leave him to get on with the task; it was management by objective. It worked best when the minister was resourceful and could innovate when faced with new, unexpected problems. My involvement in their ministries would be only on questions of policy.

All the same I had to know enough about their portfolios to intervene from time to time on issues I thought important—a fledgling airline, an airport extension, traffic jams, dispersal of communal enclaves, raising academic performance of our Malays, and law and order. Some interventions were crucial, and things might have gone wrong had I not intervened. Ultimately, responsibility for a government's failure rests with the prime minister.

## Singapore Airlines at Changi Airport

Any enterprise that promised growth and employment we had to nurture. I suspected that the Malaysians wanted to break up Singapore's joint airline with Malaysia called Malaysia-Singapore Airlines (MSA). The Tunku told the press in September 1968 that he was unhappy with Singapore's retention of all the foreign exchange earnings of MSA, the failure to establish engineering and other facilities in Kuala Lumpur, and the preponderance of Singaporeans over Malaysians on the staff.

I replied through the press that the agreement between the two governments specifically required the airline to be operated "on the basis of sound commercial principles," that the foreign exchange earned was distributed in profits in accordance with the shares held, and that the facilities and staff reflected the company's origin, namely Singapore. The real dispute was over flights to uneconomic Malaysian destinations, which we would not agree to unless the losses were borne by Malaysia.

This open quarrel came at a crucial time when Britain's commitment to the defense of Malaysia was coming to an end, and the Australian and New Zealand positions were undecided. Ghazali Shafie wrote to me about the dispute. He was an able if flamboyant permanent secretary of the Malaysian foreign ministry who had good access to the Tunku and Razak and had helped solve many difficulties when I was negotiating merger with them. I replied that the airline problem in itself was not all that important. But if we kept on bickering we would endanger our security because in the next 12 to 24 months the British, Australians, and New Zealanders would be deciding on their post-1971 defense position. I suggested that he help get the two governments on a new approach, one of quiet, commonsense accommodation. That would encourage the British, Australians, and New Zealanders to continue some commitment after 1971. Ghazali did help to moderate the public altercation. The airline carried on with a new chairman acceptable to both sides. But it was clear the Tunku wanted to split MSA and have their own airline to fly to their state capitals, so I agreed to help them build up workshops at Kuala Lumpur airport and to train their workers to repair the Fokker Friendship aircraft used on domestic routes.

I took a personal interest in MSA. I knew the Malaysians wanted to bypass Singapore wherever possible after the breakup of this joint airline. With only Paya Lebar International Airport and the three RAF airfields at Changi, Tengah, and Seletar, all on our small island republic, we had nowhere to go except international. I had earlier told the airline's management to build up international destinations. I regularly met our man in MSA, Lim Chin Beng, then the director of administration and customer services. A steady, reliable man with a good grasp of the airline industry, he was promoted to managing director in 1971. He too knew that the Malaysians wanted to break off and leave us without any flights to Malaysia except to Kuala Lumpur. He worked hard to get more landing rights on potentially profitable international routes. In the meantime, he had to keep up the morale of the pilots and workers and their confidence in the future of a Singapore-owned and Singapore-based airline. The chairman and managing director of the company faced perpetual pressures from both the Malaysians and us, which only ended when the airline split up in October 1972 into Singapore Airlines (SIA) and Malaysia

Airline System (MAS). We agreed that MAS would take over all the internal routes and SIA all the external routes.

We got landing rights to Hong Kong in 1966, Tokyo and Sydney in 1967, Jakarta and Bangkok in 1968. The most important destination was London but the British were reluctant to give us landing rights. In August 1970, before leaving for the Non-Aligned Summit in Lusaka, I asked Ngiam Tong Dow, permanent secretary (communications), about the state of negotiations with the British for landing rights in London. When he said it was very difficult, I told him to let NTUC Secretary-General Devan Nair know this. I had earlier agreed to Devan's proposal that if the British negotiators were difficult, he would get the unions at the airport to apply pressure by going slow on servicing British aircraft. As soon as the NTUC mounted a go-slow on BOAC aircraft at Paya Lebar, the British high commissioner, Arthur de la Mare, came to see me at my office. I asked him to get his government to be reasonable. A British airline could land in Singapore but a Singapore airline was denied landing rights in London. Within weeks, we obtained landing rights in London, and flew on one of the main trunk routes of the world: London-Singapore-Sydney. This opening enabled Singapore Airlines to go international. The fact that Edward Heath was then prime minister could have made it easier.

At a dinner in July 1972, with all union leaders and top management present, and before SIA was launched, I spelled out the need for a Singapore airline to be competitive and self-supporting; it would close down if it incurred losses. We could not afford to run an airline just to show the flag like other countries did. Right from the beginning, management and union clearly understood that their survival depended on being profitable. Cooperation between union and management helped Singapore Airlines succeed.

Freed from constant bickering, SIA concentrated on its international routes and flew further afield year by year. By 1996 it had one of the largest and most modern Boeing and Airbus fleets in Asia, flying to nearly all continents. It was the most profitable airline in Asia, and for its size, one of the most profitable in the world.

Central to SIA's growth was my decision to build Changi Airport. In February 1972, the cabinet had accepted the recommendation of a British

aviation consultant that we build a second runway at Paya Lebar, to be operational by 1977–1978. The Serangoon River would have to be diverted for
this to be done. There were engineering problems because of the doubtful
load-bearing qualities of the soil below the riverbed, but it would entail the
lowest land acquisition costs and require the least resettlements. The report
added that it would not be possible to have two runways ready by 1977 if
we moved from Paya Lebar to a new airport on the former RAF base at
Changi. Then came the October 1973 oil crisis. Air fares increased with the
price of fuel and the world economy slowed down. I asked for a new assessment, this time by American consultants. They recommended we keep to
the planned schedule for Paya Lebar. I was not satisfied and wanted the
option of moving to Changi reconsidered.

I had flown over Boston's Logan Airport and been impressed that the
noise footprint of planes landing and taking off was over water. A second
runway at Paya Lebar would take aircraft right over the heart of Singapore
city. A committee of senior officials again studied the alternative of building two runways at Changi by 1977 and recommended we stay with the
Paya Lebar second runway. But once built, we would be saddled with the
noise pollution for many years. I wanted a thorough reappraisal before
giving up on Changi so I appointed Howe Yoon Chong, the chairman of
the Port of Singapore Authority with a reputation as a bulldozer, to chair
a top-level committee.

When I was in Washington in April 1975, I received a letter from
Keng Swee, who was acting prime minister in my absence. The committee believed the first Changi runway could be ready by 1980 and the second by 1982, whereas the second Paya Lebar runway could only be ready
by 1984 because of the need to divert the Serangoon River and compact
the soil of the riverbed. Saigon and South Vietnam had just fallen to the
communists. Growth in Southeast Asia was likely to slow down as communist insurgencies spread throughout the region. But to base decisions
on a pessimistic scenario might well bring it about. I mulled over the
problem for a couple of days. The new airport at Changi would cost us
S$1 billion. We would still need to spend another S$400 million to
expand Paya Lebar's passenger and freight-handling facilities between
1975 and 1982. I sent Keng Swee a message to proceed.

For an airport of that size, the building period was usually 10 years. We completed Changi Airport in six. We demolished hundreds of buildings, exhumed thousands of graves, cleared swamps, and reclaimed land from the sea. When it opened in July 1981, it was Asia's largest airport. We wrote off over S$800 million worth of investments in the old airport and spent S$1.5 billion on Changi, with two runways, the second ready by 1984.

Changi is a beautiful site at the easternmost corner of the island. The approach to the city from the east coast runs along a new 20 kilometer (approximately 12 miles) expressway built on land reclaimed from the sea, with no problems of congestion, beautiful glimpses of the sea on one side, and vistas of HDB estates and private condominiums on the other. The airport and the pleasant 20-minute drive into the city made an excellent introduction to Singapore, the best S$1.5 billion investment we ever made. It helped Singapore become the hub airport of the region. The competition is keen and relentless. Newer and grander airports in Hong Kong and Kuala Lumpur with state-of-the-art equipment require Changi to be upgraded and refurbished regularly to stay competitive.

Two men played key roles in making Changi Airport a success. Howe Yoon Chong was forceful in executing policies. He had encouraged me to move the airport from Paya Lebar to Changi by assuring me he had a team that could do it in time. He did, with the resources of the Port of Singapore Authority, its chief engineer, A. Vijiaratnam, and Lim Hock San, a promising officer who implemented the project and became director of civil aviation in 1980. When I was invited to open it ceremonially in 1981, I asked Yoon Chong, then minister for defense, to go in my place. He deserved to have his name on the plaque.

The other man who played a key role was Sim Kee Boon, the shrewdest of our permanent secretaries. He organized the management of the airport. Building a fine airport has been done by many wealthy countries using foreign contractors. The challenge is in running it so that passengers have a smooth and swift passage through customs, immigration, baggage collection, and transport into the city. If they have to make a connecting flight, then there must be facilities for rest, recreation, and work. Changi has all these—rest and shower rooms, a swimming pool, business and fitness centers, and a science discovery and amusement area for children. As head of the Civil Aviation Authority of Singapore, Kee

Boon made Changi into a world-class airport, winning top ratings in travellers' magazines almost every year.

## Fighting Traffic Congestion

By 1975, traffic jams at peak hours were unbearable. I had read a paper proposing that, to reduce congestion, we charge a fee for cars entering the central business district (CBD) at peak hours. I asked our officials to examine this idea. They found it feasible. They proposed gantries with notices to warn all motorists entering the Area Licensing System (ALS), which covered the CBD at a restricted time, to display a license on their windshields. I had the plan discussed publicly in the media for several months. We refined the proposals, for example, allowing cars with four passengers to go through without a license and settling for a charge of S$3 per day, less if bought on a monthly basis. The plan eased rush hour traffic jams and was well received.

I knew this was but a temporary respite. Incomes were rising and the number of cars registered yearly was rising exponentially. I believed the answer was to limit the growth of the car population to the rate the roads could take without massive traffic jams. No matter how many underground passes, flyovers, and expressways we built, the car population would increase to clog them all up.

I proposed that a new car owner had to bid for a certificate to purchase and put the car on the road. The number of certificates available each year would depend on road capacity. We calculated that the roads then could accommodate a 3 percent annual increase of vehicles. The minister for communications took a bill for this to a parliamentary select committee to hear all representations. We settled on a scheme whereby a person had to bid for a certificate of entitlement (COE) to use a new car for 10 years.

It proved effective in limiting the yearly vehicle increase to 3 percent. Bids for COEs started low but soon rose to astronomical heights. In 1994, it exceeded S$100,000 for a car of over 2,000 cc; this was in addition to other heavy import taxes. COEs became unpopular and endless letters to the newspapers by would-be car owners argued that the bids were being manipulated by car dealers and speculators. Responding to public requests, the government prohibited car dealers from bidding for COEs in their own names for transfer to their customers and also made the certificates nontransferable. These changes made no difference. When the economy boomed and the stock market rose, so did COE bids, and vice versa, as when Singapore suffered in the economic crisis of 1997–1998.

By trial and error, I learned that if I wanted to get an important proposal accepted at all levels, I should first float my ideas with my ministers, who would then discuss them with the permanent secretaries and officials. After I got their reactions, I would have the proposal discussed among those who had to make it work. If, like the transport system, it concerned large numbers of people, I would then get the issue into the media for public discussion. Hence, before we decided on an underground mass rapid transit (MRT), we had a public debate for a year on the merits of an MRT as against an all-bus system using dedicated roads. We also had American consultants advise us on the two options. They convinced us that an all-bus system would not provide as satisfactory a solution, because in wet weather the buses would slow down and clog up the system. This would not happen with trains.

The MRT did not reduce the demand to own cars which increased every year although we slowed it down with COEs and the ALS. In 1998, we introduced electronic road pricing (ERP). Every vehicle now has a "smart card" at its windshield, and the correct toll is automatically deducted every time it passes under gantries sited at strategic points in the city. The toll amount varies with the stretch of road that is used and the time of day. Technology has made it possible to fine-tune the ALS system and extend it to all roads that have become congested. Since the amount people pay the government now depends upon how much they use the roads, the optimum number of cars can be owned with the minimum of congestion.

## Delicate Malay Issues

Some sensitive matters, however, could not be publicly debated. One such issue was what to do with the concentrations of Malays in poor conditions that from colonial days had existed in and beyond what the British had designated as "Malay settlements." At separation in August 1965, the Tunku had offered free land in Johor to Singapore Malays who felt abandoned. Few took up his offer. But their segregation had contributed to isolation and disaffection because these settlements tended to be depressed areas that had become ghettos: muddy, winding, unpaved lanes between shanty huts of wood with zinc or thatched roofs. The most troubling concentration was in Geylang Serai, which together with Kampong Ubi and Kampong Kembangan formed the biggest Malay settlement where over 60,000 Malays lived in poor conditions with no piped water or sanitation. People collected water from public standpipes sited on the side of lanes and carried it home in buckets or paid a water carrier to do so. There was no power supply although some private operators sold electricity illegally. In September 1965, one month after separation, I told residents that in 10 years all their shacks would be demolished and Geylang Serai would be another and a better "Queenstown," then our most modern high-rise housing estate.

We kept this promise. As part of our long-term plan to rebuild Singapore and rehouse everybody, we decided to scatter and mix Malays, Chinese, Indians, and all others alike and thus prevent them from congregating as they had been encouraged to do by the British. On resettlement, they would have to ballot for their new high-rise homes.

Meanwhile, to prevent another ugly situation from arising should there be another race riot, I decided to extend, in waffle-grid fashion, four roads that went through the Geylang Serai Malay settlement area, at the same time widening the existing lanes and lighting up the highways. In six to seven years, one large ghetto became nine small pockets. The most difficult part was the initial resettlement which began in February 1970. When we announced it, there was apprehension among the Malay residents. Our Malay MPs played a critical role in mediating between government officials and residents. The press and radio helped to publicize the government's compensation package and the alternative accommodation offered. By then the *Utusan Melayu* had ceased to circulate in Singapore and could not work up unfounded fears as it had done in 1964 over the resettlement at Crawford.

The most politically sensitive building to remove was a dilapidated *surau* (a small mosque). Every house of worship, however insignificant, had a committee of religious elders and activists who collected tithes and donations for its maintenance. When the time came for the *surau* to be demolished, they squatted in the premises and refused to leave. They read the government's actions as anti-Islam. Our Malay MPs arranged a meeting in September 1970 at City Hall, where my office was, for the *surau* committee and members to make their representations to senior officials from the Public Works Department and the Housing and Development Board. With the help of our Malay MPs, we persuaded them to allow the old wooden building to be demolished, giving them the assurance that a new one would be built close to the existing site. The next day, our Malay MPs and the president of MUIS, the Muslim governing body for Singapore, addressed some 200 of the congregation at the *surau* after Friday prayers. Our Malay MP, Rahmat Kenap, a doughty former trade union leader who had been unshaken when roundly denounced during the 1964 race riots as a *kafir* or infidel by UMNO leaders, reassured the congregation with the government's pledge to build a new mosque to replace an existing one. They finally agreed to move out. This paved the way for the demolition and rebuilding of some 20 other small mosques in the settlement. We offered them alternative sites and found a solution for financing their new mosques. I gave MUIS the responsibility for building replacement mosques and set up for them a building fund which received S$1 per month from each Muslim worker through our CPF system. This gave our Malays pride in building their mosques with their own funds.

Moving the house owners was less difficult. They were given compensation at set rates, according to whether the houses were built with or without government approval, plus a "disturbance allowance" of S$350 per family, which at the time was more than a month's salary for a laborer. They were given priority in the new housing estates and the freedom to choose the locality of their new homes. In spite of all these concessions, a group of 40 families refused to vacate their premises until we brought them to court.

When the roads were finally completed and brightly lit I was greatly relieved as I drove through the area one night, happy at the visibly improved security and social ambience. After Geylang Serai, it was easier to integrate the other Malay settlements.

Although we mixed the races by making them ballot for their homes, we found that they were collecting together again. When owners sold their apartments and were able to buy resale apartments of their choice, they soon recongregated. This forced us in 1989 to put percentage limits (25 percent for Malays, 13 percent for Indians and other minorities at the block level) beyond which no minority family could move into the neighborhood.

This quota ceiling limited the pool of buyers for certain resale apartments and so depressed their prices. When a Malay or Indian is not allowed to sell to a Chinese because the Chinese quota has already been filled, the apartment invariably sells at a price lower than the market rate because the smaller numbers of Malay or Indian buyers are not able to pay the higher price that the Chinese majority can. However, this is a small cost for achieving our larger objective of getting the races to intermingle.

Dhanabalan, an Indian, as minister in charge of the HDB, Jayakumar, minister for law, another Indian, and Ahmad Mattar, minister for the environment, a Malay of Arab descent, fully agreed with me that to allow resegregation would be retrograde and would reverse what we had achieved. Our other Malay and Indian MPs also shared this view. This made it easier to implement this policy.

When this task was completed by the 1980s, I decided it would be necessary to change the election laws to have joint candidates contesting two or more constituencies. After much discussion in cabinet, we took the matter to Parliament. Three or four single-member constituencies were amalgamated into single group representation constituencies (GRCs) to be contested by three or four candidates as a group or team which had to include one candidate from a minority community, an Indian or Malay. Without this arrangement, the Chinese majority in all constituencies would most likely return Chinese candidates. In the 1950s and 1960s, people had voted for the party symbol, regardless of the candidate's race. In the 1980s, after the PAP had established itself as the dominant party and was seen as likely to be returned in office, people voted more for the MP than for the party. They preferred one who empathized with them, spoke the same dialect or language and was of the same race. All candidates who have campaigned know this only too well. It was going to be difficult if not impossible for a Malay or Indian candidate to win against a Chinese candidate. To end up with a Parliament without Malay, Indian, and other minority MPs would be damaging. We had to change the rules. One advantage of a GRC is that Chinese candidates cannot make Chinese chauvinist appeals without losing the 25 to 30 percent non-Chinese vote. They need a Malay or an Indian who can win over the minority votes to be a member of their GRC team of candidates.

Another racially sensitive problem that troubled me was the consistently poorer performance in mathematics and science of a larger percentage of Malay students compared to other students. I decided that we could not keep these differences in examination results secret for long. To have people believe all children were equal, whatever their race, and that equal opportunities would allow all to qualify for a place in a university, must lead to discontent. The less successful would believe that the government was not treating them equally. In 1980, I brought the Malay community leaders into my confidence in order to tackle the problem of Malay underachievement openly and sensitively. I provided the leaders, including newspaper editors, with the examination results for the previous 10 to 15 years and highlighted the fact that the same differences in results had existed in British colonial Singapore before the war. It was not something new.

After the community and media leaders had got over their initial shock, we invited them to seek solutions with the government's full support. I told them of studies that showed a 15 to 20 percent improvement in student performance when the parents and students were motivated to make that extra effort. Their reaction was positive. In 1982, the Malay leaders with the assurance of government support formed Mendaki (Majlis Pendidikan Anak-Anak Islam—Council on Education for Muslim Children), with representatives from Malay social, literary, and cultural bodies and PAP Malay MPs. We provided them with the premises. As with the mosque building fund, to finance Mendaki we deducted 50 cents from each Malay's monthly CPF contribution. The contributions increased gradually, with increased incomes, to S$2.50. The government matched it dollar for dollar.

I invariably consulted my Malay colleagues including Othman Wok and Rahim Ishak before deciding on policies affecting the Malays. Both were practical in their outlook. I also consulted Yaacob Mohamed when Islamic issues were involved. He had been a preacher in Kelantan and was well respected as a man of some religious learning. Ahmad Mattar was a realist and accepted this as the best way to get results.

Not all my older ministers were comfortable with this move toward community-based self-help groups. Raja was the most strongly opposed to it. He was a total multiracialist and saw my plan not as a pragmatic acceptance of realities, but as backsliding. He did not want to use natural racial bonds to reach out to parents who could best motivate their children. He feared the risk of strengthening communal pulls.

While I shared Raja's ideal of a completely color-blind policy, I had to face reality and produce results. From experience, we knew that Chinese or Indian officials could not reach out to Malay parents and students in the way their own community leaders did. The respect these leaders enjoyed and their sincere interest in the welfare of the less successful persuaded parents and children to make the effort. Paid bureaucrats could never have the same commitment, zest, and rapport to move parents and their children. Chinese community leaders could not reach out to Malay parents and their children. On such personal-emotional issues involving ethnic and family pride, only leaders of the wider ethnic family can reach out to the parents and their children.

A few years after Mendaki got into its stride, the efforts of Malay community leaders plus the extra tuition in the evenings showed in a steady increase in the number of Malay students passing their examinations, with substantial progress in mathematics. In 1991, a group of young Muslim graduates formed the Association of Muslim Professionals (AMP). They had objectives similar to Mendaki's but wanted to work independently of the government. Prime Minister Goh Chok Tong encouraged them with financial support. With more of their own community leaders helping the less successful Muslim youths, the results improved.

Our Malay students scored higher than the international average in the Third International Mathematics and Science study in 1995. Of the 1987 cohort of Malay students, only 7 percent made it to polytechnics and universities. By 1999, this figure had quadrupled to 28 percent while the national percentage had only doubled. A Malay girl on scholarship graduated summa cum laude in English at Berkeley, California, in 1996. One Malay student topped his graduating architecture class in 1999 at NUS winning a gold medal. Another won a government scholarship to Cambridge where he obtained First Class Honours in physics and went on to take his Ph.D. in 1999. And a Malay was elected president of the Student Union at NTU in 1998–1999. We now have a growing Malay middle class of managing directors of MNCs, IT consultants and start-up entrepreneurs, forex dealers, bank managers, engineers, lawyers, doctors, and businessmen in tourism, food, contracting, furniture, and clothing trades.

The progress achieved by Mendaki encouraged the Indian community to form the Singapore Indian Development Association (SINDA) in 1991. The following year, the Chinese formed the Chinese Development Assistance Council (CDAC) to help their weaker students, smaller in percentage terms than the Malay underachievers but larger in total number. The Eurasian Association soon did likewise.

## Rule of Law

Law and order provide the framework for stability and development. Trained in the law, I had imbibed the principle of equality of all before the law for the proper functioning of a society. However, my experience of life in Japanese-occupied Singapore, followed by a disorderly period when the British Military Administration tried to reestablish the rule of law, made me pragmatic, not ideological, in my approach to problems of crime and punishment.

After being called to the Singapore Bar in 1951, my first case was to defend four rioters charged with the murder of an RAF sergeant during the "jungle girl" Muslim riots against whites in December 1950. I got all four men acquitted, but it left me with grave doubts about the practical value of the jury system for Singapore. Seven men, deciding by majority verdict, made for easy acquittals. The jury system had also been tried in

India, failed, and was abolished. Soon after I became prime minister in 1959, I abolished the jury system for all cases except murder. I retained this exception to keep in line with the law in Malaya at that time. In 1969, after separation from Malaysia, I asked Eddie Barker as minister for law to move a bill in Parliament abolishing the jury system for murder trials. During a parliamentary select committee meeting, David Marshall, then our most successful criminal lawyer, claimed he had 99 acquittals out of the 100 cases he defended for murder. When I asked if he believed the 99 acquitted had been wrongly charged, Marshall replied his duty was to defend them, not judge them.

A *Straits Times* court reporter who had watched many jury trials gave evidence to the same select committee that superstitious beliefs and a general reluctance to take responsibility for severe punishment, especially the death sentence, made Asian jurors most reluctant to convict. They preferred acquittal or conviction on a lesser charge. The reporter said he could predict that whenever a pregnant woman was a member of the jury there would be no conviction on a murder charge, for otherwise her child would be born cursed. After the bill was passed and jury trials were abolished, there were fewer miscarriages of justice arising from the vagaries of jury sentiments.

After what I had seen of human conduct in the years of deprivation and harshness of Japanese occupation, I did not accept the theory that a criminal is a victim of society. Punishment then was so severe that even in 1944–1945, when many did not have enough to eat, there were no burglaries and people could leave their front doors unlocked, day or night. The deterrent was effective. The British used to have whipping with a cat-o'-nine-tails or rattan in Singapore. After the war, they abolished whipping but retained caning (with rattan). We found caning more effective than long prison terms and imposed it for crimes related to drugs, arms trafficking, rape, illegal entry into Singapore, and vandalizing of public property.

In 1993, a 15-year-old American schoolboy, Michael Fay, and his friends went on a spree, vandalizing road and traffic signs and spray-painting more than 20 cars. When charged in court, he pleaded guilty and his lawyer made a plea for leniency. The judge ordered six strokes of the cane and four months in jail. The American media went berserk at the prospect of an American boy being caned on his buttocks by cruel Asians in Singapore. They raised so much heat that U.S. President Clinton appealed to President Ong Teng Cheong to pardon the teenager. Singapore was placed in an impossible position. If we did not cane this boy because he was American, how could we cane our own offenders?

After discussion in cabinet, the prime minister advised President Ong to reduce the sentence to four strokes.

The American media was not satisfied. However, not all Americans disapproved of Singapore's punishment for vandalism. While driving in New Hampshire soon after the Michael Fay story hit the headlines, my daughter Ling was arrested for not stopping when a police car flashed its blue light at her for speeding. The police officer was taking her to the police lockup when she said in reply to his questioning that she came from Singapore and that he probably disapproved of her country because of the Fay case. He said the boy deserved the caning, drove her back to her car, and wished her good luck.

Fay survived the four strokes and returned to America. A few months later the American press reported that he came home late and intoxicated one night and charged at his father, bringing him down in a scuffle. A month later he was badly burnt sniffing butane when a friend struck a match. He admitted that he had been a butane addict while in Singapore.

These measures have made for law and order in Singapore. Singapore was rated No. 1 by the World Economic Forum's Global Competitiveness Report 1997, as a country where "organised crime does not impose significant costs on businesses." The International Institute for Management Development in their World Competitiveness Yearbook 1997 also rated Singapore No. 1 for security, "where there is full confidence among people that their person and property is [sic] protected."

## Small Steps Toward IT

The digital revolution is changing the way we live and work. The Internet and its multiple offspring will require all who want to be in the mainstream of the new economy to be computer-Internet literate.

I was an early enthusiast of the use of computers, which became an important factor in increasing our productivity. In 1973, when my son, Loong, completed his Mathematics Tripos II at Cambridge, I encouraged him to do a postgraduate course in computer science because I thought it a valuable tool for calculations and storing data. I also asked the Public Service Commission to offer outstanding students postgraduate courses in computers. One of them, Teo Chee Hean, as minister for education in 1997, started a program for teachers to use computers as a teaching tool with one computer for every two students.

In 1984, I decided that the government would pay all employees through GIRO. Many clerical and manual workers preferred to receive cash, saying they did not want their wives to know their pay. I met these objections by opening Post Office Savings Bank (POSBank) accounts for them so that they could draw cash from automatic teller machines. This did away with police escorts for transporting cash on pay days, twice a month. The private sector followed suit. We then encouraged the payment of taxes and license fees by GIRO.

But while I spearheaded the early drive for computerization and payments by electronic transfer, I did not myself use a PC although they had become common. When the younger ministers e-mailed each other in the mid-1990s, I had my e-mail printed out and responded by fax.

Left "out of the loop," I decided at the age of 72 to take instructions. For the greying generation, it was not easy. It was many months before I could work my MS Word and e-mail without help every now and again from my secretaries. Even much later I would lose a file into a black hole because I had clicked on the wrong icon. Or the PC would accuse me of having "performed an illegal operation" and threaten to shut down. At the office my secretaries would help out. At home, I would ring up Loong, who after listening to my tale of woe, would guide me step by step on the phone to retrieve my hours of hard work that had been lost. When this failed Loong would come on Sunday to search through my C drive for the missing file or to solve some other mystery. It was more than a year before I was comfortable with my PC. One benefit was the ease with which I could amend and rearrange sentences and whole paragraphs on screen when writing this book. Now I would not travel without my laptop to access my e-mail.

## A Chief Justice—A President

Selecting the right man for key constitutional positions, like the chief justice and the president of the republic, is vital. A wrong choice could mean years of public embarrassment and endless problems. It is easier to decide who is the ablest than to predict who has the character to measure up to the job. I knew both the chief justice and the president intimately for many years before their appointments. One was an unqualified success; the other was an unfortunate accident that could have been avoided.

The chief justice sets the tone of the judiciary. When we were about to join Malaysia in August 1963, the last British chief justice, Sir Alan Rose, retired in order to allow me to nominate the first Singaporean chief justice. For this appointment, I looked for someone with a philosophy of society that was not at odds with mine. The inarticulate major premises of the chief justice and his understanding of the objectives of a good government are of vital importance.

I had one memorable exchange with Sir Alan. When several communist rioters were to be tried in our courts in the early 1960s, I feared that their case would be heard by an expatriate British judge who might be insensitive to the political feelings of the time. I asked to see the chief justice and explained to him that the government would be vulnerable to the charge of being a stooge of the British government if this were to happen. He looked at me quizzically and said, "Prime Minister, when I was chief justice in Ceylon I had to act as officer administering the government in place of the governor-general. He was away during a period of turmoil. You need have no fear that you will be embarrassed." He understood the need for political sensitivity.

It was with some care that I chose Wee Chong Jin to be the new chief justice. He was then a high court judge appointed by a British governor. He came from a middle-class background, was Cambridge-educated like me, a Catholic, and an anticommunist. He was strong on law and order. Sir Alan recommended him as having the firmness to keep discipline in the courts and have them follow the norms he set.

He remained chief justice till the age of 72 in 1990. I had extended his term beyond his retirement age of 65 because I could not find a suitable successor. Wee knew his law and presided with authority in his courts both at first instance and on appeals. Cast in the mold of chief justices of the British era, he concentrated primarily on his judgments and the workings of the Supreme Court but did not give as much attention to the lower courts or to the workings of the judicial system as a whole. Because of a great increase in litigation, the old system, both in the lower and higher courts, had become congested. The wheels of justice turned slowly, work piled up, and cases took 4 to 6 years to come to trial. It was nearly as slow in the lower courts which handled the majority of cases.

I had decided in 1988 to resign as prime minister at the end of 1990. Knowing that my successor, Goh Chok Tong, had no association with the legal profession and would have difficulty deciding on a suitable chief justice, I searched for the right person to appoint before I stepped down. I met all the judges separately and got each one of them to list for me, in order of merit, three persons whom he considered suitable for the office, excluding himself. Then with each judge, I went through the list of members of the bar; we also considered outstanding lawyers from the Malaysian Bar. Four judges, A. P. Rajah, P. Coomaraswamy, L. P. Thean, and S. K. Chan, placed Yong Pung How first on their list, rating him the best.

Pung How was then chairman of the Oversea-Chinese Banking Corporation (OCBC), the largest Singapore bank. After the 1969 Kuala Lumpur race riots, he had left a thriving law practice of which he was a senior partner and moved with his family to Singapore where he became chairman of a new merchant bank.

We had been fellow students at the Cambridge Law School for three years and I knew the quality of his work. I had borrowed his lecture notes for the 1946 September term which I had missed. They were comprehensive and orderly and gave me a good synopsis of the lectures. Six months later, in June 1947, I took a First in the first-year law examinations; so did Pung How. We kept in touch after we returned home. In the late 1960s, he was appointed chairman of Malaysia-Singapore Airlines by the two governments that jointly owned it. I renewed close interaction with him when he was seconded by the OCBC in 1981 to be managing director of the Government Investment Corporation which we had formed to manage and invest Singapore's reserves. He was thorough, meticulous, and scrupulously fair in his presentation of the alternatives for an investment, although he expressed his preferences. This was an important judicial quality.

I had offered to make him a judge of the Supreme Court in 1976 when he was vice chairman of the OCBC; he declined. Over lunch in early 1989, I asked him to consider becoming chief justice. My argument was that he had already reached the top position in our biggest bank and his efforts there could only benefit several thousand employees and many more shareholders. As chief justice he would be able to bring the administration of justice up to date and bring untold benefits to the whole society and our economy. If he agreed, he would first have to be a Supreme Court judge for a year to get himself back into the law before he took up the appointment as chief justice. He asked for time to think it over. It would mean a change of lifestyle. He would also lose financially. In the bank, he was paid over S$2 million a year; as a judge, he would earn less than S$300,000, one-seventh of his banker's remuneration. After a month, he accepted my offer out of a sense of duty; Singapore had given him his second home.

I made him a judge of the Supreme Court on 1 July 1989, and in September 1990, when Chief Justice Wee retired, I appointed Yong Pung How chief justice. He had suffered through the years of Japanese occupation and experienced the race riots in Malaysia. He also had strong views on the administration of the law to ensure order in society. His views on a multiracial society and how it should be nurtured and governed and his approach to law and order in such a society in this part of the world were not different from mine.

He understood that to cope with the new workload, antiquated practices had to be abandoned and new procedures adopted to deal with all cases with dispatch, in the lowest to the highest courts. I suggested that he personally visit the lower courts, even sit with the magistrates and district judges to have first-hand knowledge of their work, assess their capabilities, tighten up the system, and bring in additional talent. Work discipline needed to be restored. Lawyers had complained to me that several magistrates and district judges would leave their cars just outside the city limits to avoid paying the small fee charged during peak hours. After the licensing period was over they would adjourn their courts and drive their cars into the city center. Such was the slackness of the system.

Yong Pung How turned out to be an outstanding chief justice. He gave leadership to the judges and set a high tone for the bar. Within a few years he had reformed and updated the courts and their procedures, and reduced the backlog and the delays in cases awaiting trial. He amended the rules and practices that lawyers took advantage of to procrastinate and postpone their cases. To cope with the increased litigation he recommended the appointment of additional judges of the Supreme Court and as many judicial commissioners (senior lawyers discharging the duties of a judge) as the work required. His selection methods were systematic and fair. After meeting a large cross section of lawyers who were recognized as leading members of the bar, he shortlisted 20 and sought the assessments of each of the existing judges and judicial commissioners on their overall integrity, legal ability, and likely "judicial temperament." Then he made his recommendations to the prime minister.

For appointments to the Court of Appeal, he asked each judge and judicial commissioner to name two of their number whom he thought the most suitable, excluding himself. The two he finally recommended were the unanimous choice of all their peers. His methods, known to all the judges and senior lawyers, raised the standing and prestige of all judges and judicial commissioners.

He introduced information technology into the courts to speed up their work; lawyers can now file their court documents and make searches through their computers. By 1999, the reputation of our courts brought visits by judges and chief justices from developing as well as developed countries to study his reorganization. The World Bank recommended Singapore's system, both at high court and subordinate court levels, for other countries to learn from.

World rating agencies have given Singapore high marks for its judicial system. Throughout the 1990s, the World Competitiveness Yearbook published by the Swiss-based Institute for Management Development placed Singapore at the top in Asia for "confidence in the fair administration of justice in the society." For 1997–1998, it put Singapore within the top 10 globally, ahead of the United States, the United Kingdom, Japan, and most OECD countries. From 1995, when it began rating the legal systems in Asia, the Hong Kong–based Political and Economic Risk Consultancy rated Singapore's judicial system as the best in Asia.

I was less fortunate in my choice of the president. I had worked with Devan Nair since 1954, when I moved his election as president in Parliament in 1981. In the afternoon of 15 March 1985, I was shocked when told that Devan had acted in a bizarre manner while visiting Kuching in Sarawak, an East Malaysian state. The Sarawak state physician had phoned Nair's personal physician, Dr. J. A. Tambyah, on 14 March to ask him to take the president back because of his behavior. Nair had been uninhibited with women, including the wife of an assistant minister who accompanied him in a car, women at dinners, and nurses who looked after him. He outraged their modesty, propositioned them, fondled, and molested them. After informing our director of medical services, Dr. Tambyah flew at once to Kuching, where he found Nair had collapsed and lost control of himself, and accompanied him back on 15 March.

That same evening, at about 9:00 P.M., I saw Mrs. Nair at the Istana Lodge. To help me break the unhappy news, I brought Choo who knew her well. My note to the cabinet the following day read:

Mrs Nair was collected and could barely suppress her disgust and anger at the news that Devan had misbehaved in Kuching and collapsed. She told my wife and me that Devan was a changed man, that he had been drinking heavily from time to time, and for the last few months had consumed a bottle of whisky every night. She had sent the servants off early so that they would not know that he would get totally drunk and incapable, when he would often beat her. She knew this would happen in Sarawak and had refused to go.

In the weeks before his Sarawak visit, Devan Nair had been driving a car alone out of the Istana. He had disguised himself with a wig and had gone out without his security officer or his driver to meet a German woman. One morning, after he had been out for the night, Mrs Nair went to Changi Cottage to check. She

discovered liquor bottles, glasses with lipstick marks and cigarettes. Devan Nair had also brought the German woman to the
Istana Lodge for dinner. When Mrs Nair remonstrated, there was
a row and he had beaten her. He was not in control of himself and
his temper in his drinking bouts.

Seven of our best specialists examined and treated him. The most
senior of them, a psychiatrist, Dr. R. Nagulendran, in a report of 23
March wrote, "He (Nair) suffers from ALCOHOLISM [sic] characterised
by many years of alcohol consumption; periodic bouts of heavy and continuous drinking; psychological dependence on alcohol; lapses of memory; intermittent hallucinations; impotency; personality changes; disruption of matrimonial harmony."

Under the constitution, the president could not be charged for any
crime. If the president killed someone while driving under the influence of
alcohol, there would be public outrage. The cabinet discussed these developments at several meetings and decided that he had to resign before he was
discharged from the hospital and could resume his activities, or Parliament
would have to remove him from office. The old ministers, especially Raja,
Eddie Barker, and I, were upset at having to remove an old colleague from
so prominent a public office. We felt keenly for his family but concluded
that we had no choice; leaving him in office would cause greater harm.

On 27 March, when he had recovered sufficiently to understand the
implications of what he had done, Raja and I saw him at the Singapore
General Hospital. After some hesitation, he agreed to resign.

The following day, 28 March, Nair wrote to me: "About a year ago, I
knew myself for a confirmed alcoholic. It was only then that the DECEP-
TION [sic] began. I occasionally thought of confiding in you, but put
things off in cowardly fashion. The last time I was on the verge of confiding in you was when we met some two weeks ago in my office, before I
left for Kuching. I had missed my last chance to come clean. This proved
my undoing."

A fortnight later, in another letter dated 11 April, Nair wrote:

I could still remember a few other things besides, including some
of my aberrant conduct in Singapore during the fortnight before I

left for Kuching. What frightens me, however, is that I simply cannot recall most of the reports on how I had behaved in Kuching. And yet they must be true, because several witnesses have attested to my conduct and to the remarks I made. What confuses me further is that on at least two occasions, of which I have clear memories, the reports contradict them. I am not a liar, but then there were the witnesses. Some of them may be liars, as I tend to believe, but not all of them can be liars. In the old days they talked of one being possessed. Was I possessed? Or was it a Dr Jekyll and Mr Hyde situation?

Perhaps there has been some brain damage. Almost certainly my brain functions must have been impaired, but to what extent remains to be seen. And to what extent can what has been impaired be repaired or even restored? That too remains to be seen.

I had two roles: My first, as prime minister, was to protect the dignity of the office of president and Singapore's reputation; my second, as a personal friend, made me want to save him. After several days in the hospital we sent him off to Changi Cottage to dry him out. He insisted on going to an *ashram* (retreat) in India, to meditate and cure himself the Hindu way. I did not think he would get better that way and urged him to go for treatment. After considerable persuasion by Raja, Eddie, and some other old friends including S. R. Nathan, another close friend from NTUC days (later our president), he agreed to go to the Caron Foundation in the United States. A month later the treatment appeared successful.

Nair insisted that we give him a pension. There was no provision in the constitution for any pension for the president. The cabinet decided to offer a pension to Devan on compassionate grounds, but on condition that a panel of government doctors saw him from time to time. Eddie Barker settled it with Nair, and moved the resolution in Parliament. After it was passed Nair turned it down, denying that he had agreed to the condition. The government did not remove the condition and Nair became embittered.

One and a half years later, in a letter published in the *Far Eastern Economic Review* (*FEER*) of 29 January 1987, he denied that he was ever an alcoholic. The permanent secretary (health) sent Nair and the *FEER* a letter dated 14 February 1987, signed by all seven doctors who had managed Devan Nair's case in March and April 1985, confirming their diagnosis of alcoholism. No doctor has contradicted these findings.

In May 1988, Nair intervened in the case of Francis Seow, a former solicitor general who had admitted that he had obtained from a U.S. State Department official an assurance of asylum if he needed it. Nair attacked me, saying this was what I had done when I lobbied for international support while fighting the Malay extremists in Malaysia, meaning that I would have fled from Malaysia in case of trouble. When Nair refused to withdraw his allegations, I sued him and tabled a command paper in Parliament containing the documents relating to his alcoholism.

After these documents were published, Nair left Singapore and has not returned. Eleven years later (1999), in Canada, in an interview, he said that he had been wrongly diagnosed and that I had got the doctors to slip him hallucinatory drugs to make him out to be an alcoholic. As Dr. Nagulendran had warned us, there were "personality changes."

My mistake in Nair's appointment was to assume, without checking, that all was well with him. After his collapse, I consulted one of his closest NTUC friends, Ho See Beng. See Beng, an MP, confirmed that Nair had been drinking heavily before he was appointed president by Parliament. Asked why he had not warned me of this risk, he replied that Nair was never comatose. Had misplaced loyalty not prevented See Beng from warning me of this risk we would all have been spared much pain and embarrassment.

But all said and done, Devan Nair played a significant part in the building of modern Singapore. He stood up to be counted when the communists attacked the PAP in the 1960s, and he initiated the modernization of the labor movement that made the NTUC an important partner in the development of our economy.

# PART II

# In Search of Space—
# Regional and International

# 16. Ups and Downs with Malaysia

On 20 March 1966, eight months after separation, Tunku Abdul Rahman, the prime minister of Malaysia, visited Singapore. I called on him at Federation House near the Botanic Gardens. For three hours we talked, had a Chinese dinner, watched television, and continued talking. The only other persons present that night were his wife and the Malaysian high commissioner, Jamal Abdul Latiff. It was the way the Tunku usually conducted business. He talked of many things besides the matters most on his mind.

The Tunku proposed that Singapore ministers join his ministers for golf in Cameron Highlands in April when he would be on leave after the installation of the Agong (the king). We would then get to know each other better and all the difficulties could be sorted out. He wanted to go back to the old easy, relaxed relationship to reduce tension between his non-Malays and Malays. I said that April would not be convenient; I had to go to London and Stockholm. Perhaps in June. Over dinner he made a veiled threat by reminding me casually that Singapore's lifeline was with Malaysia, that Singapore had to work closely with it. He asked why we had stopped their unemployed from seeking jobs in Singapore. I explained that we could not have free migration to Singapore for jobs. He could not understand how this strained our economy; the same thing was happening in Kuala Lumpur. He had asked the Federal Industrial Development Agency to set up pioneer industries in Kuala Lumpur, Ipoh, Penang, and Johor Bahru. These things were bound to happen because

Singapore was a big city! I patiently explained that unemployed Malaysians were not Singapore's responsibility, that we had our own unemployed for whom we had to find jobs.

He complained about Chin Chye and Raja making speeches criticizing Malaysia. I explained that those of my ministers who came from Malaya still reacted as Malayans, emotionally unable to detach themselves from the land of their birth and upbringing. They needed time to be reconciled to being Singaporeans in a separate and independent country. Showing annoyance and impatience, he said sharply, "They must do so very quickly because I will not stand for this. These people have got other ideas and motives. In Raja's case, his loyalty may even be to India." The Tunku was wrong. Raja had been totally loyal to Malaysia although he was born in Jaffna, Ceylon.

Before I took my leave at the front door, I said that we had to reach a new working relationship and cooperate for mutual benefit, hinting ever so gently that we could not go back to the happy old days when we were the supplicants seeking merger.

I had mixed feelings about this first encounter with the Tunku after separation. He still expected me to oblige him. But I was reassured that he appeared to be still in charge. I knew he wanted a quiet life, and did not like prolonged tensions or crises.

Malaysia's leaders continued to treat us as though we were still in the early 1960s, seeking merger. For their convenience, we were out of their Parliament and their politics. Now, although Singapore was independent and sovereign, the Tunku believed that his one battalion in Singapore and his ability to cut off our water supply or close the Causeway to stop all trade and travel would compel us to comply. If he could do this just with his old-world aristocratic charm, so much the better.

In 1966, I was away for two months starting in April. Throughout this time, the Tunku, Razak, and Ghazali sniped at Toh Chin Chye, then our deputy prime minister, and me because we appeared ready to restore ties with Indonesia before Malaysia did so. The Tunku threatened reprisals. Chin Chye, as acting prime minister, had welcomed Indonesia's decision to recognize Singapore. Greatly upset, the Malaysian government issued this statement:

Singapore's decision to welcome Indonesia's decision to recognise her clearly means that Singapore would have some sort of relation or intercourse with Indonesia and this would bring Indonesian nationals to Singapore. Clearly when this happens, it will endanger our security as Indonesia has repeatedly stated and is continuing to do so that she intends to intensify confrontation against Malaysia. Malaysia must therefore continue to take whatever measure she considers necessary to safeguard her interests and her security.

Immediately after that, on 18 April, Dr. Ismail, the Malaysian minister for home affairs, imposed with immediate effect entry controls for Singapore identity card holders crossing the Causeway.

When I met the Tunku after I returned from my visit to Britain and Eastern Europe, he grumbled to me about my journeys to these communist countries, that they would open embassies in Singapore and pose a threat to Malaysia. How could I have said I wanted to be good friends with China and Indonesia, he asked. I said that although my style was different from his, I did not intend to be eaten up by the communists. I recounted how we had refused permission for the crew of a Chinese ship docked in Singapore to land because the captain refused to sign an undertaking that they would not distribute their cultural revolution propaganda material. Radio Peking had attacked our immigration department. I explained that East European countries, excepting Romania, were taking the Soviet line which was opposed to China's. Their neutrality or support would prevent us from becoming isolated, which could happen because Singapore was hosting British bases, anathema to the nonaligned countries.

Meanwhile, UMNO leaders continued to use the *Utusan Melayu,* the Jawi (Arabic script) newspaper circulating in both countries, to work up Malay sentiment against the "Chinese" government of Singapore. The *Utusan Melayu* reported that Ahmad Haji Taff, an UMNO leader in Singapore, one of Singapore's two former senators to the federal senate, had demanded that our constitutional commission write into the Singapore constitution special rights for the Malays. These special rights were in the Malaysian constitution but had never applied to Singapore.

Our news division translated the *Utusan*'s inflammatory, racist statements into English, Chinese, and Tamil, and reported them over radio
and television and in the press. This hurt UMNO leaders with non-
Malays both in Singapore and Malaysia. Ismail and Ghazali complained
about this. It was subverting Malaysia, said Ismail, and there could be no
economic cooperation until there was political disengagement. We should
not interfere in their internal affairs as we were a separate sovereign and
independent nation. Ghazali went a step further, claiming that Malaysia
had a special relationship with Singapore. He was disappointed they were
not informed of our trade agreements with Russia and other communist
countries. (Malaysia did not have any such agreements with communist
countries.) He thought these came within the ambit of our agreement
with Malaysia for economic cooperation and defense, that neither side
would take any steps or enter into any treaty or agreements that would
jeopardize the other's defense. I pointed out that he could not expect these
courtesies without reciprocating them.

Ghazali also wanted us to wait until they had restored relations with
Indonesia before we resumed barter trade with them. He insisted that we
allow only big ships of over 200 tons into our main harbor and turn away
all smaller vessels, especially sailing boats, on security grounds. Our
Special Branch, now renamed Internal Security Department (ISD), had
reported that the Malaysians themselves were openly doing barter trade
on the west coast of Malaya, allowing small sailing craft from Sumatra to
come into Johor and Malacca ports. To discuss the matter, Keng Swee
asked for a meeting of the Combined Defence Council which had been set
up after our independence. They fixed a date, but to his surprise the meeting was called off, because, the Malaysians claimed, we had accepted their
proposal. We went ahead and designated Pulau Senang, an island at the
southernmost point of Singapore, as a center for Indonesian barter traders
who came in their sailing ships from as far away as Sulawesi (Celebes).
Razak objected strenuously. Their unilateral decision making and over-
bearing demands made us resign from the Combined Defence Council.

An endless flotilla of small craft, some with outboard motors, others
with sails, brought in their crude rubber, copra, charcoal, and other produce. They departed with transistor radios, shirts, trousers, slippers, shoes,
jackets, and hats. Some even bought whole boxes of bread to take back. In

August 1966, after Confrontation had officially ended in June, we cancelled all restrictions on barter trade. Indonesian small craft once again came to Telok Ayer Basin, one of Singapore's oldest harbors.

The pressures following separation were relentless. There was never a dull moment in our relations with Malaysia. Despite our best efforts we could not reach an agreement on retaining our common currency, and the two governments announced in August 1966 that from June 1967 we would issue separate currencies. So would Brunei, which had shared the common currency, a legacy of British rule. The Singapore International Chamber of Commerce, representing British companies, the Council of the Association of Banks in Malaysia, and the Singapore Chinese Chamber of Commerce were all worried by the uncertainty of a split and appealed to the two governments to negotiate again to maintain a common currency.

Tan Siew Sin, the Malaysian finance minister, said the split would not mean the end of the world. He argued that the concessions he had made to accommodate Singapore involved a significant derogation of sovereignty on the part of Bank Negara Malaysia and ultimately the Malaysian government itself. Singapore, he said, was afraid Malaysia might not honor its undertaking to transfer the whole of Singapore's assets and liabilities as shown in the books of the central bank, but this was merely a technical, not a fundamental, reason for the break. He implied that we lacked trust in their integrity. Indeed, Singapore's reserves could not be protected simply by relying on trust.

We decided against setting up a central bank and continued with a currency board with 100 percent backing in foreign exchange reserves for every dollar we issued. Lim Kim San, as finance minister, expressed confidence in the strength and stability of Singapore's currency, which called for the tightest economic and social discipline. In Parliament, Kim San explained that "a central bank is an easy way out for a finance minister who likes to juggle [his figures] when he has a deficit in his budget. I do not think we should put such a temptation before the finance minister in Singapore." Tan Siew Sin responded, "If the central bank system is an inferior system, then it is clear that it is a mistake made by every industrialised country of the Western world and by every developing country. . . . Every independent country in the world has a central bank, or is in the process of establishing a central bank." Later, in Parliament, Tan said that the currency split was for the best, because unlike the old days, a nation's central bank was a powerful weapon for a finance minister in his monetary and fiscal policies.

Both finance ministers announced that they would keep their currencies pegged at two shillings and four pence to the dollar, or 0.290299 grams of gold. They agreed on the "interchangeability" of the two currencies: accepting each other's currency as customary tender and repatriating the currency in exchange for an equivalent amount in a convertible currency. Our two currencies continued with interchangeability from 1967 until May 1973, when it was terminated at Malaysia's request. In January 1975, the Malaysian dollar, the ringgit, dropped marginally to S$0.9998. By 1980, it had depreciated sharply by five cents against the Singapore dollar, and by 1997 it was worth less than 50 Singapore cents. Malaysian finance ministers and central bankers had run looser fiscal and monetary policies than Singapore. Not spending more than we collect in revenue has been a guiding principle from which no Singapore finance minister has departed except in a recession.

After Singapore left Malaysia in 1965, the UMNO-controlled federal government pressed ahead with Malay as the sole national and official language, and changed its education policies to bring this about. Non-Malay resentment against these changes had been increasing, and the strident communal tones of UMNO leaders did not help to assuage such feelings. In 1968, a Malaysian government white paper stated that communist subversion was being carried out in independent Chinese secondary schools. This added to the fears that they would be closed.

During their election campaign in April–May 1969, Alliance leaders made wild and groundless allegations that Singapore leaders had interfered in their politics. Tan Siew Sin, who was also the Malaysian Chinese Association (MCA) president, said he had "definite evidence" that the Democratic Action Party (DAP), formerly the PAP in Malaysia, was being financed by the PAP, if not the Singapore government. Raja, our foreign minister, registered Singapore's concern with the Malaysian high commissioner, who agreed that these remarks were counterproductive. But two days later he reported that the Tunku supported Tan's charges, claiming that, on the evidence available, they were true. The Tunku himself then pitched in at an election rally to say that Singapore's PAP leaders were hoping to win over the government in Malaysia, and "knowing that they have no chance of winning the Chinese votes, they have no alternative but to split the Malays. So they are using the Pan Malaysian Islamic Party (PMIP) as their agent." He said that the man who had provided the PMIP with funds had now been forbidden to reenter Malaysia, but refused to disclose his identity.

I was away in London when these wild allegations were made. I wrote to Lim Kim San, our defense minister: "I am a little bewildered by the crazy allegations of the Tunku and Siew Sin about our supposed interference in their elections. I also wonder when all this will explode into racial strife and guerrilla warfare. We had better build up as fast as we can. I am sure the troubles will spill over to Singapore. By the time thousands of people are prepared to openly demonstrate against them in KL, and march through the streets in a funeral procession, then the future is grim indeed." I was referring to the funeral of a Chinese youth shot and killed by police a few days earlier while he was in a group painting antigovernment election slogans.

On polling day in Malaysia, 10 May, UMNO lost 8 out of the 59 seats they held. The DAP won 14 seats in urban constituencies including Kuala Lumpur, defeating the MCA, UMNO's partner, in 13 of them. The DAP and Gerakan (another noncommunal party) held a parade in Kuala Lumpur to celebrate their victory—they had won half the seats in the Selangor state assembly. The UMNO Malay Ultras' response to this was to have a bigger parade organized by the Selangor *menteri besar* (chief minister), Harun Idris. A race riot followed on 13 May. The casualty pattern in Kuala Lumpur was similar to that in Singapore for the 1964 race riots when Singapore was under Kuala Lumpur's control. Both Kuala Lumpur and Singapore were at that time predominantly Chinese-populated cities with a minority of Malays. Yet many more Chinese were killed by this Malay minority than Malays who were killed in retaliation. The official Kuala Lumpur casualty figures were: killed 143 Chinese, 25 Malays, 13

Indians, 15 others; wounded 439. This could not have been the case if the police and military were impartial. One foreign correspondent who witnessed the riots estimated the number killed at 800.

The next day the Malaysian king proclaimed a state of emergency and suspended Parliament. The government created a National Operations Council (NOC) with Razak as chairman to govern by decree to restore law and order. Officially the Tunku was no longer in charge. This NOC marked the end of the Tunku era, and these riots changed the nature of Malaysian society. From then on Malaysia became openly a Malay-dominated society.

The riots in Kuala Lumpur had caused widespread alarm among both Chinese and Malays in Singapore, as both felt that the racial troubles would inevitably spill into Singapore. Malaysian Chinese who had fled to Singapore recounted stories of brutalities inflicted on their relatives there. As news spread of Malaysian Malay atrocities and of the bias of the Malaysian armed forces in dealing with the situation, there was anger and alarm. I was away in America, speaking to students in Yale, when I read news of these riots. Within days of the Kuala Lumpur riots, there were attacks on Malays by Chinese in Singapore. This senseless retaliation against innocent Malays was stopped by strong police action, troop deployment, and the prosecution of several attackers caught in the act. They were subsequently charged and convicted.

Four months after the riots, I called on the Tunku at his high commissioner's residence in Singapore. He looked depressed, showing the effects of a harrowing experience. He had been openly attacked in a widely circulated letter by Dr. Mahathir Mohamad (later the prime minister, then a member of UMNO's central executive council) for having sold out the country to the Chinese. I sensed he wanted Singapore to be friendly and to influence the Chinese in Malaysia not to be hostile to the UMNO leaders. I wrote this note to my colleagues: "What worries me is not whether our supporting the Tunku would lose us our non-Malay ground, but whether it would not in fact lose the Tunku his Malay ground, and so hasten his retirement."

Kim San met Razak in Kuala Lumpur a week later and reported that this time there was "no trace of the former big brother attitude. They are willing to receive advice if tactfully given without a show of upmanship. . . . It would be worth our while to prop them up for a little longer in what way we can." We were fearful that the Tunku and all his moderates would be displaced by real Ultras. Malaysia's international standing dropped precipitously, and Razak was defensive. Ironically, relations between Singapore and Malaysia improved. He needed us to help keep the Chinese in Malaysia reassured and quiescent. Our influence from Malaysia days still prevailed.

After separation, the practice of having one newspaper put out by the same editorial staff selling in both Singapore and Malaysia had continued. But after the May 1969 race riots in Kuala Lumpur, the *Utusan Melayu* became even more pro-Malay and openly hostile toward the Singapore government, belittling our efforts to help Singapore Malays. To stop it from propagating racist sentiments in Singapore, we changed the regulations to require that all newspapers must be both produced and have their editorial boards in Singapore before they could qualify for a license to print and sell here. The *Utusan Melayu* closed its Singapore office and stopped circulating. Soon thereafter, newspapers published in one territory could not be imported and sold in the other. It has remained so to this day. Both governments recognized that there were such fundamental differences of policy on race, language, and culture that what was orthodoxy in Singapore was sedition in Malaysia and vice versa.

By Malaysia's National Day, 31 August 1970, the Tunku was sufficiently weakened to announce his intention to give up his prime ministership. I felt sad for him. It was not the way to bow out after 15 years, first as chief minister, then prime minister, during which he had done much to bring Malaysia's different races together and had presided over much economic and social progress. He deserved to go out with more glory. The 1969 race riots had destroyed his dream of the happy Malaysia he had tried so hard to achieve. I was personally fond of him. He was a gentleman—an old-world gentleman with his own code of honor. He never let his close friends down. Although he did not include me among them, I continued to meet him whenever he came to Singapore for the horse races or when I visited Penang where he had retired. The last time was in Penang a year before he died in 1990. He looked frail, but when I took my leave, he saw me to the front porch and held himself up to have the press photograph us as he sent me off.

Razak, who took over as prime minister in September 1970, was a different leader from the Tunku. He did not have the Tunku's warm personality or his large and commanding presence. By comparison he appeared less decisive. Razak had been my contemporary at Raffles College from 1940 to 1942. He was the son of a Pahang chieftain. In their hierarchical society, he was much respected by the Malay students. Of medium build, with a fair, round face and hair slicked down, he looked a quiet, studious man. He was bright and hardworking. He was also a good hockey player, but ill at ease with people unless he knew them well. During Malaysia, when we were competing for the same votes, he eyed me with suspicion and unease. He probably considered me a danger to Malay dominance and political supremacy. He preferred to deal with Keng Swee with whom he was comfortable. Razak did not consider Keng Swee a rival competing for votes. Once Singapore was out of Malaysia, Razak was more at ease with me. I was no longer a competitor for votes.

He and other UMNO Malay leaders rejected the Tunku's approach to Chinese businessmen as out-of-date. Having experienced total power, both political and military, they were now completely open about their economic policies that favored the bumiputra (sons of the soil—indigenous Malays) in every sector. They implemented the New Economic Policy "to eradicate poverty" and to have "greater equality in the ownership of wealth." Malays were by regulation and administration to own 30 percent of all private capital by the year 1990, the Chinese and Indian population were to own 40 percent, and the foreign owners (mostly British) were to be reduced to 30 percent. Razak also announced a national ideology, the *Rukunegara,* that people of all races should advance together toward a just and progressive society through belief in God, loyalty to king and country, upholding the constitution and the rule of law, and the promotion of moral discipline, tolerance, and mutual respect. It was August 1970, more than a year after the race riots, before they lifted all remaining curfews and allowed political activities to resume. But sedition had assumed an extended meaning to include any challenge to the *Rukunegara* and Malay dominance.

Razak was preoccupied with getting the country back to normal after the trauma of the riots, and with fleshing out his New Economic Policy, so we had a relatively trouble-free few years. However, from time to time

1971: Putting our black labrador retriever, Bonnie—a gift from Alec Douglas Home—through her paces while Hsien Yang, Choo, and Ling look on. (*SM Lee's Collection*)

April 1955: My first election victory in the Tanjong Pagar constituency, which I continue to represent 45 years later in 2000. (*Copyright SPH*)

November 1959: Picking up the broom and leading one of many campaigns to keep Singapore clean and green. (*Copyright SPH*)

In 1964, I toured trouble spots in Tanjong Pagar and other constituencies to calm down residents terrified by racial clashes. (*Copyright SPH*)

April 1965: A French-style greeting by Prince Norodom Sihanouk in his palace in Phnom Penh. (*SM Lee's Collection*)

July 1965: Reading the riot act to K. Suppiah, president of the Public Daily Rated Employees' Unions Federation, to warn him against making excessive demands before an illegal strike. (*Copyright SPH*)

ABOVE: 1965: Visiting Bukit Ho Swee residents resettled in high-rise apartments four years after a huge fire razed their squatter colony. (*Copyright SPH*)

LEFT: January 1968: Opening the new golf course on HMS *Simbang* in Singapore. Royal Navy officers invited me to open it just before I left for London to see Harold Wilson. (*SM Lee's Collection*)

1969: A visit to the White House with President Richard Nixon and National Security Adviser Henry Kissinger; also in attendance was the Singapore ambassador E. S. Monteiro. (*SM Lee's Collection*)

May 1973: My first official visit to Suharto's Indonesia—scattering flowers on graves of two Indonesian marines executed in Singapore in 1968 for murders committed in 1965. (*Copyright SPH*)

May 1976: Meeting Chairman Mao Tse Tung in Beijing's Zhongnanhai, an enclave for China's leaders. (*SM Lee's Collection*)

November 1978: Choo and I welcoming Deng Xiaoping and his wife for dinner at the Istana. Standing behind Choo is deputy prime minister Goh Keng Swee. (*SM Lee's Collection*)

August 1982: Meeting in the White House with friends President Ronald Reagan and the U.S. Secretary of State George Shultz. (*SM Lee's Collection*)

September 1982: President Suharto greeting me at the Jakarta Airport. (*Copyright SPH*)

we had problems over both trivial and important matters. Singapore had an antilong hair campaign in 1971 as we did not want our young to adopt the hippie look. Men with long hair were attended to last at government counters and at all entry points—airport, port, and Causeway. Three youths, two Malays and a Chinese, were picked up at the Orchard Road parking lot and interrogated as suspected secret society members. They were detained for 16 hours, had their hair cut by a police barber, and released. They turned out to be Malaysians. The *Utusan Melayu* played up the story which caused a minor storm. The government apologized for the incident. In the meantime, substantial disputes were brewing over our port and the splitting of assets of our joint currency board and our joint airline.

Soon after separation, Tan Siew Sin had reportedly threatened to bypass Singapore and develop Malaysia's Port Swettenham (later called Port Kelang) and Penang, describing the 40 percent of Malaysia's trade that went through Singapore as a "relic of the colonial past." Malaysia subsequently took a series of measures to reduce the import and export of goods through Singapore. The Johor Malay Chamber of Commerce in August 1972 called on the federal government to abolish train services to Singapore as soon as Johor's port at Pasir Gudang, near Johor Bahru, was ready. Malaysia announced in October 1972 that from 1973 all goods shipped from one part of Malaysia to another had to be consigned from their own ports in order to qualify for exemption from import tax on arrival. If these goods came through the port of Singapore, they had to pay import tax. They also banned timber exports to Singapore, badly affecting our plywood factories and sawmills. After a period of disruption, we were able to source timber from Indonesia.

As Hon Sui Sen, then our finance minister, the most patient and reasonable of my colleagues, wrote to me, "The Malaysian attitude on economic cooperation is one of envy and disdain. They believe that Singapore cannot survive without Malaysia and that our prosperity is completely dependent upon them. Nevertheless, they are irritated and annoyed by the fact that despite our size and vulnerability, we have progressed beyond their expectations."

We discovered in the late 1960s that the Malaysians had formed an "S" committee to coordinate Malaysian policies on problems with Singapore.

Its chairman was the head of the Malaysian civil service and its members included the secretaries-general of the ministries of defense, foreign affairs, and home affairs. We also learned that they had coopted, from time to time, former PAP pro-communist ex-detainees including Sandra Woodhull and James Puthucheary to help them understand the thinking behind our policies. When we first heard of it, the "S" committee had sinister overtones. But we had little trouble reading their motives; they wanted to choke our economic growth wherever their economy gave them leverage over ours. Much later, when Malaysia was under Prime Minister Hussein Onn and our relations were more relaxed, I proposed an intergovernmental committee to resolve bilateral issues. Tengku Rithaudeen, his foreign minister, told me on 13 May 1980, at a meeting in Sri Temasek, that they already had an "S" committee to study problems with Singapore. By October 1986, the "S" committee had widened its focus to include bilateral relations with Indonesia, Thailand, and Brunei, and was renamed the Foreign Relations Committee (FRC). After that the Malaysians spoke openly to our officials about the FRC and its role in managing bilateral relations. The cloak-and-dagger approach of the "S" committee was abandoned.

The only Malaysian minister who was not prejudiced against Singapore was Deputy Prime Minister Tun Dr. Ismail. When he visited Singapore in April 1971 on the excuse of inspecting our housing programs, we had a good talk. He wanted more cooperation. He told the press that differences of opinion should not obstruct greater cooperation between us. At his urging, our state trading agency, Intraco, signed an agreement in 1971 to cooperate with Pernas, its Malaysian counterpart, in third country trade. Not much trade came out of this: Ismail's lone voice could not prevail against the other UMNO leaders.

To mark improving bilateral relations, I made my first official visit to Malaysia in March 1972, accompanied by Sui Sen. We discussed and settled the disposition of the currency board's surplus funds and residual assets. We negotiated in a businesslike way. The difficulty with Razak, however, was that every now and then he would change his mind and reopen an item already agreed upon.

Razak returned the visit in 1973. He wanted to terminate the interchangeability of our two currencies. I agreed. The Malaysia-Singapore Stock Exchange was also split in May 1973 into the Stock Exchange of

Singapore and the Kuala Lumpur Stock Exchange. Each kept its prevailing listing of Singapore and Malaysian stocks. Razak was happy with the current state of relations. Publicly, relations were not so close as to embarrass him with his Malay base, nor were they in such a state of acrimony as to upset his Chinese support. Razak said he anticipated troubles for both Singapore and Malaysia from the uncertainties in Thailand and Indochina, and so we should not add to our difficulties by creating problems between ourselves. I agreed. He was uneasy and concerned about his Chinese support in Malaysia and the lack of support for the MCA in the next election and asked if I could help. I had no reply. An increase in commodity prices had given him greater confidence and eased his sense of resentment at our doing better than them.

Razak invited me for a return visit. Relations were equable and stayed that way for the next three years, with quiet cooperation and few serious disagreements. Then I learned that Razak had leukemia. He flew to London frequently for treatment. In newspaper photographs and on television he appeared visibly thinner by the month. When he died in January 1976, I paid my respects at his home in Kuala Lumpur.

Hussein Onn succeeded Razak as prime minister. He was a practicing lawyer in 1968 when Prime Minister Razak brought him into active politics. They were brothers-in-law, married to two sisters.

Hussein did not look the typical Malay. He had a Turkish grandmother, spoke with a strong voice and was unusually fair for a Malay. He wore glasses, had curly hair and was taller and broader-built than Razak. He was very careful in his work. At formal meetings, he would have his brief before him with important passages neatly underlined in color, and would go through his brief methodically. He did not believe in trusting only to his memory. He was open and direct when he dealt with me, coming straight to the point, unlike Razak. I liked him. He was of the same age as Razak and me. His father, Dato Onn bin Jaafar, had been the *menteri besar* of Johor and the first leader of UMNO, which was formed shortly after the British returned in 1945 and promulgated the Malayan Union.

Hussein set out to make a fresh start. A few weeks after Razak's funeral, he visited Singapore, saying he wanted to establish good personal relations and be able to discuss and overcome bilateral problems. We had a one-on-one meeting. I told him my fears of Malay communists and their sympathizers penetrating Malaysia's mass media and their radical Malay student and trade union leadership. We talked freely and frankly about the Malay communist infiltration of his media, including the activities of Samad Ismail, an MCP member from his time in Singapore in the 1950s, and his group. When Razak was prime minister, Samad had worked his way into UMNO and become a powerful figure in the *New Straits Times* and *Berita Harian,* building up a coterie of supporters. Hussein agreed this was a danger but said that the communists and student radicals could not be arrested without upsetting the Malay ground. Later, in June 1976, the ISD arrested one of Samad's disciples in Singapore, Hussein Jahidin, a *Berita Harian* editor. He implicated Samad and several other Malay journalists in Kuala Lumpur as pro-communists. The Malaysian Special Branch arrested Samad and his Kuala Lumpur group. Hussein Onn had had the courage to act against a pro-communist Malay intelligentsia although this was likely to cost him some support.

Hussein had fond memories of Singapore. He had studied at Telok Kurau English School in 1933–1934, the years when I was also a student there. He was a little diffident at the beginning and was happy that I treated him with respect. I was impressed by his integrity and his good intentions. I took up his invitation to visit Malaysia in December 1976, when he briefed me on his internal security and Thai border problems. We also discussed economic cooperation.

Our relations had started off on a good footing but unfortunately he was influenced by the anti-Singapore feelings of Johor UMNO leaders, especially the *menteri besar,* Othman Saat, the most important UMNO leader in Hussein's home state. Othman injected his visceral dislike for Singapore into Hussein, who repeated to me Othman's complaints: We had caused a shortage of workers in their factories by attracting their workers to work in Singapore for more pay; Johor Bahru shopkeepers lost business because of competition from Woodlands New Town on our side of the Causeway. (In the 1990s, when one Singapore dollar was worth more than two ringgit, they complained that Singaporeans flocked to their shops causing prices to rise for their locals.)

The most absurd allegation of the *menteri besar* repeated by Hussein was that pig waste from our farms was polluting the straits between Johor and Singapore. And for good measure, that land reclamation on our northern coast had caused flooding in their southern coastal villages in the Tebrau area. I carefully explained that land reclamation on Singapore's northern coastline could not cause flooding in Johor; hydrologically this was impossible. And the pig waste pollution could not have come from Singapore because all our runoffs were trapped in rivers that had been dammed to form estuarine reservoirs with strict antipollution measures for the water to be potable. He accepted my explanations.

Despite amicable relations with Hussein, the Malaysians continued to take a series of actions that they thought would slow down our economy. First, the Johor state government banned the export of sand and turf. Then the federal government ruled that from 1977, all exports from Johor to East Malaysia must be shipped through Pasir Gudang port, not through Singapore. From 1980, they limited the carriage of all domestic cargo between Malaysian ports to their own vessels. They carried out these policies although their people had to pay the increased costs. Johor leaders convinced Hussein that we were out to harm Johor and prevent its economic progress. They even persuaded Hussein to tell the press in January 1979 that he was considering stopping the railway in Johor and not Singapore, in order to develop Pasir Gudang as a port.

One incident which added to this bitterness occurred in December 1976 after our general election. ISD officers found that Leong Mun Kwai, the secretary-general of the People's Front and an opposition candidate, had made defamatory remarks against me in the election that month because he had been paid to do so by the Malaysian Special Branch. We put him on television to admit this. He was convicted for criminal defamation and sentenced to 18 months in prison. Leong told the ISD that UMNO leader Senu Abdul Rahman, the former Malaysian minister of culture, youth, and sports, had personally told Leong to try to destroy my reputation.

On economic cooperation, I said we were moving away from simple manufacture into higher value-added products with more machines. We were also moving more into services—repairing of aircraft, working with computers, and so on. We would be happy if our factories, short of labor in Singapore, relocated to Johor. Nor did we want to block the growth of their port in Pasir Gudang.

Although he was influenced by his Johor UMNO leaders to be suspicious of Singapore, I found Hussein fair-minded. He wanted to do right by his country and by those who dealt with him. He was not as quick as Razak but was thorough, careful, and did not have second thoughts after a decision. He weighed his words carefully.

In 1981, Hussein flew to London for a medical checkup. He was diagnosed as having heart trouble and resigned soon after. He went back to law and died in 1990. He had won my respect as a man of integrity. Sitting at the top of an UMNO machine that was based on money politics, Hussein was completely honest. He tried to clean up the corruption, especially in the states. He authorized the prosecution in November 1975 against the *menteri besar* of Selangor, Datuk Harun Idris. Harun was convicted and imprisoned for four years. But Hussein could not widen his purge in the face of resistance from other UMNO state leaders.

In Parliament in Kuala Lumpur in May 1965, Dr. Mahathir Mohamad, as MP for Kota Star Selatan in Kedah, warned me of the consequences of challenging Malay rule. He denounced the PAP as

pro-Chinese, communist-oriented and positively anti-Malay. . . . In some police stations, Chinese is the official language, and statements are taken in Chinese. . . . In industry, the PAP policy is to encourage Malays to become labourers only, but Malays were not given facilities to invest as well. . . . It is, of course, necessary to emphasise that there are two types of Chinese—those who appreciate the need for all communities to be equally well-off and these are the MCA supporters to be found mainly where Chinese have for generations lived and worked amidst the Malays and other indigenous people, and the insular, selfish and arrogant type, of which Mr. Lee is a good example. This latter type live in a purely Chinese environment where Malays only exist at syce level. . . . They have never known Malay rule and could not bear the idea that the people that they have so long kept under their heels should now be in a position to rule them.

At a time when UMNO was demanding my detention and burning my effigy, these words were ominous. My riposte was that we had agreed to the constitution of Malaysia which provided for Malaysian, not Malay, rule. This was no light-hearted exchange in the ordinary cut-and-thrust of debate. He meant that I did not know my proper place in Malaysia.

In his autobiography, serialized by the Nihon Keizai Shimbun in 1995, he said that his "father's blood line has supposedly been traced back to Kerala State in India." His mother was a Malay born in Kedah. But he identified himself totally as a Malay and was determined in wanting to uplift the Malays.

When Hussein Onn appointed him as his deputy prime minister and minister for education I decided to hold out my hand in friendly cooperation for the future, regardless of our profound differences in the past. Through Devan Nair, who knew him well from his years in the Malaysian Parliament, I invited Mahathir to Singapore in 1978. I expected Mahathir to succeed Hussein as prime minister and wanted to put our old antagonism behind us. I knew he was a fierce and dogged fighter. I had seen the way he had fought the Tunku when the Tunku was at the height of his power. He had been expelled from UMNO but that did not deter him from carrying on the fight. I was not unwilling to clash with him when we were in Malaysia, but feuding between two sovereign states was different. I initiated this dialogue to clear away the debris of the past.

He accepted the invitation and followed up with several subsequent visits. We had long and frank exchanges of several hours each to clear the air surrounding our suspicions of each other.

He was direct and asked what we were building the SAF (Singapore Armed Forces) for. I replied equally directly that we feared that at some time or other there could be a random act of madness like cutting off our water supplies, which they had publicly threatened whenever there were differences between us. We had not wanted separation. It had been thrust upon us. The Separation Agreement with Malaysia was a part of the terms on which we left and had been deposited in the United Nations. In this agreement, the Malaysian government had guaranteed our water supply.

If this was breached, we would go to the UN Security Council. If water shortage became urgent, in an emergency, we would have to go in, forcibly if need be, to repair damaged pipes and machinery and restore the water flow. I was putting my cards on the table. He denied that any such precipitate action would happen. I said I believed that he would not do this, but we had to be prepared for all contingencies.

Mahathir was candid about his deep anti-Singapore feelings. He recounted how, as a medical student in Singapore, he had directed a Chinese taxi driver to the home of a lady friend, but had been taken to the servants' quarters of this house. It was an insult he did not forget. Singapore Chinese, he said, looked down upon the Malays.

He wanted me to cut off my links with Malaysia's Chinese leaders, in particular the DAP leaders. He undertook not to interfere with Singapore's Malays. I said we would live and let live, that I had not kept up contact with the DAP. He said clearly that he accepted an independent Singapore and had no intention of undermining it. My reply was that on this basis we could build a relationship of trust and confidence. So long as we believed they wanted to do us in, we would always be distrustful, reading sinister motives into every ambiguous move.

He was different from his predecessors. The Tunku, Razak, and Hussein Onn were from the aristocracy or the traditional ruling families associated with the sultans. Like me, Mahathir is a commoner—a trained professional doctor and a self-made politician. I believed I had satisfied him that I was not interested in outmaneuvring him, that I wanted a businesslike relationship. It was as well I initiated this dialogue and developed a working relationship. Had we carried our old antagonisms into the future, both countries would have suffered.

As prime minister, he visited Singapore in December 1981. He had advanced the time for peninsular Malaysia by half an hour so as to have one time zone for West and East Malaysia. I said Singapore would do likewise for the convenience of everyone. This put him in a good mood. He explained that he had had to educate his Malaysian officials to get them to reverse their opposition to Singapore Airlines flying to Penang. Subsequently, hotels in Penang were full and both airlines had profitable loads, benefiting from cooperation. He had asked his ministers and officers to learn from Singapore. No other Malaysian prime minister or minister had ever publicly said they had anything to learn from Singapore; Mahathir did not suffer from this inhibition. This open-minded attitude of learning from anyone whose success he wanted to duplicate in Malaysia distinguished him from his predecessors.

During our one-on-one meeting, he said people in Johor were jealous of Singapore. He advised me to lessen the envy by socializing at an official level. I said his foreign ministry, Wisma Putra, had objected to such fraternizing. He said he would tell them this was his proposal. This was a significant change of policy. In a matter-of-fact way, Mahathir said that there was resentment among Malaysia's Malays against Singapore as a prosperous Chinese city, just as they resented the Chinese in the Malaysian towns. But the people at the top in Kuala Lumpur understood this problem.

I expressed my hope to establish sound and steady relations so that our problems would not be blown out of proportion. He wanted an open and frank relationship, one that would be fair and equitable. He had ordered the lifting of the ban on the export of construction materials to Singapore. It was not being announced, but he had told the Johor authorities that this was a federal matter in which they could not interfere.

We then joined our officials and ministers. On Malaysia's claim to Pedra Branca, a small rocky island Singapore had owned for more than 100 years and where it had built a lighthouse, he said both parties should sit down and sort it out. We could exchange papers and settle the issue. I agreed. On the Straits of Johor, he wanted the Thalweg line (the line along the deepest channel between the two shores) to be fixed and not to shift with the shifting of the channel. I agreed. I requested the return of a military camp they were occupying and the acquisition of a portion of Malayan Railway land at Tanjong Pagar Station for an expressway extension. He agreed. After dinner, he said with satisfaction, "Nearly all bilateral issues have been resolved." I replied, "Let's keep it like that." It was a good first meeting. We had established a relationship.

Shortly after, our high commission in Kuala Lumpur reported a perceptible improvement in attitudes among Malaysian ministers, MPs, and civil servants toward Singapore. They were willing to learn from Singapore and were open about it. They praised Changi Airport and hoped that

Subang would be half as good. There were increased visits to Singapore to study our productivity, urban planning, and other matters.

I visited Mahathir in Kuala Lumpur the following year, in 1982. In a two-hour one-on-one meeting, we moved from just solving bilateral problems to negotiating new areas of cooperation. On the Five-Power Defence Agreement (FPDA) and the Integrated Air Defence System, Mahathir said they would counterbalance the Soviet bases in Vietnam. I told him we were buying four American E2C Hawkeye surveillance aircraft to give advance warning of any aerial attack on Singapore. Together we briefed our ministers and officials on items we had agreed upon, including Malaysia's affirmation that they would honor the 1962 Water Agreement to provide 250 million gallons per day to Singapore.

The meeting was decidedly warmer than the last. Mahathir's approach to Singapore was more pragmatic. At a press conference, I said there had been a meeting of minds, that we were on the same wavelength. Improved relations spread to warmer personal relations between officers of our armed forces where previously there had been almost no interaction.

The thaw did not last long. Antipathy for and envy of Singapore always tempted Malay leaders to seek popularity with their Malay grass roots by hitting out at Singapore. Worse, the Malaysian government resumed taking actions that hurt Singapore. In January 1984, they imposed a RM100 levy on all goods vehicles leaving Malaysia for Singapore.

I asked Malaysian Deputy Prime Minister Musa Hitam in Singapore two months later why they took action that would discourage the relocation of industries from Singapore to Malaysia by Japanese and American MNCs. These MNCs had set up electronic assembly plants in Johor to have the products sent to Singapore for more complex operations. The RM100 levy was a signal that such a relocation was not favored. Musa replied it was part of a learning process. He believed someone had suggested this as an easy way to get revenue but they would discover the wider implications. But Musa had no influence over Mahathir's policy. Instead of cancelling the levy they increased it to RM200 to discourage the use of Singapore's port.

In October that year, Malaysia reduced its import duty on a variety of foodstuffs, mostly from China, provided they were imported direct from the country of origin into Malaysia. We told their finance minister, Daim Zainuddin, that this violated GATT rules, and that we would have to report it. He amended their policy to exempt duty on goods imported via sea and airports but not via a land route, like the Causeway. It was clear that the measure was aimed against Singapore.

In 1986, our ministry of foreign affairs announced that Israeli President Chaim Herzog was to make a state visit that November on the invitation of our president. There was an outcry in Malaysia, with demonstration rallies and protests outside our high commission in Kuala Lumpur, in their states, and at the Causeway. They protested officially. Daim, who was close to Mahathir, told our high commissioner that the visit was an insult to Malaysia and the Muslims. He said that although Mahathir had said in Parliament that they would not interfere in another country's affairs, privately he was very unhappy. I told our high commissioner to explain that we had announced the visit and could not cancel it without damage to ourselves. Mahathir recalled the Malaysian high commissioner in Singapore for the duration of President Herzog's visit, saying that relations with Singapore were no longer as good, but that ties were far from tense.

From time to time, whenever the Malaysians wanted things their way, even on matters strictly within our domestic rights, relations with Malaysia were strained. What they wanted is called in the Malay language an *abang-adik* (big brother–little brother) relationship, with little brother giving way graciously. When nonvital interests were at stake, we were prepared to humor *abang,* but not when *adik* had legitimate interests to defend, as in the next issue that arose—Malays in the SAF in Singapore.

In February 1987, my son Loong, then minister for trade and industry and second minister for defense, answered a question on Malays in the SAF at a constituency function. Our Malays were asking MPs why we did not have Malay national servicemen in sensitive key positions in the SAF like the air force or armored units. The cabinet had decided to take the matter into the open. Loong said that in the event of a conflict, the SAF did not want any of its soldiers to be put in a difficult position where his loyalty to the nation might conflict with his emotions and his religion. We did not want any soldier to feel he was not fighting for a just cause, or worse, that his side might not be in the right. In time, as our national identity became more developed, this would be less of a problem. The Malaysian media read this as implying that Malaysia was the enemy. An unending stream of critical articles ensued.

The Malaysian foreign minister, Rais Yatim, raised this speech with our foreign minister. Malaysia, he said, was a "glasshouse" in the matter, because its own Chinese were represented only to a small extent in the armed forces and in the top echelons of the civil service. This, he added, was clearly understood and accepted by the MCA, that Malaysian policies were based on Malay dominance. Therefore, Malaysia could not be critical of Singapore on this issue. However, airing these problems publicly created internal pressures on UMNO leaders to respond, because it was difficult for Malay Malaysians not to associate themselves with Malay Singaporeans. But we had never criticized their policy of having Malay-dominant armed forces.

Later, in October 1987, I met Mahathir at the Commonwealth Heads of Government Meeting in Vancouver. He said that all the things he had wanted to do in cooperation with me had gone wrong. They started to go wrong with the Herzog visit, then came the issue of Malays in the SAF. In April 1987, two assault boats with four SAF personnel entered a small creek, Sungei Melayu, opposite Singapore—Malaysian territorial waters—by mistake for 20 minutes. Malaysia delivered a verbal protest. They were suspected of spying. I apologized for their mistake but pointed out that they could not have been spying as they were in uniform. Mahathir said he could not come to Singapore to see me because the atmosphere had gone sour. He suggested that we should have a few Malay pilots to show Malays in Malaysia that we trusted our Singapore Malays and that we did not consider Malaysia to be our enemy. He said all governments had to fudge; Malaysia regularly denied discriminating against the Chinese in the Malaysian armed forces. Singapore should also deny publicly our policies on Malays in the SAF. For good Singapore-Malaysia relations, he advised that we should conduct ourselves in a manner that would not make the Malays in Malaysia unhappy about Malays in Singapore.

That meeting, however, helped to restore some personal rapport. He had also asked me to help in the development of Langkawi, an island off the coast of Kedah, as a tourist resort by getting Singapore Airlines to fly in passengers. SIA launched a three-day package in Japan and Australia, but without success. I told him Langkawi could not compete with Penang and the Thai island of Phuket nearby because it did not have the infrastructure. He asked me to discuss the problems with Daim.

Daim Zainuddin is his close aide and long-standing friend from his home state, Kedah. He has a quick mind, is good at figures and decisive, and had been successful in business before he became finance minister. As finance minister, Daim initiated the policies that moved Malaysia from state-owned enterprises into profit-oriented private enterprise corporations. Without his active intervention, Malaysia's conversion to free-market policies might not have been so broad and so successful. Daim was a shrewd deal maker who honored his agreements.

Before I stepped down as prime minister in 1990, I tried to clear the decks for my successor. Drug traffickers travelling on the Malayan Railway from Johor Bahru to Singapore had been able to toss drugs out of train windows to accomplices waiting at prearranged points. I had therefore told Mahathir in 1989 that we intended to move our customs and immigration from Tanjong Pagar Station in the south to Woodlands at our end of the Causeway, to make checks at the point of entry. I anticipated that when this move was completed, passengers would disembark at Woodlands and take our MRT trains, buses, or taxis into town. Malaysians would be unhappy because, under the law, the land would revert to Singapore when it was no longer being used for the railway. I therefore proposed to Mahathir that we should redevelop this railway land jointly. Mahathir designated Daim Zainuddin to settle the terms with me. After several months of negotiations, we finally agreed that there would be joint development of three main parcels of land at Tanjong Pagar, Kranji, and Woodlands. Malaysia's share would be 60 percent, Singapore's 40 percent. The Points of Agreement (POA) was signed on 27 November 1990, a day before I stepped down. As it turned out, I did not succeed in handing over my office to Goh Chok Tong with a clean slate.

Three years after the agreement was signed, Daim wrote to me to say that Mahathir thought it was unfair because it did not include a piece of railway land at Bukit Timah for joint development. I replied that the agreement was fair in that I had given Malaysia 60 percent instead of a 50 percent share of the three parcels of land. It was a deal done between him and me, and it was difficult for Prime Minister Goh to have it reopened.

Before, during, and after Malaysia, the Malaysians have taken one step after another to restrict Singapore's access to their economy. They imposed taxes and made laws and regulations to reduce or cut off their use of our ports, airports, and other services, especially financial services. They directed their banks and other borrowers not to raise loans from foreign banks in Singapore but to use foreign banks that had branches either in Kuala Lumpur or Labuan, a tax haven they had set up on an island off Sabah. They forced us to become more competitive.

After 1990, I refrained from official dealings with all Asean governments, including Malaysia, so as not to cross lines with Prime Minister Goh. Unfortunately, for a hearing in chambers in a defamation suit in January 1997, I swore in an affidavit that Johor Bahru was "notorious for shootings, muggings and car-jackings." This caused a furor in Malaysia when made public by the defendant who had absconded to Johor.

The Malaysian government angrily demanded a retraction and an apology. I apologized unreservedly. They were not satisfied and wanted my statement withdrawn from the court document. I saw no point in refusing. I had been careless and put myself offside. In a signed statement, I repeated my unreserved apology and stated that I had instructed my lawyer to have "the offending words removed from the record." The Malaysian cabinet met and announced they had accepted my apology. We noticed, however, that they cut off all bilateral contacts and in effect froze ties. Mahathir also said that Singapore always made things difficult, as in the case of the dispute over railway land. The barrage of protests and denunciations continued for several months, and as in the past reached a crescendo in threats to cut off our water supplies.

From 1992 our customs and immigration consulted and negotiated with Malayan Railway (KTM) and Malaysian immigration and customs to move their railway line to meet our CIQ (customs, immigration, and quarantine) post in Woodlands. Prime Minister Mahathir, in April 1992, confirmed this when he wrote to Prime Minister Goh, "In fact, we feel that it would be more convenient for both countries to have the same checkpoint in Woodlands." However, in 1997, the Malaysians wrote to state that they wanted to stay in Tanjong Pagar.

Singapore replied in July 1997 that they could not remain at Tanjong Pagar because it would create serious operational problems for both countries: People would be cleared by their immigration as having entered Malaysia before leaving Singapore. Furthermore, Malaysian officials, operating in our territory without the presence of Singapore officials to lend them authority, had no power to act.

In last-minute negotiations in July 1998, Malaysian foreign ministry officials claimed for the first time that Malaysia had a legal right to have their customs and immigration at Tanjong Pagar. We gave them three months to put up their written legal arguments for proper consideration. When the time came, they asked for an extension to December 1998.

Prime Minister Mahathir did not make it any easier by the public comments he made while he was in Namibia. Shown by Malaysian journalists the reports of earlier letters and documents that his officials had written to our officials agreeing that Malaysia's CIQ would move to Woodlands, he said, referring to the POA, "In our opinion it is not enough for an international agreement to be signed by just two officials. Such agreements have to be approved by the heads of government and ratified by the cabinet and Parliament" (as reported in Malaysian newspapers on 28 July 1998). This was an unusual view of the law. Mahathir added that Malaysia would not shift its CIQ from Tanjong Pagar to Woodlands, that "That's our stand and we will stick to it." [After the dispute became public, Jayakumar, our minister for foreign affairs, in a statement in Parliament in July 1998 recounted the exchanges between the two governments.]

Older UMNO leaders have not forgotten the intense campaign of vituperation and intimidation they mounted against me in mid-1965. They had attacked me then for advocating a Malaysian Malaysia, burnt my effigy, and demanded my arrest. This was at a time when they controlled the police and army. I could not afford to give in. They then decided to get Singapore out of Malaysia. This barrage could not have been for my education. My younger colleagues knew the fireworks were intended for them. But they knew what would happen to their political standing if they wobbled. When MPs asked questions, Prime Minister Goh and Foreign Minister Jayakumar set out the facts on the railway land in Parliament, including the agreement and subsequent letters between Daim and me. Goh disclosed that he had told Mahathir the POA was a formal agreement and he could not vary its terms. However, within a framework of wider cooperation, which included the long-term supply of water, he could vary the POA. In the robust debate that followed, a younger generation of MPs stood up to be counted. Community leaders also made it clear that they were not impressed by Malaysia's methods of making friends and influencing neighbors.

While these exchanges were being traded, I launched the first volume of my memoirs, *The Singapore Story,* on 16 September 1998, my 75th birthday. For two Sundays before its launch, Singapore's newspapers carried excerpts of my description of events leading to Singapore's separation from Malaysia. This angered Malaysian leaders. A thunderous barrage of criticisms and attacks arose from them and their media, that I was "insensitive" to their economic difficulties, choosing a time of economic troubles to publish my memoirs. I had also hurt the feelings of the children of the principal actors of the 1960s, in particular Najib Abdul Razak, Tun Razak's son who was minister for education, and Syed Hamid Albar, Syed Ja'afar Albar's son who was minister for defense. They denied the truth of my account of events. Questioned at a press conference, I said I had checked and verified my facts, that my words were carefully chosen, and that I staked my reputation on the truth of what I had written. Two days after that, on 18 September, their minister for defense banned the RSAF from flying over their airspace with immediate effect. The Malaysians had decided to make it difficult for our planes to reach our training areas in the South China Sea after taking off from Singapore airfields.

The dynamics of Singapore-Malaysia relations have not changed fundamentally since our separation on 9 August 1965. Malaysia asked us to leave because we stood for a Malaysian Malaysia and they for a Malay-dominated Malaysia. A multiracial society of equal citizens was unacceptable to the UMNO leaders of Malaysia in 1965 and remained unacceptable in 1999. In May that year Malaysian opposition leader, Lim Kit Siang, revived the concept of a Malaysian Malaysia. Mahathir reacted sharply to say it was a threat to their (Malay) identity, because Malaysia was previously called *Tanah Melayu* (Malay land). Two months later (*Straits Times*, 30 July 1999) he said that if Malaysia were forced to adopt a system of meritocracy as advocated by the West, it would terminate the process implemented by the government to bridge the gap among the races. The government, through the New Economic Policy, had provided assistance to Malays in the fields of business and education, and many of them now held important positions, for example as professors and vice chancellors. He said, "If it is abolished, I am sure that the Malays and the bumiputras will become manual workers and will not be able to hold high positions they are holding today. . . . Many bumiputras will lose their jobs, their children will not be able to go to universities and will not be able to become professors and lecturers." He also lamented that Malay students shunned science-based courses in favor of Malay and religious studies.

Mahathir was determined to redress the economic balance between the races. Unfortunately, when the financial crisis struck, many Malay entrepreneurs were badly hurt because they had over-borrowed during the boom in the stock and property markets. Only Mahathir had the courage to tell his Malays (*Straits Times*, 6 August 1999):

In the past, the country had wasted a lot of resources training unqualified individuals. We had not taken into account the capabilities of those given opportunities or exposed them to enough experiences. Because of this, many of our efforts have failed and there was wastage. Although there were successes, they did not meet the investments put in. . . . In the previous two policies— the National Economic Council Policy and New Development Policy—the focus had been to churn out local bumiputra businessmen. Now we want to mould world-class entrepreneurs.

In October 1999, Mahathir called on the Associated Chinese Chambers of Commerce and Industry in Malaysia to assist bumiputras to make up the loss in their share of national wealth after the economic crisis because many bumiputra companies were saddled with debts. "Bumiputra businessmen suffered greater losses because they were new in the field and had huge loans to service, forcing some of them to sell their companies to Chinese businessmen out of desperation" (*Star*, 13 October 1999). "We not only need to help these businessmen, but also create and groom a fresh corps of bumiputra businessmen, and for this, we are asking for the cooperation of the Chinese chambers of commerce" (*Straits Times*, 13 October 1999). The group's president, Datuk Lim Guan Teik, replied, "I think it is fair, as citizens of a multiracial country, that the strong should help the weaker" (*Straits Times*, 13 October 1999).

At separation, the Tunku did not expect us to succeed. He tried to use three levers to impose his will on Singapore: the military, the economy, and water. We countered the military leverage by building up the SAF. We overcame their economic hold by leapfrogging them and the region to link up with the industrial countries. As for water, we have alternatives— our own reservoirs provide about 40 percent of our domestic consumption, and with modern technology for desalination, reverse osmosis, and recycling of used water, we can manage.

To speak of Singapore-Malaysia problems as "historical baggage" is to miss the point. If it had been only "historical baggage," then after more than 30 years as two independent states, our relations should have stabilized. But the root cause of the recurring problems in Singapore-Malaysia relations is our diametrically different approaches to the problems facing our two multiracial societies.

Singapore set out to become a multiracial society of equal citizens, where opportunities are equal and a person's contribution is recognized and rewarded on merit regardless of race, language, culture, or religion. In spite of our meager natural resources, we succeeded, and our policies have benefited all our citizens, including our Malays. We have a growing middle class of professionals, executives, and businessmen, including Malays, who have developed a strong competitive spirit and take pride in being what they are on their own merit. Each time we are rated as the best airline in Asia, the No. 1 airport, the No. 1 container port, it reminds Singaporeans what a cohesive meritocratic multiracial society can achieve, better than if we were a Chinese-dominated one and lacked solidarity.

This was not what Malaysia's leaders thought would happen when they asked us to leave in 1965.

When UMNO politicians use coded language like "special relationship," or "historic links," or "being insensitive," they are signalling that they want Singapore to be obliging and accommodating, and not to stand on its legal rights. Malaysia's ethnic Chinese and Indian ministers have told our ministers that we are too legalistic and do not know how to deal with UMNO leaders; that if we are tactful and trust the Malay leaders' words, these leaders can be most responsive. This overlooks the difference between our responsibilities to our different electorates. Singaporeans expect their government to represent their interests in a partnership of equal and independent states.

Hence, the Singapore-Malaysia relationship will continue to have its ups and downs. Singaporeans need to take these gyrations with equanimity, neither euphoric when relations are good nor despondent when relations turn bad. We need steady nerves, stamina, and patience, while quietly standing up for our rights.


Malaysia had tried to industrialize through import substitution but without success. They saw how, with investments from MNCs, we succeeded. Daim encouraged Mahathir to privatize their inefficient state-owned enterprises and invite foreign investments; he changed policies and succeeded. Mahathir wanted Malaysia to excel, with a better airport and container port, a bigger financial center, and a "Multi-Media Super Corridor." He has built up-to-date container wharves at Port Kelang and a new super airport 75 kilometers (approximately 46 miles) south of Kuala Lumpur. This made us reexamine our competitiveness, improve our infrastructure, and work smarter to increase our productivity. Suddenly, a calamitous financial crisis hit all countries in the region and decimated currencies, stock markets, and property values. The crisis will eventually work itself out and economic growth will resume.

Despite my differences with him, I made more progress solving bilateral problems with Mahathir in the nine years he was prime minister from 1981 to 1990, when I stepped down, than in the previous 12 years with Tun Razak and Hussein Onn as prime ministers. He had the decisiveness and political support to override grassroots prejudices to advance his country's interests. He had pushed the Malays toward science and technology and away from obscurantism. He had the courage to say in public that a female doctor using a pencil to examine a male patient (which the Muslim religious leaders wanted) was not the way to treat patients. Even at the height of his unpopularity during the Anwar-led unrest, the people, especially the Malaysian Chinese and Indians, knew they had no better alternative to Mahathir leading UMNO and the National Front. He had educated the younger Malays, opened up their minds with the vision of a future based on science and technology, especially computers and the Internet, which his Multi-media Super Corridor symbolized. The majority of all the Malays and all the Chinese and Indians in Malaysia want this future, not a turn toward extreme Islamic practices.

My view appeared to be contradicted by the results of the November 1999 general election, when Mahathir won with a two-thirds majority of the seats but lost the state governments of Kelantan and Terengganu to the PAS and some 20 incumbent UMNO MPs. I am not sure if this was caused by a shift toward a more Islamic society. The losses were accentuated by the dismissal in September 1998 of Anwar Ibrahim, his deputy prime minister and protégé of 17 years. Arrested three weeks later under the Internal Security Act, he was brought to court after two weeks with a black eye, charged with corruption, and sentenced to six years' imprisonment. Then he was further charged for sodomy. This change in the relationship between the two men, both held in high esteem, was too sudden. The unsavory disclosures that followed alienated many Malays, especially the young. Anwar's wife was able to contest and win election to Anwar's seat in Parliament.

When naming his new cabinet, Mahathir said this would be his last term. He has the time to put in place a successor capable of realizing his vision of Malaysia in the year 2020 as a modern, high-tech nation.


Three decades after separation, the close ties of families and friends still bind the two peoples. At the end of the day, however deep-seated the differences between the two, both sides know that if they lash out at each other without restraint, there is a risk of unscrambling the interracial harmony that holds each country's multiracial society together. Malaysia needs multiracial tolerance as much as Singapore does. A younger generation of leaders will soon be in charge in both countries. Free from the personal traumas of the past, they can make a fresh start at a practical, working relationship.

# 17. Indonesia: From Foe to Friend

When Indonesia faced separatist rebellions in 1957, Western arms dealers arrived in Singapore to sell weapons to rebels in Sumatra and Sulawesi. The Indonesian consul-general, Lieutenant-General Jatikusomo, met me in 1958 when I was an opposition leader. I assured him that if we became the government, these arms dealers would be expelled. When the PAP won the 1959 general election I kept this promise, and Jatikusomo—a dapper, intelligent, courteous, and active Javanese aristocrat—proposed that I consolidate our relationship with Jakarta with an official visit. I agreed.

In August 1960, my delegation and I were taken to the Merdeka Palace, once the residence of the Dutch governor-general, to meet President Sukarno. He wore a smart beige beribboned uniform and carried a field marshal's baton or swagger stick. It was a stifling, warm, and humid Jakarta morning, but neither fans nor air-conditioning were allowed in the palace; he disliked them. I could see sweat coming through his shirt onto the jacket of his uniform. I was in a lounge suit like the rest of my party, and was also sweating copiously.

He was an outstanding orator and mobilizer of people, a charismatic leader. Once, in February 1959, when I was driving from Singapore to Fraser's Hill, a seven-hour drive, I had listened to a broadcast as he addressed several hundred thousand Indonesians in central Java. I had tuned in at 8:30 A.M., then lost him for long periods because radio reception in a moving car was erratic. But three hours later, when I was in Malacca, he was still in full flow—a beautiful voice, so expressive that he had the crowds roaring and shouting with him. I had therefore looked forward to meeting the great man in person.

Sukarno did most of the talking for some 20 minutes. He spoke in Bahasa Indonesia, which is similar to Malay. He asked, "How big is your population?" "One and a half million," I replied. He had 100 million. "How many cars do you have?" "About 10,000," I said. Jakarta had 50,000. I was puzzled but readily conceded that he occupied first place in Southeast Asia in terms of size. Then he expounded his political system of "guided democracy." The Indonesian people wanted to revolutionize everything, including their economy and culture: Western democracy was "not very suitable" for them. He had said this in so many speeches before; I was disappointed by the insubstantial conversation.

The Dutch had not left many trained Indonesian administrators and professionals; there were few institutions that could carry the country forward, and three and a half years of Japanese occupation had wrecked whatever administration there was. Then the fighting between the Indonesian nationalists and the Dutch, which recurred intermittently between 1945 and 1949, when the Dutch finally conceded independence, had further damaged the economy and weakened the infrastructure. Nationalization of foreign enterprises and a nationalistic economic policy under Sukarno discouraged foreign trade and investments and impoverished this vast, sprawling republic.

We stayed at the Hotel des Indes in Jakarta, the equivalent of Raffles Hotel in Singapore. Alas, when it rained the roof leaked and as a matter of routine the staff immediately produced basins and pails to catch the dripping water. When I unthinkingly pulled the door of my bedroom to close it, not realizing that it had been latched to the wall, the plaster came away with the catch for the latch. When I came back that afternoon, the damage had been repaired—with a piece of paper that had been pasted over it and whitewashed.

When I asked Lee Khoon Choy, then parliamentary secretary at the ministry of culture, to buy me a few Indonesian-English and English-Indonesian dictionaries, they cost less than two dollars each. Many shops were nearly stripped of dictionaries by members of my Singapore party who bought them for friends learning Malay. The Indonesian rupiah was in a parlous state as a result of inflation.

From Jakarta we drove in a motorcade with motorcycle escorts to Bogor, formerly the summer resort of the Dutch governor-general, and then on to Bandung. From there, we flew to Jogjakarta, an ancient capital in central Java, in the president's personal twin-propeller aircraft, a gift from the government of the Soviet Union, and bigger than the commercial DC-3 I had flown in. The clock above the aisle had stopped, shaking my confidence in Russian technology and Indonesian maintenance. If that could happen to a clock on the presidential plane, what about moving engine parts?

Before my departure I issued a joint statement with Prime Minister Djuanda on trade and cultural matters. We had had several talks since he received me at Jakarta airport. He was an excellent man—able, highly educated, realistic, and resigned to the difficulties of his country. We had spoken for hours, sometimes in Bahasa Indonesia. During one exchange over dinner, I remarked that Indonesia was blessed with very fertile soil, a favorable climate, and abundant resources. He looked at me sadly and said, "God is for us, but we are against ourselves." I felt I could do business with a man of such honesty and sincerity. I left feeling that we had become friends. I could speak Malay and was to him more like an Indonesian *peranakan* (a local-born Chinese), not a *totok,* a Chinese-speaking Chinese recent immigrant who was less assimilated.

But as economic conditions deteriorated, Sukarno embarked on more foreign adventures. To support his diplomacy with the Afro-Asian world he had a sharp if opportunistic foreign minister in Dr. Subandrio. During 1963, Subandrio often saw me in Singapore, whenever he was in transit. As the formation of Malaysia became imminent, he began talking in arrogant terms. Sitting beside me on a settee in my office at City Hall one morning, he tapped my knee and waved his hand at the window to say, "Look at all the tall buildings in Singapore. They are all built with Indonesian money, stolen from Indonesians through smuggling. But never mind, one day Indonesia will come here and look after this country and put this right." By "smuggling," Subandrio was referring to exports through Singapore by their own merchants who evaded Indonesian taxes and foreign exchange requirements.

I understood his feelings, having seen for myself the deplorable conditions of life in Jakarta, where people washed themselves, their clothes, and their rice, and performed their natural functions in its *kali* or canals, in public; I did not dismiss his aspirations to take over Singapore as idle talk.

When we became independent in 1965, Indonesia was in "Confrontation" against Singapore and Malaysia. President Sukarno and Dr. Subandrio tried to exploit Singapore-Malaysia difficulties by offering Singapore the bait of immediate recognition on conditions that would have affronted and angered Malaysia. A turning point came several weeks later, on 30 September, with Gestapu, the Indonesian acronym for *Gerakan September Tiga Puluh* (movement of September 30), when General Suharto, leading the special forces, put down an attempted coup by their communists. With the support of troops under loyal commanders in the army, navy, air force, and police, Suharto warned the rebel military forces at the palace and at a radio and communication center to surrender peacefully. Daunted by a show of force, the rebel forces fled. It was the end of the coup.

At the time we did not realize how momentous this failed coup was, because we were too preoccupied with the gruesome murder of several senior Indonesian generals and the killing that followed of thousands (estimated at half a million), some of them ethnic Chinese, the alleged supporters of the communists. Suharto played it out slowly and subtly, like an Indonesian *wayang kulit,* a performance with puppets shown in silhouette as shadows on the screen. So carefully was this shadow play choreographed, so gradual the moves to strip Sukarno of authority, for some time we did not see that power had already shifted away from Sukarno to Suharto. For more than six months, Suharto did not oust the president, but acted in his name to keep up appearances as he quietly gathered the levers of power in his hands, removing Sukarno's supporters and weakening his position. Adam Malik, the new foreign minister, did not show any switch in policy. In March 1966, Sukarno signed a presidential decree that gave General Suharto power to take all necessary steps to guarantee security and preserve stability. I was still not sure that Sukarno was out, such was his charismatic hold on his people. It was only a year later, in February 1967, that Suharto was formally elected acting president by the national assembly.

By June 1966, Suharto was sufficiently entrenched to end Confrontation simultaneously with Singapore and Malaysia. Bilateral relations took some time to normalize. The Indonesians sent economic fact-finding missions to Singapore immediately in June and July 1966, more for public relations than for substance. In August, we reciprocated with a trade mission. There was some psychological movement forward in a so-called "$150 million handshake" when Singapore undertook to provide this initial sum in private commercial credit to Indonesian traders and allowed Bank Negara Indonesia, a state-owned bank, to reopen in Singapore. We agreed to resume two-way trade on a nondiscriminatory basis. They reopened all Indonesian ports to our ships. They promised that after they had made amendments to their laws, they would let our banks open Indonesian branches, but none were allowed to open until the 1990s. (Those that did open were unlucky. Within six years, by 1997, they were mired in Indonesia's financial crisis and the loans they had extended were at risk.)

There were underlying obstacles to the restoration of relations: misconceptions on politics, security, and economics; disagreements over maritime boundaries, sea passage, and the policing of bilateral trade. What they called "smuggling" was perfectly legal in Singapore because we were a free port. We could not act as their customs officers. We did not fully understand them and took a long time to learn to navigate our way through the labyrinths of their administration.

For some years there was no warmth in our relations and progress was slow. They had a tendency to adopt a big brother attitude. In March 1968, Adam Malik, speaking to the Indonesian community in Singapore, disclosed that he had assured me Indonesia was ready to protect Singapore against the communists after the British withdrew in 1971: "We shall protect them [200 million people of Asean] even if the threat comes from Genghis Khan." The language of the joint communiqué issued at the end of his visit was more diplomatic: "to strengthen existing ties on the basis of equality and mutual respect and non-interference in the domestic affairs of each other."

A few months later, in mid-October 1968, relations plunged disastrously when we hanged two Indonesian marine commandos who had been sentenced to death for killing three persons when they exploded a bomb in

1964 at the Hong Kong & Shanghai Bank branch in Orchard Road. (This was described in Chapter 2.) The Indonesian reaction was more violent than we had anticipated. A group of 400 uniformed students sacked our embassy in Jakarta and the ambassador's residence. The Indonesian troops guarding the embassy were conveniently absent. Foreign Minister Adam Malik appealed for calm, saying he had no wish to retaliate against Singapore!

There were popular calls for a total shipping and trade boycott and a review of bilateral relations. For five minutes, telecommunication services to Singapore were suspended. Student mobs also sacked the two remaining Singapore diplomatic residences. The passions aroused spilled over into anti-Chinese riots against their own citizens of Chinese origin, in Surabaya in central Java and Djambi in Sumatra.

By the end of October, however, matters seemed to cool down when Adam Malik warned that cutting off trade with Singapore would only harm Indonesia. He referred to the poor condition of their own port facilities and said, "We should think of our minimal ability." He expressed the hope that quarrels would not harm intra-Asean (Association of Southeast Asian Nations) harmony, and said that the international image of Indonesia would suffer. There was a partial lifting of the shipping ban, and by early November all curbs had been lifted. At the end of November a three-man Indonesian parliamentary delegation visited Singapore with a mandate to bury the hatchet.

The chill in relations thawed only very gradually. In July 1970, we sent Lee Khoon Choy as ambassador to Jakarta. K. C., as his friends called him, was a good linguist, fluent in Bahasa Indonesia, and interested in Indonesian arts and culture. He worked hard and successfully, befriending the top Indonesian generals who were Suharto's closest aides. They wanted to understand us and found him a friendly and well-connected interpreter. Gradually he established personal understanding and gained their confidence.

That September, at the Non-Aligned Summit in Lusaka, I met Suharto for the first time as we assembled for the meeting. Then I called on him at his villa to spend half an hour on pleasantries and to discuss the approach to be taken on Cambodia and Vietnam. He asked for my views on U.S. involvement in Vietnam and was a good listener. An American withdrawal, I said, would have grave implications for stability in the region. A communist victory in Vietnam and Cambodia was likely to lead to changes in Thailand which had a traditional policy of adjustment to and accommodation of new forces. He agreed with me. We found we shared some common views about developments and dangers in the region. It was a fair start for half an hour.

A major step forward was made when Major-General Sudjono Hoemardani visited me in April 1971. He believed in the supernatural and was one of Suharto's confidants on spiritual and mystical matters. When faced with big decisions, K. C. reported, Suharto would go to a special cave with Hoemardani to meditate before making up his mind. We discussed nothing significant for one hour in Bahasa Indonesia, but his note taker told K. C. that he was extremely satisfied with the meeting. Hoemardani had expected me to be "tough, snobbish, and arrogant" but instead found me "friendly, outspoken, and kind."

A year later, in March 1972, K. C. arranged for Lieutenant-General Soemitro, chief of the National Security Command, to drop in quietly without his ambassador's knowledge. He did not want his ministry of foreign affairs to know of his secret mission for the president. Soemitro, who spoke English, went straight to the point. Suharto wanted to clear doubts about Singapore's stand on certain problems and to hear from me personally.

He stated the Indonesian view on the Straits of Malacca, that the littoral states should have control over it. I said it had been international waters for centuries and that was the basis for Singapore's survival. We would go along with Indonesia and Malaysia on measures recommended by international bodies for its safety and security. But we would not want to be involved in any action to take control of the Straits or levy toll that could lead to conflict with the Russians, Japanese, and other big maritime nations. Soemitro replied that Indonesia would take measures to exert its sovereignty over the Straits, that if the Russians tried to get tough, Indonesia would not hesitate to have a confrontation. I must have looked unconvinced for he added in a serious tone that the Russians could try to occupy Indonesia and they would not succeed.

A month later Suharto sent General Panggabean, his most senior minister and general in charge of defense and security affairs, to see me.

He was a bluff, direct-speaking Sumatran Batak, his manner different from Suharto's quiet central Javanese ways.

He said Indonesia had wasted precious time that should have been put into economic development. Now the armed forces had to be subservient to the overall economic development of the country. He wanted Singapore, as the economically more advanced country, to complement their needs. I assured him we had a vested interest in seeing Indonesia develop.

They invited Keng Swee to Indonesia in October 1972, knowing he was my closest colleague. He found them less suspicious after my meetings with their three top generals. Further, regular intelligence contacts between S. R. Nathan, our head of intelligence, and his Indonesian counterpart, Lieutenant-General Sutupo Juwono, had convinced them that we shared their views on the big issues.

The stage was now set for my visit, scheduled for May 1973. It had been carefully prepared. K. C., quoting the Indonesian generals, reported "a serious emotional obstacle to sincere friendship." If there was to be genuine friendship with President Suharto, the episode over the hanging of the two marines had to be closed with a diplomatic gesture that addressed "Javanese beliefs in souls and clear conscience." They proposed that during the official wreath-laying at the Kalibata Heroes Cemetery, after paying my respects to the slain generals of the 1965 coup, I go to the graves of the two marines and scatter flowers on them. K. C. thought this the key to an improvement in relations because the Indonesian generals placed great store by this gesture. I agreed.

When I arrived on the morning of 25 May, I was greeted by a full-scale guard of honor of the army, navy, air force, and police, who were lined up for inspection, and a 19-gun salute. It signalled that a new page was to be turned. An editorial in one of their newspapers commented, "A long time seems to have been needed to take the one-hour flight from Singapore to Jakarta, after various visits to the UK, US, Europe, Japan and Taiwan. Only after having roamed the world does Lee Kuan Yew come to Indonesia for an official visit." The editor was right. I had first to demonstrate that Singapore could survive without living off the economies of Indonesia and

Malaysia. We were not parasites dependent only on our neighbors. We were linking ourselves to the industrial countries, making ourselves useful to them, manufacturing their products with their technology, exporting them worldwide. We had changed the survival equation.

The decisive meeting was with Suharto, one-on-one, what he called *empat mata* (four eyes). Just the two of us, without interpreters or note takers, we could speak frankly. My Malay was adequate for the purpose. Although I did not speak elegant Bahasa Indonesia, I understood him and could make myself understood. We talked for more than one hour.

Suharto made clear his determination to get Indonesia moving after 20 years of neglect. He said he appreciated that Singapore could assist in this Herculean task of rebuilding Indonesia and recognized the quality of the Singapore leadership. He gave me the impression that he was likely to treat us correctly, even cordially, based on a realistic assessment of the relative strengths and weaknesses of our two countries.

On my part, politely and tactfully, I made it clear that we expected to be part of Southeast Asia as of right, not on sufferance. We could not yield on fundamental interests like free passage through the Straits of Malacca. Economic cooperation must be on the basis of a fair quid pro quo, not the kind of relationship Indonesian leaders had with their Chinese *cukong*. (These "compradores" had to pander to the needs of their patrons in return for franchises or licenses on which they would become wealthy.) I said that at the heart of the relationship, the question was whether we trusted each other's long-term intentions.

He made clear that Indonesia had no claims to Singapore or Malaysia and claimed only those territories that had belonged to the Dutch East Indies. He was determined to concentrate on the development of Indonesia, not on foreign adventures. Most important of all, he distrusted the communists, especially Chinese communists, who had been the cause of much trouble in Indonesia. I said the Chinese communists were out to destroy us through their proxy, the Malayan Communist Party. I was determined that they should not succeed. I did not want China's influence to extend to Southeast Asia. That was the bull point with him. He accepted my good faith on this.

I saw in him a careful, thoughtful man, the exact opposite of Sukarno. He was no extrovert. He did not set out to impress people with his oratory or his medals, although he had many. He maintained a humble, friendly appearance, but was clearly a tough-minded man who would brook no opposition to what he set out to do. I liked him and felt that I could get on with him.

A year later, in August 1974, Suharto returned my visit. At the airport I reciprocated the welcome he had given me in Jakarta with a 21-gun salute and a 400-man guard of honor from the army, navy, air force, and police. The highlight of his visit was an exchange of documents of ratification relating to Singapore-Indonesia territorial sea boundaries. Once again the key meeting was *empat mata* with Suharto. He made his points in Bahasa Indonesia, without notes. He was so intent on expressing what was on his mind that two interruptions for tea and cakes irritated him. First was the "archipelago concept." Indonesia, like several other island nations, claimed territorial jurisdiction over all waters between its islands. Asean members must show solidarity and unity in support. (The Association of Southeast Asian Nations had been formed in August 1967 in Bangkok with Indonesia, Malaysia, Philippines, Singapore, and Thailand as members.) Then he gave an assessment of Indonesia's economic prospects and difficulties.

I replied that Singapore's predominant interest in the archipelago concept was freedom of passage. We were a part of Southeast Asia. We had been expelled from Malaysia. We had to create a new basis for our livelihood, and this required maritime lifelines to America, Japan, and Western Europe. Any impediment to free navigation would destroy us. Therefore, we could support the archipelago concept provided there was a public declaration by Indonesia on the traditional freedom of navigation. We made no claims to oil or other mineral resources on the seabed.

He asked for my views on the war in Vietnam. I said the outlook had turned pessimistic since we met a year ago. Nixon had resigned and whatever President Ford might want, the U.S. Congress was determined to slash aid to Vietnam and Cambodia by half. I doubted that these two regimes would last. He appeared sad at my bleak assessment.

I feared that instability in Thailand, after Vietnam and Cambodia became communist, would cause deep problems for Malaysia and Singapore. Singapore might be more than 75 percent Chinese but we were a part of Southeast Asia. I would not allow China or Russia to make use of us. He was clearly reassured by this.

The next day, addressing over 1,000 Indonesian nationals at his embassy, he said in the presence of the press that because of Indonesia's limited expertise his government was seeking technical help and investment capital from everywhere, including Singapore. By publicly accepting Singapore as an equal, independent state, one with a contribution to make to Indonesia's development, he had signalled a major change in attitude toward Singapore.

After the fall of Phnom Penh and Saigon, I met Suharto in September 1975 in Bali. The communists were on the ascendant and the tide looked like flowing over the rest of Southeast Asia. Razak had visited Beijing in May 1974 and established diplomatic relations. Malaysia had recognized the Khmer Rouge government in Phnom Penh immediately after they captured it. With disappointment in his voice, Suharto said he had told Razak of Indonesia's bad experiences with Beijing, referring to China's support for the Indonesian Communist Party's attempted coup in September 1965. He had said the same to Thai Prime Minister Kukrit Pramoj in Jakarta. Then Kukrit visited Beijing in June 1975, two months after the fall of Saigon, and established diplomatic relations. Suharto saw things getting worse in Malaysia and in Thailand. If Asean continued such disparate policies, each rushing on its own to give recognition to the new communist government in Vietnam and to the Khmer Rouge, he believed the will to stand up to the communists would be lost. He noted that Singapore and Indonesia held similar views and found themselves akin temperamentally. We were not overreacting by courting Indochina, or making flamboyant speeches as President Marcos had done recently in Beijing, praising that communist regime.

Although the security of Asean was uppermost in our minds, we agreed that Asean should emphasize cooperation in the economic and political field, and play down security. We would quietly cooperate, especially on intelligence. Indonesia and Singapore should consolidate their respective capabilities and wait for a more propitious time for Asean economic cooperation. He did not mention East Timor, which Indonesia was to occupy two weeks later. It was a good meeting. When faced with sudden reverses in the region, our reactions were similar.

But three months later, because Singapore abstained in a vote at the United Nations on Indonesia's occupation of East Timor, a second chill descended on our relations. Other Asean members had voted with Indonesia. Indonesia's army leaders boycotted our receptions in Jakarta for Singapore Armed Forces Day and National Day. Our counsellor in Jakarta reported that several generals said Suharto had been more angered than over the hanging of the two marines.

A year passed before personal rapport was reestablished when Suharto visited Singapore, unofficially, on 29 November 1976. I said Singapore would not put obstacles in the way of Indonesia's day-to-day relations with Timor; we accepted Timor as a part of Indonesia, but we could not publicly endorse its invasion and occupation. He accepted my position that if we had voted with Indonesia we would have sent the world a wrong signal about our own security.

What pleased him was an unrelated matter; I agreed to provide him, unofficially, with our trade statistics to help them curtail "smuggling," but asked that they should not be made public. He wanted these trade figures to be published. I explained that as our statistical classifications were different from theirs, publication would cause more misunderstanding. Suharto was confident he could manage the Indonesian press. Finally, he agreed to examine the long-term implications of publication before taking this step. Next, we agreed on a submarine telecommunication link between Singapore and Jakarta, with the technical details to be worked out by officials.

Although our meeting went well, our ambassador in Jakarta, Rahim Ishak, warned that Indonesians, both the leaders and the people, viewed Singapore as Chinese. He said Indonesian attitudes to Singapore were inextricably tied up with their feelings toward their Indonesian ethnic Chinese. Singapore, he warned, would be a convenient whipping boy whenever there was discontent in Indonesia. This proved to be prophetic when Indonesia went into crisis in 1998–1999.


It was our good fortune that the character, temperament, and objectives of President Suharto allowed me to develop good personal relations with him. He is a quiet man, courteous and punctilious on form and protocol. His character is in keeping with the way he carefully probed and assessed my position before my visit to Jakarta. After our second meeting, we had confidence in each other. As we met over the years, I found him to be a man of his word. He made few promises, but delivered whatever he had promised. His forte was his consistency. He is three years older than me, broad-faced, broad-nosed, with a somewhat taciturn expression until he got to know one, when he would smile frequently and easily. He enjoys his food, especially desserts, but made an effort to control his weight through walking and golf. Although he speaks calmly and softly, he becomes quite animated once he gets going on an important subject. He is not an intellectual, but he had the ability to select able economists and administrators to be his ministers. He chose Berkeley-educated economists like Professor Dr. Widjojo Nitisastro and Ali Wardhana, who opened up Indonesia to foreign trade and investments and gradually made it one of the successful emerging economies.

Our friendship overcame the many prejudices between Singaporeans of Chinese descent and Indonesians. Throughout the 1970s and 1980s, we met almost every year to keep in touch, exchange views, and discuss matters that cropped up. I would explain that language and culture were difficult emotional issues I had to handle sensitively. English was our common language, but the "Speak Mandarin" campaign was necessary because the Chinese in Singapore spoke more than seven different dialects. Similarly, Singaporeans of Malayan and Indonesian origin had given up Javanese, Boyanese, and Sundanese and were using only Malay. As for cheering for the Chinese badminton team against Indonesia, it was the stupidity of vociferous pro-China groups who had even booed their own Singapore ping-pong players when they played against players from China, the world champions. He accepted my view that over the long term the Chinese in Singapore would become Singaporean in outlook.

Suharto wanted to develop Batam, an island 20 kilometers (approximately 12 miles) south of Singapore and two-thirds its size, into a second Singapore. He proposed in 1976 that I help Indonesia to develop Batam. The infrastructure was inadequate and it had only a small population of fisherfolk. He sent his newly appointed adviser on technology, Dr. B. J.

Habibie, to see me. Habibie's mission was to develop Batam. I encouraged him to use Singapore as the dynamo, but explained that Batam needed the infrastructure of roads, water, power, and telecommunications, and the removal of administrative bottlenecks. If Habibie could get the Indonesian economic and trade ministers to finance this project, I promised to make the passage of goods and people between Batam and Singapore free of red tape so that Batam could plug itself into Singapore's economic power grid.

It took some years for the Indonesian press to recognize that investments in Batam had to be made by businessmen who would assess for themselves what was feasible and profitable. In Indonesia all major projects were the result of government investments, whether steel mills, petrochemicals, or cement plants. I had to explain repeatedly that the Singapore government could facilitate the movement of capital, material, and personnel between Singapore and Batam, and could encourage but not direct our entrepreneurs to invest.

I tried to persuade Suharto to allow 100 percent foreign equity ownership of investments in Batam when their products were entirely for export. When we met in October 1989, Suharto said he would allow firms producing entirely for export to have 100 percent foreign equity ownership for the initial five years, but after that they would have to divest a part of it to Indonesians. It was not as attractive as what Singapore offered but enough to draw some factories in Singapore that were feeling the pressure of our higher costs to move to Batam. One of our government-linked companies, Singapore Technologies Industrial Corporation, formed a joint venture with an Indonesian group to develop a 500-hectare industrial park in Batam and actively promoted it among MNCs as well as our own industrialists. It turned out a success. By November 1999, the park had generated US$1.5 billion of investments, employing over 74,000 Indonesians. It had continued growing in spite of the financial crisis that struck Indonesia in 1997.

This led to cooperation on the neighboring islands of Bintan and Karimun. Then Suharto proposed that we channel our 7 million annual tourists into Indonesia. Tourism cooperation spread throughout Indonesia with our airlines getting the right to fly to tourist destinations which we jointly developed.

As with most things, there was a negative side. Many of our Indonesian partners were ethnic Chinese, creating an undercurrent of resentment. We set out to find pribumi (indigenous) Indonesian partners. It was difficult because their successful entrepreneurs were ethnic Chinese, but we did manage to have joint ventures with several pribumi.

At all our meetings, Suharto and I would always make time to meet *empat mata,* when we could have uninhibited free-ranging discussions, and I would test out ideas which he could reject without any embarrassment. This made for rapport and confidence. I had assured him that we would not establish diplomatic relations with China until Indonesia had done so. So, before Singapore exchanged commercial offices with China, I met him personally to explain that this was an exchange of commercial representation to facilitate trade and did not amount to diplomatic representation. He accepted this.

By the mid-1980s, the Indonesians had swung around to the view that, far from being a supporter of China, we had in fact consistently stood up for our interests as Southeast Asians. Our economic relations had also improved. Indonesia had opened up all its ports to all ships and relaxed its rules for import and export. They no longer harbored suspicions of "smuggling" to Singapore. (Of course there were new complaints, that Indonesian traders were smuggling, from Singapore into Indonesia, electronic and other consumer durables to avoid paying high import duties. But this was an Indonesian customs problem for which we could not be blamed.) Also, Singapore's role as middleman for Indonesia's trade with China had ceased to be an issue because Indonesia had opened direct trade with China.

Good relations at the top between Suharto and me led Benny Moerdani, the Indonesian minister for defense and security in the 1980s, to propose and implement the development of the joint Siabu Air Weapons Range, near the Sumatran town of Pekan Baru, for use by our two air forces. It was officially opened by the two chiefs of defense forces in 1989, marking a milestone in our defense relations.

When I met Suharto at the funeral of Emperor Hirohito in Tokyo in February 1989, he informed me of a development that would lead Indonesia to restore diplomatic relations with China: China was prepared to state clearly and publicly that it would not interfere in Indonesia's internal affairs, either at party-to-party or government-to-government level. After Indonesia restored diplomatic ties with China in August 1990, Singapore did likewise when I visited Beijing that October.

A few days before I resigned as prime minister, I met Suharto when in Tokyo for the installation of Emperor Akihito in November 1990. His wife, Ibu Tien, was incredulous that I wanted to stand down when I was fit and healthy and three years younger than her husband. I explained that Singapore had never had a change in prime minister, and that it was better for me to leave at a time of my own choosing, when conditions were most favorable.

Our bilateral relations over the years from 1965 depended first on getting the measure of each other and learning to coexist. There were always problems to overcome, but we could resolve them, or work around them or set them aside, to be resolved later. In retrospect, an Indonesian president with a character and temperament more like Sukarno's would have been difficult to get close to and work with. Then the history of this period would have been different for Indonesia, and probably for the whole of Southeast Asia.

Suharto's wife died in April 1996. When my wife and I called on him that November, he looked bereft and forlorn. By June 1997, when we next saw him in Jakarta, he had regained his composure, but there was a significant change. His children had got closer to him. When we met Suharto's daughters at a royal wedding in Brunei on 18 August 1996, they were loaded with jewelry. Choo remarked to our ambassador's wife that she had not noticed this before. The ambassador's wife, who knew them well having spent years in Jakarta in her husband's previous posting, said that when their mother was alive she had restrained them, but after her death that restraint had gone, and they were showing off their jewels.

No one expected the Indonesian rupiah crisis. When the Thai central bank stopped defending the Thai baht on 2 July 1997, the contagion spread to all currencies of the region as panic swept fund managers into a sellout of the regions' shares and currencies. Wisely, the Indonesian finance minister called upon the International Monetary Fund (IMF) for help. Before he settled with the IMF at the end of October 1997, President Suharto, through an emissary, asked Prime Minister Goh for support to improve his bargaining position with the IMF. Goh discussed this with Finance Minister Richard Hu and me before taking it to the cabinet. We were fairly confident that the Indonesian economy was in better health than Thailand's. They had no big deficits either in their current account or budget, a modest reported foreign debt, and low inflation. So, we agreed to support them up to US$5 billion, but only after Indonesia had exhausted some US$20 billion of loans from the IMF, the World Bank, the Asian Development Bank, and their own reserves. Singapore also promised to intervene in the foreign exchange market to support the rupiah once Indonesia had reached agreement with the IMF. The IMF package for Indonesia amounted to US$40 billion. Japan also agreed to support Indonesia up to US$5 billion. Immediately after the agreement with the IMF was signed, the central banks of Indonesia, Japan, and Singapore, working in consultation, intervened to raise the value of the rupiah from 3,600 to 3,200 to the U.S. dollar. Before the crisis the rupiah had been 2,500 to the U.S. dollar.

This improvement was undermined when President Suharto reinstated some of the 14 major infrastructure projects that had been cancelled as agreed with the IMF. They included a power station in which his eldest daughter, Siti Hardiyanti Rukmana (Tutut), had an interest. Also, one of the 16 insolvent banks that had been closed (it was owned by the president's son) was allowed to be revived under a different name. The market reacted by selling off the rupiah. These 16 banks were only a small part of a much larger problem: There were over 200 banks, many of them small, poorly managed and inadequately supervised. Further, contrary to the agreement with the IMF, the monetary policy was eased. To add to the loss of confidence, the president of the Indonesian Chamber of Commerce announced that President Suharto had agreed to use the US$5 billion fund from Singapore to make low-interest loans available to indigenous companies suffering from the credit squeeze. Worse, Suharto became unwell in December 1997 after the exhaustion of his overseas travels.

Alarmed at the rapid decline of the value of the rupiah, I told our ambassador in Jakarta to ask Tutut if she could meet me in Singapore to convey my views to her father. I had last seen her in June 1997 when I called on her father in Jakarta. Prime Minister Goh and I met her in Singapore at the Istana Villa on Christmas Day, 1997. We explained the grave situation for Indonesia if confidence was not restored, first in her father's health and next in his willingness to implement the IMF conditions. I strongly urged her and her siblings to understand that international fund managers in Jakarta had focused on the economic privileges the president's children were enjoying; during this period of crisis, it was best if they withdrew completely from the market and did not engage in any new projects. I asked her point-blank whether she could get this message understood by her siblings. She answered with equal frankness that she could not. To make sure she understood the implications of market analysts' daily reports, I sent her through our ambassador in Jakarta a copy of the daily collection of important reports. To judge from the actions of the Suharto children, it had no effect on them.

On 6 January 1998, President Suharto delivered the Indonesian budget, which had not been discussed with the IMF and did not meet targets earlier agreed in the IMF package. In the next two days the Indonesian rupiah dropped from 7,500 to 10,000 to the U.S. dollar because both the IMF deputy managing director, Stanley Fischer, and the U.S. deputy secretary for the treasury, Lawrence Summers, had criticized the budget as not being in accordance with the IMF terms. At 9:00 P.M. on 8 January, I heard over the radio that in a frenzy of panic buying, crowds in Jakarta had cleaned out all shops and supermarkets to get rid of their melting rupiah and to stock up. I phoned our ambassador in Jakarta who confirmed the news, adding that a supermarket had been burnt down, and the rupiah was trading in the streets at a low of 11,500 to the U.S. dollar.

I alerted Prime Minister Goh, who immediately sent a message to the U.S. State Department and the IMF, suggesting that they issue statements to restore calm in the markets or risk disorder the following day. A few hours later, at 7:00 A.M. Singapore time, President Clinton phoned Prime Minister Goh to discuss the latest situation and then spoke to President Suharto. Clinton announced that he was sending Summers to help sort out the problems. Meanwhile, Fischer issued a statement that the reaction was excessive. This flurry of activity held out hopes of a possible solution and stopped what would have ended in riots and disorder.

On 15 January, President Suharto himself signed a second IMF package stipulating more reforms.

On 9 January 1998, a few days before that second agreement, Suharto's second daughter, Siti Hediati Hariyadi Prabowo (Titiek), the wife of Major-General Prabowo Subianto, commander of Kopassus (their red beret forces for special operations), saw me in Singapore. She came with her father's knowledge; she wanted our help to raise U.S. dollar bonds in Singapore. An international banker had said the dollars raised would help stabilize the rupiah. I said that in the present crisis atmosphere, when the market had doubts about the rupiah, the failure of a bond issue would cause a further loss of confidence. Then she complained of rumors from Singapore that had weakened the rupiah, and added that our bankers were encouraging Indonesians to park their money here. Could we stop it? I explained that this would be totally ineffective since Indonesians could get their money out of Indonesia to anywhere in the world by a touch of the computer key. Moreover, rumors could not affect the rupiah if the fundamentals were strong. To restore market confidence, her father had to be seen to implement the IMF reforms. If he felt that some conditions were impractical or too harsh, then he could invite a person such as Paul Volcker, the former U.S. Federal Reserve chairman, to be their adviser. The IMF was likely to listen seriously to arguments from Volcker. That message got through—a banker told me later that Volcker did go to Jakarta, but after meeting Suharto left without becoming an adviser.

Suharto's problems had been compounded by the increasing intrusion of his children into all lucrative contracts and monopolies. The IMF targeted several of them for dismantling, including the clove monopoly and a national car monopoly run by his son Tommy, the power station contract to his daughter Tutut, and banking licenses to other sons, to name just a few. Suharto could not understand why the IMF wanted to interfere with his internal affairs. In fact, these monopolies and concessions had become major issues with the fund managers. Also, his top technocrats saw Indonesia's financial crisis as an opportunity to dismantle practices that had weakened the economy and increased dissatisfaction. Most of all, the IMF was aware that the U.S. Congress would not vote for more funds to replenish its coffers if it did not stop these practices.

The crucial factor that affected the outcome was America's view, which Summers expressed to my prime minister and me on 11 January 1998, in Singapore, on his way to Indonesia. What was needed, he said, was a "discontinuity" in the way Suharto conducted his government. The privileges for his family and friends had to stop. There should be a level playing field. I pointed out that it was best to have continuity for no successor president could be as strong as Suharto to enforce the tough conditions the IMF required. So we should help Suharto implement IMF conditions and work toward the optimum outcome, namely get the president to appoint a vice president who would restore the confidence of the market in the future of post-Suharto Indonesia. This view was not shared by the Clinton administration. They were adamant on the need for democracy and an end to corruption and human rights violations. The Cold War was over. They saw no reason to "mollycoddle" Suharto (Clinton's words in his 1992 campaign).

Two months later, in March 1998, former U.S. Vice President Walter Mondale carried a message from Clinton to Suharto. He then met Prime Minister Goh and me in Singapore on his way home. After comparing notes on Suharto's likely course of action on reforms, Mondale tossed this question at me: "You knew Marcos. Was he a hero or a crook? How does Suharto compare to Marcos? Is Suharto a patriot or a crook?" I felt Mondale was making up his mind on Suharto's motivations before submitting his recommendations to his president. I answered that Marcos might have started off as a hero but ended up as a crook. Suharto was different. His heroes were not Washington or Jefferson or Madison, but the sultans of Solo in central Java. Suharto's wife had been a minor princess of that royal family. As the president of Indonesia, he was a megasultan of a megacountry. Suharto believed his children were entitled to be as privileged as the princes and princesses of the sultans of Solo. He did not feel any embarrassment at giving them these privileges, because it was his right as a megasultan. He saw himself as a patriot. I would not classify Suharto as a crook.

Prime Minister Goh visited Suharto three times, in October 1997 and January and February 1998, to explain that Indonesia's economy was in serious crisis and he had to take IMF reforms seriously or the market would sell off his currency and stocks and cause a collapse. When he came back from his final meeting in February 1998 he told me that Suharto acted as if he was under siege, believing that the West wanted him out. Goh had expressed concern to Suharto that if economic conditions worsened, there would be food shortages, social unrest, and a loss of confidence in Indonesia. The president would then face grave difficulties. Hence it was important to stabilize the economy with IMF support. Suharto's response was a confident assertion that the army was fully behind him. Goh hinted that there could be circumstances in which the people would be so hungry that the soldiers would not shoot. Suharto dismissed this possibility. He was sadly out of touch. At that time, one Indonesian general had said (this was reported in March by the U.S. ambassador to ours), "If the students were a thousand, they will be clobbered. If they were 10,000, ABRI will try to control the crowd. But if they were 100,000, ABRI will join the ranks of the students."

Several further actions that President Suharto took caused Indonesia's currency and stocks to slide downward in spite of his signing a second IMF agreement in January 1998. Later that month, news in the Indonesian press of the president's criteria for the post of vice president led people to believe that B. J. Habibie was the favored candidate. He was known for high-cost, high-tech projects like the building of airplanes. Several foreign leaders were worried by this and went to see Suharto, quietly, to advise against such a choice. They included the former Australian prime minister, Paul Keating, whom Suharto considered a good friend, Prime Minister Goh, and Malaysian Deputy Prime Minister Anwar Ibrahim. Daim Zainuddin, economic adviser to the Malaysian government, wrote to me at the end of January 1998 to ask me to see Suharto and persuade him against this appointment of Habibie because the president's ministers had said that Suharto needed to be advised by his neighbors. I could not go to Jakarta in the middle of a crisis and be seen to interfere. Instead I took a calculated risk and, in a speech on 7 February in Singapore, cautioned, "The market was disturbed by his [President Suharto's] criteria for the vice president that required a mastery of science and technology, announced shortly after the second IMF agreement. . . . If the market is uncomfortable with whoever is the eventual vice president, the rupiah would weaken again." Although I had not referred to him by name, Habibie's supporters attacked me for this statement.

When Suharto proceeded with the appointment, fund managers and foreign exchange dealers reacted as expected. They sold the rupiah short, and it skidded to 17,000 rupiah to the U.S. dollar, dragging down the regional currencies and stock markets.

In early February 1998, Bambang, the president's son, brought Steve Hanke, an American economics professor from Johns Hopkins University, to meet Suharto to advise him that the simple answer to the low exchange value of the rupiah was to install a currency board. While he publicly toyed with the currency board idea, the rupiah seesawed. The market was losing confidence in a president hitherto well regarded for his experience and judgment.

Suharto's last major military and ministerial appointments in February and March 1998 were the most disastrous misjudgments of his life. He appointed B. J. Habibie as vice president because, as he said 48 hours before he resigned, nobody would want Habibie as president. Suharto believed that no one in Indonesia and no foreign power would conspire to remove him if they knew Habibie would then be president. His golfing partner, Bob Hasan, a timber baron, was made minister for trade and industry, and his daughter Tutut, minister for social welfare. Nearly all the others appointed as ministers were loyalists either to him or his children. The most grievous error of all was his balancing act in appointing General Wiranto as chief of the armed forces while promoting his son-in-law Prabowo Subianto to be lieutenant-general and chief of Kostrad (the Strategic Forces). He knew that Prabowo was bright and ambitious, but impetuous and rash.

I had met Prabowo at two lunches in Jakarta, in 1996 and 1997. He was quick but inappropriate in his outspokenness. On 7 February 1998, he saw me and Prime Minister Goh separately in Singapore to deliver a strange message, that the Chinese in Indonesia were at risk because in any trouble—riots—they would be hurt as a minority, and Sofyan Wanandi, a well-known successful Indonesian Chinese businessman active in politics, was in grave danger as a "double minority," a Chinese and a Catholic. Sofyan had said to him and several other generals that President Suharto had to step down. When I expressed my disbelief, Prabowo insisted

Sofyan did say this, and that the Chinese Catholics were a danger to themselves. Both the prime minister and I puzzled over why he should want to tell us this about Sofyan when it was patently unlikely that any Indonesian would tell the president's son-in-law that the president should be forced to step down. We wondered if he was preparing us for something that would happen soon to Sofyan and other Chinese Indonesian businessmen.

On 9 May 1998, Admiral William Owens, a recently retired vicechairman of the U.S. Joint Chiefs of Staff, saw me in Singapore. He told me of the strange statements Prabowo had made when they met in Jakarta the day before. Over lunch, in the presence of his two young aides, both lieutenant-colonels, one a doctor, Prabowo said in effect that "the old man may not last nine months, maybe he'll die." In a happy mood, celebrating his promotion to three stars and head of Kostrad, he joked about talk going around that he himself might attempt a coup. Owens said that although Prabowo had known him for two years, he was nonetheless a foreigner. I said Prabowo had a reckless streak in him.

For several months from January 1998, student protests were confined to their campuses where faculty members and former ministers and generals openly addressed them to add their voices to the demand for reforms. To show he was in complete control, Suharto left ostentatiously in the middle of a crisis, on 9 May 1998, to attend a conference in Cairo. Inevitably the students took their demonstrations to the streets and after several clashes with riot police, on 12 May six students of Trisakti University were shot as they retreated into their campus. The outrage that followed led to a complete collapse of law and order as police and soldiers surrendered the city to mobs that rampaged, looted, and burned ethnic Chinese shops and homes and raped their women. It was general knowledge that the rioting was engineered by Prabowo's men. He wanted to show up Wiranto as incompetent, so that on Suharto's return from Cairo, he (Prabowo) would be made chief of the armed forces. By the time he returned from Cairo on 15 May, Suharto's position was lost.

One after another, the closest and most loyal of his aides and ministers deserted him after his most obedient of subordinates, Harmoko, whom he had appointed Speaker of the national assembly, publicly demanded his resignation. The drama ended on 21 May at 9:00 A.M. when Suharto appeared on television to announce his resignation and B. J. Habibie was sworn in as president.

What started as an economic problem needing an IMF rescue had ended in the overthrow of the president. It was an immense personal tragedy for a leader who had turned an impoverished Indonesia of 1965 into an emerging tiger economy, educated his people, and built the infrastructure for Indonesia's continued development. At this crucial moment, the man who had been so good at judging and choosing his aides had chosen the wrong men for key positions. His mistakes proved disastrous for him and his country.

Suharto never contemplated exile. The fortunes he and his family had were invested in Indonesia. The American journalist who had reported in *Forbes* magazine that the Suharto family had US$42 billion of assets, told me in New York in October 1998 that the bulk of it was in Indonesia. After the Indonesian meltdown, he estimated them to be worth a mere US$4 billion. Unlike Marcos of the Philippines, Suharto did not spirit his wealth outside his country in readiness for a quick exit. He remained in his home in Jakarta. After 32 years as the president, he was not about to run away. I did not understand why his children needed to be so rich. But for their excesses he would have had a different place in Indonesia's history.

General Benny Moerdani, his trusted, loyal, and long-serving head of the armed forces intelligence agency and later commander in chief of the armed forces, told me in the late 1980s that he had advised Suharto to rein in his children's endless demands for more business privileges. Had he listened to Moerdani, Suharto would not have had this tragic end.

I watched a telecast of his resignation. He deserved a more graceful exit. Suharto had concentrated his energies on stability and the economy. His policies created the conditions for strong economic growth from the 1970s to the 1990s in all Asean countries. They were golden years for Southeast Asia.

Although a president by accident, Habibie believed it was his destiny to rule Indonesia. He is highly intelligent, but mercurial and voluble. In the *Asian Wall Street Journal* (4 August 1998) he described his working style as "parallel processing on 10 to 20 issues," comparing himself to a computer. He also complained that when he took office on 21 May 1998, he received congratulations from many nations by the next day, but Singapore did not send theirs until "almost June, very late. It's OK with me, but there are 211 million people [in Indonesia]. Look at the map. All the green [area] is Indonesia. And that red dot is Singapore. Look at that." (Singapore had sent its congratulations on 25 May.) A few days later Prime Minister Goh responded in his National Day Rally speech that Singapore had only the resources of 3 million people and there were limits to what "a little red dot" like Singapore could do for its neighbors.

We knew Habibie well because he had been in charge of Batam's cooperation with Singapore. He was against the Chinese Indonesians and by extension against Singapore with its Chinese majority. He wanted to treat us as he did his Chinese Indonesian *cukong,* to be pressured and milked. This would change the basis upon which Suharto and I had cooperated as equal, independent states to an *abang-adik* (big brother–little brother) relationship. But privately, Habibie sent repeated messages to the prime minister to visit him in Jakarta and also invited Loong (the deputy prime minister) and his wife for dinner. He wanted Singapore's leaders to be seen to support him, in the belief, we were told, that Chinese Indonesian business leaders would then have confidence in him and invest. We did not see how that would result from such visits.

Two days after his reported outburst, he gave an 80-minute lecture to Teo Chee Hean, our minister for education and second minister for defense. Teo had delivered humanitarian aid to Jakarta, to General Wiranto, the Indonesian armed forces commander. In Teo's words:

Habibie was animated, his arms waving about as the expression on his face and the tone of his voice changed rapidly. He could hardly sit still, sounding passionate and looking agitated. Habibie alternated between highlighting his achievements, his special qualities, and making thinly veiled threats against Singapore. He recounted that he had lived for 25 years in Europe, from the age of 18, and had acquired values such as "democracy and human rights."

Habibie wanted Singapore to know its place and realise its vulnerability. So he proceeded to point out how "Singapore lies inside [Indonesia]." Jumping up from his seat to dash over to the map on the wall, he stretched out both arms to emphasise the green expanse of Indonesia surrounding the 'red dot' that was Singapore.

Later, on the night of 27 January 1999, as I was leaving for Davos, I was startled to hear the news on radio that Habibie had decided East Timor would be given the right to choose between full autonomy and independence. It was a sudden reversal of a policy Indonesia had strenuously upheld since 1976, that the incorporation of East Timor into Indonesia was irreversible.

In Davos, I met Stanley Roth, the shrewd, constantly travelling and indefatigable U.S. assistant secretary of state for East Asian and Pacific affairs. We agreed that Habibie's offer, once made, had permanently changed the equation, and independence for East Timor could be expected. Roth's dry comment was that prime ministers should not be so free in writing letters, especially to a president like Habibie. (Both of us had read reports that Habibie's decision had been triggered off by a letter from Australian Prime Minister John Howard, proposing a referendum for the East Timorese to decide their future.)

Shortly after this announcement on East Timor, on 4 February 1999, Mah Bow Tan, our minister for communications, called on Habibie who recounted how the Australian ambassador had informed him of the "New Caledonia" approach: to organize a referendum and be prepared to grant independence after a 15-year period of preparation. Habibie had told the Australian ambassador that Indonesia was not prepared for this approach. It had gained nothing in terms of natural resources, human resources, or gold from East Timor, and the Australians did not have the right to insist that Indonesia grant autonomy or the right of self-determination to East Timor.

"The world doesn't understand and always character-assassinates us," Habibie said to Mah. He was "fed up and tired" of this and had asked his cabinet to study the possibility of releasing East Timor—give them a choice, autonomy or independence. Should they refuse to accept autonomy but at the same time seek Indonesian help to prepare for independence, then he would have to say "sorry." He was not prepared to be East

Timor's "rich uncle." He had asked the ambassador to convey this to Australian Prime Minister John Howard. Hence the letter from Howard to him in January 1999 had contained Habibie's ideas on East Timor. When he received it, he had immediately scribbled at the sides of the relevant paragraphs commending the idea to his cabinet. Thus was set in motion a chain of events that marked a turning point in the history of Indonesia.

I had confirmation of the manner in which he decided on East Timor when I met Ginandjar Kartasasmita, the able Indonesian coordinating minister for economic affairs, on an aircraft from Singapore to Zurich, the night of the announcement. We were seated across the aisle from each other, both headed for the World Economic Forum in Davos, and got into an hour-long discussion of economic and political developments in Indonesia. But uppermost on his mind was East Timor. He recounted how the decision had been taken after the matter was raised for the first time in cabinet only that afternoon, based on Habibie's memo. The discussion lasted two hours after which all ministers including General Wiranto, the defense minister, agreed to the president's proposal. He asked with a trace of anxiety in his voice if it would have other consequences for Indonesia. I replied diplomatically that I could not say for sure but that it was a most significant policy change.

Habibie's advisers had believed this offer of autonomy or independence to East Timor would win him financial support from the IMF and the World Bank, and acclaim in the United States and the European Union as a democrat and a reformer. This would help his reelection. In fact he had agitated his generals, many of whom had spent years pacifying East Timor. Ginandjar told Prime Minister Goh in Auckland during an APEC (Asia Pacific Economic Cooperation) meeting in August that they had made a mistake in February 1999 in arming the militias. The intention had been to "persuade" the East Timorese not to vote for independence. When the East Timorese did so by an overwhelming majority of 80 percent out of nearly 99 percent of votes cast, East Timor was torched and devastated, ostensibly by the militias. Habibie's standing as an Indonesian nationalist was damaged, and the reputation of the Indonesian armed forces and the government suffered.

To help Habibie win reelection, his team of advisers had presented him as a reformer who wanted a break with the past. He released political detainees. He allowed over 50 political parties to be registered instead of the three under Suharto. He also met the press frequently and spoke freely, too freely. His choreographers reined him in and put him on a tight leash, stopping him from ad-libbing. He needed money to get support. Officials expected major changes after the elections. Fearful of being transferred out to jobs with fewer opportunities for bribes, they made the most of this interregnum. There was more corruption at all levels than during the worst of the Suharto years. The opportunities for graft were immense because many banks and large companies were insolvent and depended on government rescue schemes, opening them to pressure. One of these was Bank Bali where some US$70 million had been siphoned off by Habibie's closest associates. The IMF and the World Bank withheld funds for Indonesia until a thorough audit had been made and the wrong-doers punished. Habibie blocked the publication of the auditor's report on the grounds that it breached Indonesia's banking secrecy rules. The Indonesian media reported that the money had been traced to members of his family.

Nevertheless, for his presidential bid he mobilized all the support his Muslim reputation and presidential patronage could muster. He had aides who put a spin on his wobbly performance. He refused to give up in spite of pressure from the media, leaders of opposition political parties, and his own Golkar party. He said he was not a coward. He would only withdraw when he was rejected by the MPR (People's Consultative Assembly). He was. In the early hours of 20 October, the MPR rejected his accountability speech by 355 votes to 322. Those familiar with wheeling and dealing in Indonesian politics told me that they had never seen so much money pass to so many MPR representatives in so short a time. Habibie gave up the fight.

Habibie's withdrawal from the contest led to dramatic last-minute changes in alliances that affected the fortunes of the two main contenders for the presidency, Abdurrahman Wahid, or Gus Dur (elder brother Dur) as his followers affectionately called him, and Megawati Sukarnoputri. Gus Dur is the leader of the Nahdlatul Ulama, a traditional rural-based

Muslim organization with 30 million members. His PKB (National Awakening Party) had won 12.6 percent of the votes in the June election. Megawati, daughter of President Sukarno, led the PDI-P (Indonesian Democratic Party-Struggle) at tumultuous mass rallies to win the largest single block of 34 percent of the votes, beating Habibie (Golkar) by a wide margin. However, in the People's Consultative Assembly of 695 (of whom 200 were not elected by the electorate), at 4:00 P.M. on 20 October, Gus Dur was declared the president, winning by 373 against Megawati's 313 votes. Frenetic political maneuvring began and ended only at 3:00 P.M. the following day when the assembly started to vote for the vice president. Three candidates, Akbar Tanjung of Golkar, Wiranto, chief of the Indonesian armed forces, the TNI (Tentara Nasional Indonesia), and Hamzah Haz of the Islamic coalition had entered the contest. Megawati was reluctant to stand, fearing another humiliation. Gus Dur spent much time to persuade her and finally assured her of the support of enough parties to win. He needed her as vice president to establish his legitimacy as president. Meanwhile, violence and arson had broken out in several cities in Java and Bali where she had won nearly all the votes.

Fortuitously, Stanley Roth was in Singapore at that time to address a meeting of the World Economic Forum. He met Prime Minister Goh and me at 8:00 P.M., hours after Gus Dur had been elected president. We were as convinced as he was that Indonesia could not avoid bloodshed and more turmoil if Megawati was cheated of the vice presidency by political chicanery in the People's Consultative Assembly. Both sides resolved to do what we could to let the key Indonesian players know the effect on international investor confidence if this should happen.

On 22 October, the *Jakarta Post* reported that the U.S. secretary of state, Madeleine Albright (then in Africa), had phoned Gus Dur early the day before to "convey Washington's view" that Megawati should be elected vice-president. Megawati won convincingly by over 396 votes to 284. That saved Indonesia from a second round of disorder.

The end result was the best in the circumstances. Gus Dur, the new president, had lost his eyesight. He had suffered two strokes in 1998, but was sufficiently alert and nimble on 20 October to move swiftly to maximize his chances. After Habibie's accountability speech had been rejected by the People's Consultative Assembly, Gus Dur garnered most of the pro-Muslim votes that would have gone to Habibie. Within a week of his election, he quickly appointed a cabinet for national reconciliation in which all major political parties and the armed forces were represented. It may not be the most efficient government because of the wide power sharing, but it may help to heal the wounds self-inflicted in 17 months of bloody clashes: pribumi against Chinese, Muslims against Christians, Dayaks and Malays against Madurese, Acehnese separatists against the Indonesian military. Gus Dur and Megawati have two daunting tasks: to repair the social fabric of Indonesian society and restart the economy.

During the Suharto era, to avoid misunderstanding with the president or his aides, we did not meet Indonesian opposition leaders. Unlike the Americans and West Europeans, we did not cultivate Suharto's opponents—Megawati Sukarnoputri, Amien Rais, or even Gus Dur. Our close ties were with Suharto's ministers and the TNI. They, especially Ali Alatas, the foreign minister, and General Wiranto, the defense minister and TNI commander, helped to stabilize bilateral relations during Habibie's presidency. However, between January and April 1999, S. R. Nathan, then director of the Institute of Defence and Strategic Studies (IDSS), later, from September 1999, our president, invited Indonesian political party leaders to address his institute, with full local and international media coverage. During their visits, Singapore ministers met the speakers at lunches and dinners to understand their position and establish rapport. In this way, we got to know Gus Dur (later president), Megawati Sukarnoputri (later vice president), Amien Rais (later chairman of the People's Consultative Assembly), and Marzuki Darusman of Golkar (later attorney general in Gus Dur's cabinet).

This had angered Habibie and his aides who publicly expressed displeasure at our interfering in their internal affairs. IDSS pointed out that it had invited Golkar representatives to speak; Marzuki Darusman had done so, and IDSS had repeatedly invited Golkar's chairman, Akbar Tanjung, who had not been able to come. This did not placate Dr. Dewi Fortuna Anwar, Habibie's foreign policy adviser. She accused Singapore of being pro-Megawati.

I had met Gus Dur in Jakarta in 1997 when he addressed a private meeting where he explained the role of Islam in Indonesia and assured investors that it was not of the Middle East variety. He was a good speaker, fluent in English, well-read in Arabic, and highly intelligent. It did not occur to me then that he would become president and inherit Suharto's Indonesia after a Habibie interregnum.

The night he was sworn in as president, both Prime Minister Goh and I sent him our congratulations. We did not want any doubts about our support for their new president.

Soon after his election, he summoned all Asean ambassadors to inform them that he would visit all the Asean states beginning with Singapore. Addressing our ambassador, Edward Lee, he said pointedly, "Indonesia wants good relations with Singapore and hopes Singapore will support its recovery." He went on to explain his vision of the future: China, India, and Indonesia, three of the world's most populous countries, would come together; Japan and Singapore would provide financial and technological support. Then Asia would be less dependent on the West.

Before he came to Singapore, his foreign minister, Dr. Alwi Shihab, an able and practical man who had been a businessman and also a visiting professor of divinity at an American college, called on Edward Lee at the Singapore embassy to demonstrate that Indonesia was not taking a big brother attitude but wanted sincere cooperation. Edward Lee assured him that Singapore would help, but that there were limits to the financial and technological capabilities of 3 million Singaporeans. Singapore did not have the resources of America or Japan to restart the Indonesian economy. Alwi Shihab told him that we could act as a catalyst to bring back confidence to Indonesia. Hence, my first meeting with Gus Dur as president of Indonesia was warm and constructive.

Prime Minister Goh met President Gus Dur at the airport on 6 November 1999, and had good discussions before and during lunch. Then, before a packed audience of 500 businesspeople and diplomats, Gus Dur gave an impressive display of his political grasp and the skills expected of the new president of Indonesia in an era of greater openness and accountability. When I called on him, he invited me to be a member of his international advisory council for Indonesia's economic recovery, an honor I could not refuse. He talked of ethical standards and clean government. I said if he expected his ministers to be honest, they had to be paid so that they could live up to their status without corruption. His coordinating minister for economy, finance, and industry, Kwik Kian Gie, who was present, told George Yeo, our minister-in-attendance, that he had just discussed this sensitive issue with his president, sensitive because they could afford this only for top people, not across the board.

We had an *empat mata* meeting for an unrestrained discussion. His vitality in spite of his age, two strokes, and a hectic morning was reassuring. His sense of humor was never absent. His demeanor was that of a president in complete command of the situation. The Muslim parties that had elected him would become more realistic by having to deal with the problems and through interaction with him. They would not be the same after five years. He wanted the prime minister and me to receive his vice president, Megawati, and help her gain as much experience as possible. He said he had a good relationship with General Wiranto, and a clear view of how the military's role should gradually evolve. He knew that there were many incompatibles in the cabinet, especially in the finance and economics sectors. These problems would be sorted out. He was determined to make the government coherent and consistent.

His sense of humor was matched by a realistic appreciation of self. He joked, "The first president of Indonesia [Sukarno] was crazy about women; the second president [Suharto] was crazy about money; the third president [Habibie] was just crazy." His daughter who accompanied him asked, "What about the fourth president?" Without missing a beat, he said, "*Wayang*" (a performance, theater). In one word, he summed up his role in Indonesia. He was confident he could play the part of president of Indonesia in the new era of openness to the media and the NGOs (nongovernment organizations) that wanted *reformasi* and *democrasi.*

However, Indonesia has undergone a sea change. Power is no longer centralized in the hands of a president backed by an all-powerful ABRI, the armed forces. The election had thrown up a large number of small Islamic parties but together they did not form the majority. Megawati's party won 34 percent of the votes, the largest single bloc. Amien Rais, leader of a Muslim party with 7 percent of the votes, skillfully cobbled together a coalition of Muslim parties into a "Middle Axis" that made deals with other groups and won him the speakership of the People's Consultative Assembly against Megawati's candidate. The Middle Axis also blocked Megawati from the presidency by voting for Gus Dur, a traditional Muslim leader of central and east Java. Although a Muslim cleric, Gus Dur is acceptable to the nationalists because he has always stood for the separation of religion (including Islam) from the state. However, he was elected president only because of the votes of Muslims in the Middle Axis. Suharto had kept Islam in check until the late 1980s when he started to cultivate the Muslims to counter ABRI's influence. Habibie, as president, actively nurtured and helped them mobilize support for his reelection. Having entered the corridors of power, political Islam is now a major force in Indonesia and will remain so. The challenge for Indonesia is how to maintain a balance that will enable its people of diverse races and religions to unite as one nation based on the credo of their founding father, President Sukarno, *Bhinneka Tunggal Ika* (unity in diversity), enshrined in their national crest.

## 18. Building Ties with Thailand, the Philippines, and Brunei

My early impressions of the Thais were gathered from stopovers in Bangkok on the way to and from London in the 1950s. Later, on visits accompanying the Tunku in 1962–1963, I was impressed by the quality of the men in charge of their foreign policy. The Thai foreign ministry recruited their brightest and best, educated in British, European, and Latin American universities. It was their glamor service, highly paid and much respected because of their foreign travels at a time when travel was rare. Their domestic administrators did not match the quality of their foreign service officers. They needed their best to fend off encroachments by the British from Burma and by the French from Indochina. Thailand is the only Southeast Asian country that has never been colonized.

I met Prime Minister Field Marshal Thanom Kittikachorn in Bangkok in 1966. He was a staunch supporter of U.S. intervention in Vietnam, but by January 1973, he told me that he believed a total U.S. withdrawal from Indochina was inevitable in the long run. He wanted to see the region united by having the Indochinese countries—North and South Vietnam, Laos, and Cambodia, and also Burma, brought into Asean, but only after a genuine ceasefire by North Vietnam.

Thanom was not a complex man. He was loyal to his friends and allies. He treated me as his friend and we exchanged views frankly and freely. He was worried because of the support Thailand had given the Americans, including the use of huge air bases from which the U.S. Air Force had bombed North Vietnam—Vietnamese enmity and retribution were not to be lightly dismissed. He lamented the fact that the Americans were fighting with one hand tied behind their backs; they attacked North Vietnam only by air and fought a defensive war in South Vietnam, a no-win strategy. All they could hope for was not to lose. The Thais were adjusting to new realities.

In October that year, large demonstrations in Bangkok demanding a more democratic constitution led to Thanom's departure for the United States. He and his wife were thoroughly unhappy living in an apartment in Boston. They missed the warm tropics, their friends and relatives, and most of all their spicy Thai food.

In December 1974, Thanom flew back to Bangkok without notice. The Thai government wanted to send him back to the United States, but he refused to leave unless his ailing father accompanied him to a destination closer than America. I agreed at the Thai government's request to let Thanom take up residence in Singapore, but made it a condition that he refrain from political activities during his stay. I thought it a plus if Singapore could become a neutral sanctuary like Switzerland in Europe.

When I had him, his wife, daughter, and son-in-law, who had been with him in Boston, to dinner, he recounted the woes of being an exile in the unaccustomed cold of New England, the sense of isolation, and neighbors who complained of the pungent smells of Thai curries. In Singapore he received an endless stream of relatives and friends and our lifestyle was not too alien. But the Thai government (through the embassy staff and other officials in Singapore) kept a watchful eye for possible politicking by his Thai visitors and him.

Thanom returned to Bangkok two years later in a monk's robe, publicly declaring that he wanted to enter a monastery, and was welcomed by some members of the Thai royal family. Time had moved on, and Thanom never returned to power, but he did persuade the Thai government to return a good part of his assets which had been frozen or confiscated. This was the Thai way, never a brutal, total confrontation if a compromise was possible. Forgiving is an essential part of Buddhism.

A general election had been held earlier, in 1975, when Kukrit Pramoj, a traditional monarchist, became prime minister. He headed a coalition in which his Social Action Party had only 18 of the 140 seats.

Thailand needed him to deal with the impending North Vietnamese victory over the South. I found him shrewd and philosophical, with a keen if mischievous and malicious sense of humor. But he could be frivolous. Articulate, with expressive hands and face, he did not strike me as a man with a serious political purpose. He had acted as the prime minister in the Hollywood production *The Quiet American*. A divorcé, he lived well in a large, attractive, old-style Thai teakwood house in central Bangkok, where he entertained me to dinner alfresco.

As a formulator of policy, Kukrit worried me. I visited him in Bangkok on 17 April 1975, a week after the Khmer Rouge captured Phnom Penh and two weeks before Saigon fell. He did not have much to say about Thailand's position. Our ambassador, who had been brought up in Thailand and knew their leaders and their culture, thought they were still groping for a new foreign policy. I could not have visited them at a more tense moment. Kukrit said the U.S. bases should go within a year. He was no longer sure of the United States, and their presence, being more of a "target" than a "deterrent," compromised and embarrassed Thailand. I said we should not write off the United States. The U.S. Congress would change its attitude as developments overtook them. Singapore's view was that the presence of the U.S. Seventh Fleet made our relations with China and the Soviet Union easier. Without it, the Russian influence would be overpowering. When the Soviets wanted Singapore to allow them to store oil for their fishing fleet on one of our outer islands, we had told them to buy from the American oil companies in Singapore. If there were no Seventh Fleet, we would not be able to give them such a reply.

Two weeks after Kukrit visited Beijing in early July, he came to Singapore. He had received a North Vietnamese delegation in Bangkok. He said that the "domino theory" had been realized in French Indochina, and that the North Vietnamese wanted to be the ruler of all Indochina. I asked why Radio Hanoi was so hostile toward Thailand when their government was extending the hand of friendship. Their tactics, Kukrit said, were to coerce and frighten the Thais into establishing diplomatic relations, and they wanted the world to see that Thailand was frightened. He described his meeting with the leader of the North Vietnamese delegation to Bangkok: He did not appear to be arrogant, said they should let "bygones be bygones," and embraced him warmly when they met. Kukrit said he "shivered in the embrace." They were cold in their smiles and there was a distinct drop in temperature when the five of them sat in a room. The leader was relaxed but the rest merely sat stiffly. They pressed their claim for the return of South Vietnamese aircraft that had been flown from Vietnam to Thailand in the days before the fall of Saigon.

Kukrit's view was that we (Asean) had to be strong and firm and play "big brother to the Indochinese countries." We could help them, every now and then, in ways that would be sufficient to keep them just beyond the point of starvation. We had to show our affluence, strength, and solidarity, and occasionally ask them to join in song and dance festivals. His view on the North Vietnamese had become more robust after meeting them in Bangkok, but, more important, after his visit to China. The Thais were quick and nimble when it came to protecting their sovereignty.

He related to me what Zhou Enlai told him about me: "I am surprised at him [referring to me]. He is of my own blood. Why is he afraid of China taking over Singapore? His greater problem is to prevent the Chinese from returning to Singapore." I asked Kukrit to tell Zhou that I had no worry about the Chinese returning to Singapore, or about the Chinese in Singapore wanting to return to China, or about China taking over Singapore. Singapore was too small for China and the problems it would create would not make it worthwhile. My concern was over the messages of congratulations China sent to the Malayan Communist Party and the Indonesian Communist Party on their anniversaries. These aroused great antipathy and animosity in Kuala Lumpur and Jakarta, and I did not want that animosity reflected toward me just because I had the same blood as Zhou Enlai. I asked rhetorically whether China could help Singapore if it clashed with Indonesia. Kukrit, in a mischievous moment, disclosed this to the Bangkok press.

Our relations with the Thais became closer after the Vietnamese attacked Cambodia in December 1978. General Kriangsak, the Thai prime minister then, had no experience in foreign affairs. His foreign minister, Dr. Upadit Pachariyangkun, was an able man, highly intelligent and German-educated, but his experience did not extend to dealing with invading Vietnamese. It was a critical moment for them when the Vietnamese offered not to come within 20 kilometers (about 12 miles) of the Thai border if Thailand would stay neutral and not condemn Vietnam's attack against Cambodia. I sent Kriangsak a letter through Rajaratnam, my foreign minister, urging him not to agree. If he did, and the Vietnamese subsequently breached their undertaking, he would have no standing internationally to attack Vietnam. It was better to warn the international community of the threat the Vietnamese posed to the rest of Southeast Asia now. I believe the Chinese must have assured him that they would stand by him if Thailand was attacked because Kriangsak took a stand, protested against the invasion, and gave sanctuary to the retreating Cambodian forces and tens of thousands of refugees.

Kriangsak was not as sharp-witted as Kukrit. He got into power because he was commander in chief of the Thai army. He was prone to worrying, especially over the fallout from the conflict in Cambodia. He had placed all his bets on the Chinese. When Deng Xiaoping visited Bangkok, Kuala Lumpur, and Singapore in November 1978, before the Vietnamese attacked Cambodia, Kriangsak's welcome was the warmest. As I told Deng in the car going to the airport after our talks in Singapore, Kriangsak had taken a stand and put himself way out in front, banking on China. If China allowed the Vietnamese a free hand in Cambodia, Kriangsak and Thailand would be in peril. Deng looked grim when I described the consequences that would follow if Thailand switched sides believing that the Soviet Union was going to prevail in Southeast Asia.

Kriangsak's successor was General Prem Tinsulanonda. A bachelor, he was exceptionally honest and led a government largely free from corruption. During the eight years he was prime minister (1980–1988), Thailand prospered and economic development took off, in spite of the war in Cambodia. He was a steady and reliable leader who held to a consistent policy, a man of few words, no scholar, but practical. He enjoyed the king's trust. His command of English was not as good as Kukrit's, but he had the better strategic sense. His neat dress and manners reflected his self-discipline and an abstemious, almost austere lifestyle. The personal chemistry between us was good. From time to time, he would look closely and seriously at me to say, "I agree with you. You are a good friend of Thailand."

His foreign minister, Siddhi Savetsila, was an air marshal with a master's degree from the Massachusetts Institute of Technology. (Their air force leaders were usually very well educated.) But Siddhi had more than brains. Able and firm, he had a strong character and constancy of purpose. He was of mixed Thai and European descent, fair-complexioned, with Eurasian features, but was accepted by the Thais as a loyal Thai. He knew the Vietnamese were wily, and he saw through every maneuvre they made. Without Prem as prime minister and Siddhi as foreign minister, we would not have been able to cooperate so closely and successfully to tie the Vietnamese down in Cambodia. The two were a good team that secured Thailand's long-term security and economic development. Without them, the Vietnamese could have succeeded in manipulating the Thai government.

When General Chatichai Choonhavan became prime minister in August 1988, he talked of turning Indochina from a battlefield into a marketplace. Siddhi remained as Chatichai's foreign minister, but his position soon became untenable. Chatichai kept contradicting him publicly until Siddhi resigned. Because of Chatichai's eagerness to get Thai businesspeople into Vietnam's reconstruction, the Vietnamese hung on in Cambodia and dragged out the Paris peace talks for another three years, to 1991.

Chatichai, when he was foreign minister in Kukrit's government, once told me that when he visited his constituency in the rural northeast, he would drive up in a powerful, expensive Porsche. Asked why, he replied that if he went in an ordinary car, the farmers would not believe that he could help them. In a Porsche, they knew that he was a wealthy man with the means to help them. He did not explain what I had learned from newspaper reports, that often the headman was paid to ensure that he delivered the votes of his villagers.

Chatichai was an engaging character. After some involvement in a coup in the 1960s, he had been sent to Argentina and later Switzerland, where he owned a villa. He spent years in Europe travelling in fast cars and enjoying life. When he was prime minister, his government was reputed to be the most corrupt in Thai history. Bribery was accepted in Thailand as the natural order of things. Only in the mid-1990s, with a growing educated middle class, was there disquiet at the rampant corruption. Vast sums of money were needed to get elected. Party leaders had to finance their supporting candidates, but after elections the leaders and MPs had to recover their expenses. This was money politics the Thai way. In Japan, construction contracts paid for election expenses. In Thailand, every contract must have its payoff, otherwise there would be no funds for the next election.

On my next visit, in January 1998, in discussions, Prime Minister Chuan Leekpai, his deputy prime minister, and finance minister showed their understanding of the need to work with the IMF to restore confidence in Thailand. By 1999, they had improved Thailand's standing with the IMF and international investors.

The Philippines was a world apart from us, running a different style of politics and government under an American military umbrella. It was not until January 1974 that I visited President Marcos in Manila. When my Singapore Airlines plane flew into Philippine airspace, a small squadron of Philippine Air Force jet fighters escorted it to Manila Airport. There Marcos received me in great style—the Filipino way. I was put up at the guest wing of Malacañang Palace in lavishly furnished rooms, valuable objects of art bought in Europe strewn all over. Our hosts were gracious, extravagant in hospitality, flamboyant. Over a thousand miles of water separated us. There was no friction and little trade. We played golf, talked about the future of Asean, and promised to keep in touch.

His foreign minister, Carlos Romulo, was a small man of about five feet some 20 years my senior, with a ready wit and a self-deprecating manner about his size and other limitations. Romulo had a good sense of humor, an eloquent tongue, and a sharp pen, and was an excellent dinner companion because he was a wonderful raconteur, with a vast repertoire of anecdotes and witticisms. He did not hide his great admiration for the Americans. One of his favorite stories was about his return to the Philippines with General MacArthur. As MacArthur waded ashore at Leyte, the water reached his knees but came up to Romulo's chest and he had to swim ashore. His good standing with Asean leaders and with Americans increased the prestige of the Marcos administration. Marcos had in

Romulo a man of honor and integrity who helped give a gloss of respectability to his regime as it fell into disrepute in the 1980s.

In Bali in 1976, at the first Asean summit held after the fall of Saigon, I found Marcos keen to push for greater economic cooperation in Asean. But we could not go faster than the others. To set the pace, Marcos and I agreed to implement a bilateral Philippines-Singapore across-the-board 10 percent reduction of existing tariffs on all products and to promote intra-Asean trade. We also agreed to lay a Philippines-Singapore submarine cable. I was to discover that for him, the communiqué was the accomplishment itself; its implementation was secondary, an extra to be discussed at another conference.

We met every two to three years. He once took me on a tour of his library at Malacañang, its shelves filled with bound volumes of newspapers reporting his activities over the years since he first stood for elections. There were encyclopedia-size volumes on the history and culture of the Philippines with his name as the author. His campaign medals as an anti-Japanese guerrilla leader were displayed in glass cupboards. He was the undisputed boss of all Filipinos. Imelda, his wife, had a penchant for luxury and opulence. When they visited Singapore before the Bali summit they came in style in two DC8s, his and hers.

Marcos did not consider China a threat for the immediate future, unlike Japan. He did not rule out the possibility of an aggressive Japan, if circumstances changed. He had memories of the horrors the Imperial Army had inflicted on Manila. We had strongly divergent views on the Vietnamese invasion and occupation of Cambodia. While he, pro forma, condemned the Vietnamese occupation, he did not consider it a danger to the Philippines. There was the South China Sea separating them and the American navy guaranteed their security. As a result, Marcos was not active on the Cambodian question. Moreover, he was to become preoccupied with the deteriorating security in his country.

Marcos, ruling under martial law, had detained opposition leader Benigno (Ninoy) Aquino, reputed to be as charismatic and powerful a campaigner as he was. He freed Aquino and allowed him to go to the United States. As the economic situation in the Philippines deteriorated, Aquino announced his decision to return. Mrs. Marcos issued several veiled warnings. When the plane arrived at Manila Airport from Taipei in August 1983, he was shot as he descended from the aircraft. A whole posse of foreign correspondents with television camera crews accompanying him on the aircraft was not enough protection.

International outrage over the killing resulted in foreign banks stopping all loans to the Philippines, which owed over US$25 billion and could not pay the interest due. This brought Marcos to the crunch. He sent his minister for trade and industry, Bobby Ongpin, to ask me for a loan of US$300–500 million to meet the interest payments. I looked him straight in the eye and said, "We will never see that money back." Moreover, I added, everyone knew that Marcos was seriously ill and under constant medication for a wasting disease. What was needed was a strong, healthy leader, not more loans.

Shortly afterward, in February 1984, Marcos met me in Brunei at the sultanate's independence celebrations. He had undergone a dramatic physical change. Although less puffy than he had appeared on television, his complexion was dark as if he had been out in the sun. He was breathing hard as he spoke, his voice was soft, eyes bleary, and hair thinning. He looked most unhealthy. An ambulance with all the necessary equipment and a team of Filipino doctors were on standby outside his guest bungalow. Marcos spent much of the time giving me a most improbable story of how Aquino had been shot.

As soon as all our aides left, I went straight to the point, that no bank was going to lend him any money. They wanted to know who was going to succeed him if anything were to happen to him; all the bankers could see that he no longer looked healthy. Singapore banks had lent US$8 billion of the US$25 billion owing. The hard fact was they were not likely to get repayment for some 20 years. He countered that it would be only eight years. I said the bankers wanted to see a strong leader in the Philippines who could restore stability, and the Americans hoped the election in May would throw up someone who could be such a leader. I asked whom he would nominate for the election. He said Prime Minister Cesar Virata. I was blunt. Virata was a nonstarter, a first-class administrator but no political leader; further, his most politically astute colleague, defense minister Juan Enrile, was out of favor. Marcos was silent, then he admitted that succession was the nub of the problem. If he could find a successor, there would be a solution. As I left, he said, "You are a true friend." I did not understand him. It was a strange meeting.

With medical care, Marcos dragged on. Cesar Virata met me in Singapore in January the following year. He was completely guileless, a political innocent. He said that Mrs. Imelda Marcos was likely to be nominated as the presidential candidate. I asked how that could be when there were other weighty candidates, including Juan Enrile and Blas Ople, the labor minister. Virata replied it had to do with "flow of money"; she would have more money than other candidates to pay for the votes needed for nomination by the party and to win the election. He added that if she were the candidate, the opposition would put up Mrs. Cory Aquino and work up the people's feelings. He said the economy was going down with no political stability.

The denouement came in February 1986 when Marcos held presidential elections which he claimed he won. Cory Aquino, the opposition candidate, disputed this and launched a civil disobedience campaign. Defense Minister Juan Enrile defected and admitted election fraud had taken place, and the head of the Philippine constabulary, Lieutenant General Fidel Ramos, joined him. A massive show of "people power" in the streets of Manila led to a spectacular overthrow of a dictatorship. The final indignity was on 25 February 1986, when Marcos and his wife fled in U.S. Air Force helicopters from Malacañang Palace to Clark Air Base and were flown to Hawaii. This Hollywood-style melodrama could only have happened in the Philippines.

Mrs. Aquino was sworn in as president amid jubilation. I had hopes that this honest, god-fearing woman would help regain confidence for the Philippines and get the country back on track. I visited her that June, three months after the event. She was a sincere, devout Catholic who wanted to do her best for her country by carrying out what she believed her husband would have done had he been alive, namely, restore democracy to the Philippines. Democracy would then solve their economic and social problems. At dinner, Mrs. Aquino seated the chairman of the constitutional commission, Chief Justice Cecilia Munoz-Palma, next to me. I asked the learned lady what lessons her commission had learned from the experience of the last 40 years since independence in 1946 would guide her in drafting the constitution. She answered without hesitation, "We will not have any reservations or limitations on our democracy. We must make sure that no dictator can ever emerge to subvert the constitution." Was there no incompatibility of the American-type separation of powers with the culture and habits of the Filipino people that had caused problems for the presidents before Marcos? Apparently none.

Endless attempted coups added to Mrs. Aquino's problems. The army and the constabulary had been politicized. Before the Asean summit in December 1987, a coup was threatened. Without President Suharto's firm support, the summit would have been postponed and confidence in Aquino's government undermined. The Philippine government agreed that the responsibility for security should be shared between them and the other Asean governments, in particular the Indonesian government. General Benny Moerdani, President Suharto's trusted aide, took charge. He positioned an Indonesian warship in the middle of Manila Bay with helicopters and a commando team ready to rescue the Asean heads of government if there should be a coup attempt during the summit. I was included in their rescue plans. I wondered if such a rescue could work but decided to go along with the arrangements, hoping that the show of force would scare off the coup leaders. We were all confined to the Philippine Plaza Hotel by the seafront facing Manila Bay where we could see the Indonesian warship at anchor. The hotel was completely sealed off and guarded. The summit went off without any mishap. We all hoped that this show of united support for Mrs. Aquino's government at a time when there were many attempts to destabilize it would calm the situation.

It made no difference. There were more coup attempts, discouraging investments badly needed to create jobs. This was a pity because they had so many able people, educated in the Philippines and the United States. Their workers were English-speaking, at least in Manila. There was no reason why the Philippines should not have been one of the more successful of the Asean countries. In the 1950s and 1960s, it was the most developed, because America had been generous in rehabilitating the country after the war. Something was missing, a gel to hold society together. The people at the top, the elite mestizos, had the same detached attitude to the native peasants as the mestizos in their haciendas in Latin America had toward their peons. They were two different societies: Those at the top lived a life of extreme luxury and comfort while the peasants scraped a living, and in the Philippines it was a hard living. They had no land but worked on sugar and coconut plantations. They had many children because the church discouraged birth control. The result was increasing poverty.

It was obvious that the Philippines would never take off unless there was substantial aid from the United States. George Shultz, the secretary of state, was sympathetic and wanted to help but made clear to me that the United States would be better able to do something if Asean showed support by making its contribution. The United States was reluctant to go it alone and adopt the Philippines as its special problem. Shultz wanted Asean to play a more prominent role to make it easier for the president to get the necessary votes in Congress. I persuaded Shultz to get the aid project off the ground in 1988, before President Reagan's second term of office ended. He did. There were two meetings for a Multilateral Assistance Initiative (Philippines Assistance Programme): The first in Tokyo in 1989 brought US$3.5 billion in pledges, and the second in Hong Kong in 1991, under the Bush administration, yielded US$14 billion in pledges. But instability in the Philippines did not abate. This made donors hesitant and delayed the implementation of projects.

Mrs. Aquino's successor, Fidel Ramos, whom she had backed, was more practical and established greater stability. In November 1992, I visited him. In a speech to the 18th Philippine Business Conference, I said, "I do not believe democracy necessarily leads to development. I believe what a country needs to develop is discipline more than democracy." In private, President Ramos said he agreed with me that British parliamentary-type constitutions worked better because the majority party in the legislature was also the government. Publicly, Ramos had to differ.

He knew well the difficulties of trying to govern with strict American-style separation of powers. The senate had already defeated Mrs. Aquino's proposal to retain the American bases. The Philippines had a rambunctious press but it did not check corruption. Individual press reporters could be bought, as could many judges. Something had gone seriously wrong. Millions of Filipino men and women had to leave their country for jobs abroad beneath their level of education. Filipino professionals whom we recruited to work in Singapore are as good as our own. Indeed, their architects, artists, and musicians are more artistic and creative than ours. Hundreds of thousands of them have left for Hawaii and for the American mainland. It is a problem the solution to which has not been made easier by the workings of a Philippine version of the American constitution.

The difference lies in the culture of the Filipino people. It is a soft, forgiving culture. Only in the Philippines could a leader like Ferdinand Marcos, who pillaged his country for over 20 years, still be considered for a national burial. Insignificant amounts of the loot have been recovered, yet his wife and children were allowed to return and engage in politics. They supported the winning presidential and congressional candidates with their considerable resources and reappeared in the political and social limelight after the 1998 election that returned President Joseph Estrada. General Fabian Ver, Marcos's commander-in-chief who had been in charge of security when Aquino was assassinated, had fled the Philippines together with Marcos in 1986. When he died in Bangkok, the Estrada government gave the general military honors at his burial. One Filipino newspaper, *Today,* wrote on 22 November 1998, "Ver, Marcos and the rest of the official family plunged the country into two decades of lies, torture and plunder. Over the next decade, Marcos's cronies and immediate family would tiptoe back into the country, one by one— always to the public's revulsion and disgust, though they showed that there was nothing that hidden money and thick hides could not withstand." Some Filipinos write and speak with passion. If they could get their elite to share their sentiments and act, what could they not have achieved?

Brunei was a placid, peaceful sultanate, wealthy with oil in the mid-1950s when I was practicing law and appeared in their courts.

The sultan, Sir Omar Ali Saifuddien, invited me as prime minister, together with our head of state, Yusof Ishak, to his birthday celebrations in August 1960. He was a quiet man, soft-spoken, with a friendly, attractive smile. He had few friends, for nearly all invariably wanted to touch him for money. I met him several times in London when I was negotiating terms for Malaysia in 1962 and 1963. He was never comfortable at the prospect of becoming a member state of Malaysia. Most of his oil rev-

enue would go to the federal government, and he was not confident that
the special attention the Tunku was lavishing on him would last once he
was in Malaysia: He would become just one of Malaysia's many sultans. I
gave him my reasons why Singapore wanted to join, but left him to make
his own decision. He had legal advisers, but he made the political decision to stay out. In retrospect, it was a sound decision. The British stayed
on from 1963 until February 1984 when they gave Brunei independence.

On one of his visits to Singapore after we separated from Malaysia, Sir
Omar smiled broadly at me with his moustache twitching and his eyes
twinkling, to say, "You are now like Brunei. It is better for you." Indeed,
we shared certain common interests: small countries surrounded by bigger neighbors. I did not covet his wealth, never borrowed money from
him. I gave advice only when he asked for it. He trusted me.

In 1967, after Malaysia wound up the common currency board, its
members, Malaysia, Brunei, and Singapore, agreed that our new currencies would be interchangeable at par. When this arrangement was discon-
tinued in 1973, the old sultan decided to retain the arrangements with
the Singapore currency, interchangeability at par. He was a most frugal
sultan, completely different from other sultans in the region. He gave
Brunei a sense of financial discipline and began the accumulation of huge
assets that were managed by crown agents in London.

When the British government pressed him to institute constitutional
reforms for democracy, to delay and buy time he abdicated in 1967 in
favor of his eldest son, Hassanal Bolkiah, then a young man training at
Sandhurst. He spent a lot of time thinking of ways to keep the British in
Brunei as his protector. He refused to have anything to do with Indonesia
or Malaysia. He distrusted the Indonesians for supporting Azahari, the
leader of the Brunei People's Party who led a revolt in December 1962.
He was wary of Malaysians because Malaysian officers seconded to work in
Brunei in the late 1950s and early 1960s had patronized his Bruneian
officers, treating them like country cousins. I was careful not to have any
Singapore officer seconded for any length of time to Brunei, and when any
was sent, made sure he was properly briefed to treat the Bruneians properly and courteously.

At a private meeting in March 1979, I urged Sir Omar, the former
sultan, or Seri Begawan as he was called after he abdicated, to get half a

foot into Asean before Brunei's independence in 1984. I said President Suharto of Indonesia and Prime Minister Hussein Onn of Malaysia were both friendly and well disposed toward Brunei. He agreed to consider seeking observer status for Brunei in Asean, but nothing came of it. I explained to him how the world had changed. Sir Omar held on to his implicit faith in the British, that they would always be there to back him. He did not want to recognize Britain's changed circumstances, that there were no British naval or air task forces to come to Brunei's rescue.

Visiting British ministers frequently raised Brunei with me after Margaret Thatcher became prime minister. Her government wanted to end the protectorate by persuading the sultan to hold elections, become a more contemporary monarchy, and be independent. I did my best to urge the Seri Begawan, Sir Omar, and the sultan to move forward but they were not persuaded. The British government finally concluded that regardless of whether or not Brunei had representative government, it would have to take responsibility for its own future. Britain would continue to give support against external threat by maintaining a Gurkha battalion for which Brunei would pay. I also urged Lord Carrington in 1979, soon after he became foreign secretary, to be firm with British officers who wanted to extend their stay in Brunei. They were preventing Bruneian officials, almost all of whom had been educated in Britain, from getting the experience they needed to run their own country. There was a significant change of policy after that conversation. By 1984, when Brunei became independent, nearly all senior positions were held by indigenous Bruneians.

In 1980, I had raised with President Suharto the question of Brunei's possible membership of Asean when it became independent. Suharto said he would welcome Brunei if it wanted to join. I then persuaded the sultan to look beyond his father's view that Asean was unimportant; he should visit President Suharto and the other leaders of Asean. He finally did so in April 1981. Suharto received him warmly in Jakarta. The sultan then visited Malaysia and Thailand. When Brunei joined in 1984, Asean membership gave it an umbrella of sorts for its security and made it easier for the sultan to get along with his neighbors.

Brunei has enjoyed peace and stability since independence. The sultan has grown in self-confidence. Prince Mohamed has become a knowledgeable foreign minister and senior Bruneian officers have gained wide exposure at international conferences and grown in their jobs. The Seri Begawan, who died in 1986, would have been pleased with the results.

The friendship between the sultan's father and me has continued between the present sultan, his brothers, and ministers and Prime Minister Goh and his colleagues. It is a relationship of trust and utmost good faith.

# 19. Vietnam, Myanmar, and Cambodia: Coming to Terms with the Modern World

On 29 October 1977, a Vietnamese DC3, an old Dakota, was hijacked while on an internal flight and made to fly to Singapore. We could not stop it from landing at Seletar Air Base. We allowed the Vietnamese to send a new crew to fly the plane back with the old crew and the other passengers, after we had refuelled and refurbished it. We prosecuted the hijackers who were convicted and sentenced to 14 years' jail.

Vietnam never paid for the supplies but instead sent us a stream of warnings to return the hijackers or face the consequences. We had to stand firm and not allow ourselves to be intimidated or there would be no end of problems. Singapore's relations with Vietnam, which was reunified in 1975, had started with a standoff.

The Vietnamese cunningly exploited the fears and desires of the countries of Asean that wanted to befriend them. They talked tough over their radio and newspapers. I found their leaders insufferable. They were filled with their own importance, and prided themselves as the Prussians of Southeast Asia. True, they had suffered, taken all the punishment that American technology had inflicted on them, and through sheer endurance plus their skillful propaganda, exploiting the American media, defeated the Americans. They were confident they could beat any other power in the world, even China, if it interfered with Vietnam. For us, the puny states of Southeast Asia, they had nothing but contempt. They declared they would establish diplomatic relations with member states of Asean individually, and refused to deal with Asean as a group. Their newspapers criticized the existence of U.S. military bases in the Philippines and Thailand and spoke of collusive relations between China and Singapore.

By 1976, deepening disagreements with China made them dispatch diplomatic missions to Asean. Their deputy foreign minister, Phan Hien, brought a message of peace when he visited the countries of the region. At first he excluded Singapore from his visits, but changed his plans and came in July 1976. He said Vietnam was noninterventionist in other countries' affairs. He drew a distinction between the people and the government of the Socialist Republic of Vietnam. The people of Vietnam supported the just cause of the peoples of Southeast Asia fighting for independence, meaning the communist insurgency. The government wanted to establish bilateral relations with these countries. I pointed out that this diplomatic sophistry could not erase questions in our minds that this dual track was interference. Referring to Soviet support for Vietnam, I said great powers knew it was dangerous to clash directly with each other so they used third countries to expand their influence. Differences between Asean countries were resolved within Asean so neither the United States nor the Soviet Union could exploit them.

A year later Prime Minister Pham Van Dong also did not at first include Singapore in his proposed visits to the region, probably to make us feel insecure. We were unmoved; they could not as yet do us harm. He came on 16 October 1978. I found him arrogant and objectionable. The Vietnamese were excellent stage managers. Phan Hien had come first to show the sweet smiling face of communist Vietnam. Now Pham Van Dong, an old man of 72, showed that he was tough as nails. In discussions lasting two and a half hours, we dispensed with courtesies and euphemisms. Indeed, our forthright conversation had started in the car journey from the airport.

I began by welcoming Vietnam's desire to work together with us for peace, stability, and prosperity, but listening to Radio Hanoi and reading *Nhan Dan,* their newspaper, made me have reservations. They were unfriendly, even threatening. Dong declared Vietnam was a socialist country and he a communist. His doctrine was Marxism-Leninism. He had come to Singapore to speak as the prime minister of the Socialist Republic of Vietnam. Vietnam had to contribute to the cause of revolution and peace in Southeast Asia and the world. This should not be of concern to

Singapore. Vietnam was a country of 50 million people, a brave nation, intelligent and rich in natural resources. Both the United States and Japan had told the Vietnamese that their country would become economically a strong country, and that they, the United States and Japan, would need economic and trade relations with it.

After this confident opening, in answer to my questions he claimed that Beijing had instigated 140,000 to 150,000 ethnic Chinese in the north to leave Vietnam and return to China across the border. They could not understand why. The root cause was China's policy toward Vietnam after Vietnam's victory over the Americans. China had continued its expansionist policy against Vietnam. Beijing had made use of Khmer leaders to launch attacks into Vietnamese territory to commit atrocious crimes. China had caused the Hoa people to leave through a campaign launched by their embassy in Hanoi to train those who returned in order to send them back to Vietnam. The overseas Chinese had always been attached to their fatherland, feelings that were genuine and respectable. Beijing had exploited such sentiments.

I asked whether China would have the same policy in Singapore if it had an embassy here. He did not think it would because it did not want to bring back all the overseas Chinese. It was better to leave them where they were, to use them as instruments. Looking at me pointedly, he said that ethnic Chinese everywhere would support China, just as ethnic Vietnamese abroad would support Vietnam.

Then he turned to economic relations, with the astonishing news that Singapore could contribute to Vietnam's reconstruction. When I gently remonstrated that we must get some return for our goods and services, he bluntly said Vietnam's economy was not developed and the possibilities for trade were limited. That night, as I walked with him to dinner, he again said Vietnam could not trade but needed help; Singapore had benefited from the Vietnam War, selling the Americans war material, hence it was our duty to help them. I was dumbfounded by this arrogant and belligerent attitude.

As we drove along the waterfront the next day, he saw the many ships at anchor. Once again he charged that we had profited immeasurably from the Vietnam War and developed Singapore at their expense so it was our duty to help them. I was incredulous. I could not understand how we

were under an obligation to help them because they had been impoverished by a war we had not caused and in which we had played no part. I
said the main war materials we supplied to U.S. forces in Vietnam were
POL (petrol, oil, and lubricants) from American and British oil companies. The profits to Singapore were negligible. He looked skeptical. I said
we were prepared to trade but not to give aid. He was not pleased. We
parted civil but cold.

Twelve years later, in 1990, in Davos for a World Economic Forum
meeting, Vo Van Kiet, the first vice chairman of the council of ministers
of Vietnam, asked to see me. He hoped we would set aside outstanding
differences and cooperate. I regretted that so much time had been lost in
their occupation of Cambodia since December 1978. Until that conflict
was resolved there could be no government-to-government ties. Kiet said
there were great opportunities and he had granted over 100 investment
licenses to foreign companies. I replied that whether there were 100 or
1,000 licenses, Vietnam's economy could not take off until the United
States signalled the World Bank to extend soft loans for its rehabilitation
and the big U.S. banks decided that Vietnam was an acceptable risk. But
once Vietnamese troops were out of Cambodia, we would resume where
we had left off in 1978.

In October 1991, Vietnam and all parties signed agreements in Paris
for a comprehensive political settlement. A week later, Vo Van Kiet, now
the prime minister, visited Singapore. Although I was no longer prime
minister, we met when I attended a dinner for him given by my successor,
Prime Minister Goh Chok Tong. As the dinner was breaking up, he rose,
walked up to me, held my arms in a semicommunist embrace, and asked
whether I would help Vietnam. I asked, how? By becoming their economic adviser. I was speechless. I had been the target of their virulent
attacks since their occupation of Cambodia. Recovering from my surprise,
I said that my experience had been confined to a city state, that I had no
experience of a big country like Vietnam with a population of 60 million
people, a country devastated by many years of war and working a communist system that had to be transformed into a market system. He persisted
and followed up in two letters.

After an exchange of letters, I agreed to visit them, not as an adviser,
but to brainstorm ideas on their change to a free-market economy. It was

a totally different relationship when I went to Hanoi in April 1992. In an ornately decorated conference chamber, with Ho Chi Minh's bust as the centerpiece, I spent a whole day with Vo Van Kiet and his team of ministers and top officials. They had five questions, starting with what commodities Vietnam should focus on in its modernization, in what markets and with what partners. I replied that the questions themselves disclosed a mindset that came from long years of central planning, because they assumed there would be specific commodities, markets, or partners that could bring about a transformation for them. I suggested that they study the process through which Taiwan and South Korea had transformed themselves from agricultural into newly industrializing economies. A good strategy, I said, would be to use South Vietnam, especially Ho Chi Minh City (formerly Saigon), as the dynamo to get growth going for the whole country. Communism had prevailed in the north for 40 years, but for only 16 years in the south. People in the south were familiar with a free-market economy and could easily revert to working the old system. The best catalyst would be their émigrés—Vietnamese refugees who had left after 1975 and done well in business in America, Western Europe, and Australasia. Invite them to return and kick-start the economy in the south, since they would want to help their families and friends.

Kiet seemed attracted to the suggestion. He himself was from the south, but other, more senior leaders wanted development to be spread equally, north and south. Unstated were their apprehensions that these émigrés would return with subversive ideas or with links to foreign agencies like the CIA. After decades of fighting a hide-and-seek guerrilla war, they were suspicious of everyone.

Kiet flew to Ho Chi Minh City from Hanoi for a final meeting with me. He asked me to return every year, saying I had been a real friend because I had given honest and sincere advice, although sometimes it was painful to hear. I promised to return within two years. In the meantime, I would send a task force to study their infrastructure shortcomings and make recommendations on their seaport, airport, roads, bridges, telecoms, and power supply.

Our officers believed the Vietnamese wanted me to be associated with them to get closer to Asean and be more secure vis-à-vis China. Singapore had been Vietnam's most vocal opponent. If they normalized relations with us, foreign investors would have greater confidence. We decided to put the past behind us and help them as best we could to adjust to the market economy and become compatible partners in Asean.

In Hanoi, I asked to call on Pham Van Dong. Although he had retired, he received me at their seat of government, a 1920s stone building which had been the office of the French governors. He met me at the main door at the top of a flight of stairs. Obviously infirm, he stood erect with great effort, then walked unsteadily to his chair some distance away. They had switched off the air-conditioning because he could not stand the cold. He was frail but spoke with great firmness and determination. He recalled our meeting in Singapore, and said the past was over; Vietnam was opening a new page. He thanked me for my friendship in coming to help them. He sounded bitter and chastened. I remembered the haughty and arrogant leader who came to Singapore in 1978. Seeing how tough he was in defeat, I was thankful that Deng Xiaoping had punished the Vietnamese. They would have been unbearable as the victorious Prussians of Southeast Asia.

The Vietnamese leaders were an impressive group. Kiet was soft-spoken, but his record as a communist underground fighter belied his gentle ways. They were formidable opponents who had great determination and fighting spirit.

In my note to the cabinet I described Vietnam's terrible state, although it was six years after their opening up. In 1975, Ho Chi Minh City could vie with Bangkok; now (in 1992) it lagged more than 20 years behind. I felt that for the time being the people had lost confidence in their leaders, and the leaders had lost confidence in their system. However, they were an energetic and intelligent people, Confucianist at the grass roots. I believed they would bounce back in 20 to 30 years. Every meeting had started and ended punctually. Their leaders were serious men.

Both Kiet and the ex-general secretary of the Communist Party, Nguyen Van Linh, whom I met in Ho Chi Minh City, separately said they had to reeducate their cadres on the market economy and free themselves from wrong Marxist thoughts. A foreign banker in Ho Chi Minh City told me that because of their grievous brain drain, they suffered from a dearth of trained talent. They regarded all foreigners as potential enemies whose activities their Vietnamese employees had to report. He believed they wanted to prepare for the next war.

They were still very communist in their ways. Kiet was noncommittal after the discussions we held in the morning and afternoon of the first day. Immediately after these two meetings, I was taken to meet the Communist Party general secretary, Do Muoi, who had been briefed on the contents of the two discussions in the 20 minutes that elapsed from my parting with the prime minister. Kiet must have got the nod after my meeting with Do Muoi because that night, in his dinner speech, he picked up a point I had made, on which he had earlier been noncommittal, that Vietnam should not have too many international airports and seaports, but should concentrate on building one big international airport and one big international seaport so that they could be included in the world network of airports and seaports.

We discussed their loss-incurring state-owned enterprises (SOEs). They wanted to privatize them or sell them off to the workers and others. I explained that this method would not provide them with what was critical—efficient management. Singapore Airlines was 100 percent government-owned, but it was efficient and profitable because it had to compete against international airlines. We did not subsidize it; if it was not profitable, it would have to close down. I recommended that they privatize their SOEs by bringing in foreign corporations to get an injection of management expertise and foreign capital for new technology. A change in the management system was essential. They needed to work with foreigners to learn on the job. Privatizing within the country by selling to their own people could not bring about this result.

An infrastructure task force we sent in September 1992 submitted a report which was adopted by the Vietnamese government. We set aside a US$10 million Indochina Assistance Fund for technical training of their officials.

Do Muoi visited Singapore in October 1993. He was astonished at the high quality of buildings and infrastructure. When he visited NTUC Fairprice supermarkets, he was impressed by the variety and abundance of consumer goods available for our workers, just as Russian Prime Minister Ryzkov had been in 1990. When I returned his visit a month later, I discovered from his officials that he had instructed their agencies to learn from Singapore and wherever possible to accord preference to projects proposed by Singapore investors. However, in spite of the many agreements signed, our investors found they were not being implemented. Junior officials used them to extract better offers from other businesspeople.

Do Muoi was the most important man in Vietnam. Of heavy build, with a big face, broad nose, dark complexion, and straight hair parted at the side and combed straight toward the two sides, he looked neat and tidy. He wore the Vietnamese version of a Mao suit, unlike Kiet who dressed in lounge suits. He was not as reform-minded as Kiet, but neither was he as conservative as the president, General Le Duc Anh. He was the balancer and arbiter between the two wings of the party.

He told me he had been given two of my books when he was in Singapore. He had the book of my speeches translated from Chinese into Vietnamese, read them all, underlined the key parts on economics, and sent them to all his important cadres and ministers to read. He slept little, from midnight to 3:00 A.M., exercised for half an hour, and read until 7:30 A.M. before he started work. Our embassy staff reported that my book of speeches translated into Vietnamese was on sale. They had not heard of copyright.

When he asked how he could increase the flow of investments, I suggested they should abandon the habits they learned in guerrilla warfare. Development projects for the south that had been approved by the Ho Chi Minh authority had to be approved again in the north by Hanoi officials who knew little about conditions there. It was time-wasting. Next, projects approved by the government in Hanoi were often blocked by local authorities because of the supremacy of the local commander in charge, a legacy from their guerrilla days.

He spoke with sorrow about Vietnam's unhappy past—1,000 years spent fighting China, another 100 years fighting French colonialism and imperialism, then fighting for independence after World War II. They have had to fight the Japanese, the French, the Americans, and later the Pol Pot clique. He did not mention China's attack in 1979. For 140 years, the Vietnamese had successfully waged wars to liberate their country. Their war wounds were deep, their industries weak, their technology backward, their infrastructure deplorable. I sympathized with him, saying that the war was a tragedy for both the United States and Vietnam.

He sighed and said Vietnam would have been a developed, modern country like Singapore had it not been for the war.

I reassured him that eventually Vietnam could do better than Singapore. There was no reason why the present peace and stability should not last for a long time, for the lesson East Asia had learned from the last 40 years was that war did not pay. In two big wars, in Korea and Vietnam, and in the guerrilla war in Cambodia, there had been no victors, only victims. Do Muoi sadly agreed.

In fact, the Vietnamese had made progress. As a result of more contacts with foreigners and greater information on the market economy, ministers and officials had a better understanding of the workings of the free market. Greater street activity, more shops, foreign businesspeople, hotels—these were all signs of prosperity in Ho Chi Minh City and Hanoi.

On another visit, in March 1995, First Deputy Prime Minister Phan Van Khai led the discussions on economic reforms. He was reputed to want to move forward faster. Our investors had run into a thicket of problems. I told Khai that if he wanted to attract investors, he must make the early ones welcome. They should be helped to succeed after they had fixed their assets to Vietnam's soil. To treat investors with fixed assets in Vietnam as captives was the surest way to drive others away. Their officials dealt with investors as they had dealt with American soldiers, as enemies to be led into ambush and destroyed. Instead investors should be treated as valued friends who need guidance through the maze of their bureaucracy with its landmines and other traps.

I gave some examples of the difficulties our investors had faced. One Singapore property developer was building a hotel in Hanoi. Some 30 households around the site complained of noise and vibration nuisance. He agreed to pay each household compensation of US$48 per month. Once this was agreed, another 200 householders demanded payment. The developer decided to use a different method to bore the piles in without noise or vibrations. He was not allowed to do this because his license was for the old equipment.

Next, Singapore Telecom had a joint-venture agreement for a radio-paging service with Ho Chi Minh Post and Telecoms on a one-year trial basis, after which they could apply for a 10-year license. After Singapore

Telecom had spent US$1 million to get the system started, Ho Chi Minh Post and Telecoms proposed to buy it from them. I told Prime Minister Kiet that the sum involved was just a million dollars, but the principle was important. If they reneged on the agreement, they would lose the confidence of the Singapore business community. Kiet must have intervened to get the project through, but not without further changes to the original agreement and several outstanding issues still unresolved.

Feedback from foreign investors showed that my message did get through for Vietnamese officials became more helpful. The CEO of a large German company who visited Singapore after Vietnam told me that they had provided him with a guide. I smiled in satisfaction.

The top leaders continued to be fearful of the social ills that followed the opening up of Vietnam, and also of losing political control, and slowed down liberalization. Unlike China, where most of the mayors and provincial governors were young, tertiary-educated men, the top men in charge of Vietnam's cities and provinces were all former guerrilla commanders. They were aghast at what had happened in Moscow and the Soviet Union, and they did not approve of the social evils that had infected China's coastal cities. This was not what they had fought for.

In 1993, I had suggested to Kiet and his team that they promote these guerrilla veterans to important advisory positions and allow younger men, preferably those with exposure to the West, to take day-to-day charge. They needed to have men who understood the market economy and could relate to foreign investors. But the veterans who had fought and won the war were in charge and wanted to build the country their way. When a younger generation takes over, I believe Vietnam's economy will advance faster. Important leadership changes in September 1997 saw Vice-Premier Phan Van Khai become prime minister in place of Kiet and Vice-Premier Tran Duc Luong replace General Le Duc Ahn as president. These were steps toward a younger generation, more widely traveled and exposed to the real world, who would know only too well how far behind Vietnam was compared to its neighbors.

In November 1997, I visited Ho Chi Minh City where I met the rising mayor and secretary of the Ho Chi Minh City party committee, Truong Tan Sang. The country was in "holding" mode. Our investors in

Ho Chi Minh City and foreign bankers were aghast at the latest prohibition: no remittances out from Vietnamese Dong into foreign currency. How were they to meet their foreign debts, bank overdrafts, interest payments due for loans they had taken out in banks overseas for their investments in Vietnam? How could they carry on business? The ministry of trade and industry had been strongly against this move which they knew must discourage investors, but could do nothing. The Vietnamese central bank and ministry of finance were alarmed by the currency crisis that had hit the region and worried about their low foreign exchange reserves.

In Hanoi I explained to Phan Van Khai why such sudden changes were damaging. Many other things had also gone wrong. Singapore Telecom had settled its paging business only to run into trouble over its mobile phone business. Vietnamese Telecoms did not want to issue the license although they had promised one. The Vietnamese wanted to run it themselves. I pointed out that Singapore had to follow the trend in the developed world in privatizing its telecoms, which had to meet international competition. The only way to meet the fiercest competition was to operate as a private-sector company with foreign partners bringing in the latest technology. He understood, as did Tran Duc Luong, with whom I covered the same ground.

Once again I was taken to see Do Muoi. It was, as on previous occasions, a good discussion. But I fear its impact will again be limited. The Vietnamese will take some time to shake off their communist straitjackets and move freely and flexibly. Once they have done this, I have little doubt they can make the grade. The skill with which they used Soviet weapons and improvised to overcome critical shortages during the war, and the accomplishments of Vietnamese refugees in America and France are reminders of their formidable qualities.

My first visit to Rangoon (Yangon) was in April 1962. Prime Minister U Nu of Burma (as Myanmar was called before 1989) had asked General Ne Win to take over in 1958 because his elected government could not contain the insurgencies and rebellions of the many minority groups. After 18 months of military rule, a general election was held. When U Nu's party was returned, Ne Win handed back power. But soon U Nu was in difficulties again, and Ne Win seized power in March 1962, just before my visit.

Unlike Colombo, which I visited in 1956, Rangoon seemed dilapidated and run-down. It had been under Japanese occupation, and although spared the worst when the British fought their way back from Bengal, the damage had been considerable. Ne Win received Choo and me warmly at his house. I was disconcerted to see it ringed with guns and tanks. Obviously he took no chances. My visit was to counter the propaganda of Indonesia's President Sukarno that Malaysia was a neocolonialist plot. Over lunch, Ne Win listened to my explanations, but was not attentive. He was preoccupied with maintaining law and order, keeping down insurrections, and holding Burma together.

He lived in a medium-sized bungalow in the suburbs. He was friendly, as was his wife, Khin May Than (Kitty), a former nurse and a vivacious lady. Both were English-speaking and intelligent. Burma was one of the better-endowed countries of Southeast Asia, a rice and food exporter before the war. However, the democratic system of government did not work. The people were not of one race, speaking one language. The British had brought together into one country a whole host of different races occupying different parts of this mountainous country.

"The Burmese way to socialism" was Ne Win's motto for the Socialist Republic of the Union of Burma. His policy was simple: achieve self-reliance and get rid of the Indians and Chinese who had come into Burma with the British. The Chinese had started to leave even under U Nu, many settling in Thailand and Singapore. The larger number were the Indians, whom the British had recruited into the government service. They were slowly squeezed out.

My next visit to Rangoon was in May 1965, after attending a conference for Asian socialists in Bombay. Ne Win liked that part of my speech where I had said, "If we approach Asian problems of poverty and underdevelopment through the rosy spectacles of the Western European socialists we are sure to fail." I did not realize at that time how determined he was to be self-sufficient, to have little to do with the outside world, and to return to a romantic, idyllic past when Burma was rich and self-sufficient.

My one unforgettable conversation during that visit was with the butler at the Strand Hotel—an Indian in his late fifties, with greying hair and beard. He brought in breakfast looking forlorn and dejected, and said in English, "Sir, this is my last day, I shall not be here tomorrow." He did not know whether his Burmese assistant would be able to serve me the same breakfast: British-style tea with milk and sugar, toast and scrambled eggs. I asked why he wanted to leave. He replied, "I have to leave. I was born and have lived here all my life, but the government wants all Indians to leave. I cannot take with me more than a small sum of money and my personal belongings." Where was he going? "India." Did he have relatives there? "No." His grandparents had been brought in by the British but the government wanted to send him back. He was right about my breakfast. The next day the tray was not as neat nor the toast as crisp.

That afternoon, Ne Win played golf with me at the former British Rangoon Golf Club. It was an extraordinary game. On both sides of every fairway and surrounding us, the four players, were troops with guns, facing outward. When not swinging a club Ne Win wore a steel helmet. I hesitated to ask why. His minister, one of the players, murmured something about an assassination threat.

When Ne Win visited Singapore in 1968 and played golf, he was not security-conscious and did not wear a steel helmet. When he next came, in 1974, I suggested we should coordinate our policies to get the United States, China, and the Soviet Union to maintain a presence in the region, so as to have some power balance. He was not in the least interested, preferring to leave these matters to the superpowers.

I last visited Rangoon in January 1986. Ne Win's new wife was a doctor, well-educated and much younger than Kitty, who had died. Ne Win had an excellent recall of events that happened 15 to 30 years ago. Over dinner, I found that despite Burma's 20 years of economic stagnation, he was as distrustful of foreign powers as ever. He spoke of being locked in a "battle of wits" against elements outside Burma who wanted to make as much as they could at the expense of his country.

It was sad to see Rangoon worse than it had been since my 1965 visit. There were no new roads or buildings. Everything was in disrepair and there were potholes in the main roads. The few cars were of 1950s or

1960s vintage. There was nothing any of his ministers could do, given his policies. The English newspaper was a single-leaf, four-page tabloid. The Burmese paper was slightly less skimpy. The people in attendance at their famous Shwe Dagon pagoda looked shabby and poor. From my car, the shops looked empty.

When his prime minister, Maung Maung Kha, visited Singapore in September 1986, I tried to interest him in tourism, telling him of an article I had read in the *Singapore American* (a publication of our American community), in which two teachers from the American School described their visit to Rangoon, Mandalay, and Pagan. They had hitchhiked for part of the journey and found it a fascinating adventure. I suggested that he open up Burma, build hotels, and get safe aircraft to fly from Rangoon to Mandalay and Pagan. He would get large numbers of tourists and considerable revenue. He listened quietly but said little. Nothing happened. Ne Win did not want foreigners in Burma.

Only in 1993, when Lieutenant General Khin Nyunt, one of their key leaders, saw me in Singapore did I find a leader who was responsive, probably because Ne Win had had a change of heart. Ne Win must have told him that I was an old friend because he listened quietly as I explained that Myanmar had to adjust to the post–Cold War world, open up its economy, and develop the whole country. I pointed to China and Vietnam, two examples of former closed countries that were developing their tourism and inviting foreign investors to create jobs and wealth.

Khin Nyunt was then in charge of intelligence and the strongman of the junta or SLORC (State Law and Order Restoration Council). I asked him to reconsider his policy toward Aung San Suu Kyi, the daughter of Burma's hero and first prime minister, Aung San. She had married an Englishman but had returned to Myanmar to lead a movement against the military government. They could not lock her up forever; she would be a continuing embarrassment to their government.

Myanmar had to improve the lives of the people, co-opt capable people with experience abroad into the government. A government of military officers could never get the economy going. I suggested he should make it possible for Singapore to engage and help Myanmar economically. Singapore could defend its position internationally, if this engagement was to help Myanmar return to normalcy, not to maintain the present system. My note taker, a ministry of foreign affairs desk officer for Myanmar, was fearful that he would react strongly and was surprised when, at the end of the discussion, he thanked me for my "valuable opinion."

When General Than Shwe, the Myanmar prime minister and chairman of SLORC, visited Singapore in June 1995, I suggested that he visit Indonesia to learn how it had changed from a military leadership, with General Suharto in charge, to an elected presidency. The Indonesian constitution gave the army a direct role in government, with representation in the legislature under a system called *dwi-fungsi* (two functions). The Indonesian army had a constitutional role in ensuring the security and integrity of the country. Elections for the president and the legislature were held every five years. Myanmar had to go in that direction if it wanted to be like the other countries in Southeast Asia.

I had called on Ne Win when he visited Singapore for medical treatment a year earlier, in 1994. He talked about his peace and serenity of mind through his practice of meditation. For two years after he withdrew from government in 1988, he had been in torment, fretting and worrying about what was going on in the country. Then in 1990 he began to read about meditation. He now spent many hours each day, in the morning, afternoon, and evening, in silent meditation. He certainly looked much better than the sickly person I had met in Rangoon in 1986.

He was in Singapore again in 1997 to see his doctors. At the age of 86, he looked even better than on his last visit. This time he spoke only about meditation, giving me advice on how I could improve my meditation. I asked if he did not worry about the sickness of his loved ones, like children and grandchildren. Yes he did, but he could control, reduce, and forget these sufferings through meditation. Did he not worry when his old generals asked for his advice? No, he replied; when they did this, he told them never to talk about their work because he had retired from the troubles of this world. However, diplomats told me he commanded respect and authority within the military and could still wield influence.

The West, especially the United States, believed that economic sanctions could force the government to hand power to Aung San Suu Kyi, who had won the Nobel Peace Prize in 1991. I did not think this was likely. The army has been Myanmar's only instrument of government since Ne Win took power in 1962. The military leaders can be persuaded to share power and gradually civilianize the government. But unless the United States or the United Nations is prepared to send in armed forces to hold the country together, as it is doing in Bosnia, Myanmar without the army would be ungovernable. The West is impatient with Asean's constructive engagement and was puzzled when its leaders admitted Myanmar as a member in July 1997. But what better way was there to have the country develop, open up, and gradually change? In Cambodia, a UN force that supervized elections could not install the winner into government because the de facto government under Hun Sen controlled the army, the police, and the administration.

The generals will eventually have to adjust and change to a form of government more like their Asean neighbors'. This will come about sooner if their contacts with the international community increase.

I prefer to remember Cambodia as that oasis of peace and prosperity in the war-torn Indochina of the 1960s. Choo and I made our first visit to Phnom Penh, its capital, in 1962. Prince Norodom Sihanouk personally greeted us at the airport and had dancers in traditional costume scatter flower petals on the red carpet as we walked to the car after I had inspected a guard of honor. Phnom Penh was like a French provincial town, quiet and peaceful with wide boulevards reminiscent of the Champs Élysées in Paris lined with trees and flanked by side roads also shaded by trees. There was even a monumental archway, a Khmer version of the Arc de Triomphe, at the center of a major crossroads, the Place de e'Indépendance. We stayed at the Palais du Gouvernement, formerly the residence of the French governor general, by the Mekong River. Sihanouk himself lived in the old palace. He entertained us to dinner in grand style, then flew us in his personal Russian aircraft to see Angkor Wat.

Sihanouk was an extraordinary personality, highly intelligent and full of energy and joie de vivre. He had the airs and graces of an educated French gentleman, with all the accompanying gestures and mannerisms, and spoke English the French way. Medium in height, a little rotund, he had a broad face with flared nostrils like the stone carvings on the temples around Angkor Wat. He was an excellent host who made each visit a memorable and enjoyable occasion. His banquets of French haute cuisine, with the best French wines and beautiful cutlery to match, were a treat. I remember going to his palace in the provincial capital of Batambang, driving up to a raised entrance typical of driveways in French chateaux. As we arrived, short Cambodian guards, looking dwarfed by their thigh-high gleaming black Napoleonic boots with helmets to match, saluted with glinting swords. The reception and banquet halls were luxuriously furnished and air-conditioned. There was a Western and a Cambodian orchestra. Foreign diplomats were in attendance. It was a royal occasion.

The prince was mercurial, hypersensitive to criticism. He would answer every press article that was in any way critical. Politics for him was the press and publicity. When he was overthrown in the 1970 coup he said that he sought refuge in Beijing because he feared for his life. I believe that had he returned to Cambodia then, no soldier would have dared to shoot him on arrival at the airport. He was their god-king. He had kept Cambodia an oasis of peace and plenty in a troubled, war-ravaged Indochina by maintaining a precarious balance between the communists and the West. He sought the friendship and protection of the Chinese while he kept his ties with the West through France. When he stayed in Beijing instead of returning to defy the coup makers, the old Cambodia was destroyed.

I met him again when he came to Singapore in September 1981 for talks on forming a coalition with the Khmer Rouge. It was a changed Sihanouk. He had gone back to Phnom Penh and been a captive of the Khmer Rouge. He had been through a harrowing time; many of his children and grandchildren had been killed by Pol Pot, and he himself was in fear for his life. The old bouncy Sihanouk had been destroyed. His laughter, the high-pitched shrill voice when he got excited, his gestures—all were more muted. He was a living tragedy, a symbol of what had happened to his country and his people. The Chinese had rescued him just before the Vietnamese captured Phnom Penh at the beginning of 1979. He appeared before the UN Security Council to speak against the Vietnamese invasion, and he became the international symbol of Cambodian resistance. For a long time he was unforgiving and adamant against a coalition government with the Khmer Rouge.

After the Khmer Rouge occupied Phnom Penh, the Cambodians, or Kampucheans as they called themselves during Pol Pot's regime, were not active in the region. A senior minister, Ieng Sary, visited me in March 1977. He was soft-spoken, round-faced, and chubby; he looked the softest, kindest person, one who would look after babies tenderly. He was the brother-in-law and trusted aide of the infamous Pol Pot, the Khmer Rouge leader who had slaughtered from 1 to 2 million Cambodians out of a population of 7 million, including most of the educated, Cambodia's brightest and best. He made no reference to this genocide and I decided against questioning him. He was bound to deny, as their Khmer Rouge broadcasts did, that it ever took place. Ieng Sary was realistic. He wanted trade—barter trade. He needed spare parts for factories, pumps for irrigation, and outboard motors for their fishing boats. In exchange, he offered fish from the Tonle Sap, Cambodia's famous inland lake which flooded every year and produced excellent fish. The barter trade did not flourish (they had problems with logistics), so we had little trade or anything else to do with them.

Relations between Vietnam and Cambodia deteriorated with border clashes. Vietnam attacked Cambodia in 1978 and captured it in January 1979. Thereafter, Cambodia existed in my consciousness only through our activities in and out of the UN to garner votes to block the Vietnamese puppet government from taking over Cambodia's UN seat, and through our support for Cambodian resistance forces operating from the Thai-Cambodian border.

Sihanouk's son, Prince Ranariddh, I had met several times between 1981 and 1991. His father had placed him in charge of the royalist forces near the Thai border with Cambodia. Ranariddh resembled his father in voice, mannerisms, facial expression, and body language. He was darker-complexioned and smaller, more equable in temperament and less swayed by the mood of the moment, but otherwise much in the same mold. He had his father's fluency in French and had taught law in Lyon University before he took over the leadership of the royalist forces.

When I inspected their training camp in northeast Thailand in the 1980s I noted that it was not well organized and lacked military spirit. It was the best Ranariddh could do because, like him, his generals and officers spent more time in Bangkok than in the camp. As we were supporting them with weapons and radio equipment, I felt disappointed. After the 1991 settlement, the big aid donors took over. Ranariddh became the first prime minister (with Hun Sen as second prime minister) when his party won the 1993 UN-organized election. When we met in Singapore that August, I warned him that the coalition was a precarious arrangement. The military, police, and administration belonged to Hun Sen. If he wanted to survive, Ranariddh had to win over a part of Hun Sen's army and police officers and some of the provincial governors. Being called the first prime minister and having his man appointed defense minister were of little value when the officers and troops were loyal to Hun Sen. He probably did not take my words to heart. He might have believed that his royal blood would assure him the support of the people, that he would be irreplaceable.

I met Hun Sen in Singapore in December that same year. He was a totally different character, a tough survivor of the Khmer Rouge, a prime minister appointed by the Vietnamese in the 1980s but agile enough to distance himself from them and be acceptable to the Americans and West Europeans. He left an impression of strength and ruthlessness. He understood power, that it came from the barrel of the gun, which he was determined to hold. Once the Khmer Rouge were on the decline, and Ranariddh could no longer team up with them to challenge him, Hun Sen ousted him in 1997 and took complete control, while remaining nominally second prime minister. Sihanouk had become king again after the 1993 election, but his poor health and frequent absences from Cambodia for cancer treatment in Beijing had taken him out of the cockpit of power now occupied completely by Hun Sen and his army.

Cambodia is like a porcelain vase that has been smashed into myriads of shards. To put them together will be a slow and laborious task. As with all mended porcelain, it cannot withstand much pressure. Pol Pot had killed 90 percent of Cambodia's intelligentsia and trained personnel. The country now lacks a coherent administration. The people have been accustomed to lawless conditions for so long that they are no longer law-abiding. Only the gun is feared.

The people of Cambodia are the losers. The country is crushed, its educated class decimated, its economy devastated. Hun Sen's coup caused Cambodia's admission into Asean to be postponed. It was eventually admitted in April 1999 because no country wanted to spend US$2 billion for another UN operation to hold fair elections. Cambodia had had 27 years of war since Lon Nol's 1970 coup. Its present leaders are the products of bitter, relentless struggles in which opponents were either eliminated or neutralized. They are utterly merciless and ruthless, without humane feelings. History has been cruel to the Cambodians.

# 20. Asean—Unpromising Start, Promising Future

Asean was formed in August 1967 amid great uncertainty in the region. In a low-key ceremony, the foreign ministers of Indonesia, Malaysia, the Philippines, Singapore, and Thailand met in Bangkok to sign the declaration. The war in Vietnam was spreading into Cambodia and the region was caught up in communist insurgencies. I did not set great store by the lofty aims of the group: to accelerate economic growth, social progress, and cultural development; to promote peace and stability; to collaborate in agriculture and industry and expand trade. The unspoken objective was to gain strength through solidarity ahead of the power vacuum that would come with an impending British, and later a possible U.S., withdrawal. Indonesia wanted to reassure Malaysia and Singapore that, with the end of the Sukarno era, its intentions were peaceful and it had abandoned Sukarno's aggressive policies. Thailand wanted to associate itself with its noncommunist neighbors who were members of the Non-Aligned Movement. The Philippines wanted a forum to push its claim to North Borneo. Singapore sought the understanding and support of its neighbors in enhancing stability and security in the region.

It took 10 years before we developed cohesion and direction in our activities, time for the leaders and officials to get to know and take the measure of each other. We had a common enemy—the communist threat in guerrilla insurgencies, backed by North Vietnam, China, and the Soviet Union. We needed stability and growth to counter and deny the communists the social and economic conditions for revolutions. America and the West were prepared to help us.

The role of President Suharto was crucial for the success of Asean. After some false starts by pushy Indonesian officials, Suharto moderated the approach to one diametrically different from India's vis-à-vis the member countries of SAARC (South Asian Association for Regional Cooperation). Under Suharto, Indonesia did not act like a hegemon. It did not insist on its point of view but took into consideration the policies and interests of the other members. This made it possible for the others to accept Indonesia as first among equals.

While Asean's declared objectives were economic, social, and cultural, all knew that progress in economic cooperation would be slow. We were banding together more for political objectives, stability, and security. Asean succeeded in creating a sense of stability and security, but as expected, initially there was little tangible progress. When I addressed the fifth ministerial meeting of Asean foreign ministers in Singapore in April 1972, I drew attention to the gap between the large number of projects proposed and the few actually implemented. Each year there were 100 to 200 recommendations but only 10 to 20 were implemented.

The fall of Saigon to the communists in April 1975 increased our sense of the danger from subversion and insurgency. Asean had to undertake economic development more effectively to reduce domestic discontent. At a bilateral meeting with Suharto in Bali in September 1975, I tried to persuade him to agree to set economic targets for Asean at its first summit, which Indonesia would host, and to go for a trade liberalization policy, starting with a 10 percent reduction of tariffs on selected items by member countries and leading eventually to a free trade area. I thought he was sympathetic. To make the summit a success, we agreed to concentrate on issues that would show solidarity and put aside those that would divide us.

Ali Moertopo, Suharto's close aide, later told K. C. Lee, our ambassador, that after the president met me, his technocrats had advised him against free trade. These words conjured fears of a free-for-all competition in which Indonesia would become a dumping ground for the goods of other Asean countries, jeopardizing its chances of industrialization.

Politically, the Asean summit in February 1976 in Bali was a success. Asean had shown solidarity at a time of great uncertainty. For Indonesia, the host, there was a bonus. Held in the wake of the crisis caused by its occupation of East Timor, it improved President Suharto's international position. However, Suharto was not at ease at these formal summit meetings. He spoke only Bahasa Indonesia and could not engage in a free exchange in English. He preferred bilateral meetings. Then he would speak with animation and vigor in Bahasa Indonesia and, in the late 1980s, use English words and phrases to get his ideas across. The next summit was the following year, 1977, in Kuala Lumpur. Again I could see he was not comfortable, so the next one was not held until 10 years later, in Manila. By the time it was Singapore's turn to host a summit in 1992, I was no longer prime minister and did not attend.

We did not succeed in lowering tariffs between ourselves, but regular and frequent meetings led to easy personal and working relations between Asean ministers and officials. This helped them to solve bilateral problems informally before they became the subjects of third-party notes. Officials and ministers evolved a style of working that made it possible for disputes to be muted if not resolved, and for a more cooperative attitude to take hold. They played golf at their meetings. Between golf swings, they would test out their ideas and proposals, which could be turned down with less contention than at a formal meeting. They would also hold singing sessions after their dinners; it was obligatory for each minister to belt out one of his country's popular ditties. Singapore ministers were self-conscious and awkward. They did not do this at home. The Filipinos, Thais, and Indonesians were naturals, singing being a necessary part of their electioneering. To Western diplomats, such activities may appear inane. In fact they break the ice between people who, although close geographic neighbors, are strangers because they had been kept apart from each other for over a century by different colonial spheres of influence. Through these regular consultations and meetings, where business and recreation were equally important on the official agenda, habits of cooperation and compromise evolved. Asean officials tried to avoid confrontation, seeking consensus as the ideal. Where consensus was not possible, they settled for a compromise or a promise of cooperation.

When Asean had to deal with the developed countries, cooperation came naturally. We learned the value of political coordination when negotiating with Americans, Europeans in the European Economic Community, and Japanese. On their part, these industrial countries preferred to deal with us as a group. They wanted to encourage Asean for its rational and moderate position in international forums that led to practical outcomes. They wanted other regional groupings of developing countries to adopt Asean's pragmatic approach.

One example of Asean's value to its members was when Australia tried to change its civil aviation rules. In October 1978, it announced its new Australian International Civil Aviation Policy (ICAP) under which only Qantas and British Airways could carry passengers point-to-point between Australia and Britain and at supercheap fares. Airlines of intermediate stops, such as Singapore and the other Asean capitals, were excluded. Passengers were prevented by these special fares from making stopovers en route. The Australians also planned to reduce the capacity of the airlines of the intermediate Asean countries and cut the frequency of Singapore Airlines' flights between Singapore and both Australia and Britain. They wanted to disallow Thai International from taking passengers from Singapore, an intermediate point, on to Australia. The Australians wanted to discuss the issue only bilaterally with each affected country, but Asean economic ministers took a common stand against this. To thwart them, our Asean partners asked for time to consider the long-term implications of these changes which would cut out Asean airlines from the trunk route business and leave us with stunted regional airlines. Then we sorted out our divergent interests to present a united position.

I concluded that Boeing 747s flying from Australia to Europe would need to stop either in Singapore, Kuala Lumpur, or Bangkok en route to London. Jakarta was too close to Australia, and Colombo too far; both stops were not economic. We set out to keep the Malaysians and the Thais on our side. I instructed our officials to make enough concessions to the Malaysians and Thais so that they would join us in the fight.

I wrote to Thai Prime Minister General Kriangsak in January 1979 that Australia's move was "blatantly protectionist," that they wanted to exploit our differences by offering different inducements and threats. He supported me. My relations with General Kriangsak were close. And we gave enough concessions to Malaysian Airlines for Malaysia to stay united in Asean.

At first, the Australians nearly succeeded in isolating Singapore and dividing the Asean countries, playing one against the other. But Asean solidarity hardened after a meeting when the Australian secretary for transport spoke in tough terms to Asean civil aviation officials. This was reported to Dr. Mahathir, then Malaysia's deputy prime minister and minister for trade and industry. He was still angry over a visit to Australia with his prime minister, Tun Razak, during which they had been harassed by protesters. Mahathir stiffened Malaysia's stand against the Australians. From a bilateral dispute between Singapore and Australia, the ICAP issue escalated into an Asean versus Australia fight. Harsh words were traded in the press. Annoyed with the offhand attitudes of the Australian officials, the Indonesians threatened to deny their airspace to Australian aircraft if they insisted on ICAP. The Australian foreign minister, Andrew Peacock, visited Singapore to defuse the issue. Australia agreed to let Singapore Airlines retain its capacity and routing into Australia and allowed the other Asean airlines to increase their capacities. It was a lesson on the benefits of solidarity.

One problem that was to test Asean's solidarity from 1978 to 1991 was Vietnam's occupation of Cambodia. After the Vietnamese attacked Cambodia on 25 December 1978, Raja as foreign minister took the initiative to convene a special meeting of Asean foreign ministers in Bangkok on 12 January 1979. In a joint statement, they deplored the invasion and called for the withdrawal of all foreign forces in Cambodia. When the Vietnamese were advancing in Cambodia toward its border with Thailand, the situation became dangerous. However, the Chinese punitive expedition against Vietnam in February 1979 stabilized the position. The question then was how to prevent the Heng Samrin regime, installed in Phnom Penh by the Vietnamese, from dislodging Pol Pot's Khmer Rouge government from its seat in the United Nations. Their genocide of their own people had caused worldwide abhorrence and revulsion against the

Khmer Rouge. But if we wanted to keep the Vietnamese from getting international recognition for their puppet regime, we had no choice but to support the Khmer Rouge government.

Raja was a born crusader; the Vietnamese invasion of Cambodia provided him with a cause that stirred his idealism. He wrote powerful short memos, which we circulated to nonaligned countries, detailing how the big bullying Vietnamese, the Prussians of Southeast Asia, had pulverized and oppressed the weak and gentle Cambodians, one-tenth their size. A pleasant personality, neither arrogant nor meek, Raja was friendly, warm, and obviously sincere. His efforts made it easier for Tommy Koh in New York and ambassadors and officials from other countries to rally the votes against Vietnam at the UN and other international gatherings. Best of all, he did this without upsetting Mochtar Kusumaatmadja, the Indonesian foreign minister, who was under orders from his president not to isolate Vietnam. Suharto wanted a strong Vietnam to block any southward expansion of China. Raja and Tengku Rithauddeen, Malaysia's foreign minister, together persuaded Mochtar at least not to oppose the Thai policy and weaken the unity of Asean. The isolation of Vietnam was a decade-long saga in which Raja played a significant role.

Unexpectedly, a year later, on 24 December 1979, the Soviets invaded Afghanistan. It was a turning point; as President Carter said, the scales had fallen from his eyes. The U.S. government became more anti-Soviet and anti-Vietnam. It also changed the attitudes of our two Muslim neighbors, Indonesia and Malaysia. Both President Suharto and Prime Minister Mahathir stiffened their positions against the Soviet Union. They were suspicious of Soviet aims and their use of Vietnam. India was isolated as the only Asian country recognizing the Heng Samrin regime.

Our intelligence reports, confirmed by the Thais, showed that the Vietnamese occupation army of 170,000 were controlling all Cambodia's population centers and most of its countryside. The Heng Samrin regime's forces, some 30,000, were plagued by low morale and desertions. We were encouraged by reports of increasing popular resistance to Vietnamese occupation. The Khmer Rouge forces had withdrawn to the mountainous regions in the west, near the Thai border. Noncommunist resistance groups, which had been fighting the Khmer Rouge under commanders loyal to the old Lon Nol government, had coalesced to fight the

Vietnamese. Our officials worked hard to get Sihanouk and Son Sann to form a coalition government with the Khmer Rouge, but both feared and hated the Khmer Rouge.

Son Sann's relationship with Sihanouk was that of commoner and prince. At a meeting with his followers in Singapore in 1981, Son Sann was told by one of our officials that Sihanouk wanted to see them immediately. His whole delegation became nervous, overawed, and could not refuse to attend, even though Sihanouk no longer wielded any authority.

It took another year before Sihanouk and Son Sann were persuaded by the Chinese, Thais, and us to meet in Kuala Lumpur to sign a formal agreement for a Coalition Government of Democratic Kampuchea (CGDK). The Thais and Chinese persuaded the three parties to agree that Prince Sihanouk be the president, Khieu Samphan the vice president, and Son Sann the prime minister of the CGDK. I urged them to sign it in Kuala Lumpur, not in Beijing, because that would have made it appear a Chinese-sponsored coalition which would not receive wide support in the UN. I thought it important for the Vietnamese to see that Asean was united in support of the CGDK, that this was not just a Thai-Singapore project. Ghazali Shafie, the capable Malaysian foreign minister, was eager to take an active role. I was able to persuade Prime Minister Mahathir to support it. Once the agreement to form the CGDK had been signed in Kuala Lumpur, the Indonesians could not disavow it without risking their isolation in Asean. Sure enough, Mochtar Kusumaatmadja now agreed that Asean must support the noncommunist third force.

Sihanouk's forte was in propaganda and diplomatic maneuvring. The real power players were the Khmer Rouge leaders. Once they had broken out of their isolation as international outcasts by having Sihanouk and Son Sann associated with them in the coalition government, they built up their strength. The Chinese kept them well supplied with weapons and money. They also had income from their control of the gem mines and timber logging business along the border with Thailand.

For the Vietnamese, the formation of this coalition government was bad news. They reacted with venom, describing it as "a monster conceived by Chinese expansionism and U.S. imperialism." The Vietnamese foreign minister had repeatedly declared that the situation in Cambodia was irreversible and nonnegotiable. The Chinese challenged it and the

United States helped to oppose it. As we had hoped, international support for the coalition government increased, and any prospect of recognition for the Vietnamese puppet regime of Heng Samrin vanished.

The Vietnamese had been admired by Third World countries as great heroes after they defeated the Americans in 1975 and captured Saigon. Now they were defying world opinion, bullying a small neighbor, and becoming international villains. They were embroiled in a guerrilla war which, like the Americans in Vietnam, they could not win. They were to be bogged down in Cambodia for a further seven years until they withdrew in September 1989, but continued to be politically involved until the Paris Peace Accord in October 1991. We spent three years laboriously smoothing out differences between the Cambodians and sorting out the positions of China, Thailand, and Singapore, in order to bring along Malaysia and Indonesia and satisfy the Americans that they were not supporting the Khmer Rouge's return to power.

Raja and I worked hard to ensure that the United States remained interested in the region. Whether it was President Carter with Secretary Cyrus Vance, or President Reagan with Secretary George Shultz, I found them reluctant to play a major role. They did not want to be involved in another guerrilla war on the Asian mainland. We managed to persuade them to give modest aid, at first nonlethal, and later some lethal, to the two noncommunist resistance forces. But the Americans did help to gather votes in the UN against the Vietnamese.

Tommy Koh, our permanent representative at the UN, played a key role in lobbying and rallying votes. At the UN general assembly in 1982, Sihanouk as president of the newly formed coalition government appealed to UN members to restore Cambodia's independence and sovereignty. They responded by voting for Democratic Kampuchea with a bigger margin, a total of 105 member states. By gathering more votes in the UN each year, we made the Vietnamese feel their growing isolation.

Deng Xiaoping deterred any assault against Thailand by attacking Vietnam in February 1979. The price was paid in Chinese blood. Zhao Ziyang spelled out to me in Beijing in 1980 that by its "counteraction in self-defense" against Vietnam in 1979, China had forced Vietnam to station 60 percent of its best troops along the Sino-Vietnam border. If these men had been free to fight in Cambodia, he said, the next international conference would have been about a peaceful settlement of Thailand's problem with Vietnam, not Cambodia's. But Zhao tacitly acknowledged that China alone could not resolve the Cambodian problem. It needed the United States and Asean to muster international support.

In Washington in June 1981, at a one-on-one meeting with President Reagan, I spoke of the Soviets making trouble for Southeast Asia. I assured him that Deng Xiaoping had said that China did not want satellite states around it and was prepared to accept whoever won in a free vote in Cambodia. This helped to win Reagan's support. He was absolutely against the Vietnamese and their puppet regime.

When I proposed to John Holdridge, the assistant secretary of state for East Asia and the Pacific, in November 1981 in Singapore, that whoever won in a UN-supervised election could be allowed to take over Cambodia, and that Heng Samrin could possibly win, he interjected with vehemence, "I am not sure that that is acceptable. They are too committed to the Soviets." His expression, tone, and manner left me with no doubt that a Heng Samrin victory was as unacceptable to the Americans as to the Chinese. In August 1982, officials from the U.S. State Department and the CIA told our mission that the United States would fund the noncommunist resistance group in Cambodia by a total of US$4 million for nonlethal aid—food and medicine—to supplement Asean's efforts. It was a small beginning but an important breakthrough. The Reagan administration was getting over its Vietnam withdrawal syndrome and was prepared, in a subsidiary role, to support the noncommunist resistance. This encouraged Malaysia to supply training and uniforms. Singapore gave the first few hundreds of several batches of AK-47 automatic rifles, hand grenades, ammunition, and communications equipment.

With help from Britain, we employed British technicians and journalists to teach 14 Cambodians from the KPNLF to broadcast on shortwave radio from Singapore, and later to run a medium-wave station near the Thai border. They learned how to operate 25kW mobile Japanese transmitters. Together with the Thais and Malaysians, Singapore trained the guerrilla fighters. In 1983–1984, for the first time, resistance forces spearheaded by the Khmer Rouge continued on the offensive well into the dry season instead of retreating into Thailand.

Meeting Secretary of State George Shultz in Singapore in July 1984, I urged a reconsideration of U.S. policy of small, limited amounts of aid; the current U.S. policy would result in maximum benefits to China. We were providing the Khmer Rouge and China with political support that they could not muster on their own. Chinese military aid had ensured that the Khmer Rouge remained the strongest force. The United States should invest in the noncommunists to help them build up to their maximum potential, especially after they had shown promise of fighting capability and were enjoying more support among the Cambodian people than the Khmer Rouge. Shultz agreed it was worth a try, but pointed out that U.S. aid had to be sustainable. Unless the amounts were modest, it would be difficult to get yearly votes in Congress. He knew the sentiments in the U.S. Congress.

Shultz was right; the U.S. Congress would not support a significant aid program. Our representative on the Thai-Malaysian-Singapore-U.S. group that met regularly in Bangkok to coordinate our program estimated that the United States dispensed a total of about US$150 million in covert and overt aid to the noncommunist groups, Singapore US$55 million, Malaysia US$10 million, and Thailand a few million in training, ammunition, food, and operational funds. This was dwarfed by China who spent some US$100 million on the noncommunist forces of Son Sann and Sihanouk and 10 times that amount on the Khmer Rouge.

As it turned out, the Soviet Union was bleeding from the war in Afghanistan and its massive aid to Vietnam, Ethiopia, Angola, and Cuba. By the late 1980s, Soviet aid had stopped and Vietnam was in economic difficulties; it had an inflation rate of above 1,000 percent in 1988 and a food crisis. It had to get out of Cambodia. The Vietnamese old guard gave way to leaders who wanted to settle the Cambodian issue with China and open up their economy to save it from collapse. In July 1988, they unilaterally announced their withdrawal of 50,000 troops from Cambodia.

U.S. Congressman Stephen Solarz, in charge of Asia Pacific affairs in the House foreign relations committee, met me in Singapore and floated the proposal of a UN force to fill the power vacuum and hold elections. I encouraged him to pursue it. When Australian Foreign Minister Gareth Evans took up the proposal formally, Singapore and the other Asean members supported it. After the final agreement was signed in Paris on

23 October 1991, the UN despatched an advance peacekeeping force, followed by the UN Transitional Authority in Cambodia (UNTAC). Sihanouk returned to Phnom Penh in November 1991 from Beijing, escorted by Hun Sen who had succeeded Heng Samrin.

UNTAC was the largest and most costly UN peacekeeping mission to date—over US$2 billion for a contingent of 20,000 civilians and soldiers. It held elections successfully in May 1993. Sihanouk's party, led by his son, Prince Ranariddh, won the most seats, 58 against the 51 seats won by Hun Sen. But the Americans had changed their position on the Vietnamese puppet government: They must have been satisfied that Hun Sen wanted to be independent from Vietnam and were prepared to let him achieve power. The UN did not have the strength or will to install Ranariddh in power. It would have required disarming Hun Sen's troops and fighting the Khmer Rouge. So, the UN brokered a compromise that made Ranariddh the nominal first prime minister, but left real power in the hands of the second prime minister, Hun Sen, who was in charge of the army, the police, and the administration.

UNTAC began to leave by November 1993, its limited mission of holding elections with minimum loss of lives accomplished. Thereafter, Singapore became just an observer of the Cambodian drama. The big powers were dealing directly with each other to resolve the issue. China was the only country that had given support to the Khmer Rouge. Premier Li Peng told me in Beijing in October 1990 that although the Khmer Rouge had made mistakes in the past, they had also made contributions. In other words, they deserved a place in government. But once the Soviets agreed with the Americans to end the war in Vietnam by stopping their military aid, especially oil supplies, China's influence on the outcome diminished.

With the Vietnamese out of Cambodia, Asean solidarity weakened. Thai Prime Minister Chatichai Choonhavan wanted to seize the economic opportunities in Vietnam's rehabilitation through trade and investments. He overrode his foreign minister, Siddhi Savetsila, who said it was not yet time to make concessions. When Thailand shifted its position, the Indonesians also moved. They wanted a strong Vietnam, Laos, and Cambodia as a bloc to check any southward thrust of China's influence.

Singapore had sent a police contingent to help UNTAC. During the conflict, few countries gave aid to the noncommunist forces. We did, and our contribution in arms, ammunition, and equipment, plus political and diplomatic efforts on their behalf, helped to bring about the final outcome. But we knew the limits of our influence and went along with the UN solution for an interim government and fair elections. Both these objectives were more or less achieved. Hun Sen, his army, police, and administrators remained in firm control. Prince Ranariddh and his FUNCINPEC ministers provided Hun Sen and the former pro-Vietnam communists with the international respectability they needed to get aid. The Khmer Rouge lost out completely, so great was the international revulsion against Pol Pot for his genocidal crimes. Vietnam failed to make Cambodia its satellite despite paying a heavy price for 13 years.

We had spent much time and resources to thwart the Vietnamese in Cambodia because it was in our interests that aggression be seen not to pay. Indeed, Indonesia's costly experience in East Timor underlines this lesson. Twenty-four years after occupying it, Indonesia had to withdraw after the UN-supervised referendum in September 1999.

By the mid-1980s, Asean had established itself as a rational Third World grouping and was becoming the most dynamic region of the developing world. By opening up their economies to trade and foreign investments as recommended by the World Bank and the International Monetary Fund, the countries of Asean achieved 6 to 8 percent economic growth yearly for more than a decade. Their economic dynamism made them attractive as economic and political partners. Regular dialogue started with the Australians and New Zealanders, followed by the Japanese, Americans, and West Europeans. As Asean grew into a coherent organization with a common voice on major issues, more countries wanted to join as its dialogue partners at its annual meetings to discuss political and economic issues.

The common threat of communism from North Vietnam, China, and the Soviet Union had made for solidarity in Asean. After the collapse of communism, Asean needed a new common objective that could unite the group. By their fourth summit in Singapore in January 1992, Asean countries were ready to promote a free trade area. Singapore had long urged a greater emphasis on economic cooperation to supplement political cooperation. Our efforts had not been successful. Suggestions from Singapore for greater economic cooperation were regarded with suspicion by other Asean countries. As we had a more advanced economy, open to the world and almost totally free of both tariff and nontariff barriers, they feared that we would benefit disproportionately.

In the late 1980s, after China and later India opened up and attracted huge investments, Asean leaders changed their views. The prime minister of Thailand in 1992, Anand Panyarachun, had been a successful business-man after being head of the Thai foreign ministry. He understood the eco-nomics of trade and investment in an interdependent world. To avoid lin-gering suspicions about Singapore's motives, I advised Prime Minister Goh to get Anand to take the lead to push for an Asean Free-Trade Area (AFTA). Anand did so successfully, and the Asean summit in Singapore agreed to establish AFTA by 2008. The date was later brought forward to 2003 by the Asean economic ministers.

AFTA marked a major milestone in Asean's evolution. Asean's goal was to manage relationships between members who still jealously guarded their sovereignty, and to help resolve political problems before they erupted into conflict. AFTA will lead to a greater integration of the economies of South-east Asia.

At the 1992 summit in Singapore, Asean leaders decided that its annual postministerial conferences should be a forum for political and security matters. This led to annual meetings of the Asean Regional Forum (ARF) with Asean's dialogue partners (the United States, Japan, Australia, Canada, New Zealand, Republic of Korea, and the European Union) together with China, Russia, and India. It enabled potential adversaries to discuss in a noncombative atmosphere sensitive disputes like the competing claims to the Spratly islets. It was a change in policy from excluding to including major powers to discuss security issues in the region.

Meanwhile, Asean has to digest its enlarged membership. Vietnam was admitted into Asean in 1995, Myanmar and Laos in 1997, and Cambodia in 1999. The four have some way to go to reach the level of development of the old members, and to gain acceptability as dialogue partners of the United States and the European Union.

# 21. East Asia in Crisis 1997-1999

The sudden devastation to the economies of Asean in 1997 set back its standing and its capability to play an international role. Indonesia's President Suharto, who had built up his country and gained stature and recognition, was deposed. Prime Minister Mahathir of Malaysia was diminished by the Western media headlining his denunciations against currency speculators and Jews like George Soros. Thailand's Prime Minister Chuan Leekpai needed time to establish his international standing. What happened?

In March 1997, Richard Hu, our finance minister, told the cabinet that the Thais had asked us to defend their baht, which was under attack. We were unanimous that we should not. Nevertheless, the Thais asked him to do it for them with their funds. They did not want the market to know that only the Thai central bank was buying bahts. The Monetary Authority of Singapore did so, but warned that it would not be successful. When the attackers were repelled, the Thais thought we were proved wrong. We warned them that the attackers would return. They did, in May. By 2 July, after spending over US$23 billion of Thailand's reserves, the Thai central banker gave up. He floated the baht, whereupon it dropped by 15 percent. Thai debtors scrambled to buy dollars, driving the baht further down. We did not realize then that the meltdown in East Asia had been triggered.

Thailand, Indonesia, Malaysia, and the Philippines had their currencies closely linked to the U.S. dollar. Interest rates on the U.S. dollar were much lower than their domestic interest rates. It worked well when the U.S. dollar was weakening and their exports became cheaper and increased. When the U.S. dollar began to strengthen from mid-1995, Thai exports became dearer and declined. Thailand's companies had borrowed in U.S. dollars, assuming that their exchange rates would remain more or less the same when the time came to repay. If they had floating exchange rates, they would have weighed the risk of a possible depreciation of the baht against the benefit of a lower interest rate. And foreign lenders would not have been so confident about the borrowers' ability to repay if faced with sudden changes in exchange rates.

Several Singapore-based American bankers had discussed with me in 1996 their advice to Thai and other Asean central bankers on the hazards of trying to control both their exchange and interest rates when they no longer had restrictions on capital flows. They had recommended more flexible exchange rates. The central bankers did not heed this warning and their current account deficits increased.

Since 1995, the Thais had been having large current account deficits, importing more than they were exporting. If this continued, they would not have enough foreign currency to meet their foreign debt repayments. So, foreign exchange dealers began selling baht, anticipating the difficulties the Thai central bank would face defending the baht at its then high rate of exchange to the U.S. dollar. Once the short-sellers started to win, reputable fund managers joined them in selling down the currencies of Malaysia, Indonesia, and the Philippines as well as Thailand. All these currencies sank in value when their central banks abandoned their pegs to the U.S. dollar.

The Singapore dollar, however, was not tied to the U.S. dollar but was managed against a basket of currencies of our major trading partners. It had steadily appreciated against the U.S. dollar until the mid-1990s. Singapore dollar interest rates were much lower than U.S. dollar rates. Because it was unattractive for Singapore companies to borrow U.S. dollars, Singapore companies had little U.S. dollar debt.

Thai Prime Minister Chavalit Yongchaiyudh, an old friend of mine from the time he was a general of the Thai army, asked Prime Minister Goh Chok Tong for a loan of US$1 billion. Goh discussed this in cabinet and decided that we would agree if Thailand first sought the assistance of the International Monetary Fund. It did.

As the crisis spread, in July, Malaysian Prime Minister Mahathir denounced George Soros as the speculator responsible. Then Bank Negara Malaysia announced changes limiting the amount of Malaysian ringgit that could be swapped into foreign currencies. To check the fall in share prices, the Kuala Lumpur Stock Exchange changed its rules by requiring sellers to produce the physical share scrips within a day of any sale. They also imposed trading curbs on 100 key blue-chip stocks included in the stock exchange index computation. Fund managers dumped Malaysian and Asean currencies and stocks.

In September 1997, at an IMF/World Bank meeting of international bankers in Hong Kong, Mahathir said, "Currency trading is unnecessary, unproductive and totally immoral. It should be stopped. It should be made illegal." Another sellout of all Asean currencies and stocks followed.

Thailand and Indonesia accepted IMF rescue packages with conditions. But the Thais, after reaching agreement with the IMF in August 1997, did not implement the terms they had agreed upon: to tighten money supply, raise interest rates, and clean up their banking system, including closing down 58 insolvent finance companies. Chavalit's multiparty coalition government did not have the strength to undertake such painful reforms. Political leaders of all Thai parties both in government and opposition had close ties with bankers and businesspeople whose support they needed for fund-raising. In November, he lost a vote of confidence and resigned. In Bangkok in January 1998, he explained to me that many Thai bankers had urged him to defend the baht, that as he was a soldier, not an expert on finance matters, he had taken their advice. His banker friends might not have told him that they had borrowed over $40 billion in U.S. dollars and did not want to pay more bahts for the dollars they had borrowed.

In retrospect, what had they done wrong? By the early 1990s, the economies of Thailand, Indonesia, and Korea were already operating at full capacity. Many of the new investments were channelled into projects of doubtful value. While the euphoria lasted, everyone overlooked the institutional and structural weaknesses in these economies.

These countries would have been better off if their capital accounts had been liberalized more gradually. They would have had the time to build a system to monitor, check, and control the flow of non-FDI (foreign direct investment) capital to ensure that it went into productive investments. As it was, large amounts of capital were invested in stocks and properties, office blocks, and condominiums. These stocks and properties were in turn used as collateral for borrowing, further inflating the asset bubble. Lenders were aware of this laxness but accepted it as the way business was done in emerging markets. Some even saw the presence of politically connected business partners as implicit government guarantees for the loans and so went along with the game.

The G7 finance ministers had pressed them to liberalize their financial markets and free capital movements. But they did not explain to the central bankers and finance ministers of the developing countries the dangers inherent in today's globalized financial markets, when massive amounts can flow in or out at the touch of a computer button. Liberalization should have been more carefully calibrated according to the level of competence and sophistication of their financial systems. These countries should have installed circuit breakers—controls to cope with any sudden inflow or outflow of funds.

Although the economic conditions of each country were different, the collapse of foreign confidence affected the whole region. What began as a classic market mania with funds flowing exuberantly into East Asia became a classic market panic when investors stampeded to get their money out.

In January 1997, Hanbo, a South Korean *chaebol* (Korean conglomerate) went bankrupt in a major corruption scandal involving President Kim Young Sam's son. Many other banks and chaebols were believed to be in similar straits and the value of the South Korean won dropped. The Korean central bank defended its currency until it ran out of reserves in November and sought IMF help. In the next few weeks, the whole of East Asia, including Hong Kong, Singapore, and Taiwan, was swept up in a financial typhoon.

Hong Kong's currency had been pegged to the U.S. dollar since 1983. Because of the crisis, it had to raise its interest rates well above that of the U.S. dollar, as a risk premium to induce people to hold HK dollars. High interest rates had hurt stock and property markets. Hong Kong lost its competitiveness because the cheaper currencies of its neighbors hurt its tourist and travel industries, leaving hotels empty. Hong Kong was right to defend the peg during this crisis to maintain confidence in the territory so soon after its return to Chinese sovereignty, but the problem became acute when the crisis was prolonged.

What distinguishes East Asia's economic crisis from Latin America's underscores a basic difference in culture and social values. Unlike Latin Americans, East Asian governments had not overspent. Not all had indulged in extravagant prestige projects, or siphoned borrowed money out of their countries to park in the stock markets of New York or London. These governments had balanced budgets, low inflation, and many decades of steady high growth. It was their private sector corporations that had overborrowed short-term in the last few years to make imprudent long-term investments in properties and excess industrial plants.

Western critics have attributed this collapse to what they term "Asian values": cronyism, *guanxi,* corruption, backdoor or under-the-counter business practices. There is no question that these contributed to the crisis and aggravated the damage incurred. But were they the primary causes? The answer must be "no" because these flaws had been present, almost endemic, since the beginning of the "Asian miracle" in the 1960s, more than 30 years ago. It was only in the last few years that several of the emerging countries indulged in the excessive borrowing in foreign currencies that caused their troubles. Even excessive borrowings might not have led to such a meltdown but for their woefully inadequate systems with weak banks, inadequate supervision, and wrong exchange rate policies. Bad cultural habits aggravated the damage; wrongdoings were difficult to detect and expose where systems were not transparent.

Corruption, nepotism, and cronyism in Asia were condemned by the Western critics as proof of the fundamental weakness of "Asian values." There are many different value systems in Asia—Hindu, Muslim, Buddhist,

Confucianist. I am able to discuss only Confucian values. Corruption and nepotism are a debasement of Confucian values. A Confucian gentleman's duty to family and friends presumes that he helps them from his personal and not official resources. Too often officials use public office to do favors for family and friends, undermining the integrity of government. Where there are transparent systems to detect and check abuses of power and privilege, as in Singapore and Hong Kong (both former British colonies), such abuses are rare. Singapore weathered the crisis better because no corruption or cronyism distorts the allocation of resources, and public officers are referees, not market participants. But in the troubled countries, too many politicians and public officials have exercised power and responsibility not as a trust for public good, but as an opportunity for private gain. Making the problems worse, many political leaders and their officials refused to accept the market's verdict. For a long time they blamed speculators and conspirators for the destruction in values. Their denial made many investors pull out.

None of the leaders realized the implications of the globalized financial market of instant communications between the main financial centers of the world—New York, London, and Tokyo—and their representatives in the capitals of East Asia. The inflow of funds from the industrial countries brings not only the benefits of high growth but also the risk of a sudden outflow of these funds. Every capital—Bangkok, Jakarta, Kuala Lumpur, Seoul—has hundreds of resident international bankers supported by local staff with roots in the community. Any wrong step by the government is instantly analyzed and reported to their clients worldwide. But Suharto acted as if it was still the 1960s, when financial markets were more insulated and reaction time much slower.

Was the Asian miracle in fact a mirage? For several decades before companies in the region borrowed from international banks, these countries had high growth rates, low inflation, and prudent budgets. Backward agricultural communities had maintained stability, accumulated savings, and attracted investments from the developed countries. Their peoples are hardworking and frugal, with high savings of 30 to 40 percent. They invested in infrastructure. They concentrated on education and training. They have enterprising businesspeople, and pragmatic and pro-business governments. Their economic fundamentals have been consistently good. By 1999, after two years of crisis, recovery appeared to be on the way. High savings kept interest rates low and made for an early rebound. Foreign fund managers became optimistic and returned to the stock markets, boosting exchange rates. This may make some countries slow down their banking and corporate restructuring, which would be costly in a future downturn.

All leaders in Southeast Asia were shell-shocked by the sudden devastation of their currencies, stock markets, and property values. It will take some time to put their countries in order. This will happen, and the need to collaborate to increase the weight of Southeast Asian countries when negotiating with big powers like China, Japan, and the United States will bring them closer together in Asean. U.S. and European leaders will continue to be sympathetic and to sound helpful but their previous respect for the proven competence of the region's leaders will take some time to return.

Asean leaders will learn from this setback to build stronger financial and banking systems, with sound regulations and rigorous supervision. Investors will return because the factors for high growth will remain for another 10 to 20 years. Cronyism and corruption will be difficult to erase completely, but with adequate laws and supervision, excesses can be checked. Another meltdown is unlikely as long as the pain and misery of this crisis are not forgotten. Within a decade, the original five Asean countries will resume their growth, and from a leaner base new leaders will emerge who will gain stature and respect.

There is a deeper lesson to be drawn from this crisis. In a globalized economy, where Americans and Europeans set the rules through the WTO and other multilateral organizations, it is wasteful to use capital without regard to market forces, as the Japanese and Koreans have done. To finance the Japanese zaibatsus and the Korean chaebols in their expansion to capture market share abroad, their governments extracted the maximum of savings from their people. The savings were directed by the government through their banks for specific conglomerates to capture market share in designated products. This has often resulted in uncompetitive industries. When they were catching up with the advanced countries, it was possible to spot which industries to invest in. Now that they have caught up with the West, it is not easy to pick the winners. Like everyone else, they will have to allocate resources in response to market signals. It is a mistake to think that the Japanese and Koreans have lost their innate strengths. Judging from their past records, they will restructure and learn to operate on the basis of profitability and rates of return on equity.

# 22.  Inside the Commonwealth Club

When we became independent I assumed that Singapore would be a member of the Commonwealth. The British government was supportive, and the Tunku was keen to sponsor us. I did not know that Pakistan had initially opposed our admission; it had considered Malaysia too pro-India in the India-Pakistan conflict over Kashmir. Arnold Smith, the secretary-general of the Commonwealth, in his memoirs wrote that Pakistan's antagonism against Malaysia was carried over to the Singapore government, which had shown sympathy for India. But Smith persuaded Pakistan to abstain and not object to Singapore's admission. In October 1965, Singapore was admitted as the 22nd member of the Commonwealth. This membership was valuable. For a newly independent country, it provided links to a network of governments whose institutions were similar and whose leaders and officials shared a common background. They were all English-speaking governments, with British civil administration practices and legal, judicial, and educational systems.

Soon after we joined, the prime minister of Nigeria, Sir Abubakar Tafawa Balewa, called a conference of Commonwealth prime ministers for 11 January 1966 in Lagos, to discuss Rhodesia's Unilateral Declaration of Independence (UDI). Rhodesia was then a self-governing colony with a white minority of 225,000 in control of 4 million black Africans. I decided to go.

On the BOAC (British Overseas Airways Corporation) plane making the seven-hour flight from London to Lagos were several other prime ministers and presidents of the smaller Commonwealth countries. We made conversation. A memorable fellow passenger was Archbishop Makarios, president of Cyprus. He wore silken black robes with a tall black hat as archbishop of the Greek Orthodox Church. Once on board, he removed his robes and hat and looked a totally different person, a smallish bald man with a moustache and a mass of a beard. He sat across the aisle from me, so I had a good view of him. I watched, fascinated, as he dressed and tidied up when the plane taxied to the terminal. He diligently and carefully combed his moustache and beard. He stood up to put on his black robes over his white clothes, then his gold chain with a big medallion, and then carefully placed his hat on his head. An aide brushed him down to remove any white flecks from his flowing black robes, and handed him his archbishop's staff; only then was His Beatitude Archbishop Makarios finally ready to descend the steps in proper style for the waiting cameras. No politician could have been more PR-conscious. The other prime ministers held back and allowed him to take precedence—he was not only president, he was also archbishop.

We were greeted, inspected a guard of honor in turn, and then whisked into Lagos. It looked like a city under siege. Police and soldiers lined the route to the Federal Palace Hotel. Barbed wire and troops surrounded it. No leader left the hotel throughout the two-day conference.

The night before the meeting, Sir Abubakar Tafawa Balewa, whom I had visited two years before, gave us a banquet in the hotel. Raja and I were seated opposite a hefty Nigerian, Chief Festus, their finance minister. The conversation is still fresh in my mind. He was going to retire soon, he said. He had done enough for his country and now had to look after his business, a shoe factory. As finance minister, he had imposed a tax on imported shoes so that Nigeria could make shoes. Raja and I were incredulous. Chief Festus had a good appetite that showed in his rotund figure, elegantly camouflaged in colorful Nigerian robes with gold ornamentation and a splendid cap. I went to bed that night convinced that they were a different people playing to a different set of rules.

When the meeting opened on 11 January, Prime Minister Abubakar spoke. He was a tall, lean, and dignified figure with a slow, measured delivery. He looked every inch a chief, a figure of quiet authority, in the flowing robes of the Hausas from northern Nigeria. He had summoned this conference urgently to discuss the unlawful declaration of independence by Rhodesia, which called for action from the British. The vice president of Zambia, Reuben Kamanga, spoke next, and then Harold Wilson. It was clear Wilson was not able and not going to use force against Ian Smith's illegal independent regime. It would be politically costly in British popular support, and would also cause economic damage to Rhodesia and the surrounding African countries.

On the second day I spoke. I had no prepared script, just a few headings and notes I had jotted down as Prime Minister Abubakar and the others spoke. I took a broad philosophical approach. Three hundred years ago, the British set out to occupy North America, Australia, and New Zealand and to colonize much of Asia and Africa. They settled in the more desirable regions of Asia and Africa as conquerors and masters. But in 1966, a British prime minister was talking on equal terms with heads of government of former colonial territories. It was a continually evolving relationship. Sir Albert Margai, prime minister of Sierra Leone, had said that only an African could feel passionately and be concerned about Rhodesia. I could not agree with him that only Africans should be concerned with this problem. We were all interested parties and concerned. Singapore was closely associated with Britain in defense. If Britain were to be branded as a supporter of Ian Smith's illegal seizure of power, my position would become difficult.

I disagreed with Dr. Milton Obote, prime minister of Uganda, that Britain had been reluctant to bring the Europeans in Rhodesia to heel or to have the UN impose sanctions because of a diabolical British plot to give Ian Smith time to consolidate his regime. It was unhelpful to talk in terms of racist divisions between white settlers and immigrants. Like the peoples in Canada, Australia, and New Zealand, I was a settler. If all immigrants were racists, then the world was in for a difficult time. We had two alternative solutions to problems created by migrations that had taken place all around the world: either to accept that all men had equal rights, or to return to the rule of the strong over the weak. For colored peoples of the world to demand retribution for past wrongs was not the answer to survival. In Africa, the nub of the problem was not Rhodesia but race relations in South Africa.

I did not believe that Britain was reluctant to end the Smith regime because its survival would threaten the standing of the West with all non-European peoples. Wilson was faced with the problem of going against domestic opinion if he used force to crush a puny minority. I believed the British government was in earnest and its reluctance to bring the issue to the United Nations was because it did not want 130 members of the UN to decide what happened in Rhodesia after Mr. Smith had been brought down. Britain had to buy time for its economic interests in South Africa and Rhodesia and there was the need to preserve the Rhodesian economy in the interests of Africans as well as Europeans. When the problems of South Africa were resolved, the wider problem remained of how different races could learn to live together in a world shrunk by technological changes.

I sympathized with the Africans, but I also saw the difficulties a British prime minister faced if he had to send British troops to quell a rebellion of British settlers who had been fully self-governing for decades since 1923. The issue now was to make progress on the method and the time for achieving majority rule for Rhodesia.

One advantage of these Commonwealth leaders' meetings was that however big or small your country, when you did intervene, you were judged on your merits. Many read prepared speeches. I responded to what had just been said, and from notes. I spoke sincerely and expressed my thoughts without the euphemisms of a prepared text. This was my maiden speech at a Commonwealth prime ministers' conference and I could sense that my colleagues around the table responded favorably.

Wilson later wrote in his memoirs that "It was hard-hitting, though somewhat repetitive, as one African leader after another sought to prove how much more African he was than his neighbour. From Asia, Cyprus, the Caribbean, the message of condemnation was the same. Then Lee Kuan Yew of Singapore spoke—an off-the-cuff unprepared speech of some forty minutes at a level of sophistication rarely achieved in any of the Commonwealth conferences which I attended."

My attendance at Lagos consolidated my friendship with Harold Wilson. I had been helpful to the Africans and not unhelpful to the British. Wilson congratulated me outside the conference room and said he hoped I would attend other Commonwealth conferences. He needed a foil for difficult leaders who made long and biting speeches. The conference ended two days later after appointing two committees to review the effect of sanctions and the special needs of Zambia that required Commonwealth support.

When we left for our next stop, Accra, the capital of Ghana, there was more security along the route to the airport as tension had increased in Lagos in the four days since we arrived.

Three days after we arrived in Accra, we were told by our hosts that there had been a bloody coup in Lagos. Prime Minister Abubakar had been assassinated and so had Chief Festus. An Ibo army major from eastern Nigeria, where oil was being discovered, led the coup which killed many Hausa Muslims from northern Nigeria. The major said "he wanted to get rid of rotten and corrupt ministers and political parties." This coup put Major-General J. T. U. Aguiyi-Irons into power, but it was to be followed by many other coups.

Kwame Nkrumah, Ghana's president, did not rejoice at the news. He himself had had a narrow escape about two years before, just before I visited him in January 1964. By 1966, "Osagyefo" (Redeemer), as Nkrumah was called, had recovered enough of his bounce to give me dinner with some of his senior ministers and a bright young vice-chancellor of his university. This man, Abraham, was only about 30 years old, had taken a First in Classics at Oxford and was a fellow of All Souls' College. Nkrumah was very proud of him. I was impressed, but wondered why a country so dependent on agriculture should have its brightest and best do Classics—Latin and Greek.

On our arrival at Accra, the person who came up to the aircraft to greet me was Krobo Edusei, the minister for presidential affairs. He had gained notoriety as a corrupt minister who had bought himself a golden bedstead, a story much publicized in the world press. Nkrumah defused the scandal by restricting Krobo's portfolio to looking after government hospitality. On my second night in Accra, he took me to a nightclub in Accra. He proudly announced that he was the owner and that all VIPs would enjoy their evenings there.

We travelled by car to the High Volta dam, some three hours of travel. On the road to the dam our convoy was led by a car with loudspeakers playing music with an African beat; the lyrics had the refrain, in English, "work is beautiful." Little toddlers would appear from their huts off the road, swaying naturally to the rhythm as they made their way to the roadside to wave to us. I was fascinated to see how lithe and double-jointed they were.

I was the second guest to be entertained on a beautiful yacht that had been imported fully assembled from Miami. They told me it had been transported by rail and floated on the lake. Accompanying us on board were Krobo Edusei and Ghana's minister for foreign affairs, Alex Quaison Sackey, a well-educated and well-spoken man. When we were cruising on the lake, having cocktails and canapés on deck, Raja asked Krobo who had made his beautiful safari suit. Krobo replied, "My tailor shop in Kumasi. You must visit it one day and I will make a suit for you like mine." He then spoke of his other activities. He used to be a 30 bob (US$4) a week postal clerk; now he had two sons educated in Geneva, Switzerland. A man, he said, must have ambition. Quaison Sackey, a sophisticate who had been president of the UN General Assembly, looked most unhappy and uncomfortable. He valiantly tried to steer the conversation away from Krobo, but Krobo was not to be deterred and we were regaled with one hilarious tale after another. I wondered what would happen to these two countries. They were then the brightest hopes of Africa, the first two to get their independence, Ghana in 1957, followed shortly by Nigeria.

One month later, on 24 February, as Nkrumah was being welcomed with a 21-gun salute in Beijing, China, an army coup took place in Accra. People danced in the streets as the army leaders arrested leading members of Nkrumah's government. Alex Quaison Sackey and Krobo Edusei were with Nkrumah in Beijing. When they returned to Accra, they were placed under protective custody. My fears for the people of Ghana were not misplaced. Notwithstanding their rich cocoa plantations, gold mines, and High Volta dam, which could generate enormous amounts of power, Ghana's economy sank into disrepair and has not recovered the early promise it held out at independence in 1957.

The news I read saddened me. I never visited Ghana again. Two decades later, in the 1980s, Quaison Sackey saw me in Singapore. He had been arrested and released in one of the innumerable coups. He wanted to purchase palm oil on credit from Singapore, on behalf of the Nigerian government, which promised to pay after they had held their elections. I said that was a private business deal he had to strike. He picked up a living by using his contacts with African leaders of neighboring states. Ghana, he said, was in a mess. I asked after the bright young vice-chancellor, Abraham. Quaison Sackey reported that he had entered a monastery in California. I felt sad. If their brightest and best gave up the fight and sought refuge in a monastery, not in Africa but in California, the road to recovery would be long and difficult.

I was not optimistic about Africa. In less than 10 years after independence in 1957, Nigeria had had a coup and Ghana a failed coup. I thought their tribal loyalties were stronger than their sense of common nationhood. This was especially so in Nigeria, where there was a deep cleavage between the Muslim Hausa northerners and the Christian and pagan southerners. As in Malaysia, the British had handed power, especially the army and police, to the Muslims. In Ghana, without this north-south divide, the problem was less acute, but there were still clear tribal divisions. Unlike India, Ghana did not have long years of training and tutelage in the methods and discipline of modern government.

The next conference was in London in September 1966, when I got to know many prime ministers who had not attended the special conference in Lagos. In the two weeks there, I consolidated Singapore's position with the British public and maintained my already good relations with Wilson and his key ministers, and with Conservative party leaders.

The Rhodesia question again dominated the whole conference (as it did every conference until its settlement in 1979 at the Lusaka meeting). African leaders felt strongly for their fellow Africans in Rhodesia. They also wanted to establish their African credentials with their own people. Moreover, focusing on the Unilateral Declaration of Independence (UDI) in Rhodesia took their people's minds off their own urgent economic and social difficulties. Of the white leaders, Lester Pearson of Canada was by far the most liberal in his instincts and sympathetic to the cause of the Africans and the underprivileged.

I spoke of the problems in Southeast Asia. I said that Vietnam was a clash of two rival ideologies, each determined not to give in, knowing that the whole region would be lost if one side yielded to the other. Harold Holt, the Australian prime minister, showed discomfort when I said Australian and New Zealand armies were in South Vietnam not purely to safeguard democracy and Vietnamese freedom: They were defending their own strategic interests. He quickly recovered his balance and accepted my point when I added that their interests included my survival. I took an independent position to establish my credentials so as not to be seen as a puppet of the British, Australians, or New Zealanders whose troops were defending Singapore. I said frankly that an American withdrawal would be disastrous for all in the region, including Singapore. My language made my views acceptable, although the prevailing sentiments of African leaders were against American intervention. Singapore's standing with Africans and Asian leaders also improved.

At the next meeting, in January 1969, also in London, Wilson as chairman asked me to open the discussion on Commonwealth cooperation. I prefaced my remarks with a criticism of niggardly Western help for developing countries, then went on to explain the deeper reasons for their failure. To rally their people in their quest for freedom, the first-generation anticolonial nationalist leaders had held out visions of prosperity that they could not realize. A population explosion had increased the burden on resources. Interethnic peace, which had been enforced by the colonial overlord, was difficult to maintain after independence with power in the hands of an ethnic majority. The elite who had commanded popular support before independence had to demonstrate their continuing legitimacy, and in competing against other parties, they had been unable to resist the temptation of appeals to ethnic, linguistic, and religious loyalties. The countries suffered as their ethnic minorities, mostly Indians in Africa, were squeezed out by rioting or legislation. Often they were the shopkeepers who had acted as village bankers, since they knew who was and who was not creditworthy. This role of village banker could not be filled by their own native administrators, the U.S. Peace Corps, or British Voluntary Service officers. The layer of trained people was too thin and new states reverted back to type as soft societies without the firm hand of an overlord and a strong framework of administration. Corruption set in and became a way of life. Military coups made things worse. But most of all, most governments had favored economic planning and controls which stifled free enterprise. Fortunately, Malaysia and Singapore had not and so continued to make progress. In his book *The Labour*

*Government 1964–1970,* Harold Wilson wrote that I described "with brutal realism the economic problems of newly-emancipated countries. . . . By common consent, one of the most remarkable essays in interpretation of the post-imperial world any one of us had heard."

Wilson had proposed to alternate the biennial conferences between London and a Commonwealth country. He was keen to hold the next one in Singapore. The other leaders agreed. I was happy to host it. It would be good for Singapore to have world attention focused on it. With two years to prepare, it could be an occasion for Singapore to gain recognition as an oasis of efficiency and rationality in the Third World.

Our Commonwealth guests arrived in January 1971 to a clean and green Singapore with friendly, warm, efficient, and courteous service. The hotels, shops, taxis, and restaurants put forth their best efforts. All was neat and orderly. The families of the pro-communist political detainees staged an antigovernment demonstration outside the NTUC Conference Hall, where the meeting was being held. When the police quietly dispersed them, there were murmurs of disapproval from the British press, that we should have allowed them to carry on. The officers responsible for the delegates' security thought otherwise.

Ted Heath had announced soon after he became prime minister that Britain would resume arms sales to South Africa which had been suspended by the Labour government. This provoked a fierce reaction from black African leaders, many of whom threatened to break up the Commonwealth if Britain persisted. Soon after Heath arrived in Singapore, he agreed with me and announced that Britain would be happy to have the arms for South Africa issue treated as a separate item on the agenda. After two sessions restricted to leaders only, we agreed to a study group to consider the question of the supply of maritime arms and to report its findings to the secretary-general.

Heath was not comfortable in that Third World multiracial setting. It was his first experience of such a gathering. The African leaders set out to make him feel isolated. A little shy and guarded, he was different from Harold Wilson with his pipe-puffing bonhomie. Heath appeared stiff and ill at ease, spoke with a strong Oxford accent, and bristled when provoked. Fortunately, he knew me well and was confident that I would ensure him a fair hearing.

I called on Sir Seretse Khama, president of Botswana, as the first speaker. I knew him to be moderate, level-headed, and thoughtful. He was the son of the chief of Botswana and had married an Englishwoman when he was at Oxford. The South African government had successfully pressured the British government to block his succession to the chieftainship for many years because his black-white marriage made a mockery of their ban on black-white sex. He said Britain must be the arbiter of its own national interest, but the decision to sell arms could only damage the Commonwealth. It was a quiet and cogent speech.

Julius Nyerere, president of Tanzania, pitched his argument on a high moral plane, that South Africa was out of the Commonwealth because its ideology was inconsistent with a multiracial Commonwealth. He asked "earnestly" that Britain should not help South Africa and force African countries to react. He was unexpectedly brief. He had sized up Heath and decided it was best not to preach to him. Nyerere was the African leader I most respected. He struck me as honest and sincere. He handed over power to a successor in a constitutional manner and Tanzania never descended into the chaos of Uganda.

President Hastings Banda of Malawi said no African leader was going to leave and wreck the Commonwealth. Force would not succeed; the freedom fighters had tried since 1964 and achieved nothing. In place of force, isolation, and boycott, he called for contact and dialogue between the blacks and whites. African leaders displayed open contempt for him, but he appeared completely unmoved. I tried to check his rhetorical exuberance but once in full flow he was not to be stopped. He was quite a character, with his sunglasses even indoors and at night, and his buxom young African lady companion. He looked old but spoke with vigor, waving his fly whisk to emphasize his points. But he might as well have waved a red flag at angry bulls. I was not sure whether Heath was embarrassed or delighted.

Heath made a reasoned reply. The sale of maritime equipment to South Africa was essentially a matter of defense policy, nothing to do with apartheid. Britain depended on the free movement of goods and the freedom of the seas. Half its oil supplies and a quarter of its trade passed through the sea route around the Cape. The Soviet Union posed a maritime threat. (On 16 January, four days before Heath spoke on arms to South Africa, two Soviet warships, a cruiser and a destroyer, had ostentatiously sailed past Singapore around two in the afternoon from the South China Sea toward the Indian Ocean.)

A dramatic intervention was provided by President Kenneth Kaunda of Zambia. He warned that Britain's national interest lay not only in South Africa or the Indian Ocean, but in many parts of Africa. As he recounted cruelties Africans had suffered at the hands of white settlers, he suddenly sobbed and pressed his eyes with a white handkerchief held at one corner by his fingers. Those who saw this for the first time found it a moving experience. But he was to repeat it frequently, at almost every Commonwealth meeting whenever the subject of white domination over Africans came up. It became a familiar music hall act.

Uganda's president, Milton Obote, was different from Kaunda or Nyerere. There was deep hatred and venom when he spoke on Rhodesia, Namibia, and South Africa. I felt something sinister in his expression and the glint in his eyes. During a conference break, Obote was told that General Idi Amin had taken over his country in a coup. He looked dejected. His predicament underlined the precariousness of so many African governments.

The last speaker on South Africa was the prime minister of Fiji, Ratu Sir Kamisese Mara. A strapping, handsome six-foot-six, he looked the rugby player he was. It was unrealistic to expect the British prime minister to state that his government would not now sell arms to South Africa. To stop the sale of arms was like peeling off the outer skin of the onion. The next skin would be the sale of arms by the French, then by the Italians. On that reasonable note, we adjourned at 4:00 A.M.

I remembered how the communists in the trade unions would keep me sitting for long hours on hard wooden backless benches. Then, after all my exhausted noncommunist supporters had left and we were in the minority, they would take the vote. The Commonwealth leaders were seated in comfortable armchairs, but the thermostat was malfunctioning and the air-conditioning was too cold in the early hours of the morning. To adjourn would mean everybody getting renewed energy, building up more steam for ever longer speeches. I decided to carry on and everyone stayed. All speakers from Africa had the satisfaction of being heard; no leader was stopped from saying his piece meant for home consumption.

When discussions resumed a few hours later "on the security of the Indian Ocean," the African leaders were all absent and the work was soon done. Except for a few brief quiet periods when I got some other prime minister to take the chair, I had to sit through all 13 sessions from 14 January to 22 January. It was punishing to have to listen to repetitious speeches made at a tangent to each other. Since then, I have sympathized with those who chaired international conferences where delegates come with prepared speeches, determined to say their piece regardless of what had already been said.

Although the conference did cover all items on the agenda, the press concentrated mainly on the controversy over arms for South Africa.

Privately, over drinks, Heath expressed his disappointment at the public airing of many confidential or secret exchanges between heads of government. Canadian Prime Minister Pierre Trudeau agreed, regretting that the African leaders tended to adopt UN diplomatese. I said this was inevitable when Third World leaders were influencing each other at so many international conferences where rhetoric and hyperbole were standard fare. I added that all first-generation independence leaders were charismatic speakers, but their administrations seldom followed up with the implementation.

As chairman, I gained insights into the backstage operations of a Commonwealth conference. It was the informal, bilateral, and small caucus sessions between key leaders that determined the outcome of the conference. Arnold Smith, who in 1962 had given me dinner in Moscow when he was Canada's ambassador, had been secretary-general of the Commonwealth for more than five years. He had intimate knowledge of the personalities and positions of the leaders attending. Together we told the African leaders privately that they could never expect Ted Heath to climb down publicly. We convened two sessions, restricted to leaders, to endorse compromises Smith had brokered. The formal resolutions in the full conference were settled at these smaller meetings. At the end of the meeting, after all the histrionics, the secretary-general got the Third World leaders to understand that the guts of the Commonwealth were in economic, social, and cultural cooperation, and that depended on funding mainly from the developed old Commonwealth—Britain, Canada, Australia, and New Zealand. Commonwealth cooperation would end if the donors found the cost-benefit ratio unfavorable. With tact and skill, Smith persuaded the Africans and Asians not to push issues to the breaking point. Sonny Ramphal, the Guyanan foreign minister who took over from Smith in 1975, showed even greater skill in letting the Third World leaders have their rhetoric while he kept the road show going by making sure the cost-benefit equation kept the donors engaged.

Rhodesia and apartheid occupied much time at every conference. For most of them, unless I looked up the minutes, I would not remember the issues of the day that agitated the leaders at that time. But I have carried unforgettable vignettes of meetings and conversations from each conference. At Ottawa in 1973, I remember the chairman, Prime Minister Pierre Trudeau, a French Canadian who was completely and expressively bilingual. He told me he had an Irish mother and a French father. Trudeau had a sharp mind and a sharp tongue to match. I watched his press conference with admiration. As he switched from English to French, his facial expressions and gestures became French. He was a truly bilingual, bicultural Canadian. He had much sympathy for underdogs and was always willing to lend them a hand, but could be quite tough about cutting Canadian scholarships for Singapore students once he decided we could afford to pay.

Another person I remember from the Ottawa meeting was Prime Minister Sheikh Mujibur Rahman, the hero who had opposed Pakistan and led East Pakistan to independence as Bangladesh. He arrived in style at Ottawa in his own aircraft. When I landed, I saw a parked Boeing 707 with "Bangladesh" emblazoned on it. When I left, it was still standing on the same spot, idle for eight days, getting obsolescent without earning anything. As I left the hotel for the airport, two huge vans were being loaded with packages for the Bangladeshi aircraft. At the conference, Mujibur Rahman had made a pitch for aid to his country. Any public relations firm would have advised him not to leave his special aircraft standing for eight whole days on the parking apron. The fashion of the time was for leaders of the bigger Third World countries to travel in their own aircraft. All leaders were equal at the conference table, but those from heavyweight countries showed that they were more equal by arriving in big private jets, the British in their VC 10s and Comets, and the Canadians in Boeings. The Australians joined this select group in 1979, after Malcolm Fraser's government purchased a Boeing 707 for the Royal Australian Air Force. Those African presidents whose countries were then better off, like Kenya and Nigeria, also had special aircraft. I wondered why they did not set out to impress the world that they were poor and in dire need of assistance. Our permanent representative at the UN in New York explained that the poorer the country, the bigger the Cadillacs they hired for their leaders. So I made a virtue of arriving by ordinary commercial aircraft, and thus helped preserve Singapore's Third World status for many years. However, by the mid-1990s, the World Bank refused to heed our pleas not to reclassify us as a "High Income Developing Country," giving no Brownie points for my frugal travel habits. We lost all the concessions that were given to developing countries.

At Kingston, Jamaica, in April 1975, Prime Minister Michael Manley, a light-skinned West Indian, presided with panache and spoke with great eloquence. But I found his views quixotic. He advocated a "redistribution of the world's wealth." His country was a well-endowed island of 2,000 square miles, with several mountains in the center, where coffee and other subtropical crops were grown. They had beautiful holiday resorts built by Americans as winter homes. Theirs was a relaxed culture. The people were full of song and dance, spoke eloquently, danced vigorously, and drank copiously. Hard work they had left behind with slavery.

One Sunday afternoon, when Choo and I walked out of the barbed wired enclosure around the hotels used for the conference to see the city on foot, a passing car came to a halt with the driver shouting, "Mr. Lee, Mr. Lee, wait for me." A Chinese Jamaican, speaking Caribbean English, came up. "You mustn't forget us. We are having a very difficult time." He gave me his card. He was a real estate agent. Many professionals and businesspeople had left for America and Canada and had given him their homes and offices to sell. He had seen me on Jamaican television and was anxious to speak to me. Chinese, Indians, and even black Jamaican professionals felt there was no future under the left-wing socialist government of Michael Manley. The policies of the government were ruinous. I asked what he was going to do. He was not a professional so he could not leave or he would. But when all these big houses had been sold and there was not much real estate business to do, he might yet go. I wished him luck and cut the meeting short. I noticed the black Jamaican security officers covering me turning aggressive in their body language. Thereafter, I read the news of Jamaica with greater understanding.

To honor the queen's silver jubilee, we met in London in July 1977. It was a different relationship. Britain's economy was no longer as strong; indeed, Denis Healey had called in the IMF in 1976 to help Britain out of some difficulty. I remember standing in line behind Archbishop Makarios of Cyprus as Choo and I waited to sign the visitors' book at 10 Downing Street, before going through the back garden to watch the queen's birthday parade. His Beatitude did not use the pen proffered by a British warrant officer. He took out his own pen, signed, and walked away. As I signed, I said to the soldier, "The Archbishop signed in red." "Red as his hands were bloody," replied the warrant officer who had served in Cyprus during those bloody years when the British army had to keep down the Cypriot nationalists who were determined to get the British out and have *enosis* (union) with Greece.

In 1979, I made my third visit to Lusaka. The first, in 1964, was during my African tour of 17 capitals, and the second in 1970, was for the Non-Aligned Summit. Since 1970, Zambia's economy had declined. We were entertained at State House, where I had stayed in 1964 as the house guest of the last governor. It had lost its bloom. There were fewer deer and exotic birds in the grounds, and the big house itself did not have that spick-and-span look of British colonial government houses. We were housed in the same chalets as in 1970, dotted around the conference hall which had been built for them by Yugoslavia, a fellow member of the Non-Aligned Movement. The conference hall and chalets had not been much used since 1970 and showed it, but had just been refurbished and furnished at great expense, with furniture flown in from Spain.

The catering at the chalet where we stayed was a disaster. They had trained young students as cooks. Our cook's total repertoire was bacon and eggs or just soft-boiled eggs for breakfast, steak for lunch, and steak for dinner. There was plenty of liquor and wines, far more than we needed.

Everything was in short supply. The shops were empty. Imported toiletries were absent and there was little by way of local substitutes. Choo saw women queuing for essentials. The only souvenir she could buy was a malachite egg, to remind us that Zambia was a single-commodity economy, copper, and its price had not kept up with the prices of oil and other imports. They had no foreign exchange, and their currency was rapidly depreciating. Prime Minister Kenneth Kaunda's major preoccupation was politics, black versus white politics, not the economics of growth for Zambia. He remained as president until the 1990s when, to his credit, he conducted a fair election and lost. After Kaunda left, the lot of Zambians did not improve much.

My most memorable encounter at the Melbourne conference in October 1981 was with an Indian in the coffee room. We were the only two seeking refreshments. I asked if he was with the Indian delegation. No, he was the leader of the delegation for Uganda, representing President Milton Obote, who could not come. I was surprised (Indians had been persecuted by Idi Amin for a decade and had fled Uganda) and asked if he had returned to Uganda. No, his family had settled in London and he was the Ugandan High Commissioner in London. He had left during Idi Amin's rule. I asked what had happened to the Speaker of the Ugandan Parliament who in January 1964 had given me and my delegation a reception at Parliament House, Kampala. He was a Sikh with a turban, proud of his stone-faced Parliament House. By coincidence, the former Speaker was coming to Melbourne to meet him the next day. He had been forced to leave Uganda and had settled in Darwin, where he became a magistrate. I was sad. Uganda could have done with more such people, and not just as Speakers, to give dynamism to the Ugandan economy as the Sikhs have done in many other countries, including Singapore. He had been a casualty of the 1971 coup when Idi Amin deposed Milton Obote while he was in Singapore.

In Delhi two years later, I was seated next to Mrs. Obote at the queen's dinner. She gave me another facet of the Ugandan tragedy while recounting how in the 1971 coup she with her three children had escaped from Kampala to Nairobi. They were sent back. They escaped again and spent years in exile in Dar-es-Salaam. She returned to Uganda in 1980, a year after Idi Amin was deposed. Milton Obote, now president again, was a much sadder and more subdued man. I caught a glimpse of the magnitude of the Ugandan disaster from my conversation with his wife. She had discovered that the people had changed, no longer willing to work for what they needed. After nine years of brutalities, lawlessness, and viciousness under Idi Amin, people simply grabbed what they wanted. They had lost all the habits that made for civilized living. I was to remember this when our police contingent in the UN force reported on their experiences in Cambodia in 1991–1993. If anything, Cambodia was worse after 20 years of chaos.

That November 1983, Margaret Thatcher discussed the question of Hong Kong. Deng Xiaoping had been adamant on Hong Kong's return. She had tried to persuade him to allow an extension of the lease. He made it clear that that was completely unacceptable; China must resume sovereignty in 1997. What were my views? She had raised the matter because the governor had told her that Hong Kong leases in the New Territories were running out. I asked how far she was willing to go to press her view, given that the survival of a British Hong Kong depended upon China's attitude. She did not have a ready answer. I thought it unlikely the Chinese would agree to an extension of the lease as too much national prestige was at stake. In the case of Macau, the Portuguese simply carried on their administration without raising the matter with Beijing. She said the governor had told her he had no legal authority to extend the leases beyond 1997, so she had raised it.

Before I left Delhi, I gave my view that she had few cards in her hands. The best course would be to put the ball in the Chinese court, to tell Deng that Hong Kong could survive and prosper only if China wanted it to. The colony of Hong Kong, the island itself, and Kowloon peninsula could not survive without the New Territories, which was on leasehold. Hence it was not practical to adopt the legal position that Britain could continue to hold the colony minus the New Territories; far better to get terms for Hong Kong that would enable it to continue to prosper as it was doing, but under China's flag.

I had looked forward to the meeting in Nassau, Bahamas, in October 1985. It was the playground of wealthy Americans. Then I read in the British papers how drugs had spread throughout the Bahamas, and violent crime was rampant. The London *Sunday Times* reported that Prime

Minister Sir Lynden Pindling was involved. No libel action followed. For the queen's dinner on the royal yacht *Britannia,* Pindling offered all leaders a boat ride from our hotels to the *Britannia.* I decided to go by road. Near the wharf where the royal yacht was berthed, we passed a crowd of demonstrators with placards denouncing Pindling; several said "Chief is a Thief." The chief and his other guests took much longer by boat than we did by car. Either because the sea was choppy or the boat was slow, they kept the queen waiting for over an hour. She was usually gracious and restrained in her comments, but was not accustomed to being kept waiting. She said to me that the dishes would be overcooked. The main dish was, but the dessert was excellent.

I had lunch one day with President Junius Jayewardene of Sri Lanka and the chief justice of the Bahamas. The chief justice spoke of the widespread cocaine habit in the country and of the vast fortunes made by those in the drug network. Smugglers flew into the Bahamas from South America in small aircraft. With the connivance of customs and other officials, the drugs were taken by air and sea to the U.S. mainland. In transit, enough slipped through to the local population to ruin many a family. High government ministers had been involved. When I left Nassau, I had lost my last illusion of an island paradise anywhere in the world.

My last conference was in Kuala Lumpur in October 1989. Like the previous meeting in Vancouver, October 1987, it was uneventful and there were no "hot" issues. I spent one long evening on Langkawi island, during the "retreat" (an informal gathering of the conference members at some resort), chatting with Prime Minister Bhutto and her husband Asif Zadari, learning about Pakistani politics and culture. She had youthful good looks, a fair complexion, and a finely chiseled, photogenic face. He was an ebullient and outgoing wheeler-dealer, with no inhibitions in telling me that he was ready to consider any deal in anything—cutting a good deal was what life was about for him. He was in the fruit and other export business, in real estate and everything else. I promised to introduce him to some fruit importers to buy his mangoes, which I did when he visited Singapore accompanying his wife to some meeting in 1995. He was a likeable rogue. But I never thought him capable of murdering her brother, a charge made by the Pakistani government after she was thrown out of office by the president.

That was my last Commonwealth conference as I was preparing to step down as prime minister in 1990. The first conference in 1962 was in a different age with a different set of leaders. The Commonwealth was then a relatively small club, with deep and strong bonds of history and kinship between Britain and the old dominions. They still had close economic and political links with the newly independent countries, all still enjoying Commonwealth tariff preferences, with Britain as their main trading partner. When Prime Minister Harold Macmillan, a man of empire from the generation that had fought on the Western front in World War I, initiated Britain's entry into Europe, the old white dominions were aghast. They felt abandoned after having fought alongside Britain in two world wars. Sir Robert Menzies, the Australian prime minister, in a powerful intervention demolished Macmillan's assurances that there would be continuing close ties with the Commonwealth after Britain joined the European Economic Community.

"I run a federation. I know how federations work," he said. They were either centripetal, in which case the states would come closer and closer together as in Australia, or they were centrifugal, with the states moving further and further apart until they eventually broke away. They were never static. There could be no other dynamic at work in such groupings. If Britain joined the EEC, its ties with the Commonwealth would weaken and atrophy. Looking back over the past 40 years, I have been reminded how prophetic Menzies was.

Britain and the Europeans have got closer together. Even the old Commonwealth countries, kith and kin notwithstanding, no longer share those deep emotional bonds of the 1960s. Their destinies have gone their different ways in their separate continents. Twenty-five years later, in 1998, the British were still divided over whether to be in one currency, the Euro, and (what many fear and do not want) a federal supranational government of Europe.

Already in 1989, with over 40 leaders, there was no longer that sense of shared values. It was a club whose members came and went unexpectedly with the vagaries of elections or coups, with no time to bid farewell. There was an ephemeral quality in most of the hot topics of the day—the

New International Economic Order, North-South dialogue, South-South cooperation, Rhodesia, apartheid—they are part of history. Nevertheless each conference served a purpose. A leader could highlight certain points directly with other leaders and put the wrong party on the defensive, as happened when India supported the Vietnamese occupation of Cambodia. Face to face, Mrs. Gandhi could not, and to her credit, did not, defend India's position. This made an impression on the other leaders and influenced their stand on this problem. There was value in attending these conferences. But I had attended too many and it was time to move on.

During Commonwealth conferences, every head of government would be granted an audience with the queen as head of the Commonwealth. The only exception was the 1971 conference in Singapore, when for some reason the Heath government decided that the queen would not attend. I had first called on her in September 1966. She was amazingly good at putting her guests at ease without seeming to do so, a social skill perfected by training and experience. She was gracious, friendly, and genuinely interested in Singapore because her uncle, Lord Louis Mountbatten, had told her of his time here as Allied commander in chief, South East Asia Command.

When I saw her in London in January 1969, she said she was sorry the British had decided to withdraw from Singapore. She looked sad to see an important chapter of Britain's history come to an end. She visited Singapore in 1972 to make up for the visit she did not make in 1971. I made sure she saw all the places Lord Mountbatten had told her about, including the City Hall Chamber where he had taken the surrender of the Japanese, the Istana where he had stayed, and the Kranji Commonwealth War Cemetery. Surprisingly huge crowds gathered on the roadsides waiting to see her pass by. They surged forward to surround her whenever she got out from the car. Her assistant private secretary, Philip Moore, who had been the U.K. deputy high commissioner to Singapore in the 1960s, asked me not to have the security officers hold the crowds back as they were friendly. The queen was completely at ease, happy, and relaxed.

To commemorate her visit, the queen made me a Knight Grand Cross of the Order of St. Michael and St. George (GCMG). Earlier, Harold

Wilson as prime minister had recommended me for the Companion of Honour (CH) in the 1970 New Year's honors list. It was not usual for such a high decoration to be awarded to a young man of 47. Before I was 50, I had received two British honors much prized by those brought up in Britain's former empire. Long years of association had nurtured certain values. I have received honors from President Nasser of Egypt, Emperor Hirohito of Japan, President Suharto of Indonesia, President Park Chung Hee of Korea, and Prince Sihanouk of Cambodia among others. They do not carry the same emotional connotation. I did not think it appropriate to use the title "Sir" that went with the GCMG, but was happy to have received two coveted British trophies, even though they no longer opened doors with the British as they used to in the days of empire.

# 23. New Bonds with Britain

On 24 September 1975, the Gordon Highlanders' drums and pipes struck up in final farewell as the HMS *Mermaid* pulled out of Sembawang Naval Base. It was a mere 2,500-tonne frigate—a tiny component of the Royal Navy warships and aircraft carriers that once were based there. The last of the British troops left soon after. Their departure marked the end of 150 years of British political and military influence in the region.

The economic strength of the United States, Japan, Germany, and the European Economic Community prevailed over the region. This meant we had to build up our links with these other powers from scratch. For me personally, it was a difficult adjustment. After a lifetime of close association, I had come to know British society and its leaders well. Listening to the BBC World Service and reading British newspapers had become a habit. I had a network of friends and acquaintances in both the Labour and Conservative parties. It was easy to make contact and have a meeting of minds. After their pullout I had to learn about and get to know American leaders and the different style and standards of their media, and to gain some understanding of American society, which was so much bigger and more diverse. Doing this with the Japanese, French, and Germans was even more difficult because we neither spoke their languages nor understood their customs.

Although old ties with Britain continued even as we widened our links and established relations with these important new centers of wealth and power, it was nevertheless sad to see Britain's gradual economic displacement by Japan, Germany, and France. Time and again, its recovery was slowed down by industrial action of unions driven by class antagonism and not merely economic injustice. I believe one great obstacle to Britain's adjustment to its postimperial condition was its class-conscious society. It was slow to shed class distinctions. Without empire, Britain needed a meritocracy to retain its position as the leading nation of Europe, not a ruling class that distinguished itself from the working class by its accent, social manners, and habits, old boy network, clubs, and old school ties. Akio Morita was chairman of Sony in 1991 when he told me that Sony found it hard to get engineers in its British factories to go to the production line. Japanese engineers start from the bottom so as to fraternize with and understand the people who would be working under them. British engineers, he said, preferred their own private rooms. Aware of these shortcomings, Thatcher as prime minister downgraded class and promoted meritocracy. John Major, her successor, spoke of a "classless" Britain. Prime Minister Tony Blair's New Labour wants Britain to be rid of class consciousness.

What was worse, welfarism introduced by the Labour Party in the 1940s, and sustained by the Conservatives in a bipartisan consensus, had blunted the people's motivation to exert themselves and excel, at the expense of the economy. Most leaders in both main parties, and even in the Liberal Party, were aware of the debilitating effects of welfarism. But no one tackled this problem until Margaret Thatcher became prime minister.

As Britain's worldwide influence shrank, so did the worldview of its younger parliamentarians and ministers. Some old friends, British commanders who had fought in the last world war and had served in Singapore defending us against Sukarno's Confrontation, compared the old generation British leaders to oak trees with wide-spreading branches and deep roots. They described their younger leaders as "bonsai oak," recognizably oak trees, but miniaturized, because their root area had shrunk.

Adjusting to a different power position was difficult for Britain. It was the Conservative Party led by Margaret Thatcher, followed by John Major, that reversed the downward trend. British entrepreneurs became more self-confident and spearheaded their revival in Southeast Asia, including Singapore. The Labour Party returned to power in the 1997 election, committed to the same economic principles of the free market. It wants to cut down the government's share of total GDP (gross domestic product), encourage exports, and promote trade and investments abroad to create jobs in Britain. The triumph of Margaret Thatcher and the Conservative Party was in turning around the attitudes of the British people. This forced the Labour Party to change from Old to New Labour.

Habits and ties long established do not change easily. Our students continue to go to Britain to seek higher education. As Singapore's middle class expanded, they sent their children to Britain for their tertiary education. By the 1990s, some 5,000 Singapore students were studying in British universities and polytechnics. Oxbridge graduates still dominate the elite in Singapore. The pulls of history are responsible for this cultural lag, a delayed response to changed circumstances. After the British withdrew their forces the only power in East Asia was America. We needed to have some of our best students educated there to understand them, and to network with future leaders in their centers of excellence. Even by the 1990s, the number of our students in the United States was only two-thirds that in Britain.

History has locked us into the British educational system. Our professions are affiliated and geared to Britain's professional institutions: doctors, lawyers, accountants, architects, engineers—the lot. Professional ties endure across all echelons of our society. In some sections, however, such as medicine, because the United States spends some 14 percent of its GDP on health, more than twice what Britain does, American doctors and hospitals have excelled. We have gradually forged ties with American institutions. But our basic training in medicine is still British. So too with the other professions.

During the Thatcher years of the 1980s, Singapore-British trade grew significantly. When she freed capital movements, British investments in Singapore increased. They were of a different nature—in high value-added products such as pharmaceuticals, electronics, and aerospace. By the 1990s, Britain was again one of our major investors, the fourth largest after the United States, Japan, and Holland. Singapore investments overseas went primarily into Southeast Asia, but a significant number of our private entrepreneurs had invested in Britain, especially in tourism. One of our major companies bought a chain of hotels in Britain and our Government Investment Corporation bought into another chain of over 100 hotels, confident that the British tourist industry would continue to grow, notwithstanding the problems created by IRA bombings. Singapore's main link with Europe is still London. We have more daily flights to London than to other capitals in Europe.

When the British announced the withdrawal of their forces in 1968, there were gloomy articles, including one in the *Illustrated London News* that compared it to the retreat of the Roman legions from Britain as the Dark Ages descended over Europe. But the analogy was false. Modern communications and transportation have brought more Britons to Singapore than in colonial times. The British community now is smaller only than the American and Japanese communities. There are more British schools in Singapore now, to cater for the children of some 10,000 British families, than when we were their colony. Hundreds of Britons now come to Singapore on their own to work as engineers, architects, and technicians—no longer on expatriate terms and living in exclusive areas, but on local terms and living in the same apartments as Singaporeans. Singapore salaries have reached the levels of Britain's. Many British banking and financial institutions have set up branches in Singapore as it became one of the major international financial centers. The whole economic and political landscape has altered beyond recognition.

In 1982, the City of London made me a Freeman of the City of London, an honor which, as a former British subject, I appreciated. I was impressed to see how thorough they were about the guest list. They had invited all the British ministers and governors who had had dealings with me over Singapore. And I was asked to list the personal friends I wanted to have present. So I had the joy of having former prime ministers, secretaries of state, commanders in chief, the last governor of Singapore, and my many personal British friends, all there in the Guildhall to share that moment. Among them were Harold Macmillan, Jim Callaghan, Harold Wilson, Alec Douglas-Home, Alan Lennox-Boyd, and Duncan Sandys. It was an occasion for nostalgia. In responding to the address at the ceremony, I said,

When I was a schoolboy 50 years ago in Singapore, my teachers held this truth to be self-evident, that London was the centre of the world. It was the centre of high finance and banking, as well as of the arts, the theatre, the centre of literature, of music, of culture. It was the centre of gravity of the world, . . . as indeed it was in September 1939 when a British government decided to honour an obligation to the Polish nation, a year after it had glossed over an undertaking to the Czech nation. Thus was World War II triggered off, and the world irrevocably changed.

Part of the ceremony was a drive from Westminster to the Guildhall in a horse-drawn carriage. It had to be cancelled because a rail strike had caused traffic congestion. Industrial problems continued to bedevil Britain. Margaret Thatcher's clash with the miners' union was yet to come.

My long years in office and our historical ties with Britain gave me opportunities to know successive British prime ministers from Harold Macmillan to Tony Blair.

Harold Macmillan was of my father's generation, an Edwardian grandee in appearance and manner with a deceptively languid air and a lofty approach to young colonials like me. Sir Alec Douglas-Home was the nicest of them all—a real gentleman whose manner on television belied the shrewd geopolitical thinker he was. He might have counted with matchsticks as he candidly admitted, but he had more solid sense than many cerebral ministers on both front benches.

The most politically skillful of them was Harold Wilson. It was my good fortune that we were friends before he became prime minister. I was able to persuade him to remain east of Suez for a few years longer. Those few years made a difference because a residual British presence stayed on in Singapore until mid-1975. This gave us time to sort out our relations with Indonesia without making precipitate moves we might later have regretted. I personally owed much to Wilson for his staunch support when we were in Malaysia and after, as I have recounted earlier in my memoirs. The problems he faced in Britain were deep-seated—lowered levels of education and skills, lower productivity because unions were not cooperating with management. The Labour Party of the 1960s and 1970s was dominated by the trade unions and could not tackle these basic issues, hence Wilson was seen as going for quick fixes. To keep the party behind him, he had to zigzag, making him appear wily and devious.

In marked contrast, I found Ted Heath reliable and steadfast. I first knew him as Macmillan's minister in charge of negotiating Britain's entry into Europe and had lobbied him to protect Singapore's position. We became friends during his time as leader of the opposition after Wilson won the 1964 election. Often when I was in London, he would have me to lunch at his apartment in Albany to talk about Britain, Europe, America, and the Commonwealth. He rated Europe more important than America and the Commonwealth in Britain's future. Once he had decided on a policy, he did not lightly change his mind, and he believed in Europe before he was prime minister. If I were asked to choose one person from among the British prime ministers and ministers whom I knew to accompany me on a dangerous mission, I would choose Ted Heath. He would stay to the end to accomplish what he had set out to do. Unfortunately, he lacked the ability to enthuse and move a people. One on one, he would get animated, but on television he would appear wooden, a tremendous disadvantage in the age of electronic media. We have remained good friends, meeting occasionally in London, in Singapore, and at international meetings like Davos.

When Jim Callaghan spoke to the Cambridge University Labour Club in 1948, I was in the student audience. He was introduced as an ex-chief petty officer in the Royal Navy who had become a junior minister. He spoke confidently and well. I got to know him in the mid-1950s when attending constitutional talks in London, and we kept in touch over the years. Because he became prime minister unexpectedly and rather late in life when Wilson resigned in March 1976, he did not have his own political agenda. Indeed, Britain was in such dire economic circumstances that the IMF had to be brought in. So the agenda was set for him.

I had appealed to Jim Callaghan when he was prime minister to allow Brunei, whose foreign affairs Britain still controlled, to permit our Singapore Armed Forces to train in their jungles. The British foreign and

Commonwealth office had held up this decision to avoid involvement in our sensitive defense relations with Malaysia. I argued that Britain would soon not be in charge and we would be able to get this jungle training school anyway. Why not allow it while Britain was in charge so that it would be part of the political landscape when Brunei became independent? He agreed and we established our jungle training school in late 1976.

Faced with interminable economic problems including unemployment, Callaghan's Labour government became protectionist. In April 1977, George Thomson, by then a life peer and no longer a minister, came as Callaghan's personal envoy to ask if I intended to raise bilateral issues with British leaders during the Commonwealth conference in June. I said it would not be appropriate to raise bilateral complaints at the queen's silver jubilee celebrations, but protested that the British had persuaded the Germans to get the EEC to block the entry of Singapore-made pocket calculators and monochrome television sets. There had been no prior discussions with us. I pointed out that our pocket calculators were sophisticated models made with high-level American technology, well ahead of British technology. Stopping imports from Singapore would mean Britons paying more for the same items from America. So also with monochrome television sets built by Japanese companies in Singapore. Later the trade barriers were lifted because they did not in fact preserve British jobs.

Callaghan once asked me, "What kind of people are these Japanese? They work like ants, they keep increasing their exports but do not import." He held the Westerner's stereotype of them, forged by inhuman Japanese behavior during World War II. He did not understand them. He did not see Japanese investments, as Thatcher later did, as a way to reindustrialize Britain. He was more interested in the Africans, Indians, and other members of the Commonwealth. His worldview was focused on king and empire. During the Commonwealth Heads of Government Meeting (CHOGM), he gave African leaders every opportunity to air their views, especially on Rhodesia and South Africa's apartheid. He was the typical British Labour Party leader with a working-class background, whose instincts were to stand up for the downtrodden and the oppressed. However, he was also hard-headed when it came to tough decisions like getting his Labour government to implement rigorous IMF conditions attached to its rescue package for the sterling crisis.

Callaghan's strength was his "steady as she goes" approach to problems. He did not look for fancy solutions. He had deep loyalties to the trade unions, yet his government was brought down by the unions.

Margaret Thatcher sat next to me at a dinner in 10 Downing Street in October 1970 when Ted Heath was prime minister. She was then minister for education, and we talked about the loss to Britain when it replaced grammar schools with "comprehensives" (mixed-ability schools). The bright students lost out without any corresponding gains by the others.

When she was leader of the opposition, I asked George Thomas, then Speaker of the House of Commons, what he thought of her. In his Welsh lilt, he said, "She has great passion for Britain and would do the right things for Britain. She wants to turn the country around and I believe she is the only one with the will to do it." And when I asked Jim Callaghan, who was then prime minister, what he thought of her, his answer was, "She is the one with trousers on the front bench." These views from a Labour Speaker and a Labour prime minister reinforced my own that she was indeed a "conviction politician."

When Thatcher won the election in May 1979, I cheered for her. She was for free competition in a free market. During her years in opposition, I met her in London and on the several visits she made to Singapore, usually on her way to Australia and New Zealand. In June 1979, a month after she became prime minister, I had an hour's discussion with her before lunch at 10 Downing Street. She was brimming with ideas. In July 1980, she wrote as leader of the Conservative Party to invite me to be its guest speaker, the first ever from the Commonwealth, at the party conference in Brighton that October. I replied that I could not accept the honor because of my long association with the Labour Party, one that went back to my student days in the Britain of the 1940s.

She was an intense person, full of determination and drive, confident that she could implement her domestic economic policy, but under no illusion about the difficulties she would face from the unions. So when the coal miners' strike began in March 1984, I felt she would take the fight to the finish. But I did not expect such nastiness in the clashes between the strikers and the police to last for a whole year. Her predecessors would not have toughed it out.

In April 1985, Thatcher paid us an official visit. At dinner, I congratulated her for trimming the excesses of the welfare state:

> For nearly four decades since the war, successive British governments seemed to assume that the creation of wealth came about naturally, and that what needed government attention and ingenuity was the redistribution of wealth. So governments devised ingenious ways to transfer incomes from the successful to the less successful. In this climate, it requires a prime minister with very strong nerves to tell voters the truth, that creators of wealth are precious members of a society who deserve honour plus the right to keep a better part of their rewards. . . . We have used to advantage what Britain left behind: the English language, the legal system, parliamentary government and impartial administration. However, we have studiously avoided the practices of the welfare state. We saw how a great people reduced themselves to mediocrity by levelling down.

Thatcher responded graciously in similar vein: "I like to think that once you learnt it from Britain. And now we are relearning it from you. . . . Talent, initiative, adventure, endeavour, risk, confidence, vigour have made Singapore an example to other nations of success—an example whose clear message is that you can't enjoy the fruits of effort without first making the effort."

The next day several pro-Labour British papers carried an outburst from Labour shadow health minister Frank Dobson: "Mr. Lee should keep his stupid mouth closed." A Labour MP, Allen Adams, added, "If we are going to take his state as a model, the country would be going back to 1870 when people worked in sweatshops around the clock for virtually nothing."

This was the stereotypical Old Labour, minds that had not kept up with developments. In 1985, Singapore's per capita GDP was US$6,500 as against Britain's US$8,200. By 1995, Singapore's per capita GDP of

US$26,000 had surpassed Britain's US$19,700. Our workers earned more than the British workers. They also owned their own homes and had more savings (in Central Provident Fund and POSBank accounts) than the British workers.

When Thatcher resigned in November 1990, she sent me this farewell letter: "How unexpected life can be: who would have imagined that we should both leave the highest office in our respective countries on almost the same day, after so many years of working together. But as I leave, I just wanted to say how enormously I have benefited from our association and admired all that you stood for. One thing surely cannot be in doubt: Commonwealth Heads of Government Meetings will be much duller without either of us present!"

I had more dealings with Margaret Thatcher than with other British prime ministers because she was in power for three terms. Of all the prime ministers, I thought she offered the best hope for Britain. Her strengths were her passionate belief in her country and her iron will to turn it around. She was convinced that free enterprise and the free market led to a free society. Her basic political instincts were sound though she tended to be too self-confident and self-righteous. Her disadvantage, in a class-conscious Britain, was her background as "the grocer's daughter." It was a pity that the British establishment still labored under these prejudices. By the time she left office, Britons had become less class-ridden.

However, Thatcher could provoke great antipathy from the prime ministers of the old white dominions. At the Bahamas Commonwealth Heads of Government Meeting in 1985, both the Canadian and Australian prime ministers, Brian Mulroney and Bob Hawke, badgered and pressed her to agree to economic sanctions against South Africa. All the opening speeches at the conference, except hers, attacked South Africa's apartheid. Thatcher alone stood against imposition of further sanctions on Pretoria, calling instead for a dialogue. I respected her strength to withstand this isolation. She refused to be browbeaten and bludgeoned into submission. Unfortunately, she was on the wrong side of history.

John Major was chancellor of the exchequer when he accompanied Margaret Thatcher to the CHOGM in Kuala Lumpur in October 1989. I met

him again at 10 Downing Street in May 1996. He had a tough assign-
ment. Margaret Thatcher had thrown her weight behind his election as
Conservative Party leader and prime minister and expected him to stick
to her policies on Europe. Her influence in the party made life difficult for
him. The media too did not give him much of a grace period, writing him
off within months. And so, although the economy was doing well, it did
not help him against New Labour in May 1997.

I was struck by the youthful energy of Tony Blair when I first met him
in London in May 1995, when he was leader of the opposition. He was a
year younger than my son, Loong. Jonathan Powell, his chief of staff, took
notes and followed up. Blair wanted to know the factors that made the
difference between East Asia's high sustained growth and Britain and
Europe's more sluggish rates. I suggested that he visit East Asia before the
election and see its tremendous transformation. After he took office he
would be insulated by protocol.

The following January he visited Japan, Australia, then Singapore,
where he met our trade union leaders and saw the benefits they had
obtained for union members. He was interested in our individualized old-
age pension accounts—the Central Provident Fund (CPF), which also
provided funds for home ownership and medical services. He made no
secret of his deep Christian beliefs which made him a socialist or, as he
added when I looked askance, a social democrat. He was candid enough to
repeat "or a social democrat," something Old Labour scorned. His "New
Labour" was not a pose. He asked me what the prospects were for a successful Labour government. I said he would have a difficult time, once
Labour was in government, getting Old Labour to accept his policy. The
Labour Party was much older than he was and would not change so easily.

A few days after Blair's visit, Chris Smith, the shadow minister for
social security, came to study our system, and a few months later, Peter
Mandelson, a close aide of Tony Blair, came to look at our Medisave,
health insurance and other functions of Singapore's CPF. Blair struck me
as a serious politician wanting to learn about the developments in East
Asia and the reasons they were successful. When we met again in London
that autumn, there was an endless flow of questions over dinner.

The studied humility with which he presented himself and his party after his stupendous election victory in May 1997 was a tribute to his self-discipline. I watched the television coverage of his victory speech and his walk to 10 Downing Street. It reflected well on his team. I was in London a month after he won. We talked for an hour, and again wasted no time on pleasantries. He was focused on the tasks he had set for his government in his election promises. He was on overdrive, but not unduly elated at having been thrust into power at such a young age. We talked about China and the approaching handover of Hong Kong at the end of June. He was pragmatic in his approach in not wanting to rake over the coals Chris Patten had fired. Instead he was looking ahead to the longer-term future of Sino-British ties. As I expected, he attended the handover ceremony and had talks with President Jiang Zemin.

A year later, May 1998, when we again met at No. 10, he was all focused on the pressing issues, especially the Northern Ireland peace talks. He found time to discuss a range of other subjects, but not bilateral problems because there were none. Our circumstances had changed; Singapore was no longer as involved with Britain in matters of defense and security as with the United States, Australia, and New Zealand. My generation was Anglocentric, my son's generation is more focused on America. Loong and his contemporaries have to understand the United States. They have trained in U.S. military institutions and have done postgraduate studies in colleges like Harvard and Stanford. I lived under Pax Britannica; Loong's generation has to cope under Pax Americana.

# 24. Ties with Australia and New Zealand

Japan's sudden invasion in December 1941 dramatically changed Australia's memories of Singapore. Some 18,000 of its troops with no combat experience, together with 70,000 British and Indians, had to fight without adequate air cover against a battle-hardened Japanese Imperial Army. By the time Singapore fell in February 1942 about 2,000 Australians had been killed, over 1,000 wounded, and some 15,000 captured.

More than one-third of the prisoners of war died from malnutrition, disease, and ill-treatment, especially along the infamous Burma Railway. Many gravestones stand at the Kranji Commonwealth War Cemetery in Singapore, mute testimony to their sacrifice for king and country. The capture of thousands of their soldiers by the Japanese Imperial Army in Singapore will forever be seared into Australia's national memory, a disaster second only to Gallipoli. But Singapore is nearer home and strategically more relevant to Australia. Hence, after World War II, Australia continued its old links with Britain and its troops returned to Singapore to help put down communist insurgency in Malaya.

An Australian contingent was stationed in Malaya until Britain announced its withdrawal from east of Suez. I urged Australia's Prime Minister John Gorton, to stay on in Malaya. While in London in January 1969 for a Commonwealth prime ministers' conference, Gorton held a preliminary meeting with British Defence Minister Denis Healey, New Zealand Prime Minister Keith Holyoake, the Tunku, and myself to discuss new defense arrangements for Malaysia and Singapore. Gorton was highly strung. His fidgeting and voice showed he was not keen to take on this responsibility, which he knew would fall mainly on Australian shoulders as the British would be phasing themselves out of the region.

We agreed to postpone the decision to our next meeting, in Canberra that June. But in May, violent communal riots broke out in Kuala Lumpur, jeopardizing Australia's continued participation in defense arrangements for Malaysia and Singapore. I have described earlier how this was resolved. Gorton's doubts notwithstanding, we agreed on the Five-Power Defence Arrangement (FPDA) by an exchange of letters in December 1971. His more stout-hearted defense minister, Malcolm Fraser, was against any backing off as a result of communal riots in Kuala Lumpur. In the end, Gorton decided to withdraw his forces from Ma-laya before 1971 and move them to Singapore. The Australians feared their capabilities might not be adequate for the responsibilities. They knew that only a small contingent from New Zealand would remain with them in Singapore. Their only source of comfort in a crisis was the United States, through ANZUS, the Australia-New Zealand-U.S. treaty.

From the beginning, we had close rapport with both the Australian and New Zealand governments because there was a convergence of views on regional security; the Vietnam War was getting difficult. I had easy relations with Harold Holt and his successors, John Gorton and William McMahon. In 1972, Labor governments came into power in both New Zealand and Australia. Prime Minister Norman Kirk had a sturdy approach to security issues and did not change New Zealand's defense position. But Australia's prime minister, Gough Whitlam, was uneasy about his country's defense commitments both in Vietnam and in Malaya/Singapore. He decided soon after he won the 1972 election to withdraw his troops in Singapore from the FPDA.

In the 1970s, when we first asked Australia for permission to use their training areas for military exercises, they were not forthcoming. New Zealand, on the other hand, readily agreed. Australia changed its policy in 1980, allowing us to have land exercises, and in 1981, air force training at an RAAF base. When Paul Keating was Australia's Labor prime minister in the early 1990s, he went further and allowed expansion of Singapore Armed Forces training in Australia. John Howard's Liberal-

National coalition government has continued this policy. Australia's geostrategic goals are similar to Singapore's. We both view a U.S. military presence in the region as vital for maintaining the balance of power in the Asia Pacific region and good for security and stability, without which the rapid economic growth of the region would not have taken place. Viewed against this larger backdrop, our differences over trade and other matters were insignificant.

I spent years trying to persuade Malcolm Fraser to open up Australia's economy to competition and become part of the region. I had explained to him and his minister for foreign affairs, Andrew Peacock, that they had made Australia an important player in the region through their active involvement in defense and security and their aid programs. But their protectionist economic policies cut them off from these growing economies which could not export simple manufactures to Australia because of quotas and high tariffs. Intellectually, they accepted my arguments; politically, Fraser did not have the strength to oppose his unions or his manufacturers, both of whom wanted protection.

At the Commonwealth Heads of Government Regional (Asia/Pacific) Meeting (CHOGRM) in 1980 in New Delhi, Fraser was crusading against the European Economic Community's (EEC) protectionist policies which shut off Australian agricultural exports. I cautioned him that he would gather little support from the developing countries because they saw Australia resorting to the same policies to protect its own industries that had lost their comparative advantage. Furthermore, Australia would become increasingly irrelevant to Asean countries because when they had to decide on major policies, Australia did not appear on their balance sheets.

Succeeding Australian governments have brought their country closer to Asia. Paul Keating, who became prime minister after Bob Hawke, was convinced that economically Australia needed to plug into Asia, and personally pushed a closer-to-Asia policy. With a good mind, a strong grasp of economics, and geopolitical sense, he had served as treasurer (finance minister) for many years under Bob Hawke. But what he could do as a Labor Party prime minister was limited by the powerful influence of the Australian trade unions over his party.

One other minister who made a special effort to get closer to Asia was Gareth Evans. He had a sharp mind and, when challenged, a sharper tongue, but a good heart. As foreign minister under Hawke and Keating, Evans implemented a radical change in foreign policy. He set out to make Australia a part of the action in Asia, and so share in its economic growth. He did not want Australia to remain just an exporter of raw materials to Japan while the Japanese made cars and electronic products in Australia with Japanese technology. Evans developed close personal relations with the Asean foreign ministers. This must have been quite an effort because of their totally different habits. In Asean, serious differences were often resolved not across a table but in between hitting a golf ball. So he chased the golf ball with them.

In the early years of Hawke's Labor government, I thought his Asia policy was yet another public relations effort. When Keating also pursued this policy, I concluded this was a major policy shift. The Australians had revised their assumptions and assessments. They might have been an off-shoot of Britain and Europe, but their future was more with Asia. They saw that the economies most complementary with theirs were those in East Asia. These countries—Japan, South Korea, China, Taiwan, and Asean—would need Australia's agricultural products and minerals and would also find its wide-open spaces, golf courses, resorts, and beaches great for holidays. America, although a powerful ally for political and security reasons, would compete against Australia as an exporter of agricultural products.

At a conference in Sydney organized by the *Australian Financial Review* in April 1994, Gareth Evans, the minister for foreign affairs, invited me to speak candidly about Australia. I took him at his word. Australia, I said, was "a lucky country with an embarrassment of riches." Australia had high consumption, low savings, low competitiveness, high current account deficit, and high debt, with most of its exports in minerals and agricultural products. I believed more reform was unavoidable if they wanted to complete the restructuring of their economy and compete.

The *Financial Review* editors who had invited me gave much publicity to my frank comments. But the tabloids were indignant. They were part of the problem. The country's popular media, including a TV series produced by the Australian Broadcasting Corporation in 1991, had portrayed the economic achievements of East Asia as "a Third World hellhole of sweat shops, sex tourism and repressive regimes." They completely ignored the reality that an increasing number of Taiwanese, after studying and working in the United States, were bringing home American technology and knowledge to build their own Silicon Valley in Taiwan.

I replied to their media at the Australian National Press Club in Canberra. They had failed to inform Australians about the transformation of a region of nearly 2 billion people from agricultural backwardness to industrial and high-tech societies. These countries, including China, were producing millions of engineers and scientists. R&D in Japan had enabled the Japanese to launch satellites into space and to probe the mysteries of genetic engineering. These developments went unreported in Australia. The American media, on the other hand, had publicized the industrialization and high growth in East Asia. Although Australian academics were well-informed, the people were not. Their ignorance made it difficult for any Australian government to gain popular support for changes in its policy on economic direction and immigration.


Whether Australia's destiny is tied to Asia's suddenly came to the fore with the crisis in East Timor. It was triggered off on 27 January 1999 when Indonesian Foreign Minister Ali Alatas made a dramatic announcement after a cabinet meeting chaired by President Habibie that there would be a "popular consultation" for the people of East Timor to determine whether to accept special autonomy or become independent. That public statement changed the fate of East Timor, with long-term consequences for Indonesia and Australia. Both Alexander Downer, the Australian foreign minister, and Prime Minister John Howard were known to have easy relations with President Habibie. Unlike Suharto, Habibie spoke English and was open to persuasion, especially on East Timor.

Australia's leaders wanted to be rid of the thorn of East Timor that bedevilled Australia-Indonesia relations. They had suggested the "New Caledonia solution" to Habibie. (There the French had offered a referendum in 1998 for either continued association with France, or independence after a 15-year period of preparation.) The president had recounted to Mah Bow Tan (see Chapter 17) how the Australian ambassador, John McCarthy, had discussed the New Caledonia solution with him. Habibie had told McCarthy that he would not agree to East Timor having a 15-year transition to independence, with Indonesian economic support during this period. If they rejected autonomy, they would be out on their own. Indonesia was not going to play "rich uncle." Habibie said Howard subsequently sent him a letter that contained Habibie's ideas, whereupon he scribbled a memo to his key ministers on 21 January 1999, asking them to study whether it was wise for the MPR (People's Consultative Assembly) to decide on letting East Timor respectfully separate itself from the Republic of Indonesia. He attached Howard's letter which emphasized that East Timorese opinion was insisting on an act of self-determination. It took Habibie less than a week to decide on the choice of autonomy or independence for East Timor. In May, an agreement was signed in New York between Indonesia, Portugal, and the UN to provide for a ballot on 8 August 1999. In June, the UN Security Council adopted a resolution establishing UNAMET (UN Assistance Mission to East Timor).

But in February 1999, soon after Ali Alatas's startling announcement, the Indonesians began to arm the prointegration militias. Killings and intimidation of those favoring independence became daily occurrences. Despite all the difficulties, UNAMET conducted a ballot on 30 August, when almost all voted. When the result was announced on 4 September that nearly 80 percent had voted for independence, hell broke loose. The country was systematically devastated and its population uprooted: 250,000 were moved to West Timor, the rest fled into the hills.

Under tremendous international pressure for a week, Habibie finally invited international peacekeepers to restore order. The UN Security Council adopted a resolution authorizing the deployment of a multinational force to East Timor (InterFET). Inevitably, it had to be led by Australia; the nearest base for InterFET was Darwin. Australians learned yet again how emotional their Indonesian neighbors were.

Publicly, the Indonesians stated their preference for Asean troops. Privately, lower levels of the TNI disagreed, hinting there could be casualties. The U.S. secretary for defense announced that he would send only a communications and logistics support group, not combat troops. Australia had to lead the pack. Fearful of being seen as an army of 4,000 white troops supported by 1,000 mainly white New Zealanders, Australia sought Asian support, primarily from the countries of Asean. At an APEC meeting in Auckland in September, Prime Minister John Howard asked Singapore to participate and Prime Minister Goh agreed. So Singapore committed itself to providing a medical team, military observers, liaison officers, logistics support, and two LSTs (Landing Ship Tanks)—270 men from a population of 3 million.

The day after the UN Security Council authorized InterFET, the Singapore Armed Forces (SAF) team arrived in Darwin. Our SAF mission commander, Colonel Neo Kian Hong, flew into Dili with the InterFET commander, Major-General Peter Cosgrove, to meet the Indonesian Restoration Operations Command in East Timor. And when the first wave of InterFET forces arrived in Dili on 20 September, there was a Singapore face in Cosgrove's team.

The *Bulletin* (an Australian weekly) of 28 September 1999 reported, "The Howard Doctrine—the PM himself embraces the term—sees Australia acting in a sort of 'deputy' peacekeeping capacity in our region to the global policeman role of the U.S." This *Bulletin* report drew an immediate retort from the Malaysian deputy prime minister, Abdullah Badawi: "There is no need for any country to play a role as leader, commander or deputy. They [Australians] are not sensitive to our feeling." A Thai foreign ministry official phrased it more diplomatically, that it was not appropriate for the Australians to appoint themselves as the deputy of the Americans in protecting security in the region. The issue subsided after Howard said in Parliament (27 September) that Australia was not playing the role of a deputy for the United States or any other country, that the word "deputy" was coined by the *Bulletin*'s correspondent.

To add heat to the controversy, while attending a UN General Assembly meeting in New York, Malaysian Prime Minister Mahathir criticized Australian troops as "rather heavy-handed" in the way they had pointed guns at the heads of suspected militiamen. He added, "Indonesia had been pouring in a lot of money into East Timor and the international community should allow Indonesia to practise democracy and show the

East Timorese they can gain from being integrated with Indonesia." East Timorese leader Jose Ramos-Horta, joint Nobel Prize winner with Bishop Carlos Belo, responded that Malaysia had "an extremely poor record in upholding human rights in East Timor. No one would cooperate with the Malaysian commander. There could be even total civil disobedience."

Ramos-Horta wanted to scotch an earlier proposal by the UN secretary-general to put a Malaysian in command of the UN peacekeeping force that would replace InterFET in January 2000. He added, "East Timor doesn't want to be part of Asean. We want to be part of the South Pacific Forum." East Timorese leaders had concluded that Australia was the most reliable of their neighbors.

Australia had been drawn into the East Timor conflict. In World War II, Australian troops fighting the Japanese there were helped by the local population who were then brutally punished by the Japanese. To add to Australia's sense of guilt, Prime Minister Gough Whitlam had during several meetings with Suharto acquiesced in his intention to occupy and annex East Timor. (Indonesians say Whitlam encouraged Suharto.) At the UN in 1976, Australia had voted for Indonesia in the resolution on East Timor. Singapore had abstained. When repression followed the occupation in 1975, East Timorese resistance fighters based themselves in Australia. For 24 years, this issue had simmered away.

When Paul Keating met me in September 1999, he predicted that Australia would be drawn into a prolonged conflict with Indonesia. He added that Howard's letter to Habibie would undo the good relations with Indonesia that he had painstakingly built up, culminating in the security pact he had signed with Suharto in 1995. As he had foreseen, the Indonesians tore it up on 16 September 1999, the day after the UN Security Council approved InterFET.

East Timor developments were driven by the Australian media and popular sentiments, by the Portuguese government getting the European Union to pressure Indonesia at every international gathering, and by the U.S. media, NGOs, and congressional aides. They were constantly barking and nipping at Indonesia's heels, making it an issue that dogged Indonesia at every international forum. Habibie thought he could be rid of this burden by his proposal. But neither Australia, the European Union, nor the United States had asked for or wanted an independent

East Timor. Habibie did not realize that he would never be forgiven by Indonesian nationalists for offering a ballot that could only lead to independence.

Whether or not it was wise to have proposed self-determination for East Timor, Australia did right in leading InterFET into East Timor to put a stop to the inhumanity being perpetrated. While no Asian leader voiced support for Australia as it led InterFET troops into East Timor, all knew that Australia was saving an ugly situation from getting worse. It was an operation costly in political and economic terms for Australia, a task no country in the region would have undertaken. If Australia had not acted after the part it had played leading to the vote for independence, it would have earned its neighbors' contempt. As it turned out, the quiet and firm manner in which Major-General Cosgrove commanded InterFET troops won the quiet respect of many leaders in the region. As expected, Indonesian crowds demonstrated daily outside the Australian embassy in Jakarta. Australian nationals working in various towns of Indonesia had to be evacuated.

I had watched with fascination as the East Timor crisis developed. Howard and Downer based their policy on Habibie's responses. Habibie wanted to persuade the Indonesian people to reelect him as their president by showing that international leaders like John Howard thought highly of him as a democrat and a reformer. The Australian leaders had overlooked the powerful forces that Habibie had to contend with: the more than 5,000 graves of Indonesian soldiers in East Timor; the large coffee and other plantations that had been parcelled out to previous serving TNI officers; the fear of TNI senior officers that East Timor's independence could aggravate separatist movements in Aceh and other provinces. Habibie was not in a position to give up East Timor without serious repercussions.

I had expected the militias to try to influence the votes by fair means or foul. But I never imagined they would systematically devastate the country in the two weeks between the announcement of the referendum results and the arrival of InterFET forces. It did not make sense for the TNI to allow them to do this, but then many things that did not make sense had happened, which is why Singapore, like the others in Asean, had stayed out of the East Timor issue.

When Abdurrahman Wahid was a candidate for president, he said on 13 October that Australia had been "pissing in our face" and proposed freezing relations. Ten days after his election as president, he said, "If Australia needs to be accepted by a nation of 210 million people, we will receive [them] with an open heart. If they want to separate from us, it's okay." The Australian ambassador had been hard at work to moderate the rhetoric, but it will be some time before relations return to what they were before this crisis.

The Australians have had a baptism of fire in an Asian crisis. Prime Minister John Howard may not have understood the danger of dealing with a transitional president like Habibie, but when the defining moment came, Howard acted as a prime minister of Australia should. With strong support from the Australian media and public, he sent Australian troops to lead InterFET forces into East Timor, despite threats by the militias to inflict casualties on the Australians. These events confirmed the obvious, that Australia's destiny is linked more to Asia, than to Britain or Europe.

My first meeting with Gough Whitlam after he became prime minister was at the 1973 Commonwealth Heads of Government Meeting (CHOGM) in Ottawa. Whitlam was a handsome man, and very conscious of his good looks. He was quick-witted but also quick-tempered and impulsive in his repartees. He proudly told the assembled leaders that he had changed Australia's restrictive immigration policy and would not require Asians who were educated in Australian universities to leave after their graduation. I took him to task over this "new look policy," pointing out that he only accepted skilled and professional Asians and that this created a serious brain-drain for Singapore and his other poor Asian neighbors. He was furious.

He also announced in dramatic fashion his change of direction to be a "good neighbour" in the region and a "good friend" of the Afro-Asian countries. I challenged his claims and cited examples like his quota restrictions on the import of shirts into Australia and on traffic rights for Singapore Airlines. He took this as a personal slight and his exchanges became acerbic. He was a new boy whereas I had old friends around the table in Britain's Ted Heath, Canada's Pierre Trudeau, Norman Kirk of New Zealand, Julius Nyerere of Tanzania, and Errol Barrow of Barbados. They spoke up to support my point of view. One result was that Prime Minister Norman Kirk of New Zealand emerged as the representative voice of the South Pacific supported by Western Samoa, Tonga, and Fiji.

Whitlam then attacked me publicly to say that Singapore had a large ethnic Chinese population and therefore Soviet ships would not come to Singapore. The Soviet Union immediately diverted four Soviet tenders (feeder ships) to Singapore for repairs to test whether we were Chinese or Singaporeans. I replied that Whitlam should not provoke the Soviets again, for the next time they would send a missile destroyer or a nuclear submarine.

When I returned to Singapore from Tokyo, I learned that an Australian representative at the UN had asked the UN high commissioner for refugees to get us to allow some 8,000 Vietnamese refugees who had arrived in many boats to disembark in Singapore on humanitarian grounds. The following day, 24 May 1973, I summoned the Australian high commissioner to tell him that this was a most unfriendly act. Once they landed, we would never be able to get them to leave. He explained that out of the 8,000 boat people, the Australians were prepared to take about 65 who had been educated in Australia. Only by disembarking them could he sort out the 65 or 100 that Australia would accept. I asked what would happen to the balance of the 8,000 who would have disembarked and would refuse to go back to the ships. He mumbled a vague reply. I said his action showed that his present government was unfriendly to Singapore. At a reception in Canberra, his prime minister had unjustly ticked off the No. 2 in our high commission for this refugee problem. Far from Whitlam being the aggrieved party, I was prepared to expose his moves and show him up as a sham white Afro-Asian. The Australian high commissioner was sweating with discomfiture. The refugees were not allowed to land. We accepted 150 fishermen and their families. The rest sailed on to Indonesia, some to Australia.

It was a time of considerable stress for both Australia and Singapore or these exchanges would not have been traded between friends. The American withdrawal from Vietnam and the exodus of Vietnamese boat people were traumatic events. It was a relief when their governor-general removed Whitlam for some alleged constitutional irregularities in November 1975 and appointed Malcolm Fraser to form a caretaker government to hold a general election, which Fraser won handsomely.

Malcolm Fraser was huge even for an Australian. I came to know him well when he was Gorton's defense minister. When we met in Kuala Lumpur at the funeral of Tun Razak in mid-January 1976, I took the opportunity to discuss with him the deployment of Australian forces in peninsular Malaysia and Singapore. He said there was no question of pulling out. He decided to leave his Mirage squadrons and Orion aircraft in Butterworth. I felt reassured by his hard-headed approach to security and stability, and his determination not to give things away.

With my encouragement, Fraser saw Prime Minister Mahathir in 1982. Mahathir said that the Vietnamese foreign minister, Nguyen Co Thach, had declared openly that he would provide bases for Soviet forces in Vietnam if necessary, and it would be foolish for Malaysia to dismantle its bases for foreign countries. It was perfectly acceptable to Malaysia if the Australians wished to stay, but if they wanted to leave there was nothing Malaysia could do about it. Fraser was satisfied and left his planes at Butterworth.

Fraser had conservative views but was never able to undo the damage Whitlam had done in less than three years by precipitately bringing in the welfarism that has burdened Australian budgets ever since. We became and remained friends, although I disagreed with his protectionist economic policies. He was reluctant to open up an economy that cosseted its workers at the expense of its consumers. Eventually Labor governments in the late 1980s and 1990s had to face the difficult task of gradually opening up the country to imports and abandoning uneconomic industries.

When the Australian Labor Party won the general election in March 1983, I was apprehensive that the troubles we had had with Whitlam would resurface. But Bob Hawke was a completely different personality from Whitlam, and the Labor leadership had learned from the excesses of the Whitlam years. Hawke had his heart in the right place and wanted to do the right thing, but every time he took something away from the workers in one sector, he gave it back in subsidies in some other sector. He was Australia's second longest serving prime minister. He presented himself and his arguments well and was always conscious of how he would appear on television.

He withdrew one of the two Mirage squadrons, but deferred decision on the second squadron. In March 1984, he decided to run down the remaining Mirage squadron gradually between 1986 and 1988. I was able to persuade him to keep rotational deployments of his F18s from Darwin totalling 16 weeks a year. This arrangement has continued to the present. By staying on in Butterworth until 1988, the Australians added to the security of Malaysia and Singapore, giving us more than 30 years of stability and growth. After the race riots in Singapore in 1964 and in Kuala Lumpur in 1969, the Australians had been apprehensive about getting involved in clashes between Singapore and Malaysia, or in conflicts between Indonesia and Malaysia or Singapore. By 1988, the Australians had revised their defense assessment; they now considered that the risks of such catastrophes were not high and saw strategic and political value in staying engaged in the region through the Five-Power Defence Agreement.

Looking back, their prime minister who most impressed me was Bob Menzies. Perhaps it was because I was a younger man and more impressionable. I watched his virtuoso performance at the Commonwealth prime ministers' meeting in September 1962 in London. He had a commanding presence, a strong booming voice coming from a large head on a big, broad figure, hair turning white, bristling eyebrows, and an expressive ruddy face. He exuded the confidence and authority of a generation that had been loyal to king and empire. When, despite his best efforts to dissuade it, Britain decided to join the Common Market, he knew that the world had changed irrevocably, that sentiments and ties of kinship could not displace the realities of geopolitics and geoeconomics in the post-imperial world.

Another impressive Australian leader was Paul Hasluck, the external affairs minister (1964–1969) who later became governor-general (1969–1974). He was quiet, soft-spoken, observant, well-read, and well-briefed.

I met him on my first visit to Australia in 1965 when he was in Menzies's cabinet. When Singapore was facing Indonesian Confrontation and, after that, British withdrawal, I met him frequently. He steered Australia's foreign policy with a steady hand and a deft touch. He did not want to abandon Malaysia and Singapore but was careful not to upset the Indonesians or make them feel that "they were being ganged up against," as he said frankly to me. His values, stressing the importance of family, education, and hard work, were those of the prewar generation before Australia came to regard itself as the "lucky country."

Like Australia, New Zealand's links with Singapore were through Britain. Because they are further away from Asia, New Zealanders did not feel so threatened during World War II by the possibility of Japanese invasion and were less suspicious of Asians. They took their share of Vietnamese refugees and were less nervous about boat people pouring onto their shores. This attitude was to undergo a change by the 1990s after they had experienced more Asian immigration.

On my first visit to New Zealand in April 1965, I was surprised to see how British they were in their habits and manners. I stayed in small hotels where maids still wore aprons, as British maids did just after the war, and brought in "morning tea" before breakfast. Their accent was nearer to British accents. There was more courtesy and reserve, less of the Australian backslapping mateyness. The country was green, in contrast to brown and dusty Australia. For many years, the younger sons of the gentry who did not inherit their fathers' estates in England went out to own huge farms in New Zealand, rearing sheep and cattle and growing wheat for the mother country. It was a gracious way of life that gave them a high standard of living. New Zealand developed an advanced system of welfare benefits that gave the people one of the best standards of living and a high quality of life before World War II. After the war, they became wealthy.

They held on to this agriculture-based society for longer than was wise. The Australians industrialized; they did not. So their bright and ambitious young people left in large numbers for Australia, Britain, and America. In the 1980s, New Zealand set out on a different course to develop an economy to offer opportunities for the talented so that they need not emigrate. They also brought in well-educated Asian immigrants, and they began to market the natural beauty of their countryside, promoting tourism on a large scale. It was a belated effort to compete.

One of their longer-serving prime ministers was Keith Holyoake. I first met him when he arrived at Singapore airport in 1964, when we were in Malaysia. He was a stout man with a strong, deep voice resonating from a barrel of a chest. He was down to earth and had no pretensions. He was a farmer and proud of it. He did not pretend to be an intellectual, but had the common touch, which must have been one reason why he won four successive elections and was prime minister from 1960 to 1972. I liked him and respected his integrity. Under pressure, I found him steady and unflappable.

After Britain's Commonwealth secretary, George Thomson, saw me in Singapore in 1967 to tell me of Wilson's decision to withdraw their forces, I phoned Holyoake. It was November, New Zealand's summer. He said he did not think the British would change their minds: He had already tried. He wished me luck in my attempt to get more time. He ended the conversation, saying, "I am in my holiday home by Lake Taupo. It's a sunny day, beautiful and peaceful. You must come and take a holiday here. It'll be a break from your work." He had a different sense of danger, way down in the South Pacific. Years later, I took up his invitation. Huka Lodge near Lake Taupo was indeed tranquil.

When Norman Kirk became New Zealand's Labour prime minister, we met at the 1973 Ottawa Commonwealth conference. He stood out as sincere, straight-speaking, not given to persiflage. On his way back to New Zealand in December 1973, he visited me. We sat on the front lawn of Sri Temasek one evening before dusk, exchanging thoughts on the future. The Vietnam War looked like it was coming to an unhappy close. I asked how he, from outside the region, saw Singapore and its prospects for stability and growth, and where the dangers would come from. His reply was direct and pithy. New Zealand was "the odd man out," rich, white, democratic. Singapore was "the odd man in," a completely Western city and democratic in the center of Southeast Asia, yet different and unique. Its success was its danger; Singapore had become exposed.

We got on well. I was sad when he died a few months later, in August 1974. Twenty-plus years after he said this, when Australia and New

Zealand wanted to join the Asia side of the Asia Europe Meeting (ASEM) of heads of government in Bangkok in 1996, Prime Minister Mahathir objected, saying they were not a part of Asia. It was his visceral reaction, one not shared by most of the other leaders. I believe before too long the logic of geography and economics will prevail against old prejudices, and Australia and New Zealand will be included in ASEM.

Robert Muldoon won the election in December 1975 and remained prime minister until 1984. He was stout, with a big bald head, pugnacious face, and a combative temperament to match. He stood up to and freely traded verbal punches with his Australian counterparts, Malcolm Fraser and Bob Hawke, to remind them that Australia could not take New Zealand for granted.

He wanted to separate sports from politics, and strenuously defended New Zealand's All Blacks rugby team for playing in South Africa and receiving a South African rugby team in New Zealand. To his surprise there were violent protests against them in New Zealand. Over the next few years, I watched him discover at Commonwealth meetings that New Zealand would be isolated if he continued his policy. So, after a strenuous defense of his position, at the 1977 CHOGM in London, he agreed to a declaration boycotting South Africa in sports because of apartheid. It was not worth the fight. He did not hide his sentiments. In 1979, he was one of the few at the Lusaka CHOGM who sympathized with Thatcher on her stand on Rhodesia and South Africa. But he saw sooner than Thatcher that the tide of history was against white domination of Africa. Unlike Whitlam, Muldoon never postured as a white Afro-Asian. Instead he focused his time and resources on the South Pacific islands. He was a chartered accountant, with a mind that could master details and crunch numbers. His analysis of economic problems sounded tough-minded but he was soft when it came to policy implementation. When farm prices fell, he maintained price supports for his farmers. When the manufacturing sector faced problems, he gave them more protection.

It was left to his Labour Party successor, David Lange, to begin the difficult process of trimming down subsidies, causing enormous pain to those who had been cosseted. Lange was an unusual character, of medium height but considerable girth. He had an easygoing manner, a quick mind, and a good memory. Soon after he won the 1984 election he visited me in Singapore on his way to Africa to increase trade with them. I expressed my doubts whether this was likely. He chided me for being skeptical, but conceded later that I was right. He had a good sense of humor and an infectious laugh.

When the Australians announced in 1972 that they would withdraw their battalion from Malaysia in 1973, the New Zealanders decided to remain and did so for another 17 years. Their sturdier nature earned them the nickname "Gurkhas of the South Pacific." However, New Zealanders underwent a sea change in July 1984 when they elected Lange and his Labour Party. His party decided they did not want a nuclear Pacific and took a strong antinuclear stand. They were prepared to jeopardize their ANZUS treaty with the United States by refusing to allow any nuclear-powered ship or any ship carrying nuclear weapons to sail through New Zealand waters or dock in its ports, in effect blocking off the U.S. Navy. It was an astonishing reversal of their traditional attitudes. In October that year, when I met Lange in Singapore, I told him that nuclear warships frequently passed through the Straits of Malacca and the Straits of Singapore, that we recognized the risks of nuclear accident but the U.S. naval presence in the region had given us 30 years of stability. He remained unconvinced. For him and his party, a non-nuclear world was the only way to a secure future.

In Canberra in 1986, Bob Hawke asked me to convince Lange that their long-term interests were best served by ANZUS. When I visited Wellington, I again argued with Lange that his antinuclear policy was overcautious, but did not change his mind. Jim Bolger, then the opposition leader, however, agreed with me that small countries like Singapore and New Zealand would have room to maneuvre and make progress only if the United States continued to maintain the world balance. He added, "New Zealand's anti-nuclear stand would only hasten its disintegration." But when he became prime minister in November 1990, public opinion made it impossible for him to reverse this policy. New Zealanders had decided to opt out of the troubles of the world, for the time being.

As a Labour prime minister, Lange instinctively felt he had to champion the underdog. But on economic reforms and opening up the economy to market forces, he could be persuaded. That was because his finance minister, Roger Douglas, was a convinced free-market man and carried his prime minister with him during his first term of office.

However, during his second term, Lange, under pressure from his cabinet and party colleagues, backed away from the more unpopular reforms. This delay prolonged the agony for New Zealand farmers, manufacturers, and consumers.

In December 1984, Lange announced, without any prior consultation, the cancellation of Singapore's General Scheme of Preferences (GSP) status for our exports. In doing so, New Zealand had moved sooner than America and the European Community. When our foreign minister explained to him that while our loss through the cancellation of GSP in New Zealand would be marginal, we would suffer grievously if the Americans or Europeans followed them and did the same, Lange accepted the argument and restored our GSP status.

Without a large store of gold, diamonds, coal, uranium, and other minerals that provide Australians with a comfortable living, New Zealanders did not have the "lucky country" mindset. When the price of the food they exported fell in the 1980s, Lange and Douglas reduced price supports for farmers and made New Zealand more competitive. It was to the great credit of Prime Minister Jim Bolger that when his National Party returned to power in 1990, he continued these liberalization policies.

I never had any dispute with the New Zealand leaders, not even Bob Muldoon, who could be aggressive and heated in arguments. In my experience the New Zealanders can be depended on to honor their undertakings.

# 25. South Asia's Legends and Leaders

As a young student, I admired Nehru and his objective of a secular multi-racial society. Like most nationalists from British colonies, I had read his books written during his long years in British jails, especially his letters to his daughter. They were elegantly written, and his views and sentiments struck a resonant chord in me. Together with other democratic socialists of the 1950s, I had wondered whether India or China would become the model for development. I wanted democratic India, not communist China, to win. But despite achievements such as the green revolution, population growth has kept down India's standard of living and quality of life.

I visited Delhi for the first time as prime minister in April 1962. I was driven to Pandit Jawaharlal Nehru's home to meet him. It had been the residence of one of the British military commanders—two storys, wide verandas, spacious grounds beautifully laid out. We had a half-hour discussion.

For lunch, we were seated at a long table, probably inherited from British times. Each guest had a large silver tray as his dinner plate, and picked what he fancied from a wide array of rice, chapatis, curries, vegetables, meats, fish, pickles, and condiments that were brought to him. What was unusual was that everyone ate with their fingers. Choo and I had had no practice at this. While they held their food neatly and daintily with their fingertips, we rummaged through ours, the gravy reaching up to our knuckles. We felt and looked messy. I was relieved when silver finger bowls of water with slices of lime came for guests to wash their greasy fingers before eating the sweets, which were delicious. Nehru, sitting opposite me, noticed our awkwardness. I explained that besides chopsticks we usually used forks and spoons. Fortunately, they provided us with cutlery at other meals in Delhi.

Nehru was sufficiently interested in what I had told him to invite me to a second meeting the next day, when he gave me 90 minutes. I explained the demographics of Singapore and of Malaya, and the hold the communists had on the Chinese population because of their enormous success in transforming China from a corrupt, decadent society into a disciplined, clean, and dynamic if regimented one. But communism was totally unsuited to Southeast Asia. Moreover, an independent Singapore would be a disaster, as it would be bound to incur the hostility of its neighbors—Malays in Malaya, and Javanese and other Malay racial groups in Indonesia. I believed the best solution was to merge Singapore with Malaya and the Borneo territories since the Tunku did not want to take Singapore alone because then the Chinese would become equal to the Malays in voting strength. Nehru was pleasantly surprised to find a Chinese so determined not to have Singapore under communist control and the influence of Beijing.

I visited Nehru again in 1964 when I stopped in Delhi on my way back from a tour of Africa. He was a shadow of his former self, weary, weak in voice and posture, slumped on a sofa. His concentration was poor. The Chinese attack across the Himalayas had been a blow to his hopes of Afro-Asian solidarity. I left the meeting filled with sadness. He died a few months later, in May.

My meetings with Nehru in the 1960s allowed me to meet his daughter, Indira Gandhi. When we became independent, we asked the Indian government to help Singapore gain acceptance into Afro-Asian organizations; their diplomatic missions gave us unstinting assistance. A year later, I visited India to thank Gandhi and to interest her government in Southeast Asia. A young, energetic, and optimistic Indira Gandhi met me at the airport with a guard of honor, and drove with me to the former Vice-regal Lodge, now called Rashtrapati Bhavan.

Gandhi was frank and friendly toward the end of my three-day stay in 1966. She said it was difficult for her to carry on with a cabinet not of her own choosing. Ministers were going in different directions. Although she had been appointed in a most cynical manner by the Congress Party bosses who wanted to use Nehru's image for the next election, I thought that if she won by a handsome majority, she had every intention of governing in her own right.

It was sad to see the gradual rundown of the country, visible even in the Rashtrapati Bhavan. The crockery and cutlery were dreadful—at dinner one knife literally snapped in my hand and nearly bounced into my face. Air conditioners, which India had been manufacturing for many years, rumbled noisily and ineffectively. The servants, liveried in dingy white and red uniforms, removed hospitality liquor from the side tables in our rooms. Delhi was "dry" most days of the week. On one occasion, returning to the Rashtrapati Bhavan after a reception given by our high commissioner, my two Indian ADCs in resplendent uniforms entered the elevator with me with their hands behind their backs. As I got out, I noticed they were holding some bottles. I asked my secretary who explained that they were bottles of Scotch. It was the practice at our high commission's diplomatic receptions to give bottles of Johnnie Walker Scotch whisky to deserving guests, and each ADC received two. They were not obtainable in India because they could not be imported. There was a hypocritical pretense at public egalitarianism, with political leaders wearing homespun clothes to identify themselves with their poor, while they quietly amassed wealth. This undermined the morale of the elite officers, civil and military.

My few days' stay in the Rashtrapati Bhavan and my meetings with their top leaders at receptions and in various settings were a sobering experience. On my earlier visits in 1959 and 1962, when Nehru was in charge, I thought India showed promise of becoming a thriving society and a great power. By the late 1970s, I thought it would become a big military power because of its size but not an economically thriving one because of its stifling bureaucracy.

Indian officials were more interested in getting into the joint communiqué, a commitment from Singapore to join it in its "great concern over the danger to the world in general and Southeast Asia in particular arising from prolongation of the conflict in Vietnam." Its nonalignment policy was tilted toward the Soviet Union; this was the price to ensure a regular supply of weapons and military technology.

Indira Gandhi visited Singapore two years later, in May 1968. We had a wide-ranging exchange during which I concluded that India did not have the wherewithal to extend its influence in Southeast Asia. Nevertheless, when I visited India in 1970, I asked her whether India intended to extend its naval interests into Southeast Asia. Their foreign minister, Swaran Singh, who was present, intervened to say India was interested in increasing economic ties but its greater interest was in keeping its western sea lanes open. I sensed that India's primary defense concern was Pakistan, fearing a U.S.-China-Pakistan line-up.

When Morarji Desai became prime minister in 1977, I soon established rapport with him. I had known him when he was India's deputy prime minister in 1969. During the London Commonwealth conference in June 1977, I lunched with him at his high commissioner's residence. He was in his eighties, a strict vegetarian who ate only raw nuts, fruit, and vegetables, nothing cooked. His meal that day consisted of raisins and nuts. The chocolates heaped in front of him were untouched. His high commissioner did not know of his strict diet. Even his milk had to come straight from a cow, not from a bottle. Indeed, at a regional Commonwealth conference in Sydney the following year, Australian Prime Minister Malcolm Fraser had a milk cow at hand. Desai assured me he had more than enough nourishment from his diet, that vegetarians were long-lived. He proved his thesis by living till age 99. He had a dry sense of humor and a capacious memory, but some unusual ideas. In December 1978, in the car taking us from Delhi airport to the Rashtrapati Bhavan, he said that thousands of years ago Indians had made a space journey and visited the planets, which the Americans were then doing. I must have looked skeptical, so he emphasized, "Yes, it is true. It is by reincarnation. It is recorded in the *Bhagavad Gita*."

Indira Gandhi lost the election of 1977 but was returned to power in 1980. When I met her at the Commonwealth Heads of Government Regional Meeting (CHOGRM) in Delhi in September 1980, she had lost some steam. India's basic policies had not got off the ground. Its alliance with the Soviet Union prevented any close collaboration with the United States and Europe. This, plus a system dominated by inefficient state enterprises, not many private sector enterprises, and little foreign investment had made India's economy limp along. Its achievement was to feed its huge population, growing faster than China's.

When India in 1980 condoned the Vietnamese occupation of Cambodia by recognizing the Vietnamese-installed regime, we became contestants at international conferences. We were on opposite sides of an issue crucial to peace and stability in Southeast Asia. At the New Delhi CHOGRM that year, Indira Gandhi in her opening remarks as chairperson dismissed the value of condemning armed intervention across frontiers. I quietly put the contrary view that the Vietnamese and Soviet occupations of Cambodia and Afghanistan respectively were establishing a new doctrine of justifiable intervention outside the framework of the UN Charter, setting precedents for open and armed intervention. There were endless arguments between our officials on the drafting of the communiqué. The agreed draft avoided any mention of either the Soviet Union or Vietnam as aggressors, but did call for a political solution to uphold the independence and sovereignty of Afghanistan and Cambodia. In her closing remarks, she promised India would play its part to persuade people (in Moscow) to withdraw from Afghanistan. But on Cambodia, India recognized the regime because it controlled all major parts of the country, "one of the usual norms for recognition."

When she wrote to invite me to the 7th Non-Aligned Summit in Delhi scheduled for March 1983, I declined, stating, "In striving for true unity, the Non-Aligned Movement cannot be indifferent to the recent violations of the basic principles of national independence, integrity and sovereignty, particularly of its member states. . . ."

But I did attend CHOGM, the full, not regional, Commonwealth meeting in Delhi later, in November 1983, when we again argued over Cambodia. Despite this sparring, because of our long association and good personal relations, there was no personal animus between us.


Indira Gandhi was the toughest woman prime minister I have met. She was feminine but there was nothing soft about her. She was a more determined and ruthless political leader than Margaret Thatcher, Mrs. Bandaranaike, or Benazir Bhutto. She had a handsome face with an aquiline nose and a smart hairstyle with a broad streak of white against a jet black mass of hair combed back from her forehead. And she was always dressed elegantly in a sari. She affected some feminine ways, smiling coquettishly at men during social conversation; but once into the flow of an argument, there was that steel in her that would match any Kremlin leader. She was unlike her father. Nehru was a man of ideas, concepts he had polished and repolished—secularism, multiculturalism, rapid industrialization of the state by heavy industries in the fashion of the Soviet Union. Right or wrong, he was a thinker.

She was practical and pragmatic, concerned primarily with the mechanics of power, its acquisition, and its exercise. A sad chapter in her many years in office was when she moved away from secularism, and to win the Hindi-Hindu vote in North India, consciously or otherwise brought Hindu chauvinism to the surface and allowed it to become a legitimate force in Indian politics. It was to lead to the recurrence of Hindu-Muslim riots, the burning and destruction of the ancient mosque at Ayodhya, and the emergence of the Bharatiya Janata Party (BJP), a Hindu chauvinist party, as the single major party in Parliament in 1996 and again in 1998. She was at her toughest when the unity of India was threatened. There was outrage throughout the Sikh world when she ordered troops into the Sikh holy temple at Amritsar. Watching how incensed the Sikhs in Singapore were, I thought it was politically disastrous: She was desecrating the innermost sanctuary of the Sikh religion. But she was unsentimental and concerned only with the power of the state which she was determined to preserve. She paid for it with her life in 1984, assassinated by her own Sikh bodyguards.

Our divergent policies on Cambodia kept me away from India until March 1988, when I tried to establish contact with her son Rajiv Gandhi, then the prime minister. His deputy foreign minister, Natwar Singh, was with him—a sharp mind and a good presenter of difficult Indian positions. Rajiv suggested that the United States should establish diplomatic relations with Vietnam and stop its economic sanctions because he believed Vietnam intended to withdraw from Cambodia and focus on economic reconstruction. He knew, as we did, that the Vietnamese were then in severe economic difficulties. Vietnam, I replied, had to pay a price for occupying Cambodia, but I hoped that in 10 years there would be a different Vietnam, one which Singapore could work with and welcome as an economic partner. When there was a settlement in Cambodia, India and Singapore would again be on the same side. Both events did happen.

After our discussions, Rajiv Gandhi and his wife Sonia gave Choo and me a private lunch at his residence. Rajiv was a political innocent who had found himself in the middle of a minefield. Because his mother had been assassinated in her own home, Rajiv's security cover was overpowering. He said he found it oppressive but had learned to live with it. I saw him as an airline pilot with a straightforward worldview. In our discussions, he often turned to Natwar Singh. I wondered who guided him through Indian politics but was certain many would want to hold his hand and lead him their way.

Only a well-meaning prime minister would have sent Indian troops to Sri Lanka to put down a rebellion by Jaffna Tamils. These were descendants of Tamils who had left India over 1,000 years ago and were different from India's Tamils. Indian soldiers spilled blood in Sri Lanka. They withdrew and the fighting went on. In 1991, a young Jaffna Tamil woman approached him at an election rally near Madras, ostensibly to garland him, and blew them both up. It was not fair. His intentions had been good.

In 1992, Narasimha Rao's minority Congress government was forced to change India's economic policies radically to comply with an IMF rescue package. Rao got on well with my prime minister, Goh Chok Tong, when they met at the Non-Aligned conference in Jakarta in 1992, and persuaded him to visit India with a delegation of Singapore businesspeople. His finance minister, Manmohan Singh, and his commerce minister, P. Chidambaram, visited Singapore to brief me on their changes in policy and attract investments from Singaporeans. Both ministers were clear on how to improve India's economic growth and knew what had to be done. The problem was how to get it done with an opposition that was xenophobic on free enterprise, free markets, foreign trade, and investments.

Rao visited Singapore in September 1994 and discussed India's opening up with me. The most difficult obstacle, I said, was the mindset of Indian civil servants toward foreigners—that they were out to exploit India and should be hindered. If he wanted foreign investments to flow into India freely, as in China, they must change their mindsets and accept that it was their duty to facilitate, not regulate, the activities of investors. He invited me to visit India for a brainstorming session with his colleagues and his top civil servants.

In January 1996, I visited Delhi and spoke to his civil servants at the India International Centre, and also to businesspeople from their three chambers of commerce, on the obstacles that blocked India's path to higher economic growth. In a separate one-on-one meeting with Rao, he acknowledged that age-old fears of Indians that economic reforms would lead to unequal distribution of wealth had made it difficult for him to proceed with further changes. He had injected large amounts of money to benefit the people but had been accused by his opposition of selling and mortgaging the country. He highlighted two social issues: India's slow rate of public housing because funds were lacking and its high birth rate. He wanted my prime minister to help him in his housing program. I had to dampen his high expectations that because of our successful housing program we could solve India's housing problems. Singapore could provide India with planning but they had to raise the resources to implement the plans themselves.

When I met Rao in the 1980s, he was foreign minister in Indira Gandhi's government. He was of the generation of independence fighters, in his late seventies and on the verge of retirement. When Rajiv Gandhi was assassinated in 1991 in the middle of an election campaign, the Congress Party agreed on Rao as leader. A sympathy vote gave his party the largest number of seats, although short of a majority. Rao became prime minister and for the first two of five years carried out radical economic reforms; but he was not an energetic young man chasing his own ideas. The impetus to the Indian economy came from Manmohan Singh, his finance minister, who ironically had started his career as a central planner. Rao did not have the conviction to persuade the people of India to support these reforms over the heads of an obstructive opposition.

With slow economic but high population growth, India is not about to be a wealthy nation for some time. It has to solve its economic and social problems before it can play a major role in Southeast Asia. It is in Asean's interest to have India grow stronger and help maintain peace and stability on the Indian Ocean side of Southeast Asia.

India has so many outstanding people in all fields of scholarship, but for a number of reasons it has allowed the high standards the British left them to be lowered. There is less insistence now on meritocracy by examinations for entrance into top schools and universities, the professions, and the Indian Civil Service (ICS). Cheating at examinations is rampant. Universities allot their quota of places to MPs of their state, who either give or sell these places to their constituents.

The ICS in British days was selected from the crème de la crème of all India. An Indian had to be outstanding to be admitted into this elite British service. During one of my visits in the 1960s, I stayed at the Rashtrapati Bhavan. Before golf one morning, two Indian officers who had been members of the original ICS, not the IAS (Indian Administrative Service) which it had since become, came for breakfast. They were impressive. One of them explained how a few hundred ICS officers governed 450 million Indians in British India and governed well. He spoke with nostalgia of the quality of the men selected for the ICS, and regretted that the entrance examinations, which used to be conducted only in English, could now be taken in English or in Hindi. Populist pressures had lowered standards of recruitment and had also led to poorer communications within the service.

It was a gradual slide in quality of a once elite service, now caught up in the throes of a social and economic revolution which had reduced living standards. During the days of the British Raj, they had lived up to a certain lifestyle. Generals, admirals, air marshals, and senior ICS officials played golf. In the India of the 1960s and 1970s, they could not buy good (i.e., imported) golf balls because their import was forbidden. I remember one excursion to the Delhi Golf Club. Our high commission had advised me to bring several boxes of golf balls to distribute to the committee members of the club. It was depressing to see top brass and civil servants breaking up the packages and taking fistfuls of golf balls to stuff into their golf bags.

Indeed, golf balls were so precious that caddies would dash into any house or rough to find them. Once, at the former Bombay Royal Golf Course in 1965, I sliced my ball into a squatter area and heard the loud clatter as it fell on a zinc roof. My caddie dashed off, I thought to find out who was hurt. But no—a little boy emerged with the golf ball, not to complain of injury but to bargain over the price of the ball. I was sad to see how the caddies had collected broken plastic and wooden tees, sharpened their ends and reused them to tee up the balls of the players. In the locker rooms, bearers (menservants) put on and took off your socks and shoes. There were too many hands with too little work.

Perhaps the fault lies in the system. India has wasted decades in state planning and controls that have bogged it down in bureaucracy and corruption. A decentralized system would have allowed more centers like Bangalore and Bombay to grow and prosper. Another reason could be their caste system. It has been the enemy of meritocracy—each caste demands its quota in all institutions, whether recruitment into the IAS or entrance to the universities. A third reason is the endless conflicts and wars with Pakistan that make both poorer.

The Delhi I visited in the 1960s was a big, sprawling city with many open spaces, not polluted and without too many squatters. The Delhi of the 1990s was an environmental mess. It was January and the air smelled foul with the fumes from coal burning in power stations and in homes. There were squatters everywhere. For security, they placed a whole company of soldiers in front of the Sheraton Hotel where I stayed. And traffic was clogged up. It was not the spacious capital it once was.

By the time Narasimha Rao's Congress Party lost the election in 1996, a 13-party coalition including several communist parties had come together to keep the Hindu nationalist BJP party out of power. Indian democracy had moved from its secular base. It was difficult to pursue further liberalization of the economy. But the deeper problem was never solved. Prime Minister Inder Kumar Gujral in a public statement referred to the findings of a survey that India was the second most corrupt country in Asia. He said in 1997 to his Confederation of Indian Industry, "I sometimes feel ashamed, and I hang my head in shame when I am told that India is one of the ten most corrupt countries in the world." India is a nation of unfulfilled greatness. Its potential has lain fallow, underused.

My first visit to Sri Lanka was in April 1956 on my way to London. I stayed at the Galle Face Hotel, their premier British-era hotel by the sea. I walked around the city of Colombo, impressed by the public buildings, many with stone facing undamaged by war. Because Mountbatten had based his Southeast Asia Command in Kandy, Ceylon had more resources and better infrastructure than Singapore.

That same year, Solomon West Ridgeway Dias Bandaranaike won the election as leader of the new Sri Lanka Freedom Party and became prime minister. He had promised to make Sinhalese the national language and Buddhism the national religion. He was a brown "pukka sahib," English-educated and born a Christian; he had decided on nativism and converted to Buddhism, and had become a champion of the Sinhalese language. It was the start of the unravelling of Ceylon.

Singapore's then chief minister, Lim Yew Hock, invited me to meet him at dinner. A dapper little man, well-dressed and articulate, Bandaranaike was elated at having obtained an election mandate from the Sinhalese majority to make Ceylon a more nativist society. It was a reaction against the "Brown Sahib" society—the political elite who on inheriting power had modeled themselves on the British, including their lifestyle. Sir John Kotelawala, the prime minister whom Bandaranaike succeeded, went horse riding every morning. Bandaranaike did not seem troubled that the Jaffna Tamils and other minorities would be at a disadvantage now that Sinhalese was the national language, or by the unease of the Hindu Tamils, the Muslim Moors, and the Christian Burghers (descendants of Dutch and natives) at the elevated status of Buddhism as the national religion. He had been president of the Oxford Union and he spoke as if he was still in the Oxford Union debating society. I was not surprised when, three years later, he was assassinated by a Buddhist monk. I thought it ironic that a Buddhist monk, dissatisfied with the country's slow rate of progress in making Buddhism the national religion, should have done it.

In the election that followed, his widow, Sirimavo Bandaranaike, became prime minister on the sympathy vote. She proved to be a less voluble but much tougher leader. When I met her in Ceylon in August 1970, she was a determined woman who believed in the nonaligned ideology. Ceylon favored the withdrawal of all U.S. troops from South Vietnam, Laos, and Cambodia, and a Nuclear-Weapons Free Zone in the Indian Ocean, free of big-power conflicts. As a younger man, I patiently explained my different foreign policy objectives, that Singapore would be gravely threatened if South Vietnam were to fall into the hands of the communists, threatening Cambodia, Laos, and Thailand. The insurgency would spread into Malaysia, with serious consequences for Singapore. We could not subscribe to this high-minded ideology when it had serious consequences for our future. Other great powers in the region, China and Japan, would in time expand their naval buildup. Therefore Singapore found it necessary to continue with the Five-Power Defence Agreement, which gave us some security.

Her nephew, Felix Bandaranaike, was her éminence grise on international affairs. Bright but not profound, he claimed good fortune of geography and history had blessed Ceylon with peace and security so that only 2.5 percent of its budget was spent on defense. I wonder what he would have said in the late 1980s when more than half its budget went into arms and the defense forces to crush the Jaffna Tamil rebellion.

Ceylon was Britain's model Commonwealth country. It had been carefully prepared for independence. After the war, it was a good middle-size country with fewer than 10 million people. It had a relatively good standard of education, with two universities of high quality in Colombo and Kandy teaching in English, a civil service largely of locals, and experience in representative government starting with city council elections in the 1930s. When Ceylon gained independence in 1948, it was the classic model of gradual evolution to independence.

Alas, it did not work out. During my visits over the years, I watched a promising country go to waste. One-man-one-vote did not solve a basic problem. The majority of some 8 million Sinhalese could always outvote the 2 million Jaffna Tamils who had been disadvantaged by the switch from English to Sinhalese as the official language. From having no official religion, the Sinhalese made Buddhism their national religion. As Hindus, the Tamils felt dispossessed.

In October 1966, on my way back from a prime ministers' conference in London, I visited Colombo to meet Prime Minister Dudley Senanayake. He was a gentle if resigned and fatalistic elderly man. When we played golf on the former Royal Colombo golf course, he apologized for the encroaching squatter huts and the goats and cows on the fairways. He said it was inevitable with democracy and elections; he could not justify keeping these green open spaces in the center of the city. He sent me by train to

Nuwara Eliya, their once beautiful hill station. It was a most instructive lesson on what had happened after independence. The food on the train (in a special carriage) was poisonous. The crab was badly contaminated and stank. I went immediately to the restroom and spewed it all out. This saved me. In Nuwara Eliya, I stayed at the former British governor's hill residence, "The Lodge." It was dilapidated. Once upon a time it must have been well maintained, with roses (still some left) in the garden that looked like an English woodland. About 5,000 feet above sea level, it was pleasantly cool. I played golf on a once beautiful course; like the one in Colombo, this also was encroached upon by huts, goats, and cows.

At dinner, a wise and sad-looking elderly Sinhalese explained that what had happened was inevitable with popular elections. The Sinhalese wanted to be the dominant race; they wanted to take over from the British as managers in the tea and coconut plantations, and from the Tamils who were the senior civil servants. They had to go through this tragedy of making Sinhalese the official language for which they had paid dearly, translating everything from English into Sinhalese and Tamil, a slow and unwieldy process. The universities taught in three languages: Sinhalese to the majority, Tamil to the Jaffna Tamils, and English to the Burghers. At the university in Kandy, I had asked the vice chancellor how three different engineers educated in three languages collaborated in building one bridge. He was a Burgher, and wore a Cambridge University tie so that I would recognize he had a proper Ph.D. He replied, "That, sir, is a political question for the ministers to answer." I asked about the books. He replied that basic textbooks were translated from English into Sinhalese and Tamil, always three to four editions late by the time they were printed.

The tea plantations were in a deplorable condition. The locals who had been promoted were not as good supervisors as their British predecessors. Without strict discipline, the tea pluckers were picking not only young shoots but also full-grown leaves, which would not brew good tea. Their coconut plantations had also suffered. It was, said the old Sinhalese, the price people had to pay to learn how to run the country.

I did not visit Ceylon for many years, not until I had met their newly elected prime minister, Junius Richard Jayewardene, in 1978 at a CHOGRM conference in Sydney. In 1972, Prime Minister Sirimavo

Bandaranaike had already changed the country's name, Ceylon, to Sri Lanka, and made it a republic. The changes did not improve the fortunes of the country. Its tea is still sold as "Ceylon" tea.

Like Solomon Bandaranaike, Jayewardene was born a Christian, converted to Buddhism, and embraced nativism to identify himself with the people. In his 70-odd years, he had been through the ups and downs of politics, more downs than ups, and become philosophical in his acceptance of lowered targets. He wanted to move away from Sri Lanka's socialist policies that had bankrupted it. After meeting me in Sydney, he came to Singapore, he said, to involve us in its development. I was impressed by his practical approach and was persuaded to visit Sri Lanka in April 1978. He said he would offer autonomy to the Tamils in Jaffna. I did not realize that he could not give way on the supremacy of the Sinhalese over the Tamils, which was to lead to civil war in 1983 and destroy any hope of a prosperous Sri Lanka for many years, if not generations.

He had some weaknesses. He wanted to start an airline because he believed it was a symbol of progress. Singapore Airlines employed a good Sri Lankan captain. Would I release him? Of course, but how could an airline pilot run an airline? He wanted Singapore Airlines to help. We did. I advised him that an airline should not be his priority because it required too many talented and good administrators to get an airline off the ground when he needed them for irrigation, agriculture, housing, industrial promotion and development, and so many other projects. An airline was a glamour project, not of great value for developing Sri Lanka. But he insisted. So we helped him launch it in six months, seconding 80 of Singapore Airlines' staff for periods from three months to two years, helping them through our worldwide sales representation, setting up overseas offices, training staff, developing training centers, and so on. But there was no sound top management. When the pilot, now chairman of the new airline, decided to buy two second-hand aircraft against our advice, we decided to withdraw. Faced with a five-fold expansion of capacity, negative cash flow, lack of trained staff, unreliable services, and insufficient passengers, it was bound to fail. And it did.

It was flattering to have Sri Lanka model their country after Singapore. They announced that they would adopt the Singapore-style Area

Licensing Scheme to reduce traffic entering the city, but it did not work. They started a housing program in 1982 based on ours, but there was no adequate financing. They set up a free trade zone only slightly smaller than the area of Singapore that might have taken off but for the Tamil Tigers whose terrorist tactics scared investors away.

The greatest mistake Jayewardene made was over the distribution of reclaimed land in the dry zone. With foreign aid, he revived an ancient irrigation scheme based on "tanks" (reservoirs) that could store water brought from the wet side of the mountains. Unfortunately, he gave the reclaimed land to the Sinhalese, not the Tamils who had historically been the farmers of this dry zone. Dispossessed and squeezed, they launched the Tamil Tigers. Jayewardene's private secretary, a Jaffna Tamil loyal to him, told me this was a crucial mistake. The war that followed caused 50,000 deaths and even more casualties, with many leaders assassinated. After more than 15 years, it shows no sign of abating.

Jayewardene retired in 1988, a tired man. He had run out of solutions. Ranasinghe Premadasa, who succeeded him, was a Sinhalese chauvinist. He wanted the Indian troops out of the country, which was not sensible. They were doing a nasty job for Sri Lanka. When the Indian troops left, he was in a worse position. He tried to negotiate with the Tamil Tigers and failed. He was not willing to give enough away.

I met him on several occasions in Singapore after he became president and tried to convince him that this conflict could not be solved by force of arms. A political solution was the only way, one considered fair by the Jaffna Tamils and the rest of the world; then the Tamil United Liberation Front, the moderate constitutional wing of the Tamil home rule movement, could not reject it. I argued that his objective must be to deprive the terrorists of popular support by offering the Tamils autonomy to govern themselves through the ballot box. He was convinced he could destroy them. In 1991 and 1992, he sent the Sri Lankan army to fight major battles against the Tamil Tigers. They did not succeed. In 1993, at a May Day parade, a suicide bomber approached him in a street procession. He and many others died. His successor, Sirimavo Bandaranaike's daughter, President Chandrika Kumaratunga, tried negotiation and war. She recaptured the Jaffna peninsula but did not destroy the Tamil Tigers.

The fighting goes on. It is sad that the country whose ancient name Serendip has given the English language the word "serendipity" is now the epitome of conflict, pain, sorrow, and hopelessness.

We established diplomatic relations with Pakistan in 1968 but for many years had little trade or other links. We did not share common positions in international affairs until the 1980s when the Afghan and Cambodian conflicts, both funded by the Soviet Union, brought us together.

President Zia ul-Haq visited Singapore in 1982 as part of a tour of Southeast Asia. He told me his sole purpose in visiting Singapore was to meet me as the person responsible for modern Singapore. I gave him my standard reply, that modern Singapore was the work of a team. We discussed Indo-Pakistan relations. Singapore relations with India then were strained because of differences over Cambodia. I agreed with Zia that Soviet strategy and objectives had created the war in Afghanistan and Cambodia.

He invited me to visit Pakistan, which I did in March 1988. He welcomed me in style as President Marcos had done in 1974. Once our commercial aircraft crossed the India-Pakistan border near Lahore, six F-16 fighter planes escorted us to Islamabad. He mounted a huge guard of honor for inspection, a 19-gun salute, and hundreds of flag-waving children and traditional Pakistani dancers to greet me at the airport. I was impressed to see Islamabad noticeably cleaner and better maintained than Delhi, with none of the filth, slums, and streets overflowing with people in the city center. Standards at their guesthouses and hotels were also higher.

Zia was a heavyset man, with straight black hair carefully combed back, thick moustache, a strong voice, and a confident military manner. He was a strict Muslim and made Pakistan's military officers go dry like the rest of the country. As his guests, we were provided with locally brewed beer at the guesthouse. At dinner, Zia made an off-the-cuff speech to compliment me, not just on Singapore, but especially for standing up to the Western press. He had been following the Singapore government's exchanges with the Western media and cheered for us. He had suffered in their columns and was delighted we were not taking it lying down. He conferred on me Pakistan's "Order of the Great Leader" (Nishan-I-Quaid-I-Azam).

In a press conference before departure, I praised President Zia for his courage in undertaking the dangers of giving logistics support to the Afghans. Had he been a nervous leader who preferred to look the other way, the world would have been worse off. Unfortunately, a few months later, before our relations could progress, Zia was killed in a suspicious plane crash.

Ties with Pakistan again stagnated until Nawaz Sharif became prime minister in November 1990. He was a stout man of medium height, short for a Pakistani, already bald although only in his late forties. Unlike the Bhuttos, Nawaz Sharif came not from the landed property feudal elite but from a middle-class business family in Lahore. He had built up steel, sugar, and textile companies during the years when Pakistan was ruled by military leaders, including Zia ul-Haq. He visited Singapore twice in 1991—in March, quietly, to study the reasons for our economic progress; in December, to ask me to visit his country and advise on the opening up of its economy. Pakistan, he said, had started on bold reforms, using Singapore as a model.

He struck me as keen to change and make Pakistan more market-oriented. I agreed to go the following year. At my request, he sent the secretary-general of his finance ministry, Saeed Qureshi, to Singapore to brief me. We met for three sessions of three hours each, to discuss facts and figures he had sent earlier. It was soon obvious that they faced dire and intractable problems. They had a low tax base, with income tax yielding only 2 percent of their GDP. Many transactions in land sales were not documented and tax evasion was widespread. They subsidized agriculture, railways, and steel mills. Defense took 44 percent of the budget, debt servicing 35 percent, leaving 21 percent to administer the country. Hence their budget deficits were 8 to 10 percent of their GDP and inflation was reaching double-digit figures. The IMF had drawn their attention to these parlous figures. The solutions were obvious but political will was difficult to exercise in a country without an educated electorate and with the legislature in the grip of landowners who controlled the votes of their uneducated tenant farmers. This made land and tax reforms near impossible. Corruption was rampant, with massive thievery of state property, including illegal tapping of electricity.

I spent a week in Pakistan from 28 February 1992. I had two meetings with Prime Minister Nawaz Sharif and his key cabinet colleagues, including his finance and economics minister, Sartaj Aziz, an irrepressible optimist. After I returned, I sent Nawaz Sharif a report together with a personal letter to summarize the actions he should take.

He was a man of action with much energy. He sympathized with the plight of taxi drivers and lowered taxes for taxis even though that raised problems of fairness to other car buyers. His business background made him believe in private enterprise as the solution for slow growth and he was eager to privatize state enterprises. But in Pakistan they were not sold by inviting open tenders. Friendship, especially political ones, determined who got what. He always believed that something could be done to make things better. The problem was that often he had neither the time nor the patience to have a comprehensive study made before deciding on a solution. On balance, I believed he was better able to govern than Benazir Bhutto, the leading opposition leader who was later to succeed Nawaz Sharif. He knew more about business, with or without patronage, than either she or her husband, Asif Zadari.

On my journey home, I stopped in Karachi to meet Benazir Bhutto. She was full of venom for Nawaz Sharif and President Ghulam Ahmed Khan. She said her party had been unfairly treated; the government had tried to discredit her and her party by prosecuting her colleagues and her husband. The corrupt police were abetting the government, and a troika of the military, the president, and the prime minister ran the country. She also claimed she had started their current push for deregulation and had passed the legislation for privatization.

Nawaz Sharif visited Singapore in December 1992 on his way home from Japan. He wanted me to make a followup visit to assess progress in implementing my recommendations. He had privatized 60 percent of targeted enterprises and foreign investments had increased. Again Saeed Qureshi briefed me. I discovered many of my recommendations had not been implemented. I had feared this would happen. Before I could visit Islamabad again, confrontation between President Khan and Prime

Minister Nawaz Sharif led to the resignation of both and fresh elections. Benazir Bhutto became prime minister.

Shortly after the election, I met Benazir Bhutto in Davos in January 1994. She was elated and full of ideas. She wanted Singapore to participate in a road project from Pakistan to Central Asia going through Afghanistan. I asked for a detailed proposal for us to study. She also wanted us to look into the viability of sick enterprises in Pakistan and take them over. Her husband was even more ebullient. He was going to build an island off Karachi to develop as a free port and a free trade zone with casinos. It was totally uneconomic. Pakistan had so much unused land, what need was there to build an island? Their approach was simple: Singapore was successful, had lots of money, and therefore could invest in Pakistan and make it as successful.

In March 1995, Bhutto and her husband visited Singapore. She said she had heeded my advice in Davos and ensured that all her proposals had been well thought through. She invited Singapore to transfer its labor-intensive industries to Pakistan. I said she would first have to convince our businesspeople. When investors saw on television every night Muslims killing other Muslims in Karachi with heavy weapons and bombs, they must ask themselves, why should they be involved? I did not visit Pakistan. She was dismissed from office in 1996 by Leghari, a president she herself had appointed. Nawaz Sharif won the subsequent election in February 1997, to return as prime minister.

Pakistan's deep economic and political problems remained. Too much of their budget went into defense. Their politics continued to be poisoned by implacable animosities between the leaders of the two main parties. Asif Ali Zadari was charged with the murder of his wife's brother, Murtaza Bhutto. And husband and wife were both charged for corruption involving vast sums of money, some of which was traced to Switzerland.

To compound Pakistan's problems, in May 1998, India conducted several nuclear explosions. Two weeks later, Pakistan conducted its own tests. Both were economically stretched, Pakistan more than India. When I met Pakistani Prime Minister Nawaz Sharif during his visit to Singapore in May 1999, he assured me that he had had good discussions with India's Prime Minister Vajpayee the previous month and that neither side intended to deploy missiles with nuclear warheads. He ventured the view that because both had nuclear capabilities, an all-out war between them would no longer be possible. It is an outcome devoutly to be wished.

The Pakistanis are a hardy people with enough of the talented and well-educated to build a modern nation. But unending strife with India has drained Pakistan's resources and stunted its potential.

# 26. Following Britain into Europe

My views of the Europeans had been much influenced by British attitudes of the 1950s and 1960s. The Europeans seemed different and somewhat strange, not as cohesive as nations nor as constitutional-minded as the British: The French were prone to riots and revolutions and the overturning of constitutions; the Germans tended to use force to settle disputes. But once Harold Macmillan as prime minister made his bid in 1962 to join the European Economic Community (EEC, now the European Union) and was rebuffed, I believed it was only a matter of time before a second application or a third would succeed. After Britain announced its withdrawal from east of Suez in 1968, Prime Minister Harold Wilson made an overture to President Charles de Gaulle. Again it failed, but it underlined how important Europe had become for Britain.

Britain wanted to join to get out of its recurring economic difficulty of slow growth compared to the faster growth of Germany, France, the Benelux countries, and even Italy—all members of the EEC. It was clear that the larger market spurred growth. I wanted to build ties with this new Europe and not have Singapore shut out when Britain joined.

As with most bureaucratic organizations, statements of principle from the top are no assurance of a smooth relationship. I encountered protectionist policies of "Fortress Europe" in the 1970s over our exports. In October 1977, I went to Brussels to see the president of the European Commission, Roy Jenkins, with whom I had kept in touch since the 1960s when he was British chancellor of the exchequer. I had written to him earlier that their application to Singapore of GSP rules (the General Scheme of Preferences which gave developing countries limited import duty-free entry) had caused problems for our exports of electronic calculators, umbrellas, projectors, and plywood. Recently, even fresh orchids were meeting objections from Dutch and Italian flower growers. I added that I had expected problems with textiles and umbrellas but not with electronic calculators and fresh orchids. Jenkins was sympathetic and promised to look into this, but he could do nothing about the umbrellas. It seemed they were produced in President Giscard d'Estaing's constituency.

With the other commissioners, I discussed how to avoid manufacturing those products that the EEC countries would find sensitive because of persistent high unemployment. I discovered to my dismay that the list was unlimited. Any member country with any influence on Brussels, feeling the slightest pain, could appeal to Brussels for protection and would invariably get it. Yet the EEC denied it was the most protectionist of all the trading blocs. I cited the experience of Philips and Siemens, two of the best-known European MNCs; they had found it more difficult to export their Singapore-made electronic products to Europe than to America and Asia.

I raised two matters: first, that "graduation" leading to the removal of GSP benefits should not be applied prematurely to Singapore; and second, that selective safeguards blocking imports were unlikely to be effective in solving EEC problems. I tried to convince Jenkins, as president of the EEC, that he should formalize the promising EEC-Asean relationship in an agreement for economic cooperation, and that a visit by him to the countries of Asean would put the imprimatur of the commission on this goal. Instead, he sent Viscount Davignon, the commissioner of industrial affairs. Jenkins was not fond of travelling to the East, whose prospects he did not rate highly. Finally, with the help of the German foreign minister, Hans-Dietrich Genscher, Asean succeeded in getting the EEC to sign an agreement in 1980 for a Joint Cooperation Committee to promote and review activities. Asean countries, however, still faced endless protectionist problems with this multimember organization. Its agricultural subsidies and tariffs worked against palm oil exports; its health and safety regulation on rubber products and eco-labelling and other forms of labor and environmental standards effectively checked Asean exports. As for Singapore, in 1986, as part of its review of the GSP privileges, the EEC imposed a quota on Singapore ball bearings.

European MNCs were less agile and dynamic than the Americans and Japanese. They were missing the opportunities for global integrated production, manufacturing different components of a product in different countries. That was the situation in the 1980s and it was still largely true in the 1990s.

To establish ties with the French who were the moving spirit behind the EEC, I arranged in May 1969 to meet President de Gaulle whom I had long admired as a great leader. Just before the visit, French students took to the streets and demanded constitutional reforms and more university places, in fact challenging de Gaulle's legitimacy. The visit was postponed. De Gaulle called a referendum, lost it, and retired. I never got to meet this stern, tall, unbending man who had restored French pride in themselves and their country, and whose autobiography impressed me even in an English translation.

Instead I met his successor, Georges Pompidou, in September 1970. He was friendly and jovial, a man who enjoyed an exchange with a visitor from a strange faraway place called Singapore. He emphasized that France was more than just high fashion in clothes, exotic perfumes, and great wines. He wanted French quality chemicals, high-tech machinery, engineering, and aircraft to be the image the world had of 1970s France. He had a philosophical bent and engaged me for 20 minutes on Asian attitudes toward gold. Would it still be highly priced and treasured if it became no more than a commodity and no longer a backing for currency? I was strongly of the opinion that it would. Over the millennia, historical experience of devastation and famine caused by drought, floods, wars, and other calamities had taught the Chinese people the value of gold, indestructible, immutable, and fungible. The three-and-a-half year Japanese occupation of Singapore was a recent reminder. I told him that with one *tahil* (slightly more than one ounce) of gold, regardless of hyper-inflation, you could feed a family for a month as well as buy medicine and other essentials. My account seemed to confirm his own beliefs. I said it was a primeval instinct in man. His interpreter, Prince Andronikov, a French Russian émigré, translated this as *primitif*. I protested, "No, primeval, going back to earliest times." The interpreter looked coldly at me to say, "Yes, in French primeval is primitif." I felt duly chastened.

Valéry Giscard d'Estaing was elected president in May 1974, succeeding Pompidou. I was in Paris on a private visit but he received me within a few days of his election. It was a good meeting for over an hour at the Élysée Palace. Unlike Pompidou, who knew English but insisted on speaking in French, President Giscard decided to use English. Tall, with a long patrician face, a bald high dome of a skull, he spoke with a strong French accent, choosing his words carefully and with great precision.

He was very French in his approach, cerebral, logical, and systematic: Why did Singapore develop and not the others, what was missing in the others? I could only tell him what I thought were three primary reasons: first, stability and cohesion in society; second, a cultural drive to achieve and a thrifty, hardworking people always investing in the future, with high savings for a rainy day and for the next generation; third, a great reverence for education and knowledge. He was not satisfied that that was the complete answer.

Giscard's prime minister, Jacques Chirac, had a totally different set of interests. He did not spend time on philosophical discussion about what was happening in Asia but wanted to know what more could be done between France and Singapore. I tried to interest him not just in Singapore but in the wider region, using Singapore as the stepping stone. It took another 10 years, under a different president and after several prime ministers, before I convinced the French government and entrepreneurs that Southeast Asia was a promising part of the world to invest in.

Raymond Barre succeeded Jacques Chirac as prime minister in August 1976. Barre, a rotund man of medium height, was a professor of economics and a sympathetic listener. He favored the establishment of French joint ventures and investments abroad. He supported my proposal to develop Singapore into a technological servicing center and said that France could cooperate with us in sales and services in the region. He proposed a five-year Singapore-France bilateral cooperation agreement on trade, investments, technical assistance, and cultural cooperation with specific set targets. He was practical and systematic in tackling problems, keen on results. But his French industrialists were not ready for this enterprise. I spoke to a group of them in the French National Employers' Federation (CNPF). At the end of an hour's discussion, their spokesman told the press that investors were aware of the opportunities in Singapore but many appeared disinclined to get up and go "as it is too far away and English-speaking," adding that France could not be everywhere as it was concentrating on Africa. Indeed, the French were focused on Francophone Africa. Even in Asia, they were drawn toward Vietnam, believing it would still be French-speaking and French-inclined. It was not until the mid-1980s, when a socialist President Mitterrand and his Gaullist prime minister, Jacques Chirac, both decided that Africa was not as ready for development as Asia, that my efforts came to fruition.

In July 1981, on my way to London to attend the wedding of Prince Charles, I stopped in Paris hoping to meet the newly elected president, François Mitterrand. But the Quai d'Orsay, the French foreign office, was starchy and did not approve of a stopover visit. The president was busy, but as he also was going to the wedding, he would meet me in London at the residence of their ambassador. To soften the rebuff, Prime Minister Pierre Mauroy gave me lunch.

At my departure from Paris, I was driven speedily through heavy traffic, escorted by their police outriders from my hotel to Charles de Gaulle Airport. It was a beautiful summer's day. The expressways lined with trees and the embankments covered with creepers were a glorious sight. Charles de Gaulle Airport was modern and efficiently laid out. Then I arrived in Heathrow, all higgledy-piggledy; a labyrinth of roadways took me from the plane to the VIP lounge, then out to scruffy streets with roundabouts and grass verges unkempt and overgrown with weeds, on to my Knightsbridge hotel. The contrast between Paris and London was stark.

My mind went back to my first visit to Paris in June 1948 with Choo. It was a scruffy, down-at-heel, postoccupation city, a poor relation compared to bomb-scarred but neat and tidy London, a city of confident people, proud of their record of standing up to the Nazis and saving humankind from tyranny. I remembered also the chaos in Paris in May 1958 just before Charles de Gaulle came back as president to form the Fifth Republic. Through his culture minister, Malraux, he cleaned up

Paris, scrubbed the soot from the buildings, and made it a city of lights. They restored French pride and injected fresh hope, while London muddled on as the British economy stumbled from one crisis to the next. I believed there were advantages in revolutionary change as against Britain's slow and gradual constitutional evolution. The British held endless meetings over new airports around London including Stansted and Gatwick, all leading to nothing, as planning authorities were stymied by local interests determined to preserve their amenities at the price of the nation's progress. Even after the Thatcher years, Heathrow still stands as an ancient monument to symbolize a lack of dare and dash.

Of the French leaders I met, the most perceptive in assessing political trends and the nature of different societies was President Mitterrand. He talked about the threat posed by the aggressive intervention of Soviet forces in Afghanistan. He conceded the Soviets had had successes in Vietnam and the Middle East, particularly Syria, but its influence everywhere else had declined. They had given a lot of arms but had few friends. He was confident that, united, the West had the ability to restore the general balance of power.

During his first two years as president, with Pierre Mauroy as prime minister, Mitterrand followed standard socialist policies. He lowered interest rates, expanded credit to mop up unemployment, and nationalized several major industries and banks. The French economy suffered. Old as he was, in his seventies, Mitterrand's ideology was not set in stone. He changed his prime minister and pursued more conventional economic policies to control money supply and inflation, and restored steady if unspectacular growth. One achievement of his 14 years as president was to educate the French socialists and make them a party of government.

We had a more substantial discussion for over an hour in September 1986 when his Concorde made a refuelling stop at Changi Airport. Protocol did not require me to meet him, but I had found him a serious man. His was a *tour d'horizon.* With great insight, Mitterrand said that the Soviet empire was in such a state that one mere accident would be enough to split central Europe from the Soviet Union, that Soviet control was based on a balance of power that had been in its favor. However, history had shown that the balance always shifted and the ideological power of the Soviet Union was beginning to decline. A third generation of communists believed that they could benefit from the experience of the Western world, and this was causing weaknesses in the Soviet system.

He wholeheartedly agreed with me that Europe would be a much stronger force in international affairs if it could speak in one voice. This was his great ambition—a Europe of 320 million with great technological capabilities. He believed English and French could serve as common languages in Europe, with French equally powerful. But the unification had to be a slow process. If it were a question of survival, Europe would undoubtedly be totally united. On the other hand, Europe would always resist being swallowed by the American civilization; it would fight to maintain its distinct European identity. Americanization, with its fast foods, pop music, and movies, was invading the basic European lifestyles.

He asked about the Cambodian situation, which he said appeared frozen. I disagreed with his view because there was now cause for optimism. Communism had been checked in the region, having reached its peak when North Vietnam captured Saigon. Since then, the emptiness of the communist system, Vietnam's invasion and occupation of Cambodia, and its own grinding poverty had destroyed the image of idealism that communism had hitherto projected. Mitterrand was surprised to learn that living standards in Vietnam were so dreadfully low that, as I told him, they were happy to get food parcels from relatives in America and France. The Vietnamese, I said, had made a grievous strategic error in fighting China. By continuing its occupation of Cambodia, Vietnam had to forego economic growth while the Asean countries were forging ahead. Vietnam was already one generation behind Asean, and by the time they found a solution to their Cambodian burden, they would be lagging by two generations.

I met Mitterrand again on an official visit in May 1990. He came out to the steps of the Élysée to greet me, an honor our ambassador noted. He again expressed surprise at the failure of the Vietnamese who were "courageous, imaginative and resourceful people." I added that the Vietnamese knew that they were able and could see that the Thais who were less hardworking and less organized were the more successful, that it was their system that was at fault. To put right the system, they would need a generation change at the top. Could there be a grassroots movement in Vietnam to overthrow the system as had happened in Eastern Europe? I did not think so, because Vietnam had a long-established tradition of emperors and strong leaders.

Mitterrand returned to the subject of the collapse of the Soviet empire and with uncanny prescience predicted the reemergence of "all sorts of nationalistic forces that had long been suppressed."

One able French prime minister was Edouard Balladur who led a Gaullist government that cohabited with socialist President Mitterrand. We had met on several previous occasions. His diplomatic adviser had been ambassador in Singapore and a friend, so I knew Balladur was a man of considerable ability. I was surprised, therefore, that he had some strange theories about trade. In his office, with note takers, he expounded his theory that liberalization for free trade could take place only between countries of similar social and economic structures, otherwise the differences could lead to distortions and unfair competition. He gave as example the French textile industry, which would be lost in another 10 to 15 years because of competition from China, Taiwan, and South Korea. I disagreed with him and argued that protection of any country's industry was no longer possible except at great cost. Companies were global in reach, an irreversible result of progress in technology, especially in global communications. Firms sourced material from one country, used labor from another, set up production plants in a third, and marketed their products in a fourth.

Although he agreed with my views in general, he could not help but take a protectionist position, because of fears over the loss of jobs whenever companies relocated their production plants out of France. He agreed that economic competition should be honest and fair, adding that Japanese car manufacturers did not compete fairly as they possessed certain advantages. I found this an eccentric and odd explanation from a man of undoubted intellect.

A similar view was put to me by Jacques Chirac when, as mayor of Paris, he met me in Singapore at the end of 1993. He had read the speech I made at the Asahi Forum that October when he was in Tokyo. He found my proposition that Europe was protectionist absurd. Europe was the most open market in the world with the lowest tariffs. The real protectionists, he argued, were Japan and the United States. It was unfair to blame France or the European Commission for blocking the Uruguay Round negotiations because it refused to give up Europe's Common Agricultural Policy. I countered that if there were no free trade, then the world must prepare for another war. The Chinese had built their ancient empire because they needed to establish order over a wide expanse of territory and its many peoples so that goods and services could be exchanged freely within their empire. When all parts of the globe were carved up into various empires as before World War II, war resulted from competition for more raw materials, more markets, and more wealth.

We next discussed French agriculture and the Uruguay Round. I had listened to a BBC program on the plight of the French farmers and how the French countryside had suffered. But this was part and parcel of the technological revolution. French farmers could not be protected forever and ever to keep their way of life unchanged. Chirac retorted that France needed to protect its agriculture, but he wanted me to know that he shared my views on free trade. For its own long-term interest, there was no way other than free trade, hence France was the least protectionist.

I quoted former GATT Director General Arthur Dunkel as an expert witness that France was protectionist. The then director general, Peter Sutherland, also said so. Chirac interjected to say that he had no confidence in Sutherland. I said the EEC president, Jacques Delors, had confidence in Sutherland, to which Chirac promptly replied that he had no confidence in Delors as well!

Chirac said we could not convince each other, so it was best if we agreed to disagree. In the end, he did move the position of Balladur's government so that a settlement was reached on the Uruguay Round. Since we first met in 1974, Chirac and I had become friends and could talk freely and frankly to each other without giving or taking offense.

I was struck by the deep interest both Chirac and the German chancellor, Helmut Kohl, had in China and East Asia. I discussed this with Prime Minister Goh Chok Tong and suggested that he launch an initiative for regular meetings between leaders of the European Union (EU) and East Asia. The Americans had regular meetings with East Asia through APEC, and with the EU through many organizations. But the EU and East Asia had no formal meetings that could foster trade, investments, and cultural exchanges. Goh took it up with French Prime Minister Edouard Balladur, and the first Asia-Europe meeting of leaders was held in Bangkok in February 1996. Visiting Asian countries on their way to or after that meeting, many European leaders discovered the extent of the East Asian industrial transformation, and decided on biennial meetings of EU and East Asian leaders.

My first encounter with Germans was at the Frankfurt airport in April 1956. The British Overseas Airways Corporation "Argonaut" had stopped in Rome where I heard mellifluous if languid announcements over the loudspeakers as Italian porters trundled baggage leisurely. On arrival at Frankfurt a few hours later, I felt the air appreciably cooler and crisper, as if to match the peremptory *Achtung-Achtung* over the loudspeakers, followed by instructions that were compelling and insistent as German porters briskly went about their business. It reminded me of the difference between the German and Italian armies described in dispatches from the battle fronts of World War II. I had read them in reports carried by Allied news agencies when I was editing their cables during the Japanese occupation.

I visited Willy Brandt in Bonn in September 1970 when he was the German chancellor. We had met earlier in Brussels, in 1964, during the centennial of the Socialist International. After my speech at that meeting, he came up and sympathized with me over the communal riots in Singapore that had been organized by supporters of the central government out to intimidate the Chinese. He invited me to visit him. I likened Singapore to a West Berlin without the advantage of the Federal Republic of Germany to back it. As a former mayor of West Berlin he understood my predicament. He was the most sympathetic of all European leaders to Singapore's plight. I tried to convince him not to write off Southeast Asia because I was confident we would overcome the communist insurgencies threatening so many countries in the region. Brandt was attractive—tall and broad-framed, with a friendly, handsome face and a good voice. He was more visceral than cerebral in his reactions. Perhaps he allowed his heart to rule his head. He was a good old-fashioned socialist, always in favor of equalizing opportunities and rewards.

Helmut Schmidt, who took over from Brandt in 1974, was clear-headed and tough-minded, with definite views on all key issues. He had contempt for the equivocation on East-West issues of developing countries' leaders who were afraid to criticize the Soviet Union. Having been defense minister, then finance minister, as chancellor he had a thorough grasp of economic, defense, and strategic issues.

He and his wife, Loki, visited Singapore in October 1978. In the three days they spent here, we took the measure of each other and found much common ground. When we recorded a television interview for a German television station, the interlocutor was surprised that we seemed to think and talk alike on so many issues.

I proposed to Schmidt that he set up a German-Singapore Institute to run courses on advanced manufacturing and information technology, to help German businesses set up in the region. He agreed. The institute turned out to be of great benefit to German investors who were able to recruit technicians trained to German standards. Later, Singapore became host for the training of other Third World workers at this institute.

After my visit to Bonn and Berlin the following autumn, I wrote in a note to the cabinet:

> Berlin looked more prosperous than in 1970, my last visit. But it lacked the relaxed and free spirit of Bonn. The communists have a choker on the people of West Berlin. They stifled the vibrancy of life, not enough to give cause for protest, or to make newspaper headlines, but enough of a constant and nagging pressure to remind Germans generally that they have hostages in West Berlin. As I passed the Russian war memorial with their guards standing like statues, I was reminded that they were suppliers of weapons which were causing so much suffering in Indochina and threatening Thailand. Without the flow of these weapons, there would be no Vietnamese troops in Cambodia nor Cambodian refugees in Thailand. . . . Our saving grace is that their system is

so damnably inefficient in providing the goods and services the people want. Regimentation has left their people shabbier in spirit and poorer in everything, except the capacity to make war. This inferiority, over time, will become increasingly clear to everyone including their own people. If the West does not give the Soviets any opportunity to exploit their military superiority, their system will be under profound stress by the 1990s.

So it turned out.

I next met Schmidt in Bonn in January 1980, after the Soviet invasion of Afghanistan. I was with a group of leaders, including Henry Kissinger, Ted Heath, and George Shultz, for a free-ranging discussion. We were unanimous that the Soviet Union had to be resisted at all costs and the Afghan people supported.

Schmidt stepped down from office in 1982 because his Social Democrat Party (SPD) would not support the policies he thought necessary to restore financial discipline. He remained active, writing in *Die Zeit,* a newspaper, and chairing conferences of the InterAction Council, a group of former world leaders who met annually to discuss long-term world problems in a totally dispassionate and nonpartisan manner. I became a member of his group after I stood down from office in 1990.

Schmidt's successor, Helmut Kohl, was a giant of a man, probably the largest and tallest leader in the world then. On my visit to Bonn in May 1990, he was eloquent on German reunification, then about to happen. It had to happen, he said, and in the context of European unity. He was confident and optimistic that he could manage the costs and problems of reunification. He dismissed any suggestion of a "Fortress Europe." Germany would not condone protectionism and he was confident the German industry would be able to compete against the Japanese.

I expressed concern that German reunification would consume so much resources, energy, and manpower that there would be little left over for the Asia Pacific region. He assured me that he would not lose interest in East Asia. He was most conscious that a reunified Germany, with some 20 million East Germans added to 60 million West Germans, would raise fears among its neighbors. He said that everybody wanted a united

Germany to remain in NATO, and although their motives for wanting this were not always "friendly," the end result was positive: "European unity and German unity are two sides of the same medallion."

He had equally strong views on China. There were many *dummkoepfe* (blockheads) in the Federal Republic of Germany who wanted to isolate China because of Tiananmen. It was the wrong approach. He agreed with Singapore's policy of engaging China. China wanted a foot in Europe, particularly in Germany, which had the highest number of Chinese students in Europe, and they would be the future modernizers of China.

Unlike the French, German industries and banks had been active in Singapore and the region from the early 1970s, long before Chancellor Kohl developed a personal interest. After the Dutch, the Germans were the largest single European investor in Singapore, and our largest European trading partner. Kohl visited Singapore in February 1993, two and a half years after German reunification. He admitted the cost of integrating East Germany was more than he had expected. Nevertheless he was accompanied by over 40 top German industrialists. I urged him not to leave East Asia to the Americans and the Japanese. Germany, Kohl said, was essentially outward-looking. He wanted more economic and cultural links with the area. He invited me to visit Germany to keep in touch. He wanted Singapore and German entrepreneurs to invest together in China, Vietnam, and other East Asian markets. I visited him in May 1994 to keep him abreast of events. He also spoke of Russia, that the European Union was not treating the leaders in Moscow with the respect that was due. The Russians were a proud people and felt belittled and slighted by this. If the correct approach was not maintained, he was convinced Russian nationalists and militarists would get back into power and "the whole cycle would start again."

In November 1995, Kohl visited Singapore again and repeated his concern over Russia. His European partners did not understand that Russia was crucial to peace in Europe. They had to help Russia become stronger and more democratic and not go back to dictatorship and expansionism. Europe would need Russia as a balance against China. For these reasons, Germany was Russia's top aid donor with US$52 billion in 1989, more than half of all international assistance. He despaired of the Americans.

They were becoming inward-looking. The Republicans were "as bad if not worse." No Republican candidate had been to Europe during a presidential election year as they had done in the years of the Cold War.

He wanted my personal assessment to check against his official reports on China, Japan, Vietnam, Indonesia, Malaysia, India, Pakistan, Bangladesh, and the Philippines, and I gave him frank answers with no varnish. When I said that such and such a country was a hopeless case, he would concur to say he would not invest there. He was hard-headed and our assessments often matched.

In June 1996, Kohl took Choo and me over the Rhine in a helicopter to visit Speyer, with its splendid eleventh-century cathedral, in his home state, Rhineland-Palatinate, in the heart of Europe. He had brought Mitterrand, Gorbachev, Thatcher, and others on this sentimental journey to the wine district of the Rhineland. His wife joined us at his favorite restaurant, Deidesheim Hof, where we tried some of his favorite dishes. During dinner he regaled me with accounts of his encounters with East Asian leaders he liked and some whom he found prickly. He found Suharto an unassuming man and they became close friends. Before he became chancellor, he had visited Suharto at his home. As he waited in the hall admiring fish in an aquarium, a man wearing a sweater and a sarong came out; together they watched the fish and then got into conversation. The German ambassador who accompanied Kohl did not take notice of him. Only after some time did Kohl realize this was the president himself. Suharto invited him to stay for lunch and they spent four hours together. On another occasion, Suharto took him to his farm to see his cattle, after which Kohl arranged for a German stud bull to be sent. The next time he met Suharto, the president shook his hand and said the bull had done a first-class job.

Kohl showed that he placed little weight on form and much on substance when we travelled around Speyer, all six of us, not in Mercedes limousines, but in a Volkswagen people mover. When I gave him lunch in Singapore, he arrived in a tour coach, in order, he told me, to have a better and more comfortable view of the city.

Helmut Schmidt and Helmut Kohl were not the best of friends and the German media were intrigued that I got along well with both. When they asked me, I replied it was my business to get on with whoever was the leader of Germany, that I did not take sides. Kohl was often unfavorably compared with Schmidt, his immediate predecessor. Schmidt is an intellectual, always tossing out interesting ideas which he expounded with trenchant force and clarity in *Die Zeit* after he retired as chancellor. Kohl, on the other hand, has been described by the media as dull and uninspiring. This led many to underestimate him. When he first came to power, no one expected him to become the longest-serving German chancellor since Bismarck. When I got to know him better, beneath the outward bulk and apparent clumsiness I discovered a good mind with keen political instinct. He was a strong character, resolute and consistent in pursuing his objectives. His great vision enabled him to come to terms with Germany's past and he was determined that the past would never again be repeated. Hence his single-minded pursuit of the European Monetary Union (EMU) which he referred to as a question of war and peace. He believed the Euro would make the process of European integration irreversible.

Kohl lost the election in September 1998. He will go down in history as a great German who reunified Germany and as a greater European who wanted Germany as part of a supranational Europe to avoid the disastrous European wars of the last century. He consolidated Franco-German ties and set the Euro for a successful launch on 1 January 1999, despite much skepticism and opposition. The Euro weakened against the U.S. dollar in its first year. If the Euro eventually succeeds, Kohl's contribution to European unity will have been historic. His admission that he had managed secret donations to his party that should have been declared, cannot diminish his contribution to Germany and the EU.

French leaders impressed me by the quality of their intellect and political analysis. They had a greater ability than the Germans to project themselves onto the world stage, making use of the resources of the Germans in the European Community. A reunited Germany would challenge this arrangement. But Chancellor Kohl knew too well the fears that could be aroused if Germany appeared to throw its weight.

One serious obstacle to European cohesion and unity is the absence of a common language. Schmidt spoke to Giscard in English and told me they could establish a close rapport. Mitterrand and Chirac communicated with Kohl through an interpreter. I have always found it difficult to feel the texture of another person's mind when an interpreter stood in between. Schmidt, Giscard, and Chirac all spoke to me in English and I could feel the grain of their thinking better than with Mitterrand and Kohl, who spoke through interpreters. When I had to wait for interpreters to tell me what they said, it was more difficult to read their body language. When a person speaks in English, even if it is not grammatical or idiomatic, I get the feel of the way his mind works. Pauses and hesitations in the middle of a sentence sometimes change the nuance of a sentence; an interpreter would have smoothed out these pauses and given me the substance without the wrinkles that would indicate the person's reservations. Until the Europeans settle on a common language, they cannot equal the uniformity and the benefits of scale that America enjoys. Every EU country teaches English as the second language. None is prepared to give up its language for English or any other language. EU engineers and managers will therefore not be so easily interchangeable as Americans when working on major projects.

French aspirations to have their language as one of the leading languages of international diplomacy have had to yield to pragmatism. By the late 1980s, French speakers at international conferences began to speak in English for greater impact on the international audience. With the Internet, the supremacy of the English language can be ignored only at a heavy price. It is common in the 1990s to listen to French and German CEOs having discussions in English.

# 27. The Soviet Union: An Empire Implodes

I was in Jesselton (now Kota Kinabalu) near the jungles of British North Borneo for a court case when news broke in October 1957 that the Russians had sent a sputnik into space. It was a spectacular demonstration of the superiority of Soviet technology. I took the challenge of the communist system seriously. The Soviets were aggressive everywhere in Asia and together with communist China were fueling guerrilla insurrections. They loomed even larger in my mind after they sent the first man into space in April 1961. It lent credence to their claim that history was on their side.

I was curious to know what they were like as a people and took the opportunity to visit Moscow in September 1962 after a Commonwealth conference in London. I was given the standard official tour of Moscow including a night at the Bolshoi, where I watched Stravinsky on his first return to Russia conducting the orchestra for the ballet *Petrushka.* The officials insulated me from people in the streets, shops, and hotels and I met no one other than themselves.

My lasting impression of Moscow and its officials is one of drabness and dourness. There was a *bábushka,* exactly as I had read in books—a big, fat lady sitting outside the elevator on my floor of the National Hotel (their best, where Stravinsky was also staying), doing little else. They served me an enormous breakfast—caviar, smoked sturgeon, slabs of ham and meat, an assortment of bread, butter, coffee, tea, vodka, and cognac— on a table covered with a dark velvet tablecloth. When I returned that night from the ballet, the food was still uncleared. And as I had been warned, the bathtub and washbasin had no stoppers. I had brought a solid rubber ball expressly for this purpose. It did not work for the washbasin but fortunately did for the bathtub. The Chaika car (a medium-size saloon) was dreadful. The officer who took me around was from the ministry of culture in charge of Southeast Asia, and the highest official I got to see was deputy foreign minister Kuznetsov. In Moscow, I had the impression of menace in the air, but that was perhaps my imagination. That the Soviets were a great power was a reality.

I therefore encouraged my elder son, Loong, to study Russian, reasoning that since he was keen on mathematics, he could then read the publications of many excellent Russian mathematicians. I thought Russia was going to be a powerful influence in the lives of my children. Loong spent five years studying the language with a Czech émigré professor teaching at our Nanyang University, followed by the Tass correspondent, and then a succession of young Russians who were studying Chinese there. Finally a British diplomat taught him Russian for the O-level examination, for which he got a distinction.

Singapore established full diplomatic relations with Russia in 1968 but contacts were minimal. They had nothing we wanted to buy except the catch of their fishing fleet that trawled the Indian and Pacific Oceans. They formed a joint venture with one of our companies to can their fish, and they also repaired their vessels in our dockyards and took on provisions. The Soviets, however, were interested in Singapore because of its strategic location. This point was brought home to me during an enforced stopover in Moscow in January 1969.

Choo and I were on our way to London, flying on Scandinavian Airlines System via Bangkok, Tashkent, and Copenhagen, when the pilot announced that the plane was unable to land at Tashkent because of weather conditions and had to land instead in Moscow. The weather looked fair as we flew over Tashkent. Waiting on the tarmac of Moscow airport were their foreign ministry officials with Ilia Ivanovich Safronov, the Russian ambassador-designate to Singapore. It was a freezing night. Choo slipped and nearly fell on the icy tarmac, quite unprepared for these conditions. My secretary shivered with the cold but warmed up in the VIP room with cognac. What they wanted from this elaborate exercise was for me to meet the man coming to Singapore as their first ambassador. It was also a simple way to impress upon me their size, their might, and their reach.

Safronov, who spoke Mandarin, had served in China and his duty obviously was to make a close study of the potential influence that China could muster in Singapore. Soon after he arrived in Singapore, he brought me an invitation from Prime Minister Aleksei Nikolayevich Kosygin to visit the Soviet Union.

In September 1970, I arrived in Moscow past midnight on an Aeroflot flight from Cairo, to be welcomed by a guard of honor of tall Russian guardsmen under floodlights. They moved like robots and shouted back in unison when I was prompted to say "Hello" to them in Russian. The inspection of the guard of honor ended with the men marching past close to me in an intimidating show of aggressiveness and strength. It was designed to impress, and I was impressed.

I called on a corpulent President Nikolai Podgorny at the Kremlin for discussions and lunch. He spoke of improving cultural and economic relations. A nondescript character, he left no impression on me. The next day, they flew us to Sochi then drove us from their guest dacha over two miles of a hilly road by the Black Sea to a large holiday home in Pitsunda, where a serious-looking but not unfriendly prime minister greeted us. Kosygin proudly showed us the facilities of his resort dacha, in particular his heated indoor pool with a large sliding door, which worked at the press of a button. I spent some two hours talking with him before dinner.

Kosygin showed keen interest in the circumstances under which we had separated from Malaysia. He asked "whether Singapore had in fact made serious efforts to live together in the Federation." I assured him we had tried our best but that there was a fundamental difference in our political beliefs on communal issues and policies. He asked if he was right to assume that the idea of federation with Malaysia had not been abandoned. I referred to ties of geography and family between the two countries, but after the Kuala Lumpur May 1969 race riots, I did not think it was productive to talk about rejoining the Federation. The leaders there were suspicious of Singapore. He then asked about the support enjoyed by the communists (i.e., Maoists) in Singapore. I said this peaked at about 33 percent in 1961–1962 and was now probably 15 percent.

It was clear to me from his body language and his questions on the influence of Beijing on our Chinese-educated that he did not think an independent Singapore was in the Soviet interest. He referred pointedly to our military repair facilities used by U.S. aircraft and ships, and also the rest and recreation visits of U.S. servicemen from Vietnam. I countered that our repair facilities were open to all on a commercial basis. He was interested in using our dockyards and, with an eye to the former British naval facilities, said he hoped to expand bilateral relations in the political and economic fields. He was prepared to send all types of vessels, including Soviet warships, for repairs. His deputy minister for foreign trade would visit Singapore to assess the prospects of enhancing trade.

He struck me as a man of some subtlety and gravitas. He did not raise the Soviet proposal for an Asian collective security system that President Podgorny had put to me in Moscow. Since I had shown no enthusiasm, Kosygin simply said that they were both a European and an Asian country, and naturally interested in what went on in Southeast Asia, although some chose to deny them the right to be Asians.

A foreign affairs officer who accompanied me, a China specialist, Mikhail S. Kapitsa, did most of the talking and probing throughout my visit. Soviet hospitality was overwhelming. On the aircraft from Moscow to Sochi, they served caviar, smoked sturgeon, vodka, and cognac soon after breakfast. When I said that British habits made me drink only tea in the morning, the liquor and food were removed. Their minister who accompanied us said he was also a tea drinker and sang its praises.

I was impressed by the huge war memorial at Volgograd (Stalingrad during World War II) to commemorate their heroic defense of the city under siege. As a cable editor in Japanese-occupied Singapore, I had read war correspondents' dispatches during that long battle in 1943–1944. Magnificent wall bas-reliefs commemorated the many acts of bravery of Russian troops and civilians during the siege. Nearly as memorable were their war memorial and cemetery at Leningrad (now St. Petersburg). These were a brave, tough, and enduring people who had absorbed the heavy punishment the German Wehrmacht had inflicted, turned the tables on their enemy, and finally driven them all the way back to Berlin.

Friendly and hospitable though they were, Choo and I suspected that our rooms were bugged. After dinner on our first night in Moscow, she said in our bedroom at the guest dacha, "Strange, they paid so much attention to me. They must think I have a great deal of influence over you. They gave very little attention to Raja." The next day, Rajaratnam, my foreign minister, received much more and Choo much less attention from our hosts. It was so obvious that I wondered if they wanted us to know they were eavesdropping. For the rest of the trip, even in the bathroom, I felt that they were monitoring my thoughts.

After 1970, we had no more high-level contacts except for four visits from Soviet Deputy Foreign Minister N. P. Firyubin to Singapore between 1974 and 1980. I chided him for not supporting Asean when even mainland China had voiced its support. They were suspicious of Asean as an anti-Soviet pro-U.S. organization. Firyubin was highly intelligent and pleasant to talk to, but had no power to decide policy. When we met for the last time in April 1980, he tried to burnish the poor reputation of the Soviets after their support for Vietnam's occupation of Cambodia and their own invasion of Afghanistan. He said the Soviet Union wanted détente with the rest of the world and referred to the recent visits of Vietnamese leaders to Southeast Asian capitals as an indication of their new mood for peace. Vietnam was willing to discuss the establishment of a zone of peace, freedom, and prosperity. The Soviet Union supported this and would do everything to maintain peace, security, and mutual trust. I was blunt in contradicting his views. If they wanted peace, they should get Vietnam to reverse its aggression in Cambodia, which had alarmed all the other countries in Southeast Asia. I emphasized that the Soviet Union's invasion of Afghanistan in December 1979 had made all countries in Southeast Asia fearful of Soviet intentions.

We also discovered around this time that our cypher officer in Moscow had been compromised by a Russian woman and had handed her the embassy's decoded messages. They must have done this routinely for all embassies, whether friend or foe. What they hoped to learn from reading our communications with our embassy puzzled me, for all we wanted was to stay out of trouble with them.

After Vietnam invaded Cambodia, Russian propaganda had turned hostile against Singapore, speaking of 25 million Chinese who lived outside the People's Republic of China as China's proxies, a dangerous Fifth Column in their countries of residence. I reminded Firyubin that the

Soviet Union had an embassy in Singapore but China did not, that he knew I disapproved of the Chinese government's attempts to appeal to overseas Chinese in the region over the heads of Southeast Asian governments. However, Vietnam's aggression and occupation of Cambodia had succeeded in stifling fears the Thais and others had of China. The Soviet Union had to make a fundamental decision to change its policy. The less trouble it created in Southeast Asia, the fewer the opportunities for China to get closer to these countries.

After the Soviet invasion of Afghanistan, we joined the boycott of the 1980 Moscow Olympics, froze the cultural exchange program and deferred all visits by their economic delegations. We also denied repair facilities and even bunkering to their naval and auxiliary vessels in our civilian dockyards, and overflight and technical stopover facilities for Soviet aircraft flying to Indonesia.

Relations remained frozen for nearly a decade until Gorbachev introduced glasnost and perestroika. When Prime Minister Nikolai Ryzhkov visited Singapore in February 1990 he represented a different government and country. He had none of the self-confidence and swagger of a leader of a big power. He had approached Deputy Prime Minister Ong Teng Cheong for a $50 million loan to buy Singapore consumer goods. I did not agree and told Ong Teng Cheong not to respond. By the time the prime minister of the Soviet Union had to approach tiny Singapore for a $50 million loan, they must have exhausted their credit with all the big countries. A sovereign debt from the Soviet Union was worthless.

He was taken to an NTUC-owned "Fairprice" supermarket. When I gave him dinner that night at the Istana, he expressed his amazement that our workers could afford the wide variety he saw of meats, fruits, and vegetables imported from all over the world. That the Soviet Union was suffering from food shortages at the time brought this subject to the forefront of his thoughts.

Ryzhkov was pleasantly soft-spoken and friendly. He admitted that Stalin's imposition of the command economy and the isolation of the Soviet Union under conditions of autarky had done damage. His government had since made a turnaround. They had now seen how closely interrelated the world had become and had decided to get intensively involved in international economic relations irrespective of the country's system.

He invited me to visit the Soviet Union, which I did in September that year. This time, the welcoming ceremony at Moscow airport was very different. Their guard of honor was no longer of uniformly tall six-foot-three guardsmen. They were a mixed lot of the tall, short, and medium, and the bandsmen were similarly an odd mix. The clockwork military precision was missing. They no longer bothered to create that sense of awe in their visitors.

Ryzhkov was late for his meeting with me and apologized profusely. He had been held up in the Supreme Soviet trying to find a compromise between two divergent sets of proposals for a transition of the Soviet economy to an open-market system. He displayed a total loss of confidence in their system and bewilderment at how to get into a market system. He said his government had watched Singapore with great interest because they were now embarking on a transition to a market economy and were attracted by the remarkable changes in Singapore. They were also studying the experiences of many countries to extract the positive elements of how others had managed their economy. I thought how disastrous it was for a huge country like the Soviet Union to be talking of learning about the market economy from other countries at this late stage of disintegration.

My meeting with President Mikhail Gorbachev was postponed several times because he was caught up in a series of intense discussions on the next step into a market economy. Soviet protocol officers were apologetic, but I told my ambassador not to worry. We were witnessing the end of an empire. I had the advantage of having seen an earlier one, the collapse of the British Empire in February 1942 as the Japanese captured us. I was taken to his office at the Kremlin when he broke away from one of the interminable meetings to meet me for half an hour. All formalities were put aside as we met in a small group, he with only his *chef de cabinet* and one interpreter, and I with only my deputy prime minister, Goh Chok Tong, and my foreign minister, Wong Kan Seng.

He was uncertain what his next steps should be to solve almost insoluble problems. I thought to myself that he had made a fatal mistake going for glasnost (openness) before perestroika (restructuring), that Deng Xiaoping had been wiser doing it the other way around. Gorbachev looked composed, calm, and sincere when he said that each nation was unique and no country must dominate another militarily. He said the Soviet Union was engaged in perestroika, grappling with the question of choice, the choice of political and economic reform, and how it should proceed. The Soviet Union had begun its perestroika in 1917 but that had not worked out the way it was supposed to. Now he was trying all over again. He understood that Singapore's perestroika had started many years ago. He valued the development of bilateral relations.

It was a miracle, I said, that the transformation of the Soviet Union was so peaceful. If he could get through the next three to five years without violence, he would have scored a great triumph. I complimented him for not using military might to solve his problems since otherwise it would have been disastrous for the world. He replied that no matter what stage of economic or cultural development a country was in, no one could say which was first-rate and which was second-rate because each nation was unique in its own way.

As we walked out of the Kremlin, I marveled that such a decent man could reach the top of so evil a system. A lesser leader would have sought to resolve the problems of the Soviet Union by using its huge military capabilities, which would have caused untold damage to the rest of the world. It was a stroke of good fortune for the United States and indeed the world.

In my discussions with China's leaders, I discovered their totally different view of Gorbachev as a superpower leader who had listened to the siren calls of his enemies. He should have been on guard when his enemies' media praised him. Instead, he followed their exhortations and by glasnost (openness) brought about the disintegration of his country, exactly what his foes wanted. Therefore, when the American media referred to Vice Premier Zhu Rongji as China's Gorbachev, Zhu quickly distanced himself from anything that might be seen to be like Gorbachev. The accolade he or any Chinese leader preferred was to be seen as a Deng Xiaoping with his socialist realism, that black cats or white cats both caught mice. Few Chinese, leaders or ordinary people, commiserated with Gorbachev when he was repudiated by his own people with less than 1 percent voting for him in the 1996 Russian presidential election. They saw him as having dismantled the Soviet empire in a way the CIA would have been proud to have done.

The Soviet Union's disintegration did not affect Singapore as we had few economic links with it. The first sign of its system breaking down was when the visits of its fishing fleet became irregular. Ships' captains were selling their fish elsewhere, sometimes on the high seas, to pay their crew and the dockyards that repaired their vessels cheaper than we could. Central control from Moscow had broken down. Aeroflot, the Soviet airline, was in similar difficulties. It did not have the hard currency to pay for aviation fuel and had to beg for petty cash from Moscow Narodny Bank's branch in Singapore to pay for fuel to fly back to Moscow.

Despite this growing chaos Aeroflot brought in plane-loads of Russian tourists who shopped for electronic goods they could sell at several times their cost once past Moscow customs. They were profitable excursions for these freelance traders. Soon more Russian women than men arrived. Word had got around that all they needed was their air ticket and taxi fare to our hotels where male clients would provide them with the resources to pay for the electronic goods to take home at the end of their short stay. Our ambassador in Moscow was a moral man who disapproved of this and approached the Soviet interior ministry to get them not to issue passports to such women. But the flow of these enterprising young Russian women amateurs continued.

When I visited the Soviet Union that September of 1970 and met Premier Kosygin at his holiday dacha on the Black Sea, the Soviet leaders were expansive and assertive, confident that the future belonged to them. To watch this massive, tightly controlled empire shudder, become ungovernable, and then break up, was an awesome spectacle. Something like this must have happened to China in the last decades of the Qing dynasty. The difference is that Russia still has nuclear capability, an ultimate deterrent against any predator out to dismember it. And anyone who believes that the Russians are finished as a powerful people should remember the nuclear and space scientists, chess grandmasters, and Olympic champions they nurtured despite a crippling centrally planned economy. Unlike their communist system, the Russians are not a people to be consigned to the dustbin of history.

# 28. America: The Anticommunist Anchorman

In late August 1965, within days of the trauma of separation from Malaysia, I was suddenly faced with a personal problem. Choo had a worrying medical condition that required surgery. Her gynecologist, Dr. Benjamin Sheares, recommended an American specialist who was the best doctor in this field. I tried to get him to come but could not persuade him to do so. He wanted Choo to go to Switzerland where he was going for some other engagement. I enlisted the help of the U.S. consul-general and, through him, the U.S. government. They were unhelpful; either they could not or would not help. I approached the British to get their top specialist named by Sheares. He agreed and immediately flew to Singapore, expressing understanding for my not wanting her to travel abroad when I could not leave Singapore. This incident reinforced my gut feeling that I would find it difficult to work with the Americans whom I did not know as well as the British.

I was angry and under stress. In a television interview with foreign correspondents a few days later, I fired a broadside at the Americans. I expressed my unhappiness that the U.S. government had not been able to help in persuading an American medical specialist to come to Singapore to treat someone dear to me. Then I disclosed publicly for the first time the story of how, four years earlier, a CIA agent had tried to bribe an officer of our Special Branch (our internal intelligence agency).

In 1961, the CIA offered this officer a fantastic salary and guaranteed that if his activities were discovered or he got into trouble, they would remove him and his family to America and his future was assured. Their proposition was so attractive that the officer took three days to consider it before deciding he had to tell his chief, Richard Corridon, about it. Corridon immediately reported to me and I told him to lay a trap. He did and caught three Americans red-handed in an apartment on Orange Grove Road as they were about to administer a polygraph lie-detector test on our Special Branch officer to check his honesty. One was a member of the U.S. consulate here and claimed diplomatic immunity; two were CIA officers, one based in Bangkok, the other in Kuala Lumpur. They were caught with enough evidence to send them to jail for 12 years. The American consul-general, who knew nothing about it, resigned.

After discussing the matter with Keng Swee, Chin Chye, Raja, and Pang Boon, I told the British commissioner, Lord Selkirk, that we would release these men and their stupidity would not be made public if the Americans gave a hundred million U.S. dollars to the Singapore government for economic development. They offered US$1 million, not to the Singapore government, but to the PAP—an unbelievable insult. The Americans had been buying and selling so many leaders in Vietnam and elsewhere that they believed they could buy and sell leaders everywhere. We had to release one American who had diplomatic immunity but we held the two CIA officers on detention orders for one year under Emergency Regulations. At Selkirk's repeated urgings, we released them a month later with a warning never to do this again. We hoped the warning would be heeded, but feared it would not.

In response to this public disclosure, the U.S. State Department denied that any bribe had been offered, and deplored my statement as "unfortunate, unhelpful and simply playing into the hands of the Indonesians." "The Americans stupidly denied the undeniable," I replied, releasing details and a letter dated 15 April 1961 signed by Dean Rusk:

Dear Prime Minister:

I am deeply distressed to learn that certain officials of the United States government have been found by your government to have been engaged in improper activities in Singapore. I want you to know that I regret very much that this unfortunate incident has occurred to mar the friendly relations that exist between our governments. The new administration takes a very serious view of this matter and intends to review the activities of these officials for disciplinary action.

Sincerely yours,

(Sgd Dean Rusk)

My attitude in 1961 to America and Americans was summed up in my instructions to Corridon: "Investigate this matter thoroughly, every aspect of it. Leave nothing unturned until you get to the heart of the matter. But remember all the time that we are not dealing with an enemy, but the bloody stupidity of a friend."

Besides venting my anger on the Americans for being unhelpful, my objective in exposing this incident that August 1965 was to signal to the West that if the British pulled out, there would be no American bases in Singapore, but we would "go along with Australia and New Zealand." I wanted the British to remain. I was fearful that after our sudden separation from Malaysia, Britain would want to withdraw as soon as Indonesian Confrontation ended.

I viewed Americans with mixed feelings. I admired their can-do approach but shared the view of the British establishment of the time that the Americans were bright and brash, that they had enormous wealth but often misused it. It was not true that all it needed to fix a problem was to bring resources to bear on it. Many American leaders believed that racial, religious, and linguistic hatreds, rivalries, hostilities, and feuds down the millennia could be solved if sufficient resources were expended on them. (Some still do. Hence their efforts to build peaceful, multiracial, multireligious societies in Bosnia and Kosovo.)

Their methods of countering communism in Asia did not impress me. They were unprincipled in their dealing with Ngo Dinh Diem, South Vietnam's nationalist leader, backing him until he refused to do America's bidding, then looking the other way when Diem's generals assassinated him. They meant well but were heavy-handed and lacked a sense of history. I also feared they would consider all ethnic Chinese likely communist supporters because China was communist.

But America was the only country with the strength and determination to stem this relentless tide of history and reverse the erosion of people's will to resist the communists. So I wanted the British, Australians, and New Zealanders to be a buffer. Life would be difficult if Singapore were to become like Saigon or Manila. By themselves, the British in Malaysia and Singapore could not have blocked the communist advance into Southeast Asia. It was the Americans who stopped the Chinese and Vietnamese communists from spreading guerrilla insurgency into Cambodia and Thailand. The United States supported President Sukarno in Indonesia until the communists attempted a coup in September 1965. It was an irreplaceable backstop against further communist expansion.

I was relieved the Americans were prepared to oppose communists wherever they threatened and whatever the cost. Because Americans were resolutely anticommunist and prepared to confront them, Nehru, Nasser, and Sukarno could afford to be nonaligned. This was a comfortable posture and one I had adopted without at first realizing that it was a luxury paid for by Americans. Without them out front, together with the British, Europeans, Australians, and New Zealanders, checking the Russian and Chinese communists, Singapore could not have been critical of China or Russia.

I had made clear my support of American intervention in Vietnam. In May 1965, while Singapore was still in Malaysia, I spoke to a left-wing audience at an Asian Socialist Leaders' Conference in Bombay. At a time when Indians were neutral and critical of American action in Vietnam, I told them that "As Asians we must uphold the right of the Vietnamese people to self-determination and to be free from any hint of European domination. As democratic socialists we must insist that the South Vietnamese have the right not to be pressured through armed might and organised terror and finally overwhelmed by communism. So we must seek a formula that will first make it possible for the South Vietnamese to recover their freedom of choice, which at the moment is limited to either communist capture or perpetual American military operations."

In many speeches I had emphasized that the governments of Southeast Asia must use the time the Americans were buying for us by their intervention in Vietnam to solve the problems of poverty, unemployment, and inequity in our societies. Unknown to me, the U.S. assistant secretary for East Asia, William Bundy, had read my speeches. We met for the first time in my office in March 1966. He assured me that the

United States intended to play a quiet role and did not wish to maintain a military presence in Malaysia. They had been drawn into Vietnam deeper than intended and were not anxious to get involved elsewhere in East Asia.

The Americans wanted the British to stay in Malaysia for historical reasons, and because of a "division of labor." They would leave the major running of policy to the British, who were the only European power able to do it. If Malaysia turned to them for economic help, they would be happy to help but would take a low posture.

I asked about U.S. reactions to a hypothetical communist-inspired communal conflict between Singapore and Malaysia. Bundy insisted that they would not like to get involved. I stressed that they should not view the entire Chinese diaspora as some monolithic group steered by the communists on the mainland. If American policy treated all Chinese in Southeast Asia as potential mainland Chinese agents, they would have no alternative but to become Chinese chauvinists. Asked about Vietnam, I said the will to resist was the critical factor. This was absent. The people of South Vietnam must be persuaded that there was a reasonable prospect that they could win the fight.

Early in 1966 we agreed that American troops serving in Vietnam could come to Singapore for their rest and recreation. The first batch of 100 arrived in March 1966 and stayed for five days in a rental apartment block in a suburban area. They flew in from Saigon three times a week in civilian chartered Pan American flights. About 20,000 came in a year, 7 percent of the total number of tourists of that time. The financial benefits were small. It was a quiet way of showing support for America's effort in Vietnam.

Bundy saw me again in March 1967. I felt I could trust him; he was open and straight-talking. He was not out to impress anyone and was careless about his clothes—I noticed that he wore torn socks. But he had an air of quiet confidence. He knew I had been pressing the British to stay. That was also American policy. He assured me that the United States would continue to slog it out in Vietnam, that the results were heartening: 20,000 Vietcong had defected. He was confident that the Republicans, then out of government, had no alternative. The problems might become messy but President Johnson was very determined and would not give up because the United States was convinced their action in Vietnam was a major contribution to stability in Southeast Asia.

Bundy invited me for an informal visit to Washington in the late autumn, away from the crush of visitors around the annual opening of the UN session. I would have a chance to meet and talk with the people who made their policies, and those in the wider circle who were part of their establishment. I said that while the British were running down their bases in Singapore, my visit to America would look like I was scared.

In July 1967, he wrote to me and referred to reports from London that I might have made "a real dent amongst the Labour Party MPs who did not have an adequate understanding of the facts of life in Southeast Asia." He also welcomed my brief but forthright reference in a BBC television interview to the critical importance of what the Americans were doing in Vietnam. America was getting such bad press that they were relieved when someone other than a client state stood up to voice support for their unpopular policy. He proposed an official visit. Raja was unhappy at having to announce so soon after the British defense white paper had been published that I would visit Washington. It would show that we were nervous. I decided to go. Bill Bundy must have had a reason for wanting me to go to Washington that year.

I had not been to America except in 1962, to appear before the UN decolonization committee in New York. Singapore did not have a mission in Washington until that year, 1967. So I cast around for a crash course on the thinking and mood in Washington and the major personalities. I drew on the British, Australian, and New Zealand high commissioners. I wrote to Louis Heren, a good friend since the 1950s who was then the London *Times* correspondent in Washington. Of all the briefings, his was the most valuable. He wrote, "For a superpower such as the United States, all countries except the Soviet Union and China are small. You will not mind my saying that in comparison Singapore is a tiddler. Outside the State Department's bureau for East Asian and Pacific affairs, very little attention is paid to it." He was reassuring, however, that I had a "reputation for being a sane, rational and steady sort of bloke," mainly because of my position on Vietnam. The fuss over the CIA incident had been largely forgotten. "The problem in America was three-dimensional: the administration, Congress, and the press. The latter two tend to react in simple East-West terms. Are you a Commie or are you with the

U.S.? The administration is very different. Heaven knows there are enough simpletons in it, but there are also first-rate men. The obvious ones below cabinet level are William Bundy and Robert Barnett, one of Bundy's deputies, an acknowledged China expert, Walt Rostow, the president's special assistant for national security affairs." Other people I should look out for were Averell Harriman, ambassador at large, and Mike Mansfield, the majority leader in the senate, "well-informed and quietly influential."

He gave a thumbnail sketch of Johnson, the best I read before seeing the president. "A strange man, devious, manipulating, and occasionally ruthless. Having said that, I must admit to being one of his few if qualified admirers. He has fire in his belly, in the old Biblical sense. He wants to do well by his country, especially the poor and the Negroes. . . . Rusk and McNamara you can trust. Both are honest and rather nice men, good in the old-fashioned sense of the word."

In October 1967, I flew to Kennedy Airport, New York, and then on to Williamsburg, where I stayed in one of those restored homes with antique furniture of the time when Williamsburg was the capital of Virginia. Choo and I were taken on a sightseeing tour of Williamsburg in a horse carriage with a black coachman dressed in period costume. It was historical Disneyland. The following day, we flew by helicopter to the White House. The protocol officer had asked me to shake President Johnson's left hand because his right hand was bandaged. When I landed on the White House lawn for a full state welcome with guard of honor, I shook Johnson's left hand like a good boy scout.

Johnson used superlatives, describing me as "a patriot, a brilliant political leader, and a statesman of the new Asia," and Singapore as "a bright example of what can be accomplished, not only in Asia but in Africa and Latin America—wherever men work for a life of freedom and dignity." I was embarrassed by the extravagant praise, most un-British. In response, I obliquely endorsed what he was doing in Vietnam but asked whether Americans believed that their progeny would inherit the brave new world if they did not persevere (in Vietnam).

Immediately after the welcoming ceremony, Johnson had a one-on-one session with me. He was a tall, huge Texan with a booming voice. I felt dwarfed standing by his side. He was moody and troubled, but wanted to hear my views. He was relieved to find someone from Southeast Asia and near Vietnam who understood, sympathized, and quietly supported what he was doing to contain the communists and prevent them from capturing South Vietnam and causing more mischief beyond Vietnam.

Johnson was very direct. Was the war winnable? Was he doing right? I told him he was doing right but the war was not winnable in a military sense. He could prevent the communists from winning. This would allow a Vietnamese leadership to emerge around which the people would rally. That would be a victory because that government would have the support of the people and it would be noncommunist. I had no doubts that in a free vote the people would vote against the communists. He was cheered, if momentarily.

At dinner in the White House that night, Johnson replied to my question on American staying power, "Yes, America has the resolution and the restraint to see this struggle through in Vietnam. . . . I cannot put it more clearly or with more confidence. You have a phrase in your part of the world that puts our determination well. You call it 'riding the tiger.' You rode the tiger. We shall."

After dinner, a few senators took me out to the upstairs porch overlooking the White House lawn. A tall, pale, lean Mike Mansfield, a Democrat from Montana and senate majority leader, asked me a direct question: Did I think the assassination of Diem did good or harm? It did harm, I said. There was no one to replace him who was more able to lead. There could have been other ways to get Diem to change his policy or his method of ruling. Bumping him off had produced instability, and worse, uncertainty as to whether any leader who stood up for Vietnam and refused to follow American advice could survive. He pursed his lips and said, yes, it was bad. He asked what the solutions were. I told him there were no easy ones, no quick shoot-outs at high noon. It was going to be a long, hard slog, unglamorous. Just to tough it out and prevent the communists from winning while a South Vietnamese leadership emerged— that would be victory enough. It meant a long stay. I could see from his face that Americans would find that difficult.

Dean Rusk, the secretary of state, was a quiet, thoughtful man, looking more an academic than a politician. I told him I hoped the next

American president would win his election in a way that would convince Hanoi that the American people had the patience and resolve to see the war through. If America disengaged, the tide would go against all non-communist countries. Thailand would change sides and Malaysia would be put through the mincing machine of guerrilla insurgency. After that, with fraternal communist parties in control, the communists would cut our throats in Singapore. The Chinese army would not have to march into Southeast Asia.

Vice President Hubert Humphrey spoke with little reservation. He was convinced that apart from a minority who were either hawks or doves, 70 to 80 percent of the senate supported the president's Vietnam policy. The opposition was from a generation of Americans who had grown up 22 years after the Second World War. They had not known war or real economic hardship. They were the hard core of opposition in the universities. It was important that people like me, who were nonaligned and known to be politically independent, should speak up and stop the erosion of public opinion in the United States. His fear was that unless people like me could help keep the carpet under Johnson's feet, he would be beaten in America, not Vietnam. Humphrey was a likeable man and politically shrewd, but I doubted his toughness.

Robert McNamara, the defense secretary, was bright-eyed, eager, and full of energy. He thought American and Singapore objectives were exactly the same; we both wanted the British to stay in Singapore. The American people did not want to see the United States standing alone. He said Britain's purchase of F-111s showed its very strong ties with the United States and its intention to fullfil British commitments in Southeast Asia. This was October 1967, one month before Britain devalued the pound and decided to abandon east of Suez.

With both the House foreign affairs committee and the senate foreign relations committee, the main topic was Vietnam. I gave them answers that brought little relief to their concerns. They wanted to hear answers that could be executed within a year or less, before the next presidential election. I offered no such solutions.

At Harvard, I spoke to some students and also met Professor Richard Neustadt, director of the Institute of Politics in Harvard and a specialist on the American presidency. I had asked Bill Bundy if it was possible for me to spend a short sabbatical to get to know Americans and their system. I felt I had to understand them. They had different strengths and weaknesses from the British. Theirs was a vast continent. They had no single tightly knit group of decisionmakers all clustered around either Washington or New York as the British had in London. American decisionmakers were scattered over 50 states, each with differing interests and different pulls. Bundy arranged for me to meet Neustadt, who promised to tailor a course for me at the Institute of Politics for one term in the fall of 1968.

I was on the go every day, talking endlessly to the media and to different groups—the Asia Society, the Council of Foreign Relations in New York, students in Harvard and in St. Louis, the Foreign Relations Council in Chicago, and the press and television in Los Angeles. Even in Honolulu, where I stayed as the house guest of the commander in chief, Pacific, I had to talk. Only at the resort of Mauna Kea on the big island of Hawaii could I relax, play golf the whole day, and watch the manta ray at night after dinner.

Reports from our missions in Washington, Canberra, and Wellington were good, but Keng Swee and Raja were disturbed that I sounded too pro-American, defending Johnson's intervention in Vietnam. This might alienate our grassroots Chinese-speaking base. They advised me to move back to a more neutral position. When I returned to Singapore, I discussed this with them and changed my language to a more critical stance, but still gave clear support to the American presence in Vietnam. I was convinced that to knock U.S. policy in Vietnam would hurt President Johnson and cause damage to his position in America. I was not prepared to do what was against Singapore's interest.

My 10-day visit left me with some strong impressions. As I told my cabinet colleagues, our relationship with the United States was superficial, unlike our relationship with Britain. The Americans thought in terms of numbers and size. In Southeast Asia, Malaysians and Singaporeans were nothing compared to the Indonesians.

Events moved unexpectedly and decisively after my return. The British devalued the pound and in January 1968 announced early withdrawal—by 1971. Two weeks later, the North Vietnamese launched their Tet (New Year) offensive. They surged into more than a hundred cities and towns, including Saigon. The American public was shaken by television reports of this offensive. In fact, the Vietnamese offensive was a failure, but the media convinced Americans that it was an unmitigated disaster for them and that the war was lost. Two months later, on 31 March, Johnson announced, "I shall not seek and I will not accept the nomination of my party as president." From then on it was a despondent America hanging on grimly, waiting for a new president to seek a not dishonorable withdrawal from Vietnam.

From October to December 1968, as planned, I took a short sabbatical in the University of British Columbia (UBC) and Harvard and left Goh Keng Swee in charge. I spent several weeks at UBC. From their faculty club, where I was a guest, I watched the U.S. presidential election campaign on television. After Nixon won, I flew from Vancouver to Ottawa to meet Pierre Trudeau, who had become prime minister earlier that year. Then on to Boston and Harvard where I was a visiting fellow at the Institute of Politics, which was attached to the John F. Kennedy School of Government.

At Harvard's Eliot House, where I stayed with some 200 students and 10 fellows, I had an immersion course on American culture. Neustadt had arranged for me a wide exposure to American scholars in various fields, mainly American government and politics, development economics, motivation, and productivity. It was a full program of morning discussions with one group, a working lunch with another, an afternoon seminar, and social dinners at night with distinguished scholars. At the annual Harvard versus Yale football game, I had a taste of American youthful exuberance complete with pom-pom-waving cheerleaders. The efficiency of the arrangements was impressive. A graduate student attached to me chased up materials or arranged any meetings I wanted in addition to what had been fixed. The Secret Service caused quite a disruption to the normal life of Eliot House, parking their center of operations in the senior common room to give me 24-hour security. I dined in the hall with the students, fellows, and the master, Alan Heimert. I was struck by the easy informality between teachers and students. The students were extremely bright; one teacher confessed that it could be quite unnerving to argue with some of them.

The academics in Cambridge, Massachusetts, were different from those in Cambridge, England. British dons of the 1940s to 1960s were happy to be in their ivory tower, separated from the hurly-burly of London and Westminster. American professors, on the other hand, increased their stature by being associated with the government. In the Kennedy administration many of the professors would take the Boston-New York-Washington shuttle. The forte of British academics of that period was in rigorous study of the past, not of the present or the future, which involved conjecture. They did not have the direct interaction with business and industry that the Harvard Business School provided. The Americans, unlike the British, did not confine themselves to a critical examination of the past. Investigating the present to predict the future is a strength of American scholarship. Their think tanks have made futurology a respectable subject under the title "futuristic studies."

My greatest benefit was not more knowledge but the contacts and friendships I made with scholars who were not only expert on contemporary affairs but also had access to the nerve centers of American government and business. I was a curiosity in Harvard, an Asian politician taking time off to recharge his batteries and seek knowledge in academia at the age of 45, after 10 years in office. They readily hosted dinners for me to meet interesting people including economist John Kenneth Galbraith, Japan specialist and former U.S. ambassador to Japan Edwin Reischauer, China specialist John Fairbank, MIT political science teacher Lucien Pye, who had done research on guerrilla communism in Malaya in the 1950s, and MIT's Paul Samuelson, famous for his economics textbook, who explained to me why Americans still kept low-value-added industries like textiles. My most valuable discussions were with Ray Vernon of the Harvard Business School. He gave me such practical insights into the workings of the contemporary economies of Hong Kong and Taiwan (described earlier) that I returned every four years to learn more from him.

I found many other fresh ideas and picked the brains of other highly intelligent people who were not always right. They were too politically correct. Harvard was determinedly liberal. No scholar was prepared to say or admit that there were any inherent differences between races or cultures or religions. They held that human beings were equal and a society only needed correct economic policies and institutions of government to succeed. They were so bright I found it difficult to believe that they sincerely held these views they felt compelled to espouse.

Harvard faculty members I met across a dinner table were sharp, witty, and stimulating, even though I did not always agree with them. Galbraith had the most acerbic tongue of all. At one dinner, I met Henry Kissinger. It was pure serendipity that at that dinner where many liberal Americans voiced strong criticisms of the Vietnam War, I took the contrary view and explained that America's stand was crucial for the future of a noncommunist Southeast Asia. Kissinger was circumspect in his choice of words to justify American intervention. Surrounded by doves, he was careful not to appear a hawk. Speaking slowly in his heavy German-accented English, he gave me the impression of a man who was not going to be swept along by the mood of the moment. Shortly afterward, Nixon's office announced that Kissinger would be the national security adviser. By then he had left Harvard. Before I flew home that December, I met him in New York to encourage him to stay the course in Vietnam, and said that preventing the communists from winning was within America's capability.

I wanted to call on President Johnson. Bill Bundy was surprised that I wanted to see a lame duck president and not the president-elect. I said Nixon needed time to sort out his staff and agenda and I could come back after he had settled into his job. It was a forlorn and melancholy Johnson I met. He said he had put everything he had into Vietnam. His two sons-in-law were in the armed forces and both had served in Vietnam. No man could do more. I left a disconsolate Lyndon Johnson.


My next visit to America was in 1969. I called on President Nixon on 12 May. He had met me in Singapore in April 1967 when on a tour of Southeast Asia to prepare himself for the presidential election the following year. He was a serious thinker, knowledgeable about Asia and the world. He always wanted the big picture. For over an hour in my office, I answered his questions. The Cultural Revolution was then at its height. He asked me what I thought was going on. I said that the only direct knowledge we had was from debriefing our older folk whom we allowed to visit their relatives in Guangdong and Fujian provinces in southeast coastal China. As far as we could make out, Mao wanted to remake China. Like the first Chinese emperor, Qin Shihuang, who had burnt all the books of the time to wipe out what had gone before, Mao wanted to erase the old China and paint a new one. But Mao was painting on an old Chinese picture imbedded in mosaic; the rains would come, Mao's paint would be washed off, and the mosaic would reappear. Mao had only one lifetime and did not have the time or power to erase over 4,000 years of Chinese history, tradition, culture, and literature. Even if all the books were burnt, the proverbs and sayings would survive in the folk memory of the people. Mao was doomed to fail. (Years later, in his retirement, Nixon quoted what I had said in a book. He also quoted me on the Japanese, that they had the drive and the ability to be more than just makers and sellers of transistor radios. Only then did I learn that, like me, Nixon had the habit of making notes after a serious discussion.)

Asked about U.S.-China enmity, I said there was no natural or abiding source of enmity between China and the United States. China's natural enemy was the Soviet Union with whom it shared a 4,000-mile boundary which had been shifted to China's disadvantage only in the last 100 years. There were old scores to settle. The boundary between America and China was an artificial one drawn on water across the Straits of Taiwan. It was ephemeral and would pass with time.

When we met in Washington in 1969, Nixon again questioned me on China. I gave him basically the same replies. I did not know then that his mind was already focused on China to improve America's position vis-a-vis the Soviet Union.

The subject that took the most time was Vietnam. America, he said, was a large, rich, powerful nation engaged in a guerrilla war with Vietnam, a poor country, underdeveloped and with practically no technology. Billions of American dollars had been spent on the war which had cost 32,600 American dead and 200,000 casualties. This had nearly exhausted the patience of the American people and members of Congress. Pressures were mounting daily for an American pullout as soon as possible. But he had to consider the effects of the pullout on the South Vietnamese people, government, and military, on Vietnam's neighbors in Southeast Asia, on America's allies, including Australia, New Zealand, the Philippines, South Korea, and Thailand, and on the world in general. The issue was the credibility of American promises. Despite pressure from American public opinion in Congress, he had to ensure the best solution to the problem. I sensed that he wanted to end the Vietnam War because of domestic opposition, but was not about to be the first American president to lose a war. He wanted an honorable exit.

I expressed my amazement at the Americans' loss of confidence. A precipitate ending of the Vietnam War would have dangerous and unpredictable consequences not just in Vietnam but also in neighboring countries, especially Thailand, which had totally committed itself in support of the United States. Any withdrawal should be purposeful and gradual so that South Vietnamese soldiers could take on more of the war—they must be pushed to take on their share of the fighting. The solution was to get a group of dedicated South Vietnamese leaders to tackle their problems with the dedication and sense of purpose the Vietcong displayed. The aim should be for South Vietnam to be like South Korea, where some 30,000 to 50,000 American soldiers were stationed to enable the South Korean armed forces to increase their capability year by year. For such a withdrawal to succeed, Hanoi and the Vietcong had to get the message that America had all the time in the world for a slow, deliberate withdrawal and the president would not be pressured into a hasty and calamitous pullout. Hanoi was fighting the war in Washington and was helped unwittingly by many in Congress, egged on by the media. The U.S. role should be to help the South Vietnamese fight for themselves, so that if they fought and lost the United States could not be held responsible, provided they had been given enough time and equipment; in other words, to Vietnamize the war. He showed interest. The scheduled half-hour meeting went on for one and a quarter hours. He wanted reasons to believe that he could get out in a way that would not mean a defeat. I believed it was possible. That cheered him.

When I next met Nixon on 5 November 1970, he appeared fatigued after a strenuous midterm election campaign. He went over the Vietnam options. Then he turned to China. I suggested that he open America's doors and windows to China and begin trade on nonstrategic goods. When two-thirds of the UN members supported China's admission, the United States should not be seen to be blocking it. America should not be discouraged by Mao's negative attitude. I repeated, the United States had no common frontier with China as the Russians had.

At a separate meeting in the White House annex, Henry Kissinger asked me about the proposed Russian use of the dockyard at the naval base in Singapore. As I expected, he had heard from Ted Heath of Kosygin's interest in the use of the naval base after the British left. I had earlier told Heath this to encourage him not to leave the naval base in a hurry. I assured Kissinger that I would not make a decision without first informing the British and him. The Russian move had given me a card to play. I hoped the Americans would encourage the Australians to remain in Singapore. I was comfortable with Britain, Australia, New Zealand, and Malaysia in the Five-Power Defence Arrangement. I orbited around Australia and New Zealand and they orbited around the United States—a happy situation for Singapore. "And for the U.S.," Kissinger added. I said that because Singapore did not receive U.S. aid, I could speak as an objective, nonaligned voice from Southeast Asia. Kissinger agreed that this was best for both of us.

Meanwhile, Kissinger had contacted the leaders in Beijing through the Pakistanis. He secretly visited Beijing in 1971 to prepare for Nixon's visit in February 1972. When Nixon announced it in January 1972, it astonished the world. I was uneasy that he should have done this without first telling any of his Asian allies, neither the Japanese nor the government of the Republic of China, their other ally in Taiwan. That visit was indeed "a week that changed the world," as Nixon said.

The war situation in Vietnam appeared unpromising when I next visited America, in April 1973. Casualties continued with no victory in sight, and the U.S. Congress was pressing the administration to disengage totally from Southeast Asia. Choo and I had lunch with Robert McNamara, then World Bank president, and his wife at their home in Georgetown. Looking grave, McNamara said there were disturbing reports that Nixon was involved in the coverup of Watergate and things might get very difficult.

I had a premonition of trouble ahead, both for Nixon and for Southeast Asia.

When I arrived at the White House on the morning of 10 April, the president was at the front porch to greet me. He was warm and friendly and went out of his way to show his appreciation for my consistent public backing of his lonely position on Vietnam and Cambodia. For photo opportunities, he strolled with me in the White House rose garden and talked of the roses and the crabapple trees in full bloom. Inside the White House, Nixon said he did not see China as an immediate threat; it would be a force to reckon with only in 10 or 15 years when its nuclear program had matured. He asked about Vietnam and the ceasefire terms under which the United States had promised aid to reconstruct North Vietnam. I replied that it was the best possible arrangement under the circumstances. It was right to woo the North Vietnamese away from dependence on Russia and China. If America did not give any aid for reconstruction, the North Vietnamese would become more dependent on Russia and China.

In spite of his many preoccupations so soon after his reelection as president and with Watergate brewing, Nixon gave a White House dinner in my honor. There is a ritual at White House dinners which makes for presidential grandeur. Choo and I walked down the staircase of the White House with the president and his wife accompanied by several ADCs resplendent in bemedalled uniforms and gold aiguillettes. We paused at the landing as a fanfare of trumpets drew everyone's attention. A hush fell as we walked down the final flight of stairs with the assembled guests looking up at us. Then we lined up—the president, Mrs. Nixon, myself, and Choo—to receive the guests. It was the same ritual as when Lyndon Johnson gave me dinner in 1967. But Nixon's style was different. He shook every hand with enthusiasm and the appropriate greeting: "Glad to see you again." "How nice to see you." "How good of you." In between he would insert a few words of praise or comment on particular guests as I shook hands with them. In the midst of all this, he said in an aside, "Never use the wrong expression, like 'How do you do.' You may have met the man before. It will show you did not recognize him and he will be offended. Always use a neutral phrase like 'How nice to see you.' 'How good to see you.' 'It is good to see you.' And if you recognize him, 'Ah, it is a long time since we last met. How good to see you again.' " He was a professional but had little small talk and never told jokes, unlike Ronald Reagan whose conversation was rich with such social lubricants.

Marshall Green, assistant secretary of state for East Asian and Pacific affairs, asked for my views on America's China initiatives, meaning Nixon's visit to China in February 1972. I said they could not be faulted except for the element of surprise. If it had been done with less surprise, the favorable results would have been even better. The surprise factor had planted apprehension in Japanese and Southeast Asian minds that big powers were prone to sudden policy switches which could leave them on the wrong side.

Green explained that the Japanese had great difficulty in keeping secrets; they said so themselves. He stressed that the new relationship with China had not changed America's policy toward any other nation in the area. Taiwan had been concerned at the outset. But it was now clear that the United States was maintaining its treaty commitments. Korea had also been worried but now realized that their relationship with the United States had not been altered at all. In short, normalization of relations with the People's Republic of China had been taken at no one's expense. The end result was more stability for all in Asia.

Increased contact with Western civilization and technology, I said, was bound to have an effect on China. Its present isolation could not be sustained. For example, because of the total insulation of the Chinese people from the outside world, their ping-pong team that visited Singapore was unwilling to talk of anything but ping-pong. I believed once the Chinese economy was past the "line of barest necessities," they would face the problems the Soviets now had. The Chinese people would want choices in the products available to them, and with choices they would lose their egalitarian fervor.

Green assured me that the United States fully intended to continue to play an important stabilizing role in Asia. "We will keep our forces in the area and we will meet our treaty commitments." I was reminded of Harold Wilson and Denis Healey's earlier assurances that Britain would stay in Singapore. I consoled myself with the thought that because America, unlike Britain, had never depended on a colonial empire to be a world power, it would not be under the same economic pressure to withdraw from Asia.

When Nixon resigned on 9 August 1974, to avoid impeachment for Watergate, I feared for South Vietnam. As one of his last acts as president, Nixon had signed into law a bill that imposed a ceiling of US$1 billion on American military aid to South Vietnam for the next 11 months. Within days of his resignation, the House of Representatives voted to trim it to US$700 million. The axe was falling and the neck on the chopping block was President Thieu's.

On 25 April 1975, Thieu left Saigon. On 30 April, as North Vietnamese troops were advancing into the city, an American helicopter took off from the embassy roof, a moment captured in that indelible photograph of panic-stricken South Vietnamese hanging on to the helicopter skids. Later that day, North Vietnamese tanks drove up to the presidential palace and ceremonially knocked its gates down.

Although American intervention failed in Vietnam, it bought time for the rest of Southeast Asia. In 1965, when the U.S. military moved massively into South Vietnam, Thailand, Malaysia, and the Philippines faced internal threats from armed communist insurgencies and the communist underground was still active in Singapore. Indonesia, in the throes of a failed communist coup, was waging *konfrontasi,* an undeclared war against Malaysia and Singapore. The Philippines was claiming Sabah in East Malaysia. Standards of living were low and economic growth slow. America's action enabled noncommunist Southeast Asia to put their own houses in order. By 1975, they were in better shape to stand up to the communists. Had there been no U.S. intervention, the will of these countries to resist them would have melted and Southeast Asia would most likely have gone communist. The prosperous emerging market economies of Asean were nurtured during the Vietnam War years.

In the weeks before Saigon fell, a huge armada of small boats and ships packed with refugees set out across the South China Sea, many headed for Singapore. Quite a few of them were armed. Keng Swee, acting as prime minister, sent an urgent report to me in Washington that the number of refugees had reached several thousands in nearly a hundred boats. He wanted an immediate policy decision. I signalled that we should refuse them landing and get them to move on to countries with more space to receive them. A massive exercise started on 6 May. The Singapore Armed Forces repaired, refitted, refuelled, reprovisioned, and sent out to sea a total of 64 vessels carrying more than 8,000 refugees. Many of the captains of these vessels had deliberately disabled their engines to avoid being sent off.

As this operation was taking place, I called on President Gerald Ford at noon on 8 May 1975, eight days after the fall of Saigon. Kissinger, as secretary of state, was with him. Ford looked troubled but not despondent. He asked for the region's reaction to the fall of Vietnam. I had been in Bangkok in April, just before Saigon fell. The Thais were nervous, as were people in Indonesia. Suharto was quietly and firmly in control. I said congressional intervention to stop the bombing of the communists had contributed to the fall of South Vietnam. If Watergate had not happened and the bombing had continued, the South Vietnamese forces would not have lost heart and the outcome could have been different. Once the bombings stopped and aid was significantly reduced, the fate of the South Vietnamese government was sealed.

Ford asked where America should go from there. I said it was best to let the dust settle and watch how events unfolded in Laos, Cambodia, and Vietnam. I believed the Pathet Lao would take over Laos and come under Vietnamese control. In Cambodia, the Khmer Rouge was engaged in killing thousands of anticommunists. (I did not know then how indiscriminately they would kill, including all who were educated or were not part of their peasant revolution.) Thailand would get the People's Republic of China on its side as an insurance against invasion by the Vietnamese communists. Kissinger asked whether the PRC would help the Thais. I thought it would. I suggested it was best to keep cool and watch how events evolved. If at the next election a president like McGovern were to be elected and gave in to the communists, the situation could become hopeless.

Ford had been portrayed as a bumbler and stumbler, an American football player who had injured his head too many times. I found him to be a shrewd man with common sense who knew how to size up the people he had to deal with. He was genuinely friendly with an easy informality. After dinner, when I asked to be excused to go to the restroom, he insisted on bringing me to his private quarters. So up the elevator we went, followed by his secret service bodyguards. There, in a vast private bathroom, was a whole array of exercise equipment, the latest of body-building and keep-fit instruments, and all his toiletries and shaving gadgets spread over the washbasins. I could not imagine any European, Japanese, or Third World leader bringing me to his private bathroom to freshen up. He was just a friendly man, happy to have me as his guest and grateful that there was one person from Southeast Asia who spoke up for America as its stocks went down with the hasty evacuation of Saigon. He was not out to impress me, but he did—as a solid, dependable man.

# 29. Strategic Accord with the United States

When President Jimmy Carter took over from Gerald Ford, there was an abrupt change of emphasis in U.S. foreign and defense policies. He was more interested in Africa than Asia. To the dismay of America's friends and allies in Asia, he announced that there would be a rundown of U.S. troops in Korea. Carter believed Americans were tired after the Vietnam War and wanted to forget Asia. He concentrated on the reconciliation of black and white Americans. He also saw his role as a builder of bridges across the great divide between the whites and the blacks in southern Africa. His emphasis was on human rights, not defense and security. Asean leaders braced themselves for four difficult years as they waited to see what he would actually do.

When I met him in October 1977, he had budgeted his time meticulously. There would be a 5-minute photo opportunity, then a 10-minute tête-à-tête followed by a 45-minute discussion between the two delegations. He kept to this schedule almost to the second. What astounded me was the subject he raised during the 10-minute tête-à-tête—why did Singapore want high-tech weapons like I-Hawk (Improved Hawk) ground-to-air missiles? It was not an item in my brief. No previous president had ever queried me on our modest purchases of weapons, let alone defensive ones. High on Carter's agenda was the stopping of arms proliferation, especially high-tech weapons, and I-Hawk was considered high-tech for Southeast Asia. I said that Singapore was a very compact urban target which had to be thickly defended. Our Bloodhound missiles were out of date, but if he had difficulty selling I-Hawks to us, I would buy British Rapier missiles; it was not a matter of great importance. To cut the matter short, I said we would not apply to buy them. Two years later, they sold us I-Hawk missiles after the U.S. ambassador in Singapore, a former Democratic governor of North Dakota and a Carter supporter, intervened with the White House.

The official delegations met for 45 minutes and finished to the second. He had a laundry list which he pulled out from his shirt-pocket some 15 minutes before the end to check if he had covered all the items. Without rereading the minutes of the meeting, I would have had no recollection of what we discussed. They were all inconsequential matters. His predecessors, Johnson, Nixon, and Ford, had always covered the broad picture: how did Asia look—Japan, South Korea, and Taiwan, then the communist countries of China and Vietnam, then U.S. allies Thailand and the Philippines.

Carter did not raise these subjects. Nevertheless, I decided to give him a broad-brush picture of how important America was for the stability and growth of the region, and how it should not lose its focus as this might weaken the confidence of noncommunist countries who were its friends. I am not sure I made any impression. Had I not met Richard Holbrooke, assistant secretary of state for East Asia and the Pacific, earlier in May in Singapore, I doubt if I would have had a meeting with Carter. Holbrooke wanted someone from the region to get him to concentrate on Asia, and thought I could be that someone.

When I was leaving, he gave me a green leather-bound copy of his campaign autobiography, *Why Not the Best?* He had already inscribed it, "To my good friend Lee Kuan Yew. Jimmy Carter." I was flattered but surprised by my elevation to "good friend" even before he had met me. This must have been standard practice during his election campaign.

I scanned his book, hoping to get some light. I did. He was from the Bible belt, a born-again Christian. Two items stick in my mind. His father had given him a coin on his way to Sunday school. He came back and put two coins on the dressing table. When his father discovered this, he was given a whipping. He never stole again! I was puzzled how this helped him win his campaign. The other was when Admiral Rickover interviewed him for duty on a nuclear submarine. Rickover asked him what his position was in his class at Annapolis Naval Academy. He proudly said 59th. Rickover asked, "Did you do your best?" He replied, "Yes, Sir," then changed it to "No, Sir, I didn't always do my best." Rickover said, "Why not?" Carter said he was shaken. Hence the title of his book, *Why Not the Best?* And Carter set out to live by this motto. One day, I saw him on television staggering at the end of a marathon race, near exhaustion and collapse. He was driven by this ambition to do his best, regardless of his physical condition at that time.

I met him again briefly in October 1978. Vice President Walter Mondale received me and Carter dropped by for a photo opportunity. We did not have much of an exchange; he was still not interested in Asia. It was fortunate that his advisers persuaded him not to withdraw U.S. troops from Korea.

His great achievement was to get Egyptian President Anwar Sadat and Israeli Prime Minister Menachem Begin to settle their war. I was amazed that he had memorized every disputed well, hedge, and border between the two countries. I thought of the Shell appraisal system—helicopter quality, seeing the broad picture and having the ability to focus on relevant details. Carter focused on every detail.

Three major events in 1979 concentrated Carter's mind on Asia toward the end of his term of office. First, Deng Xiaoping visited him in late January to establish diplomatic relations and alerted him on China's intention to punish Vietnam for occupying Cambodia. Second, Carter advised the Shah of Iran to leave his country in the face of a popular revolt. Instead of a democratic human rights government, the ayatollahs took over in February. Third, on 24 December, the Soviet Union invaded Afghanistan in support of a communist regime unable to sustain itself. Carter was so shocked that he said, "The scales fell off my eyes." He had not seen the Soviet regime for what it was. He had embraced Brezhnev at Vienna in 1979 after signing the SALT treaty and had believed that the Soviet leaders were reasonable people who would respond to sincere gestures of peace.

Carter's national security adviser, Zbigniew Brzezinski, was a reassuring figure at the power center. He had a broad strategic mind and saw the value of China in the overall balance against the Soviet Union and as a check on Vietnam's becoming too much of a tool of the Soviets. He could put his views forcefully across in any forum, but was wise enough to carry out his president's foreign policy, not his own. Aid from the United States and many Muslim nations poured arms, money, and fighters into Afghanistan to strengthen the resistance groups that eventually bogged down the forces of the mighty Soviet Union.

Holbrooke was able to moderate Carter's early impulses to cut U.S. commitments in Asia, especially in Korea where he wanted to pull out 40,000 U.S. troops after losses in Vietnam. As I wrote to Holbrooke in December 1980 before he left his post, ". . . During a period when many in the Administration, in Congress, and in the media wanted to forget Southeast Asia, you worked ceaselessly to rebuild and to restore confidence in U.S. strength and purposes. The future appears less in jeopardy than it did in 1977 when we first met."

Carter was a good, God-fearing man, perhaps too good to be president. Americans voted for him on the rebound after the excesses of Watergate. But after four years of pious musings about America's malaise, they were ready to embrace Ronald Reagan whose bright and upbeat view of Americans and their future was to carry them forward in good spirits for two presidential terms. Reagan was a man of simple, straightforward ideas, a strong and successful leader. He turned out to be good for America and the world. It was as well that in November 1980 Americans voted for a Hollywood actor instead of a peanut farmer.

I first met him when, as governor of California, he visited Singapore in October 1971. He had a letter of introduction from President Nixon. California was Nixon's home state and Reagan must have played a key role in Nixon's election. In a 30-minute discussion before lunch, I found him a man of strong convictions, resolutely anticommunist. He talked about the Vietnam War and Soviet troublemaking all over the world. At lunch for him and his wife, young son, and personal aide, Mike Deaver, he kept the conversation on the Soviet peril. He was so interested that he wanted to continue the discussion after lunch. His wife and son left and I took him back to my office where we spent another hour on strategic issues relating to the Soviet Union and China. Some of his views were startling and vivid. He said that during the Berlin blockade, the United

States should not have flown supplies in but should have confronted the Russians with tanks and demanded that the road to Berlin be opened, as required in the Four-Power Agreement. If they did not open the road, then war. I was taken aback by his black-and-white approach.

Ten years later, in March 1981, former President Gerald Ford visited Singapore to tell me that President Reagan, who had been inaugurated that January, wanted to meet me, and soon. I received a second message to ask if I could go in June, and I did. When I arrived at the White House about noon on June 19, Reagan was at the porch of his office wing and received me warmly. We had a one-on-one meeting for 20 minutes before lunch. He wanted to talk about Taiwan and China.

I told Reagan that it was in America's interest to have a Taiwan which was successful to provide a constant contrast to conditions on the mainland. This would have far-reaching and worldwide impact through the media and VIPs who visited both sides. He then asked me whether President Chiang Ching-kuo needed new-generation aircraft. Chiang was pressing for them at a sensitive time in Reagan's presidency. Reagan had been highly critical of the People's Republic of China (PRC) during his election campaign and had made known his staunch support for Taiwan. I knew that any sudden switch of policy would be difficult for him. However, to allow sales to Taiwan of new-generation aircraft would up the stakes with China. I gave him my opinion that there was no immediate threat to Taiwan from the mainland, and that Taiwan's present F-5s were adequate. China was not increasing its armaments. Deng Xiaoping wanted more consumer goods for his people who were demoralized and starved of creature comforts after a decade of the Cultural Revolution. Taiwan's aircraft would need to be upgraded later, not immediately.

His key advisers joined us for lunch: Caspar Weinberger from defense, Bill Casey from the CIA, Jim Baker, his chief of staff, Mike Deaver, and Richard Allen, his national security adviser. The key subject was China—China vis-à-vis Taiwan and China vis-à-vis the Soviet Union.

He asked about the PRC's overture to the Soviet Union on their common border problems immediately after Secretary of State Alexander Haig had visited Beijing. In my view, this move by the Chinese was to give notice to the United States that they should not be taken for granted. I did not, however, believe that the PRC and the Soviet Union could make much headway given their deep and abiding conflict of interests. Both were communist evangelists, each maneuvring against the other to win Third World support. Furthermore, Deng had to accommodate those around him who did not want to get too close to America. I believed Deng was quite set on his policy, which was to give low priority to military spending and high priority to consumer goods the people needed.

Referring to the unrest in Poland, Reagan said the Russians must be worried about being overextended. I said they were prepared to let the economy go down to preserve their "empire which extended across Eurasia." Reagan's ears pricked up at the word "empire." He told Richard Allen to use that word more frequently when describing the Soviet domain. Reagan's next speech referred to the "evil empire" of the Soviets.

In the last 10 minutes, in a one-on-one discussion after lunch, he asked me to convey a message to President Chiang not to press him at that moment for high-tech weapons as it was a difficult time for him. He asked me to assure Chiang that he would not let him down. Reagan knew that I was close to Chiang and would help to soften the disappointment his message would cause. I met Chiang a few days later to give him Reagan's message that the time was inappropriate for Taiwan's purchase of high-tech weapons such as aircraft. Chiang asked me why his good friend Reagan could not be more helpful. I hazarded a guess that America needed the PRC to maintain a global balance of forces against the Soviet Union. As the West Europeans and Japanese were not willing to spend on armaments as decisively as America wanted, Reagan was considering whether to upgrade China's military capabilities with small injections of technology, which with China's huge manpower would mean added pressure on the Soviet Union. Chiang nodded his agreement. He accepted that Reagan had a valid reason, and asked me to tell him, "I understand you." Chiang was satisfied. He trusted Reagan.

Like Chiang, Reagan went by his gut instincts. He either trusted you or he did not. He was also a man of deep and abiding loyalties, both to his friends and to his cause. His advisers, including his first secretary of state, Al Haig, had told him of the importance of communist China in the grand strategy against the Soviet Union. He accepted this analysis but was not comfortable with the Chinese communists. He had inherited a relationship with China he knew he had to maintain.

I left Washington feeling more confident than when Carter was president. Reagan had a natural optimism that infused all those around him with the same "can do" spirit. He looked at the sunny side of every issue and was prepared to stand up for his beliefs. More important, he was able to carry the American people with him, often in spite of the media. When I wrote to thank him for the lunch, Reagan's reply was substantive. One paragraph read: "I want [U.S.] relations with Peking to improve and will work hard to achieve this, but not at the expense of our old friends on Taiwan. Nor do I want you, our partners in Southeast Asia, to view our association with Peking as taking precedence over our relations with you." When his administration announced its decision on U.S. arms sales to Taiwan, it did not include the sale of advanced fighter aircraft on the grounds that "no military need for such aircraft exists."

Ten months later, in April 1982, Vice President George Bush saw me in Singapore before going to China. He wanted my views on how to approach the PRC-Taiwan issue. I said the issues were so complex that I was sure the Chinese did not believe they could be resolved by his visit. What was important was for the forms to be observed. The PRC would have studied Reagan's character and views thoroughly. They knew of his many trips to Taiwan and of his friendship with President Chiang Ching-kuo. Because Reagan was what he was, for the Chinese, form was as important as substance. They knew they could not get Taiwan back for a long time. However, the principle that Taiwan is a part of China should not be challenged or there would be trouble. I was sure that Deng needed America—he had visited America in January 1979 to settle normalization because he needed America on China's side, or at least to be neutral in any conflict with the Soviet Union. Deng also knew that he was dealing with a tough-minded leader in Reagan.

Bush asked whether there was domestic opposition in China to the PRC's relationship with the United States. I believed China's relationship with America had received the imprimatur of Mao himself, so few would openly oppose having good relations with America. Deng had not only normalized relations but gone one step further by opening up the country. This would have important long-term consequences. The leaders' sons were studying in the United States, as were many other Chinese. There would be a brain drain, maybe 20 percent or more, but those who returned would come back with fresh ideas. The Chinese knew they were running a risk in opening up, so the decision they had made was significant. They were prepared to have the students come back with radical ideas, carrying with them the germs of change. A difficult problem was that as a presidential candidate Reagan had made strong statements in support of Taiwan. And he had repeated them even after George Bush went to Beijing in August 1980 to tell the Chinese they should understand and respect the U.S. position, that it had to move gradually on Taiwan. Yet I believed the Chinese placed great importance on fidelity. They knew that people who betrayed their friends would also betray them. They would be surprised if the United States were to give way if they pushed on Taiwan. What they wanted from the United States was a reaffirmation of the principle that there was one China. Bush assured me that Reagan was not going to set the clock back by having two separate states and two ambassadors.

I suggested that the United States invite Premier Zhao Ziyang to visit Washington and then President Reagan should visit Beijing to put his position in the way Bush had expressed it. The Americans should convince Beijing of their one China policy. The way to do this was for Reagan to meet and convince Deng that that was America's basic position. Bush agreed, as Reagan could say what he meant in a convincing way. There was much common ground between China and the United States, Bush added. Reagan was "paranoid and uptight about the Soviet Union" and events in Poland and Afghanistan had reinforced this. Reagan did not like communism but saw the strategic value of a relationship with China.

By my next visit to Washington in July 1982, George Shultz had succeeded Al Haig as secretary of state. I knew Shultz when he was secretary of the treasury under President Nixon in the early 1970s and we had become friends. Haig had gone all out to forge a "strategic consensus" against the Soviet Union and had agreed to reduce arms sales to Taiwan gradually. Shultz had to settle the form of words that would spell out this promise. He tossed a few questions at me. I said there was little value in leaving Taiwan militarily naked and at China's mercy in order to use China's weight against the Soviet Union. China would be against the Soviets anyway. Shultz had a more sober assessment of China's value in the balance against the Soviets. He implemented a much more calibrated and measured policy that did not require the United States to abandon its obligations to an old ally.

Again, Reagan took me aside before lunch for a one-on-one discussion with no note takers. He discussed China and Taiwan, and China and the Soviet Union. I said he did not have to sell out the Taiwanese, even though he needed China against the Soviet Union. The two objectives were not irreconcilable. They could be managed and contained.

He knew that I had met the top Chinese leaders both on the mainland and in Taiwan. He also knew I was anticommunist but a realist. So he tested his ideas on me. I told him to put the Taiwan issue aside as a dispute which could not be resolved for the time being and should be left for the next generation, as Deng had suggested to the Japanese regarding their dispute over the Senkaku/Diaoyu Islands. I suggested Reagan should explain to Beijing that he had been a very old friend of Taiwan and could not simply write them off. He asked if he should visit China. He was personally reluctant to go and felt he would be obliged to visit Taiwan on the same trip if he did decide to go. I was astounded to hear this. I advised against a visit to Taiwan, especially on the same trip. As I had earlier said to Bush, Reagan should first invite either Premier Zhao Ziyang or General Secretary Hu Yaobang to Washington before he visited China. After one or both of them had visited the United States, a return visit by him would be an appropriate response.

Reagan later wrote to say, "Our private talk before lunch on 21 July was of great benefit to me. I have come to expect wise counsel and advice from you and that is just what I received on that occasion. Your frankness and candor really proved the strength of our friendship which I value so highly."

In early 1984, Premier Zhao visited Washington and stressed that China wanted closer economic relations. In May, Reagan visited China. Soon after that, Paul Wolfowitz, assistant to Shultz, came to Singapore to brief me on Reagan's visit and to discuss certain aspects of the visit the Americans had found difficult to understand. It had been a good trip with real progress made in the economic field. Reagan had not yielded on global issues when the Chinese disagreed with him. Deng had emphasized that Taiwan was a knot in U.S.-PRC relations that had to be untied. I said it was good that Deng had had an opportunity to get a feel of

Ronald Reagan. The Chinese would have realized that they had to live with Reagan, not just for one but for two terms. Indeed, Reagan did win a second term.

After Reagan's reelection, Shultz proposed that I make an official visit to Washington in early October 1985. I found Reagan in good form. He looked youthful, with a good head of hair and a strong voice none the worse after four years in office and a bullet through his chest that had narrowly missed his heart. Reagan did not have a mind for detail. Indeed, he made clear that he did not want to be bothered with details which could confuse the big picture. His strengths were constancy and tenacity of purpose. He knew what he wanted and set out to achieve it by surrounding himself with able people who shared his thinking and were successful in their chosen fields. And he exuded confidence and optimism. The eight years of the Reagan presidency were good years for America and the world. His "Star Wars" program confronted President Gorbachev and the Soviet Union with a challenge they could not hope to meet. That helped to dismantle the Soviet Union.

As before, in a one-on-one meeting, he sought my views on China and Taiwan. He said he had been walking a careful line between the PRC and Taiwan. He had made clear to the PRC that the United States would not walk away from Taiwan: "The U.S. was a friend of both and would remain in that position." Then he asked me to persuade President Chiang to have Taiwan remain in the Asian Development Bank (ADB) after its designation was changed to "Taipei, China" when the PRC was admitted to the ADB. Chiang had wanted to withdraw from the ADB, and Congress had threatened to withhold American contributions if Taiwan was "expelled." Later, I had a difficult time in Taipei putting Reagan's case to Chiang but in the end good sense prevailed. In January 1986, the PRC became an ADB member and Taiwan was renamed "Taipei, China."

Reagan had observed during his visit to China the previous year that the Chinese had begun to recognize that they must give opportunities to their people to create a better life. I said this was a tribute to what the United States had achieved in Taiwan through the free flow of capital, technology, expertise, goods, and services. I was certain Deng had read of the tremendous economic development of Taiwan and must have wondered how people whom he regarded as a gang of "effete, corrupt and useless bandits" were able to make the grade. Deng must have thought that the United States had helped these "bandits" with capital, technology, and know-how and he would dearly like to have this formula passed on to China. Deng knew America could be invaluable for China's modernization.

During my official visit, I was given the honor of addressing a joint session of the U.S. Congress. The legislators of the world's most powerful nation gave time to a leader of a tiny island. Tommy Koh, our ambassador, reported that both Reagan and Shultz had encouraged Speaker Tip O'Neill to invite me. I spoke on an issue then at the top of the American agenda—protectionism to safeguard jobs and check growing U.S. trade deficits with newly emerging economies of East Asia. In 20 minutes, I described how the issue of free trade was really the question of war or peace for the world.

Nations wax and wane. I argued that if a nation on the rise, with an excess of energy, was not allowed to export its goods and services, its only alternative would be to expand and capture territory, incorporate the population, and integrate it to make for a bigger economic unit. That was why nations had empires which they controlled as one trading bloc. It was a time-honored way for growth. The world had moved away from that after the end of World War II in 1945. GATT, the IMF, the World Bank, and new rules made possible a prosperous and dynamic Germany in spite of large numbers of Germans returning from the East into a shrunken land area. So also with the Japanese, who had to leave Korea, China, Taiwan, and Southeast Asia and be packed into a few Japanese islands. The Germans and the Japanese were able to stay within their boundaries and grow through trade and investments. They cooperated and competed with other nations and were able to prosper and flourish without wars. But if trade in goods and services was blocked, then China would revert to its historical solution of small warring states conquering one another to gain control of more territory and people until they became one colossal continental empire. This tight, logical exposition may have convinced the legislators intellectually, but many found it emotionally difficult to accept.

Another problem Reagan raised during our discussions was the Philippines. President Marcos had been in difficulties ever since exiled opposition leader Benigno Aquino was shot and killed at Manila Airport on his return from the United States in August 1983. Marcos had been Reagan's good friend and political supporter. When Shultz earlier discussed the matter with me, I said Marcos was now the problem, not the solution. He asked me to speak frankly to Reagan who was most unhappy at the prospect of abandoning an old friend. So, as gently as I could, I described to Reagan how Marcos had changed from the young anticommunist crusader of the 1960s to become a self-indulgent aging ruler who allowed his wife and cronies to clean out the country through ingenious monopolies and had put the government heavily in debt. The credit ratings of the Philippines and his government had plummeted. Reagan was most unhappy to hear my assessment. I suggested the problem was how to find a neat and graceful way for Marcos to leave and have a new government installed which could begin to clean up the mess. He decided to send an emissary to express U.S. concern to Marcos at the deteriorating situation.

The Philippines blew up on 15 February 1986, after the Marcos reelection as president was challenged as fraudulent. The American ambassador, Stapleton Roy, was instructed to seek my views. I said that the United States had to deal with Marcos whether he was constitutionally installed or not, but should not alienate the bulk of the Filipino people, many of whom had voted for Corazan Aquino. I said America should not accept a fraudulent election but should put pressure on Marcos, not to lead to a showdown but to fresh elections. Aquino should be kept "mobilised and in a dynamic state" because she was a "force for good." She should not be allowed to despair.

The next day, 16 February, Corazon Aquino claimed victory and announced a program of nationwide nonviolent protest to bring down the Marcos regime. In a joint move, the Philippines' five Asean neighbors issued similar statements to express their concern over the critical situation in the Philippines which could lead to bloodshed and civil war, and called for a peaceful resolution.

I told Ambassador Roy that Marcos should know the door was open for him to leave. If he felt he had no place to go to, he might fight it out. On 25 February, Roy told me his government agreed with my views and asked whether I would be willing to undertake the task of coordinating an Asean approach to offer Marcos asylum. Raja, our foreign minister, said it would be difficult to get all five Asean members to agree. I immediately sent Marcos, through our ambassador in Manila, an invitation to come to Singapore. It was an offer that, if accepted, would help diffuse the dangerous situation that then prevailed. At the same time, Reagan sent a private message to him not to use force and said he had arranged for him, his relatives, and associates to be given asylum in Hawaii. Marcos accepted asylum in Hawaii in preference to Singapore. That same day, 25 February, Aquino was sworn in as the new president of the Philippines.

A few days after he arrived in Honolulu, Marcos had his baggage, which included cases of new peso banknotes, inspected by American customs. He sensed trouble and sent me a message that he wanted to come to Singapore. Aquino, who had already taken over as president, objected. Marcos stayed on in Hawaii to face multiple lawsuits.

One problem the United States had with President Aquino was the renewal of the lease for the U.S. military bases in the Philippines. She had taken a strong antibases stand hoping to get more concessions. This was to rebound on her. When she finally came to an agreement with the United States, the Philippine senate rejected it; the senators said that the U.S. bases diminished their sense of nationhood.

Senator Richard Lugar, the senior Republican leader in the senate foreign relations committee with special interest in defense, visited me in Singapore in January 1989 after discussions with President Aquino in Manila. He asked whether we could help if the United States had to leave Subic Bay. I said we could offer the use of our base facilities but warned that the whole of Singapore was smaller than what the United States had in Subic. We did not have the space to accommodate U.S. servicemen. I urged him to have U.S. bases remain in the Philippines, adding that Singapore would publicly offer the United States the use of our bases if that would make the Philippine government feel less isolated internationally and more willing to allow U.S. bases to stay.

Our ambassador in Manila raised this question with the Philippine foreign secretary, Raul Manglapus, who said he would welcome such a public statement. I asked our minister of state for foreign affairs, George Yeo, to state publicly in August 1989 that we would be willing to give

U.S. forces increased use of our bases. After this statement, Manglapus replied that "Singapore must be singled out and appreciated for its forthright position." Later, President Aquino told me my stand was helpful.

Malaysia and Indonesia were unenthusiastic. The Malaysian defense minister, Rithauddeen, said that Singapore should not jeopardize the status quo by allowing an increase of foreign forces in the region. The Indonesian foreign minister, Ali Alatas, hoped Singapore would continue to support the idea of a nuclear weapons–free zone in Southeast Asia, adding that Indonesia would oppose the offer if it amounted to a new base.

At a televised National Day Rally on 20 August 1989, I said that there would not be any new bases with large numbers of U.S. troops. Singapore did not have the space. We were offering access to our existing bases which would remain under the control of the Singapore government; they would not become American bases. I, too, was in favor of a nuclear weapons–free zone and of a zone of peace, freedom, and neutrality, proposed by Indonesia and Malaysia, respectively. But if oil and gas were found in the Spratlys, it would not be such a zone of peace. Earlier that August I had met both President Suharto and Prime Minister Mahathir in Brunei and clarified the size and nature of my offer.

The U.S. government took up the offer. While in Tokyo for the installation of Emperor Akihito, I signed a memorandum of understanding (MOU) with Vice President Dan Quayle on 13 November 1990, two weeks before I resigned as prime minister. It turned out to be of more value than either the United States or Singapore had foreseen. When the Americans left their bases in the Philippines in September 1991, Singapore's facilities gave U.S. forces a toehold in Southeast Asia.

Regional perceptions of the value of American access to Singapore facilities underwent a sea change after China published maps in 1992 that included the Spratlys as part of China. Three Asean countries (Malaysia, Brunei, and the Philippines) had also claimed these islands. That November, Ali Alatas said that Indonesia had no difficulty in seeing the merits of U.S. access to Singapore's military facilities.

I first met George Bush in June 1981 when he was vice president to Reagan. Our excellent relations did not change when he became president. I knew him as an exceptionally warm and friendly man. Back in 1982, when he knew I was travelling to Washington to meet Reagan, he invited me to stay with him at Kennebunkport, Maine, where he was vacationing for the summer. I thanked him but declined because I was meeting my daughter Ling, then in Boston working at the Massachusetts General Hospital. He sent back a message to bring her along and clearly meant it. So we all stayed the weekend with him. Ling and I went jogging with him together with his secret service squad. We talked freely on politics and generally had a relaxed time. Barbara Bush was as friendly as her husband—outgoing, hospitable, and warm, with no pretensions. Like him, she was genuinely happy to have friends stay with them for a long weekend and made us feel welcome.

After Iraq invaded and occupied Kuwait in 1990, to build up their forces in the Gulf, the United States had to move half a million troops to the Gulf area swiftly. The MOU had not yet been signed but we allowed U.S. aircraft and naval vessels carrying troops and matériel across the Pacific to transit through Singapore. We also sent a medical team to Saudi Arabia to show our support for this action in the Gulf. Indonesia and Malaysia stayed neutral. Their Muslim majorities wanted solidarity with and sympathy for Saddam Hussein and the Iraqis.

I visited President Bush in the White House on 21 January 1991 as Operation Desert Storm was moving toward its spectacular conclusion with American, British, and French forces encircling Iraqi forces. We spent the evening in his private quarters with Brent Scowcroft, his national security adviser, discussing the broader Arab-Israeli situation. I congratulated him on his success in marshalling the broad coalition of forces in support of this operation, including the Arab states of Egypt, Syria, Morocco, and the Gulf. I cautioned, however, that the Muslim world had rallied to Saddam Hussein even though he was in the wrong. The Israelis kept building more settlements on the West Bank, and this had inflamed Arab and Muslim opinion. America's allies and friends were alarmed. Somewhere down the road there would be an explosion. I urged America's public support for a Middle East solution fair to both Palestinians and Israelis, to show that it was not supporting the Israelis, whether they were right or wrong.

We next met when Bush visited Singapore in January 1992 on his way to Australia and Japan. His problems with China had increased after

Tiananmen on 4 June 1989. It was election year and he was under pressure, including from liberals in his own Republican Party. To maintain his China policy, he needed concessions from China in areas such as the release of detained Tiananmen protest leaders, nuclear proliferation, long-range missiles, and trade. He was facing increasing difficulty in upholding his veto on Congress's resolution to withdraw China's Most Favored Nation (MFN) status. As President Yang Shangkun was coming to Singapore, Bush wanted me to ask him to take unilateral action in releasing prisoners to show conciliation.

I saw President Yang two days later and conveyed the message. Yang said U.S. pressure on human rights was an excuse to impose on China its political system and its values of freedom and democracy. This was not acceptable.

When Bush lost the election to Bill Clinton that November, I felt we were in for a change of attitudes and styles. Clinton had promised "an America that will not coddle tyrants, from Baghdad to Beijing." Many of Clinton's supporters acted as if China were a Third World aid recipient country amenable to diplomatic and economic pressure. Life was not going to be easy for China or for America.

# 30. America's New Agenda

Singapore's relationship with the United States falls neatly into two parts—during and after the Cold War. When the Soviet Union posed a threat to America and the world, we had good relations with both the Democrat and Republican administrations from Johnson in the 1960s to Bush in the 1990s. Our strategic interests coincided completely. The United States was against the Soviet Union and communist China. So were we. Furthermore, we were strongly in support of a U.S. military presence in East Asia.

The fall of the Berlin Wall in 1989 marked the beginning of the end of the Cold War, but the effects of this geopolitical change were felt only in the Clinton presidency from 1993. With the arrival of an anti–Vietnam War generation in the White House, human rights and democracy, which had been subsidiary issues, became all-important. The U.S. government supported a Russian Federation under President Yeltsin that said it wanted to democratize. It spoke of Russia as its friend and ally, and of China as its potential adversary. We were not at odds with the United States over Russia, whatever our doubts about its democratic future. But we distanced ourselves from its hostile rhetoric against China. We feared that talking and acting as if China were an enemy would make it into one. We did not want this to happen; no country in Southeast Asia wanted to go out of its way to make China an enemy. This was a time when America wanted to scale down its presence in Southeast Asia, and Singapore was no longer as useful as before.

Many Americans thought that with the collapse of communism in the Soviet Union, China's communist system would not endure, and that it was America's moral duty to bring about its end. There were two approaches: one, favored by President Bush, to encourage gradual change through a process of constructive engagement; the other, favored by the U.S. Congress, to impose sanctions and apply political and economic pressure for human rights and political reform. Bush imposed some sanctions on China after Tiananmen, but was soon under pressure to deny MFN (Most Favored Nation) status for Chinese goods imported into America. Congress passed resolutions to deny MFN to China until it improved its human rights performance. Bush vetoed them, and this became an annual ritual that has persisted.

The promotion of democracy and human rights has always been a part of U.S. foreign policy. But during the Cold War, a shared strategic interest in resisting communist expansion in Southeast Asia set the tone in bilateral relations. Singapore had its differences with the Carter administration over democracy and human rights, and with the Reagan and Bush administrations on issues of press freedom, but these differences were not pursued in a confrontational and aggressive manner.

For example, Patricia Derian, assistant secretary of state for humanitarian affairs and human rights in the Carter administration, met me in January 1978 to urge the abolition of detention without trial. I told her the law had been challenged by the opposition at every election and each time an overwhelming majority of the electorate had voted for us and for the law. Singapore was a Confucianist society which placed the interests of the community above those of the individual. My primary responsibility was the well-being of the people. I had to deal with communist subversives, against whom it was not possible to get witnesses to testify in open court. If I followed her prescription, Singapore would come to grief. What could the United States do to rescue Singapore more than they were doing for the boat people of South Vietnam, who were then sailing out into the perils of pirates and the weather in the South China Sea? If the United States would give Singapore the status of a Puerto Rico and underwrite Singapore's future, I would follow her prescription. Then the United States would have to pick up the pieces if Singapore failed. Derian was so stressed that she asked if she could smoke, in spite of having been told by her ambassador that I was allergic to it. As she could not bear her deprivation any longer, I took pity on her and brought her upstairs to an open veranda where she relieved her frustrations with long puffs on her cigarettes. It did not improve her arguments. Twenty years later, Ambassador John Holdridge, who had been present at our 1978 meeting, wrote in his memoirs,

> Lee Kuan Yew, whom I heard on several occasions describe himself as 'the last Victorian,' certainly was and is a staunch Confucianist as well. He and his followers have attempted to inculcate Singapore's younger generation with Confucian virtues. Derian, on the other hand, is a veteran of the civil rights movement in the American South, with its frequent clashes between civil rights demonstrators and local authorities, a struggle that epitomized the 'rights of man' beliefs inherent in the U.S. Constitution. She completely dismissed Lee's view that the well-being of society takes precedence over individual rights and that detainees in Singapore only needed to forswear violence to be released. The two talked past each other for the better part of two hours and never came to a meeting of the minds.

Because we shared overriding strategic concerns, this disagreement was not brought into the open.

Another instance was in June 1988 when we asked for a U.S. embassy diplomat to be removed for interfering in Singapore's domestic politics. The diplomat had instigated a former solicitor general to recruit disaffected lawyers to contest the coming elections with him against the PAP, and had arranged for one lawyer to meet his superior officer in the State Department in Washington, who gave the lawyer an assurance that he would get asylum if he needed it. The State Department denied these allegations and in retaliation asked for a newly arrived Singapore diplomat to be withdrawn. In a debate in Parliament, I proposed that the matter be resolved by a competent neutral international committee of three experts. If this committee found that what the U.S. diplomat had done was legitimate diplomatic activity, the Singapore government would withdraw its protest and apologize. The State Department spokesman welcomed my reaffirmation that Singapore wanted to put an end to the dispute, but remained silent on my proposal. No more was made of this.

The issues that Americans put at the top of their agenda in the 1990s were human rights and democracy, and Western versus Eastern values. The Japanese were being pressed by the Americans to link their aid programs to recipient countries' democracy and human rights record. The *Asahi Shimbun,* a liberal, antiwar, pro-democracy Japanese newspaper, invited me to a forum in Tokyo in May 1991 to discuss the subjects of human rights and democracy with prominent Japanese and American opinion formulators. I said it was 50 years since the British and French first gave independence with Western-type constitutions to over 40 former British colonies and 25 former French colonies. Unfortunately, both in Asia and Africa the results have been poor. Even America had not succeeded in leaving a successful democracy in the Philippines, a former colony it freed in 1945 after nearly 50 years' tutelage. I suggested that a people must have reached a high level of education and economic development, must have a sizeable middle class, and life must no longer be a fight for basic survival, before that society could work such a democratic political system.

The following year the *Asahi Shimbun* forum again discussed democracy and human rights, and their effect on economic development. I said that since different societies had developed separately for thousands of years in disparate ways, their ideals and norms were bound to be different. Therefore, it was not possible to insist that American or European standards of human rights of the late twentieth century be imposed universally. However, with satellite television, it had become increasingly difficult for any government to hide its cruelties to its own people. Slowly but inevitably, the community of nations would find a balance between noninterference in another country's internal affairs and the moral right to insist on more civilized and humane treatment by all governments of their own peoples. But as societies became more open, there would be convergence toward a common world standard of what was acceptable. Inhuman, cruel, or barbaric methods would be condemned. (In the case of Kosovo some six years later, although NATO and a large majority of the UN could not accept Yugoslav President Milosevic's barbarism against the Albanian Kosovars, there was no unanimity that this was sufficient ground for intervention without the sanction of the UN Security Council.

Russia, China, and India, representing 40 percent of humanity, condemned the bombing of Serbia by NATO in 1999.)

One interview I gave to the respected American journal, *Foreign Affairs,* was published in February 1994, causing a minor stir among Americans interested in the Asian versus Western values debate. In my answers, I avoided using the term "Asian values," of which there are many different kinds, and instead referred to Confucian values, the values that prevail in the cultures of China, Korea, Japan, and Vietnam, countries that used the Chinese script and had been influenced by Confucian literature. There are also some 20 million ethnic Chinese among the peoples of Southeast Asia whose Confucian values are not the same as the Hindu, Muslim, or Buddhist values of South and Southeast Asia.

There is no Asian model as such, but there are fundamental differences between East Asian Confucian and Western liberal societies. Confucian societies believe that the individual exists in the context of the family, extended family, friends, and wider society, and that the government cannot and should not take over the role of the family. Many in the West believe that the government is capable of fulfilling the obligations of the family when it fails, as with single mothers. East Asians shy away from this approach. Singapore depends on the strength and influence of the family to keep society orderly and maintain a culture of thrift, hard work, filial piety, and respect for elders and for scholarship and learning. These values make for a productive people and help economic growth.

I stressed that freedom could only exist in an orderly state, not when there was continuous contention or anarchy. In Eastern societies, the main objective is to have a well-ordered society so that everyone can enjoy freedom to the maximum. Parts of contemporary American society were totally unacceptable to Asians because they represented a breakdown of civil society with guns, drugs, violent crime, vagrancy, and vulgar public behavior. America should not foist its system indiscriminately on other societies where it would not work.

Man needs a moral sense of right and wrong. There is such a thing as evil, and men are not evil just because they are victims of society. I said in *Foreign Affairs* that many of the social problems in the United States were the result of the erosion of the moral underpinnings of society and the diminution of personal responsibility. Some American liberal intellectuals had developed the theory that their society had advanced to a stage where everyone would be better off if they were allowed to do their own thing. This encouraged Americans to abandon a moral or ethical basis for society.

During the Cold War, this interview would have passed unnoticed as an intellectual discourse. Without the solidarity forged out of our common opposition to communism, my views brought into the open the deep differences between American and Asian attitudes to crime and punishment, and the role of government.

Some Americans believe that I formed these opinions only after China became economically buoyant following its open-door policies. In fact, they arose from my experiences in the early 1950s when I discovered the cultural gulf between the Chinese-educated and the English-educated in Singapore. A people steeped in Chinese values had more discipline, and were more courteous and respectful to elders. The result was a more orderly society. When these values were diluted by an English education, the result was less vigor and discipline and more casual behavior. Worse, the English-educated generally lacked self-confidence because they were not speaking their own native language. The dramatic confrontations between the communist-led Chinese middle school students and my own government brought home these substantial differences in culture and ideals, represented by two different value systems.

American liberal academics began to criticize us for our attitudes to the Western press circulating in Singapore. We were not following their pattern for development and progress, that as a country developed its free-market economy and enjoyed prosperity, it should become more like America, democratic and free, with no restrictions on the press. Because we do not comply with their norms, American liberals will not accept that our government, which Singaporeans have repeatedly voted for, can be good.

No critic has been able to fault the Singapore government for corruption, nepotism, or immorality. For many years in the 1990s, business risk-assessment organizations such as Political and Economic Risk Consultancy based in Hong Kong have rated Singapore as the least corrupt country in Asia; Transparency International based in Berlin rated Singapore as the seventh least corrupt in the world, ahead of Britain, Germany, and the United States. Singapore was and is different from the banana

October 1985: Addressing the joint session of the U.S. Congress on free trade. Behind me, Vice President George Bush and Speaker Tip O'Neill. (*Copyright SPH*)

June 1988: An important agreement with PM Mahathir in Kuala Lumpur to build the Linggui dam on the Johore River. (*Copyright SPH*)

September 1988: Chinese Communist Party General Secretary Zhao Ziyang hosting dinner at Diaoyutai, Beijing, on my 65th birthday. (*SM Lee's Collection*)

January 1990: President Lee Teng-hui receiving me in Taipei. (*SM Lee's Collection*)

May 1990: With Margaret Thatcher and her grandson at Chequers on my last official visit. "Who would have imagined that we should both leave the highest office in our respective countries on almost the same day," she wrote later that November. (*Copyright SPH*)

September 1990: Goh Chok Tong, Wong Kan Seng, and I met a harassed President Mikhail Gorbachev in the Kremlin. (*Copyright SPH*)

1990:
Receiving
Chinese
Premier Li
Peng at
the Istana.
(*Copyright
SPH*)

1990: With
President
François
Mitterrand
at the Élysée
Palace, Paris.
(*Copyright
SPH*)

1994: With Jiang
Zemin at the
Istana poolside
barbecue dinner.
Loong is in the
background. (*SM
Lee's Collection*)

1995: Posing for a hand-shake with the Plen (Fan Chuang Pi) in Diaoyutai Beijing. (*SM Lee's Collection*)

February 1996: Greeting French President Jacques Chirac in Singapore. (*Copyright SPH*)

September 1999: With Chinese Premier Zhu Rongji at Zhongnanhai, Beijing. (*SM Lee's Collection*)

September 1999: Cabinet meeting with Prime Minister Goh Chok Tong in the chair. (*Copyright SPH*)

A family portrait taken during Chinese New Year's Eve, February 4, 2000. (*Copyright SPH*)

republics that they usually label "authoritarian." To show their disapproval the American press describes Singapore as "antiseptically clean." A Singapore that is efficient is called "soullessly efficient."

Harvard political science professor, Samuel Huntington, in an address in Taipei in August 1995, contrasted the Singapore model with the democratic model in Taiwan. He quoted a *New York Times* headline which summed up the difference between "clean and mean" Singapore and "filthy and free" Taiwan. He concluded, "The freedom and creativity that President Lee has introduced here in Taiwan will survive him. The honesty and efficiency that Senior Minister Lee has brought to Singapore are likely to follow him to his grave. In some circumstances, authoritarianism may do well in the short term, but experience clearly shows that only democracy produces good government over the long haul."

Americans and Europeans were justifiably triumphant and exultant after their success in helping to dissolve the Soviet Union by pressing for human rights and democracy under the Helsinki Accords. But they were unrealistic in hoping to repeat the process in China. Unlike the Russians, the Chinese did not accept the cultural norms of the West as superior and to be emulated.

One evening over dinner in Singapore in March 1992, former German Chancellor Helmut Schmidt asked me whether China could become democratic and observe human rights like the West. Choo, who sat next to Schmidt, laughed outright at the idea of 1.2 billion Chinese, 30 percent of them illiterate, voting for a president. Schmidt noted this was her spontaneous reaction to the absurdity of it. I replied that China's history of over 4,000 years was one of dynastic rulers, interspersed with anarchy, foreign conquerors, warlords, and dictators. The Chinese people had never experienced a government based on counting heads instead of chopping off heads. Any evolution toward representative government would be gradual. Nearly all Third World countries were former colonies that, after decades of colonial rule without either elections or democracy, received democratic constitutions fashioned after those of their former rulers. But the British, French, Belgian, Portuguese, Dutch, and U.S. democratic institutions had taken hundreds of years to evolve.

History teaches us that liberal democracy needs economic development, literacy, a growing middle class, and political institutions that support free speech and human rights. It needs a civic society resting on shared values that make people with different and conflicting views willing to cooperate with each other. In a civic society, between the family and state, there are whole series of institutions to which citizens belong, voluntary associations to promote specific common interests, religious institutions, trade unions, professional organizations, and other self-help bodies.

Democracy works where the people have that culture of accommodation and tolerance which makes a minority accept the majority's right to have its way until the next election, and wait patiently and peacefully for its turn to become the government by persuading more voters to support its views. Where democracy was implanted in a people whose tradition had been to fight to the bitter end, as in South Korea, it has not worked well. South Koreans battle it out on the streets regardless of whether they have a military dictator or a democratically elected president in charge. Brawls in the Legislative Yuan of Taiwan, plus physical clashes in the streets, are reflections of their different cultures. People will evolve their own more or less representative forms of government, suited to their customs and culture.

In 1994, soon after the fall of the Soviet Union, when Americans were in a confident mood, they tried to bring instant democracy to Haiti by reinstalling an ousted elected president. Five years later, the Americans quietly slipped out of Haiti and privately admitted defeat. Writing in the *New York Times,* American author Bob Shacochis asked, "What went wrong? Setting aside for the moment the culpability of the Haitian leadership, Washington's policymakers might acknowledge that *in vitro* democratization is a risky procedure. Haitian democracy, born prematurely, will not survive without a genuine multiparty system, which won't exist without a secure middle class, which can't evolve without a viable economy, which won't exist without credible leadership strong and wise enough to wrench the country out of its tailspin." Because the American administration did not publicly acknowledge this failure and its reasons, this will not be the last time it makes this mistake.

At our discussion in March 1992, I had emphasized to Schmidt that it was different with human rights; technology had brought the peoples of the world into a global village, all watching the same atrocities on television as they happened. Because all peoples and governments want the respect and esteem of others, they must gradually move away from behavior that made them disreputable. The next time Schmidt was in China, I noted that he pressed for universal standards of human rights, not of democracy. Later, Schmidt wrote in his newspaper, *Die Zeit,* that China could not become an instant democracy, but that the West should press for its human rights to become acceptable.

The interest of America, the West, and even Japan in democracy and human rights for Asia springs from their concern over the outcome in China, not in Taiwan, South Korea, Hong Kong, or Singapore. America wanted these East Asian "tigers" to be examples to China of free societies that had prosperous economies because of democratic political institutions. The *New York Times,* in the article Huntington quoted in 1995, had pointed out that Taiwan and Singapore were the two most successful Chinese societies in 5,000 years of Chinese civilization, and that one or the other was likely to be the model for the future of mainland China. This is not the case. China will chart its own way forward. It will select and incorporate those features and methods of government that it finds valuable and compatible with its own vision of its future. The Chinese people have a deep and abiding fear of *luan* (chaos). Because of their country's immense size, their leaders are extra-cautious, and will carefully test, adjust, and adapt before incorporating new features into their system.

The fight between the United States and China over human rights and democracy focused on Hong Kong's return from Britain to China. The United States has economic leverage on China through Hong Kong. If it is not satisfied that Hong Kong is administered separately from China, it can cut off the separate export quotas and other benefits to Hong Kong. The fate of 6 million Hong Kongers will not affect America or the world. But the destiny of 1,200 million Chinese in China (likely to become 1,500 million by the year 2030) will determine the balance of forces in the world. Americans have joined issue with China over Hong Kong's "democracy" more to influence the future of China than that of Hong Kong. Similarly, American liberals criticize Singapore not because they are concerned about democracy and human rights for our 3 million people but because they believe we are setting the wrong example for China.

From 1993 to 1997, Clinton's policy on China underwent a sea change. This was the result of a crisis caused by China's missile exercises in the Straits of Taiwan in March 1996 and the United States' response of sending two aircraft carrier groups to the waters east of Taiwan. This standoff led to a reexamination of positions by both China and the United States. After intense discussions between their top security officials, relations stabilized. President Jiang Zemin made a successful state visit to Washington in October 1997, and President Clinton made a return visit to Beijing in June 1998 when he was agreeably surprised to find Jiang ready to reciprocate their live TV press conference in Washington. When he arrived in Hong Kong on his way out, he said President Jiang Zemin was "a man of extraordinary intellect, very high energy, a lot of vigor. He has a quality that is profoundly important at this moment of our history: he has a good imagination. He has a vision, he can visualize a future that is different from the present."

Yet within months, this warmth turned cold as the Cox Report of the Senate committee investigating the loss of nuclear missile secrets blamed it on Chinese espionage. Leaks of the Cox Report created such a hostile mood in Congress that President Clinton did not seize the offer to close a WTO deal with Chinese Premier Zhu Rongji in Washington in April 1999. Within two weeks, in May, American bombs hit the Chinese embassy in Belgrade, a tragic error. Relations turned sour. This roller-coaster relationship between the world's most powerful and the world's potentially next most powerful nation is unsettling to all in Asia.

U.S.-China relations took a promising turn in November 1999 when they agreed on the terms for China's entry into the World Trade Organization. China's entry will greatly increase its economic links, based on a framework of set rules, with the United States and other member countries. This will lead to mutually beneficial relationships.

From time to time, American administrations can be difficult to deal with, as during President Clinton's first term (1993–1996). After the Michael Fay incident, Singapore suddenly became persona non grata because we were not following the American liberal prescription for how to become a democratic and developed country. But our relations warmed up again after the currency crisis in July 1997. The United States found us a useful interlocutor. Singapore was the only country in the region where the rule of law and sturdy banking regulations with rigorous supervision had enabled it to withstand a massive capital outflow from the area. At an APEC meeting in Vancouver in November 1997, President Clinton accepted Prime Minister Goh Chok Tong's proposal for a special meeting of the affected countries and G-7 members to discuss the economic crisis and help them put their banking systems right and restore investor confidence. The first meeting of G22 finance ministers was held in Washington in April 1998.

As the crisis worsened in Indonesia, there were close consultations between key U.S. Treasury and State Department officials and ours as we tried to halt the meltdown of the Indonesian rupiah. President Clinton phoned Prime Minister Goh before he sent out Deputy Treasury Secretary Larry Summers to see President Suharto in January 1998. In March 1998, Clinton sent former Vice President Mondale as his personal representative to explain the gravity of the situation to Suharto. Their efforts failed because Suharto never understood how vulnerable Indonesia had become after he opened up its capital account and allowed Indonesian companies to borrow some US$80 billion from foreign banks.

In the middle of this financial crisis, Singapore further liberalized its financial sector. What we did was out of our own convictions, but it coincided with the IMF and U.S. Treasury prescription on how to develop a financial free market. We were commended by the Americans as an example of a free, unfettered economy.

There will be ups and downs in Singapore's relationship with the United States because we cannot always follow their formula and act as their model for progress. Singapore is a densely populated, tiny island located in a turbulent region, and it cannot be governed like America. However, these are small differences compared to the value of U.S. presence in Asia, which has ensured security and stability and made economic growth possible. America accelerated this growth by opening up its markets to exports from noncommunist countries. If Japan had won the war, we would have been enslaved. If the United States had not entered World War II and the British had continued as the major power in Asia, Singapore and the region would not have industrialized so easily. Britain did not allow its colonies to get ahead industrially.

When China entered the Korean War, threatening peace and stability in East Asia, the Americans fought North Korean and Chinese forces to a standstill at the 38th parallel. They helped to rebuild Japan with aid and investments, and made possible the industrialization of South Korea and Taiwan. The United States expended blood and treasure in Vietnam from 1965 to 1975 and checked the spread of communism. American companies came to Southeast Asia to set up repair facilities to support the U.S. forces in Vietnam. Then they built manufacturing plants unrelated to the Vietnam War, and exported their products to America. This triggered off the industrialization of Southeast Asia, including Singapore.

America's generosity of spirit grew out of an innate optimism that it could give and still have more to give. Unfortunately, this spirit weakened in the late 1980s because of trade and budget deficits. To correct the deficits, America demanded that Japan and the other NIEs open up their markets, revalue their currencies upward, import more American products, and pay royalties for intellectual property.

After the collapse of the Soviet Union, Americans have become as dogmatic and evangelical as the communists were. They want to promote democracy and human rights everywhere, except where it would hurt themselves as in the oil-rich Arabian peninsula. Even so, the United States is still the most benign of all the great powers, certainly less heavy-handed than any emerging great power. Hence, whatever the differences and frictions, all noncommunist countries in East Asia prefer America to be the dominant weight in the power balance of the region.


My reservations in the 1960s about dealing directly with Americans were because they acted as if their wealth could solve all problems. Many of their officials then were brash and inexperienced, but I found them easier to work with than I expected. I did not need interpreters to understand them. They too could read me easily. Had I made my speeches only in Chinese or Malay, Bill Bundy, the assistant secretary of state for East Asia, would not have read them and initiated the relationship with successive administrations that began with my meeting with President Johnson in October 1967. I was fortunate in getting on with most of the U.S. presidents and their principal aides, especially their secretaries of state. Several have kept up our friendship even after they left office. Working together for shared objectives, we learned to trust each other and became good friends.

America's political process, however, can be unnerving for its friends. Within 25 years, I have seen impeachment proceedings started against two American presidents—Nixon in 1974 and Clinton in 1998. Fortunately, no great harm was done to the state of the union. Just as great a source of anxiety is the speed at which policies in Washington change with changes in the principal players. It makes for unpredictable relationships. According to friendly diplomats in Washington, these new faces bring fresh ideas and act as a "flushing mechanism" to prevent the consolidation and fossilization of a ruling elite. I believe only a wealthy and solidly established nation like America can roll with such a system.

Notwithstanding the openness of the American political process, no country knows how America will react to a crisis in its part of the world. Were I a Bosnian or a Kosovar, I would never have believed that Americans would involve themselves in the Balkans. But they did get involved, not to defend America's fundamental national interests, but to uphold human rights and put an end to crimes against humanity committed by a sovereign government against its own nationals. Is such a policy sustainable? And applicable worldwide? In Rwanda, Africa, it was not. Hence American friends keep reminding me that their foreign policy is often driven not by considerations of strategic national interest, but by their media.

In spite of many mistakes and shortcomings, America has succeeded, and spectacularly so. In the 1970s and 1980s, its industries were going down in comparison to Japanese and German industries, but they came back with unexpected vigor in the 1990s. American corporations lead the world in the use of computers and information technology. They have exploited the digital revolution to restructure and flatten their organizations, and have increased productivity to previously unheard of levels while keeping inflation low, increasing profits, and staying ahead of the Europeans and Japanese in competitiveness. Their strength is in their talent, nurtured in their universities, think tanks, and in the R&D laboratories of their MNCs. And they attract some of the brightest minds from the world over, including many from India and China, to new, high-growth sectors like Silicon Valley. No European or Asian nation can attract and absorb foreign talent so effortlessly. This gives America a valuable advantage, like having a magnet to draw in the best and brightest from the world.

It has taken some time for Europeans to acknowledge the superiority of the American free-market economy, especially its corporate philosophy of concentrating on rates of return on equity. American executives are driven by their ceaseless search for increased shareholder value through higher productivity and competitiveness. The cost of this high performance–high reward system is an American society more divided than European or Japanese society. These two societies do not have the equivalent of the American underclass. European corporate culture puts much importance on social unity and harmony. German companies have trade union representatives on their management boards. But they pay a price in lower rates of return on capital and poorer shareholder value. The Japanese have life-long employment and place high value on loyalty to and from their employees. The drawback is over-manning and loss of competitive edge.

However, in the 1990s, many European companies have listed themselves on the New York Stock Exchange. This requires them to focus on quarterly returns and shareholder value. Acceptance of American standards of corporate governance is the accolade Europeans have paid to Americans.

As long as its economy leads the world, and America stays ahead in innovation and technology, neither the European Union nor Japan nor China can displace the United States from its present preeminent position.

# 31. Japan: Asia's First Miracle

My impressions of the Japanese have undergone several changes over the last 60 years. Before World War II, I knew them as polite and courteous salesmen and dentists. They were a clean, neat, disciplined, and self-contained community. I was thus completely unprepared for the cruelties they inflicted from February 1942 as conquerors of Singapore. They were unbelievably cruel. There were exceptions but systematic brutalization by their military government made them a callous lot. We suffered three and a half years of privation and horror. Millions died in Japanese-occupied territories in Southeast Asia. Prisoners of war, British, Dutch, Indian, and Australian alike, rotted away or were worked to death.

Unexpectedly, on 15 August 1945, came the emperor's order to surrender. From being our lords and masters, the Japanese transformed themselves into model prisoners of war, conscientious and hardworking, cleaning up the city, applying themselves to their changed role seriously and diligently. Then they disappeared from the scene. I read of their distant hardships as they rebuilt Japan.

In the 1960s, good-quality Japanese electrical goods flowed into Singapore. By the 1970s, the Japanese were up and running again. Their mastery of industrial production of textiles, petrochemicals, electronic goods, television sets, tape recorders, and cameras, plus modern management and marketing methods, had made them a formidable industrial power. As they grew stronger, they bowed less low.

For me and those of my generation, the deepest and strongest imprint the Japanese left on us was the horror of the occupation years. Those memories are indelible. I have since come to know many Japanese in a broader range of relationships—ministers, diplomats, businesspeople, editors, writers, and academics. Some became good friends. They are well-educated, knowledgeable, and very human. I know the people much better than I did in my youth. Because of fear and hate arising from the suffering of the occupation years, I had felt the satisfaction of *schadenfreude* when I read of their hunger and suffering in their bombed and burnt cities. This feeling turned into reluctant respect and admiration as they stoically and methodically set out to rebuild from the ashes of defeat. Skillfully, they evaded most of the MacArthur military occupation policy objectives and preserved many key attributes that had made old Japan strong. A few were sent to the scaffold for their war crimes. The majority rehabilitated themselves and, as democrats, some won elections and became ministers. Others continued as patriotic, hardworking bureaucrats dedicated to the rebuilding of Japan as a peaceful, nonmilitary nation—but one which neither repented nor apologized.

My first postwar dealing with the Japanese was over a cold-blooded massacre committed when they captured Singapore in 1942. By chance, bones in a mass grave were discovered during earthworks in February 1962 in Siglap, a suburb in the eastern end of the island. There were 40 such sites. They revived all the memories of *Sook Ching* (a WWII site) some 20 years earlier when the Japanese *Kempeitai* (military police) rounded up and slaughtered 50,000 to 100,000 young Chinese men during the first fortnight after they captured Singapore. I had to be seen to raise the matter with the Japanese government and decided to see for myself this revitalized Japan. In May 1962, I made my first visit to Japan, then not completely recovered from the ravages of war.

The Japanese foreign office put us up at the Imperial Hotel, a building designed by American architect Frank Lloyd Wright, later demolished. It was a gracious, spacious, low-rise structure that looked Western yet was very Japanese. From my suite, I had glimpses of the old Tokyo, which I imagined must have been a charming city. The new bustling Tokyo showed clear signs of an economy revving up, but was higgledy-piggledy, rebuilt hastily from the ashes of the fire storms that had devastated it when the American B-29s carpet-bombed it with incendiaries. The Japanese paid a heavy price for its urgent and haphazard reconstruction. The road system was bad and streets were narrow, not laid out on a grid and already jammed with traffic which would get worse as cars proliferated. For a people with such a superb sense of the aesthetic, they had rebuilt an unattractive city, and thrown away the opportunity to rebuild an efficient, elegant capital, as was well within their capabilities.

The national passion for golf, the prestige game, was very much in evidence. Foreign Minister Kosaka took me to play at his "300 Club," one of the most expensive in Japan, with only 300 members from their political and business elite. The top executives had expensive imported American golf clubs and golf balls. The clubs made in Japan were inferior, with shafts that had no whip or feel. I thought that that was the limit of their technology and their ability to imitate. Twenty years later, Japanese golf clubs were some of the best and most expensive in the world.

The only important business I raised with Prime Minister Hayato Ikeda was the "blood debt," a request for compensation for their wartime atrocities. He expressed his "sincere regrets"—not apology—for what had happened. He said the Japanese people would like to make amends for the "wrong done to the spirits of the departed"; he hoped these events would not prevent the growth of friendly relations between the people of Japan and Singapore. The question of compensation was left open. They wanted to avoid making a precedent that would lead to a deluge of claims from other victims elsewhere. He and his officials were most polite and were anxious to resolve the issue before it stirred up past bitterness. We eventually settled this "blood debt" after independence, in October 1966, for $50 million, half in grants and half in loans. I wanted to establish good relations to encourage their industrialists to invest in Singapore.

Although my next visit to Tokyo in April 1967 was unofficial, Prime Minister Eisaku Sato saw me. He knew I had not been keen to press for compensation and thanked me for having resolved the "bones" issue. He accepted my invitation to visit Singapore and came in September that year, accompanied by his wife. He was the first Japanese prime minister to visit Singapore after the war.

Sato was dignified and serious-looking until he broke into a friendly smile. When he laughed it was with a hearty guffaw. Sato looked like a samurai warrior. He was medium in height, broad-built, and sturdy and strong both in the expression of his face and in his posture. Choo once asked him over lunch if it was true that he was descended from samurais. He proudly answered yes, adding, so was his wife. He spoke in a deep voice and did not waste words. For every three sentences by his foreign minister, Takeo Miki, he uttered one, the more telling one. He held a place of honor among his country's postwar leaders as the first Japanese leader to be awarded the Nobel Peace Prize.

We were comfortable with each other. After our meeting in Tokyo, he knew that I was not anti-Japanese, that I wanted to cooperate with Japan to industrialize Singapore. The only reference he made in his speech to the Japanese occupation was "There were times in the history of Asia when we had a number of unhappy incidents," a monumental understatement.

I paid a return official visit a year later, in October 1968. Japanese protocol was extremely particular, insisting that I wear a black homburg, grey gloves, and a dark suit for the welcome and send-off ceremonies at the airport. They were sticklers for formal Western dress forms.

Japanese officials and ministers, including the prime minister, expected me to solicit aid, as the British withdrawal from Singapore was then in the news. They knew the magnitude and urgency of our problems, and were much surprised that I did not seek aid as other visiting leaders from developing countries had done. From discussions with Sato and Miki, I concluded that they viewed Singapore, with its efficient port facilities and other infrastructure, as a useful starting point for their economic activities in Southeast Asia. For this role, they needed Singapore to have good relations with Indonesia and Malaysia.

Sato also formally thanked me for the recent successful visit to Singapore of Crown Prince Akihito and Princess Michiko. I had entertained them to dinner and taken them to the roof of the Istana to see the Southern Cross, a constellation they could not see from Japan. As both were fluent in English, the conversation flowed easily. Choo and I were later to enjoy their gracious hospitality on several of our visits to Tokyo.

Because it was an official visit, the emperor and empress of Japan gave us lunch at the Imperial Palace. The main palace had been bombed, so they received us in one of the outer buildings. We were brought into a drawing room, beautifully carpeted and simply but elegantly furnished with a few pieces of furniture—chairs and tables, including some exquisite small tables on which gifts were placed. Coming face to face with this demigod was a memorable moment in my life. For three and a half years in Japanese-occupied Singapore, he was god. Working for them as a cable editor in 1943–1944 in Singapore's Cathay Building, many times I had had to bow deeply toward the Imperial Palace in Tokyo in homage. Here before Choo and me was this small man with a spare stooped frame. He looked utterly harmless. Indeed, he was friendly and courteous, speaking in a very low whisper. The empress was larger-built, soft and gentle-looking with a pleasant round face. We were ushered by protocol officers into position for a ceremonial photo-taking. Then we sat down for a conversation, inconsequential except that at the appropriate moment he expressed his regrets for any suffering caused to the people of Singapore during the war. I nodded but did not say anything. I was not prepared for it, and thought it best to stay silent.

That old reverence of the Japanese for their emperor will be difficult to re-create now that they have stripped the royal household of its myth of divinity. There remains no mystery about what the throne represents. To sit and make small talk in subdued tones across the luncheon table with this former god-king was an anticlimax. I wondered what Sato, who sat close to him at lunch, thought about his emperor, for he belonged to the generation that had revered him as a god.

Choo and I were to call on the emperor and empress on several other occasions. One of my last acts as prime minister was to attend his funeral in February 1989. Dignitaries from all over the world came to Tokyo to pay tribute to the head of a resurrected industrial power. It was a solemn traditional ceremony. In Shinjuku Imperial Garden was this magnificent wooden Shinto shrine specially made for this funeral from beautiful white pine without using a single nail. Everybody was in a dark suit with overcoat, muffler, and gloves, or in traditional dress. We were under an open tent, seated facing this shrine, shrivelled by a wind blowing out from Siberia. It was two and a half hours of biting, bitter cold. The Japanese arrangements were meticulous. There was an adjoining enclosed reception area which was warm and accessible, with hot refreshments, snacks, and restrooms with heated seats. Every guest present was provided with warm rugs and special packets, large and small, which acted as heat pads when the plastic wrapping was torn off and oxygen started the chemical process. I put the small pads in my shoes under my instep, and large ones in each pocket of my jacket, trousers, and overcoat. Poor Choo had no pockets whatsoever in her Chinese dress. I saw my neighbor put several heat pads on his seat to keep his bottom warm. It was a more severe test than bowing to him from the rooftop of the Cathay Building in Singapore. I could not have imagined then that I would represent Singapore to pay my respects to the Japanese emperor at his funeral, together with U.S. President George Bush and Britain's Prince Philip, representing the two big powers his forces had attacked without warning on 7 December 1941. All the major countries and many of the aid recipient countries were represented by their president or prime minister, and in some cases also by their monarch. The world came to pay tribute to Japan's outstanding success.

Over the last 35 years, I have come to know Japan and its leaders better. We needed them to help us industrialize. They in turn saw Singapore as a strategic location in Southeast Asia from which they could expand their economic activities into the region. We also straddled the sea route from the Gulf states to Japan, critical for their oil tankers. Issues that regularly arose in my discussions with Japanese prime ministers were free passage through the Straits of Malacca, Japanese investment in Singapore and Southeast Asia, the security of the region including China's role in it, and economic cooperation in the Asia Pacific region.

The right of free passage through the Straits of Malacca was uppermost in the minds of almost all the Japanese leaders I met in the 1960s and 1970s. Sato had first expressed his concern in 1967 that big tankers might not be able to pass the Straits of Malacca because of its shallowness in certain parts. I said there would be no danger if those parts could be properly demarcated with lighted buoys or lighthouses. With advanced technology, the straits could be deepened and lighted buoys could mark out the lanes. He was encouraged by my positive approach. He was preoccupied with their sea access to raw materials, especially oil, and to their markets. These issues had led them into World War II. Then they had the military capability to strike out. After the war they did not. The next prime minister, Kakuei Tanaka, also raised this issue in May 1973 when I went to Tokyo. When I told him that we could work together to resist any proposal by other countries in the region to collect tolls from ships passing through the straits, he was visibly reassured.

Two years later, when I called on Prime Minister Takeo Miki, he expressed his sincere appreciation for our help in two accidents in the Straits of Singapore involving Japanese oil tankers, which had caused a furore with our neighbors. In January that year, the *Showa Maru* had run aground at Buffalo Rock, a few kilometers from Singapore, causing an oil slick 20 kilometers (approximately 12 miles) long. There were fears of considerable pollution to the coastlines of Indonesia, Malaysia, and Singapore. Our port authority had immediately dispatched antipollution barges to contain and disperse the oil slick with detergents. Then in April, the *Tosa Maru* collided with another tanker off St. John's Island, even nearer to Singapore, and broke in two. Fortunately, it had off-loaded its cargo of oil and so caused no pollution. Nevertheless, the Indonesian and Malaysian governments publicly called for toll fees from ships to compensate for damage to the littoral states, and also for a limit on the tonnage of ships allowed to sail through the Straits of Malacca. It was so vital an issue for Japan that during that visit both Deputy Prime Minister Takeo Fukuda and Foreign Minister Kiichi Miyazawa separately thanked me for our help.

The Japanese government, more than other major powers, rates the importance of a developing country according to its economic value to Japan. Singapore has no natural resources. It therefore rates us poorly. To get the Japanese to help us, for example, in investing in a petrochemical plant, we had to remind them that their ships passing through the Straits of Malacca would have problems with toll collectors if Singapore were to join the other littoral states, Indonesia and Malaysia. Japan's concern over the Straits of Malacca only abated after the UN Convention on the Law of the Sea (UNCLOS) in 1982 spelled out the right of free passage through international straits.

During my years as prime minister, I encouraged Japanese investment in Singapore. When Prime Minister Sato visited Singapore in September

1967, I said to him publicly that Singaporeans had no inhibitions over Japanese capital, technology, managers, or expertise, that Japan was set to lead the rest of Asia to greater industrialization. I told their industrialists in the Keidanren, their association for big industrialists, that we would welcome any industry with a wage or freight advantage in Singapore. A year later, our Economic Development Board (EDB) set up an office in Tokyo, but in the early 1970s the Japanese were not so ready to relocate their factories abroad. They were building up their industrial capacity in Japan itself. Only in the 1980s, when pressed by the Americans over their increasing trade surpluses, did they begin manufacturing in America. And when Europe shut out their products, they started to manufacture there, especially in Britain to export to the EEC.

Typical of the careful and thorough manner in which Japanese companies invested abroad was the way Seiko decided to build its plant in Singapore. It took us more than three years in the early 1970s to persuade Seiko to build a watch factory in Singapore. Our EDB man in Tokyo, Wong Meng Quang, had been educated in a Japanese university and understood well their language and culture. Seiko did not believe that there was any place in Southeast Asia with the supporting industries and a sufficiently well-educated and trained workforce to meet their demands for precision engineering. Wong worked hard to convince them that to prepare for the day when cheaper quartz watches would make it uneconomic to manufacture in Japan, they should consider Singapore. He cultivated the director in charge of technology and production. After several study missions, many feasibility reports, and innumerable assurances that we would give every assistance necessary, they finally decided to invest. I opened their factory in 1976. If they were thorough and careful before deciding to invest, after that decision they went all out to ensure its success. They soon shed their doubts over the standards of our workers and upgraded into the manufacture of precision instruments, industrial robotics, and automation systems.

In 1969, we were interested in a petrochemical project. I first asked Miki for his government's support as we knew that unlike the Americans or Europeans, the government in Japan played an important role in these investments and its support was often decisive. In May 1975, I met Norishige Hasegawa, the president of Sumitomo Chemical Corporation.

He was willing to commit his company to such a project but said his government did not support it. He asked me to get Japan's prime minister to make a public commitment in support. Prime Minister Miki was reluctant to do this because Indonesia, an oil producer, wanted a petrochemical project for themselves. I urged Miki not to allow Japan to be pressured by resource-rich countries to desist from making a sound investment. I reminded him of the help Singapore had rendered over the two leaking Japanese oil tankers and hoped he would support the Sumitomo project. He then issued a short statement that although it was a private investment project, the Japan government had a deep interest in it and was ready to promote it.

It was another two years, in May 1977, before Miki's successor, Takeo Fukuda, endorsed the Singapore-Japan petrochemical project with Sumitomo as the leader of the project for the Japanese. Without him, the project might never have materialized. An investment of over US$1 billion was considered massive in 1977, and petrochemicals too capital-intensive and high-tech for Singapore. Even so, it took the intervention of Prime Minister Yasuhiro Nakasone when he visited Singapore in 1983 to get it really going. Shortly afterward, the project proceeded on a 50:50 basis. It had a slow start coming on-stream in a period of oversupply but it became profitable and spawned several major investments in downstream products.

The Japanese prime ministers I met, from Ikeda in 1962 to Miyazawa in 1990, were all men of considerable ability. One stood out as a rough diamond—Kakuei Tanaka, whom I met in May 1973 in Tokyo. He had a reputation as a bulldozer, a man with a powerful computer-like mind, a construction contractor who had fought his way up from the ranks. Of average height for a Japanese, broad and burly, he was a bundle of energy. A brusqueness and bluntness in his approach distinguished him from other Japanese prime ministers. They were mostly graduates of Tokyo Imperial University or some other renowned institution who became bureaucrats, and after rising to the top of their civil service had joined the leadership of the Liberal Democratic Party (LDP). Tanaka never went to university but was more than equal to his job.

It was refreshing to talk to a Japanese leader who was ready to express his views without inhibitions, even on sensitive subjects like anti-Japanese sentiments in Southeast Asia. Japan was then in trouble with Thai students in Bangkok demonstrating against their economic exploitation. I said it was not enough to send their trade and industry minister, Nakasone, to pat the Thais on their backs; if Tanaka did not want such problems to fester, he had to show the Thais, Indonesians, and Filipinos that the Japanese were interested beyond extracting their raw materials, for example by offering them industrialization. I was to repeat this argument with other Japanese prime ministers with not much effect.

Within eight months, in January 1974, I received Tanaka in Singapore. When he descended from his plane, his face was crooked with his lips and cheek puckered to one side. He was not self-conscious, explaining in a matter-of-fact way that he had a nerve problem which would take some time to clear up. He exuded enormous self-confidence.

He resigned at the end of 1974 because of a bribery case against him over the purchase of Lockheed aircraft, but remained a powerful figure in the LDP, a king-maker, until he died in 1993.

Takeo Fukuda was a slight, trim, wiry man with a puckish expression on a small, delicately formed face. I met him in May 1977 after he became prime minister. From previous meetings with him as a minister, I knew he had a sharp, capacious mind and wide-ranging interests. Once, to show how disadvantaged Japan was, he took out a bulky pocketbook from his breast pocket to read out the size of Japan's Extended Economic Zone (EEZ) compared to America's. He had kept all useful facts and figures, including the number of square miles that each country had as its EEZ according to the Law of the Sea.

In August, Fukuda visited Singapore after attending the Asean summit in Kuala Lumpur. We had one and a half hours of "belly talk" (Japanese for letting one's hair down). Our ministers agreed to set up a Japan-Singapore training center and to make contributions by Japanese firms to the center tax-deductible. The Japanese asked us to support a five-year transition period before the UKC (Under Keel Clearance or draft of a ship) at 3.5 meters (approximately 4 yards) was enforced for Japanese tankers coming through the Straits of Malacca. Although Indonesia, Malaysia, and Singapore had agreed that it be implemented in three and a half years, I promised to try to extend it to five. We succeeded.

Then I protested to Fukuda that his officials had spoken of Singapore not as a developing country but as an industrialized one not entitled to soft loans from Japan. If they treated us as already industrialized when we were not, the EEC and the United States would soon do the same. We would lose our General Scheme of Preferences (GSP) and other advantages before we could compete on equal terms. Fukuda took note and they ceased to raise this. Years later, in mid-1980, it was the European Commission in Brussels that questioned Singapore's status as a developing country.

Fukuda remained a force in Japanese politics after he retired as a Diet member. His son won the seat he vacated, so deep and personal were the loyalties of Japanese voters. When he died in 1995, Japan lost a shrewd, experienced, and wise leader. He had a grasp of the problems of the world at the end of the twentieth century and understood Japan could not live in isolation.

I made an official visit in October 1979 after Masayoshi Ohira succeeded Fukuda. Japanese protocol had moved with the times and no longer insisted on a black homburg and grey gloves. We were put up at the Asakasa (guest) Palace. We had lunch given by Emperor Hirohito and the empress, and a formal black-tie dinner with the prime minister.

Ohira had a broad, smiling face and puffed cheeks and laughed easily. A Hitotsubashi University graduate working in the ministry of finance, he was a cautious, capable leader. I drew his attention to the demonstration effect on our neighbors of Singapore-Japan cooperation in projects like the Japan-Singapore training center, the computer software training center, the Japanese studies department of the University of Singapore, and the pairing of the University of Singapore's engineering faculty with its Japanese counterpart. These were carefully studied by our neighbors. Because Singapore had succeeded, they realized the value of training and knowledge and were more likely to cooperate with Singapore and Japan. He agreed to my request for help in human resource development, adding that this subject was close to his heart. When Ohira died suddenly a year later, I lost a friend.

Zenko Suzuki, who succeeded Ohira, visited Singapore and the other Asean countries in January 1981. I urged him to give special attention to Asean the way Europe did to Africa at the Lomé Convention. Suzuki emphatically agreed. He had decided to visit Asean first, although traditionally the first overseas call of a Japanese prime minister was on Washington. Only later would he go to Washington, and then to the G-7 summit in Ottawa. Japan was a true member of Asia, he declared, and as its only highly industrialized country, had a special responsibility for and intended to work with Asia.

His change in posture was significant. It was unthinkable for a Japanese prime minister to make such a major shift without the support of their all-powerful bureaucrats. To underline his emphasis on Asean, he recounted how the Soviet Union had approached Japan for help in Siberia's economic development. Unless the Soviets changed their policies in Afghanistan and Vietnam, Japan would not give economic assistance for Siberia, although the Soviets had asked Japan to separate economics from politics. I encouraged him in this firm stand; if Japan, Europe, and America helped the Soviets to cover up the failures of their system, they would continue to create trouble for the world. Without outside help, in 15 to 20 years they would face problems more severe than Poland's. Suzuki agreed.

A graduate of the Fisheries Training Institute (now Tokyo University of Fisheries), he was an expert on the subject. I had an enjoyable dinner with him discovering the mysteries of fisheries and the fishing industry of Japan. Many of the metaphors he used were fish-related. When I proposed that Japan should concentrate on human resource development, training Southeast Asians to be skilled and productive workers like the Japanese, he agreed, saying, "If you give a man a fish, he has but one meal; if you teach him how to fish . . ." He would set aside a hundred million dollars for a training center in each Asean country, and one in Okinawa. The key to a modern economy, he said, was through training, not grants and soft loans.

Because most Japanese prime ministers after Sato did not remain in office more than two years, it was difficult to establish deep personal relations with them. Changes of prime minister and ministers made little difference, for Japan continued to achieve high growth rates. Foreign commentators attributed this to the power and competence of the bureaucracy. I believe they underestimated the competence of the men who took turns to become prime minister and cabinet ministers. They were drawn from the same pool of leading members of the LDP factions, all of them able, experienced, and sharing a common outlook.

Yasuhiro Nakasone, Suzuki's successor, was able to stay as prime minister for five years from 1982. He could speak English but with a strong Japanese accent. He spoke in a resounding voice with emphasis and vigor. He had been a lieutenant (paymaster) in the Japanese Imperial Navy and was proud of it. Tall and strapping for a Japanese at five-foot-eleven, with a high dome of a balding forehead, he exuded energy and self-discipline. He meditated for two hours at a temple once a week, sitting with back straight and legs crossed in lotus position, and recommended I take it up. I took his advice and with the help of a friend, a Buddhist and a Western-trained doctor, I learned to do it, but only for half an hour at a time. Later, I made it a daily routine. It has been more beneficial than tranquillizers.

He had none of the self-effacing ways of most Japanese leaders. When I visited him in March 1983, he welcomed me, saying how happy he was to have realized his hope to greet me in the prime minister's office. He was concerned over Asean's reaction to what he termed "a slight increase in Japan's defence expenditure." When he was in charge of the Defence Agency he had made known his hawkish views, that Japan must be ready to defend itself. Now he had the excuse that the American senate had passed a resolution calling upon Japan to increase its defense expenditure. He wanted to assure apprehensive neighbors that Japan was not becoming militaristic simply because it improved its self-defense forces so as to be able, in an emergency, to defend the three straits (Soya, Tsugaru, and Tsushima) around the Japanese islands. This, he claimed, had been the policy of previous cabinets, although it had not been publicly declared.

When he visited Singapore in 1983, I recounted that 10 years previously, in that same cabinet room, General Ichiji Sugita (retired), who as a lieutenant colonel had helped to plan General Tomoyuki Yamashita's invasion of Malaya, had apologized to me for his role. He had returned in 1974 and 1975 together with his surviving officer colleagues to brief Singapore Armed Forces officers on their experiences during the campaign in Malaya and their final assault on and capture of Singapore. Much had taken place in the Istana since General Yamashita stayed there after he captured it. We must not allow ourselves to be blinkered by the past but work toward a future free of suspicions. He expressed in English his "heartfelt gratitude" for my position.

The deep-seated fears of the Japanese people of getting embroiled in another unwinnable and punishing war slowed down Nakasone's strong defense policies. Opinion polls showed the people favored a low posture on defense. Because of his forthright nature, we talked freely when we met over lunches and dinners in Tokyo long after he was no longer prime minister.

The grip of the LDP on power started to slip from the late 1980s. The system that had worked well for 35 years could no longer cope with the changed domestic and international circumstances. The LDP came under increasing attack for corruption, with the media reporting one scandal after another. The Japanese media had decided to break up the cozy partnership between LDP politicians, big businessmen, especially construction contractors, and top bureaucrats.

Noboru Takeshita, who succeeded Nakasone as prime minister in 1987, was a dapper little man who had graduated from Waseda University, not Todai. He was always soft-spoken and formal in his social interaction. His often smiling face belied the shrewd political infighter he was. He had a cautious leadership style compared to Nakasone's, but could deliver on his promises.

Takeshita was prime minister at a time of excitement and hope among the Japanese of getting the Kurile islands back from the Soviets. Gorbachev needed international financial assistance. The Japanese were prepared to be generous, provided they got back their four islands or at least a firm undertaking to return them. In Tokyo, at the funeral of Emperor Hirohito in February 1989, Takeshita told me that the Soviet Union had not relented in its occupation of the islands. Later, he sent me a message asking me to put in a word of support for the return of the islands when Soviet Prime Minister Ryzhkov visited Singapore in early 1990. I once asked Prime Minister Takeo Miki why the Soviets, who had so much of the world's territory in Euro-Asia, would want four islands off the

Kamchatka Peninsula. Miki's face darkened when he said with deep anger and passion that the Russians were greedy for territory. What had happened to the Japanese inhabitants of the Kurile islands? He replied with disgust, "Every single Japanese was removed and sent back to Japan." Takeshita shared this passionate desire to get back the four islands. When Ryzhkov visited Singapore, I raised the subject of the four islands. His response was totally predictable: There was no dispute over the four islands; they were Soviet.

During Takeshita's two-year term of office, a scandal connected with an employment company called Recruit blew up. His right-hand man was alleged to have received funds for political purposes and committed suicide, to the great sorrow of Takeshita who resigned as prime minister.

After a series of scandals, the public demanded a clean figure as prime minister. Although he led one of the smallest LDP factions, Toshiki Kaifu became prime minister in 1989. He was a pleasant, gregarious man known as "Mr. Clean." While not as scholarly as Miyazawa, or decisive like Nakasone, or an infighter like Takeshita, he had the common touch.

During his full two-year term, he faced problems which Nakasone would have been happy to deal with in his decisive manner. The Americans wanted Japan to send troops to the Gulf for action against Iraq. Kaifu consulted all faction leaders and ended up not sending any, instead paying US$13 billion as Japan's contribution to this operation.

The West had recognized Japan's economic power and, beginning from 1975 with Rambouillet, had invited its leaders to the G-5 summits. But Japan faced obstacles in its search for a role as a major economic power, the most serious being the attitude of Japanese leaders to their war-time atrocities. They compare badly to the West Germans who openly admitted and apologized for their war crimes, paid compensation to victims, and taught younger Germans their history of war crimes so they would avoid making the same mistakes. In contrast, Japanese leaders are still equivocal and evasive. Perhaps they do not want to demoralize their people or insult their ancestors and their emperor. Whatever the reason, successive LDP prime ministers have not faced up to their past.

Kaifu made the first break with the past in a memorable speech in Singapore in May 1990. He expressed "sincere contrition at past Japanese actions, which inflicted unbearable suffering and sorrow upon a great many people in the Asia Pacific region. . . . The Japanese people are firmly resolved never again to repeat those actions, which had tragic consequences. . . ." It was just short of an apology. He spoke with candor and realism.

I highlighted to Kaifu the difference between the German and Japanese attitudes to their war records. When German industrialists and bankers gave me their CVs, they would invariably list their experiences during the war—fighting in campaigns in Stalingrad or Belgium, where they had been captured as POWs by the Soviets or Americans or British, the rank they attained, and the medals won. But Japanese CVs left the years 1937 to 1945 blank, as if those were nonyears. It was a signal that they did not wish to talk about them. Not surprisingly, a curtain fell between the Japanese and people they dealt with, building suspicion and distrust. I suggested that the Japanese study the German way of educating the next generation on their history, so as not to repeat the same mistakes. Kaifu said he was encouraged by my comments and stressed that Japan was changing. He was the first postwar prime minister, he said, who did not have a military background. In 1945, he was still a young student; in the 1960s, he had participated in the democratization process. He would look into the task of educating the young about the facts of World War II and would revise their school textbooks. He did not stay long enough in office to follow through before he was replaced by Kiichi Miyazawa.

Short and sprightly, with an inquiring expression on his round face, Miyazawa's broad brow would wrinkle when he pondered over a question. He would purse his lips before he delivered a cautious and carefully thought-out position. He struck me as more of a scholar than a politician, and could easily have stayed on as a professor in Todai, where he graduated, had he chosen a career in academia. Instead he became a finance ministry bureaucrat.

The media had quoted me in 1991: Letting the Japanese rearm for UN peacekeeping operations in Cambodia was like "giving liqueur chocolates to an alcoholic." At a lunch with other LDP leaders in Tokyo shortly before he took over as prime minister, Miyazawa asked me what I had meant. I replied that it was difficult to change Japanese culture. The Japanese have a deeply ingrained habit of wanting to achieve perfection

and going to the limits in whatever they do, whether in flower arrangement, sword-making, or war. I did not believe Japan could repeat what it
had done between 1931 and 1945 because China now had the nuclear
bomb. But if Japan wanted to play its part as a permanent member of the
UN Security Council, its neighbors must feel it was trustworthy and
dependable as a force for peace. Miyazawa asked whether Kaifu's expression of "contrition" was not in itself a catharsis. I said it was a good start
but not an apology. As prime minister, Miyazawa's first statement in the
Diet in January 1992 expressed his "heartfelt remorse and regrets" at the
unbearable suffering and sorrow the people of the Asia Pacific region had
endured. Unlike Nakasone, who was a hawk, Miyazawa was a dove. He
had always supported the U.S.-Japan alliance and was against any rearm-
ing. His English was fluent with a wide vocabulary, making a frank
exchange of views easy. He was quick to take up and counter any point he
did not accept—but ever so politely. We had been good friends for many
years before he became prime minister.

Miyazawa was concerned about the kind of China that would result
from its high growth rates. Like Sato in 1968, Miki (1975), and Fukuda
(1977), Miyazawa discussed China at length. Even when China was closed
to the world with its economy stagnant, Japanese leaders paid it careful
attention. After Deng Xiaoping's open-door policy, the Japanese were
increasingly focused on a neighbor that was growing at 8 to 10 percent
yearly and could challenge Japan's preeminence in East Asia. Miyazawa's
concern was that a strong China, without the checks and balances of a
democratic system and a free press, would affect the security of Japan and
East Asia. Most Japanese leaders believed that their arrangements with the
United States would ensure security for 20 years. It was the long-term
future that troubled Miyazawa and all Japanese leaders. Their unspoken
fear was that one day the Americans would be unable to maintain their
dominant military presence and would be unwilling to defend Japan. They
were uncertain whether China would be a force for stability or tension.

I argued that it was best to draw the Chinese out to become a part of
the modern world. Japan should get bright Chinese students to study in
Japan and develop close relationships with young Japanese. The exposure
of China's best and brightest to the United States, Japan, and Europe
would make them less inward-looking and would get them to understand

that if China wanted to grow and prosper, it had to be a law-abiding member of the international community. If the Chinese were isolated and thwarted in their efforts at economic reform and progress, they would become hostile to the advanced countries.

Most Japanese leaders believed that in a crunch, Asean countries would line up with Japan, but were unsure how Singapore would react. They accepted that despite being ethnic Chinese my views and policies toward China were those of a Singaporean whose interests were in Southeast Asia, and that I would not necessarily support China in any conflict. However, they were uncertain how Singapore's majority Chinese population and its future leaders would react under Chinese pressure. I do not think I succeeded in dispelling their doubts.

During Miyazawa's term as prime minister a powerful faction led by a young Tanaka protégé, Ichiro Ozawa, brought the government down in a critical vote. Unlike other LDP faction leaders, Miyazawa was not a tough, ruthless infighter. In the election that followed, the LDP lost power. One outcome of this break in the LDP hold on government was that Morihiro Hosokawa became the first prime minister to admit in unambiguous language Japan's aggression in World War II and apologize for the sufferings caused. He did not have the LDP mindset, to hang tough over their war crimes. This unqualified apology came only after a nonmainstream party leader became prime minister.

The following year, Prime Minister Tomiichi Murayama of the Social Democratic Party of Japan also apologized, and did so to each Asean leader in turn during his visits to Asean countries. He said publicly in Singapore that Japan needed to face up squarely to its past actions of aggression and colonialism. On the 50th anniversary of the end of the war (1995), he expressed once again his feelings of deep remorse and his heartfelt apology. Japan, he said, would have to reflect on the sufferings it had inflicted on Asia. He was the first Japanese prime minister to lay a wreath at Singapore's civilian war memorial. We had not asked him to do so. He said he did it to maintain future peace and stability in the region. He was aware of latent anti-Japanese sentiments around the region and saw the need to deepen political, economic, and cultural exchanges. The apologies of two non-LDP prime ministers, Hosokawa and Murayama, irrevocably dented the hard-line no-apology stance of previous Japanese governments.

Although the LDP as such did not apologize, it was part of the Murayama coalition government that did.

When Ryutaro Hashimoto of the LDP became prime minister in 1996, he visited the Yasukuni Shrine in July that year, on his birthday, in a personal, not official, capacity. He paid his respects to the spirits of the war dead, including General Hideki Tojo, the wartime prime minister, and several other war criminals who had been hanged for war crimes. This ambivalence in attitudes leaves a big question unanswered. Unlike the Germans, the Japanese have not had a catharsis and rid themselves of the poison in their system. They have not educated their young about the wrong they had done. Hashimoto expressed his "deepest regrets" on the 52nd anniversary of the end of World War II (1997) and his "profound remorse" during his visit to Beijing in September 1997. However, he did not apologize, as the Chinese and Koreans wished Japan's leader to do.

I do not understand why the Japanese are so unwilling to admit the past, apologize for it, and move on. For some reason, they do not want to apologize. To apologize is to admit having done a wrong. To express regrets or remorse merely expresses their present subjective feelings. They denied the massacre of Nanjing took place; that Korean, Filipino, Dutch, and other women were kidnapped or otherwise forced to be "comfort women" (a euphemism for sex slaves) for Japanese soldiers at the war fronts; that they carried out cruel biological experiments on live Chinese, Korean, Mongolian, Russian, and other prisoners in Manchuria. In each case, only after irrefutable evidence was produced from their own records did they make reluctant admissions. This fed suspicions of Japan's future intentions.

Present Japanese attitudes are an indication of their future conduct. If they are ashamed of their past, they are less likely to repeat it. General Tojo, who was executed by the Allies for war crimes, said in his last will and testament that the Japanese were defeated only because superior forces overwhelmed them. For a country of its size and population, Japan can become a very considerable power in high-tech warfare. True, it will suffer severe disadvantages if a conflict between Japan and China escalates beyond conventional weapons. This is unlikely, but if it does happen, Japan's capabilities should not be underestimated. If the Japanese feel threatened, deprived of their means of livelihood as a nation by being cut off from oil or other critical resources, or shut out from their export markets, I believe they will again fight ferociously as they did from 1942 to 1945.

Whatever the future may hold for Japan and Asia, to play their role as an economic modernizer and UN peacekeeper, the Japanese must first put this apology issue to rest. Asia and Japan must move on. We need greater trust and confidence in each other.

# 32. Lessons from Japan

After World War II, a few men at the top of Japanese society were determined to rebuild Japan and its industrial sinews. This elite had not been disbanded by General MacArthur's occupying forces. When communist China intervened in the Korean War, the Americans switched their policy to one of rebuilding Japan. Japanese leaders realized this was their chance and kept a low, humble posture while they caught up with Americans, first in textiles, steel, ships, motorcars, and petrochemicals, then electrical and electronic goods, cameras, and finally computers. They had an elitist system. Like the French with their Grandes Ecoles, their former imperial universities as well as the top private ones selected the best and honed their talent. That talent found its way to the top of the bureaucracy and their corporations. Their elite, both administrators and corporate leaders, are equal to any in the world. However, the Japanese miracle was not the work of just a few at the top. The Japanese people as a whole shared a determination to prove that they were able to make the grade. At every level they strove to excel.

I saw an unforgettable example of how they took pride in their work during a visit in the late 1970s to Takamatsu, a city on the island of Shikoku. The Japanese ambassador gave me dinner at their best, albeit three-star, hotel. The food was excellent. For fruit and dessert, a chef in his thirties appeared in immaculate white to demonstrate his skill with a sharp knife, peeling persimmons and crunchy pears. It was a virtuoso performance. I asked about his training. He had started as a kitchen helper, cleaning plates, peeling potatoes, and chopping vegetables. Five years later he graduated as a junior cook; ten years later he became a chief chef in this hotel and was proud of it. Pride in their job and the desire to excel in their given roles, whether as cook, waiter, or chambermaid, makes for high productivity, and in manufacturing, near-zero defect products. No nation in Asia can match them, not the Chinese, Koreans, Vietnamese, or Southeast Asians. They consider themselves a special people. You are either born a Japanese and therefore in that magic circle, or you are not. This myth of being special makes them a formidable force as a nation, a corporation, or a team in any workplace.

Indeed, the Japanese have admirable qualities. Theirs is a unique culture, where they fit into each other snugly like Lego bricks. One-to-one, many Chinese can match the Japanese, whether it is at Chinese chess or the game of *Go.* But in a group, especially a production team in a factory, they are difficult to beat. When I presented an award to Nobuo Hizaki, the managing director of Nichison company in the 1980s, I asked how Singapore workers compared to their counterparts in Japan because both worked identical machines. He assessed the Singaporeans' productivity at 70 percent. The reasons: Japanese workers were more skilled and multi-skilled, were more flexible and adaptable, and had less job-hopping and absenteeism. They accepted the need for life-long learning and training. All workers considered themselves grey-collar workers, not white- or blue-collar. Technicians, group leaders, and supervisors were willing to soil their hands. How long would it take for Singapore workers to catch up? He thought in 10 to 15 years. When pressed, Hizaki said Singapore workers would never catch up 100 percent. He gave two reasons. First, Japanese workers would cover for workmates who had to attend to other urgent business; Singapore workers looked only after their own jobs. Second, there was a clear division in Singapore between the rank and file and the officer cadre, which was the British system, where a polytechnic or university graduate came straight into the officer grade. This was not so in Japan.

When I was in Japan in 1967, I visited the Yokohama shipyards of shipbuilders IHI (Ishikawajima-Harima Industries), our joint venture partner in Jurong Shipyard in Singapore. The vice president, Dr. Shinto, was a stout, energetic, able man and an outstanding engineer. Like the other workers, he wore his company's uniform. He wore rubber boots and a hard hat and provided me with the same before we toured the dockyard. He knew every inch of it and gave a running commentary in English. The Japanese workers were disciplined, hardworking, united, and efficient.

Back in his office, over a working lunch, he explained the difference between British and Japanese managements. Japanese executives and engineers start work on the factory floor. They had to understand the low-level workers before they could rise from the ranks to lead them effectively. The British dockyard executive sat in his carpeted office and did not visit the workers on the shop floor or in the dockyards. That was bad for morale and productivity.

Later that year, I visited Swan Hunter's shipyards on the Tyneside. Sir John Hunter took me through his dockyard. The contrast was stark. Sir John wore a beautifully tailored suit with highly polished shoes. We drove up together in a Rolls Royce. When we walked through the greasy shop floor the muck stuck to our shoes. I had not noticed such grease at the IHI dockyards in Yokohama. As we were about to enter the Rolls, I hesitated. Sir John did not. He scraped the soles of his shoes against the floor and went into the car where he wiped the remaining grease on to the thick beige carpet. I was invited to do the same. I must have looked surprised for he said, "They will shampoo it." We were driven off, not to an office working lunch but to the Gosforth Hotel, where we had an excellent meal before playing 18 holes of golf. The British executive lived in style.

May 1975 was my first visit to Japan after the oil crisis of October 1973. I had read of the comprehensive steps the Japanese had taken to save energy and their success in reducing oil consumption per unit of industrial output. I found that all offices and public buildings, including their top hotels, had reduced power use. That summer, the temperature in my air-conditioned hotel room could not be brought below a minimum 25°C which was warm; there was a polite notice asking guests to be forbearing. The chambermaids assiduously switched off all lights and air conditioners every time we left our rooms.

I asked our Public Utilities Board officials to study how the Japanese had been so successful in conserving energy. Their report showed how seriously they, unlike the Americans, had tackled the problem. Factories consuming more than a certain amount of electricity had appointed energy managers to rationalize energy use and report their progress to the Ministry of International Trade and Industry (MITI) yearly. The construction industry took conservation measures to prevent heat loss through external walls and windows. Manufacturers improved the efficiency of domestic appliances like air conditioners, lighting, and water heaters and so lowered electricity consumption. They did the same for industrial machines and were required to display the power efficiency of each.

The government gave tax incentives for installing energy-saving equipment, while banks financed the purchase and installation of heat insulation and other such equipment at special low rates of interest. They created an Energy Conservation Center in 1978 to spread information on conservation technology through exhibitions, factory energy audits, and research. No wonder Japan achieved the lowest electricity consumed per unit of industrial production.

I asked our ministries to adopt similar measures wherever practical. We managed to cut down our use of electricity but nowhere as effectively as the Japanese.

By the late 1970s, Japan was greatly admired for its recovery from the oil crisis. It enjoyed high rates of growth while Western Europe and America slowed down. Numerous articles and bestselling books extolled its virtues. But the Japanese could not erase the widely held stereotype that they worked like ants, lived in rabbit hutches, closed their markets, and exported an endless flow of steel, cars, and zero-defect television sets and electronic products.

I learned from the Japanese the importance of increasing productivity through worker-manager cooperation, the real meaning of human resource development. We had formed a National Productivity Board (NPB) in 1972. We made progress, especially after Wong Kwei Cheong, a PAP MP and the managing director of a joint venture Japanese electronics company, educated me on the virtues of Japanese-style management. He helped us form a National Productivity Council with members drawn from the private sector to advise the NPB. I approached the Japan Productivity Center to help us set up a center and saw the chairman, Kohei Goshi, a dry old man of very few words in his mid-seventies. He was an ascetic who exuded sincerity and earnestness. He described productivity as a marathon with no finishing line. With his help over the next 10 years, we built up an effective productivity organization that gradually got the unions and management working together on improving productivity.

Japanese managers are totally dedicated to their jobs. In the 1970s, a Japanese engineer at Jurong Shipyard failed to secure an important oil storage tank project because of an error he had made in calculating costs. He felt deeply responsible for the drop in his company's profits that year and killed himself. We were shocked. We could not imagine any Singaporean feeling such a heavy sense of personal responsibility.

In every major city I visited in China and Vietnam, the major Japanese trading companies had stationed representatives to study what could be purchased and sold to other parts of the world, and what goods these places needed which Japan could bring in from elsewhere. They beavered away assiduously and kept Japanese companies well-informed. Singapore companies, on the other hand, have trouble getting young executives to take hardship postings in developing countries like China and Vietnam.

Because they demand so much of themselves, Japanese companies seldom find Singapore managers as good as their own. In Jurong Shipyard, after 20 years of a joint venture operation started in the 1960s, the CEO, chief financial officer, and chief engineer were all Japanese. Nearly all American MNCs had appointed local CEOs within 10 years of starting operations. Singapore executives and engineers know that promotions and acceptance are most difficult in Japanese MNCs.

High Japanese standards of responsibility, reliability, professionalism, and competence in the Japanese language made for hurdles difficult to cross. This is changing, but slowly. In the 1990s, one major Japanese MNC, NEC (Nippon Electric Company), appointed a Singaporean as its CEO. By then, more than 80 percent of the American companies and 50 percent of European companies operating in Singapore had done so. Their different culture has created problems for Japanese companies overseas.

They do not absorb non-Japanese easily into their corporate system. In a global economy, the Japanese will be at a disadvantage unless they can change and become more like the Americans and Europeans and absorb foreigners into their corporate cultures.

After living in Japan for decades, Chinese Singaporean bankers and businesspeople rarely develop deep friendships with their Japanese associates, in spite of speaking fluent Japanese and conforming to Japanese social norms. They meet over dinner and at social gatherings in public places, almost never in their homes.

The Japanese do not give business to foreign banks. Singapore banks in Japan depend entirely on Singaporeans and other foreigners. When big Japanese firms invest in Singapore, they bring their supporting companies to cater to their needs, including Japanese supermarkets, restaurants, and other suppliers of their way of life.

Because they were cut off from Western technology and had a difficult time reaching the top, depending much on reverse engineering, the Japanese are miserly in passing on their technology, as Taiwanese, Koreans, and Southeast Asians have found. Having earned their newly found wealth the hard way, they are loath to part with it to spendthrift Third World regimes, to benefit, not the people, but a few leaders. It is a minor miracle that under American suasion, they have become the world's largest aid donor. Singaporeans have also come up the hard way, so I understand Japanese sentiments. We have always preferred to give aid in the form of training and technical assistance, not in grants which could be misused.

In 1980, officials from our ministry for trade and industry visited their counterparts in Japan's formidable Ministry for International Trade and Industry (MITI) which had charted the course for Japan's postwar industrial progress. Their report was illuminating. The Japanese were focused on the future. They were not harking back to an idyllic Japan of sailing ships and samurais. Their agenda was energy conservation, alternatives to oil, and a strategy to overcome protectionism in steel, cars, and electronic products by moving to creative knowledge industries. So far their progress had been a catching-up process. Now they had to move forward on their own by creating new technology and new products. MITI's vision for the 1980s was of a technology-based Japan that embarked on the continuous acquisition and exploitation of new knowledge to serve the needs of people and societies.

MITI's advice to our officials in 1980 was, given Singapore's geographic position and environment, to prepare for a possible role as a center for knowledge and information, to complement Tokyo. The Japanese believed that for such a center to succeed, the people had to be reliable and trustworthy. We took their advice to heart. After a careful study of what it took to be such a knowledge and information center, we redoubled our emphasis on the teaching of the sciences, mathematics, and computers in all our schools. We computerized the whole government administration to set the pace for the private sector. We gave income tax incentives by allowing rapid depreciation for computers. That decision has given us a lead over our neighbors. It seeded our plans for an "intelligent island," completely linked up with fiberoptics and directly connected with all the main centers of knowledge and information—in Tokyo, New York, London, Paris, and Frankfurt, and also our neighbors, Kuala Lumpur, Jakarta, Bangkok, and Manila.

At my meetings with the Japanese Chamber of Commerce in Singapore, I learned how they continuously rejuvenate their enterprises with fresh investments. In order to compete worldwide, they set out to acquire the most advanced technology for their industries. What impressed me most was their emphasis on investing in the people who work these machines and manage the company. To make the best use of state-of-the-art machines, they have continual training and retraining of their staff. This philosophy ensured that they would always be out in the forefront.

MITI officials explained to me that the fundamental strength of any enterprise lay in its people. Hence, they invested in their workers who had life-long employment. We Singaporeans were immigrants. Our workers were accustomed to the British system where workers moved to the employer who paid best.

Also uniquely Japanese was their way of paying workers fringe benefits in allowances, overtime, bonuses, and company welfare. These amounted to more than the basic wage, unlike the practice in Singapore. Because supplementary benefits were high, a company faced with a recession could immediately trim bonuses and allowances to save as much as 40 to 50 percent of their wage bill, and restore them later when company profits recovered.

This made life-long employment possible. Management and workers shared the profits, and also shared the hardships in lean years when the company did not make profits. Workers were conscious that the company's long-term well-being was crucial for their life-long employment. Their companies provided medical and dental care, housing, including hostels for bachelors and housing loans at highly subsidized rates, family recreational facilities, education for employees' children, farewell and welcoming parties, long-service gifts, stock options, and congratulatory and condolence allowances. The ties that bound them to their company were many and strong. Of course, only the big companies and the public sector could afford this life-long employment system. They were able to pass on the burden of retrenchments in a downturn to their suppliers, the smaller companies. I wanted to emulate them but gave up after discussions with Singapore employers. We did not have their culture of strong worker loyalty to their companies. Moreover, many of our big employers were American and European MNCs with different company cultures.

I have tried to identify those Japanese strong points which we could adopt because they were system- or method-based. In the 50 years since I first knew them as military overlords, I have had many meetings with Japanese engineers, CEOs, ministers, and formidable bureaucrats. I have come to believe reports of some Western psychologists that their average IQ, especially in mathematics, is higher than that of Americans and Europeans.

In spite of my experiences during the Japanese occupation and the Japanese traits I had learned to fear, I now respect and admire them. Their group solidarity, discipline, intelligence, industriousness, and willingness to sacrifice for their nation make them a formidable and productive force. Conscious of the poverty of their resources, they will continue to make that extra effort to achieve the unachievable.

Because of their cultural values, they will be among the survivors after any catastrophe. From time to time they are hit by the unpredictable forces of nature—earthquakes, typhoons, and tsunamis. They take their casualties, pick themselves up, and rebuild. The behavior of the people of Kobe after a massive earthquake in 1995 was exemplary and impressive. Riots and looting followed in Los Angeles in 1992 after a less devastating earthquake, whereas the Japanese in Kobe reacted stoically. There was no looting or rioting. Japanese companies mounted their own rescue effort to provide food, shelter, and clothing; voluntary organizations came forward to help without any prompting. Even the yakuza (Japanese mafia) pitched in. The government's rescue efforts were slow. Railways and roads were unusable, and telephones, water, and power were cut. But there was no wringing of hands, however terrible their losses in family and property.

I was amazed at how life was returning to normal when I visited Kobe in November 1996, one and a half years after the earthquake. They had taken this catastrophe in their stride and settled to a new daily routine. They are indeed different in culture. But they will have to change enough to fit into the world of many peoples with many different cultures.

The Japanese paradigm of catching up with the West has run its course. It climaxed in the late 1980s when the Tokyo stock market capitalization was equal to that of the New York Stock Exchange and land values in Tokyo exceeded those of New York. However, when the Bank of Japan pricked the bubble in 1990, the economy went on a long slide downhill.

Meanwhile, in the 1990s, the American economy transformed itself through downsizing and restructuring, and exploiting the digital revolution, especially the Internet. It has left both the Japanese and the European economies far behind. The Japanese are working out a new paradigm. It has to embrace the digital revolution; it must also emphasize rates of return on equity and concentrate on shareholder value as American corporations do. As the economy has globalized, Japan has been forced to open up its domestic market. Many time-honored practices, like life-time employment, will have to change. But I have seen the strength of the Japanese people, and the quality of their education. While they may not have encouraged as many entrepreneurs in new start-ups as Americans have done, their young men and women do not lack imagination, creativity, or innovative ideas. Within five to ten years, the Japanese will come fighting back.

# 33. Korea: At the Crossroads

I did not have happy memories of the Koreans because the first ones I met were in Japanese uniform. They were one of two groups of auxiliaries the Japanese brought to Singapore, the other being Taiwanese. The Koreans were the toughs and as heavy-handed as the Japanese soldiers. The Taiwanese were used as interpreters, speaking Hokkien, Singapore's major Chinese dialect.

After the war, South Korea's economic dynamism overrode my past prejudices. I visited the country in October 1979 when President Park Chung Hee received me in his official residence, the Blue House. Park was an ascetic-looking man, small and wiry with a sharp face and a narrow nose. He had been chosen and trained as a military officer by the Japanese. He must have been among the best of his generation.

He wanted close relations with Asean and hoped I would help. He said the prospects of peace in the Korean peninsula were not good. The South did not want another war, placing peace first and reunification second. The North wanted to reunify by force. I asked if the American commitment would go beyond 1981, the date President Carter had announced for the withdrawal of U.S. forces. He replied that Carter's Defense Secretary Brown had promised security after 1981 and had stated publicly that the security of South Korea was vital to the United States. I said Carter's 1976 election pledge to withdraw troops from Korea was popular with Americans; if it again became popular, Carter could change. He agreed, saying he was uneasy over U.S. policy which was affected by four-year election cycles.

He had no small talk at dinner that night. His daughter, in her twenties and English-speaking, kept the conversation flowing. Park said his training was that of a military officer, and his job was to take the advice and recommendations of the experts whom he had appointed as ministers and top officials, and decide policy.

His prime minister, Choi Kyu Hah, was an able man, Japanese-educated. Choi's wife was equally intelligent and well-educated in Japanese. She and her husband still read Japanese novels and newspapers. The Korean intelligentsia, like the Taiwanese, were as much influenced by the Japanese as I was by the British. Park had been in power for 18 years and had got the economy thriving with a disciplined and united people, all of whom were determined to achieve economic modernization. Following Japanese practice, he jealously protected his domestic market and exported aggressively. He encouraged, even forced Koreans to save, denying them luxuries like color television sets which they were exporting in increasing numbers. I was impressed by his strong will and grim resolve for Korea to succeed. Without Park, Korea might never have made it as an industrialized nation. Five days after I left Korea, Park was assassinated by his closest aide, the chief of intelligence. According to the government, it was part of a plot to seize power. Their press reported that the intelligence chief had feared being replaced after Park criticized him for his failure in handling unrest when students and workers fought police in Pusan.

My visit confirmed my assessment that the Korean people were tough and capable of enduring great hardships. Successive invaders had swept across the steppes of central Asia and come to a halt in the peninsula. They were of Mongolian stock with distinctive facial and physical features, easily distinguishable from the Japanese or Chinese. They were proud of their history and took me to Kyongju, their ancient cultural center where the tombs of Shilla dynasty kings had yielded elaborate artifacts of gold and precious stones.

Their hatred for the Japanese was intense. Thirty-five years of merciless Japanese suppression of any rebellious activity had left deep scars on their soul. They remembered the Japanese invasions over the last 500 years, each of which they repelled. Even among the most Japanized of the Korean elite, including Prime Minister Choi and his wife, both completely at home in Japanese language, literature, and culture, there was an underlying antipathy toward their former rulers. The Japanese were hard on the Koreans because they resisted colonization and domination. They had also resisted Chinese overlordship for a thousand years, but they did not have that same deep antipathy for the Chinese. They had adopted the Chinese script and with it had imbibed the teachings of Confucius.

Korean students in American universities have shown that they are as bright as the Japanese or Chinese. But although physically Koreans are hardier, they cannot equal the Japanese in cohesiveness and dedication to their companies. Korean workers and unions were quiescent as long as there was martial law. When it was lifted, the unions became militant with go-slows, sit-ins, and strikes. They demanded more pay and better conditions regardless of what was happening to their export markets. Korean employers and unions never achieved the cooperative relationship that Japanese companies and their unions enjoy. Japanese unions never damaged their companies' competitive position however sharp their disputes with their employers over who got what.

The Koreans are a fearsome people. When they riot, they are as organized and nearly as disciplined as the riot police who confront them, policemen who resemble gladiators in their helmets with plastic visors and plastic shields. When their workers and students fight in the streets with these policemen, they look like soldiers at war. Their strikers squat on the ground to listen to speeches and pump fists into the air rhythmically. They are an intense people not given to compromise, and when they oppose authority, they do so with vigor and violence.


I made two more visits to South Korea in the 1980s to meet Presidents Chun Doo Hwan and Roh Tae Woo. President Kim Young Sam I met in Singapore in 1996. All four Korean leaders, from Park to Kim, were deeply concerned over their country's geopolitical vulnerability, caught between three huge and powerful neighbors, China, Russia, and Japan.

When I met Chun in Seoul in 1986, I was struck by his preoccupation with and fear of North Korea. I found this strange. The South's population was twice that of the North. They were immensely richer and had access to better military equipment from America. The traumatic experience of the communist invasion must have left deep scars and an abiding fear of the ferocity of their northern brethren. The Korean foreign ministers I met all spoke with awe of the military might and prowess of the North, despite its parlous economy.

Another issue which dominated my discussions with South Korea's leaders was trade and investments between the newly industrializing economies (NIEs), which included South Korea and Singapore, and the developed countries of Europe and America. With President Chun, in 1986, I raised my concern at the growing protectionist sentiments in America and Europe. If we, the NIEs, did not open up our markets to reciprocate the free access we had to America and Europe, they would find it unbearable and protectionism would grow. He agreed that the NIEs should liberalize. Korea was doing so in a systematic and steady way, to be completed in two years. I pointed out that after his liberalization, Korea's tariffs would still be high at 16 to 20 percent. Chun's response was that Korea was not a rich country. It had a per capita income of only US$2,000, less than Singapore's, and it had a debt of US$46.5 billion besides the burden of defense.

When I spoke to their four major business associations over lunch in Seoul in 1986, I found them most reluctant to open up their markets. Two years later, at lunch with the same four associations, I discussed the need to increase their imports, urging that they and other NIEs should discuss with the industrial nations in the OECD (Organization for Economic Cooperation and Development) ways to narrow trade imbalances. This time they were more receptive, realizing that their position was not tenable in the longer run.

During Chun's presidency, massive demonstrations and riots brought Seoul to a standstill from time to time. Toward the end of his term, they were endemic. Roh, as his key aide, moved skillfully to lower tensions and gathered support to run and win the next presidential election.

Roh Tae Woo was a quiet and serious man. When we first met in July 1986, he was a minister in Chun's cabinet. He spoke highly of Singapore's clean government. His president had tried to eliminate corruption but had found this not easy. How had we tackled it? I explained our system:

first, good intelligence; next, an impersonal, not a subjective approach; third, solid backing from the top for anticorruption investigation and prosecution. As his Democratic Justice Party (DJP) was not a communist party, I said he could not dispense with the existing bureaucracy and start afresh, but had to use it. He could slowly ease out older senior officials and bring in younger people who were untainted, and ensure they maintained high standards. They should be paid well. I emphasized, however, that unless the top leaders were beyond reproach, and the higher echelons cleaned up before the lower, it would be a waste of time.

I next met Roh in 1988 when he was president. He asked how I had stayed in power for so long, winning successive elections. Because, I replied, people knew I did not lie and was sincere in advancing their interests. Ordinary people could not follow the intricacies of an economic or a political problem, so they learned whom to trust. To win such trust, I never said anything which I did not believe in, and people slowly recognized that I was honest and sincere. This was my most powerful asset. It was also U.S. President Reagan's strength. He had good speechwriters. He worked on their drafts, using their ideas, but putting them into his own words. He did not allow himself to be "voiced over" by his speechwriters, so when he delivered a speech, he came across as a man of sincerity and conviction. I advised Roh not to compete with Kim Dae Jung in making powerful speeches. Roh had shown the people that he could keep cool in a crisis with massive riots and disorder before the election, and had shown humility. These were assets he should build on.

Roh had coopted Kim Young Sam, one of the two major opposition leaders, into his party. This enabled Kim to become the first elected civilian president in 1992. He made cleaning up corruption his major campaign issue. He sacked three cabinet ministers within weeks of their appointment for various corrupt practices, removed several senior judges, and sacked and imprisoned a number of senior military officers. The army acquiesced. Several Korean television and newspaper groups visited Singapore to do documentaries and articles on our anticorruption law and enforcement system.

In 1996, I met President Kim Young Sam when he visited Singapore. A dapper, well-dressed man, he proudly told me that he jogged many kilometers every morning. He said that we shared common values like the importance of the family unit and a social network to support the family. I added that our most important common interest was the strategic importance of the U.S. presence in Asia.

The situation in the North had changed dramatically. Kim described the leaders of North Korea as crazy and capable of irrational acts. They had an armed force of 1.1 million soldiers but their weapons were outdated, supply lines weak, and logistics vulnerable.

Kim had said when he took office that he would not reopen old issues. But as domestic pressures increased, he reversed his position in late 1995 and got the national assembly to pass a special law to lift the statute of limitations for the 1979 coup and for murder, sedition, corruption, and other crimes related to the 1980 Kwangju massacre, when the military had killed several hundred civilian protestors. His two predecessors were arrested and charged. I was startled to see them on television brought to court in remand prison clothes, handcuffed and humiliated. Chun was sentenced to death and Roh to 22 years and 6 months in prison for their role in the 1979 coup and 1980 Kwangju killings. Both were also fined for taking bribes during their presidential terms. On appeal, these sentences were later reduced to life sentence for Chun and 17 years for Roh.

Soon after, President Kim Young Sam himself was engulfed in a huge corruption scandal when a large chaebol (conglomerate), the Hanbo Group, collapsed, owing billions of dollars to several government-controlled banks. Kim's son was prosecuted for taking some US$7 million and sentenced to three years' jail, with a fine of US$1.5 million. The opposition alleged that Kim himself had received bribes from the Hanbo Group and that he had grossly exceeded the legal spending limits for his election. President Kim made a public apology on television, but refused to disclose details. The standing of the incumbent president and his ruling party collapsed after the widely publicized scandals of corruption and mismanagement of the economy. Because of the ensuing economic crisis, South Korea required the assistance of the IMF.

In December 1997, Kim Dae Jung, a veteran opposition leader standing for the fourth time, won the presidential election. He had forged an electoral alliance with Kim Jong Pil, the first Korean Central Intelligence Agency (KCIA) chief who had once ordered his capture.

As a prominent dissident, Kim Dae Jung had spent many years in the United States and become an advocate of the universal application of human rights and democracy regardless of cultural values. As an opposition leader, he had written an article in the magazine *Foreign Affairs* in response to my interview with the editor, Fareed Zakaria. He did not agree that history and culture made for different attitudes of a people and different norms of government. *Foreign Affairs* invited me to reply. I chose not to. The difference in our views cannot be resolved by argument. It will be settled by history, by the way events will develop in the next 50 years. It takes more than one generation for the political, economic, social, and cultural implications of policies to work themselves out. It is a process of attrition, of social Darwinism.

As the president-elect, Kim Dae Jung agreed to Kim Young Sam's pardon of the two former presidents then serving long terms of imprisonment for treason, bribery, and, in the case of Chun, murder. They were freed in December 1997 and attended the presidential swearing-in ceremony in February 1998. After his swearing-in, President Kim Dae Jung shook hands with Chun and Roh, a gesture of "reconciliation and harmony" in Korean society, as the presidential spokesman put it. It was staged before a crowd of 40,000. Whether this political theater restored the people's confidence in their system of government is open to question.

South Korea's political institutions would have suffered less damage if, like Mandela's government in South Africa, they had closed all past accounts. The Truth and Reconciliation Commission in South Africa forgave all those who had committed atrocities during the apartheid regime if they declared their previous wrongdoings. While it might not have achieved reconciliation, the commission did not worsen the divide.

Their trials not only destroyed Chun Doo Hwan and Roh Tae Woo, they also diminished the men who had helped to create modern Korea, leaving the people cynical and disillusioned with all authority. It will be some time before Koreans regain their esteem for their leaders. Chun and Roh had played by Korean standards of their time, and by those rules they were not villains. Pressured by American public opinion against having another military man as successor, Roh had allowed power to go into the hands of Kim Young Sam. These events have sent the wrong signals to military leaders in charge of other countries, that it is dangerous to hand over power to civilian politicians who seek popular support.

In 1999, I attended a meeting in Seoul as a member of the International Advisory Council (IAC) to the Federation of Korean Industries. At a forum on 22 October, IAC members had a discussion with the leaders of Korean chaebols. These chaebols are Korean versions of Japanese zaibatsus. In every major industry where zaibatsus have been successful, chaebols followed to compete with cheaper labor and lower costs. Like the Japanese, they went for market share, ignoring cash flow and the bottom line. As in Japan, the whole Korean domestic economy, especially the high savings of their workers, provided the base for chaebols to get capital at low interest rates and target specific industries.

With the end of the Cold War, the external situation changed. Like Japan, Korea had to open its domestic and especially its financial markets. Their chaebols had borrowed about US$150 billion in foreign currency for rapid industrial expansion in Korea and abroad—in China, the former communist countries in eastern Europe, the Russian Federation, and the central Asian republics of the former Soviet Union. These investments were not based on expected returns on equity but on aggressive expansion to capture market share. When they were unable to repay the interest due, toward the end of 1997 the Korean currency, the won, collapsed. The IMF came to their rescue. Three weeks later, Kim Dae Jung won his election as president.

I told the chaebol chiefs that Korea was at a crossroad. They could not continue with the old paradigm based on the Japanese model, because the Japanese themselves had hit the wall. Korea and Japan were now part of an integrated global economic and financial system, and would have to abide by the rules that the United States and the European Union had settled for the IMF, World Bank, and WTO. This required them to be as competitive in their investments, with the eye on the bottom line, as any American or European corporation. The question was how to get from where they were to where they must be if they were to be competitive.

Chaebols had grown into widespreading conglomerates. Now they should concentrate on what they had done best and make those their core businesses, hiving off their noncore businesses. Next, they needed managers who had entrepreneurial drive if their businesses were to thrive.

The chaebol leaders were pleased that I thought Confucianist culture had not caused their collapse, but that their weakness was their informal system of doing business and their disregard for the rate of return on equity and the bottom line. This was made worse by their not having open, transparent systems, level playing fields, and standard international accounting practices. Hong Kong and Singapore, both Confucianist societies, had withstood the financial storm because both had British systems of law, business methods that were transparent, accounting practices of international standard, open tenders and binding contracts negotiated on level playing fields, and bank loans made at arm's length. Korea had to adopt these practices. Korean business practice followed that of the Japanese, based more on informal relations and less on formal rules and the law. The chaebol leaders understood the need for such restructuring but were reluctant to give up family control of the corporate empires they had built up in the last four decades, and hand over the destinies of their constituent companies to managers who had been accustomed to leaving the entrepreneurial decisions to the founders.

After the IAC meeting, I called on President Kim Dae Jung at the Blue House. In his mid-seventies, he was broad-built and above-average in height for a Korean of his generation. He walked slowly with a limp, the result of an injury sustained from an attempt on his life in 1971, reportedly by KCIA agents. He had a serious, even solemn, expression, until he broke into the occasional smile. He posed a series of issues, starting with North-South relations. Methodically, he went through the items he had in mind. He wanted a critique of his policies, beginning with his "sunshine policy." The aims of this policy were, first, to prevent war by maintaining a strong deterrent stance; second, to reunify the two Koreas without damaging or threatening the North Korean regime; third, to create an environment in which the two could cooperate in economics and business at the private level.

I said it made sense to help the North Koreans change from within by transferring technology, management, and know-how and encouraging them to develop. North Korea could raise its standard of living and be less of a burden on the South. However, this must be accompanied by more people-to-people contact, particularly exchanges between think tanks, universities, and opinion formulators, to change their mental outlook.

He then asked for my assessment of Chinese–North Korean relations. I did not believe the chemistry between old leaders like Deng Xiaoping and Kim Il Sung existed between Jiang Zemin and Kim Jong Il. The older generation had fought together as comrades in arms in the Korean War. The present generation of leaders did not share that camaraderie. It was not in China's interest to have war and disorder in the Korean peninsula. What China wanted was a status quo that would enable trade with and investments from the South to continue. Neither was it in China's interest to have the two Koreas reunited. Then China would lose the North Korean card against the United States and South Korea. Kim had thought through his problems; he simply wanted my confirmation or contradiction of his views.

Kim impressed me by his stand on East Timor. The recent crisis and the Internet age, he said, had brought northeast and southeast Asia closer together. Although East Timor was geographically far from South Korea, the conflict had indirectly affected them. It would be better if all countries in Asia could cooperate as one, on a bigger scale. That was why he had decided to send combat troops (a battalion of 420) to East Timor, even though his opposition in the national assembly was against it. He had another reason: In 1950, 16 countries came to South Korea's aid and hundreds of thousands died in the Korean War. South Korea would have failed in its responsibilities if it did not help the UN in East Timor. Making northeast and southeast Asia one region, I believed, was a matter of time. The two subregional economies were increasingly intertwined.

The Korean media had expected us to discuss our differing views on Asian (i.e., Confucianist) values, and on democracy and human rights. I told them the subject was not discussed; we were both in our late seventies and unlikely to change our views. History will decide who had a better reading of Confucian culture.

In Kim I found a man who had been tempered through many a crisis. He had learned to control his emotions in order to achieve his higher purposes. He had been captured by the KCIA when he was in Japan and tortured, and would probably have been killed but for the intervention of the Americans. Yet in order to win the election in 1997 he formed an alliance with a former KCIA director, Kim Jong Pil, and made him his prime minister when he won the election.

A significant reason for South Korea's present political, economic, and social difficulties was that the transition from martial law to free-for-all democratic politics had been too sudden. They had no established tradition of law enforcement to control public assemblies or rules to regulate trade unions and require them to hold secret ballots before going on strike or taking industrial action. In Singapore, when we took office in 1959, the British had left us a whole set of subsidiary legislation for minor offenses, so when Emergency rule ended there were other means to keep public protests from going beyond tolerable limits and upsetting law and order. If the Koreans had democratized more gradually and had first put in place the necessary legislation to modulate demonstrations and protests, the people might have been less prone to excesses in their protests, especially the angry confrontations of workers and students with the police.

It will take some time to renew the social contract between leaders and people. They need to restore people's confidence that there will be fair play between the successful and the less successful, between the better and the lesser educated, between management and labor. In their dash for rapid growth, successive presidents allowed a policy that favored high rewards for industrialists, managers, and engineers as against workers, widening the wealth gap as their GDP rose. Once restored in a new social contract, Koreans will forge ahead with vigor again. They are a dynamic, industrious, resolute, and able people. Their intense culture makes them achievement-oriented.

After several false starts, the North and South Korean presidents finally met at a summit in Pyongyang on 13 June 2000. The live telecast of their meetings astonished South Koreans. The much maligned North Korean leader, Kim Jong Il, demonstrated warmth, humor and friendliness. A wave of euphoria swept South Koreans. Even the most skeptical were impressed. But doubts remain. Was this not the man who ordered the assassination of South Korean ministers at a wreath-laying ceremony in Rangoon in 1983 and the bombing of a South Korean airliner in 1987?

Within days, U.S. Secretary of State Madeleine Albright visited Beijing and Seoul. In Seoul, she said U.S. forces would remain in Korea. But if the thaw continues, she must expect the North to press for their withdrawal and the South to agitate in support. And if North Korea stops its missile development, it will remove the need for America's national missile defense system, which is to guard against a missile attack by a "rogue" state like North Korea, not China.

I met President Jiang Zemin in Beijing on the afternoon of that Korean summit. He was in high spirits, recounting with pleasure the handshake of the two leaders he had watched on television. Jiang had much to be satisfied about, Kim Jong Il having made a rare visit to Beijing to discuss the matter with him two weeks before the event.

# 34.  Hong Kong's Transition

I first visited Hong Kong in 1954 on an Italian liner, the *Asia.* She stayed three nights in Hong Kong, allowing Choo and me to wander around the colony on foot. It was a charming city on the island fronting the harbor, with a growing township across the water on the Kowloon side. It was attractive because behind the town center was the Peak, some 1,000 feet high with roads and houses dotting the hillside.

The people were hardworking, goods were cheap, service was excellent. I was taken to a shop one morning, had myself measured by the tailor, and ordered two suits. In the afternoon, I went back for a fitting. That night, the suits were delivered to my cabin, something Singapore tailors could not have done. I did not understand then that when the communists "liberated" the mainland in 1949, with the influx of some 1 to 2 million refugees from China had come some of the best entrepreneurs, professionals, and intellectuals from Shanghai and the provinces of Zhejiang, Jiangsu, and Guangdong. They formed a thick layer of talent that was to transform Hong Kong into one of the most dynamic cities in the world, helped by the more enterprising and resourceful of the Chinese workers who had decided to leave China rather than live under communist rule.

To the world at large, Hong Kong and Singapore are two similar Chinese cities of approximately the same size. To me there were as many contrasts as similarities. Hong Kong has twice the land area and twice the population packed on the island, Kowloon peninsula, and the New

Territories. Hong Kong had a bleaker economic and political environment in 1949, totally dependent on the mainland's restraint. China's People's Liberation Army could march in any time they were ordered to. But despite uncertainty and the fear of a disastrous tomorrow, or the day after, Hong Kong thrived.

Singapore did not then face such dire prospects. I was relieved we were not living so precariously under such intense pressures, as Hong Kong was. Even after Malaya became independent in 1957, Singapore was still linked economically and physically to the peninsula, with people and business to-ing and fro-ing. Only in 1965, after we were asked to leave Malaysia, did we face as bleak a future. But unlike Hong Kong we did not have a million and a half refugees from the mainland. Perhaps if we had, and with them had come some of the best entrepreneurs and the most industrious, resourceful, and energetic people, we would have gained that extra cutting edge. Indeed, a similar refugee inflow from the mainland in 1949 also helped Taiwan. Without it, Taiwan would not have had the top talent that had governed China until 1949. Their administration, with American aid, transformed Taiwan. When all this happened in 1949, I did not understand the importance of talent, especially entrepreneurial talent, and that trained talent is the yeast that transforms a society and makes it rise.

I next visited Hong Kong in May 1962. In eight years, it had moved way ahead of Singapore, judging from the buildings and shops I saw. After independence in 1965, I made a point of visiting Hong Kong almost every year to see how they handled their difficulties, and whether there were any lessons I could learn from them. I saw Hong Kong as a source of inspiration, of ideas of what was possible given a hard-driving society. I also wanted to attract some of their businesspeople, especially their manufacturers, to set up textile and other factories in Singapore. The Hong Kong media did not look kindly upon my efforts and wrote highly critical reports of Singapore to dissuade their people from leaving.

In February 1970, the University of Hong Kong conferred on me an honorary degree of Doctor of Law. In my address, I said, "As pioneers in modernisation, Hong Kong and Singapore can act as catalysts to accelerate the transforming of traditional agricultural societies around them. . . ." I hoped that "they may become dissemination points, not simply of the sophisticated manufacture of the developed world, but more vital, of social values and disciplines, of skills and expertise." A decade later they both did.

After this visit, I wrote to our Economic Development Board that with the political uncertainty because of China and the expiry in 1997 of the 99-year lease of the New Territories to Britain, Singapore could attract some of their brains and their skilled workers. We could also lend Hong Kong our skills and credit when they were short.

My admiration for Hong Kong's people and their capacity to bounce back after each setback never diminished. They suffered as grievously in the 1970s as Singapore did because of the oil crisis, but they adjusted more quickly. Their shops cut prices, their workers accepted pay cuts. The few trade unions they had did not fight market forces. In Singapore, we had to soften the blow of inflation and recession and buffer our workers from a sudden drop in living standards, helping to sort out problems between management and unions.

People in Hong Kong depended not on the government but on themselves and their families. They worked hard and tried their luck in business, hawking or making widgets, or buying and selling. The drive to succeed was intense; family and extended family ties were strong. Long before Milton Friedman held up Hong Kong as a model of a free-enterprise economy, I had seen the advantage of having little or no social safety net. It spurred Hong Kong's people to strive to succeed. There was no social contract between the colonial government and them. Unlike Singaporeans, they could not and did not defend themselves or their collective interests. They were not a nation—indeed, were not allowed to become a nation. China would not have permitted it, and the British never tried it. That was the great difference between Hong Kong and Singapore.

We had to be a nation or we would cease to exist. We had to subsidize education, health, and housing even though I tried to avoid the debilitating effects of welfarism. But the Singaporean cannot match the Hong Konger in drive and motivation. In Hong Kong when people fail, they blame themselves or their bad luck, pick themselves up, and try again, hoping their luck will change. Singaporeans have different attitudes to government and to life. They prefer job security and freedom from worry.

When they do not succeed, they blame the government since they assume its duty is to ensure that their lives get better. They expect the government not only to arrange a level playing field but, at the end of the race, to give prizes even to those who have not done so well. Singaporeans vote for their MPs and ministers and expect them to distribute whatever prizes there are.

A Hong Kong entrepreneur who settled in Singapore summed it up for me succinctly. When he established textile and garment factories in Singapore in the early 1970s, he brought his Hong Kong managers with him and hired several more Singaporeans. The Singaporean managers were still working for him in 1994, while his Hong Kong managers had set up their own businesses and were competing against him. They saw no reason why they should be working for him when they knew the trade as well as he did. All they needed was a little capital, and the moment they had that, off they went. The Singaporean lacks that entrepreneurial drive, the willingness to take risks, succeed, and be a tycoon. In recent years there have been encouraging signs of change. When the region was enjoying rapid growth, more young professionals and executives ventured out, first as salaried managers with incentive share options, and later on their own, when they knew the risks and were confident of making it.

We were able to attract some entrepreneurs in textiles, garments, plastics, and jewellery, a few jade and ivory carvers, and some furniture makers from Hong Kong. In the 1960s and early 1970s, they were most welcome for the jobs they created and the optimism they generated. The best stayed on in Hong Kong where they could make more profits than in Singapore. But they set up branches as we had hoped, and sent their younger sons to look after the Singapore branch.

After the 1984 Joint Declaration between the United Kingdom and China settling the colony's future was announced, I invited a group of their leading businesspeople and professionals to visit us during the week of our National Day celebrations that August. As a result, a group of Hong Kong tycoons together invested over S$2 billion in Singapore's largest convention and exhibition hall and office complex called Suntec City where we hosted the first ministerial meeting of the World Trade Organization in December 1996, a year after the building was completed. It was one of their many nest eggs scattered across the Pacific coastal cities, mainly of North America and Australasia. Their media believed Singapore wanted to cream off their talent, but it was in our interest to have Hong Kong succeed after it returned to Chinese sovereignty. To raid and deplete Hong Kong of talent is a one-off exercise. A thriving Hong Kong will be a continuing source of business and benefits.


Hong Kong's British rulers had governed in the old imperial tradition— haughty, aloof, condescending to the locals, and even to me, because I was Chinese. The earlier governors were promoted from the ranks of the British colonial service. This changed after 1971. Murray MacLehose was from the British foreign service, a superior service. He decided to visit Singapore before he took up his appointment. Hong Kong was plagued by corruption; he wanted to see how we had kept it under control. He wanted also to see what we had done in education, especially our poly-technics. Hong Kong had none; they had spent almost nothing on techni-cal education. He wanted to see our public housing; he wanted to improve their housing before conditions became critical.

The British provided an honest administration, except for some 10 years before MacLehose became governor. Corruption then was so bad that he had to introduce strong measures based on Singapore's anticorrup-tion laws and practices. Of course the colonial rules of the game favored the British business community. Hong Kong & Shanghai Bank and Chartered Bank were note issuers. The British hongs (big trading compa-nies, later to become conglomerates) enjoyed a privileged position, but their privileges were gradually diminished as British rule reached its last decade when many hongs were bought out by Hong Kong Chinese.

Before the next governor, David Wilson, took up his appointment in 1987, he too visited Singapore to see how a majority ethnic Chinese com-munity had organized itself and sought to resolve its problems. He was also a foreign service officer, a China specialist. Wilson wanted to know about Singapore's experience in gaining independence. I told him our cir-cumstances were different. We had been part of Malaysia, then unintend-edly became independent and had to manage our own destiny. The Special Administrative Region (SAR) of Hong Kong would be part of China. Any Hong Kong chief executive would have to understand China and learn to live with its leaders, while protecting Hong Kong's interests. He would not have complete freedom to act.

Until 1992, British policy was to consult and negotiate with China any basic change they proposed to make in policy before they announced it publicly. This was to achieve what the British called a "through train." In other words, there was to be no change of either engine or carriages when it came to the crossing point between British Hong Kong on 30 June 1997 and Chinese Hong Kong on 1 July 1997. After the shock of Tiananmen in 1989, the British government felt it should do something beyond what was agreed with the Chinese in the 1984 Joint Declaration. The British wanted to satisfy their conscience that they had done their best to protect the way of life of Hong Kong people after Hong Kong was returned to China.

Six weeks after Tiananmen, we offered to give 25,000 Hong Kong families Approval In-Principle (AIP) permanent residence, without their having to move to Singapore until the need arose. This AIP would be valid for five years and could be extended for another five. It did not draw talent away from Hong Kong at a time of great uncertainty. Huge queues formed outside our Singapore Commission in Hong Kong to get the application forms, and nearly caused a riot. When I met Governor Wilson in Hong Kong in January 1990, I assured him that I had no intention to damage Hong Kong by the offer of AIPs, that we would lend Hong Kong our skills and credit when they were short, and vice versa, and each would profit from the capital, skills, and talent of the other. We had not expected such a tumultuous response. Many who applied did not qualify, because they did not have the necessary education or skills. After a year, we had granted a total of 50,000 AIPs, double the intended number. By 1997, only 8,500 had moved to Singapore. Hong Kong soon recovered from the shock of Tiananmen and was doing well. The people earned good money in Hong Kong, more than they could in Singapore or elsewhere. Indeed, many who had emigrated to Canada, Australia, and New Zealand later returned to work in Hong Kong, often leaving their families behind.

Chris Patten, like his predecessors Wilson and MacLehose, stopped in Singapore in July 1992 on his way to take up his appointment in Hong Kong. After an hour's discussion, I sensed he wanted to stretch the limits of what the British had agreed with the Chinese and asked, "What cards do you have? What's new?" Instead of answering he simply repeated my question, "What's new?" I felt uneasy that he was contemplating reforms that would breach the agreement. Hong Kong journalists had come to Singapore to interview me after my meeting with Patten. To prevent any misreporting, instead of meeting them I issued a statement: "I believe if the objectives he [Patten] decides upon are within the framework of the Joint Declaration and the Basic Law, he will have firm grounds to govern and build upon . . . the best measure of his success will be that the system he leaves behind continues to work well for Hong Kong beyond 1997."

In October 1992, after a visit to China, I went to Hong Kong. Patten had announced that he would expand the electorate for functional constituencies representing businesspeople, professionals, and other special interest groups by including as voters all their employees. Interviewed by the press, I said, "Patten's proposals were very imaginative about increasing the depth of democracy. . . . Very ingenious. His proposals slip into the blank spaces of the Basic Law and the Joint Declaration." But I added, "[Patten's] blueprint resembled more an agenda for action of a nationalist leader mobilising his people to fight for independence from a colonial power, than a valedictory programme of a departing colonial governor." Privately, I cautioned Patten when I met him in Government House, that he had negated the meaning of "functional constituencies" because he had widened it beyond these functional groups of professionals or businesspeople for whom they were intended, to include all workers employed by them.

In mid-December, I returned to Hong Kong for a lecture at Hong Kong University. Patten, as chancellor of the university, took the chair. In answer to a question from the audience on his proposed reforms, I read out portions of speeches made in the House of Lords by two former governors, Lord Murray MacLehose and Lord David Wilson, and an interview by Sir Percy Cradock, Thatcher's political adviser who had negotiated with the Chinese. All three had made clear that Patten's course of action was contrary to what they, on the British team, had negotiated and agreed with the Chinese government. I thought it better to state my position in his presence so that he could reply if he wanted to. He did not.

Patten spent the last five years of colonial rule entangled in controversy with the Chinese government. The Chinese reacted to Patten's move with anger. If Britain wanted it that way, they were prepared to scrap the whole agreement. They announced that they would negate Patten's changes. In July 1993, the Chinese formed a preliminary working committee to prepare for the post–1 July 1997 period. In August 1994, the standing committee of the National People's Congress voted to replace the Legislative Council (Legco) and the urban and regional councils and district boards. The governor and the British government in London did not take this rejection seriously. Patten held elections in September 1995; he included nine new functional constituencies and had widened the electorate to include the whole working population of 2.7 million voters. The Chinese leaders declared that it would not recognize the electoral results, that the political structures being set up by the British were not in accordance with the Basic Law and the Joint Declaration and would be scrapped, and the legislative council reconstituted. The governor believed that the Chinese government would eventually acquiesce because not to do so would be to go against the people's wishes and would be costly internationally.

I had a glimpse of official British thinking after a discussion in May 1993 with Malcolm Rifkind, then under-secretary of state of defense, later foreign secretary. The British felt a sense of obligation to ensure that democracy was a basic way of life in Hong Kong by 1997, and they believed, even without a referendum, that that was the colony's desire. I said what many Hong Kong people wanted was to have nothing to do with China till the end of time. Since this was not possible, surely the best way forward, if they were to continue to thrive and prosper, was to get Hong Kong's administrators and potential leaders to get to know and understand their counterparts in China and learn to protect the island's special needs. Rifkind said they were trying to build an entrenched constitutional structure in Hong Kong to make it more difficult for China to destroy democracy, in effect to build a system of guarantees for freedoms which the West took for granted, such as freedom from arrest and freedom to travel. If that system were entrenched, it would be more difficult for China to destroy it. I said it would be an exercise in futility. Hong Kong's chief executive had to adjust and accommodate China's overriding interests. With only four years left, it was not possible to imbue Hong

Kong people with democratic values and cultural impulses which had never existed there. This was a test of wills that Britain could not win.

I came to the conclusion that the British were banking on the Americans to pick up the cudgels against China on human rights and democracy. America had the leverage in its trade deficit of US$20 billion for the year 1992, which was to balloon to US$40 billion by 1997. Another leverage was its yearly grant of Most Favored Nation (MFN) status for Chinese exports. But China could counter this by not cooperating on nonproliferation of nuclear material and missile technology capabilities.

The Western media wanted to democratize China through Hong Kong, or at least put pressure on China through democratic changes introduced into Hong Kong. So they backed Governor Patten's belated and unilateral political reforms. This encouraged some of the territory's politicians to believe they could behave as if Hong Kong could be independent.

More important than all these political moves between the British and Americans on one side and the Chinese on the other, was the dramatic, unexpected economic development that took place in China. After Tiananmen in 1989, when investors from the Western countries stayed away, Chinese entrepreneurs from Hong Kong, Macau, and Taiwan had ventured into China. In three years, they were doing well. They showed a skeptical world that *guanxi* or personal relationships—speaking the same language, sharing the same culture, and not following the rules—would make up for deficiencies in the rule of law. These overseas Chinese were so successful that in November 1993, at the second World Chinese Entrepreneurs' Convention in Hong Kong, I warned them that if their investments in China disadvantaged their own adopted countries, they would exacerbate their relations with their own governments.

Hong Kong stock and property markets had collapsed after the shock of Tiananmen at the prospect of the colony's return to China. Eight years later, China had achieved a complete turnaround in its economy, and Hong Kong was looking forward to continuing growth with a thriving China. As 1 July 1997 approached, the Hong Kong property markets and stock markets went steadily upward, demonstrating a confidence which no one could have predicted. Hong Kong businesspeople who had decided to stay, and nearly all did, had accepted the reality, that their future depended upon good relations with China. China's business done through Hong Kong would make the territory prosper until such time as Shanghai and other coastal cities built up their facilities.

I was in Hong Kong for the week before the handover on 30 June 1997 and met Tung Chee-hwa. In the six months since he had been chosen as chief executive-designate of the Hong Kong Special Administrative Region, he had undergone a sea change. From a very private person who had spent his life in the family shipping business, he found himself suddenly under the glare of the media, frequently questioned by tough journalists. He accepted that for Hong Kong to succeed, China must succeed. It was a sound basis for governing Hong Kong. I found the business and professional elite had adjusted psychologically to becoming a special region of China. So had the Hong Kong Chinese language media. Even the most irreverent of the Chinese newspapers, run by a maverick businessman who had abused and insulted Premier Li Peng, had toned down. The press knew what was out of bounds.

Governor Patten, however, continued his bickering with Beijing to the very end. British leaders boycotted the swearing-in of the provisional legislature, declaring it was in breach of the Joint Declaration. Chinese leaders were not invited to the British farewell, but would not have attended in any case. The Chinese had wanted their contingent of uniformed troops to be in Hong Kong before the arrival of Jiang Zemin for the handover ceremony at midnight on 30 June. At first the British refused but eventually they allowed some 500 troops with light arms to come in at 9:00 P.M. When the Chinese announced the day before the deadline that they would send some 4,000 more troops to Hong Kong at 4:00 A.M. on 1 July, the departing governor denounced this "appalling news." It was pointless. Sovereignty would have reverted to China at midnight on 30 June, and Hong Kong would already be Chinese territory.

In the early hours of 1 July after the handover ceremonies, I heard a crowd using battery-powered megaphones shouting slogans for 10 to 15 minutes. Later, I learned that some 3,000 demonstrators had done this with the police clearing the way for them in empty streets. Martin Lee, leader of the Democratic Party, was addressing crowds on continuing their fight for democracy from the balcony of the legislative council building. It was no revolutionary situation. The international media reported this ritual protest.

Strangely, the mood in Hong Kong was muted. People had had 13 years since the 1984 Joint Declaration to prepare for this moment. There was no jubilation at being reembraced by the motherland. But neither was sadness visible at the departure of the British, no fond farewells from the multitude at the farewell parade or when the royal yacht *Britannia* cast off its moorings to carry the last governor away. Patten had filled the last five years of British rule with acrimony. He had derailed the "through train" the Chinese had agreed to whereby the Legco elected in 1995 would have continued beyond reunification in 1997, and left behind a legislature with a less liberal set of rules for elections than if he had not unilaterally changed them.

As they took charge on 1 July 1997, Chief Executive Tung and his top officials ran into the East Asian financial crisis, although they did not know this until 1998. Thailand devalued its baht on 2 July, triggering off a rot that spread through the region, on to Russia, and then Brazil. The Hong Kong dollar's peg to the U.S. dollar forced Hong Kong to increase its interest rates. That brought down property, share, and all asset prices, causing a recession and unemployment. Dissatisfaction with the government increased. The expectations of Hong Kong people had changed. Under a foreign, colonial government they expected nothing but protection from the Chinese communists. Under a Chinese government of Hong Kongers, they expected much more. Hong Kong suffered from chicken flu, a rare virus that particularly threatened old people and young children. A million birds had to be killed; their owners demanded compensation and got it. When red algae destroyed the stock of fish farmers, they too demanded and were given compensation. Then an investment house went bankrupt; investors who had deposited their share scrips with it were compensated.

In Hong Kong for a conference in June 1999, I met many troubled people, including some old friends and several new acquaintances. They analyzed their problems with clarity but could not see the solutions. They recounted that at the tail end of empire, the British had relaxed their governance of Hong Kong. Rather than arouse protests and confrontations by implementing unpopular policies, they gave in to pressure groups, such as taxi drivers who had threatened a strike when the government wanted to phase out diesel for taxis to cut down pollution. Pressure groups have learned to counter and abort hard policies by mounting protests. Now with Hong Kong a part of China, their chief executive had no political strength to counter such action. Unlike the British governors, who took support from their Legislative Council (Legco) for granted, Tung faced legislative councilors, none of whom felt any obligation to support his policies. His civil service secretaries had no electoral mandate to back their views when challenged by the elected members in Legco.

Patten's attempt to strengthen the democratically elected legislative council failed. The Legco that was elected when Hong Kong was still under colonial rule was dissolved. There are deep divisions within the educated elite on how to go forward and make the present system work. The old system the British ran had been weakened and cannot cope with the new political situation. On one side are the pragmatists, businesspeople, and professionals who wanted to have a working relationship with the government in Beijing and were bitterly opposed to Patten's policies. On the other side are the academics, media, and professionals who wanted to build up as strong a constitutional defense against any heavy hand from Beijing as possible and, by garnering international support, especially from the United States, put pressure on China not to interfere in the affairs of the SAR. The pragmatists were not prepared to enter the political fray themselves, relying instead upon politicians in whom they had little confidence to stand up for them against Beijing. It was an unhappy situation. Few were prepared to come out and lead. To do so would mean having to face the reality that Hong Kong's interests can be advanced only if its leaders can win the confidence of the leaders in Beijing.

Hong Kong people will have to reconcile the competing sectional interests—employers like Li Ka Shing versus politicians playing for union and workers' votes, professionals and managers versus lower-paid white-collar workers—over who pays what taxes and who gets what subsidies for health, housing, and education. After balancing their competing sectional interests, they face the more difficult part, to define their basic collective interests and fight for them, not as a separate independent state, but as a

Special Administrative Region in China. This task is made doubly difficult because people in Hong Kong do not identify themselves as Chinese. Those born on the mainland tell pollsters that they are Hong Kong Chinese, those born in the colony call themselves Hong Kong people. When the SAR government proposed that the Chinese national flag be raised and the national anthem sung daily at all schools, 85 percent of parents opposed it. On the other hand, the tenth anniversary of Tiananmen drew some 50,000 people to a candlelight vigil. I suspect they were fearful more for what could happen to them in Hong Kong than a repeat of what took place at Tiananmen. In contrast, when the Chinese in China protested with outrage at the bombing of their embassy in Belgrade in 1999, only a handful of Hong Kongers put on a token demonstration outside the U.S. consulate.

One controversial decision Tung made was to seek the help of the National People's Congress (NPC) to overturn a judgment of Hong Kong's court of final appeal. A provision in the Basic Law gave the right of entry and abode in the territory to children born in China to Hong Kong residents. The court held that children, including illegitimate ones, of Hong Kong residents and the offspring of a mainland parent who only subsequently acquired permanent residence in Hong Kong, had this right of abode. The people of Hong Kong were alarmed when the government disclosed that over one and a half million people would eventually be entitled to enter Hong Kong.

In March 1999, the secretary for justice sought an interpretation of this provision of the Basic Law from the NPC standing committee in Beijing. The standing committee limited the right of abode to children of at least one parent who was a Hong Kong resident at the time of birth. The legal fraternity, the academics, and the media were critical, fearing that the government had created a precedent for the NPC to interfere in their judicial process. But most people supported the government's move and were not interested in legal niceties.

On 21 October 1999, at the 4th anniversary lecture of the Hong Kong Policy Research Institute, a think tank that does some work for the SAR government, I spoke of the problems of transition that had proved more difficult than anyone had expected. Hong Kong had been taken through a crash course on democracy and human rights by Governor Patten, supported by the U.S. and U.K. media. The aim was to etch in the minds of the people the principles of freedom of expression—especially of the press, popular elections with the widest franchise, a bill of rights to protect fundamental liberties, the rule of law, and independence of the judiciary—and to hand over to China an irreversibly democracy-minded Hong Kong. This led many in Hong Kong to assume that the economy would look after itself, that if they protected democracy and human rights, all would be well. It turned out otherwise.

Like every other country, Hong Kong people found their primary need to be their survival and well-being. People felt frustrated that the old system, where everybody worked hard for himself and nearly everybody succeeded, was no longer working. But there could be no return to the old system. Expectations and attitudes had changed. They had to move forward. As long as electoral politics was responsibility-free, their Legco was a chamber for political posturing to win votes in the next elections. The promises of their political leaders would never be tested because they did not have the responsibility to deliver on their pledges.

There were two ways forward. First, their legislators could become more realistic and work within the framework of a Special Administrative Region which was a part of China, and signal their acceptance of China's overriding national interests; in that case Beijing would probably allow a majority party to assume power after 2007 when the constitution would be reviewed. Or second, by a process of attrition, Beijing would wear down the recalcitrant politicians. Hong Kong people had up to 2007 to decide which way to go. The Hong Kong of old was history. Its future depended upon how its people acted to promote their group interests.

In one hour of questions and answers, I stated the obvious to the audience at the international convention center—1,200 of Hong Kong's political, business, and media elite—that if Hong Kong became just another Chinese city, it was of no value to China. What made Hong Kong useful to China was its strong institutions, management expertise, sophisticated financial markets, the rule of law, the transparency of legislation and regulations, a level playing field for all, plus a cosmopolitan lifestyle with English as the language of business. These made Hong Kong different.

Hong Kong faced two contrary pulls. To be useful to China, it must learn to work with Chinese officials and understand their different social, economic, and political system and mindset. But it must never allow those attitudes to affect Hong Kong for otherwise it would become just another Chinese city. It had to retain the characteristics that made it an indispensable intermediary between China and the world, as during British rule.

I expected much media criticism for stating hard facts. The response of the audience was warm; that of the media the next day was mild. Their reports caused professional groups to reflect on the choices they faced. They were in a situation completely different from the one Chris Patten had envisaged. The heavy hand of China was nowhere in evidence, but the heavy heart of the people of Hong Kong had immobilized them from moving ahead to define and work toward goals that were practical and achievable in their new circumstances. When British officials governed them, Hong Kong people did not have to act cohesively as a community. They were great individualists and daring entrepreneurs, willing to take high risks to earn big rewards for themselves and their families. Now they are faced with serious alternatives for their future; they must make these choices together as a special subgroup of the Chinese nation.

For the present, between the aspirations of the people of Hong Kong, who want more democracy to protect their comfortable, prosperous way of life, and the expectations of China's leaders, who want a Hong Kong that will be useful and mischief-free, there is a wide and deep gap. Over the next 47 years, both sides must move toward each other and converge. It may not be as difficult as Hong Kong people now fear. It will be two more generations before they meet in one country, one system. If the changes that have taken place in the one generation since Chairman Mao died continue at the same pace, the convergence should not be too uncomfortable.

# 35. Taiwan: The Other China

Their isolation made the Taiwanese keen to develop ties with Singapore in the early years. On our part, we were anxious not to be completely dependent on the Israelis for military training. Initial discussions began in 1967. They sent a top-level representative who saw Keng Swee, then defense minister, and me. By December, they had submitted a proposal for building up an air force. We were keen to train our pilots and naval officers in Taiwan; the Israelis could not offer such facilities. The Taiwanese defense ministry was helpful, but every now and again would hint that when their foreign ministry got wind of their defense assistance, they would require some form of diplomatic recognition in return. We made it clear that we could not give way on this.

When the Taiwanese did set up the "Office of the Trade Representative of the Republic of China" in Singapore in 1969, it was clearly agreed that this exchange of trade missions was not recognition of either state or government by the other. We did not want to get entangled with the mainland's claim to be the sole government of China, including Taiwan.

When the UN resolution for the admission of the People's Republic of China (PRC) came up, we voted for the resolution to admit China but abstained on the resolution to expel Taiwan. Our policy was to remain consistent: There was "one China," and the reunification of the PRC and Taiwan was an internal matter to be resolved between the two.

The links between Taiwan's National Security Bureau and our ministry of defense had resulted in their lending us some Taiwanese flying instructors and several technicians and mechanics to get our aircraft maintenance section started. When the director of their National Security Bureau proposed that I visit Taiwan to meet their premier, Chiang Ching-kuo, son of President Chiang Kai-shek, in Taipei in May 1973, I agreed. Premier Chiang and his Russian wife met Choo and me at the airport, drove with us to the Grand Hotel and showed us to our suite. The following day, we flew with him in his VIP Boeing 707 to an air base, where he put on a half-hour scramble-and-take-off demonstration by an airforce unit. Then we drove together to Sun Moon Lake, a holiday resort, where we spent two days getting to know each other.

At a dinner in Taipei, I met his foreign minister, finance minister, economic affairs minister, chief of general staff, and director of National Security Bureau, and so made the acquaintance of his top trusted aides. Apart from my good personal chemistry with Chiang Ching-kuo, the foundation of our relationship was that we were both against communism. The Chinese Communist Party was his mortal enemy and the Malayan Communist Party, which was linked to the Chinese Communist Party, was mine. We had a common cause.

He spoke English haltingly and his Mandarin was difficult to understand because of his heavy Zhejiang accent. He understood my English, and together with my Mandarin we were able to do without an interpreter. This was crucial in establishing empathy which later developed into rapport. I explained the geopolitical situation in Southeast Asia, how Singapore was viewed as a third China, after China and Taiwan. We could not deny our racial, cultural, and linguistic links, but the fact that we were against the Malayan communists reassured our neighbors that we would not be a Trojan horse for a communist China.

Our trade representative in Taipei reported later that the premier had a good opinion of Singapore and of me, and was pleased to have met me. One factor definitely helped: My daughter, then a young medical student, had accompanied us. She is Chinese-educated and speaks Mandarin fluently. Her demeanor identified her immediately as Chinese. It made a crucial difference to how Chiang Ching-kuo perceived my wife, my daughter, and me, and helped determine relations between Singapore and Taiwan. A close friendship developed between Chiang and me in an exchange of correspondence.

There was a total news blackout on my visit, both in Taiwan and Singapore. It was at my request, to avoid international attention and controversy.

When I visited Taiwan again in December 1974, Premier Chiang took a personal interest in my program. He lined up navy and marine corps units for a ceremonial drive-past, as for a visiting head of state, all without publicity. He also accompanied me to view his country's progress, including major construction works like the East-West Highway built through difficult mountain terrain.

During this second visit, I broached the subject of training our armed forces in Taiwan, because of Singapore's limited space. We had discussed it with his military staff several months earlier. He was sympathetic. By April 1975, we had reached agreement for Singapore Armed Forces training in Taiwan under the code name "Exercise Starlight." Valid initially for one year, it allowed us to train infantry, artillery, armor, and commando units, dispersed all over Taiwan in areas used by their equivalent forces. They charged us only for what we consumed and no more.

Chiang had a fair, round face, wore thick horn-rimmed glasses, and had a fairly rotund figure. He was calm and quiet, with a soft voice. He did not pretend to be an intellectual but had a practical mind and keen social intelligence. He was a good judge of character and surrounded himself with trustworthy people who would give him honest advice even when unwelcome. When he spoke, it was after careful reflection because he was not given to casual commitments. He could not travel freely abroad and found me an additional source of information on developments in America and the wider world. He would ask keen, searching questions on changes in the geopolitical scene. Until he became infirm in the mid-1980s, Chiang would accompany me around Taiwan on each of my visits of three to four days. In a free-ranging exchange, he would test on me his assessments and views of political events formed from reading reports. He felt his international isolation keenly.

From 1973 to 1990, I visited Taiwan once or twice a year, nearly always stopping over in Hong Kong. It was instructive and inspiring to see the economic and social progress of the Chinese in Taiwan, with 8 to 10 percent annual growth. From a low-wage, labor-intensive economy based on agriculture and manufacture of textiles, garments, and sports shoes, they moved steadily upmarket. At first, they pirated expensive medical, legal, and other textbooks which they sold at ridiculously low prices. By the 1980s, they were printing them under license on quality paper and in hard covers. By the 1990s, they were making computer chips, motherboards, PCs, laptops, and other high-tech products. I had observed a similar upgrading of the economy and living standards in Hong Kong. The rapid progress of these two maritime Chinese communities gave me great encouragement. I picked up useful pointers. If they could make it, so could Singapore.

The Chinese in Taiwan, without the straitjacket of communism and a centrally planned economy, were racing ahead. Taiwan, like Hong Kong, had minimal welfare. This was to change with the introduction of popular elections in the early 1990s. Their opposition in the legislature pressed for and got the government to implement medical, pension, and other social security benefits, so the budget ran into deficit. With a rambunctious opposition in the legislature, the government in the 1990s had difficulty increasing taxes to balance the budget. Fortunately, so far Taiwanese workers remain better motivated than their Western counterparts.

Chiang and his ministers were proudest of their advances in education. Every student was educated at least to junior middle school, nine years, and by the 1990s some 30 percent were university graduates. Their finance minister, K. T. Li, lamented the brain drain. From the 1960s, out of some 4,500 graduate students who went to America for PhDs every year, only 500 would return. As Taiwan rose in the economic league tables, Li set out to attract some of their best to return, those who had worked in top research laboratories and in the big electronic multinationals. He built a science park near Taipei and provided them with cheap loans to start their businesses in semiconductors. Their computer industry took off. These people had built up networks with Americans in the computer industry and acquired the knowledge and expertise that enabled them to keep abreast of the latest developments and to market their products. They were supported by locally educated Taiwanese engineers and technicians.

The 2 to 3 million mainlanders who came over with General Chiang Kai-shek's forces had included a thick layer of intellectuals, administrators, scholars, and entrepreneurs. They were the catalyst that transformed Taiwan into an economic powerhouse.

However, the mainlander elite in Taiwan knew they were in a difficult position in the long term. They were a minority of about 10 percent. Gradually but inexorably, both the bureaucracy and the officer corps of the armed forces, originally manned by mainlanders or their children, came to have increasing numbers of Taiwanese. It was only a matter of time before the Taiwanese, 90 percent of the population, swung their political weight. Chiang and his senior aides recognized this. They were selecting from among the Taiwanese those they considered the most reliable and dependable—people who would continue their policy to stand firm against the communists on the mainland, yet never go for an independent, separate Taiwan, which was anathema to the mainlanders.

By the mid-1980s, a younger generation of educated Taiwanese had risen through the ranks of officialdom. We changed our trade representative, who was from Chiang's own province of Zhejiang, to one who could speak the local Min-nan dialect, a subdialect of Fujian province. We could see a different Taiwan emerging. We had to know the Taiwanese in the bureaucracy associated with the Kuomintang (KMT), but steered clear of Taiwanese dissidents who wanted independence. Their organizations were illegal, and several were imprisoned for sedition.

In the mid-1980s, I noticed Chiang's health had declined markedly. He could no longer accompany me around Taiwan. From our conversations, I gathered he was being pressed by the U.S. media and Congress to democratize the political system. Chiang lifted martial law and began this process. His son Hsiao-wu, their trade representative in Singapore, had filled me in on his father's thinking. I told Chiang that to ensure Taiwan's security he had to retain the support not only of President Reagan, but also of the U.S. media and Congress because Reagan needed the backing of both. Later, Chiang allowed the unofficial opposition, which had been illegal, to participate in elections for the Legislative Yuan.

Chiang died in January 1988. He had enjoyed enormous domestic prestige which helped to manage the forces unleashed by his recent lifting of martial law. I attended his funeral. Also present to pay their respects were many Japanese and American leaders, former prime ministers and high office holders, but no current incumbents. It was a traditional

Chinese-style funeral. His body was taken to a temporary resting place outside Taipei, to be kept, like his father Generalissimo Chiang Kai-shek's, for eventual interment in their county in Zhejiang province, south of Shanghai.

Vice President Lee Teng-hui then took over. I had met him first as mayor of Taipei, then as the governor of Taiwan province. Occasionally, we played golf. He was competent, industrious, and deferential to his superiors, especially the president and the mainlander ministers. He was then a friendly self-effacing official, tall, with greying hair, thick glasses, and a wide smile. Before Chiang Ching-kuo chose him as vice president in 1984, several other native Taiwanese KMT leaders had been considered but thought less suitable. I assumed Chiang must have been absolutely satisfied that he was reliable and could be trusted to continue Chiang's policies never to allow an independent Taiwan.

For a few years President Lee Teng-hui continued the KMT's settled policy of one China and no independent Taiwan. He set out to win over enough of the old guard and a few of the young guard mainlanders in the KMT to take complete control of the party. All those in key positions who gave contrary views or unwelcome advice were soon removed, including Hau Pei-tsun, the premier, and Fredrick Chien Fu, his foreign minister who had advised against his visit to America in 1995. Lee rapidly democratized the system to place more Taiwanese in key appointments and strengthen his hold on the KMT and the country. The KMT old guard had earlier told me they expected and accepted the inevitability of this. But they did not know how swiftly President Lee would shift political power to the 90 percent majority through popular elections to the national assembly and Legislative Yuan. He transformed the KMT itself until eventually many left it to form the New Party, a move which seriously weakened the KMT's grip on power.

Once he had consolidated his position, President Lee began to express his feelings in words which caused the leaders in Beijing to conclude that he wanted to keep Taiwan separate from China for as long as possible. In 1992, President Lee announced his terms for reunification. He defined "one China" as the Republic of China, not the People's Republic of China. National reunification would only be achieved under a "free, prosperous and democratic China"—in other words, communist China must first become as democratic as Taiwan. I did not know then that this was intended as a fixed, unbridgeable position, not a starting point for negotiations.

In April 1994, President Lee gave an interview to Ryotaro Shiba, a well-known Japanese journalist. It was published in a Japanese magazine and never denied. In it, he said the KMT was a party of outsiders, that the Taiwanese people had suffered greatly under the occupation of outsiders, which included the KMT government, and that "Difficulties will lie ahead of Moses and his people. . . . 'Exodus' may be a kind of fit conclusion." For a president of Taiwan to talk of Moses leading his people to the Promised Land was a statement China could not ignore.

Native Taiwanese harbored a deep grievance against the mainlanders for the "2-28" incident. Around 28 February 1947, thousands of native Taiwanese were killed by Nationalist troops for expressing their resentment against the mainlanders who behaved not as liberators but as overlords. All public reference to this tragedy was suppressed, but it lived on in the memory of the local population and broke into the open when a Taiwanese became president. To his credit, President Lee kept in check any attempt to settle past scores.

Popular elections tend to reopen these old wounds and accentuate the divide between native Taiwanese and mainlanders. To appeal to the 90 percent majority, politicians emphasize their indigenous identity. They campaign in the local Min-nan dialect and ridicule mainlander opponents for their inability to speak the language. Some even question the allegiance of mainlanders to Taiwan.

Older mainlander leaders felt hurt by these divisive attacks. Mainlander scholars had helped build universities and nurtured many able native Taiwanese. Outstanding mainlander leaders like Premiers Y. S. Sun and Yu Kuo-hwa and Finance Minister K. T. Li had crafted the policies that transformed Taiwan from an agricultural into an industrial economy. They laid the foundation for Taiwan's considerable success.

A more grievous result of electioneering has been the growing involvement of triads (Chinese mafia or secret societies). The KMT's triad links date from prewar Shanghai days, when General Chiang Kai-shek used them to fight the communists. They accompanied him to Taiwan. A Taiwanese mafia has flourished and taken root. As long as elections did not lead to real power, the government was able to control them.

When the political system opened up in the late 1980s and elections became contests for real power, the triads soon discovered that they could get themselves elected into positions of power. By 1996, when 10 percent of the national and 30 percent of the local legislatures were secret society members, they were a political force. Corruption and vote buying have become entrenched. Once in office, they have to recoup their expenditure.

A free press has not been able to check corruption ("black gold") or suppress the triads which it has compared to the Sicilian mafia. They have become so powerful that when a notorious triad leader was killed by a rival gang in 1996, the secretary-general of the office of President Lee Teng-hui paid public homage by sending a traditional funeral scroll to win over his followers. The deputy legislative speaker and other prominent legislators were present at the funeral, as were several opposition leaders. The mafia has penetrated the construction industry, agricultural cooperatives, and even the baseball league. It has muscled its way into annual general meetings of listed companies and cash-rich temple committees, and even started recruiting members in schools.

In June 2000, two weeks after his appointment, the first non-KMT Justice Minister, Chen Ding-nan, said: "In the East Asia region, Taiwan has the most serious cases of corruption and has failed to do anything about it for the past 50 years. Lee Teng-hui is the source of Taiwan's black-gold politics. He knew where it was and did little more than talk about the need to combat it. That was the reason why former justice ministers were forced to step down because they took Mr. Lee's words to heart and tried to clean up. The atmosphere, the culture, the people—it can easily influence judges and police and even the legislative officials. We need them to take responsibility."

I received President Lee in Singapore in 1989, the first visit by a Taiwanese president to Southeast Asia. I extended him all the personal courtesies due to a visiting head of state. But although we had not then established diplomatic relations with the PRC, I decided the protocol level would not be that for a head of state. There were no flags, no guard of honor, no ceremonial trappings of a state visit. In all public statements, we referred to him as President Lee "from Taiwan," not "of Taiwan." Nevertheless, that visit raised his political profile in the region.

Because I had acted as a channel for messages between the two sides, the PRC and Taiwan chose Singapore as the venue for their first-ever talks, in April 1993. The Chinese named it "Wang-Koo Talks" after the surnames of the leaders who officially represented "unofficial" organizations on both sides. I met both delegation leaders separately and knew that they were entrusted by their respective presidents with different agendas. Koo Chen-fu, representing Taiwan, wanted to settle only technical matters like authentication of documents and the verification of lost registered mail; his president did not want any discussions on liberalization of trade, let alone reunification. Wang Daohan wanted these preliminaries to lead to substantive discussions on reunification. As expected, the talks did not improve relations.

President Lee is a voracious reader with an enormous capacity for absorbing information. He had been educated in Japanese schools in Taiwan when it was Formosa, a Japanese colony. During the war, he was among the few Taiwanese chosen to be educated in Japanese universities, in his case Kyoto Imperial University, second in prestige only to Tokyo Imperial University. He returned to Taiwan after the war to complete his university education in Taipei. Later, he went on to America for two stints, the second of which was in Cornell where he did a PhD in agricultural economics.

By preference, he proudly told me, he read four top Japanese papers every day and watched NHK TV by satellite from Tokyo. Even for books, he preferred to read Japanese translations rather than the English originals because he found them easier reading. Steeped as he was in Japanese history and culture, he did not think much of the mainland, either its history and culture or its present communist leaders, viewing them with the eyes of a Japanese-trained elite. He had a disdain for the communist leaders, and publicly called them "blockheads," "stupid," and "damaged brains." The Chinese leaders never returned these compliments, but I felt sure some desk officer in Beijing dutifully recorded them.

I found him self-confident, well-read, and well-briefed on every subject that interested him. But because of Taiwan's isolation, he could not understand why world leaders did not sympathize with Taiwan as the Japanese did. He considered Japan's sympathy and support for Taiwan of great importance. He also believed that if he followed the prescriptions of American liberals and the U.S. Congress for democracy and human rights, the United States would defend him against communist China.

I could not understand President Lee's position. An old friend of his explained that his Japanese training had imbued him with the bushido spirit of the Japanese warrior, and he considered it his mission to lead the people of Taiwan to the "promised land." Lee, this friend added, was also a devout Christian who would do God's will at all costs, fired by the bushido spirit.

In June 1995, after powerful lobbying, President Lee got the U.S. Congress to pass a unanimous resolution to give him a visa to visit Cornell, his alma mater. That visit and the speech he made at Cornell had a far graver impact than the U.S. Congress expected. I had feared some reaction, but did not realize the depth of China's distrust of President Lee and the implications they read into the U.S. president's decision to allow the visit. Later that year, in October, I asked Premier Li Peng why he was so convinced that Lee Teng-hui wanted independence. Li Peng said they had watched the whole video recording of Lee Teng-hui's speech at Cornell. Lee did not refer at all to one China, but emphasized Taiwan, and called it the Republic of China on Taiwan. This conviction led in March 1996 to the most serious confrontation between the two sides since the 1958 crisis in Quemoy. The Chinese deployed troops and conducted military exercises in Fujian province opposite Taiwan, and fired missiles that landed in waters near important seaports on Taiwan's west coast.

To moderate the situation, on 3 March 1996, I made this plea, "China's leaders have referred to me as an old friend. I am an older friend of Taiwan. If either one is damaged, Singapore will suffer a loss. If both are damaged, Singapore's loss will be doubled. Singapore benefits when both prosper, when both co-operate and help each other prosper." Vice Premier Qian Qichen, China's foreign minister, at a press conference said this was an internal matter, that although I knew more about Taiwan than most outsiders, this was not a matter that involved outsiders. This gentle rebuff did not surprise me as it was in keeping with their basic stand that this was an internal "Chinese" problem to be resolved directly between the leaders on both sides.

Meanwhile, President Lee began to deemphasize Taiwan's Chineseness. From the end of the war in 1945 until the death of Chiang Ching-kuo in 1988, their schools and universities taught in the national language (Mandarin). Students learned the history and geography of mainland China of which Taiwan was a province. Now, schools teach more of the history and geography of Taiwan, and less of China. As early as 1989, soon after Chiang died, I could sense the embarrassment of Premier Yu Kuo-hwa, a mainlander, who accompanied me on a visit to Taitung, an old Japanese hot spring resort. After dinner, in a karaoke session, the local Taiwanese ministers sang Minnan songs, which Yu did not understand.

During his 12 years as president, Lee voiced separatist sentiments that had lain dormant in Taiwan. He underestimated the will of the leaders and people of the Chinese mainland to keep Taiwan firmly within its fold. Lee's policies could only prevail with the support of the United States. By acting as though such support would be forthcoming for all time, he led the people of Taiwan to believe that they did not need to negotiate seriously on Taiwan's future with China's leaders. His contribution to Taiwan's future has been to turn the reunification issue into the most important item on Beijing's national agenda.

China's leaders closely watched the election campaign for the next president in March 2000. They were concerned with the rising support for Chen Shui-bian, candidate of the Democratic Progressive Party. Native Taiwanese nationalists who formed this party had long fought for Taiwan's independence and been imprisoned and punished by the KMT government under President Chiang Kai-shek and his son, President Chiang Ching-kuo. On February 22, 2000, Beijing media published a State Council white paper to warn that if Taiwan refused to discuss reunification indefinitely, China would have to use force. It was directed at Chen. On March 15, three days before the vote, Premier Zhu Rongji in a live television press conference warned the Taiwanese that China would shed blood to protect its territory.

Chen Shui-bian won with less than 40 percent of the vote against independent candidate James Soong, with 36 percent. The KMT candi-

date Lien Chan, the incumbent vice president, lost badly. President Lee
Teng-hui was seen to have abandoned Lien Chan by a perfunctory campaign speech in Lien's support. Several of Lee's closest friends endorsed
Chen. This added to the distrust of China's leaders for Chen. Beijing said
it would wait and see, listen to what Chen would say and watch what he
would do. Chen made conciliatory statements after he was declared the
winner but none of the statements committed him to eventual reunification. President Jiang Zemin said talks could only resume under the principle of One China. Chen said One China could be an item for discussion.
At his inauguration on 20 May, Chen said "both sides possess enough wisdom and creativity to jointly deal with the question of a future 'One-
China.' " He gave no cause for any precipitate action against Taiwan, but
did not say enough to shake the mainland leaders' beliefs that he would
continue the "Lee Teng-hui era, without Lee Teng-hui." Two hours after
the speech, the mainland said he lacked sincerity. Beijing will probably
wait until after they know in November 2000 who will be the next U.S.
president before deciding on their course of action. The stage may be set
for a dramatic face-off. If the new president equivocates and does not
agree to accept that Taiwan and the mainland are parts of one China, however defined, the situation will become volatile. No Chinese leader can
survive if he is seen to "lose Taiwan."

The new president has two choices: carry on where Lee Teng-hui left
off, which means conflict, or close that chapter and start a new one on a
realistic basis. Taiwan has been separated from the mainland for over a
hundred years since 1895. No Chinese in Taiwan relishes being reab-
sorbed into this huge mass of 1.2 billion. They prefer their different way
of government, lifestyle, and higher standard of living, which they have
worked hard to achieve. Even the mainlanders who have been in Taiwan
since 1949 and support reunification, do not want it in the near future.

The United States may be able to stop China from using force for
another 20 to 30 years. Within that time, China is likely to develop the
military capability to control the straits. It may be wiser, before the military balance shifts to the mainland, to negotiate the terms for an eventual,
not an immediate, reunification.

Assume that the worst has happened, that the mainland has used
force and caused the United States to react and decisively defeat the PLA

by superior technology. "Is that the end of the story?" I asked three American think-tankers soon after the elections in Taiwan. One replied, "That is the beginning of the story." He had thought through the problem. If superior U.S. technology frustrates them, it is not difficult to imagine 1,200 million Chinese being fired by one powerful urge, to show Americans they are not cowards and inferior.

For President Chen Shui-bian to continue Lee Teng-hui's policy of creating a separate and distinct Taiwanese national identity will confirm Beijing's suspicions that he has set Taiwan's course of independence. This will increase the danger of a precipitate solution to the issue of reunification. If Taiwan becomes an independent nation, Lee Teng-hui will go down in Taiwan's history as a hero. If Taiwan is reunited with the mainland by force, history will not be so kind to a man who brought unnecessary pain and suffering on the Chinese people in Taiwan.

The Chinese people on both sides of the straits can lessen their problems by establishing easier relations over the years. If there is to be a peaceful reunification, there has to be a gradual blurring, not an accentuation of the differences that at present divide and distinguish the two societies. Both need time to work and narrow the social, economic, and political gap. The sense of belonging to the Chinese nation is weaker in Taiwan than in Hong Kong. The mainland has the weight and girth to accept this and adopt an open and magnanimous approach to help this process of reconciliation. Reunification achieved by force will leave indelible scars. On the other hand, Taiwan's leaders have the responsibility not to move toward independence or deliberately widen the differences between the two societies.

# 36.  China: The Dragon with a Long Tail

No foreign country other than Britain has had a greater influence on Singapore's political development than China, the ancestral homeland of three-quarters of our people. The Singapore-China relationship has been long, complex, and unequal. From the founding of Singapore in 1819 until 1867, Qing dynasty China did not recognize the existence of the overseas Chinese. This changed in the 1870s when China set up consulates in Nanyang (the South Seas), then under the colonial control of the British, French, and Dutch. These consulates, including one in Singapore, were intended not so much to protect the Chinese as to harness their loyalty to China by promoting Chinese culture and education, and to obtain their financial support.

In the 1920s, the Chinese Communist Party (CCP) sent an agent to Singapore to build up a communist movement in Nanyang. When the communists held a secret meeting in Singapore in 1930 to found the Malayan Communist Party (MCP), Ho Chi Minh, the legendary Vietnamese communist leader, was present. The rivalries and conflicts between the Kuomintang Nationalist Party (KMT) and the CCP in China extended to their supporters in Singapore and Malaya. During the war both the KMT and CCP fought against the Japanese in China. Because of their stronger anti-Japanese resistance activities, the CCP enjoyed greater support from Chinese workers and farmers.

The rise of communist China in 1949 inspired an intense patriotic pride that surged through the Chinese-educated community in anticipation of the emergence of a powerful China, one that would banish their sense of humiliation and subjugation at the hands of the British and other Europeans. On the other hand, it aroused deep-seated fears among Malays, Indians, English-educated Chinese, and a minority of the Chinese-educated who supported the KMT. In 1949, both the KMT and the CCP were proscribed in Singapore, but the division of the community between the two remained.

The People's Republic of China (PRC) aimed to increase the loyalty of the overseas Chinese to Beijing. In 1949, it formed the Overseas Chinese Affairs Commission and began radio broadcasts. It supported Chinese education overseas and encouraged the Nanyang Chinese to send home to China their sons for education and remittances for their relatives. It also appealed to qualified doctors, engineers, and teachers to return and help rebuild the motherland. It was a subversive challenge to the colonial governments and to the newly independent governments of Southeast Asia in Indonesia and, later, Malaya. Radio Beijing, the *People's Daily,* and the *Beijing Review* regularly denounced Malaysia as a neocolonialist plot to persecute people of Chinese descent.

The Tunku and other Malay leaders feared Beijing's influence over the MCP and over the bulk of their Chinese-speaking population. When in 1963 Zhou Enlai wrote to me a letter similar to that addressed to many other heads of government, calling for the removal and destruction of nuclear weapons, I gave him a bland reply that such a solution would be welcomed by all. This was while we were a self-governing colony and not a state in Malaysia. When my letter to Zhou was made public by China in 1964, after we were in Malaysia, the Tunku publicly reprimanded me for having "entered into direct correspondence with a government which Malaysia does not recognise and which has proved by word and deed to be hostile to Malaysia."

In January 1965, Premier Zhou Enlai had condemned the formation of Malaysia in a speech to an Indonesian delegation in Beijing. After independence, we had no diplomatic contact with the PRC. Indeed, up to 1970, Beijing did not recognize the existence of an independent Singapore. PRC broadcasts and publications referred to Singapore as "a part of Malaya." Malaysia, too, did not exist because it was "a neocolonialist plot." Their propaganda regularly condemned "Singapore authorities" for their "criminal armed suppression of Singapore people." In 1966, the All China Federation of Trade Unions sent a telegram to left-wing unions in Singapore expressing the indignation of Chinese workers at the "barbarous acts of suppression of the workers perpetrated by the Singapore authorities who are tailing behind U.S. and British imperialism." I was attacked by name in 1968 when Radio Beijing reported Lee Kuan Yew as a "running dog of U.S. and British imperialism."

When the Cultural Revolution in China was at its height, we used to confiscate large quantities of Chinese stamps bearing "Thoughts of Mao" imported by some Chinese-language bookshops, and also thousands of copies of Mao's little red book brought in by Chinese seamen who wanted to distribute them. Even the Singapore branch of the Bank of China joined in this madness and gave out Cultural Revolution propaganda pamphlets to customers at their counters. We arrested and prosecuted our own citizens who indulged in this frenzy, but left Chinese nationals alone to keep open the trade with China.

In late 1970, Beijing quietly changed its stance toward Singapore. In those capitals where we were represented, our heads of mission were invited to China's national day receptions. China's priority then was to get as many governments as possible to close ranks against the Soviet Union and check the expansion of its influence into Southeast Asia. The Soviet intervention in Czechoslovakia in 1968 and border clashes between Chinese and Russian forces across the Amur River in 1969 had rendered China's revolutionary antics dangerous. They were weakening China's capability to resist Soviet aggression.

By 1971, China stopped public attacks on the Singapore government. That year, the Bank of China's branch in Singapore hoisted the Singapore flag on our national day, something it had not done before. Trade between our two countries had always been in their favor. Singapore then was China's second biggest foreign exchange earner after Hong Kong. We were not concerned over this adverse balance of trade because we were an entrepôt economy. But we required all Singapore Chinese firms that dealt with China to be registered with a government agency that controlled trade with communist countries. Thus, a franchise from the Chinese side had to be matched with a permit from the Singapore government.

The first contact came through "ping-pong diplomacy" in 1971. We allowed a Singapore ping-pong team to accept an invitation to play at the

Afro-Asia Table Tennis Friendship Games in Beijing. A few months later, a second delegation went for the Asian Table Tennis Union. We then accepted a Chinese offer to send their ping-pong team for a friendly visit to Singapore the following year, a few months after President Nixon had been to China. We had refused two previous offers, one of a troupe of acrobats, the other a Beijing trade mission. Raja as foreign minister thought a third rebuff would be unnecessarily offensive. During the friendly ping-pong matches I was angered when a large part of the audience jeered at the home team and shouted slogans in praise of Mao. I publicly castigated these infantile left-wingers as Singapore's "mini-Maos."

The PRC had also altered its position toward the overseas Chinese. Malaysian Prime Minister Razak had sent a delegation to Beijing in May 1974, a year before the fall of Saigon. After its return, the Malaysian government sent us an aide-mémoire on their discussions. The leader of their delegation had posed two questions to Premier Zhou Enlai: first, on their policy toward the overseas Chinese; second, on their support for the MCP. Zhou replied that the term "overseas Chinese" was not accurate as many had already taken up citizenship of their countries of residence. They were conservative by nature and had become a great problem in the PRC's relations with these countries. The "new China" had a new revolutionary policy toward the "so-called overseas Chinese." It had dissolved the Overseas Chinese Affairs Commission to discourage Chinese overseas from thinking of returning to China. China would not interfere if any country with a Chinese population abolished Chinese newspapers and Chinese schools. As for the MCP, the question had to be "viewed from an historical perspective." The PRC had always supported "liberation movements" to free themselves from colonial oppression. But only support from inside the country, and not support from the PRC, could make such a movement succeed. Therefore, if countries of Southeast Asia and China had a forward-looking view, relations could be improved and they could have diplomatic relations.

Since 1969, China had required overseas Chinese who visited China to apply for visas, where previously they had been allowed free entry. They had decided it was not possible to have their cake and eat it. If they wanted normal diplomatic relations with the countries of Southeast Asia that had Chinese populations, they had to give up their principle of jus sanguinis (the law of the blood), that any person descended from a Chinese father was automatically a Chinese national.

In October 1971, our permanent representative at the United Nations, when voting for the admission of the PRC, said, "There is one China and that Taiwan is a part of China. . . . It follows therefore that the Taiwan question is an internal matter to be settled by the Chinese peoples including those of Taiwan." But we still did not have official exchanges with the PRC. After the Malaysian government established relations with the PRC in May 1974, I thought it was time for Singapore to initiate formal contacts with the PRC government. I agreed to Raja's visiting China in March 1975.

We believed that uppermost in Chinese minds was Singapore's relations with their bitter adversary, the Soviet Union. Qiao Guanhua, the Chinese deputy foreign minister, had met Raja in October 1974 at the UN, and asked about Russian ships repaired in Singapore. Raja explained that we did not discriminate against any country that wanted to have its ships repaired; we were an open port. But he assured Qiao that we would not allow Singapore to be used for subversive activities against neighboring countries, and our neighbors included China. Raja repeated this position to Zhou Enlai when they met, adding that as our neighbors were hypersensitive over Singapore's Chinese majority, we would establish diplomatic relations with China only after Indonesia had done so. We had to avoid any suspicion that Singapore was influenced by kinship ties with China. Premier Zhou said China respected Singapore as an independent state. We had a more compelling reason which they might have guessed; we wanted to first weed out communist subversives in our Chinese middle schools and Nanyang University. We also needed time to reduce the number of those born in China and vulnerable to chauvinist appeals who were in positions of influence in various associations including the Chinese Chamber of Commerce. We had seen how susceptible the China-born were to pulls of sentiment and blood.

Premier Zhou sent me an invitation to visit China through Thailand's Premier Kukrit Pramoj who visited Beijing in June 1975. I did not respond. In September 1975, when I was visiting the Shah in Teheran, his prime minister, Hoveida, also conveyed Premier Zhou's invitation to me, adding that time was short. I took this to mean that I should come soon if we were to meet. There had been numerous press reports of Zhou being in hospital for long periods. I decided to go. But before we could settle on a date in May 1976, Zhou died. We announced the proposed visit in mid-April. A few days later Raja restated the government's position, that Singapore would be the last Asean country to exchange diplomatic representations with China.

This trip to China was my most thoroughly discussed and prepared foreign visit. We knew from other delegations that the Chinese were systematic and would probe every member of the delegation for information. We settled a common line on key issues for all senior members of my delegation. First, the question of recognition and diplomatic relations: We could not change our basic position, that we would move only after Indonesia had established relations; we had to be the last in Asean. Second, Soviet activities in Singapore: We would not allow the Soviet Union to engage in any anti-China activity, but as a free economy we had allowed the Soviets to open a branch of their Moscow Narodny Bank to conduct trade relations. The Chinese feared the Russians were buying the support of Chinese business leaders. We decided to assure the Chinese that we did not view a strong China with suspicion. We were neither pro-Soviet Union nor pro-China. We were pro-West because that was in the interest of Singapore and its neighbors. We were fully aware of Soviet activities in Singapore and the region and would keep such activities under close watch.

We expected them to push for liaison offices or trade representatives and decided to make it clear that this had to wait until they had established similar offices in Jakarta. However, we would concede one PRC representative of the Bank of China to work in its Singapore branch. While we wanted to encourage them to expand their trade with Singapore and were willing to allow relatively innocuous cultural and sports exchanges like ping-pong and basketball teams or acrobatic troupes, we did not want to hold out any false hopes for more; nor did we wish to antagonize the Soviet Union. On Taiwan, we would reaffirm our policy of recognizing only one China, namely the PRC. Most important of all, as we expected them to characterize Singapore as a "kinsman country," we decided to emphasize our distinctiveness and separateness from them.

I asked for a lengthy visit to see as much of China as possible. They fixed it for 10–23 May 1976. To make doubly sure that no one doubted we were not going in as kinsmen Chinese, we had in our 17-member delegation a Jaffna Tamil foreign minister (Rajaratnam) and a Malay parliamentary secretary (Ahmad Mattar), who would be present at all meetings, which would be conducted in English.

There was no direct flight from Singapore to Beijing. We flew to Hong Kong, took the train to Lo Wu at the border with China, and walked across the frontier to board the Chinese special train for Canton. That afternoon we were flown in their British-built Trident to Beijing where a welcome ceremony awaited us at the airport. I inspected a guard of honor mounted by units of the People's Liberation Army, the navy, and the air force after the PLA band played the Singapore and Chinese national anthems. Then some 2,000 schoolgirls in colorful costumes waved Singapore and Chinese paper flags and flowers, chanting "*Huan ying, huan ying*" (welcome, welcome) and "*Re lie huan ying, Re lie huan ying*" (warmly welcome, warmly welcome). There was a large banner in Chinese which read *jian jue zhi chi xin jia po ren* (resolutely support the people of Singapore). They did not express support for the *government* of Singapore. Unlike their usual reception for heads of government of countries with whom they had diplomatic relations, there was no welcoming editorial in the *People's Daily* and the diplomatic corps were not at the airport to greet me. Otherwise, they laid on full protocol honors for my visit.

Premier Zhou had died that January. Deng Xiaoping had been rusticated and was not in Beijing. I was received by Hua Guofeng. He looked and acted like the tough chief of security of a communist country that he had been. Our public positions were made at the formal state banquet on the night of 11 May. He complimented us: "In international affairs, Singapore opposes hegemonism and power politics, stands for peace and neutrality of Southeast Asia, actively develops relations with other Third World countries and has contributed positively to promoting economic exchanges and trade among nations." Then he read out his standard denunciation against superpower hegemony, referring indirectly but obviously to the Soviets who were carrying out infiltration and expansion in Southeast Asia after the American withdrawal from Vietnam.

I replied, "History brought together Chinese, Malays and Indians in Singapore. We are proud of our own heritage. Sharing a common experience, we are developing a distinctive way of life. By geography, our future will be more closely interlinked with those of our neighbours in Southeast Asia."

We had three formal meetings for a total of seven hours. At the first three-hour meeting in the Great Hall of the People on 11 May, Hua Guofeng invited me to speak first. I spelled out the basic facts concerning Singapore. Malaysia and Indonesia suspected Singapore of being pro-China because we were 75 percent Chinese. The Americans and Russians were also suspicious. Singapore had its work cut out not to be seen in these simplistic terms—that because we had a Chinese majority we must therefore be pro-China. The problem was that there were sections of our Chinese who were chauvinistic, the old generation born in China, but they were an aging and diminishing group. In addition there was a younger generation, completely Chinese-educated, who were unable to master the English language and unable to get good jobs; although not as emotionally attached to the fatherland as those born in China, they tended to be pro-China, and some of them pro-communist. We had to prevent them from doing Singapore harm.

Singapore would not be anti-China, I continued. The stronger China became, the better and more equal the balance between the United States, the Soviet Union, and China. This would be safer for the world and for Singapore. If China concluded that an independent Singapore was not against China's interest, then many of the differences between our two countries would diminish. On the other hand, if they believed that an independent Singapore was against its interest or if China therefore wanted to help install a communist government, then disagreements were bound to increase.

Instead of answering my points, Hua launched into his script, an analysis of the "Three Worlds" which was then China's standard exposition of the international situation. It was couched in strong revolutionary language. The current international situation would speed up the decline of the superpowers and promote the awakening of the Third World. The

United States and the Soviet Union belonged to the First World, developing countries in Asia, Africa, Latin America, and other parts of the world (China and Singapore included) belonged to the Third World, and the developed countries were the Second World. The United States and the Soviet Union were competing for world hegemony. The United States was overstretched and the Russians wanted to dominate the world. As long as they both continued this contest, the world was heading for another war. All countries should therefore be prepared for such an eventuality. However, China viewed both the United States and Russia as "paper tigers"; their strength did not match their ambitions. In carrying out their policy of expansionism and aggression the Russians were bound to be defeated. China was concerned that one wolf (U.S.) should not be replaced by a tiger (Russia) at Asia's backdoor. His speech was in the stilted language their radio and newspapers used when berating imperialists and revisionists.

On 12 May, just before the second talks were to begin that afternoon, their protocol officer suddenly rushed to the guesthouse to tell us that Chairman Mao would receive us. Visiting VIPs were usually not given any appointment to see the chairman. After they had sized up the visitor, if they thought it appropriate they would inform him at short notice that he would be given this signal honor of meeting their great leader. My wife and daughter were summoned back from sightseeing at the Summer Palace of the Empress Dowager without being told the reason. Select members of the delegation—myself, my wife and daughter, Rajaratnam (foreign minister), Hon Sui Sen (finance minister), and K. C. Lee (minister of state for culture)—were driven in a convoy to Mao's secluded residence.

The cars turned into an old walled-off enclosure opposite the Great Hall of the People, called Zhongnanhai, near Tiananmen Square. We went through lacquered gates into a complex of Chinese-style low-rise villas sited around a lake, stopped at one of the villas, and were ushered in. In the drawing room was "the great helmsman," Mao Zedong, in a light grey Mao suit, supported by two female aides. We shook hands. Then we all sat down, correctly and properly, taking care not to cross our legs, a gesture of disrespect. For some 15 minutes, Mao spoke indistinctly and a middle-aged woman repeated his words in Mandarin in a high-pitched voice. On several occasions, she wrote down some large Chinese characters to show to Mao who confirmed that that was what he had said. Then it was translated into English. It was not a substantial conversation. They had extended a courtesy to the Singapore delegation to signal that they considered us important enough. He no longer possessed the sharp intellect which Nixon and Henry Kissinger had described so eloquently after their meetings in 1972. I thought Mao had difficulty articulating not just his words but also his thoughts. I guessed he had Parkinson's disease. At 82, he looked mentally and physically frail.

The next day their major newspapers, including the *People's Daily*, carried a front page photo of him with me seated on his left. The photo showed him better than he was face-to-face. Years later, I kept being asked by journalists and writers what he was like. In all honesty I could only say I did not know. What I had seen was a shadow of the man who had led the Long March, built up a guerrilla army into a powerful fighting force, fought the Japanese in guerrilla actions until their surrender in August 1945, defeated the KMT Nationalist Army, and ultimately made the Communist Party supreme in China from 1949. He did liberate China from poverty, degradation, disease, and hunger, although famine killed millions because of his Great Leap Forward in 1958. But he did not liberate the Chinese people from ignorance and backwardness. Yes, "the Chinese people have stood up" as Mao proclaimed at Tiananmen on 1 October 1949, but they do not yet stand tall.

I had my second meeting with Hua at the Great Hall of the People for two hours later that afternoon. He continued in the same language of the day before, that as a socialist country China firmly supported the struggle of Third World countries in opposing imperialism, colonialism, and hegemonism. Likewise, it supported the revolutionary struggles of all countries, and the Chinese Communist Party (CCP) had relations with many Marxist-Leninist parties in the world but did not interfere in the internal affairs of other countries. Party relations were one thing and state relations were another. I said I did not understand the logic of these statements. Instead of meeting my argument directly, he said how the Malaysian government dealt with the MCP and its activities and what their relations with each other should be were "altogether an internal matter of the Malaysian government."

On Indochina, he emphasized China's "international duty" to support the peoples of Vietnam, Laos, and Cambodia in resisting "U.S. aggression." Soviet efforts to interfere and sow discord were unlikely to succeed as these countries would not give up their hard-won independence to another big power. It was a hint of the Sino-Soviet contest and impending problems with Vietnam.

This ended the two formal meetings in my program. The following afternoon could be "talks or rest." We spent the morning of 13 May visiting the Great Wall and the Ming tombs. It was warm, dry, and dusty. We were all thirsty. We ended up with a full Chinese lunch which I washed down liberally with beer at a restaurant near the Ming tombs. As we drove back in the Red Flag limousine without air-conditioning, I felt drowsy.

When we arrived at the Diaoyutai guesthouse, the protocol officer was standing at the door to say that Premier Hua was waiting to have a meeting with me. They had given us no notice during the whole morning that there would be a meeting that afternoon, or I would not have gone on that long, tiring excursion. The program had stated either a meeting or tour of the Temple of Heaven. Since they had taken us on such an exhausting journey to the Great Wall and the Ming tombs, we had assumed that the afternoon was free. I was fatigued from the walk up the Great Wall and drowsy from the beer at lunch and the hot, dusty, 90-minute drive back. Their tactics reminded me of those of the communist cadres in Singapore who often tried to wear us down. I went upstairs to wash with cold water, drank several glasses of Chinese tea, and freshened up as best I could. I went down at 4:00 P.M. to what was to be a two-hour meeting.

We spent some time fencing over the niceties of party-to-party and government-to-government relations. I asked, "Will you support an Indonesian communist party which sets out to liberate Singapore or consider that an unjust war?" He replied, "The question is hypothetical and does not exist. The Indonesian invasion of East Timor was wrong. The people of East Timor should have the right to choose their own social systems and government." I persisted, "Is the Malaysian Communist Party, calling itself the Malayan Communist Party, right or wrong to want to liberate Singapore?" He replied, "It is for the people of Singapore to choose their own social system and their own form of government." I asked, "Then am I right that China will not support the liberation of Singapore by the Malayan Communist Party, because such a liberation should be by the people of Singapore, not the people of Malaysia?" He looked puzzled because he did not know that the Malayan Communist Party wanted to liberate both Malaya and Singapore.

At this stage, Qiao Guanhua scribbled furiously and passed him a note. Like the tough security chief he was, he ostentatiously pushed aside the note without reading it, and said he did not know what the situation was, but wherever communist parties fought for liberation, they were bound to win because that was the tide of history.

I explained that the MCP claimed to be the communist party to liberate both peninsular Malaya and Singapore. So it would be useful at some stage for the PRC to make its position plain: that government-to-government relations with Singapore would be correct; however, any party-to-party relations should be between the Chinese Communist Party and a communist party of Singapore that sought to liberate Singapore, not a party of Malaysia or Malaya like the MCP.

Hua repeated that it was not possible for a foreign power to impose a socialist system on another country, if that was what I feared. I pressed him to clarify China's stand on principle that it was wrong for a Malayan communist party to liberate people in Singapore. He fudged, saying he had not studied the matter. I repeated my question but he still refused to clarify his position.

Instead he went on the offensive, raising the main purpose of the meeting, Singapore's military links with Taiwan. He began softly, that there existed long-term traditional friendship between the peoples of China and Singapore, a "kinsman-like relationship" between the Chinese people and the people of Chinese descent in Singapore. He hoped relations would further improve after my visit. Then he became stern and in a serious tone said we had developed a "military relationship" with the "Chiang clique from Taiwan." This was in contravention of the one China position of the Singapore government and not beneficial to the development of relations.

I refused to be defensive. Yes, Singapore recognized that there was one China and that Taiwan and the mainland were one country. However, for the time being, the Nationalist government that retreated from the mainland was in charge of Taiwan. I had to deal with the de facto authority in Taiwan. If the PRC were in physical charge of Taiwan I would have approached the PRC for training facilities. Singapore must have the ability to defend itself. Because of our limitations of air, sea, and land space, we have had to do our training in Thailand, Australia, and New Zealand. Before starting full-scale training in Taiwan in 1975, our foreign minister, Rajaratnam, had informed their foreign minister, Qiao Guanhua, that this move did not in any way reflect a change in our position of recognizing one China. Qiao Guanhua had not responded to Raja.

Hua Guofeng concluded by stating that given the different social systems of the two countries, important differences existed. These did not matter, because both sides had found many common points through a frank exchange of views. Hua had pressed me as far as he could.

I said the front page publicity in the *People's Daily* of my meeting with Chairman Mao would not be received with joy in Southeast Asia. It was better for China not to send a trade mission to Singapore until our neighbors' suspicions from this publicity had subsided. The more China embraced us as "kinsman country" the greater would be our neighbors' suspicions. It was difficult because Singapore's neighbors had significant Chinese minorities who played a disproportionate role in the economy and their economic success had aroused the jealousy and resentment of the indigenous peoples. Where they were of different religions, there was little intermarriage as with the Muslims in Malaysia and Indonesia. This was a never-ending problem that China had to take into account. It was an important underlying factor in the relationship between China and the other countries in Southeast Asia.

Hua said he had already made it very clear that "the Chinese government recognises and respects the independence and sovereignty of Singapore." China's policy toward the people of Chinese descent living abroad was clear. It did not approve of dual nationality. It encouraged these people to take the nationality of their country of residence of their own volition. All those who did so would automatically lose their Chinese citizenship. He was happy that the overwhelming majority of people of Chinese descent in Singapore had already become citizens, and together with peoples of other nationalities (meaning "races"), were building up their own country. The traditional friendship and "kinsman-like" relationship between the peoples of Singapore and China were beneficial to the development of relations. His turgid, clichéd rhetoric jarred. Raja thought he lacked the sophistication and subtlety of Zhou Enlai, who, Raja believed, would have handled the discussions differently and without communist jargon. I was disappointed that the leader of such a huge country looked tough and strong but lacked finesse. He merely trotted out the standard party line when dealing with questions of race and kinship, and indulged in sophistry differentiating government-to-government from party-to-party relations to justify China's interference in our internal affairs. And he would not admit the contradiction between his theory that liberation must come from within and China's material and propaganda support for the Communist Party of Malaya to liberate Singapore by force. Qiao Guanhua and his foreign ministry officials familiar with Southeast Asia were uncomfortable as they watched their premier trying to browbeat, without success, the Singapore ministers.

In my return banquet speech two nights later, I emphasized, "China and Singapore agreed that they should conduct their bilateral relations by concentrating on those matters on which there is agreement and not those on which we have different views because of different basic assumptions. . . . Premier Hua says that being a socialist country, China supports the revolutionary struggle of all countries. But Premier Hua also states that China does not interfere in the internal matters of other countries, and that how the Singapore government deals with its communists is a matter for the Singapore government to decide. Based on this noninterference, I believe that we can develop our relations." This public statement was to reinforce my hand against the communist united front elements in Singapore.

That night after dinner, Premier Hua Guofeng drove with me in the Red Flag car from the guesthouse in Diaoyutai to Beijing Central Railway Station. It was a ceremonial send-off with thousands of schoolchildren waving colored paper flowers and chanting their farewell. They put me and the whole delegation, together with all the security, protocol, and baggage officers, on a special train for our provincial tour to the west.

The train left Beijing at 10:15 P.M. In my carriage was a bathtub, the largest I had ever seen. I wondered why anyone would want a bathtub instead of a shower in a railway carriage that jolted and shook. Perhaps it had been fitted out for Chairman Mao. We woke up in Yangchuan in Shaanxi province. After breakfast on the train, we were driven along a winding uphill road to Dazhai. There we were briefed by the revolutionary committee who had much experience in receiving VIP visitors. We listened to a well-practiced recitation of how revolutionary fervor conquered all. We slept overnight on the train and woke up at Xian to see the recent discoveries of the tomb of Emperor Qin Shihuang. They had just begun excavating the terracotta warriors there.

Later, at a welcoming dinner given by the Shaanxi provincial revolutionary committee, we listened to the first of many speeches that followed Hua Guofeng's line in denouncing the "capitalist roader," someone who had sneaked into the Communist Party and was striving to restore capitalism. I had read that Deng Xiaoping had been removed from his position as second in command of the government and condemned as a "capitalist roader." When I first heard Hua use this term, I paid little attention, but from its constant repetition at every place we visited, I concluded that this must be a serious matter; this man who remained unnamed had to be an important person if he needed to be condemned again and again.

The next morning we left for Yenan, the legendary base of the Eighth Route Army, and the loess cave which had been Mao's study. At the museum of memorabilia, the guide, a young woman, spoke like a zealous evangelist. She referred to Mao with religious fervor as if he were God and Zhou Enlai and the other immortals of the Long March his archangels. A small white horse had been stuffed and put into a glass case because Zhou Enlai had ridden on it for part of the Long March. The guide's recitation was so oppressive that both Choo and Ling wandered off, leaving me to show interest and make polite responses.

We stayed the night at Yangchialing, the biggest town near Yenan. Again we heard the compulsory denunciation of the "capitalist roader" by the prefectural revolutionary committee chairman. We flew back to Xian and stayed in the spacious guesthouse complex where I was given a suite with an enormous bathroom and dressing room. They said it had been specially built for Chairman Mao. These plush guesthouses were perks for provincial and Beijing leaders.

We flew to Shanghai, to be greeted once more by dancing schoolgirls in gay-colored clothes carrying paper flags and flowers. At dinner, the chairman of the Shanghai municipal revolutionary committee, a young man, denounced the "capitalist roader" with some vehemence and passion. We learned that Shanghai was the most leftist of all the cities and provinces and the base of the radicals around Mao's wife, Jiang Qing, and the Gang of Four who were to be arrested and imprisoned soon after Mao died.

Toward the end of our provincial tour, some fraternization took place between their officials and members of my party who could speak Mandarin. They bantered as they helped each other to the dishes at dinner, saying ironically, *"zi li geng sheng,"* one of the slogans Mao promoted: "self-reliance, self-help," meaning, I will help myself to the food, there is no need for you to serve me. The ice was breaking. Behind the disciplined exterior of the communist cadre was a human being who appreciated good food and good wines, which they enjoyed only when VIPs came visiting.

Then a last dinner by the Guangdong provincial and the Guangzhou (Canton) municipal revolutionary committees. Mercifully only one speech and one last denunciation of the "capitalist roader," delivered with absolutely no passion or conviction.

The next morning they gave us a colorful send-off at the Canton railway station before we boarded the special train for Shenzhen. For the final time, hundreds of schoolgirls bounced up and down carrying paper flags and flowers, chanting goodbye. I wondered how they could allow students to miss classes for such displays. Two hours later we were at Lo Wu. As we walked across the border away from China we breathed a sigh of relief at leaving behind the chants and slogans.

All of us had been eager to see this new mysterious China. For ethnic Chinese in Nanyang it had a mystical appeal as their ancestral homeland. The Chinese put their children in their best clothes to greet and send us off at airports, railway stations, kindergartens, and other places we visited. Their bright-colored frocks, jumpers, and sweaters were worn only on special occasions and then carefully put away. The mass of the Chinese people wore drab dark blue or dark grey ill-fitting unisex Mao jackets. We did not know it then, but these were the last few months of the Mao era. He was to die four months later, after the Tangshan earthquake that September. Later, I was glad to have seen the country before Deng Xiaoping opened up China, to have witnessed the enforced uniformity of dress and speech and listened to their mind-numbing propaganda.

Everyone we met gave the same answers to our questions. At Beijing University I asked students what they would do after they graduated. The answers came pat, "Whatever the party decides, how I can best serve the people." It was disturbing to listen to parrot-like responses from highly intelligent young people. The answers were all politically correct but not sincere.

It was a strange world. I had read about China, especially after the Nixon visit. But the relentless assault of the huge slogans—painted or pasted on walls, on giant placards planted in the middle of wheat and rice fields, all in the fiercest revolutionary terms—was a surrealistic experience. To have these slogans blaring forth from loudspeakers in railway stations and public parks and on the radio numbed the senses. We found little of such fervor in the people, except when they had to speak to us about the Cultural Revolution in simulated animated tones of praise. It was a kind of Chinese Potemkin village.

Dazhai was their model commune in mountainous, infertile Shaanxi in the northwest. For years it was frequently praised in their media for regularly producing miracle harvests. Daqing in the northeast was where the oilfields were. Mao's slogan was: To learn about agriculture, study Dazhai. To learn about industry, study Daqing—*Nong ye xue Dazhai. Gong ye xue Daqing.* So, I had asked to see Dazhai.

Ten years later, they disclosed that Dazhai was a fraud. Its higher outputs were due to special inputs that made its agricultural yield so high. In the Daqing oilfields the model workers did not extract the maximum from the ground because of poor technology, and their yields were going down. Revolutionary fervor could not make up for expertise, whether in agriculture or in mining. The belief in the Mao era, "Better Red than Expert," was a fallacy, a fraud practiced on the people.

At every provincial capital, the chairman of the revolutionary council (or governor, as he was known after the Cultural Revolution had officially ended) gave me a welcoming dinner. Each uttered the same denunciation and vituperation of "the capitalist roader," the code name for Deng

Xiaoping. We could make no sense of it, not understanding then the coded language they used to denounce him. I watched the solemn faces of the men who read out the speeches deadpan. The interpreters knew by heart what was coming and simply repeated the stock phrases in English again and again. I wondered what their real feelings were, but none betrayed their thoughts.

There was such a welter of impressions that it took us some time to sort them out. I compared notes with Choo every night. If they were eavesdropping as the Russians did in Moscow in 1970, they did not show it. My daughter Wei Ling, then a third-year medical student, accompanied us. She had been completely Chinese-educated in Nanyang Girls' High School up to O levels, 10 years of formal education in the Chinese language before she switched to English for her A levels to study medicine at our university. She had no difficulty with the language, but she had immense difficulty in really understanding them, their inner thoughts. When she wandered about on her own in the provincial cities we visited, crowds would gather around her out of curiosity. Where was she from? Singapore. Where was that? Their women at dinners were equally interested in Ling. She looked Chinese, spoke their language, yet was unlike them in her behavior—not shy, talking freely in adult company. She was well-dressed compared to them, forward and outward-going, like a girl from the moon. She herself felt different from them. Like me, she found the constant barrage of propaganda from the loudspeakers and the radio a deafening and deadening experience.

My daughter's reactions were a revelation. She had studied precommunist Chinese history and literature in a Chinese school and looked forward to seeing the historic monuments, cultural artifacts, and scenic wonders, especially those referred to in the purple passages she had memorized. But seeing their poverty juxtaposed against mountains and temples with those romantic-sounding names convinced her that China's emphasis on being the world's oldest continuous civilization was an obstacle to its catching up with the developed world; that Singapore was better off because we had no such stumbling block.

She was surprised to see how different China was from even the East European countries she had visited with me—more isolated from outside influence—and how thoroughly the people had been indoctrinated to produce politically correct standard answers however junior the official, from whatever province. She had few opportunities to interact with ordinary people. Wherever she jogged or walked, her security escort accompanied her and sealed her off. What she tired of seeing were the big-character slogans, several in fashion then: "Criticize Confucius—Criticize Deng Xiaoping," "Crush bourgeois economism [sic]," "Long live the ever-victorious Mao Zedong thought." She was amazed at the people's unquestioning obedience to authority. By the end of the visit she was glad her ancestors had chosen to seek their fortunes in Nanyang.

Before this visit, our government had been strict in refusing Singaporeans under the age of 30 permission to visit China. On my return I instructed that this ruling be reviewed, convinced from my own observations and Ling's reactions that the best way to eradicate romantic ideas about the great fatherland was to send them on a visit, the longer the better. Soon thereafter, we removed this restriction.

I was impressed by the size of China and the vast differences between their 30 provinces. What I was not prepared for was the gaggle of different accents I came across. It was difficult to understand many of them. Premier Hua was a Hunanese with a thick accent. Very few of the people I met spoke standard *pu tong hua* (the common language, Mandarin). The range of dialects and accents when they spoke "Mandarin" was so great that when we got to Guangzhou their interpreter who accompanied me, an excellent interpreter, could not understand the elderly member of the revolutionary council who came from Hainan island, even though he was speaking what he thought was Mandarin. I understood him because we had many Hainanese in Singapore who spoke Mandarin like his, so I interpreted their Hainanese revolutionary council member to their interpreter! This is a small example of the problem of unifying China through a common language. China is one and a half to two times the size of continental Europe in population and area. The Chinese are 90 percent Han Chinese using the same script. But they have different consonant and vowel values for the same written word and have developed different idioms and slang in their various provinces and even in adjoining towns in the same province. They have been trying to unify their language since the overthrow of the Qing dynasty in 1911, but it will be a very long time before they succeed. With satellite TV, radio, and cellular telephones, they may be able to achieve it in another one to two generations, but only for the better-educated of their younger population.

For a fortnight in China we were on the move every day, accompanied by different hosts in the different provinces, attended to by their Southeast Asia desk officers, interpreters, and protocol, baggage, and security officers who accompanied us all the way from Beijing to Guangzhou. Toward the end it became a strain to always be on our best behavior. They had officials in their team who spoke every language and dialect we did. Whether we spoke Hokkien, Malay, or English, they had officials who had lived in Southeast Asia, or had served in Indonesia for many years, and spoke Malay, Bahasa Indonesia, or Hokkien like a native, and could eavesdrop and understand us. So we could not switch languages to cut them out. On the few nights we had dinner by ourselves we had a hilarious time comparing notes.

At every stop the Beijing officials who looked after us and our needs would engage members of our party in conversation to gauge our attitudes on various issues and our reactions to them. They were very thorough. Our press writers told us that late every night they were seen discussing the day's findings and writing up detailed reports of the day's conversations and observations. I wondered who would read them—obviously somebody must, because they took their reporting seriously. I concluded one reason they wanted me to visit was their desire to meet me face-to-face and assess my character and attitudes.

As we bade them goodbye at the railway station in Guangzhou, the desk officer in charge of Southeast Asia and Singapore, a tall, consumptive-looking man in his fifties, told K. C. Lee that after observing me for two weeks, he found me hard and tough. I took that as a tribute. When they clapped their hands in unison to welcome me, I waved back. I did not clap back, as was their form. I felt it ridiculous to clap in response. I made a point of being Singaporean and different. We reacted alike: Neither Choo, Ling, nor I felt we were one of them. In fact, we had never felt more un-Chinese than on that first visit.

It was also embarrassing, when visiting a factory or exhibition, to be offered, as was their custom, a brush, Chinese ink on a slab of slate, and a sheet of rice paper or a clean page in a book to write my comments. Since my acquaintance with a Chinese brush was limited to a few months in primary school, I had to decline and ask for an ordinary pen to write my comments in English.

This feeling of not being Chinese became less intense as I got to know them better and was no longer distracted by the differences of speech, dress, and manners. But on that first visit, we found them and their manners alien. With the Chinese in the south, we could have passed off in appearance as one of them. But even so we felt keenly that we were not one of them.

I was to discover that many of our young Chinese students who went back to China in the 1950s to contribute to the revolution were never accepted into Chinese society. They were always separate, *hua qiao* or overseas Chinese, different, "softies" who did not quite belong. It was sad; they had gone back because they wanted so much to contribute and belong. They were, or perhaps had to be, treated differently with perks and privileges not available to the locals, or life would have been too difficult for them. And because of those perks and privileges, they were resented. It was difficult for both sides. Sentiments of kinship were fine provided the overseas relative lived abroad and visited occasionally bearing gifts and greetings. But to stay and be part of China was to be a burden unless the relative had special skills or knowledge. Many who went back with romantic revolutionary ideals ended up as émigrés in Hong Kong and Macau, where they found life more congenial, more like that in the Singapore and Malaya they once despised and abandoned. Many of them had petitioned to be allowed to return to Singapore. Our Internal Security Department strongly recommended against this, suspecting plants by the MCP who would create trouble. It was a total misreading of the true position. These people had been thoroughly disillusioned with China and communism and would have been our best inoculation against the virus of Maoism.

We are so much like the Chinese in the southern provinces in physical appearance. We have the same cultural values, in attitudes toward relationships between the sexes, relations within the family, deference due to our elders, and other social norms regarding family and friends. But we are so different in our outlook and view of the world and of our place in this world. Theirs is so huge a country that they feel absolutely confident there will be a seat for them at the top table once they have put themselves right, and it was only a matter of time. No Chinese doubts their ultimate destiny after they have restored their civilization, the oldest in the world with 4,000 years of unbroken history. We, the migrants who have cut our roots and transplanted ourselves on a different soil, in a very different climate, lack this self-confidence. We have serious doubts about our future, always wondering what fate has in store for us in an uncertain and fast-changing world.

# 37.  Deng Xiaoping's China

My meeting with Vice Premier Deng Xiaoping was unforgettable. A dapper, stocky man of 74, not more than five feet tall, in a beige Mao suit came down from a Boeing 707 at Paya Lebar airport in November 1978. Walking briskly, he inspected the guard of honor, then drove with me to the Istana Villa, our guesthouse in the Istana domain. We met that afternoon for formal discussions in the cabinet room.

After seeing the spittoons in the Great Hall of the People, I had arranged for a blue-and-white porcelain spittoon to be placed next to Deng. I had read that he regularly used one. I also placed an ashtray ostentatiously for him alone although there was a no-smoking rule for air-conditioned rooms in the Istana. It was a gesture to a great figure in the history of China. I made sure that the exhaust fan serving the cabinet room was switched on.

I welcomed him as a great Chinese revolutionary. He replied that Singapore could be said to be an old place for him. Fifty-eight years before, in 1920, he had visited it for two days on his way to France. When I visited Beijing in 1976, he had not been able to meet me; at that time he had been "shoved aside." He had been defeated by the Gang of Four, but in the end they were defeated. He spent the next two and a half hours on the dangers the Soviet Union posed to the world. All countries and peoples who did not want war had to form a united front against the warmongers. He quoted Mao: We should all unite to cope with the *wang ba dan* (literally "tortoise egg" but translated by his interpreter as the S.O.B). He gave a comprehensive survey of Soviet maneuvres in Europe, the Middle East, Africa, South Asia, and finally in Indochina. The Soviets had scored immensely in Vietnam. Some people did not understand why relations between China and Vietnam were so bad, and why China had taken action such as cutting off aid, which pushed Vietnam toward the Soviet Union instead of winning it over. The question to ask was, why did Vietnam see fit to fall completely into the lap of the Soviet Union when it was not in their interest? The answer was Vietnam's "fond dream for many years of the Indochina federation." Even Ho Chi Minh had had such an idea. China had never agreed to it, and Vietnam regarded China as the greatest obstacle to its realization of this federation. China had concluded that Vietnam would not change and would become more anti-China. The expulsion of ethnic Chinese from Vietnam was one such manifestation. After careful consideration China had decided to cut aid.

Deng said China's total aid to Vietnam had been over US$10 billion, at current value worth US$20 billion. When China cancelled aid to Vietnam, the Soviet Union had to carry this burden alone. When they could not satisfy Vietnam's needs, they got it admitted to COMECON (the communist bloc counterpart to the EEC), to shift the burden to the East European countries. The Vietnamese were also putting out their begging bowls before Japan, America, France, Western Europe, and even Singapore. In 10 years' time, he said, China would consider pulling Vietnam from the Soviet Union again. I thought to myself that Deng took a very long view, totally different from American leaders.

He said the real and urgent problem was a possible massive invasion of Cambodia by Vietnam. What would China do? he asked rhetorically. What China would do would depend on how far the Vietnamese went, he answered himself. He repeated this a few times, not committing himself outright to a counterattack on Vietnam. He said if Vietnam succeeded in controlling the whole of Indochina, many Asian countries would be exposed. The Indochina federation would expand its influence and serve the global strategy of the Soviet Union to move southward into the Indian Ocean. Vietnam's role was that of a Cuba of the East. The Soviets were drastically increasing their Pacific fleet. The world had witnessed great turbulence in the last two years as was evident from events in Vietnam, Afghanistan, Iran, and Pakistan, all pointing to a southward thrust by the Soviet Union. China's policy was to counter the strategic deployment of the Soviet Union, whether in Zaïre or Somalia. Wherever the Soviet Union attacked, China would help to repel the attack. To have peace, Asean had to unite with China and repel the Soviet Union and its Cuba in Southeast Asia, Vietnam. His two interpreters did not take notes diligently; they only made a few squiggles. I concluded he must have made the same presentation in Bangkok and Kuala Lumpur and they knew it by heart. It was past sunset when he finished. I asked whether he would like me to respond or adjourn till the next day to give him time to change for dinner, and for me to think over what he had said. He preferred not to let the dinner get cold.

At dinner, he was sociable and friendly, but still tense. Vietnam's invasion of Cambodia was very much on his mind. When I pressed him— what would China do, now that General Kriangsak, the prime minister of Thailand, had committed himself on China's side by giving Deng such a warm reception in Bangkok—he again muttered that it depended how far they went. My impression was that if the Vietnamese did not cross the Mekong River, it would not be so dangerous, but if they did, then China would do something.

He invited me to visit China again. I said I would when China had recovered from the Cultural Revolution. That, he said, would take a long time. I countered that they should have no problem getting ahead and doing much better than Singapore because we were the descendants of illiterate, landless peasants from Fujian and Guangdong while they had the progeny of the scholars, mandarins, and literati who had stayed at home. He was silent.

The next day I made my points in one hour—actually half an hour, without the translation. I summarized what he had said about the Soviet threat by referring to well-documented studies of their military capabilities by the International Institute of Strategic Studies in London. I pointed out that Germany's Chancellor Helmut Schmidt, France's President Valéry Giscard d'Estaing, and American leaders in Washington had given me different conclusions on the dangers the Soviet Union posed. Some of them believed the Soviets were wasting too much of their resources on armaments. Anyway, small countries like Singapore could only take note of these world trends but could not influence the outcome.

We had to analyze the situation from a regional, not a global, viewpoint. The problem after the end of the Vietnam War was that American troops had withdrawn from Vietnam and Thailand. It was clear that they would never again engage communist insurgents on the Asian mainland. The next question was how long American forces would stay in the Philippines to balance the growing Soviet fleet in the Indian and Pacific Oceans. Singapore wanted the United States to stay in the Philippines.

To allay Deng's concern about Singapore's attitude to the Soviets, I listed our main trading partners—Japan, the United States, Malaysia, and the European Union, each with 12 to 14 percent of our total world trade. China was only 1.8 percent and the Soviet Union a mere 0.3 percent. Soviet contribution to our economic life was negligible. I also needed no lessons on the hegemonistic behavior of the Russians. I recounted to him how in 1967, after visiting Abu Simbel and Aswan, when I was returning to Cairo on an Egyptian aircraft accompanied by an Egyptian minister, there was a commotion in the cockpit as the plane was about to land. The minister excused himself to go to the cockpit. After the plane landed, I discovered that the Soviet pilot of another plane had told airport control he did not understand English, and demanded priority to land ahead of the VIP plane. The Egyptian minister had to bark his order from the cockpit to ensure that the VIP plane landed before the Soviet plane. I needed no lessons on the arrogance of the Russians.

China wanted Southeast Asian countries to unite with it to isolate the "Russian bear"; the fact was that our neighbors wanted us to unite and isolate the "Chinese dragon." There were no "overseas Russians" in Southeast Asia leading communist insurgencies supported by the Soviet government, as there were "overseas Chinese" encouraged and supported by the Chinese Communist Party and government, posing threats to Thailand, Malaysia, the Philippines, and, to a lesser extent, Indonesia. Also, China was openly asserting a special relationship with the overseas Chinese because of blood ties, and was making direct appeals to their patriotism over the heads of the governments of these countries of which they were citizens, urging them to return and help China in its "Four Modernizations."

A few weeks earlier, in October, Vietnamese Prime Minister Pham Van Dong had visited us and where Deng was now seated. I had asked

Pham Van Dong the reason for Vietnam's trouble with the overseas Chinese, or Hoa people; his blunt answer was that, as an ethnic Chinese, I should know that ethnic Chinese would always support China all the time, just as Vietnamese would support Vietnam, wherever they might be. I was less concerned with what Pham Van Dong thought than with the impact of what he must have told the leaders of Malaysia. I recounted another incident where the Vietnamese permanent representative to the UN had told the four Asean permanent representatives that the Vietnamese had treated the Hoa people equally, and yet they turned ungrateful; that was the main cause of the exodus of 160,000 ethnic Chinese from Hanoi to China across their border, while other Chinese fled from the south in boats. The Indonesian permanent representative, forgetting that his colleagues from the other three Asean countries—Philippines, Thailand, and Singapore—were ethnic Chinese, told the Vietnamese that they had been too kind and generous to the Hoa people, and that they should learn from the Indonesians. I left Deng in no doubt as to the visceral suspicions of its neighbors Singapore faced.

Pham Van Dong, I added, had placed a wreath at Malaysia's National Monument. Deng had refused to do this. Pham Van Dong had also promised he would not help subversion. Deng had not. The Malaysians must be suspicious of Deng. There were underlying suspicions and animosity between Malay Muslims and Chinese in Malaysia, and between Indonesians and their ethnic Chinese. Because China was exporting revolution to Southeast Asia, my Asean neighbors wanted Singapore to rally with them, not against the Soviet Union, but against China.

Asean governments regarded radio broadcasts from China appealing directly to their ethnic Chinese as dangerous subversion. Deng listened silently. He had never seen it in this light: China, a big foreign power, going over the governments of the region to subvert their citizens. I said it was most unlikely that Asean countries would respond positively to his proposal for a united front against the Soviet Union and Vietnam and suggested that we discuss how to resolve this problem. Then I paused.

Deng's expression and body language registered consternation. He knew that I had spoken the truth. Abruptly, he asked, "What do you want me to do?" I was astonished. I had never met a communist leader who was prepared to depart from his brief when confronted with reality, much less ask what I wanted him to do. I had expected him to brush my points aside as Premier Hua Guofeng had done in Beijing in 1976 when I pressed him over the inconsistency of China's supporting the Malayan Communist Party to foment revolution in Singapore, not Malaya. Hua had answered with bluster, "I do not know the details, but wherever communists fight, they will win." Not Deng. He realized that he had to face up to this problem if Vietnam was to be isolated. I hesitated to tell this seasoned, weather-beaten revolutionary what he should do, but since he had asked me, I said, "Stop such radio broadcasts; stop such appeals. It will be better for the ethnic Chinese in Asean if China does not underline their kinship and call upon their ethnic empathy. The suspicion of the indigenous peoples will always be there, whether or not China emphasizes these blood ties. But if China appeals to these blood ties so blatantly, it must increase their suspicions. China must stop radio broadcasts from south China by the Malayan and Indonesian Communist Parties."

Deng said simply that he needed time to think about what I had said, adding that he would not learn from Pham Van Dong. He, Deng, had also been asked to lay a wreath at the National Monument which commemorated those who had killed Malayan communists. As a communist, it had been impossible for him to do this. Pham Van Dong could do such a thing because he was "that kind of a communist." He was "selling his soul." China, he emphasized, spoke honestly. The Chinese had never concealed their views, and what the Chinese people said counted. During the Korean War, China had issued a statement that if the Americans approached the Yalu River, the Chinese people could not sit idly by. But the Americans took no notice. On foreign policy, China always spoke what it thought. As for communist parties, he had nothing to add, so the interpreter said. But in his Mandarin, what Deng actually said was, he had "lost interest in stating it again."

The reiteration of their overseas Chinese policy, he said, was for two reasons: The first was the anti-Chinese activities of Vietnam; the second was the internal considerations of China, the result of the activities of the Gang of Four in the Cultural Revolution. Relatives in China of the overseas Chinese had suffered badly, with many persecuted and imprisoned. He wanted to restate China's position on ethnic Chinese abroad: that China favored and encouraged them to take up the citizenship of the country of residence, that those who wanted to remain Chinese would still have to abide by the laws of the country of residence, and that China did not recognize dual nationality.

On Cambodia, he assured me that China's approach would not be affected by the conclusion of the Soviet-Vietnamese treaty of friendship and cooperation. China was not afraid that Vietnam might ask the Soviet Union to threaten China, adding that the Soviet Union would not dare to engage China in a big way. He looked deadly serious when he added that China would punish the Vietnamese if they attacked Cambodia. China would make them pay a heavy price for it, and the Soviet Union would discover that supporting Vietnam was too heavy a burden. Then he asked what advice China's friends (meaning Singapore) would give on the problems confronting both countries (China and Singapore).

I replied that Cambodia's leaders must be sensitive to international opinion as they needed the sympathy of the world. They were behaving in an irrational way with no feeling for their own people. Deng's response was that he also did not "understand" some of the things done in Phnom Penh; he made no defense of the Khmer Rouge's genocide.

Winding up, I said Deng had stated that China needed 22 years for modernization. In these 22 years, if there were no unnecessary problems created in Southeast Asia, conditions should improve. If there were such problems, the consequences would be adverse for China, as they had been for Vietnam and Cambodia. Deng agreed with me. He hoped there would be unity and stability in Asean. He was saying this "from the bottom of my heart."

He was the most impressive leader I had met. He was a five-footer, but a giant among men. At 74, when he was faced with an unpleasant truth, he was prepared to change his mind. Two years later, after they had made alternative arrangements for their fraternal communist parties in Malaysia and Thailand, the radio broadcasts stopped.

During dinner, I had urged him to smoke. He said, pointing to his wife, that the doctor had told her to get him to stop. He was trying to cut down. That night, he did not smoke or use the spittoon. He had read that I was allergic to smoke.

Before his departure I called on him at the Istana Villa to talk for some 20 minutes. He was glad he had come and seen Singapore again after 58 years. It was a dramatic transformation and he congratulated me. I replied that Singapore was a small country with two and a half million people. He sighed and said, "If I had only Shanghai, I too might be able to change Shanghai as quickly. But I have the whole of China!"

He said he had wanted to visit Singapore and America before he joined Karl Marx—Singapore, because he had seen it once when it was a colonial territory, while on his way to Marseilles after the end of the First World War to work and study; America, because China and America must talk to each other. It was not until after Vietnam occupied Cambodia that I understood why he was keen to visit the United States.

During the drive to the airport, I asked him point-blank what he would do if the Vietnamese attacked Cambodia. Would he leave the Thais vulnerable and watch them being intimidated, and then forced to bend toward the Soviet Union? He pursed his lips, and his eyes narrowed as he whispered, "It depends how far they will go." I said he would have to do something after the Thai prime minister had so openly and whole-heartedly received him in Bangkok. Kriangsak had to rely on China to maintain some balance. He looked troubled and again whispered, "It depends how far they will go."

At the airport he shook hands with the VIPs and ministers, inspected the guard of honor, walked up the steps to his Boeing 707, then turned around and waved goodbye. As the door closed on him, I said to my colleagues that his staff were going to get a "shellacking." He had seen a Singapore his brief had not prepared him for. There had been no tumultuous Chinese crowds, no rapturous hordes of Chinese Singaporeans to welcome him, just thin crowds of curious onlookers.

A few weeks later I was shown articles on Singapore in their *People's Daily.* Its line had changed. Singapore was described as a garden city worth studying for its greening, public housing, and tourism. We were no longer "running dogs of the American imperialists." Their view of Singapore changed further in October the following year, 1979, when Deng said in a speech, "I went to Singapore to study how they utilised foreign capital. Singapore benefited from factories set up by foreigners in Singapore: first, foreign enterprises paid 35 percent of their net profits in taxes which went to the state; second, labour income went to the workers; and third, it [foreign investment] generated the service sectors. All these were income [for the state]." What he saw in Singapore in 1978 had become a point of reference as the minimum the Chinese people should achieve.

At the end of January 1979, Deng visited America and restored diplomatic relations with President Carter without the United States abandoning Taiwan. He was making sure the United States would not align itself with the Soviet Union when China attacked and "punished" Vietnam. That was why he was keen to visit the United States.

At the governor's lodge at Fanling in Hong Kong for a golfing holiday, I met David Bonavia, a China expert, formerly of the London *Times*. He dismissed Deng's warning as an idle threat because the Soviet navy was in the South China Sea. I said that I had met Deng three months ago and he was a man who weighed his words carefully. Two days later, on 16 February 1979, Chinese forces attacked across the border with North Vietnam.

China declared that the objectives of the military action were limited, and urged the UN Security Council to take immediate and effective measures to stop Vietnam's armed aggression against Cambodia and bring an end to Vietnam's occupation of Cambodia. The operation lasted one month. They incurred heavy losses but showed the Vietnamese that, whatever the cost, they could make deep incursions into Vietnam, destroy towns and villages in their path, and withdraw, as they did on 16 March 1979.

During China's invasion of Vietnam, Deng said publicly that China was prepared for a possible war with the Soviet Union, and that a lesson for Vietnam was also a lesson for the Soviet Union. The Soviet Union did not attack China. The Western press wrote off the Chinese punitive action as a failure. I believe it changed the history of East Asia. The Vietnamese knew China would attack if they went beyond Cambodia on to Thailand. The Soviet Union did not want to be caught in a long-drawn-out war in a remote corner of Asia. They could afford a quick decisive action against China, but the Chinese denied them this by declaring that their military action was a "punitive" action and was not intended to capture Vietnam. As Deng had predicted, the Soviet Union was saddled with the burden of supporting Vietnam, which they did for 11 more years until 1991, when the Soviet Union disintegrated. When this happened, the Vietnamese agreed in October 1991 to withdraw from Cambodia—after 12 years of costly and futile occupation.

On my second visit to China in November 1980, I found many changes. The men who had got "helicopter" promotions during the Cultural Revolution had been quietly shunted aside and their keen, zealous attitudes were no longer on display. Our protocol officer's perpetual eager-beaver look was an enduring impression I had carried away from my first visit in 1976. With the Cultural Revolution officially denounced, the people appeared greatly relieved.

Premier Zhao Ziyang met me for talks. He was a different character from Hua Guofeng or Deng Xiaoping. Of medium build, he had the complexion of someone with a light suntan over his fine features. I had no difficulty understanding his Mandarin because he had a good, strong voice without any heavy provincial accent. He came from Henan, a province south of Beijing that had been the cradle of the Chinese civilization, a huge, once-rich agricultural area now poorer than the coastal provinces.

We discussed the Cambodian issue and how we had to find an alternative to the Khmer Rouge guerrillas who were doing the bulk of the fighting. Zhao nodded his head, acknowledging that Pol Pot would be unacceptable to the world. I conceded that unfortunately the Khmer Rouge was the best fighting force against the Vietnamese. Zhao had just taken over as premier and lacked the confidence to settle issues on Cambodia and Vietnam without referring to Deng. I found him a reasonable, balanced, and rounded man, not ideologically blinkered.

An advance copy of my dinner speech had been given to their protocol. They wanted me to remove a passage critical of their policy toward the Communist Party of Malaya and its radio broadcasts from China. The passage read, "For years China instigated and helped guerrilla insurgency in Thailand, Malaya and Indonesia. Many Asean leaders have put these unfortunate events behind them. Unfortunately, a residue of China's past policies continues to trouble relations between China and Asean."

When we resumed talks that afternoon, I referred to this. Their protocol had said that this part was unacceptable and had to be left out if the speech was to be delivered, otherwise there would be no speeches. This was most unusual. I had already given copies to the Singapore press and they would have released it to the foreign correspondents, so it was not possible to delete anything. Zhao replied that the Chinese people would not forgive him if I delivered this speech and he did not respond to some of the points made by me. He did not want to turn "a grand and friendly banquet" held in my honor into an occasion for a hard exchange of words which would have an adverse international effect. There was no question of wanting to tell me what I should not say at the banquet; he was merely suggesting that both sides cancel the speeches. If my views were nevertheless made known to the public, he would understand. I agreed to no speeches.

He launched into the Chinese view of Soviet global strategy. He assured me that China would do its part to allay the suspicions and fears of Malaysia and Indonesia toward China. Soviet objectives were to control oil resources and sea lanes, including the Straits of Malacca, in order to strangle Japan and Western Europe, and to some extent the United States; the collaboration between the Soviet Union and Vietnam was not one of fortuitous expediency but a strategic collaboration. He said Malaysia and Indonesia could never win over Vietnam away from the Soviet Union unless either Vietnam renounced regional hegemony, in which case it would not need the Soviet Union, or the Soviet Union renounced global hegemony, in which case it would not need Vietnam.

As for party-to-party relations, it was a historical problem of a global nature and China was sincerely making efforts as far as possible so that it would not affect its relations with Asean countries. The problem would take some time to solve. He would say formally to me that China would solve the problem, but not overnight.

The overseas Chinese question was another problem left over from history. China was not in favor of dual nationality and had encouraged Chinese living abroad to take up the nationality of their host countries. But if ethnic Chinese abroad remained Chinese nationals, China could not cease to have contact with them. As for the contributions made by ethnic Chinese abroad to China's modernization, this did not represent the policy of the government of the People's Republic of China. China would make an effort to reduce the suspicion of other countries over the question of overseas Chinese. However, both sides should be concerned with more important issues than the policy of China toward overseas Chinese. On Cambodia, I would be meeting Deng Xiaoping, who would deal with all the points I would wish to raise; in other words, Deng was the final authority.

The next morning I met Deng Xiaoping for over two hours in a different room in the Great Hall of the People. He looked lively and vigorous. He had been well-briefed and did most of the talking. He said my talks with Zhao had gone well, adding that General Ne Win also had not delivered a speech at the banquet in his honor at the Great Hall of the People, but had "good talks" with the Chinese. This was his reassurance that the cancellation of my speech would make no difference to the outcome of our talks.

Deng argued that China was a huge country with a large population. It did not need the resources of other countries. It was preoccupied with the problem of uplifting its people out of poverty and backwardness, "a great undertaking that might take half a century." China was too populous. There were just too many things to do. He hoped I would explain China's "genuine and clear" position to Indonesia and Malaysia. China wanted to see a strong Asean, "the stronger, the better." China had a "global strategy" in handling its relations with Asean countries, the United States, Japan, and Western Europe. He fully understood Singapore's position regarding establishing diplomatic relations with China, that we would do so after Indonesia. Singapore's calculations were correct and in conformity with Singapore's "strategic considerations."

On Cambodia, he said, there were two basic points that must be met: First, a political settlement of the Cambodian question must be based on Vietnamese withdrawal from Cambodia, otherwise there was nothing to talk about; second, there had to be unity among all resistance forces inside Cambodia. The Khmer Rouge was willing to unite with other resistance forces; it was prepared to accept Sihanouk or, if Sihanouk was not willing, Son Sann as head of state. But neither was willing, I said. He stressed there was no alliance to speak of without the Khmer Rouge forces. Pol Pot's policies were wrong, but any political settlement in Cambodia must be based on "prevailing realities."

One such reality, I said, was that except for the PRC the rest of the world believed that Pol Pot was murderous and mad, and Sihanouk and

Son Sann were right in not working with the Khmer Rouge. Thailand and Singapore were in danger of being seen as stooges of China for supporting the DK (Democratic Kampuchea) government's seat in the UN.

In my view, two major problems had to be solved: first, international representation at the UN, because a vacant seat would eventually be filled by Heng Samrin; second, how to intensify resistance fighting in Cambodia. Much of the fighting was by the Khmer Rouge, but this must not be forever. Malaysia and Indonesia must be satisfied that continued support of the DK government would not lead to the restoration of China's influence in Cambodia. Both believed Vietnam's argument that Asean's actions helped China to weaken Vietnam and would allow China to increase its influence in Southeast Asia. President Suharto had told me that in 10 years China could create great problems for the region.

Instead of answering my points, Deng asked how the Malaysians and Indonesians could drive the Vietnamese out of Cambodia. I replied that neither was troubled by the Vietnamese occupation of Cambodia; they believed a strong Vietnam could oppose any southward expansion by China. The problem was one of perspectives. The question was not what China intended to do, but what China was capable of doing, and whether it was in China's interest. Malaysia and Indonesia saw China as the supporter of communist forces that had troubled them for the last 30 years.

Deng repeatedly asked me to play a role in promoting an alliance between the Cambodian resistance groups. China had built a "palace-like residence" for Sihanouk in Beijing. There was friendship between him and Sihanouk, but they deliberately avoided talking politics. I recapitulated his position: first, that China would support and encourage the establishment of a noncommunist force to resist the Vietnamese; second, that China would accept the emergence of an independent Kampuchean government after a Vietnamese withdrawal from Cambodia, even though China did not have any hold on such a government. He confirmed it. At a press conference in Beijing with foreign correspondents I made these two points. Their reports were never contradicted by the Chinese.

Deng asked me to tell my Asean neighbors that they should not believe that any power which was communist would naturally have good relations with China. The Soviet Union was the biggest threat and one needed to have a good and clear understanding of the damaging effects of its global policy. He asked rhetorically what Indonesia would gain by thwarting China's policy of opposing Soviet global strategy. Making concessions to Malaysia and Indonesia would not solve the problem, because they had the wrong strategic assessments.

On that note, we went to lunch where they served a Chinese delicacy, the fabulous *xiong zhang*—bear's paws, braised tender in a rich gravy. It was the best gourmet meal I ever had at the Great Hall of the People. The chef had made a special effort for Deng's guests. (Bears are now an endangered species in China.)

Chinese protocol was correct in taking me to see Hua Guofeng last. He was still chairman of the Communist Party and therefore ranked higher than Deng, a vice chairman. But from the importance of the officials in attendance, I had no doubt whose words carried the day.

Premier Zhao Ziyang met me again in Beijing in September 1985. He referred to me as an "old friend of China," their label for those they want to put at ease. Then he asked for my impressions of the places I had visited on my way to Beijing.

His manner encouraged me to speak up. I said I could give inoffensive observations, leaving out the critical, but that would be of no value to him. I first gave him my positive impressions. Shanghai had younger leaders than in 1976, vigorous and dynamic; people looked happier and more prosperous in colorful clothes; there was construction everywhere; and the traffic problem was still manageable. I was impressed by the governor of Shandong province, a vigorous go-getter, full of ideas and great ambition to upgrade the infrastructure of Shandong. He had plans for airports in Jinan and Yantai, and had proposed three business projects to our businesspeople; his staff was well-organized.

Then I gave the negatives: Bad old practices were unchanged. As prime minister for over 20 years, I had stayed in many guesthouses, and could guess the nature of the administration from their condition. Jinan's huge guesthouse complex gave an impression of waste; I was told my suite with its giant-size bathtub had been built specially for a visit by Chairman Mao. The labor to keep this complex in good condition could be put to better use running a top-class hotel. Because guests in residence were few and far between, the staff were out of practice.

Next, the poor road system. Parts of the 150-kilometer (approximately 90-mile) road from Jinan to Qufu, the birthplace of Confucius, were just mud tracks. The Romans built roads that lasted 2,000 years. China had labor and stones in abundance and there was no reason why there should be mud tracks linking Jinan, the provincial capital, to Qufu with its tourist potential.

Singapore had little culture or history and a population of two and a half million, but it had three million tourists a year (in the mid-1980s). China's monuments and ruins resonated with history. Selling scenery, fresh air, fresh food, laundry services, curios, and souvenirs to tourists would give much employment and put money into the pockets of many people. China, with a population of about 1,000 million, had only 1 million tourists a year—800,000 overseas Chinese and 200,000 foreigners.

Hesitantly, I suggested that they might like to send some of their supervisors to Singapore. They would not encounter language and culture differences and could observe our work ethics and attitudes. Zhao welcomed my proposal. He suggested that our managers and experts at top, middle, and grass-roots level visit China to assess their workers in a Chinese context. I said their workers might not respect our supervisors, because they were "descendants of coolies from Fujian province." Later, they sent several delegations of managers of their state-owned enterprises to Singapore. They saw a different work culture that placed importance on the quality of work.

He said China had three major economic tasks: first, build up infrastructure like roads and railways; second, upgrade as many factories as possible; and third, improve the efficiency of their managers and workers. He described the problem of inflation. (This was to be one of the causes of the trouble in Tiananmen four years later.) He wanted more trade, economic and technical cooperation between China and Singapore. China was ready to sign a three-year agreement with us to process not less than 3 million tons of Chinese crude oil per year, and would import more chemical and petrochemical products from Singapore as long as they were at international prices. Thus began their participation in our oil industry.

Their state oil company set up an office in Singapore to handle this business and also do oil trading.

On Cambodia, Zhao disclosed to me that the Vietnamese had offered to enter into secret negotiations with them. They had refused Vietnam's offer: It was not sincere and was designed to split China from Asean and from the Cambodian resistance groups. There could be no improvement in Sino-Vietnamese relations before the Vietnamese committed themselves to withdrawing from Cambodia. China had repelled repeated Vietnamese intrusions into Chinese territory; 700,000 soldiers, or 60 percent of Vietnam's forces, were tied down on the China-Vietnam border but China had several hundred thousand men and would continue to pressure Vietnam. Unlike his hesitancy in 1980, Zhao now spoke confidently on Cambodia and Vietnam and did not refer me to Deng.

I was taken to meet Deng. He bantered about his advanced age of 81 compared to my 62. I assured him that he did not look old. He was not worried about age. China had made satisfactory arrangements for personnel changes: "Even if the heavens collapsed, there would be people in China to shoulder it." China's domestic development, in every aspect, was reasonably good, with many changes in the last five years. Ten old leaders had retired from the politburo, their posts taken by younger leaders. Many leaders over the age of 60 had resigned from the central committee and 90 new, younger ones had been elected. These leadership changes had been in progress for seven years, but were still not completely satisfactory and needed further reshuffling. By right, he, Deng, should also retire, but there were a few problems he first had to solve.

He repeated that he was already 81, ready to meet Marx, that it was a law of nature and everyone should be aware of it, except Mr. Chiang Ching-kuo. He asked when I had last met Chiang and whether he had solved the leadership problem. Only then did I realize that his opening remarks on age were not casual banter but a lead to Chiang and Taiwan. I said I last met Chiang in January, eight months earlier, that Chiang had diabetes, which was generally known, and that he was aware of his mortality. Deng wondered aloud whether Chiang had made any personnel arrangements after him. As best as I could see, he had, I replied, but could not say who would replace him eventually. Deng feared chaos and confusion in Taiwan after Chiang's departure. At the moment, at least both sides shared a common feeling that there was only one China. Chaos could lead to the emergence of two Chinas. I asked how. He explained that there were two possible developments: First, there were forces in the United States and Japan which supported Taiwan's independence; second, the United States would continue to regard Taiwan as one of its unsinkable aircraft carriers. The present U.S. government (with Ronald Reagan as president) had not completely changed its policy on Taiwan. It regarded Taiwan as an important military base and wanted to keep it in its sphere of influence. Deng had discussed Taiwan with President Reagan the year before and had tried to persuade him to give up this aircraft carrier policy, pointing out that the United States had 10 other unsinkable aircraft carriers around the world. Taiwan was of crucial importance to China.

He had asked U.S. Defense Secretary Caspar Weinberger his reaction to eventualities. If Taiwan refused to negotiate on reunification, what should China do? And if Taiwan became independent, what then? Because of these eventualities, China could not renounce the use of military force to solve the Taiwan question, but it would make every effort to solve the problem and achieve reunification by peaceful means. He had told both President Reagan and Secretary of State George Shultz that Taiwan was the crux of relations between China and the United States. The previous December, he had asked British Prime Minister Thatcher to convey a message to President Reagan to help China achieve the reunification of Taiwan in his second term. He had also told Shultz and Weinberger that if they failed to handle the question properly and allowed the U.S. Congress to intervene, it would give rise to conflict in Sino-U.S. relations. China might not be able to attack Taiwan but could block the Straits of Taiwan. The United States could be drawn into the conflict. He had asked U.S. leaders what they would then do, but the response was that the United States did not answer hypothetical questions. There was a real possibility of such an eventuality.

Knowing that Chiang Ching-kuo and I were good friends, he then requested me to convey his personal regards to "Mr. Chiang" when I next met him. I agreed. He hoped to be able to cooperate with Chiang, as both had been in the same university in Moscow in 1926 although not in the same class. Chiang was about 15 or 16 and Deng was 22 in 1926. (A month later I personally passed Deng's message to Chiang in Taipei. He listened in silence and did not reply.)

As for the Cambodian situation, Deng said it was not unfavorable. I responded that what he had said in 1978, before Vietnam invaded Cambodia, had come about. The Vietnamese were stuck in Cambodia. We should continue to help the guerrilla forces to ensure that they stayed mired, with no trade, investments, or economic development and totally dependent on the Soviets. China's success in economic reforms, I said, would not be lost on the Vietnamese: They could have built up their own country and traded with the world instead of occupying their neighbor and suffering for it.

Deng regretted that the Vietnamese leaders were not prepared to follow China's way. He said "some friends" in Southeast Asia believed in Vietnam's publicity stances and empty promises. The true motive of Southeast Asian leaders (referring to Indonesia and Malaysia) was to use Vietnam and sacrifice the Cambodian nation in order to counter China whom they regarded as their real enemy. Deng then referred to Gorbachev; China had demanded that he remove three obstacles in the way of Sino-Soviet relations, the first of which was to stop military aid to Vietnam and to get the Vietnamese to withdraw from Cambodia. China had seen no sign of this.


When I next met Zhao Ziyang, on 16 September 1988, he had been promoted to general secretary. He saw me at my villa in Diaoyutai, their guesthouse complex, to speak about China's economic problems. He was disturbed by a wave of panic buying throughout China a few weeks earlier, in late August and early September. They had had to reduce construction, control the growth of money for consumption, and slow down economic growth. If other measures did not work, the government would have to stress party discipline—I took this to mean "punish high officials." The panic buying must have reminded him of the last days of the Nationalist government in 1947–1949.

Then he took me to the restaurant in the Diaoyutai complex to celebrate my 65th birthday. During dinner, he asked for my views on a recent television series he had sent me, the "Yellow River Elegy," produced by some younger members of his reform program think tank. It had depicted a China steeped in feudal tradition, tied down by superstitions and bad old habits, a China that would not make a breakthrough and catch up with the modern world unless it abandoned its old conformist attitudes.

I thought it overpessimistic. China need not abandon its basic cultural values and beliefs in order to industrialize and modernize. Taiwan, South Korea, Japan, Hong Kong, and Singapore had all sought to preserve their traditional values of thrift, hard work, emphasis on scholarship, and loyalty to family, clan, and the wider nation, always placing community interest above individual interest. These Confucian values had resulted in social cohesion, high savings, and investments, which led to high productivity and growth. What China needed to change was its overcentralized system of administration and the attitudes and mindset of the people, so that people would be more receptive to new ideas, whether Chinese or foreign, and be willing to test them out and adapt them to China's circumstances. This the Japanese had done successfully.

Zhao was concerned that China's economy was not taking off like those of the NIEs without being plagued by high inflation. I explained that this was because, unlike China, the NIEs never had to deregulate planned economies with prices for basic commodities controlled at unrealistically low levels.

He exuded the quiet confidence of a good mind that took in briefs swiftly. Unlike Hua Guofeng, he was a gentleman, not a thug. He had a pleasant manner, neither abrasive nor bossy. But one needed to be tough and ruthless to survive at the top in China, and for the China of that period he was too liberal in his approach to law and order. When we parted, I did not know that within a year he would become a nonperson.

The next day, 17 September 1988, I had my last meeting with Deng. He was suntanned after several weeks at Beidaihe, the seaside resort for China's leaders to the east of Beijing. He looked vigorous and his voice was strong. I praised China's economic progress. Yes, there had been "pretty good results" during the last decade, but good economic development had created new problems. China had to curb inflation. It was important to strengthen discipline. The central government had to exercise effective control but not contradict the opening up to the outside world. Good management was more important after opening up, otherwise there would be anarchy and "great chaos under Heaven." China was a large country but backward in technology and even in culture. In the past decade, they had solved the problem of food and clothing. Now they wanted to reach a *xiao kang* (comfortably off) stage, quadrupling their 1980 per capita GDP to between US$800 and US$1,000. China had to learn from others, "including you and even South Korea."

I complimented him on the considerable changes in China, not only in new buildings and roads but, more importantly, in people's thinking and attitudes. People were more critical and questioning, but optimistic. I said his 1979 visit to the United States, telecast in daily half-hour programs, had shown U.S. conditions, changing Chinese perceptions of America forever.

Deng remarked that the Americans had treated him very thoughtfully. He had told Secretary Shultz that Sino-U.S. relations were developing smoothly but the main problem remained Taiwan. He then asked whether I knew that "my schoolmate and your good friend" Chiang Ching-kuo had on many occasions said that he (Chiang) would "justify himself to history." Deng obviously wanted an answer to the message he had asked me to give to Chiang. I did not respond, because Chiang had not given any reply. Deng said that although the United States had publicly declared it did not want to get involved in the reunification question, the U.S. government had intervened in the handling of this question. There were many obstacles to reunification but the "largest obstacle" was the United States. He repeated the point he had made when I last saw him, that the United States was using Taiwan as an "unsinkable aircraft carrier." When he normalized relations during his 1979 visit to Washington, President Carter had agreed that the United States would do three things: abrogate the joint defense treaty with Taiwan; withdraw U.S. troops from Taiwan; and sever diplomatic relations with Taiwan. These commitments had been carried out. But the United States intervened many times on the Taiwan question through its Congress, which passed the Taiwan Relations Act and various resolutions interfering in China's internal affairs. He had told Reagan and Shultz that they had to reconsider their policy of maintaining "unsinkable aircraft carriers." Deng said he dearly wanted to ensure the reunification of Taiwan with the mainland before he went to meet Karl Marx.

# 38. China Beyond Beijing

In the 1980s and 1990s, I visited China almost every year to better understand its leaders' motivations and ambitions for China. Because we had started from antagonistic positions, we needed time and deeper interaction to develop a relationship of confidence with China. China had been exporting revolution to turn Singapore into a communist state. When they had a fight with Vietnam on their hands, they needed better relations with Asean. It was during this period, from 1978 to 1991 when we worked in our different ways against Vietnam's occupation of Cambodia, that our perceptions of each other changed.

On each visit, I would spend over a week touring the provinces, accompanied by a junior Chinese minister. Travelling with him across China for some 8 to 10 days on the same VIP aircraft, spending many hours together, I gained a better understanding of the thinking and background of their leaders. His wife would keep Choo company.

On one such visit in 1980, I found China a very different country. My daughter Wei Ling was agreeably surprised. She had been sightseeing in Beijing and had noticed the more relaxed mood of Chinese people she met, now that Mao had died and the Gang of Four had been removed. Both officials and *lao baixing* (the 100 surnames, Chinese for *hoi polloi*) were freer and more at ease when speaking to her. I still remember some of the spectacular sights we visited including Chengde, the summer capital of Qing Emperor Qian Long, and the Yangtze River's Three Gorges. The trip down the Yangtze from Chongqing (formerly Chungking,

Chiang Kai-shek's World War II capital in Sichuan) to Yichang at the exit of the gorges took one and a half days. To look up and see, high up on the perpendicular surface of sheer rock, huge Chinese characters carved thousands of years ago to commemorate events and ideas was to be awed. It resonated with the history of a people struggling against immense odds. Even more startling was the sight of human beings working as beasts of burden, towing barges and small ships as they had done from time immemorial. Whole rows of men with ropes on their shoulders and backs pulled boats upstream for miles. It was as if time had stood still and the machines used in the rest of the world had missed them.

On that trip the vice minister for foreign affairs, Han Nianlong, and his wife accompanied us. Both were able, well-informed and good company. Ten years my senior, he had a lively temperament and a nimble mind to match. He was a small man, well-groomed with good taste in Western clothes, often sporting a waistcoat. He understood English and had a keen sense of humor. He added to my education and enjoyment of my second visit. He had been in charge of the Vietnam conflict. In him the Vietnamese faced a formidable opponent. He had detailed knowledge of everything that concerned Vietnam and Cambodia. China was going to pin Vietnam down and exhaust it in the coming years, however long it might take. He was absolutely confident that the Vietnamese would, as President Ronald Reagan would say, "cry uncle." We spent several hours talking over meals on that ship. They had simple tastes in food, and after days of rich party food it was a relief to join them for a plain bowl of noodles. We had been offered banquet food but asked for their simple fare. He came from one of the poorest provinces in China, Guizhou, which produced Maotai, their most famous liquor, more powerful than vodka. I have a healthy respect for its potency—its delayed kick is tremendous and even a heavy meal does not buffer its effect. Maotai flowed freely but I asked for beer.

Our visit to the university in Wuhan, one of China's major industrial cities along the Yangtze River, was a saddening experience. Some of the professors we met were American-educated. Although advanced in age and their English rusty, they were obviously men of erudition and quality. In the library, Ling, then a medical student, spoke to a young man who was reading an English-language biology textbook. She asked to see it and found that it was printed in the 1950s. She was incredulous. How could they be reading a biology book 30 years out of date? But they had been shut off for more than 30 years; having just opened up to the West, they had no foreign exchange to buy the latest textbooks and journals. And they had no photocopying machine. It would take a long time closing the knowledge gap that had widened between them and the developed world. The Cultural Revolution had set them back by a whole generation. The present students, recovering from the Cultural Revolution, were taught with outdated textbooks by teachers using outmoded teaching methods and without audiovisual aids. This would be another semilost generation. True, the most brilliant of them would make it regardless of the disadvantages. But an industrial society requires a well-educated total population, not just the brilliant few.

After the welcoming dinner in Wuhan, our host and all the officials accompanying us disappeared. We wondered what had happened and sent our aides to find out. They reported that they were all clustered around a television set in a sitting room, watching the Gang of Four in the dock, on trial. It was the moment of retribution for the people who had terrorized them for years now about to get their just desserts. We went to our guest drawing room to watch. It was a Chinese version of what I had read of Soviet trials in Stalin's time, except that no executions were expected and there were no long self-incriminating confessions. On the contrary, Jiang Qing, Mao's widow, looked defiant and ferocious, talking, almost screaming in a high-pitched, shrill voice, as she pointed to all her judges and berated them. When Mao was in charge, they were his dogs who barked when he told them to. How dare they sit in judgment over her! She was as bold and defiant a shrew as when she cracked the whip while Mao was alive.

For the rest of our journey, the Gang of Four and their evil deeds were subjects of innumerable conversations between the Chinese officials and members of our party. Some had sad stories to tell of their experiences. It was frightening that an ancient civilization could be reduced to such madness, proudly referred to then as the Cultural Revolution.

Other things had also gone wrong. A friendly senior provincial official from Fujian, a southern province, accompanying me on a drive through Wuhan, pointed to a building nearing completion and said, *tai zi lou,* a high-rise building for "princes." I did not understand. He explained that "princes" meant the sons of important officials in the province and the city. He shook his head and said it was bad for morale, but there was little he could do about it. Without saying so, he acknowledged that it was a slide back to the old China where power had always meant privilege, and privilege meant perks for family, relatives, and friends.

Of the other stops, Xiamen and Gulangyu (Amoy and Kulangsu in the Fujian dialect) were memorable. For the first time in China, we heard the familiar dialect sounds of Singapore. I had spent years learning it to fight elections and it was a joy to hear them speak it the way I had been taught by my teacher, with the Xiamen accent of the prewar sophisticates in the Fujian province who came into contact with Western business-people and missionaries.

At Gulangyu, an island next to Xiamen, they showed us two bungalows belonging to the Singapore government. They had been purchased by the colonial government before World War II to house British colonial officers sent to Amoy to learn Hokkien. What we saw were two dilapidated buildings, each occupied by four or five families, many times the number of persons it was meant to house. They hastened to assure us that they would restore and return the buildings to us. (Hon Sui Sen, my finance minister, later told me he had heard horror stories of landlords who had taken back possession of their properties and been asked to pay arrears of salaries to caretakers for all the years since 1949.) Gulangyu was remarkable as a relic of European dominance. Every style of European architecture was represented. Some of the big houses were owned by wealthy overseas Chinese who had returned before the war to retire there. They had used French and Italian architects to build these once beautiful homes with curved staircases and banisters of travertine marble, and marble statues indoors and outdoors as if they were in Florence or Nice. Gulangyu must have been an oasis of luxury before the Japanese captured it in 1937 together with Shanghai.

Our hosts pointed across the straits in the direction of Jinmen (Quemoy), an island under Taiwanese control. On a clear day it could be seen with the naked eye. That was exactly what President Chiang Ching-kuo had told me earlier that year when he took me to Jinmen and pointed across the same stretch of water to Gulangyu. Only a few years ago, the

Taiwanese had been sending over balloons from Jinmen to Gulangyu carrying food parcels, cassettes of Taiwan pop singers including Teresa Teng, their top-of-the-chart pop star, and propaganda leaflets. In the 1950s and 1960s they had exchanged artillery barrages. In the 1980s, they traded insults over loudspeakers.

The difference between the standards of living of Taipei in Taiwan and Xiamen in Fujian was stark. One was linked to the outside world, particularly America and Japan, with capital, technology, knowledge, foreign experts, and their own returned students from America and Japan building a modern economy. The other was plodding along, proud of its agricultural prowess based on knowledge of the 1950s and hardly any farm machinery, with deplorable communications and a low standard of living.

The cuisine was familiar but different. At lunch they produced the original *baobing* (popiah), stir-fried shredded bamboo shoots wrapped in a pancake to make a spring roll with the necessary garnishes and condiments. It was different from the Singapore version. They had all the familiar candies, such as delicious crushed peanut brittle, rolled up like a mini Swiss roll, tastier than what we had in Singapore. All of us knew this was where most of our ancestors came from. Wherever their village in Fujian province, for their journey to the South Seas, most would have come to Xiamen, the international settlement, to board the big ships that would take them south to Nanyang.

From Xiamen we flew on to Guangzhou (Canton), then went back to Hong Kong by train. They had stopped the constant exhortations over loudspeakers, monotonous and repetitious speeches about the "capitalist roader" and other clichés of the Gang of Four. The Chinese were also less rigorous in their dress code. Once we left Beijing, the women interpreters who accompanied us wore floral blouses with slacks or skirts, which they did not do in 1976. Maoist China was fading into history. The old habits of the Chinese would return; a few good ones, and more than a few bad ones, as we were to discover on my next visit in 1985—growing corruption, nepotism, and favoritism, the ills that have always beset China.

This time we left with more favorable impressions. Our hosts were relaxed, enjoyed the meals and conversation, and were ready to talk of the disastrous decade of *wen ge*—their shorthand for *wen hua da ge ming,* the great Cultural Revolution. The leaders and officials we met were more open and at ease, willing to discuss their past mistakes and future problems. There were fewer of the slogans that used to be plastered all over Beijing and other cities, and of the giant square placards in rice and wheat fields. The few modest slogans now exhorted people to work hard for the Four Modernisations. They were becoming more natural, more like other societies.

China's leaders were conscious of having lost a generation because of the Cultural Revolution. They had turned away from Mao's belief in perpetual revolution. They wanted stable relations with other countries to get economic cooperation and help China recover. I thought it unlikely that there would be a modern China for another generation.

Every province of China is different in geography, economy, education, and standard of efficiency. The preoccupations of their governors are different. I did not realize how dry, dusty, and barren north China was until I visited Dunhuang, the beginning of the Silk Road, to see the famous Buddhist grottoes which had been abandoned for many centuries. When the governor of Gansu province sent me on a camel ride to the "Singing Sands" not far from Dunhuang, I realized that we were on the edge of the Gobi and Taklamakan Deserts. Their Bactrian camels were splendid double-humped shaggy creatures more elegant than the single-humped dromedary of the Arabian peninsula. The scenery with its high sand dunes was beautiful if bleak; but life was and still is hard.

These tours showed us why provincial loyalties were strong in such a vast and densely populated country. Their accents, diets, and social habits vary. The elite could not know each other as well as their counterparts did in Europe, Japan, and the United States. America may be a continent, but the population is not as large, and excellent communications allowed their elite to meet and interact regularly. China is too populous, and until the 1980s when they built up their airports and imported Western aircraft, communications were so poor that they lived in separate worlds. Hence every leader who rose to the top in Beijing brought with him as many of his provincial colleagues as was decent without arousing resentment from those excluded. Fellow provincials understood and could best read their leader's mind.

There is strong interprovincial rivalry. Every governor will rattle off the basic statistics of his province—land area, population, cultivable land, rainfall, annual production of agriculture, industry services, and its ranking among the 30 provinces for each individual item, including total GDP. There is equally keen intercity rivalry; each city mayor will recite its vital statistics and ranking among cities. The ranking is settled by the central government to encourage competition, which appears overkeen as leaders try to improve their position by all means, even resorting to trade wars. A fast-growing province such as Guangdong needed to import food for the influx of "floating" workers from other provinces; its neighbor would refuse to sell it grain. A province with a successful motorcycle manufacturing plant could not export its products to adjoining provinces that wanted to protect their own motorcycle plants.

I had assumed that the communist system made for complete unified central control. This never was so in China. From the earliest dynasties, provincial authorities have enjoyed considerable independence in interpreting imperial edicts, and the further away from the center a province was, the greater its independence. Five words, *shan gao, huang di yuan* (mountains are high, the emperor is far away), express the cynicism and skepticism of generations of the disaffected who have been shortchanged by the local authorities. We were to have firsthand experience of this when we embarked on an ambitious project in the city of Suzhou in the 1990s.

I gained some insights into how their government works: cumbersome and multilayered, with four layers of authority—central, provincial, city or county, and district. In theory, written directives from the center apply equally across a whole continent. In practice, their battles over turf are fierce and tenacious, each ministry jealously guarding its rights and trying to extend its powers. Intraministry contests and gridlocks are frequent. There is no distinction between a civil servant and a political appointee. The Chinese Communist Party is supreme and anybody of any consequence must have a position in the party. To rise as an official or do well in private business, party membership is invaluable.

The quality of the people in charge of China is impressive. With training and exposure to free-market economies, they could equal top executives in America, Western Europe, and Japan. They have capacious minds, analytical and quick on the uptake. Even in casual conversation the subtlety of their presentation shows a sharpness of intellect that can be fully appreciated only if one understands the Chinese language.

I had expected this of the leaders in Beijing, but was surprised to discover the high caliber of their provincial officials, party secretaries, governors, mayors, and senior officials. The thick layer of talent spread over the continent is impressive. Those who get to the very top are not necessarily a class apart from those who just missed it. In a populous country like China, the luck of the draw plays a considerable part in getting to the top even though they have a careful and thorough process of selection, with the emphasis on ability and character, no longer on ideological purity or revolutionary fervor as during the disastrous years of the Cultural Revolution.

One former activist gave me an insight into how the personnel section of the Communist Party of China selects their top talent. Everyone has a file or dossier, which starts with his primary school report, containing not only his academic performance but his teachers' assessments of his character, behavior, values, and attitudes. At every stage of his career, there are records of judgments of his peers and superiors. At every level for promotion, all suitable candidates are assessed before appointment. At the top echelons of the pyramid is a core of between 5,000 and 10,000 who have been chosen and carefully graded by the organization department of the Communist Party, not the government. To ensure that gradings are correct, inspection teams from the center visit provinces and cities to assess the assessors and interview an activist before he is promoted. In case of disagreement, the matter would be reviewed in Beijing. The selection process is thorough, searching, and comprehensive. Finally, at the very top, promotion is done by the leader himself who has to judge not only the merit but also the loyalty of the candidate. It was Deng Xiaoping who chose Zhao Ziyang to be general secretary of the Communist Party and nominally no. 1 in China. It was Deng who reversed his decision after Tiananmen in 1989.

# 39. Tiananmen

In May 1989, the world watched a bizarre drama unfold in Beijing. It was shown live on satellite television because the Western media were there in strength with their cameras in position to cover the Deng-Gorbachev summit. Students had gathered in large numbers in orderly fashion at Tiananmen Square in front of the Great Hall of the People. They carried banners and placards to protest against corruption, nepotism, and inflation. The police were benign. The general secretary of the Chinese Communist Party (CCP) himself, Zhao Ziyang, made encouraging noises, that the students wanted the party and the government to reform, and had good intentions. As the crowds swelled, the banners and slogans became more critical, antigovernment, and strident. They started to denounce the government and Premier Li Peng by name. When nothing happened, they targeted Deng Xiaoping, ridiculing him in satirical doggerel. When I saw this on television, I felt that this demonstration would end in tears. No emperor in China can be lampooned and ridiculed and continue to reign.

Tiananmen was a strange episode in China's history. Li Peng was telecast reading out the declaration of martial law. I watched excerpts of Beijing television relayed by satellite via Hong Kong to Singapore. One vivid premartial law episode showed representatives of the students in the Great Hall of the People arguing rudely with Premier Li Peng. They wore jeans and T-shirts. Li Peng was in an immaculately pressed Mao suit. The students scored heavily against Li Peng in that TV encounter. The drama reached a climax when soldiers tried to march into the square and were repulsed. Finally, on the night of 3 June, tanks and armored personnel carriers rolled in while the world watched on television. Some researchers who have sifted through the evidence were persuaded that there was actually no shooting in Tiananmen Square itself, that the shootings took place as troops accompanying the tanks and armored personnel carriers were forcing their way through the streets leading to the square.

It was unbelievable. The People's Liberation Army (PLA) had turned its guns on its own people. I felt compelled to issue a statement the following day, 5 June:

> My cabinet colleagues and I are shocked, horrified and saddened by this disastrous turn of events. We had expected the Chinese government to apply the doctrine of minimum force when an army is used to quell civil disorder. Instead, the fire power and violence used caused many deaths and casualties. They were totally disproportionate to the resistance unarmed civilians offered.
>
> A China with large sections of her people, including her best-educated, at odds with the government means trouble, with people resentful, reforms stalled, and economy stagnant. Because of her size, such a China could create problems for herself and her neighbours in Asia.
>
> We hope wiser counsels will prevail to pursue conciliation, so that the Chinese people can resume the progress which the open-door policies have brought them.

I did not condemn them. I did not regard them as a repressive communist regime like the Soviet Union. A certain momentum had been built up by those mass demonstrations in those two months.

The reactions of ethnic Chinese communities in Hong Kong, Taiwan, and Singapore were markedly different. People in Hong Kong were distressed and terrified. They had watched the tragedy unfold on television almost 24 hours a day. They identified themselves with the students. Some Hong Kong youths had even camped with them in Tiananmen Square. That was a time when China had encouraged Hong Kong and

Taiwan journalists and visitors to get closer to China. When the shooting took place, Hong Kongers were distraught at the prospect of coming under the control of such a cruel government. There were spontaneous outpourings of grief and rage. A million people took to the streets soon after the scenes appeared on television. For days, they continued demonstrations outside the Xinhua News Agency, the unofficial PRC presence in Hong Kong. They helped protesters escape from the mainland through Hong Kong to the West.

In Taiwan, there was sadness and sympathy for the students but not fear. There were no mass demonstrations of protest or grief. They were not about to be governed by China.

Singaporeans were shocked. Few believed that such firepower was necessary, but nobody demonstrated. People knew China was different, a communist country. A delegation of students from the universities presented a protest letter to the Chinese embassy.

It was an instructive moment, highlighting the different positions, perceptions and emotional involvement of these three groups of ethnic Chinese, placed in varying degrees of political proximity to communist China.

But for his part in ordering the PLA to clear Tiananmen, Deng would have been eulogized in the West when he died in February 1997. Instead every obituary was laced with heavy criticism of the brutal crackdown on 4 June and every TV soundbite included a playback of the same scenes of Tiananmen. I do not know how Chinese historians will evaluate his role. I consider Deng a great leader who changed the destiny of China and of the world.

He was a realist, practical and pragmatic, not ideological. Twice he had been purged by Mao, but he came back to power to save China. Twelve years before the Soviet Union collapsed he had known that the centrally planned economy did not work. He opened up China to free enterprise and the free market, starting with the special economic zones on the coast. Deng was the only leader in China with the political standing and strength to reverse Mao's policies. Like Mao, Deng fought to destroy the old China. But he did what Mao did not do. He built the new China, using free enterprise and the free market "with Chinese characteristics."

A veteran of war and revolution, he saw the student demonstrators at Tiananmen as a danger that threatened to throw China back into turmoil and chaos, prostrate for another 100 years. He had lived through a revolution and recognized the early signs of one at Tiananmen. Gorbachev, unlike Deng, had only read about revolution and did not recognize the danger signals of the Soviet Union's impending collapse.

Twenty years after Deng's open-door policy, China shows every promise of becoming Asia's largest and most dynamic economy. If it avoids disorder and conflicts, either domestic or international, it will become a giant economy in 2030. When he died, Deng left the Chinese people a huge and promising legacy. But for him, the People's Republic of China would have collapsed as the Soviet Union did. If China had disintegrated, the Western media would have sympathized with the Chinese people as they have done with the Russians. Instead, the West has to weigh the prospect of a powerful China in 30 to 50 years.

Three months after Tiananmen, on 24 August, Hu Ping, China's minister of commerce who had accompanied me on my provincial tour in 1988, called on me. Premier Li Peng wanted him to brief me on the "6-4" incident ("6-4," June 4th, is a Chinese shorthand—they refer to big events by the month and day on which they occurred). The situation was now stable, but the impact on China had been great. During the 40 to 50 days of turmoil, China had lost control of the situation. The students had used the problems of corruption and inflation to rally people to their cause. Their police lacked experience and were not able to deal with such demonstrations as they did not have water cannons and other riot control equipment.

He said that by early June, the students had militarized themselves by robbing weapons and equipment from the PLA. (I had not read of this.) The troops tried to enter Tiananmen Square on 20 May but were obstructed. They were withdrawn and "re-educated." On 3 June, the troops began another push. Some were armed, but many were not. All had orders not to fire. In fact, the ammunition pouches of many of the troops contained biscuits. They had no rubber bullets. The day after the incident, he himself had toured Chang-An Road (road of eternal peace), the stretch from the Military Museum to the Diaoyutai guesthouse, and seen the smoking wrecks of 15 tanks and armored cars. The troops had acted with great restraint, abandoning their vehicles and firing shots into the air. His ministry was located near the square and he saw the million-strong demonstration. In fact, 10 percent of the staff of his ministry and of other ministries had joined the demonstrators. They were also against corruption and were sympathetic to the students. Casualties, Hu Ping insisted, were caused when the troops were trying to get to Tiananmen Square, not in the square itself as the foreign press claimed.

Since then, foreign businesspeople and their Chinese staff had returned to work. He believed that their foreign friends would gradually understand. Some young Chinese had links with an intelligence agency of a Western country and had spread Western opinions and information through advanced equipment. (I took this to mean the fax machine.) Although Western countries had now imposed sanctions, China would never allow foreign interference in its internal affairs. But most of these countries, including international banks, had not taken sanctions further. Contacts were being restored. He hoped Singapore-China bilateral relations would stay good because they were on firm foundations.

"6-4" was a shock to me and the people of Singapore, I replied. We had not expected to see the use of such tremendous firepower and force. We were accustomed to seeing on television, almost nightly, clashes between South Korean police and workers and students, white South African police beating up blacks, and Israelis using tear gas, rubber bullets, and other weapons against Palestinians, with occasionally one or two deaths; tanks and armored cars were never used. Singaporeans could not believe what they had seen—a Chinese government that had been so reasonable, forbearing, and tolerant in May, suddenly turned brutal, using tanks against civilians. Singaporeans, especially ethnic Chinese, could not understand this and felt deeply shamed by such an uncivilized action. There were deep mental scars.

China had to explain to Singapore and the world why it was necessary for the demonstrations to be put down in this way, why there was no other way. To go overnight from "soft" to "hard" was not explicable. China's real problem was not with countries in Southeast Asia, which had neither the wealth nor technology to help China modernize. Its problem was with the United States, Japan, and Europe. The United States especially, through the World Bank and the IMF, had done China many good turns. China had to erase the bad impression it had created. I suggested they get some American public relations firm to help in this task. Americans were an emotional people. Television had a tremendous impact on them. Senators and members of Congress controlled the president and money; China must pay close attention to them. Fortunately for China, President Bush had lived in China for several years and knew it better than most Americans. He had been trying to calm down Congress.

I cautioned that if China stopped sending students abroad because of the added problems they had caused through faxing their ideas to their friends in Beijing, China would shut itself off from knowledge and technology. The loss would be incalculable.

He assured me that their policies on students and on opening up would not change. Many businesspeople from Taiwan were coming in to invest. Their policy toward Hong Kong and Taiwan also would not change. But the situation in Hong Kong was more complicated, he said. The slogans people had coined in Hong Kong had changed from "Hong Kong people rule Hong Kong" to "Hong Kong people *save* Hong Kong." He did not refer to the enormous outpouring of fear and sympathy in street processions of a million Hong Kong people in protest against "6-4."

A sad memory I have of Tiananmen Square, packed with demonstrators sporting slogans on headbands, is of Zhao with a megaphone, almost in tears, pleading with the students to disperse, telling them that he could no longer protect them. That was on 19 May. It was too late. The CCP leaders had decided to declare martial law and use force if necessary to break up the demonstrations. At that stage, the students had either to disperse or be forcibly removed. Zhao had not shown that toughness needed in the leader of a China on the verge of *luan* (chaos). Orderly protesters had been allowed to become defiant rebels. If not firmly dealt with, they could have triggered off similar disorder throughout the vast country. Tiananmen is not London's Trafalgar Square.

Communist China has adopted the Soviet practice of the "nonperson." However powerful a leader has been, once he is out he becomes a nonperson and is never mentioned in public. Although I would have liked to meet Zhao Ziyang on my later visits to China, I could not raise the subject. A few years after Tiananmen, I met one of his sons and was given a glimpse of what life had been like for Zhao and his family after his fall from grace. Zhao had had to move out of Zhongnanhai, where all party leaders lived, to a house occupied by Hu Yaobang (the former general secretary of the party) when Hu was a director of the organization department of the CCP. For the first few years, Zhao had a sentry at the entrance and his movements were monitored. Later, the surveillance was relaxed. He could play golf at a Chinese-owned golf course in a Beijing suburb but not on a foreign joint-venture golf course. He could visit inland but not coastal provinces, to minimize contact with foreigners and the resulting publicity. Zhao's children were overseas, except for one daughter who worked in a Beijing hotel. His living conditions were comfortable. His family could visit him. By Soviet standards of treatment for nonpersons, he was not badly off. He was better-treated than Krushchev had been by Brezhnev, or Gorbachev by Yeltsin.

The man who publicly carried the international and domestic odium for the declaration of martial law and the forcible dispersal of the crowd at Tiananmen was Premier Li Peng. In fact, the decision was made by Deng, supported by several of the Long March veterans. I first met Li Peng in Beijing in September 1988. He had taken over as premier from Zhao Ziyang who had become general secretary. Li was not as outgoing as Zhao. A Russian-trained engineer in his mid-sixties, he had a good, capacious mind and was always well-briefed and careful with his words. He was not the back-slapping type and could take offense when none was intended. I adjusted to his temperament and we got on. After I came to know him better, I found him a sensible if conservative man.

He is the son of a leading communist and had been adopted by Premier Zhou Enlai. He has no provincial accent at all, because he lived where the CCP headquarters were, with the Zhou family in Yenan, and later in Beijing. His wife is more outgoing, an easy conversationalist with an attractive personality. Unlike most Chinese leaders' wives who kept in the background, she frequently played hostess. She spoke English for social purposes. Choo found it easy to talk to her in English without interpreters.

At our formal discussion, Li Peng asked about Singapore's business developments in China. I said Singapore investors faced many difficulties.

Too many had lost money and become discouraged. The word had got around that there was confusion in China, so investments had slowed down. They could not understand why Chinese managers and supervisors could not exercise discipline over Chinese workers. Singapore- and Hong Kong–owned hotels needed to employ their own Chinese as supervisors to discipline the staff. Even so, there were problems. For instance, workers fired for removing materials from a hotel had to be reinstated because other workers created trouble. Labor relations had to change if China wanted progress. They should allow investors to manage their own enterprises, including hiring and firing workers.

He replied that foreign investors were welcome to make money, but China's policy was to ensure that they did not make too much money. (I took this to mean that, whatever might have been agreed, if in their opinion profits were too high, they would find some way of making the division of profits more equitable.) China's taxation policies in the special economic zones were better than those in Hong Kong. But he admitted that foreign investors faced low efficiency in the government and much red tape. China had great difficulty solving this. Many state-owned enterprises were overstaffed and making losses. They had to care for retired workers. With the free market, China's wage system had become absurd. A senior professor in a well-known university had a salary of about 400 yuan. The professor's daughter, an attendant in a foreign enterprise, received as much. No one could say that the contribution of the daughter was as large as that of the father. The entire wage system would have to be changed, but he could not raise the salary of the professor because the government had insufficient resources. China had achieved much since it initiated the policy of opening up to the outside world, he said, but inflation had been very high and had to be controlled by slowing down the rate of investments in construction. China would not reverse the reforms. He was confident they would overcome their difficulties.

Asked for an assessment of the security situation in East Asia, I painted an optimistic picture of growth and stability, provided there were no security upsets. The Soviet Union was contained by both the United States and China. The U.S. policy was to co-opt Japan with its economic strength to supplement its own while providing security for Japan. As long as this arrangement prevailed, there was no need for Japan to rearm.

Japan did not have nuclear capability, but it was possible that Japan would go it alone if the United States proved no longer dependable. In that case, the threat to all countries in Southeast Asia would increase. Most Japanese leaders of the older generation wanted to continue this partnership with the United States which had brought them prosperity and the good life. There was a danger that a younger generation of leaders, having no experience of the last war, might think differently, especially if they revived their myth that they were descendants of the sun goddess.

Li Peng thought I had underestimated the Japanese danger. China had to be vigilant over the resurrection of the Japanese military. Despite Japan's self-imposed ceiling of 1 percent of GNP, its military expenditure was some US$26–27 billion more than China's. There were some Japanese leaders who wanted to reverse the verdict of history that Japan had committed aggression against China, Southeast Asia, and the South Pacific. He cited two examples: the way they wrote their textbooks and visits to Yasukuni shrine by top Japanese leaders. (The Yasukuni shrine honors soldiers who died in war.) Japan's economic success had created the wherewithal to make it a major political and military power. At least some Japanese leaders were thinking along those lines. His concern at a possible revival of Japanese militarism was real. At the same time, China "was consistently on guard" against danger from the Soviet Union.

Two years later, on 11 August 1990, Premier Li Peng visited Singapore. He had just reestablished Sino-Indonesian diplomatic relations in Jakarta. We met with only note takers and an interpreter. I had said on many past occasions that Singapore would be the last country in Asean to establish diplomatic relations with China. Now that Indonesia had restored diplomatic relations, I wanted to resolve this before I stepped down as prime minister in November that year. Li Peng noted that during my long years as prime minister, relations between Singapore and China had developed well. He too would like to settle this matter before I stepped down. Hence, he invited me to visit China in mid-October.

I then referred to the issue that had bogged down discussions at the official level on the agreement to exchange embassies—our troops training in Taiwan. I did not see a final date for our training there. Singapore was deeply indebted to Taiwan, in particular to the late President Chiang

Ching-kuo who had enabled us to break out of our limited space for military training. We could not forget our debt. We paid only for what we consumed or used and had not paid a single extra dollar. It was a special relationship. We felt close to each other because we were both noncommunists and shared the same language, culture, and ancestry. Li expressed understanding of our position, that Singapore was prosperous but not big. Finally, he said China would not insist on a specific time frame for Singapore training in Taiwan to end.

After that meeting, a thorny issue over which negotiations had been stalled for many months was on its way to resolution. Unlike in 1976, I was no longer concerned that a Chinese embassy in Singapore could pose problems for our security. Our domestic conditions had changed. We had solved some basic problems in Chinese education. All our schools had converted to a national system with English as their medium of instruction. Nanyang University no longer taught in Chinese and its graduates could easily find employment. We had stopped breeding successive generations of disadvantaged graduates.

At a full delegation meeting after our discussion, Li referred to Tiananmen as the "turmoil in China last summer." Some countries had imposed sanctions that caused China some difficulties but also hurt themselves. The Japanese had eased their sanctions after the G-7 meeting. I said that, unlike the Western media, Singapore did not consider Tiananmen to be the end of the world, but it was a great pity that China had lost out in public relations. Li said, "The Chinese government lost total control of the situation." As premier, he "could not even go into the streets. This chaos lasted for 48 days."

Li Peng is not a man for lighthearted jests. That day he surprised everyone when he said he would like to "crack a joke" on our troop training in Taiwan: They could train in China on terms better than in Taiwan. There was a burst of spontaneous laughter around the table. When that day arrived, I said, peace would have broken out in Asia.

Two months later, I paid my last visit to Beijing as prime minister, to formalize and establish diplomatic relations on 3 October. After this was done, we discussed the Iraqi occupation of Kuwait. Li Peng said Iraq could not be defeated easily in a blitzkrieg. (When with sophisticated weaponry Desert Storm tore through Iraq's defenses in a matter of days, it must have come as a surprise to China's civil and military leaders.)

He disclosed that a few weeks before our meeting, at Vietnam's request, its leaders, Nguyen Van Linh (premier), Do Muoi (party secretary), and Pham Van Dong (senior leader and former prime minister who had visited Singapore in 1978), had held talks in Chengdu, Sichuan province, with General Secretary Jiang Zemin and him. They had agreed that Vietnam would unconditionally withdraw from Cambodia under UN supervision, and that a national security council would govern Cambodia until the elections. China was now ready to improve relations with Vietnam.

In October 1990, I met President Jiang Zemin. He received me warmly, quoting from the *Analects* of Confucius: "It is a pleasure to receive friends from afar." He had missed me when he visited Singapore in the early 1980s, and when I visited Shanghai in 1988 when he was mayor there. He had visited Singapore twice, on the first occasion for two weeks to study how the Economic Development Board (EDB) got investments into Singapore and how we developed industrial estates. He was then tasked with setting up special economic zones in Guangdong and Fujian. The second visit was a transit stop. He had carried away a deep impression of Singapore's city planning, orderliness, traffic conditions, cleanliness, and standard of service. He remembered our slogan, "Courtesy is our way of life." He was pleased he could speak Mandarin with ordinary people in the streets, which made it easy for him to get around.

Jiang said that after the "6-4" incident, the West claimed that through television it was possible for them to interfere in Chinese affairs. The West acted in accordance with their value system. He could accept that there were different views, but not that only one view was correct. There was nothing absolute in these concepts of democracy, freedom, and human rights. They could not exist in abstraction, but were linked to a country's culture and level of economic development. There was no such thing as freedom of the press. Western newspapers belonged to and were controlled by various financial groups. He referred to Singapore's decision in 1988 to restrict the sales of the *Asian Wall Street Journal* and said China should have done the same during Gorbachev's visit. Many Western media reports on the "6-4" incident were not accurate.

Deng's policy of opening to the world and adhering to socialism remained unchanged. Since I had expressed concern about the continuance of this open-door policy, Jiang assured me that it would be "accelerated." They had decided to break away from the Soviet centrally planned system. He had studied in the Soviet Union for two years and visited the country on 10 occasions, so he knew the difficulties of their system. China wanted to establish a mixed economy, to combine the best of the centrally planned economy and market regulation.

China wanted to maintain contact with other countries. It faced difficulties in feeding 1.1 billion people. It was an enormous effort to supply the whole country with grain alone. As mayor of Shanghai, with a population of 12 million, he had found it difficult to supply 2 million kilos of vegetables daily. For an hour he spoke of China's colossal needs. At dinner the conversation was lively. He would quote couplets and verses from his immense mental anthology memorized since childhood. His comments were peppered with literary allusions, many beyond my limited knowledge of Chinese literature, which added to the work of the interpreter.

Instead of the stereotyped grey communist apparatchik that I had expected, I found a medium-height, stocky, fair, bespectacled, broad-faced, black hair combed straight back, ready-smiling party chairman. He was the No. 1 man in China, chosen by Deng Xiaoping in a matter of days after "6-4" to take the place of Zhao Ziyang. He was highly intelligent and well-read and had a gift for languages. He was fluent in Russian, spoke English and German, and could quote Shakespeare and Goethe. He told me he also spoke Romanian, having worked in Romania.

Jiang was born in 1926 into a scholarly family in Yangzhou town, Jiangsu province. His grandfather was a renowned physician and a talented poet, painter, and calligrapher. His father was the eldest son. An uncle who had joined the Communist Youth League at 17 and been killed at 28 in the civil war against the Nationalists in 1939 was considered a revolutionary martyr. His father gave Jiang Zemin, then 13, to the widow of this uncle who had no son. So Jiang had impeccable revolutionary antecedents when he joined the communist student groups in the universities in Nanjing and Jiaotong in Shanghai.

He was brought up in a home with books, paintings, and music. Jiang sings, plays the piano, and enjoys listening to Mozart and Beethoven. There were significant differences in academic performance between people of the various provinces. Jiangsu was the "Lake District" of China where, over the millennia, its pleasant microclimate had attracted retired mandarins and literati. Their progeny have raised the academic level of the population there. Suzhou in Jiangsu province, once the capital of one of the states in the Spring Autumn period (about 770–476 B.C.), has one street called Zhuang Yuan Jie. *Zhuang Yuan* was the title given to the candidate who came first in the imperial examinations that used to be held in the capital city once every three years. Suzhou leaders proudly claim that quite a number of them came from that street.

Although I had been well-briefed, Jiang was a surprise. I had not expected to find so extroverted a Chinese communist leader. When Jiang spent two weeks in Singapore in 1980, Ng Pock Too, an EDB director, was his liaison officer. After Jiang was made general secretary, Ng gave me a thumbnail sketch. He was surprised Jiang had been placed in this top position. He remembered him as a serious, hardworking, conscientious, and thorough official: Jiang would study every problem in detail, take notes, and ask searching questions. Ng thought highly of him because, unlike other Chinese officials who stayed in five-star hotels, Jiang chose a three-star hotel off fashionable Orchard Road. He travelled modestly—in Ng's car, by taxi, or on foot. Jiang was a thrifty, honest official, but did not appear to be a political animal.

Toward the end of the two weeks, Jiang had looked Ng Pock Too in the eye and said, "You have not told me everything. You must have a secret. China has cheaper land, cheaper water, cheaper power, cheaper labour. Yet you get so many investments and we don't. What is the secret formula?" Nonplussed, Ng explained the key importance of political confidence and economic productivity. He pulled out his copy of the Business Environment Risk Index (BERI) report, and pointed out Singapore's rating as 1A on a scale of 1A down to 3C. China was not even included in the rating. Singapore was safe and favored for investments because of safe political, economic, and other factors. There was no danger of confiscation. Our workers were industrious and productive, and there were minimal strikes. Our currency was convertible. He went through the BERI measurements. Jiang was not altogether convinced, so he gave Jiang the BERI report to take home. They had a summing-up discussion in Jiang's small hotel room before they left for the airport. Jiang finally said he understood the magic formula, that the EDB had the "unique knowhow to sell confidence"! Ng concluded, "I never thought he would be the No. 1 man in China. He was too nice."

Our personal chemistry was good. Jiang was gregarious. I was open and direct. Whereas with Li Peng I had to be careful not to speak even half in jest, Jiang knew I meant well and did not take offense. He also had a very un-Chinese habit of holding his guest's forearm and looking him earnestly in the eye when he asked a direct question. His eyes were his lie detector. I assumed he must have been satisfied that I was not being evasive when he asked some very probing questions about Taiwan, America, and the West, and about China itself.

Personal chemistry does make a difference to the ease with which business can be done on difficult and sensitive issues. I could not have talked as freely with either Hua Guofeng or Li Peng as I did with Jiang Zemin. It might have been possible with Zhao Ziyang, but not in the same free-ranging manner.

Many, myself included, underrated Jiang's staying power because of his bonhomie and his penchant for quoting poetry at every opportunity. But there must be a tough infighter side of him that his opponents would have discovered to their detriment when they thwarted him. There is no question about his integrity and dedication to the high cause placed upon him by Deng Xiaoping, to carry China's modernization forward and make China a prosperous, industrial society with "a socialist market economy." He explained its meaning to me at some length, that China had to be different from a Western free-market economy because the Chinese were socialists.

When I met Jiang again two years later, in October 1992, we talked about the international situation. It was a few weeks before the U.S. elections. I suggested China would need to buy time for itself if Clinton won. He should give Clinton room to maneuvre and do a U-turn on some of his policies, like China's Most Favored Nation status, to avoid a head-on confrontation. A new, young president eager to show his supporters that he was ready to live up to his election speeches could result in problems for both China and America.

Jiang listened. He answered indirectly. He had read my speeches, those delivered in China and elsewhere. During Deng's tour of the southern provinces in January that year, Deng had referred to the rapid development of Southeast Asia and especially Singapore. The 14th party congress to be held the following month would carry out Deng's policy of "socialism with Chinese characteristics." For this, China needed a peaceful and stable international and internal environment. The market economy would expand in China but would take a long time. As for democracy for China, the East had been influenced by the teachings of Confucius and Mencius. Any "shock treatment" (of sudden democracy) for China, like that in the Soviet Union, was out. As for the present unhappy state of U.S.-China relations, the fault was not China's. By selling fighter planes and weapons to Taiwan, America had violated the principles of the 1982 communiqué agreed between China and the United States. But China had not made a big issue of it because it did not want to embarrass President Bush during his election campaign.

He described China's economic situation. Then he asked me what would be the most satisfactory rate of GNP growth for China. Their previous target was 6 percent. In the next congress, their proposed target was 8 or 9 percent. The four Little Dragons and Japan, I replied, had achieved double-digit growth with little inflation for sustained periods during the early phases of their industrialization. Before the oil crisis, Singapore had achieved 12 to 14 percent growth rates with little inflation. The optimum rate of growth for Singapore did not depend on any magic figure, but on how much of our labor and production capacity was underused and also on our rates of interest and inflation. I added that Dr. Goh Keng Swee (my former finance minister, who had been advising the Chinese on their special economic zones) believed China's most important problem was the inability of the People's Bank of China (PBOC), their central bank, to control credit. Each PBOC branch in the provinces responded to pressure from provincial governments when creating credit. Furthermore, data on money supply at any given time was insufficient. China had to control money supply to keep inflation under control, and not allow the provincial branches of the PBOC to create credit without the knowledge and permission of the central bank.

He made a note of this. He said he had graduated as an electrical engineer but had begun to learn economics and was reading the works of Adam Smith, Paul Samuelson, and Milton Friedman. He was not the only Chinese leader studying market economics. I advised him to study the workings of the U.S. Federal Reserve Bank and the German Bundesbank, two successful central banks. Of the two, the Bundesbank had been more successful in fighting inflation. The chairman of the Bundesbank was appointed by the chancellor, but once appointed he had independence and the chancellor could not order him to increase money supply or lower interest rates. China must get credit creation under control and not be overconcerned about not exceeding a putative ideal rate of growth. For example, if Guangdong province could grow faster than other provinces because of inputs from Hong Kong, then he should let it do so, and encourage that growth to spread to neighboring provinces through improved road, rail, air, river, and sea transportation. He said he would study these points.

When I next met Jiang in Beijing in May 1993, he thanked me for having facilitated the Wang-Koo talks in Singapore between "unofficial" representatives of China and Taiwan. It was the first time since 1949 that the two sides of the civil war had met, albeit "unofficially." Jiang said, however, that he felt "very strange and disappointed" with the numerous reports that Taiwan wanted to join the UN. He thought it was unwise for the West to treat China as a potential enemy.

I said that Taiwan's push to join the UN was not encouraged by the United States. Dick Cheney, the former U.S. secretary for defense under Reagan until 1992, and Jeanne Kirkpatrick, the former U.S. permanent representative to the UN, also under Reagan, had said in Taipei recently that it was not realistic for Taiwan to join the UN, that Taiwan could join UNESCO, the World Bank, and other technical organizations, but not the UN itself. I believed Taiwan's wish to join the UN was a passing phase with President Lee Teng-hui, who wanted to break away from the old KMT position, which was not to join any international body because Taiwan was not a full member of the UN. (I was to discover later that I was wrong; it was not a passing phase. Lee Teng-hui really hoped to join the UN and to assert Taiwan's separateness as the Republic of China on Taiwan.)

The best outcome of China-Taiwan relations, I believed, was a peaceful and gradual interlocking of economic, social, and political relations between the two. For example, in 1958 the mainland had exchanged artillery fire with Taiwan across the narrow Straits of Quemoy and Matsu. If China had succeeded in reuniting with Taiwan then, China would now be in a less advantageous position. Because it did not, it could now tap the resources of some 20 million Taiwanese who had acquired economic and technological assets through their association with America. He nodded in agreement. Would it not be better to have Taiwan carry on as a separate entity, I suggested. Then America and Europe would continue to let Taiwan have access to their technology and know-how for another 40 to 50 years, and China could benefit further from what Taiwan could put into the mainland. He shook his head in disagreement.

I next argued that if he wanted the United States to have less leverage, he should open up China to more European MNCs. Then American businesspeople would lobby their government against actions that jeopardized their interests in China for fear of losing out to European and Japanese MNCs. He thought this a good point. I added that America and Europe could not tolerate another Japanese-style closed-market economy in a China that only exported and did not import. For China to develop, it must use its potentially huge market to attract foreign investors who can sell their products in China and thus "lock them into China's growth." Jiang agreed that as a big country it was not realistic to have a wholly export-oriented economy. China must increase its exports, but not to the United States alone, and China had to develop an open market. He agreed more with the view of Vice Premier Li Lanqing (in charge of trade) than with that of Vice Premier Zhu Rongji (in charge of industries). Zhu held the view that local industries must have a certain degree of protection. Jiang said China's policy was to learn from various countries and pick up their strong points, not only in know-how, science, and technology but also in cultural experience.

One animated meeting I had with Jiang was in October 1994, about Taiwan. Earlier that year, in May, Taiwan's President Lee Teng-hui had stopped over in Singapore to ask Prime Minister Goh to convey a proposal to President Jiang. This was to set up an international shipping company, to be jointly owned by the PRC, Taiwan, and Singapore (with only a nominal Singapore shareholding), to handle trade between China and Taiwan. All ships trading with the PRC would be put under this company.

Goh had written to Jiang to convey the proposal. Jiang had not accepted it. Then Goh and I had decided to put up a Singapore proposal to bridge the gulf between the two, by forming a company for both shipping and airline, to be registered in Singapore and jointly owned by the PRC, Taiwan, and Singapore in more or less equal shares. This company would wet-charter ships and aircraft (lease ships and aircraft with their full crew complement) in equal numbers from China and Taiwan. After three years, the two would buy out Singapore's share. President Lee had agreed to this proposal when we met in Taiwan in mid-September 1994.

I met Jiang a few days later, on 6 October, in the Great Hall of the People. He proposed that we talk in a small group, he with his deputy director, state council (Taiwan affairs), I with our ambassador. Jiang said, "I have an interpreter but let us not waste time. You'll speak in English, I can understand you. I'll speak in Chinese, you can understand me, and when you don't, my interpreter will help." We did save time.

President Lee, I said, had agreed to our proposal but believed there would be many difficulties in the details, so he would want Singapore to be involved in resolving them. The Taiwanese foreign minister wanted the shipping line to start first. They had designated a special zone at Kaohsiung as their international transit cargo port. After it had been run successfully for a year, the airline could start.

Jiang said Prime Minister Goh's proposal had been made with good intentions, but was not appropriate. There was no reason for any camouflage for the two sides to get together. He had heard these same views from many sources. He then referred to Lee Teng-hui's interview with Ryotaro Shiba, published in a Japanese magazine in April. (In it, Lee had referred to himself as Moses leading his people out from Egypt to the Promised Land.) Jiang added that Lee's attempt to attend the Hiroshima Asian Games showed him as totally unreliable. Lee wanted two Chinas, or one China and one Taiwan. The more talks there had been, the wider the gap between them. Lee had been saying one thing and doing another. Lee should not assume that he (Jiang) was a fool and could not read his true position. China's leaders weighed their words carefully and stood by them, he said, suggesting Taiwan's leaders did not. China's leaders placed great importance on trust and righteousness, he said, implying Lee did not have these qualities. Jiang showed anger when he said that Lee was cozying up to his former colonial masters (meaning Japan).

He was in such full flow that even when I did not understand specific phrases he used and only caught the gist of his meaning, I did not stop him for clarification. He spoke with great passion, to underline the seriousness of his position and the depth of his convictions.

At the time, I did not understand his controlled anger. Later, I discovered that three days before our meeting, while I was in Henan province, President Lee had said in the *Asian Wall Street Journal,* "There is no leader strong enough in Beijing, nobody able to give the final say. Deng Xiaoping is still around, but we don't think he is in any condition to exercise his brains. Mr. Deng had tried to establish Jiang Zemin as top leader wearing all the hats. . . . After Mr. Deng has gone, we may find the true leader taking the stage. We don't know if there is someone we can see now or someone hiding who will come out."

# 40. China: To Be Rich Is Glorious

Deng Xiaoping went on a well-publicized tour of south China in February 1992. At Shenzhen he said that Guangdong should catch up with Asia's Four Dragons (Hong Kong, Singapore, South Korea, and Taiwan) in 20 years, not only in economics but also in social order and social climate. China should do better than these countries in these matters. Only then would it have the distinguishing characteristics of Chinese socialism. Deng added, "There is good social order in Singapore. They govern the place with discipline. We should draw from their experience, and do even better than them." In China, commendation from Deng was the ultimate word on what was good.

I had told Deng over dinner in 1978 in Singapore that we, the Singapore Chinese, were the descendants of illiterate landless peasants from Guangdong and Fujian in south China, whereas the scholars, mandarins, and literati had stayed and left their progeny in China. There was nothing that Singapore had done that China could not do, and do better. He stayed silent then. When I read that he had told the Chinese people to do better than Singapore, I knew he had taken up the challenge I quietly tossed to him that night 14 years earlier.

After Deng's endorsement, several hundred delegations, most of them unofficial, came from China armed with tape recorders, video cameras, and notebooks to learn from our experience. Singapore had been given the imprimatur of their supreme leader. They put us under their microscopes and studied those parts they considered attractive and wanted to reproduce in their cities. I wondered what my communist adversaries of the 1960s, the Plen, the Malayan Communist Party leader in Singapore, and Lim Chin Siong, the communist united front leader, would say. The Chinese Communist Party had been their source of inspiration.

China's leaders had been troubled by the "social pollution"—proliferating prostitution, pornography, drugs, gambling, and crime—in the special economic zones. Ideological purists criticized the wisdom of the open-door policy. Deng's answer was that when windows were opened, with the fresh air some flies and mosquitoes were bound to fly in, but they could be dealt with.

Soon after Deng's speech, the head of the International Liaison Department of the Chinese Communist Party asked our ambassador in Beijing if we would brief them on "how we had maintained strong moral standards and social discipline." Specifically, they wanted to know "if Singapore had experienced contradictions in the process of absorbing Western technology that was needed to develop the economy, and how to maintain social stability." They had been observing us for some years. Reports had been appearing in their media commending Singapore for its infrastructure, housing estates, cleanliness, orderliness, and greenness, its social stability and harmony, and the courtesy of its people.

A delegation led by their vice minister of propaganda, Xu Weicheng, came for a 10-day briefing. "Vice minister of propaganda" was a misnomer: He was actually vice minister of ideology. We explained our belief that social control could not depend on discipline alone. People had to have a decent life with reasonable housing and social amenities if they were to lead moral and upright lives. They had to accept the basic principles of our system of government, like obeying the law and observing their duty to help the police in the prevention and investigation of crime.

The delegation visited all departments connected with social order—the police (especially those sections dealing with drugs, prostitution, and gambling); the agencies in charge of censorship of undesirable videos, films, books, and magazines; newspaper offices and radio and TV stations to ask about their role in informing and educating the public; and the NTUC and the People's Association to see organizations that catered to workers.

I met Xu at the end of his visit. He told me he was interested in how we had used the free market to achieve rapid economic growth; how we had blended Western and Eastern culture as we absorbed Western science and technology; and, most important, how we maintained racial harmony. His delegation was responsible for ideology and wanted to learn how to eradicate social vices.

We were candid about the problems we could not solve. Vices such as prostitution, gambling, drug addiction, and alcoholism could only be controlled, not eradicated. Singapore's history as a seaport meant prostitution had to be managed and confined to certain areas of the city where the women were given regular health checks. Gambling was impossible to suppress. It was an addiction Chinese migrants had carried with them wherever they settled. But we had eliminated the triads or secret societies and broken up organized crime.

As for corruption, Xu expressed his doubts whether agencies like Singapore's Corrupt Practices Investigation Bureau and the commercial affairs department could deal with the large "grey areas" in a society like China where *guanxi* (personal relationships) was all-pervasive. The definition of corruption in China was different. Moreover, he stressed, the party was supreme and its members could only be disciplined internally within the party. (This meant that some 60 million party members are not subject to the ordinary law of the land of China. Since then several very senior party activists have been sentenced to death for smuggling, and others to long prison terms for corruption. But the party leaders can intervene and reverse judicial decisions.) Xu said that not all Singapore's methods could be replicated as China's system was very different. Perhaps small new cities like Shenzhen could usefully follow Singapore's experience. China would always remain socialist. Their only way was to try out policies one at a time, for unlike Singapore, China had to adapt its policies to differing conditions in its 30 provinces.

He was struck by our clean and efficient administration. How had we preserved the people's social and moral values? All we did, I replied, was to reinforce the cultural assets the people had, their inherited values and sense of right and wrong. Confucian virtues such as being filial to one's parents, honest and upright, hardworking and thrifty, sincere to one's friends, and loyal to the country were important supports for the legal system. We reinforced these traditional values by rewarding behavior that conformed to them and punishing contrary behavior. At the same time, we set out to eradicate such weaknesses as nepotism, favoritism, and corruption, which were the dark side of Chinese Confucianism—the obligation to help one's family. Singapore is a compact society and its leaders had to set the example in honesty and upright conduct. We considered it vital that the people feel confident the government would not cheat or harm them. Then, however unpopular government policies might be, the people accepted that they were not the result of immorality, nepotism, or corruption.

Xu asked how a government should deal with foreign influences out to change a country's internal system. The problem, I said, was not foreigners directly interfering with our internal policies, but indirectly and insidiously, through their media and through personal contact, influencing and changing our people's attitudes and behavior. This would become increasingly difficult to control because satellite broadcasting technology would improve. We could only mitigate the harm to our social fabric by inculcating and strengthening the traditional values of our people. The family, I believed, had the greatest influence on a child's values in the first 12 to 15 years of life. Sound values, if rooted early in life, could later resist contrary influences and pressures. Roman Catholic priests, if entrusted with a child for the first 12 years of its life, could usually ensure the child would remain Catholic for life.

When the delegation returned to China, their report was circulated as "Reference News" and read by party members. In a paperback published to give an account of Singapore, Xu quoted what he considered my approach: "It requires prolonged efforts to administer a country well, and to change the backward habits of the people; a certain amount of administrative pressure is necessary at the beginning, but what is most important is education." Li Ruihuan, the politburo member in charge of ideology, told me when I visited Beijing a year later that he had initiated the study mission. He had visited Singapore when he was mayor of Tianjin, and considered it worth a study.

Another area they were interested in was our legal system. Qiao Shi, chairman of the National People's Congress standing committee and third-ranking leader of China, was also responsible for settling the necessary legislation to establish the rule of law. He visited Singapore in July 1993 to study our laws. The Chinese communist leaders, he said, had abolished all existing laws when they promulgated the People's Republic of China on 1 October 1949. Thereafter, they had governed by edicts. Party policies became the law. Only after Deng Xiaoping's open-door policy did they recognize the need for laws to govern commercial relations. Qiao Shi said no one would cooperate with China if it was seen as unstable and fractured. China needed the rule of law to maintain long-term stability. I said China should be able to get a system of laws established in 20 to 30 years, but it would take longer for people as a whole to accept the rule of law and act in accordance with it. He replied that not everyone had to understand it. As long as the top people practiced it, the rule of law would work. He came across as a serious man who had thought through his problems.

China under Deng was more open and willing to learn from the world than it had been for centuries. Deng was courageous and strong enough in the party and the nation to admit openly that China had lost many years in pursuit of a revolutionary utopia. It was a refreshing time of open minds and enthusiastic progress, a radical change from the years of wild slogans and disastrous campaigns. Deng initiated the fundamental changes that laid the foundations for China to catch up with the rest of the world.

In September 1992, together with Deputy Prime Minister Ong Teng Cheong, I visited Suzhou, China's Venice. It was in a dilapidated condition, with its canals filthy and polluted. But the idea struck us that we could redevelop Suzhou, make it into a beautiful city, and build a new industrial and commercial section next to it. It had beautiful Chinese gardens built around villas so that every window and every veranda looked out on to rock gardens, water, and plants. Traces of its old grandeur could still be seen in some of the mansions that had been restored.

Suzhou's mayor, Zhang Xinsheng, drew me aside after lunch one day to say, "Singapore has US$50 billion in reserves." "Who told you that?" I asked. He had read it in World Bank reports. He added, "Why don't you invest 10 percent of it in Suzhou? Get us industrialised like Singapore? I will guarantee you special treatment so that your investments will succeed." I said, "Able and energetic mayors soon get promoted; then what?"

He paused and replied, "Well, you may have trouble with my successor, but after a while he will have no choice but to go along the route that I would have laid down. People in Suzhou want what they have seen of Singapore on television and in the newspapers—jobs, housing and a garden city." I replied, "You have no power to give us a fresh site on which we can build a miniature Singapore. You need the central government's authority to do that."

I gave no more thought to this. That December, he turned up at my office to say that he had approached Deng Xiaoping's office with his proposition. There was a good chance it would go through. Could I put up the proposal in a plan? He was close to Deng Xiaoping's son, Deng Pufang. So Ong Teng Cheong did some artist's impressions of what old Suzhou could be like after restoration, with a modern industrial township next to it. A few months later, when Deng Pufang visited Singapore, I showed him sketch plans of a restored city together with an adjoining new industrial township. He was enthusiastic. His input through his father's office gave this project a push. When Prime Minister Goh visited Beijing in April, he discussed the proposal with Premier Li Peng and Jiang Zemin.

In May 1993, I met Vice Premier Zhu Rongji in Shanghai. I had earlier written to him on the Suzhou project. I explained my proposal for cooperation: a government-to-government technical assistance agreement to transfer our knowledge and experience (what we called "software") in attracting investments and building industrial estates, complete with housing and commercial centers, to an unbuilt site of about 100 sq. km in Suzhou. This would be backed by a business consortium of Singapore and foreign companies in a joint venture with Suzhou authorities. The project would take more than 20 years to complete, and there would be difficulties adapting our methods to the different conditions of China.

At first Zhu thought my proposal was another money-making idea on behalf of our investors. I explained that my proposal was in response to many delegations that had come from China to study us in a piecemeal manner but would never understand how our system worked. With Singapore and Chinese managers working together side by side, we could transfer our methods, systems, and know-how. Zhu agreed it was worth trying. He pointed out that Suzhou had access to the Yangtze River and was near Shanghai (90 kilometers, or about 56 miles, to the west), China's largest international center.

Four days later, I met newly promoted Vice Premier Li Lanqing in Beijing. He was from Jiangsu province, born in a town not far from Suzhou. He fully supported the project because Suzhou had high-quality people and could absorb and adapt Singapore's experience. Li said Singapore-China cooperation had the advantages of a common culture, tradition, and language. A pragmatist, he acknowledged that the project must be economically viable and yield a reasonable return. When he was vice mayor of Tianjin, his basic principle for cooperation had been "equality and mutual benefit."

Beijing sent two delegations in October 1993 to study Singapore's system—one from the state council, the other from Jiangsu province. Only after they were satisfied that parts of our system were suitable for China did they agree to this "software transfer."

In February 1994, I signed the Suzhou Agreement with Vice Premier Li Lanqing in Beijing, witnessed by Premier Li Peng and Prime Minister Goh. I met Jiang Zemin to confirm that the work in Suzhou would start soon but would take more than 10 years to reach a significant level of development. Jurong Industrial Township in Singapore, only 60 sq. km, had taken us 30 years.

The project, Suzhou Industrial Park (SIP), took off with great enthusiasm on both sides, but we soon ran into difficulties. There was a divergence of objectives between the center (Beijing) and the locals (Suzhou). The top leaders in Beijing knew that the essence of the project was to transfer our knowledge of how to plan, build, and administer a comprehensive industrial, commercial, and residential park that could attract high-quality foreign investors. The officials in Suzhou moved away from this core objective and were sidetracked by their parochial interests. We wanted to show them how to do things the Singapore way, with our emphasis on financial discipline, long-term master planning, and continuing service to investors—our software. They wanted the "hardware"—the buildings, roads, and infrastructure that we could build and the high-value investments we could attract using our worldwide connections and reputation. They were not focused on learning how to create a probusiness climate; nor did they select their most promising officials to be trained to take over from us. "Hardware" brought direct and immediate benefits to Suzhou and credit to its officials; Beijing wanted "software" so as to spread its benefits to other cities through adopting Singapore's probusiness practices.

Instead of giving SIP their full attention and cooperation as was promised, they used their association with Singapore to promote their own industrial estate, Suzhou New District (SND), undercutting SIP in land and infrastructure costs, which they controlled. This made SIP less attractive than SND. Fortunately, many of the large MNCs valued our interface and chose SIP in spite of its higher land costs. Hence, despite these difficulties, SIP made significant progress and within three years had attracted over 100 projects with a total investment commitment of almost US$3 billion. It ranked top in China in terms of the average value of each investment project. These projects would create over 20,000 jobs, 35 percent of which would be for the tertiary-educated. The chairman of the Office of the Special Economic Zone commented that "in merely three years from inception, SIP's speed of development and the overall standard are first-class in China."

This progress was made in the face of increasing difficulties. The rivalry between SND and SIP confused potential investors and diverted the attention of the Suzhou officials from the objective of software transfer. Things came to a head in mid-1997 when the vice mayor of Suzhou, who ran SND, told a meeting of German investors in Hamburg that President Jiang did not support SIP, that they were welcome to SND and did not need Singapore. This made our position untenable. We were wasting too much time, energy, and resources fighting with the local authorities.

I raised the problem with President Jiang in December 1997. He assured me that SIP remained his top priority and that the problems at the local level would be resolved. But notwithstanding this assurance from the very top in Beijing, Suzhou did not stop promoting SND in competition against SIP. We had reasons to believe they had borrowed so heavily that to stop promoting SND would cause severe financial difficulties. After much discussion we agreed in June 1999 that there would be a change in responsibilities in the existing joint venture between the Singapore consortium and the Suzhou authorities. The Singapore consortium would remain the majority partner in control of the project and complete the first 8 sq. km by the end of the year 2000; the Suzhou authorities would then take over majority partnership, control the project and complete the rest of the 70 sq. km using the first 8 sq. km as a reference model. We would remain for at least a further three years until 2003 as minority partners and help guide a Chinese management team in servicing investors in SIP.

It was a chastening experience. Both sides had believed that because of apparent language and cultural similarities there would be fewer problems in dealing with each other—each side expected the other to behave like itself. Unfortunately, while language was no problem, our business cultures were totally different. Singaporeans take for granted the sanctity of contracts. When we sign an agreement, it is a full and final undertaking. Any disagreement as to the meaning of the written document is interpreted by the courts or an arbitrator. We took great care that the documents we prepared were both in English and Chinese, with both versions authoritative. For the Suzhou authorities, a signed agreement is an expression of serious and sincere intent, but one that is not necessarily comprehensive and can be altered or reinterpreted with changing circumstances. We depended on laws and systems. They were guided by official directives; often these were not published and their interpretation varied with the official in charge.

For example, power supply. Although the Suzhou government had in a written agreement promised to provide a certain quantity of electricity, it failed to get the relevant authority to deliver on its promise. To resolve this, we got the Suzhou government's permission to build a diesel power plant. After the plant was built, we were told that diesel plants were discouraged by the power authority and were prohibited from operating it. The municipal officials explained that they had no control over the power authority. When they agreed to let us install the diesel power plant, they knew the power authority had overriding control on energy but did not tell us we needed the latter's concurrence. It took months of negotiation and only when the problem threatened to shut down the park was it resolved. The five years in Suzhou educated us on the intricacies of their multilayered administration and flexible business culture. We acquired a more intimate understanding of their system and learned how to work around its blocks and obstacles to get them finally to wrap up our project as a partial success, not a total failure.

China has an immensely complex government. After two centuries of decline that began with the Qing dynasty, China's leaders face the formidable task of installing modern management systems and changing the mindsets and habits of officials steeped in the traditions of the imperial mandarinate.

China is still a poor country with many backward provinces. Their domestic problems require sustained economic growth to resolve. As China's development nears the point when it has enough weight to elbow its way into the region, it will make a fateful decision—whether to be a hegemon, using its weight to create its sphere of influence in the region for its economic and security needs, or to continue as a good international citizen because it can achieve better growth by observing international rules.

China has repeatedly stated that it will never become a hegemon. It is in everyone's interest that before that moment of choice arrives, China be given every incentive to choose international cooperation, which will absorb its energies constructively for another 50 to 100 years. This means China must have the economic opportunities to do this peacefully, without having to push its way to get resources like oil, or to have access to markets for its goods and services. There are fair and equitable rules in multilateral organizations like the WTO for a free exchange of goods and services so that each country can stay within its borders and improve its people's well-being through trade, investments, and other exchanges. This was the way the Germans and the Japanese were able to rebuild after World War II. Their territories shrank even as they had to accept their nationals expelled from territories they had occupied and colonized. Despite smaller territories and reduced natural resources, both flourished as never before because they had access to markets through the IMF and GATT. If such a route is not open to China, the world must live with a pushy China. In that event, the United States will not be alone in being concerned about what China will do when it is able to contest the present world order settled by America and its partners in Europe.

The Chinese Communist Party faces a profound challenge. Communism has failed worldwide and the people of China know it. But the

CCP has not failed. It has liberated China, unified it, and enabled the people to feed and clothe themselves. Despite the disasters of the Great Leap Forward (1958) and the Cultural Revolution (1966–1976), the Chinese are proud that foreigners can no longer violate China's sovereignty with impunity as they did when they exercised extraterritorial rights in the foreign concessions.

I had an interesting sample of the rapid change in China when in September 1994 I arrived at Zhengzhou Airport in the inland province of Henan. A line of their old Red Flag limousines was waiting. I knew Henan was not as prosperous as the coastal provinces but had not expected them to be still using the Red Flag limousines. To my surprise, they ushered me and the party secretary, Li Changchun, to a brand new Mercedes 600. I was intrigued to hear the familiar way in which he and the driver conversed with each other. Later, when I was alone with the driver, I asked how much he earned as a driver. He replied that he was really the owner of the car. Party Secretary Li had wanted to borrow it for my visit and he decided to drive it to meet me. Six years ago, he was a supervisor in a factory, but after Deng's exhortation to get rich, he had gone into business. He now had three factories employing some 5,000 workers assembling electronic products. He owned three cars including this Mercedes 600. China was changing fast and irrevocably.

The government and the CCP are also changing, but not as fast as the economy and society. To demonstrate popular support, the CCP has allowed elections at village and county levels. In provincial elections for high officials, Communist Party members who have not been nominated by the party can stand against the official candidates. The governor of Zhejiang province in 1994 was a candidate who had defeated the Communist Party nominee. The legitimacy of the CCP now rests upon the benefits that Deng Xiaoping's reforms initiated in 1978 have brought to the farmers and workers: more food, clothing, homes, and consumer goods—and more wealth than they ever had. But the people also know that the Chinese in Taiwan, Hong Kong, and Macau have done better than the mainland Chinese because they have free markets. As long as the CCP can produce results and improve the people's lives, its legitimacy will not be challenged. This could go on for another generation. The CCP policy is to absorb the best and the brightest into the party. Many have joined to avoid the disadvantages of not being a member, but the study of Marxist-Leninist-Maoist theories by party members is perfunctory.

In the next 50 years, the Chinese will have to complete three transitions: from a planned to a market economy, from a rural to an urban base, from a tightly controlled communist to an open civic society. Several factors can derail China from its present track of catching up with the industrial nations. The first and most important is Taiwan. If Chinese leaders feel that Taiwan is going to go independent and could be lost, they will not be so detached and calculating and could act with unpredictable consequences. The next factor is rapid urbanization. At present, 30 to 35 percent of the 1.3 billion Chinese live in small towns and cities. By 2050, they will be 80 percent, well-informed and able through electronic means to mobilize for mass action. They will be able to do this with more ease than the Falungong, a cult that, through the Internet, organized some 10,000 of its followers to gather peacefully in Beijing in April 1999 to squat around Zhongnanhai, the residence of the Communist Party leaders. China's political structures must allow its citizens more participation and control over their lives or there will be pressures that could destabilize society, especially during an economic downturn.

A third factor would be the widening differences in incomes, growth rates, and quality of life between the wealthy coastal and riverine provinces and the disadvantaged inland provinces. However extensive the roads, railways, airfields, and other infrastructure the central government may build to bring industries, trade, investments, and tourism inland, they will still lag behind. This could increase peasant discontent, causing serious tensions and massive migrations. Furthermore, as more Han Chinese populate the border provinces of Tibet, Xinjiang, and Qinghai, there could be problems between them and the minority races.

The fourth and most profound factor will be the different values and aspirations of the next generation. The people and government want to build a modern, strong, and united China, whatever that takes. Better education and wider global exposure will result in a people who are knowledgeable about the world, with frequent and multiple links with their counterparts in other societies. They will want Chinese society to be equal to other advanced countries in standard of living, quality of life, and individual freedoms. This desire is a powerful force that the leaders are harnessing to drive the nation forward. In particular, how Japan, Korea, and Taiwan, with cultures and traditions similar to the Chinese, are governed will have a great influence on the thinking of the Chinese intelligentsia.

Several problems can cause serious disruptions: a breakdown of the banking system, huge unemployment following reforms of state-owned enterprises without adequate social security nets, an aging population that will place a heavy burden on the one-child family generation having to support their elderly parents, and serious environmental pollution.

However, the most pernicious problem is corruption. It has become embedded in their administrative culture and will be difficult to eradicate even after economic reforms. Many Communist Party members and government officials in the provinces, cities, and counties are not above corruption. Worse, many officials who are expected to uphold and enforce the law—public security officers, procurators, and judges—are also corrupt. The root cause of the problem was the destruction of normal moral standards during the Cultural Revolution. Deng's open-door policy in 1978 enlarged the opportunities for corruption.

The leaders want to establish a legal system with proper institutions. Because they know the institutions necessary for the rule of law in a civil society cannot exist in a moral vacuum, they are reemphasizing Confucianist teachings among the population. They have also launched the "three-stresses" campaign in an attempt to clean up the party's rank and file: to talk about learning, to talk about politics, and to talk about honor and dignity. But so long as officials are paid unrealistically low wages, such exhortations will have little effect, regardless of the severity of the punishment meted out, not even death and long prison terms.

Nevertheless, pragmatic, resolute, and capable leaders have steered China through these perils since 1978. They command authority and credibility. They have successors in place as competent and resourceful and even better-educated than themselves. If these future leaders remain pragmatic, they should be able to overcome these difficulties.

In the two and a half decades since my first visit in 1976, I have seen China transformed. I find most astonishing not the physical structures, new buildings, expressways, and airports, but the different attitudes and habits of the people and their willingness to speak their minds. Books are written and published that would have been sedition in the 1970s or 1980s. The free market and modern communications have brought more openness and transparency. They will make China as different again in another two decades.

I place my hope for China's progress on their best and brightest who have studied or travelled extensively abroad in their impressionable years. More than one hundred thousand of them are now studying in the United States, Western Europe, and Japan. The present leaders in their late sixties and seventies are products of the anti-Japanese war and did their postgraduate work in Russia. Their mindsets will not change much. Many of their children who have Ph.D.s from American universities have vastly different outlooks. Vice Premier Qian Qichen, formerly the foreign minister, has a son, Qian Ning, who worked for the *People's Daily* and shortly after Tiananmen went to the United States to study journalism in Ann Arbor. He stayed in America for four years and on his return wrote a candid book that was published and sold in China. The observations of a man with such an impeccable background are significant, reflecting the thinking of a younger generation in their thirties: "I realised a simple truth, we Chinese, at least the younger generation, can have another way of life. . . . Chinese women are liberated once again—what they have lost are only the chains of tradition, but what they have gained is their freedom." I believe it is not only Chinese women who lose their fetters after a stay in America. These men and women in their twenties and thirties who studied in the West are the best-equipped intellectually to meet the needs of China's modernization. They have been exposed to new ideas and knowledge in societies vastly different from their own. In 20 to 30 years, their generation will change the shape of China. They probably already realize that even after China has been restored as a great industrial power, it will not be a Tang or a Han "Middle Kingdom," the center of the universe, but one of several advanced nations.

Americans would do well to keep their options open. The Chinese are a different people with a different culture and a different history. They will change at their own pace in their quest for technology and a modern economy, preserving their values and traditions, and maintaining continuity with their past. China-bashing by constantly denigrating them for their lack of democracy and human rights will only antagonize a whole generation of Chinese and make them anti-American and xenophobic. This is not far-fetched. When the tragic bombing of the Belgrade Chinese embassy took place in May 1999, I thought at first that the demonstrations, with slogans reminiscent of the Cultural Revolution, were orchestrated. But our mission in Beijing reported that the Chinese were genuinely outraged and angered by what they saw as a bullying America out to put China down. To foster such a reaction will not contribute to peace and stability. The Americans will have to learn that some reforms require time to make them possible. And such changes will be made by the Chinese for Chinese purposes, not in order to comply with American norms, under American economic or moral sanctions.

Even before the bombing, bilateral relations had already been strained when President Clinton did not accept major concessions made by Premier Zhu Rongji in April in Washington to join the WTO. When I met him in Beijing in September, Zhu dwelt at length on this subject. He would not back away from the offers he had made, but required serious concessions in return. Four days later, while in Shanghai for a meeting of the Fortune Global Forum, Henry Kissinger and I urged Robert Rubin, the treasury secretary who had just resigned in July after an illustrious six-year term, to speak to President Clinton. And I made the same points a few days later to the U.S. secretary for defense, William Cohen, when he visited Singapore. Cohen, who needed no persuasion on the merits of bringing China into the WTO, brought it up with his president.

After five days of strenuous bargaining in Beijing, China and the United States reached agreement on 15 November 1999. It was a relaxed Premier Zhu who visited Singapore a fortnight later. He attributed the success of the negotiations to the intervention of President Jiang. Joining WTO was not without its dangers, he said to me, but if China's leaders did not believe they could overcome the problems, Jiang would not have agreed to it. Zhu's responsibility was to implement Jiang's decision. The painful measures necessary will be less difficult to execute because it was the president who made the decision to join.

For both China and the United States, strategic considerations must have been as important as economic benefits in reaching this agreement. China's WTO membership will help it restructure its economy to gain in competitiveness and long-term growth, but it will have to become a rule-abiding member of the international community.

Over the last 40 years, I have seen how Koreans, Taiwanese, and Japanese officials and business executives have changed. From a reserved, inward-looking, and nationalistic elite, they are now self-confident and at ease with American and Western ideas. Many of them have been educated in the United States and are not ill-disposed toward its people. This is not to say that Chinese on the mainland, conscious of their potential big-power status, will evolve just like the Taiwanese. America has a choice, to have them neutral or friendly instead of becoming hostile. When dealing with an old civilization, it is wise not to expect swift changes. The biggest problem between America and China will be Taiwan.

It is an imponderable leftover from the unfinished Chinese civil war. With Taiwan under Chen Shui-bian, a new president whose party stands for independence, the danger of miscalculation by the three parties directly involved—the Mainland, Taiwan, and the U.S.—has increased. Any mis-step could upset growth and development in China and East Asia. This problem can be contained if the status quo is not changed, and eventual reunification is an aspiration for both sides.

Meanwhile, through the WTO, the Chinese economy can become integrated into the rest of the world. With broad and deepening people-to-people contacts, stereotyped perceptions of each other will be replaced by more realistic appraisals. When the Chinese people's livelihood is inter-dependent with that of the world through trade, investments, tourism, and the exchange of technology and knowledge, there will be a better basis for a stable world.

China has the potential to realize its goal of becoming a modern econ-omy by 2050. It can be engaged as an equal and responsible partner in trade and finance, and become one of the major players in the world. If it is not deflected from its present concentration on education and economic development, China could well be the second largest, if not the largest, trading nation in the world, with greater weight and voice in interna-tional affairs. This is one vision of China in 50 years—modern, confident, and responsible.

# PART III

# Winding Up

# 41. Passing the Baton

When I reflected on the predicament of Suharto in 1998 when he was forced to resign and hand power over to a vice president he considered inadequate to succeed him, I was glad that I had resigned as prime minister in November 1990. I was still in command of the political situation and of a humming economy. I was physically still vigorous. But had I not stood down, I might have found myself trapped in the financial crisis, with my faculties less acute and my energy levels down. Instead, for the past nine years I helped to ease the way for my successor, Goh Chok Tong, and his team of younger ministers to take full charge of the Singapore government. Prime Minister Goh retained me in his cabinet as senior minister. Without the pressure of daily decision making, I was able to reflect on the bigger and longer-term issues and contribute toward more rounded solutions.

My experience of developments in Asia has led me to conclude that we need good people to have good government. However good the system of government, bad leaders will bring harm to their people. On the other hand, I have seen several societies well-governed in spite of poor systems of government, because good, strong leaders were in charge. I have also seen so many of the over 80 constitutions drafted by Britain and France for their former colonies come to grief, and not because of flaws in the constitutions. It was simply that the preconditions for a democratic system of government did not exist. None of these countries had a civic society with an educated electorate. Nor did their people have the cultural tradition of acceptance of the authority of a person because of that person's office. These traditions take generations to inculcate in a people. In a new country where loyalties are to tribal leaders, they must be honest and not self-serving or the country is likely to fail whatever the constitutional safeguards. And because the leaders who inherited these constitutions were not strong enough, their countries went down in riots, coups, and revolution.

The single decisive factor that made for Singapore's development was the ability of its ministers and the high quality of the civil servants who supported them. Whenever I had a lesser minister in charge, I invariably had to push and prod him, and later to review problems and clear road-blocks for him. The end result was never what could have been achieved. When I had the right man in charge, a burden was off my shoulders. I needed only to make clear the objectives to be achieved, the time frame within which he must try to do it, and he would find a way to get it done.

It was Singapore's good fortune that we had, for a small, developing country, a fair share of talent, because our own had been reinforced by the talented men and women who came here for their education, and stayed on for employment or business opportunities. Because of our relentless and unceasing search for talent both at home and abroad to make up for the small families of the well-educated, Singapore has been able to keep up its performance. Our greatest task was to find the people to replace my aging ministers and myself.

My colleagues and I had started to search for younger men as possible successors in the 1960s. We could not find them among the political activists who joined the PAP, so we scouted for able, dynamic, depend-able, and hard-driving people wherever they were to be found. In the 1968 general election, we fielded several Ph.D.s, bright minds, teachers at the universities, professionals including lawyers, doctors, and even top administrators as candidates. In by-elections in 1970 and 1972, we fielded several more. We soon discovered that they needed to have other qualities besides a disciplined mind able to marshal facts and figures, write a thesis for a Ph.D., or be a professional. Leadership is more than just ability. It is a combination of courage, determination, commitment, character, and ability that makes people willing to follow a leader. We needed people who were activists with good judgment and interpersonal skills. The search became more urgent at each subsequent election because I could see that my colleagues were visibly slowing down.

One day in 1974, Hon Sui Sen, then our finance minister, told me that he hoped I would let him stand down at the next general election. He was feeling his age. I was astonished. He was only 60. How could I let him go? Who would do his job? Over lunch, just the two of us, this conversation had more impact on me than any other exchange I have ever had. He said investors had been confident because they were comfortable with the ministers in charge, especially with me. But they could see that he was getting on and were looking beyond and behind him to see who would replace him. They could not see a younger minister with the potential to be minister for finance. I had many more years to go, but he did not think he could carry on for much longer. He had met many CEOs of American corporations. They had to retire at 65. Several years before a CEO's retirement, he had to put before the board one or more candidates for them to choose one as his successor. I resolved that I must not be found wanting in this respect, and that I must place Singapore in competent hands before I retired.

To do this I had to find and get into office a group of men to provide Singapore with effective and creative leadership. Had I left it to chance, depending on activists coming forward to join us, I would never have succeeded. We set out to recruit the best into government. The problem was to persuade them to enter politics, get themselves elected, and learn how to move and win people over to their side. It was a slow and difficult process with a high attrition rate. Successful, capable professionals and executives are not natural political leaders, able to argue, cajole, and demolish the arguments of opponents at mass rallies, on television, and in Parliament.

To see how wide the net must be cast for talent, I had only to remember that the best ministers in my early cabinets were not born in Singapore. Three-quarters of them had come from outside Singapore. The net that brought in my generation of leaders was thrown in a big sea that stretched from South China across Malaysia, to South India and Ceylon. Now we were fishing in a small pond and getting fewer big fish.

For years my colleagues and I had assumed that in the ordinary political process, activists from universities, trade unions, and party branches would throw up the people who could carry on our work. By 1968, we recognized this was not going to happen. The original team had been thrown up by the traumatic events of World War II, Japanese occupation, and the communist insurgency. The weak, the timid, and the irresolute were eliminated by natural process. By surviving, they proved they could stay on top of the opposition and govern. Their convictions pitted them against the British, and later the communists and the Malayan Malay Ultras. During repeated crises, we had forged deep and abiding bonds between ourselves and the people. These bonds endured. Our final task was to find worthy successors. Mao tried to solve this problem of suitable successors by arranging a Cultural Revolution as a substitute for the Long March. It was not possible for us to simulate a Japanese invasion and occupation, and the subsequent struggle for independence. Our solution was to look for men with the right character, ability, and motivation, and hope that when they encountered the inevitable crises, they would emerge tested as leaders.

The general election of 1968 was a political landmark with 18 new candidates out of 58. We won all the seats and improved the quality of our MPs and ministers. Over 40 percent were university-educated either in English or Chinese, while 55 percent had secondary or higher secondary education. Those without much education were trade unionists who had left school early because their families were too poor. The loyalists who had been with us from the difficult early days had to give way to fresh talent when I made promotions to office. At a meeting of MPs in April, soon after the election, I compared the party to an army where there had to be constant recruitment. Most would join as privates, some as officers. Some would not be more than sergeants. It did not follow that all who joined as officers would become generals. Those who proved their worth, whether or not they had university degrees, would be promoted. I had to prepare the ground for a thorough change of office holders. I protected the interests of the faithful by a Parliamentary Pensions Act. All those who had served for not less than nine years as MPs, parliamentary secretaries, and ministers would be entitled to pensions.

Of all my ministers, Hon Sui Sen was the best at talent scouting. It was he who chose Goh Chok Tong to run Neptune Orient Lines, our national shipping line, when it was making a loss; Goh turned it around in a few years. Sui Sen also brought in Dr. Tony Tan, who later became our deputy prime minister. He was a physics lecturer at the University of Singapore, then was the general manager of Singapore's largest bank, Oversea-Chinese Banking Corporation. Sui Sen talent-spotted S. Dhanabalan, who had worked with him in the EDB and was in the Development Bank of Singapore; he was later to be a minister in charge of several important portfolios.

I systematically scanned the top echelons of all sectors in Singapore—the professions, commerce, manufacturing, and trade unions—to look for men and women in their thirties and forties whom we could persuade to stand as our candidates. Ability can be assessed fairly accurately by a person's academic record and achievement in work. Character is not so easily measured. After some successes but too many failures, I concluded that it was more important, though more difficult, to assess a person's character.

In 1970, when the American spaceship *Apollo 13* malfunctioned nearly 300,000 miles out in space, I watched the unfolding drama, fascinated. One false move by any one of the three men on board would have left them drifting into outer space, never to return. They remained calm and collected throughout the ordeal, entrusting their survival to the judgment of the people at ground control whose instructions they followed meticulously. I saw this as proof that NASA's psychological and other tests conducted on the ground, simulating the weightless and isolated conditions in spaceships, had successfully eliminated those who were prone to panic in a crisis. I decided to have one psychologist and one psychiatrist test our candidates.

They put prospective PAP election candidates who had the potential to be ministers through psychological tests designed to define their character profile, intelligence, personal backgrounds, and values. These tests were not conclusive but they helped to eliminate the obviously unsuitable and were an advance on gut reactions during a two-hour interview. From time to time I would disagree with the conclusions of the psychologists, especially where I felt the candidate had been smarter than the interviewer and been able to "fake good" without appearing to do so.

Professor H. J. Eysenck, a psychologist from London University who visited Singapore in 1987, reinforced my view that testing for IQ and personality and character traits was useful. He cited an American oil MNC that employed 40 psychologists for the recruitment and promotion of 40,000 employees. We did not have enough trained psychologists to assess the candidates for important appointments. After a discussion with him, I got the NUS to train more behavioral psychologists to help in selecting people with the right attributes for various jobs.

I also checked with corporate leaders of MNCs how they recruited and promoted their senior people, and decided one of the best systems was that developed by Shell, the Anglo-Dutch oil company. They concentrated on what they termed a person's "currently estimated potential." This was determined by three qualities—a person's power of analysis, imagination, and sense of reality. Together they made up an overarching attribute Shell called "helicopter quality," the ability to see facts or problems in a larger context and to identify and zoom in on critical details. A panel of assessors, at least two of whom must know the person being assessed, could accurately rank executives of broadly similar abilities for helicopter quality. After trying out the system and finding it practical and reliable, I adopted it for our public service in 1983, replacing the British system we had inherited.

Some people are naturally better than others in seeing into or through a person, and make excellent interviewers and assessors. One such outstanding person was Tan Teck Chwee, the chairman of our public service commission from 1975 to 1988. No candidate for recruitment or officer for promotion succeeded in deceiving him. It had nothing to do with Tan's undoubtedly high IQ. It had much to do with a different part of his mind that enabled him to read a person's character from facial expressions, tone of voice, and body language. Another with this gift is Lim Kim San, a former senior cabinet minister. I put him on every panel for the selection of PAP candidates for election. His assessments were more visceral than cerebral and most times correct. His exact opposite, a cerebral person lacking this gift, was Goh Keng Swee. Often he would pick an officer or an aide and rave about his excellent qualities based on the person's paperwork. Six to 12 months later, he would be looking for a replacement. He simply could not see through a person. Psychologists call this ability social or emotional intelligence.

My attempt to inject new blood into the leadership was not without stress. Several old guard ministers were concerned about the pace at which they were being replaced. Toh Chin Chye said that I should stop talking about the old guard getting old because they were not getting old that fast, that I was demoralizing them. I disagreed. We were all slowing down and visibly aging, including me and Toh himself. In cabinet, he would put an electric heater under the cabinet table to blow warm air over his feet. I could see myself in the mirror. I did not feel the same inexhaustible enthusiasm and zest to see and find out things for myself. More and more I relied on reports, photographs, and videos.

Toh and several of the old guard wanted our successors to come up the same way we had done, as activists, not by head-hunting and direct recruitment. Keng Swee, Rajaratnam, Kim San, and Sui Sen did not believe there was much chance of reproducing ourselves in that way. After the December 1980 election, I decided to send a clear signal to all the old guard that the course of self-renewal was irreversible, although the pace would depend on how successful the new MPs proved to be. I left Toh out of the new cabinet. I was concerned that several of the old-timers might rally around him to slow down the pace of self-renewal. I sensed that one old guard minister, Ong Pang Boon, shared Toh's unease, as did a number of the older ministers of state and parliamentary secretaries including Lee Khoon Choy, Fong Sip Chee, Chan Chee Seng, and Chor Yock Eng. I had to drop Toh to preempt any split in the leadership. It was painful after so many years working together. The support of the old guard had made possible what we had achieved, but it was our joint responsibility to ensure that Singapore continued to be governed by able, honest, and dedicated men. The original team had peaked and was running out of steam.

The new MPs, bright young men who had won scholarships to renowned universities overseas and in Singapore, were taking over key jobs within three to four years of joining the PAP. The veterans felt that they should not have such an easy path to office, but should learn and wait. I did not think young and talented men would sit and wait; either they were going to make it or they would want to move on.

Toh was bitter. I offered to make him our high commissioner in London, but he did not want to leave Singapore because of his young daughter's education. He found another appointment for himself. He stayed on in Parliament for another two terms, sniping at me and the

PAP, never enough to be accused of disloyalty, but enough to be a mild embarrassment. I did not want to put him down publicly.

After I dropped Toh from the cabinet, I told Pang Boon that I would appoint him for another term, but I could not allow any obstruction to self-renewal. He understood and we avoided a clash. When he retired in December 1984, I wrote to him expressing my appreciation for his work from 1959 to 1984, adding,

> I also thank you for helping in the selection of candidates for self-renewal. You had certain reservations. You pointed out that only time and crises can reveal latent defects in a person. I agree with you. You also had misgivings, as had Chin Chye, over the speed of self-renewal and the effect it was having on the morale of old guard MPs. I must take the responsibility for both the method and the pace of self-renewal, though it is reassuring to me that Goh Keng Swee and Rajaratnam supported me. A younger team of ministers and MPs have now become the majority both in cabinet and in Parliament. There is no turning back. I am confident that the younger leaders will be equal to the task, but if not, the responsibility will be mine, shared with Keng Swee and Rajaratnam.

The one retirement I felt most keenly was Keng Swee's. In mid-1984, he told me that he had decided, for personal reasons, to step down at the end of the term and would not contest the next election. He had done enough and it was time to go. For several years after he left, he was invaluable as deputy chairman of the Monetary Authority of Singapore. He also set up the Government of Singapore Investment Corporation as a separate organization to handle our national savings and reserves.

The old guard took some time to accept the new blood, and some were never reconciled to seeing them promoted over their heads. I understood their feelings. Fong Sip Chee had been a stalwart PAP member from the 1950s when the PAP was an endangered party. He became an MP in 1963 and was a minister of state from 1981 to 1985. He never understood why he was not more deserving of promotion and believed, wrongly, that it was because he had not been to university. Others like Ch'ng Jit Koon, a minister of state, and Ho Kah Leong, a parliamentary secretary, both Nanyang graduates, supported and worked with the new ministers. It was an emotionally difficult but necessary changeover. I had to do it, whatever my own feelings.

After the 1980 party conference, I promoted six young ministers of state to the cabinet. This encouraged other young talent to join and be tested as ministers of state. Besides high helicopter quality, they needed to have political sense and the temperament to establish rapport with grassroots leaders. Those with these extra qualities I took into cabinet.

For every person who made it we would have interviewed more than 10. The attrition rate was high because, despite all the psychological tests, we could never accurately assess character, temperament, and motivation. To succeed, the man (or woman) and his spouse and family had to be prepared for loss of privacy and time. Nursing a constituency and attending official functions, plus a lower income than they could earn outside, made political office unattractive. Most of all, the person must have that extra quality, the capacity to work with people and persuade them to support his policies.

I decided 1988 would be the last election I would lead as prime minister. After I won, I asked the younger ministers to decide among themselves whom they would support as prime minister. I had helped to select them as MPs and appointed them as ministers. I wanted my successor to have the support of his peers. I had seen how Deng Xiaoping had failed with his appointees, Hu Yaobang and Zhao Ziyang. I also remembered how Anthony Eden, chosen by Winston Churchill, failed. The younger ministers chose Goh Chok Tong.

Chok Tong was not a natural politician. He was tall, gangling, and awkward, and spoke English with a heavy Hokkien accent. When he became an MP in 1976 he was self-conscious and without the gift of speech-making. But he had ability, dedication, and drive, and was interested in people. Soon after I brought him into the cabinet I advised him to take lessons to improve his public-speaking skills. We found an English woman to teach him and some of the other new ministers to speak in a more relaxed, natural way. From my own experience in learning Mandarin and Hokkien, I knew it was not easy to change childhood speech patterns. I described to Chok Tong my own experience, how for years I spent hours in between work practicing Mandarin and Hokkien with teachers to improve my fluency. My old teachers introduced Mandarin teachers to him. He applied himself with determination and became a much more effective communicator.

In the 1990 cabinet, together with Chok Tong, were Ong Teng Cheong, S. Dhanabalan, Tony Tan, Yeo Ning Hong, Lee Yock Suan, S. Jayakumar, Richard Hu, Wong Kan Seng, Lee Hsien Loong, Yeo Cheow Tong, Ahmad Mattar, and George Yeo. I had brought together men of integrity and ability with strong commitment to society. After several years of experience working together with the old guard in cabinet, they were as prepared as could be. I resigned that November.

I had been prime minister for 31 years. To have stayed on for another term would have proved nothing except that I was still fit and effective. On the other hand, if in the years that I had left, I was able to help my successor get a grip on his job and succeed, that would be my final contribution to Singapore. I did not suffer any withdrawal syndrome. Chok Tong did not want to move into my old office in the Istana Annexe, which I had occupied for 20 years since I moved from City Hall, but chose to create a new office on the floor above mine. I continued to make a contribution through discussions in cabinet and in bilateral meetings with the prime minister and other ministers.

Chok Tong's style, the way he worked with his team, was different from mine. He carefully planned the various steps he needed to swing public opinion slowly toward the desired goal. It worked. In the January 1997 election, the PAP increased its percentage of votes from 61 percent to 65 percent for the 36 constituencies contested. It won back two of the four seats lost in 1991. Prime Minister Goh and his ministers were in full command.

A crisis tested Chok Tong and his team in mid-1998 when our currency went down in value, and stock and property prices fell by 40 percent following the collapse of our neighbors' economies. Many MNCs retrenched workers in Singapore and transferred their operations to our lower-cost neighbors. The problem was similar to the recession in 1985 when we had overpriced ourselves by allowing higher wages, fees, and taxes and other costs. The solution then was a raft of cost-cutting measures, 15 percent decrease in the employers' contribution to the workers'

CPF and lower fees and taxes. Chok Tong's team worked out a similar package that reduced costs by cutting taxes and lowering employers' contribution to the CPF from 20 percent to 10 percent. Retrenchments slowed down. By the middle of 1999, the economy had revived. Their steady and competent management of the crisis won them the confidence of international fund managers and investors.

# 42. My Family

The communists impressed me by the great importance they placed on the woman a prospective supporter was attached to. They knew a wife could make an enormous difference to a man's reliability and commitment to the cause. They had objected to my political secretary, Jek Yeun Thong's steady girlfriend, whom they regarded as not politically suitable. He ignored this objection and without his knowledge they dropped him from their cell network. They were right; she was not supportive of their cause.

I was fortunate. Choo never had any doubts or hesitation about my going on with the fight, whatever the consequences. She told me she had absolute confidence in my judgment. She was a great source of strength and comfort. She has a keen intuition when judging people. While I make up my mind more on analysis and reason, she decides more on "feel" and has an uncanny knack of sensing the real feelings and positions of a person behind the smiles and friendly words. She was often right about who not to trust, although she could not quite explain why—maybe it was the expression on a person's face, the way he smiled, the look in his eyes, or his body language. Whatever it was, I learned to take her reservations about people seriously. Early in 1962, when I was negotiating with the Tunku to join Malaysia, she expressed her reservations over whether we could work with the Tunku, Razak, and the other UMNO and MCA leaders. She said they were different in temperament, character, and social habits, that she could not see the PAP ministers getting along with them.

I replied we simply had to work with them, because we needed to. We had to have a merger and a broader base to build a nation. Within three years, by 1965, she was proved right. We were incompatible and they asked us to leave Malaysia.

Meeting the wives of foreign leaders, she would give me a good reading of their husband's friendliness or otherwise from the way the wife acted or talked to her. I never took her views as the last word, but I did not dismiss them.

She saved me much time and tedious work, correcting the drafts of speeches that I dictated and the transcripts of what I said in Parliament and in interviews. She is familiar with my vocabulary and can guess my dictated words that my stenographers cannot make out. I made a point, however, not to discuss the formulation of policies with her, and she was scrupulous in not reading notes or faxes that were sensitive.

For my part, the knowledge that she had her profession as a lawyer and if necessary could look after herself and bring up the children on her own freed me from worries about their future. They were a source of joy and satisfaction. She brought them up well-mannered and self-disciplined, never throwing their weight around, although they had grown up as the prime minister's children. Our home at Oxley Road was only a seven-minute drive from her office at Malacca Street. She hardly ever attended business lunches with clients. Instead she would return home to have lunch with the children and keep in touch. When she was away at the office she had reliable, long-serving "black-and-white" Cantonese maids, so named for their black pants and white blouses, to mind them. Choo used a cane when the children were particularly naughty or disobedient. I did not physically punish them; a stern rebuke was effective enough. Having a violent father turned me against using physical force.

We had decided in 1959, when I first took office as prime minister, not to live at Sri Temasek, my official residence in the Istana domain. They were very young and we did not want them to grow up in such grand surroundings with butlers and orderlies to fuss over their needs. It would have given them an unrealistic view of the world and their place in it. Watching them grow up constantly reminded me of the need to build a safe and wholesome environment for our children to live in.

All three—Hsien Loong (born 1952), Wei Ling (1955), and Hsien Yang (1957)—were educated in Chinese schools, first Nanyang kindergarten, then Nanyang Primary School for six years. The boys went on to Catholic High School and then to National Junior College. Ling continued in Nanyang Girls' High School, then went to Raffles Institution. They were similar in their academic performance—good at science and mathematics, fair in Chinese, poor at drawing, singing, music, and handwork.

We made it a point, and so did they, that they had to make it on their own. All three won the President's scholarship, awarded to the 5 to 10 best A level students of their year. The two boys were also awarded SAF scholarships. This required them to undergo military training during their university summer vacations, and to serve in the Singapore Armed Forces for at least eight years upon graduation. Choo and I did not encourage them to do law; we left them to decide what they were good at and interested in doing. Loong enjoyed mathematics and wanted to do it at university but was quite sure he did not want it as his career. So, he studied mathematics at Trinity College, Cambridge, became a "Wrangler" (first-class honors in maths) in two instead of the usual three years, then took a postgraduate diploma in computer science with a star for distinction. He was trained in field artillery at Fort Sill, Oklahoma, later spent a year at the Command and General Staff College at Fort Leavenworth, Kansas, then a year on public administration at the Kennedy School of Government in Harvard.

Yang liked engineering. Not intimidated by his brother's record, he also went to Trinity College, Cambridge, and took Firsts in both parts of the engineering Tripos. He went to Fort Knox for armor training, later to Camberley, England, for Staff and Command, and to Stanford University, California, for a year in business administration.

Ling was fond of dogs and wanted to be a vet. Choo dissuaded her by citing what a vet friend did in Singapore: inspecting pigs at the slaughterhouse before and after slaughter to make sure they were fit for human consumption. That settled her choice. When she won the President's scholarship, she chose to do medicine in the University of Singapore and graduated as the Honors student, the top student of her year. She specialized in pediatric neurology and was attached for three years to Massachusetts General Hospital and later spent a year at Toronto's Children's Hospital.

Loong was always interested in what was going on in the country and in government. As a schoolboy of 11, he accompanied me when I went on constituency visits to rally ground support in the months before we joined Malaysia. He was old enough at 12 to remember the panic and turmoil of the 1964 race riots, including a sudden curfew that caught him at Catholic High School in Queen's Street wondering how he was to get home. The family driver had the wit to drive my father's small Morris Minor to take him home in chaotic traffic. Loong had been studying Malay since he was 5, and after Singapore joined Malaysia, had started learning to read Jawi, Malay written in the Arabic script. For practice he read the *Utusan Melayu,* Umno's Jawi newspaper, which published wild communal accusations against the PAP and me. Politics was a part of his extracurricular education.

From his student days in Cambridge, he knew he wanted a part in deciding what Singapore was to become and was willing to enter the political arena. After his Maths Tripos examinations, his tutor in Trinity College had urged him to reconsider returning to serve in the SAF, and pursue instead a career in mathematics in Cambridge, since he had done exceptionally well. The president of Oxford and Cambridge Society of Singapore, when presenting him with the prize as the best Singapore student of 1974 class, referred to a letter from another tutor of Trinity College. He wrote that Loong had obtained "50% more alpha marks than the next first class candidate" and that "in the recorded history of the Mathematical Tripos such a difference between the top man and the next has never been known before."

When I met his tutor at his graduation, he told me that Loong had written to him a most rational, thorough, and thoughtful letter explaining why he would not go on with mathematics no matter how good he was at it. Later, I asked his tutor for a copy of this letter that Loong had sent him in August 1972:

Now the reasons for not becoming a professional mathematician. It is absolutely necessary that I remain in Singapore, whatever I do, not only because in my special position if I "brain-drained" overseas the effect on Singapore would be disastrously demoralising, but also because Singapore is where I belong and where I want to be. . . . Further, a mathematician really has little say in what goes on in the world around him, in the way things are going on in the country. This does not matter at all in a large developed country like Britain, but in Singapore it would matter very much to me. It does not mean that I have to go into politics, but an important member of the civil service or the armed forces is in a position to do a great deal of good or harm. . . . I would prefer to be doing things and perhaps be cursed by other people than have to curse at someone else and not be able to do any more.

He was then only 20 but he knew his mind and where his commitments were.

Life is not without its tragedies. Loong married in 1978 Dr. Wong Ming Yang, a Malaysian he had met when she was in Girton College studying medicine at Cambridge. In 1982, she gave birth to their second child, a boy, Yipeng. He was an albino and visually handicapped. Three weeks later Ming Yang died of a heart attack. Loong's world collapsed. His mother-in-law looked after his two children, with Choo pitching in. They had the help of a maid whom Pamelia (my brother Suan's wife) had immediately sent over to meet this emergency. Later, we worried that Yipeng was slow in learning to speak and did not relate to people. When Ling returned from her training in pediatric neurology at the Massachusetts General Hospital, she diagnosed him as autistic. After some years in a preparatory school followed by a school for the visually handicapped, Yipeng's socialization skills improved and he was able to join a mainstream secondary school. Ling rediagnosed him as having Asperger's Syndrome (a mild form of autism) and he is intellectually normal. He has turned out to be good-natured and the best-behaved and most likeable of my grandchildren.

While Loong was still unsettled after his bereavement, Goh Chok Tong, then the minister for defense and assistant secretary-general of the PAP, invited him to stand for Parliament in the December 1984 general election. At that time Loong was a colonel on the general staff and the joint staff in the SAF. Chok Tong, as his minister, had a high assessment of Loong's potential in politics. Loong was concerned that, as a widower with two young children, he would find it difficult to manage the family as he would have to be absent much of the time on political work. He discussed it with Choo and me. I told him that if he missed the coming election he would have to wait for four to five years before he would have another chance. With every passing year he would find it more difficult to change and adjust to political life, especially learning to work with people in the constituencies and the unions. Most of all, he had to feel deeply for people, be able to communicate his feeling for them, and move them to go with him. At the age of 32, Loong left the SAF and contested the election in December. He won one of the highest majorities of any candidate in the election.

I appointed Loong a junior minister in the ministry of trade and industry. His minister immediately put him in charge of a private sector committee to review the economy just as we entered a severe recession in 1985. The committee's proposals that the government take strong steps to reduce business costs and strengthen competitiveness were a major political test for Loong and the other ministers. In November 1990, when I resigned as prime minister, Loong was appointed deputy prime minister by Prime Minister Goh Chok Tong.

Many of my critics thought this smacked of nepotism, that he was unduly favored because he was my son. On the contrary, as I told the party conference in 1989, the year before I resigned, it would not be good for Singapore or for Loong to have him succeed me. He would be seen as having inherited the office from me when he should deserve the position on his own merit. He was still young and it was better that someone else succeed me as prime minister. Then were Loong to make the grade later, it would be clear that he made it on his own merit.

For several years, Chok Tong had to endure the jeers of foreign critics that he was a seat warmer for Loong. But after Chok Tong won his second general election in 1997 and consolidated his position as his own man, the jeering stopped. As Chok Tong's deputy, Loong has established his standing as a political leader in his own right—determined, fast, and versatile in ranging over the whole field of government. Almost every difficult or taxing problem in any ministry had his attention. Ministers, MPs, and senior civil servants knew this. I could have stayed on a few years longer and allowed him to gather support to be the leader. I did not do so.

When Choo and I were in Johannesburg in October 1992, Loong phoned from Singapore while I was addressing a conference. I immediately rang back, fearing bad news. It was, devastating. A biopsy of a polyp found in his colon had been diagnosed as cancer, a lymphoma. Subsequent news gave us some grounds for relief; the form Loong suffered from was intermediate grade lymphoma which usually responded to chemotherapy. Loong underwent a three-month course of intensive chemotherapy. It cleared up his cancer cells and brought him a remission. The specialists advised that if it did not recur within five years his remission could be considered a cure. We waited anxiously for the five years to elapse. October 1997 came and passed without mishap. Loong had gone through two major crises.

In December 1985, Loong married Ho Ching whom he had known as an engineer in the ministry of defense. She had won the President's scholarship in 1972 and taken first-class honors in engineering at the University of Singapore. She is now a hands-on chief executive of a government-linked company, Singapore Technologies. It was a happy choice. They have two sons and Ho Ching embraced Loong's two other children as her own.

Yang married a girl from Singapore, Lim Suet Fern, who was studying law at Girton College, Cambridge, and also took a First. They have three sons. After 15 years in the SAF, Yang was seconded to Singapore Telecom. He had been asked by his permanent secretary to join the civil service as an administrative officer with the prospect of soon becoming a permanent secretary, and the potential to be head of the civil service. He preferred the challenge of the private sector, and opted to join SingTel. When he was promoted to CEO, my critics again alleged nepotism. It would have been a disaster for him and for the system of meritocracy that I had set up if he had been promoted because of me. The officers he served with and his peers knew better. So did the fund managers. SingTel shares did not weaken. After several years dealing with chairmen and CEOs of major international telecom companies, all talk of favoritism evaporated.

When our children were still in school, years before I raised the unmarried graduate women issue in 1983, Choo and I had told them that when they marry they must be happy to have their children as bright only as their spouses. They married their equals.

Ling, a neurologist, is a deputy director (clinical services) of the National Neuroscience Institute at Tan Tock Seng Hospital. She is unmarried, like many other graduate women of her generation. She lives with us, as is normal in Asian families, and travels extensively to conferences on neurology, pursuing her interest in epilepsy and learning disabilities in children.

The family has remained close. When they come for lunch on Sundays, the younger boys work each other up and create boisterous bedlam in the dining room. Most people dote on their grandchildren, spoiling them in the process. We are fond of ours, but feel that their parents are overindulgent. Perhaps we were too strict with their parents, but it has served them well.

My three brothers, Dennis, Freddy, and Suan Yew, a sister, Monica, and I have all benefited from a strong, resourceful, and determined mother who ensured that we were educated to the best of our abilities and her resources. Dennis followed me to read law at Fitzwilliam House in Cambridge. Later, together with Choo, we practiced law in partnership as Lee & Lee, and after a year Eddie Barker, an old friend at Raffles College and in Cambridge, joined us. Freddy became a stockbroker. Suan went to Fitzwilliam to study medicine and came back to build a successful practice. Monica married early. They rallied around to help in many ways when the family was in trouble, as when Loong lost Ming Yang in 1982, and again when he had cancer in 1992.

My siblings and I are especially close to each other. I was not just the eldest brother but also the one who helped our mother to make the major decisions. My father was carefree by nature and early in my teens my mother had co-opted me as the substitute head of the family. My brothers and sister still regard me as head of the family as much as the eldest brother. The extended family meets at least twice a year, on Chinese New Year's Eve for a reunion dinner and on New Year's Day at my home in Oxley Road. We keep in touch whenever there is anything important, like the arrival of new grandchildren. Now in our sixties and seventies, we are reminded how much we share of our parents' genes as with each illness our doctors check to confirm that our siblings are not similarly afflicted. We are grateful that three of us have already exceeded the biblical three score and ten.

# 43. Epilogue

As a boy of six, I rode in a bullock-cart on wooden wheels bound in a metal strip, without springs or shock absorbers, enjoying a hilariously bumpy ride on a dirt track to my grandfather's rubber estate. Fifty years later, in 1977, I flew in a supersonic Concorde from London to New York in three hours. Technology has changed my world.

I have had to sing four national anthems: Britain's *God Save the Queen,* Japan's *Kimigayo,* Malaysia's *Negara Ku,* and finally Singapore's *Majulah Singapura;* such were the political upheavals of the last 50 years. Foreign troops have come and gone—British, Australian, and Indian, then the Japanese, with their auxiliaries, the Taiwanese and Koreans. The British returned after the war and fought the communist insurgency. Then came independence for Singapore. Indonesia mounted Confrontation against Malaysia. The swirling currents of political changes swept me along.

Would my colleagues and I have embarked on our journey had we known the hazards and perils we would face when we formed the People's Action Party in November 1954? Had we known how complex and difficult were the problems that lay ahead, we would never have gone into politics with the high spirits, enthusiasm, and idealism of the 1950s. We could feel the swelling pride of the Chinese in both Singapore and Malaya at the success of communist China. Yet, there we were in the 1950s, a small group of English-educated colonial bourgeoisie, without the ability to reach the Chinese dialect-speaking masses who were the majority, going headlong into the fray. How could we ever hope to compete against the Malayan Communist Party? We did not think in those terms. We just wanted the British out.

We pressed on, oblivious of the dangers ahead. Our visceral urges were stronger than our cerebral inhibitions. Once plunged in, we were sucked ever deeper into the struggle. We had to fight the communists sooner than we expected, contending against their open-front labor, student, and cultural organizations, all backed by their armed underground. We solved that problem by merger with Malaya in 1963 to form Malaysia, only to discover that the Ultras in the UMNO Malay leadership wanted a Malay-dominated society. This led to communal riots, endless conflict, and eventually separation and independence in 1965. We found ourselves facing Confrontation by Indonesia. After that ended in 1966, the British announced in 1968 the withdrawal of their armed forces. We overcame one problem only to be faced with an even more daunting one. There were times when it looked hopeless.

We learned some valuable lessons in those early years as apprentices in the exercise of power. We never stopped learning because the situation kept on changing and we had to adjust our own policies. I had the advantage of several ministers who read widely and were attracted to new ideas but not mesmerized by them—Keng Swee, Raja, Sui Sen. We passed interesting books and articles we had read to each other. When we started, we were ignorant and innocent, but we were saved by being careful to probe and test ideas before we implemented them.

My colleagues and I forged our camaraderie under these intense pressures. In successive crises, we had to put our lives in each other's hands. We trusted each other, knew each other's strengths and weaknesses and made allowances for them. We did not take any straw polls to tell us what popular sentiment wanted us to do. Our task was to swing the people around to support what had to be done so that Singapore could survive as a noncommunist, noncommunal, viable society.

I was fortunate to have had a strong team of ministers who shared a common vision. They were able men determined to pursue our shared goals. The core team stayed together for over two decades. Keng Swee, Raja, Sui Sen, and Kim San were outstanding. They were all older than I was and were never inhibited from telling me what they thought, especially when I was wrong. They helped me stay objective and balanced, and saved me from any risk of megalomania which could so easily come with long years in office. I also had Toh Chin Chye, Ong Pang Boon, Eddie Barker, Yong Nyuk Lin, Kenny Byrne, and Othman Wok—capable men of integrity, dedicated to the cause.

When we started in 1959, we knew little about how to govern, or how to solve our many economic and social problems. All we had was a burning desire to change an unfair and unjust society for the better. To do that, we had to win political power. Having gained it, we had to retain the support of our people to continue our unfinished job.

I sought out able men and placed them in positions of authority as ministers and top public officers to administer an honest, efficient system and be responsive to the needs of the people. We had to keep the workers on our side and at the same time tend to the needs of investors whose capital, knowledge, management skills, and overseas markets would enable us to make a living without our traditional hinterland, Malaysia.

We learned on the job and learned quickly. If there was one formula for our success, it was that we were constantly studying how to make things work, or how to make them work better. I was never a prisoner of any theory. What guided me were reason and reality. The acid test I applied to every theory or scheme was, would it work? This was the golden thread that ran through my years in office. If it did not work, or the results were poor, I did not waste more time and resources on it. I almost never made the same mistake twice, and I tried to learn from the mistakes others had made. I discovered early in office that there were few problems confronting me in government that other governments had not met and solved. So I made a practice of finding out who else had met the problem we faced, how they had tackled it, and how successful they had been. Whether it was to build a new airport or to change our teaching methods, I would send a team of officers to visit and study those countries that had done it well. I preferred to climb on the shoulders of others who had gone before us.

In retrospect, it was our good luck that Singapore did not come to greater harm from some of the high-risk policies and actions that we embarked on. We worked with the communists in a united front; we could have been chewed up and swallowed as happened to social democrats in Poland and Czechoslovakia after World War II. We acted in the naïve belief that the force of electoral arithmetic would gradually bring about a less communal Malayan society; time has shown that racial loyalties cannot be overcome by the pulls of common economic interests. When faced with bleak economic prospects, I allowed an oil refinery at Keppel, thus placing a great fire hazard next to our major economic asset, the main harbor. And Chinese middle school student riots in the 1950s made such an indelible impression on us that we postponed implementing a national education policy with English as our working language from 1965 until 1978, and so reduced the economic prospects of many cohorts of Chinese students.

I learned to ignore criticism and advice from experts and quasi-experts, especially academics in the social and political sciences. They have pet theories on how a society should develop to approximate their ideal, especially how poverty should be reduced and welfare extended. I always tried to be correct, not politically correct. Foreign correspondents representing the Western media in Singapore preached their theories and criticized my policies, hoping to influence the voters and the government. It was just as well that the people were as pragmatic and realistic as the government.

Would I have been a different person if I had remained a lawyer and not gone into politics? My work experience would have been more limited and my horizons narrower. In politics I had to range over the whole gamut of the problems of human society. As the Chinese saying goes, "the sparrow though small has all five organs." Small though we may be, our needs are the same as those of any large country, domestically and internationally. My responsibilities gave me a wide perspective of human societies and a worldview that a lawyer would not have.

But I never allowed myself to forget Singapore's unique situation in Southeast Asia. To survive, we had to be better organized and more efficient and competitive than the rest of the region or there was no reason for our role as a nodal point between the advanced and the developing countries. After everything had been analyzed and argued, I went by my gut instinct of what would work in Singapore. I had persuaded our people to oust the British and join Malaya. Then we found ourselves thrown out of Malaysia. Thereafter, it was our duty to make Singapore succeed and give our people a future.

A united and determined group of leaders, backed by a practical and hardworking people who trusted them, made it possible. Did I expect an independent Singapore, with a GDP of S$3 billion in 1965, to grow 15 times to S$46 billion in 1997 at 1965 dollars and to have the 8th highest per capita GNP in the world in 1997 according to the World Bank? I have often been asked this question. The answer is "no." How could I have foreseen that science and technology, especially breakthroughs in transportation, telecommunications, and production methods, would shrink the world?

The story of Singapore's progress is a reflection of the advances of the industrial countries—their inventions, technology, enterprise, and drive. It is part of the story of man's search for new fields to increase his wealth and well-being. Stamford Raffles of the East India Company found an island of 120 fishermen in 1819 and turned it into an emporium on the sea route from India to China. As the commercial center of the British Empire in Southeast Asia, it prospered through international trade. When steamships replaced sailing ships, and again when the Suez Canal opened in 1869, traffic increased and added to Singapore's growth.

During the Japanese occupation (1942–1945), shipping was drastically reduced by the war, amounting to a blockade. Trade declined precipitately, food and medicine became scarce, and half the population of 1 million left for peninsular Malaya and the Riau islands. Many who remained were half-starved. After the victory of the Allies in August 1945, shipping resumed, bringing food, medicine, and other essentials, and the dispersed population returned. Trade and investments brought recovery.

With each technological advance, Singapore advanced—containers, air travel and air freight, satellite communications, intercontinental fiberoptic cables. The technological revolution will bring enormous changes in the next 50 years. Information technology, computers, and communications and their manifold uses, the revolution in microbiology, gene therapy, cloning, and organ reproduction will transform people's lives. Singaporeans will have to be nimble in adopting and adapting these new discoveries to play a role in disseminating their benefits.

People in Singapore learned quickly from their interaction with foreigners. We sent our brighter students abroad to study in developed countries, at first on scholarships given by these countries, later on scholarships given by the Singapore government. We also noted the increasing social difficulties these advanced societies faced because of their liberal social and welfare policies. I benefited from the lessons others paid for. I met many able foreign leaders who educated me and added to my understanding of the world.

Getting together a team to succeed my colleagues and me was almost as difficult as getting Singapore off the ground after independence. The second generation leaders brought a fresh burst of energy and enthusiasm into the government. Their experiences and ideas are more in tune with the younger generation and can lead Singapore in the new millennium. I derive immense satisfaction watching them gain in confidence and get into their stride.

What does the future have in store for Singapore? City-states do not have good survival records. The Greek city-states no longer exist as states. Most have not vanished physically, but have been absorbed by the hinterland in a larger entity. The city-state of Athens has disappeared. But the city of Athens survives in Greece, with the Parthenon to bear witness to the achievements of the original Athenians. Other cities in big countries have been sacked and destroyed, their people decimated or dispersed, but the nations they were part of have endured and new people have repopulated and rebuilt them. Will Singapore, the independent city-state, disappear? The island of Singapore will not, but the sovereign nation it has become, able to make its way and play its role in the world, could vanish.

Singapore has existed for 180 years since its modern founding by Stamford Raffles, but for the 146 years before 1965 it was just an outpost of the British Raj. It thrived because it was useful to the world. It is part of the global network of cities where successful corporations of advanced countries have established their businesses. To remain an independent nation, Singapore needs a world where there is a balance of power that makes it possible for small states to survive, and not be conquered or absorbed by larger countries.

Peace and stability in the Asian Pacific depend upon a stable triangular relationship between the United States, Japan, and China. China and Japan have competing geopolitical interests. The Japanese invasion and occupation of China still trouble their relationship. The Japanese share more interests with the Americans. A balance between the United States and Japan on one side and China on the other will set the structure and context for other relationships in East Asia. If there is an overall balance, the future of the region is more than fair and Singapore can continue to be useful to the world.

I did not know when I started my political life in the 1950s that we would be on the side of the winners of the Cold War and that Singapore would enjoy economic and social progress that flowed from stability, enterprise, and links with the West. We were living through a period of immense political, social, and economic change. The most difficult years were from independence in 1965 to British withdrawal in 1971. Only when the main units of the British forces had left and we did not suffer severe unemployment did I feel we were less vulnerable.

The future is as full of promise as it is fraught with uncertainty. The industrial society is giving way to one based on knowledge. The new divide in the world will be between those with the knowledge and those without. We must learn and be part of the knowledge-based world. That we have succeeded in the last three decades does not ensure our doing so in the future. However, we stand a better chance of not failing if we abide by the basic principles that have helped us progress: social cohesion through sharing the benefits of progress, equal opportunities for all, and meritocracy, with the best man or woman for the job, especially as leaders in government.

# Index